A HISTORY OF HULL

D1354469

THE
UNIVERSITY
OF HULL
PRESS

A HISTORY OF
HULL

Edward Gillett
and
Kenneth A. MacMahon

THE UNIVERSITY OF HULL PRESS
1989

© The University of Hull Press

British Library Cataloguing in Publication Data

Gillett, Edward, *1915* - and 11. MacMahon, Kenneth A.
(Kenneth Austin), *1914* - *72*.

A History of Hull - 2nd Edition
1.   Humberside. Hull. History
I.   Title
942.8'37

ISBN 0 85958 481 X

Published 1980 by Oxford University Press (Hardback)
Reprinted 1985, 1986, 1988 by Hull University Press
(Paperback)

Second and extended edition 1989
First and second reprint 1990 by Jacee Print
Third reprint 1993 by The University of Hull
Fourth reprint 1995 by Jacee Print

Preface and Acknowledgements

This book is not intended to compete with the massive and authoritative Victoria County History volume on Hull. It is, nevertheless, a work of original research, intended to give a compact account of the history of the town both for the specialist in urban history and for the general reader, and as far as possible an attempt has been made to include topics not dealt with elsewhere.

My friend and colleague, the late Kenneth MacMahon, did not contemplate my joining him in this work, which was to be done by the late Dr F. W. Brooks, once our mentor, and himself. Illness prevented Brooks from making any direct contribution and MacMahon died leaving most of what he had done in only a semifinal form. I can in a sense claim this book, especially in this second edition, as mostly mine; but I must strongly emphasise that unless he had started it there would probably have been no book such as this, though I much regret that neither of us ever suggested that we should collaborate. It was only chapters 20 and 21 which MacMahon clearly regarded as ready for publication. He had done most of the work needed for eight of the twentysix chapters. I did the rest, rewriting six of his eight chapters, using his version wherever possible. I have now made additions to all chapters, making this a rather longer work.

I can do no better than repeat the acknowledgements from the first edition:

This book would not have been written without the advice and encouragement of the Publications Committee and the help of the Librarian and staff of the Brynmor Jones Library in the University of Hull. Facilities for research were most generously afforded by Mr G. Oxley, Archivist to Hull Corporation, and Mr N. Higson, Archivist to the University. Much help in consulting eighteenth- and nineteenth-century newpapers was given by Miss J. Crowther of the Local History Library, Hull Central Library. The chapter on the twentieth century owes a great deal to the work of the late Richard Evans, whose achievements in this and other fields have never been sufficiently appreciated, and it should be acknowledged that both authors learnt the craft of local historian with the advice and example of Dr F. W. Brooks. Throughout the writing of this work I had the constant help and sympathy of my wife, who virtually became my research assistant. She also corrected the proofs.

Thanks for the permission to reproduce the illustrations are due to Mr Martin Lonsdale; the Vicar and churchwardens of Holy Trinity Church, Hull; Mr B. S. Ayers, Deputy Director of the Hull Archaeological Unit; and the *Hull Daily Mail*. Last of all I should particularly like to thank Mr A. Marshall, University Photographer of the University of Hull, who gave generously of his time in producing the illustrations.

For this revised edition I would also like to add the names of the Revd Peter Stubley and Mr Bernard Foster for their valuable hints and Mr R. Wheeler-

Osman, University Photographer, for additional photographic work. For permission to reproduce the cover illustrations I am indebted to the City Record Office and the Ferens Art Gallery. I want also particularly to thank Miss Jean Smith, Secretary to the University Press and her helpers. They have removed the flaws which disfigured the first edition which, at the request of Philip Larkin, I produced (to use his words) 'with all possible and reasonable speed'.

Edward Gillett
Cottingham
1988

Contents

Illustrations

Maps

Abbreviations used in Notes of Sources

Readers are asked to note that the numbers in the text refer to the sources, which are listed at the end of each chapter. Where an asterisk appears additional information will be found with the source note. Where op. cit. is shown this refers to a work already given in full earlier in the same chapter notes.

Where necessary the following abbreviations have been used:

APC	*Acts of the Privy Council* (HMSO).
Apprentices, 1883	Report of a Committee to inquire into the Masters, Owners and Crews of Fishing Vessels, Cmd 3432, 1883. Microfilm in Hull Central Library. (Not to be found in BPP).
BB	Bench Book, Kingston upon Hull Record Office.
Bellamy	J. M. Bellamy, *The Trade and Shipping of Nineteenth Century Hull.*
Boyle	J. R. Boyle, *Charters and Letters Patent granted to Kingston upon Hull.*
BPP	British Parliamentary Papers (Irish Universities Press, 1970).
BTC	British Transport Commission.
Carleton Monckton	Carleton Monckton MSS (Hull Central Library).
CCR	*Calendar of Close Rolls* (HMSO).
Chamb.	Chamberlains Rolls, Kingston upon Hull Record Office.
CIM	*Calendar of Inquisitions, Miscellaneous* (HMSO).
Collier	B. Collier, *The Defence of the United Kingdom.*
CPR	*Calendar of Patent Rolls* (HMSO).
CSPD	*Calendar of State Papers, Domestic* (HMSO).
CTB	*Calendar of Treasury Books* (HMSO).
D.	Deeds, Kingston upon Hull Record Office.
DNB	*Dictionary of National Biography.*
ECH	*Eastern Counties Herald.*
EHR	*English Historical Review.*
EMN	*Eastern Morning News.*
ERB	*Hull and East Riding Red Book, 1898.*
ERCRO	East Riding County Record Office (now Humberside Record Office).
Evans	R. Evans, 'The Social and Economic Structure of Hull' (Unpublished thesis in the Brynmor Jones Library, University of Hull).
Fisheries, 1863	Royal Commission on Sea Fisheries, 1863. *Minutes of Evidence* (BPP).
Fisheries, 1893	House of Commons Paper, No. 377, 1893. *Minutes of Evidence* (HMSO).
Fuller	T. Fuller, *The Church History of Britain.*

Gawtress	W. Gawtress, *The Corporation of Hull* (1833).
HA	*Hull Advertiser.*
Hadley	G. Hadley, *A History of Hull* (1788).
HDM	*Hull Daily Mail.*
HMC	Historical Manuscripts Commission.
HN	*Hull News.*
HP	*Hull Packet.*
Hull Critic	*Hull and East Riding Critic.*
Jones	H. A. Jones, *History of the Great War . . . The War in the Air* (1922-37).
JTH	*Journal of Transport History.*
KHRO	Kingston upon Hull Record Office.
L.	Letters, KHRO.
Leg.	P. Legouis, *Andrew Marvell.*
LPH	*Letters and Papers, Foreign and Domestic of the Reign of Henry VIII.*
MC	*Reports from Commissioners on Municipal Corporations in England and Wales* (1833).
n.p.	no pagination.
Oldfield	T. H. B. Oldfield, *The Representative History of Great Britain and Ireland* (1816).
OUP	Oxford University Press.
PHA	*Port of Hull Journal.*
Plan	E. Lutyens and P. Abercrombie, *A Plan for the City and County of Kingston upon Hull* (1945).
PM	G. Shaw, *Life of Parkinson Milson.*
PRO	Public Record Office.
R	*Hull Rockingham.*
Sheahan	J. J. Sheahan, *History of the Town and Port of Kingston-upon-Hull*, 2nd ed. 1866. [Where the first edition, published in 1864, has been used this is indicated].
SM	*Lincoln, Rutland and Stamford Mercury.*
TC	*Trade and Commerce of Hull* (1878).
TGSEY	*Trans of the Georgian Society for East Yorkshire.*
Tickell	J. Tickell, *A History of the Town and County of Kingston-upon-Hull.*
Woolley	W. Woolley, *A Collection of Statutes relating to Kingston upon Hull.*
VCH	*Victoria County History.*
YAJ	*Yorkshire Archaeological Journal.*
YASRS	Yorkshire Archaeological Society, Record Series.
YC	*York Courant.*

Archaic Words used in the Text

Assize	The regulation of the price, weight etc. of bread, ale and other essential articles.
Bearward	Keeper of a performing bear.
Brazill	A Dyestuff.
Composition	Agreement.
Crayer	A small sailing-ship.
Deodand	Any object which caused the death of a human being. Used also as an adjective. A thing declared deodand was forfeited to the Church, or, subsequently, to the King.
Feoffee	Trustee. This usage is still familiar at Nafferton and Bridlington.
Fother	A weight: in the case of lead equal to 19½ hundredweights.
Grampus	A small marine mammal resembling a whale; a killer whale.
Hulk	The largest type of medieval ship.
Kidds	Bundles of twigs or faggots.
Lagan	Wreckage etc. lying at the bottom of the sea.
Last	A measure, varying with the commodity—twelve sacks in the case of wool.
Mark	160 old pennies up to c. 1700.
Miniver	Fur of a small animal resembling an ermine.
Pinder	The man who was responsible for detaining stray animals.
Prise	A right to take various types of goods without payment.
Quarrel	A missile used with crossbows and similar weapons.
Springald	A large catapult.
Stockfish	Unsalted cod dried in the sun and air.
Thew	A kind of small pillory.
Train-oil	Whale-oil.
Wainscot	High quality Baltic oak.
Walker	A fuller who, originally, had to full the wet cloth by stamping on it.

I

Beginnings of the Medieval Town

Like Hedon, New Malton and Ravenspurn (Ravenserodd) Hull was a medieval 'new town', at first with an area of no more than about 80 acres; but it alone among the new towns of Yorkshire grew into a city. Hull does not appear in Domesday Book; but it is possible that there was some kind of settlement near the mouth of the River Hull even in 1066. There was a ferry, bringing salt from the coastal salterns of Lindsey, apparently across the Humber, from Grimsby. In later times this ferry went to Hull which perhaps had its origins in the claims of the Archbishop of York to extensive privileges in the water of Hull derived from his lordship of the borough of Beverley. Domesday Book clearly shows that the lands of this liberty enjoyed special privileges and although the account which Alfred of Beverley gave in the twelfth century of the origins of these privileges, granted by Athelstan in gratitude to St John of Beverley for his victory at Brunanburh, seems fictitious, it is reasonable to regard them as having existed before the Norman Conquest.[1]

It is not here argued that Hull existed in or before 1066, but that there was trading near the confluence of the River Hull and the Humber, as, for example, on the estate of the archbishop at Drypool, and that this trade was an extension of the trade of Beverley merchants. As late as 1313, long after the foundation of the borough of Kingston, a group of Beverley merchants sent £4000 worth of goods to Flanders in three Flemish ships which had arrived at Hull, and Beverley long remained a larger place than Hull. Whereas in 1377 there were only ten towns in England bigger than Beverley, there were nineteen bigger than Hull, though this gives no indication of the large extent of the trade carried on at the latter, which was probably financed by capital of Beverley and York men.[2]

The probability that there was trading at Hull before anything which could properly be called a town existed, is increased by the case of Boston, not certainly known to have existed until 1130: but it is fairly plain that there was a harbour in Skirbeck, from which Boston was subsequently separated, since in Domesday Skirbeck appears as by far the wealthiest place in the parts of Holland (Lincolnshire) accounting for more than a quarter of its population and almost a ninth of its value. Again, Scarborough may have existed, if Kormak's saga can be trusted, in about 965 and almost certainly was burned by Harald Hardrada in 1066; but in Domesday it is concealed in the manor of Falsgrave, which it was later to annex.

It has long been known that in 1203-4 Hull, perhaps the river rather than the town, if there was one, ranked sixth among the ports of the east and south coasts of England, considerably behind Lynn, which ranked fifth, but with about twice as much trade as York or Newcastle. That there was probably nothing which could be recognised as a town is indicated by the absence of roads even a hundred years later. There was simply a point of trans-shipment where vessels from Beverley and York met the larger craft capable of crossing the North Sea and entering the Baltic. But in 1239 there certainly was a settlement out of which the future town was to grow; for on 2 June of that year Archbishop Gray granted to the burgesses of his borough on the Humber — no name is given to it in the register — that their properties should be 80 feet wide and 160 feet long and they should enjoy the same privileges as his burgesses of Beverley. For each of these very large plots the rent demanded by the archbishop was no more than 4*d* a year — about two days' wages. This settlement must relate to Wyke, in which his claims were soon to conflict with those of the monks of Meaux.

To reinforce his position Archbishop Giffard in 1267 petitioned the Crown for all the liberties granted to St John of Beverley by Athelstan in the water of Hull 'which the heart may think of or the eye may see'. For us this certainly does not prove the existence of an Athelstan charter or of the precursor of Kingston upon Hull in the tenth century; but it does reinforce the view that in all probability there was traffic at the mouth of the river in pre-

Conquest times, and that in the thirteenth century the archbishop felt that such a claim was respectable, or almost. An official inquiry for the Crown then found that from time out of mind — the legal definition of which was any time prior to 3 September 1189 — the archbishop had been able to take prises of wine in the River Hull, taking a tun from before the mast and another aft. This was ratified by letters patent of 20 March 1267 confirming that Archbishop Walter Giffard and all future archbishops should take the prises in the haven of Hull, which he held, as Archbishop Walter de Gray had done.[3]

The thirteenth-century references to Hull, at any rate before the time of the first charter, are to the haven. After the defeat of the younger Simon de Montfort at Northampton in 1264 knights of his faction fled to Hull — Norman and Roger de Arcy, Roger Marmion and two others. They were arrested, and the constable of Scarborough Castle was ordered to bring them to the King. It may well have been because this command went to a royal official and not to his bailiffs at Hull which, when the war was over, prompted the archbishop to seek a royal confirmation of his rights. Thereafter his bailiffs were not ignored by the Crown. In 1274 they were under suspicion of having neglected to enforce the prohibition on the export of wool and to have allowed three merchants of Pontefract to ship their wool in the haven. And about the same time it was found that John Playbote of Hessle had shipped 40 sacks and the Abbot of Meaux 129 sacks. These, of course, were illegal exports. As soon as the legal trade can be traced from the customs returns the real volume of the trade is seen to be immensely greater. In 1281-2 over 3000 sacks of wool were exported through Hull, which in this trade ranked as the fourth port, running almost equal third with Southampton.[4]

In all probability the trade in wool had been going on continuously throughout the thirteenth century and earlier. It is not possible to point to a beginning, or to know whether the trade was helped or hindered by the change in the course of the River Hull which may be dated as taking place in or about 1253. In disastrous floods along the whole of the east coast, of which the Louth Park chronicler speaks in that year, floods came as far inland as Cottingham and the Meaux chronicler, apparently speaking of the same floods, records that much of the abbey land at Myton 'collapsed into the Humber and was never recovered'. The main course of the River Hull had previously been through Myton to the west of the present river, possibly leaving it about the point in Wincolmlee known at the present day as High Flags. It now shifted its channel into Sayer Creek and followed its present course; but the old channel remained and was frequently referred to in the medieval records of the town. As late as 1303 the current in the Old Hull, as it was already called, was thought to be still strong enough for a water mill; and although it often was feared that the dumping of ballast might in course of time render the new haven unnavigable, it has remained a permanent feature in the topography of the town. It was probably this change in the course of the river which frustrated the attempt of the Archbishop to create his borough on the Humber.[5]

By the time that this change took place Wyke, the future Kingston upon Hull, and Myton, immediately to the west of it, had fallen largely into the hands of the monks of Meaux, against whom the Archbishop of York completely failed to vindicate his claims. Archbishop Walter Giffard (d. 1279) in a dispute with Meaux concerning property at Wyke, insisted on his ancient right to have the case heard in an ecclesiastical court in the porch of Beverley Minster. But the King's judges decided that the land in dispute was not in the liberty of St John of Beverley, and Meaux therefore kept its land. This was a triumph for Robert de Thornton, the twelfth abbot (1270-80), and it must have been he, and not his successor as the chronicler believed, who was able to raise a loan of 800 marks on the security of the Meaux property in Wyke and Myton, in a devious transaction in which quite clearly some of the parties involved were guilty of serious frauds, camouflaged by the devices employed to conceal usury which was contrary to canon law. In the end Meaux lost over £1000. What is significant for the history of Hull is that the original money-lender was William de Hamelton, along with Adam his brother. William was already high in the King's service and was later to be his Chancellor and Dean of York, and it may have been this business which made it known to the Crown that Wyke and Myton formed a highly desirable investment where much could be gained, if the King had his own bailiff instead of having to rely on those of the archbishop.

On 31 January 1293 the Abbot and Convent of Meaux granted to Edward I all their property in Wyke and the grange of Myton, and received from him an unspecified 'great profit whereof we are well content'. Whatever they had been promised failed to come up to expectations and the chronicler considered that they lost heavily on the deal. His view may be unreliable. The finances of Meaux were in any case in a critical and complicated state; his chronology is vague; and the motive he attributes to the King — 'the establishment of a haven suitable for ships and merchandise' — seems an unlikely one since such a port already existed. It is clear that Wyke was enclosed in a defensive ditch but that the grange of Myton was not. There were about forty tenants who had buildings on their plots in Wyke, including Geoffrey de Hotham and Walter le Celererman who had the building in which the abbot had sometimes held his court. Most of these tenants and about a dozen others also had plots on which there were no buildings, and there were also seven acres and one rood of grassland used for the fair.[6]

The new town had grown up in an area of rough common land, much of it subject to flooding, shared between the villagers of Ferriby, Swanland, Anlaby, Hessle, Westella, Kirkella, Willerby and Wolfreton, an area which in the fifteenth century was to be almost identical with that of the newly created county of Kingston upon Hull. The rural origins of Wyke itself were reflected in the existence of a few plots held by villein tenure. The last traces of this were extinguished with the charter of 1 April 1299 which turned Wyke into the free borough of Kingston upon Hull, governed by a warden appointed by the Crown, but sworn to protect the interests of the burgesses, who gained privileges similar to those of Scarborough.[7*] By this charter they gained freedom throughout the King's dominions in France as well as Wales, Scotland, England and Ireland, from the payment of various tolls; they could freely dispose of their land by will (and presumably by sale) and, as well as markets each Tuesday and Friday, they were to have a fair starting on 26 May each year and lasting for thirty days. The King's warden was to have a court in the town and virtually all non-criminal disputes arising within the town were to be tried there. Above all, the sheriff was deprived of all jurisdiction in the borough — a supremely important privilege since the almost contemporary Hundred Rolls shows us the acts of torture and extortion of which the sheriff's underlings in most counties were capable. The rights of infangenthef and utfangenthef granted in the charter probably meant that the warden could still exercise

the ancient right of immediately executing criminals caught red-
handed, but for the others there was to be a town gaol in which
they were to await trial. Since some uncertainty remained as to
who was to try these prisoners, letters patent of 1302 granted that
whenever the need arose the King would appoint commissioners of
gaol-delivery to try them. Further, a mint was set up.[8]

The new borough prospered. Usually Hull occupied the third
place among ports exporting wool, but as early as 1297-8 it
exported 4636 sacks and was second only to London. In the first
twenty years of the fourteenth century the export of wool from
Hull dropped below 2000 sacks only in two years and was above
4000 sacks in nine. Wool exports from England were increasing
almost everywhere. In 1312 the burgesses secured an important
exemption from an ordinary feature of customary law which could
be a serious hindrance to trade: henceforth no person whether he
was English or alien could be arrested or his goods detained at Hull
for any grievance which any party might have against a third
unless he were his surety. This privilege was for seven years only,
but as soon as the town became self-governing under its mayor, he
and the principal burgesses could decide whether or not to arrest
the goods of, for example, a Scarborough man in a case where a
Hull man had a claim against a different Scarborough person, and
they seem to have acted with great discretion in this matter.[9]

Edward I had been able to discard the King's Jews, who, since
the Conquest had been used by the Crown as the unhappy
instruments of extortion; since he could now use the customs of
the ports and the genius of Italian and other continental financiers
as a means of expanding and anticipating his revenue. And the
new status of Hull is shown in the interest taken in it by men of
Lucca and Florence. As early as 1287 Richard Guydichionis, a
merchant of Lucca, of the society of the Bardi, was appointing
Hamo Box of London to take the King's prises of wine in Hull.
The name of Hamo Box appears among the lists of tenants in the
Meaux charter granting Wyke to the King, and by 1309 he had so
far prospered that he had a private oratory in his house and was
farming those tithes in Hull which were the property of the parish
church of Ferriby. In the last decade of the thirteenth century
much of the wool trade at Hull was in the hands of the Bardi, the
Frescobaldi and other merchants of Florence and Lucca. In 1306
certain Lombard merchants and others of the society of the Bardi

dispatched 120 sacks of wool from the port in a ship which was wrecked on the Norfolk coast on its voyage to Flanders — an indication that much of this Italian trade was between Hull and Flanders. In 1300 the exchange of Hull, along with those of Newcastle and Exeter, was in the hands of the Frescobaldi. In 1311 the Ballardi of Lucca were to collect all the customs at Hull on hides and sheepskins until they had recompensed themselves for the £1513 which they had lent to the King, and in the following year Gascon merchants were allowed to recoup themselves for £88 due for wine supplied to the King out of the Hull customs. Three merchants of the Bardi in 1317 were allowed to collect £2000 out of the Hull customs until they had recovered the amount of the loan which they had advanced to Aymer de Valence, Earl of Pembroke. The Perucchi in 1322 had 1000 marks out of the Hull customs, in which the Bardi of Florence also had an interest; but soon the de la Poles took over.[10]

In the late thirteenth century there were no roads to the new town, a deprivation less serious than it might appear to be since country roads were so bad and river transport much easier. Because of the absence of roads it was necessary that dead bodies should be taken along the Humber bank to the churchyard at Hessle. Archbishop Corbridge in 1301 therefore ordered that a graveyard should be consecrated near the chapel already existing at Hull. Burial processions had been particularly dangerous in winter. An order from the King two years later explicitly said that there were no roads, and new ones were therefore to be laid out. At the time of writing, from about a mile away it can be seen that Anlaby and Hessle Roads point straight at the church of Holy Trinity, a consequence of the surveys made in 1303. The Crown in acquiring Wyke also had the right to make roads sixty feet wide over any of the Meaux lands. A new road was made from the ferry over the Hull to the bridge at Bilton, through Drypool and the pasture called *Suttecotessomergang* to the cross of *Somergangg* and the cross of *Sutcoates*. These names still exist in Southcoates Lane and Summergangs Road which existed long before there were any buildings on them — though Sutcotes was a hamlet. The road continued through the meadows of Sutton, over a new bridge at *Lambeholmesikes*, to the bridge at Bilton. This road was forty feet wide. Another of the same breadth was made from Aldgate, now Whitefriargate, through *Milnecroft* and *Oxecrofte*, through the commons shared by Myton, Ferriby, Swanland and Anlaby, through Anlaby itself westwards until it joined the King's highway from Hessle to Beverley. *Milnecroft* was probably where Prospect Street now joins Spring Bank, and from that point a road sixty feet wide was made via the *Graycock* across *Derynghamdyke* (probably where Queens Road and Sculcoates Lane now cross Beverley Road) through *Bordenbrig* and the land of the lady of Cottingham which then extended up to the River Hull, through the ings of Skidby and through Thearne and Woodmansey to Beverley.

The men of Swanland in 1315 complained that ever since the time of Richard Oysel the keepers of the King's town had restricted their pasture rights. Loretta, lady of Swanland, believed in direct action and consulted with her family and her neighbours. She was a rather flighty person who in 1304 had some difficulty in clearing herself of accusations of sins of the flesh with a chaplain. Now, with her stepson John de Usflet and other people of Swanland and Westella, by night she broke the banks and ditches made for the protection of Myton and Hull so that the King's corn and meadows were flooded.[11] On the east side of the river Sir John de Sutton was aggrieved not only by the building of a road through his land to Bilton, but also by the loss of his ferry over the Hull. The burgesses now had their own ferry for which no toll was charged, only sixty feet away from his, which accordingly went out of use, and he lost 40*s* a year. To make his power felt he prevented the men of Hull from using the new road, but, having Edward I to deal with, found himself in prison with his brother Nicholas and was not released until he had paid a fine of 100 marks which may well have been the greater part of his income for one year.[12]

The earliest lists of the burgesses of the new town show them as predominantly local, though soon there were to be families with a branch in Bordeaux as well as in Hull. About half of all those who had property in Wyke in 1293 had surnames derived from the names of places within twenty-five miles, and the four knights with Wyke property, Sir Robert de Percy, Sir Gilbert de Briddeshale, Sir William St Quinton and Sir John de Karletone, all belonged to the East Riding. The archbishop was the only magnate of real power with Hull property, but although he never lost it in the middle ages — Bishop Lane was part of it — his claims to special privileges derived from St John of Beverley were soon extinguished.

His first setback came in 1298. Among the Easterlings or Hanse merchants who arrived at Hull in May there was one so ill that he was given the last rites by the priest of Drypool on the east bank of the river Hull and died ten days later. The body remained on board the ship overnight in accordance with custom. When the crew were taking him to be buried they were stopped by John Haget and others, with a large crowd of the archbishop's villein's from Skidby, Woodmansey and Thearne. The archbishop's bailiff then held an inquest, arrested the ship, and demanded £20, which was probably not much less than she was worth, for her release. The Crown was determined, however, to maintain its rights which were now based not only on sovereignty but also on the King's lordship's in Hull and Holderness. An inquiry found for the King that the archbishop had usurped his rights. the haven from the junction of the old course of the river, here called *Veilhull*, was part of the lordship of Holderness. Since Walter de Gray was archbishop (1215-55) all the rights which he and his successors had exercised in the River Hull were usurpations. Here it seems that 'Hull' means the new course of the river, and the verdict is a further confirmation that the change of course had happened in 1253.[13]

John and Richard de la Pole were wine merchants with interests in Hull by 1308, and until 1327 Richard acted for the archbishop in Hull as well as being deputy-butler for the King. In 1327 he became butler of the realm. There was some confusion caused by this promotion and in 1328 he took no customs on wine in Hull for the King. The burgesses resented the claims of the archbishop and it was probably as a result of their petition that Edward III ordered Richard de la Pole to take the customs of wine and prevent the archbishop from taking his prises. The latter, however, continued to exercise his rights and Hull merchants found that their wine trade was having to pay tribute once to the King and again to the archbishop. To defeat the latter, whose claim only extended to vessels carrying twenty tuns of wine or more, they tried the effect of leaving three vessels carrying wine in the Humber, and landing the cargo in batches of less than twenty tuns. The dispute was driving the wine trade away, until in 1334 the Crown lawyers found a flaw in the patent of 1267 on which the archbishop based his claims. The patent had granted prises to him but had not specified that they were prises of wine. In matters of common law the King's judges had the last word, and however frivolous this proof of a flaw may have been, it virtually put an end to the archbishop's claims in the river.[14]

A rental made in 1347 shows that most of the streets of Hull already existed, though some in course of time were to change their names, Hull Street becoming High Street, for example, Aldgate — Whitefriargate, and Lisle Street — Mytongate. It is not known with certainty whether they were metalled in the earliest days, but they probably were, since they were maintained in the fifteenth century with stone and sand, and from time to time the Crown gave grants of pavage which enabled the town to levy a toll on some of the traffic entering the town by land — some would be exempt if it belonged to persons privileged as burgesses — for the maintenance of its roads. The first of these grants, for five years, was made in 1300, and another, for seven years, in 1317. The traffic probably consisted of no more than a dozen or so pack-horses on an ordinary day and rather more on a market day and during the fair. Carts were very rarely seen and sometimes prohibited, and a very small flow of road traffic would serve all the needs of a place which as regards population was about an average town with fewer than 2000 inhabitants.[15]

Developments taking place in the last quarter of the twentieth century are rapidly erasing the pattern of medieval streets and it is therefore necessary to record that the town, soon to be walled, was entirely on the west side of the River Hull. Its northern boundary can still be envisaged as following, very roughly, the centre of Queen's Gardens, and its western boundary as passing through the 'town docks', running north from the Humber. This, at any rate, was the area which was to be enclosed by the fourteenth-century walls; but since Hull lay among common land largely without boundaries, in its early days there was a part of the town near the River Hull outside the northern gate and the ditch extending some distance to the north and consisting mainly of the long, ploughed strips which were characteristic of open-field farming. All this northern extension, with much property inside the town, belonged to the de la Poles.[16]

The King had acquired Myton, immediately to the west of the

town, but though the town was affected by the existence of Myton and the burgesses probably hired grazing there for their horses and cows, it did not become part of Hull until Tudor times. If the orders received by Robert de Sandale, warden of Hull and Myton, were carried out, by 1314 the hall of the manor of Myton had a new porch with a chamber over it. There was a kitchen, other chambers and other buildings, all enclosed in a moat with a bridge and gate-house. When the Crown acquired the Meaux property in Myton it was worth £24 8s a year derived almost entirely from rather less than 200 acres used for sheep-farming. There were two windmills and there was also the Hull windmill of Arnold de Gretford somewhere outside Myton in the ploughed fields and meadows. The Myton Manor also appears to have had a watermill on the Old Hull.[17] When the King first acquired the town he had yet another windmill, leased to Thomas Baron, Rector of Kirkella. Like all buildings of timber it was easily dismantled and reassembled on a different site. Richard Oysel had agreed to allow the rector to move the mill, but he had gone off to the North Riding to be Rector of Great Smeaton and as the Crown had not performed its side of the bargain and provided timber for maintenance, by 1312 the mill on its new site was beyond repair, and the foundations of the Myton watermill were so weak that it was in danger. Nevertheless *c.* 1300 there were more windmills than the inhabitants needed and some must have existed to serve the needs of mariners in the port. It is significant that orders were given for the remaking of the ruined windmill with oaks from Burstwick.

It may be that the grant of a ferry across the Humber was of more importance to the inhabitants, and certainly to trade, than the laying out of new roads. It was granted by the Crown in 1315 with tolls for which the keeper was to account at the exchequer yearly: ½*d* for a man on foot, 1*d* for a man with his horse, 2*d* for a cart with two horses with a further 1*d* for each horse. The maintenance of the south ferry-boat, as it was always called, soon became an important responsibility of the borough officers, and the ship was stout enough to have made a sea voyage.[18]

Sources

1.   E. Gillett, *A History of Grimsby*, 7; F.W. Brooks, *Domesday Book and the East Riding*; *Historians of the Church of York* (Rolls Series), ii, 350; i, 294.
2.   *CCR* 1313-18, 7; R.B. Dobson, *The Peasants' Revolt of 1381*, 55-7.
3.   C. Frost, *Notices Relative to the Early History of the Town and Port of Hull* (Appendix, 31); A.L. Poole, *From Domesday Book to Magna Carta*, 96; *Archbishop Gray's Register* (Surtees Society), 251.
4.   Frost, op.cit., citing *Foedera* iv, 237; *CPR* 1266-72, 47; E. M. Carus-Wilson and Olive Coleman, *England's Export Trade 1275-1547*, 36.
5.   *Patent Rolls* 1227-32, 88; *CPR* 1258-66, 360; *CIM*, ii, No. 967; *Rotuli Hundredorum* (Record Commission), 106.
6.   *Chronicon de Melsa* (Rolls Series), ii, 91; Lincolnshire Record Society, *The Chronicle of Louth Park Abbey*, 52; *CCR* 1302-7, 91; *Chronicon de Melsa*, ii, 153-5, 183-5; *DNB* s.v. HAMILTON, WILLIAM, d. 1307.
7.*   Hull University Archives: Boyle's *Transcripts* (Exchequer T.R. Misc. Book, 274, f.170, f.172); *Chronicon de Melsa*, ii, 186-92. But villein tenure continued in Myton, where in comparatively recent times there was much copyhold (i.e. former villein) property.
8.   J.R. Boyle, *Charters and Letters Patent granted to Kingston upon Hull*, 1-5; M. Powicke, *The Thirteenth Century*, 634.
9.   Carus-Wilson, op.cit., 40-43; *CPR* 1307-13, 415.
10. *Archbishop Greenfield's Register* (Surtees Society), iii, 153; *CPR* 1301-7, 538; *CPR* 1292-1301, 504; *CPR* 1307-13, 386, 457, 9; *CPR* 1321-4, 159, 129.
11. *Archbishop Corbridge's Register* (Surtees Society), 161-2; YASRS *Yorkshire Inquisitions*, iv, 47; *CPR* 1301-7, 91.
12. *CPR* 1313-17, 317, 409, 609; *Archbishop Corbridge's Register*, 196-7; G. Poulson, *The History and Antiquities of the Seignory of Holderness*, ii: 344-5; *Yorkshire Inquisitions*, iv, 147.
13. *CIM*, i, No. 1781.
14. A.S. Harvey, *The de la Pole Family of Kingston upon Hull*, 7; Frost, op.cit., 126-9.
15. *CPR* 1292-1301, 514; *CPR* 1317-21, 32; BB2, f.149.
16. BB2, f.148-9.
17. *CCR* 1313-18, 118; *CIM*, ii, No. 1313; *CCR* 1307-13, 407.
18. *CPR* 1313-17, 344.

2

The Medieval Trade of Hull

As the exports of wool from England increased, the new town prospered. In the 1270s, when statistics first become available, Boston and London, and occasionally Southampton, shipped more wool than Hull. In the years 1279-99 there were probably never fewer than about 2000 sacks a year leaving Hull. In five years there were 3000-4000 a year, and in three years more than 4000 a year. This was at a time when the whole of the wool sent out of the country was usually about 20,000 to 30,000 sacks each year. In the first decade of the fourteenth century the Hull shipment never fell below 3000 sacks a year except in one year. In six years the figure rose above 6000 sacks and in one of these years it was above 7000. By now the total export from England was usually over 30,000 sacks and in three years over 40,000; and Hull ranked as the third wool-exporting town, well behind London, but usually not far behind Boston. In a few years in the fourteenth century more wool left Hull than Boston, and in most years the amount leaving Boston was not very much greater than that leaving Hull.[1]

Most and possibly all of the wool from Hull went to Flanders, Brabant and Artois. Flemings were caught ignoring a prohibition on exports and in 1271 the bailiffs of Hull and Boston were to arrest their goods. Even Italian merchants, usually interested in the Hull customs as security for their loans to the King, engaged in the Hull wool trade. In 1306 Lombard merchants and others of the society of the Bardi and the Peruchi sent 120 sacks to Flanders, but their ship was wrecked on the coast of Norfolk. The wool came from those places having access to the rivers which flowed into the Humber, but the origin of the wool sent from Hull usually does not appear except when smuggling was detected. In 1274 merchants of Pontefract were sending it to Hull and it was suspected that the bailiffs were conniving at unlawful shipments. In 1320 it was thought that the officers of the customs were at fault. John Rotenheryng got his wool in Lincolnshire and for £29 3*s* 4*d* bought eight sacks in Lincoln. John de Haynton, of Beverley, was probably from Lincolnshire, where Robert Jolyf and William Kelstern, both Beverley merchants, with Roger de Ormesby of Louth bought twenty-one sacks. John le Goldbeter and John Cokelare of York in 1341 loaded their wool at Turnheved, west of Selby. John le Goldbeter in the previous year, and Richard de Acastre, also of York, bought wool from John de Ellerker of Ellerker and the Prior of Ferriby, loaded it at Thevesflete near Hessle and sent it to Flanders. In 1341 John Swarteghe, a Dutch mariner, took uncustomed wool from Ravenserodd. Most of it came from Blackhowe Moor, the usual name then for the North York Moors, but some was taken on board at Grimsby. But all the wool we have been dealing with was either loaded into a Hull ship or was in the end shipped from Hull.[2]

With one and possibly two notable exceptions Hull families do not appear as actively engaged in the wool trade. When Hull merchants took to smuggling they kept away from Hull. John de Selby and William Wele, both of Hull, in 1365 joined with Thomas Goldeman of Preston and John Wright of Paull to hire a Hedon ship which illegally took ten sacks of wool from Paull to Flanders, a cargo worth nearly £40, whereas the value of the ship was only £5. It may be that few Hull merchants had sufficient capital to engage in either the legal or the illegal branch of the trade; but it seems clear that the new regulation made in 1343 had made it, for the time being, too difficult to smuggle from Hull. The new regime was no sooner instituted than some York wool-merchants had their wool shipped without payment of custom at Ferriby in John Swerd's round-ship, the *Johan* of Hull.[3]

At the beginning of January 1343 the Sheriff of Yorkshire had received orders to go to Hull and there assemble the inhabitants including the mayor and acquaint them with new regulations for the handling of wool. Because much wool had been shipped without the payment of duty, none was to be stored in any house of which the back or the side was open to the water. All wool was to be publicly weighed in a place to be fitted up for that purpose and in the presence of those who would be able to declare if there was any fraud involved. Once it was weighed the wool could not normally be returned to the warehouse. Except in bad weather it must immediately be loaded into the ship; but if the weather made this impossible it was to go to a warehouse guarded and sealed by the officers of the customs. Only those porters sworn for the purpose could carry the sacks to the ship, where officers would supervise the stowage. To enable them to do this properly only one ship was to be loaded at a time. No ship was to leave the haven until she was fully loaded, because it had become common for partly loaded ships to leave and then secretly take on board un-customed wool in the roadstead or at sea. But even with a fully loaded ship some smuggling was possible. Peter de Grymesby had his ship, the *George*, fully loaded at Hull with wool and other goods, paying the full duty; but without his knowledge the crew hid wool in their beds and their sea-chests. The cargo reached Flanders, but by some means the news of this small-scale smuggling reached the authorities and in 1362, after his ship had been declared forfeit, he had to petition for her return.[4]

In the course of the next century the system was greatly modified. By 1442 wool as recorded by the officers of the Crown was no longer being shipped on such a scale, but smuggling of un-customed wool was still common. This time the Bench (the term by which we shall normally describe the mayor and aldermen) tried to set matters right without the intervention of the Crown. No one was to keep in his house more than one hundred sheepskins or a sack of wool without notifying the mayor, who was then to go to the house with an alderman and there take note of the wool and its destination. All wool not belonging to Hull men was to be kept in the wool-house, the place on the river bank where it was weighed and the duty paid, and so long as there was any room there, no wool was to be taken into any house in the town or in the recently created county of Hull.[5] The effectiveness of these orders depended entirely on the willingness of the bench to stop an illicit trade of such great advantage to the port.

The rise of the de la Pole family into the higher aristocracy of England is connected with Hull, but as the importance of the family grew, though its Hull property remained, its connection with the affairs of the town became more tenuous. Richard and

William de la Pole were both deeply involved in the Hull trades in wine, wool and corn, and both were knighted and rose high in the service of the Crown, the first named dying in 1345 and the second in 1366. Sir William's son, Sir Michael, was never a Hull merchant but an active soldier and courtier fully ten years before his father's death, after which he held baronial rank and was finally created Earl of Suffolk in 1385. The real connection of the family with Hull was therefore limited to the first half of the fourteenth century; but Sir William, the first mayor in 1332, was beyond all doubt the most important man in Hull with concerns extending far beyond the town. For the history of the town his importance lies in the fact that his career shows how great a fortune could be made in it. Because of the loans which he and Richard had made to Edward III, with Reginald Conduit of London he was able in 1337 to form a consortium of English wool-merchants which was able to obtain a monopoly of the export of wool. There had been an embargo on wool for the Netherlands for almost a year. This caused an accumulation of wool in England, enabling merchants to buy at a low price, and sell at a higher price than usual in the Netherlands because of the shortage thus artificially, but not exceptionally, created. Unfortunately, they were not all men of equal integrity. The smaller merchants felt that they were being cheated by the greater, and some again took to smuggling. This situation existed in all the wool ports and not in Hull only. In February 1338 Edward III, determined that he would not be the loser, seized 10,000 sacks which the consortium had accumulated at Dordrecht, giving bonds in exchange to those having claims on the wool. As there was delay in redeeming the bonds, men of large means were able to buy bonds at a discount from merchants of smaller capital. When the bonds were finally redeemed in July 1343, sixty-nine of them were to be converted to cash out of the customs of Hull, and it seems probable that to a certain extent the holders of the bonds were those who customarily traded in wool at Hull.[6]

There were sixty-nine of these merchants or partnerships. One or two merchants, who belonged to Durham, probably never had their wool on vessels in the Hull haven. Most of the rest probably did. The biggest was William de la Pole, who got £2039. Walter Prest of Melton Mowbray got only £3 less. Fourteen of these merchants were of Beverley, two of York and four from places accessible along the Trent. At least three or four belonged to

Barton or other places of Lincolnshire, Hugh Cokheved of
Appleby being the most prominent of these, with £700. Apart
from William de la Pole the list does not disclose how many
belonged to Hull. Nearly all who are identified by name only had
surnames derived from place names of the East Riding, and six of
them may well have belonged to Hull.

In 1322 Richard Fitz Dieu of Hull — where his name appears in
the records as Godesone — obtained a protection from the Crown
for his ships carrying wine, corn and victuals from the south to
York, Newcastle and the north. This would ensure that his ships
were not arrested for the King's service. Coal from Newcastle
seems to have been one of the staple Hull trades from the
beginning. The town charged a toll of 20*d* on each 20 tons of coal
coming from Newcastle, and 6*d* a ton on vessels going overseas, as
well as smaller tolls on keels, ketches and Hull cogs. A ship could
be bought outright for as little as £5 and still be useful for a North
Sea crossing; but most vessels in the continental trade cost much
more. In 1304 John Scaile and Nicholas Putfra bought a foreign
ship for £20 and spent another £20 on re-rigging her. She was
arrested in Flanders at Swyne, the port of Bruges, and as requests
from the Crown for justice to be done were ignored the mayor and
bailiffs of Hull were authorised to arrest goods of Bruges.[7]

Connections with the Netherlands appear to have been more
frequent than with any other part of the Continent. In 1309 there
was a similar case regarding the arrest of goods. Because Wynand
Moraunt, a merchant, probably a foreigner, residing in Beverley,
could not obtain payment of a debt of £100 or more due to him in
Gröningen, cloth to this value brought into Hull by two Gröningen
men was arrested. But cloth had long been manufactured in the
East Riding and woad from Flanders and Brabant was needed for
dyeing it. In 1328 a ship loaded with woad bound for Hull from
Sluys was driven by storms to Scotland. The ordinary medieval
ship with a single mast and a square sail could make no progress to
windward, and this is what would often happen if strong westerly
winds prevented a ship from entering the Humber and heavy seas
made it too dangerous to anchor. The *Godewhile* in 1368 brought
a large cargo to Hull and then took on board two pilots for the
passage to Newcastle for coal before returning to Middelburg in
Zeeland. The master was allowed to take £6 10*s* in money with him
for this purpose, but when he was searched he was found to have

£25 10s hidden under his arm, which he was intending to take out of the country illegally.[8]

But even in early times there was a good deal of trade with more distant ports. Timber essential for masts and spars came from Norway and the Baltic. Geoffrey de Hamby, trading with Norway, had failed to obtain redress for wrongs done to him there, and it was proposed to arrest Norwegian goods and ships in Hull. There were also ships from the Baltic. In 1339 and again in 1340 the mayor and bailiffs were to arrest £100 of goods from Lübeck, Rostock, Stralsund or other places in north Germany for trespasses done there to merchants of Hartlepool and Yarmouth. And because an English merchant had been robbed at Königsberg, Hull was to arrest goods from East Prussia up to the value of £90.[9]

Florentine merchants in 1314 took wool from Hull in a ship of Bayonne, which probably had made her outward passage with wine, a cargo of even higher value than the wool which was exported. Men of Winchelsea in 1300 were, as an exceptional favour, allowed to bring wine of Bergerac and St Emilion to Hull free of custom, and in 1310 vintners and other merchants came under a safe-conduct. It may have been the lack of such a document which caused the arrest of vintners from Besatz. Wool and corn were taken with other goods to the Bay of Biscay ports and wine was taken on board there. William de la Pole in 1338 was ordered to arrest for the King, ships in Hull and ports west of Hull, to take wheat, wool and other merchandise to Aquitaine, joining the fleet which was being sent principally to bring back wine. The merchants trading in wine can sometimes be traced from the licences granted to them to take money overseas, which they very probably did illicitly in other years. In 1364 those licensed to take money from Hull to bring back wine were Henry de Selby in the *Katerine*, Robert de Selby in his ship strangely named *Hallehalugh*, Richard Bate, John Baynbrigge who was a vintner of York, Walter Box, a Hull vintner, Robert de Fangfoss, another York vintner and Adam and William de Coppendale, both Beverley vintners. Box was allowed to take £50 from Southampton or Plymouth. The total amount of money which could be taken from Hull is not clear, but was certainly more than £300, roughly equivalent to a baronial income for one year.[10]

Because duty was payable on wine, like wool it could be handled only by porters sworn for the purpose. The wine trade was clearly a large one in the fourteenth century, but it is not until the fifteenth century that customs' returns enable us to trace the fluctuations of the trade. In the first half of the century, in most years more than a thousand tuns were landed at Hull and the maximum of 1838 tuns was in 1413-14. In another nineteen years more than 1200 tuns arrived, but in twenty-three years there were fewer than 1000 tuns though usually more than 500. In the second half of the century the trade was smaller and it was only in 1453-4 that more than a thousand tuns arrived. No reliable figures are available after 1481-2, but in eight years there were more than 700 tuns and fewer than 500 tuns in five years only. Though most of the imports were French, German wine was sold in Hull and the bench in 1440-1 spent £29 0s 9d on Rhenish wine, more probably for the entertainment of important persons than for themselves.[11]

In most years when there was no failure of the corn harvest, ships bringing wine from Gascony had sailed with corn. Three Bordeaux merchants were licensed to return from Hull with 500 quarters of corn, which ordinarily could not be sent out of the kingdom without a licence, in 1337, in the ship of William de Briel; Robert de Denton of Hull was licensed to take 600 quarters to Gascony in 1333 and Michael de Redeness of York was allowed to take 500 quarters so long as he gave a bond to be forfeited if he took it to Scotland instead of Gascony. Roger Swerd in 1337 took 400 quarters of wheat, peas and beans, joining the wine fleet at Portsmouth; and William atte Halle of Beverley with Adam de la Botlerie of Driffield and Walter de Echingham of York combined to load 400 quarters of corn into a Zeeland ship bound for Middleburg. John de Dringhouses of York in 1341 obtained a protection for the corn which he was sending to Hull in his ship the *Eleyne*, possibly because it was in danger of being requisitioned if he did not. A merchant of Bruges came to Hull in 1343 for 1000 quarters. Two Spanish merchants in 1347 from Bilbao, probably bringing iron, left with 600 quarters of wheat for Bordeaux, and earlier in the same year John Swerd had taken 600 quarters of wheat to Gascony in the *Seynt Johan* of Hull. The connections with Bordeaux were of such importance that some Hull families were also established in Bordeaux. In 1347 eleven merchants obtained a licence to ship 2600 quarters from Hull to Bordeaux, and three of them who were also Hull men were citizens of Bordeaux — Thomas de Sereby, Richard Upsale and Henry

Taverner.[12]

It would appear from this that it was more usual to export corn to Gascony than to the Netherlands, and that merchants of York, Beverley and Driffield as well as aliens and Hull men were involved in the trade. The quantity licensed for export sometimes exceeded 1000 quarters in one year. In 1354 there were licenced for 1000 quarters, including wheat; in 1355 for 800 quarters only; in 1356 for 3200 and in 1357 for 1000. In 1358 the licence for 1000 quarters — there was no other — went to the King's daughter Isabel, who was to send it from her manors in Holderness. All the licences except one which specified no destination, were for corn to be sent to Gascony, Calais, Holland or Zeeland, and for Hull merchants except in the case of four ships from Zierickzee in Zeeland, which were to load 800 quarters. It was possible for an area as small as Holderness to provide a surplus of 1000 quarters for export. The total area under corn in Lincolnshire and Yorkshire having reasonable facilities for river transport to Hull was probably about 300,000 acres and the quantity sent overseas was therefore rarely more than a fifth of one per cent of the harvest.[13*]

In the second half of the fourteenth century considerable amounts of cloth began to pass through the port. The first recorded export of English cloth from Hull was in 1350-1 when London and Bristol were the leading cloth ports and Hull exported nine cloths only. Ten years later 700 were shipped, but Hull was no more than sixth in importance among the places exporting cloth. Hanse merchants were interested in the trade, but even so Bristol handled ten times as much. In the 1360s the number of cloths passing through Hull was usually more than a thousand a year, and all the time the trade was tending to increase, with Hull usually third after Bristol and London. Piracy, foreign affairs and the low cost of transporting cloth by land (in relation to its value) produced strange fluctuations in the trade and Hull was twice top of the list, with 3400 cloths in 1400-1 and 4200 in 1382-3. In six years in the 1390s more than 4000 went through Hull which was now in most years second only to Bristol, which handled between 5000 and 10,000 cloths.[14].

A fourteenth-century scale of charges fixed for the handling of goods in the town by porters and sled-men correlates closely with a fifteenth-century list and with customers' accounts of imports and therefore shows the kind but not the quantity of goods arriving at the port. These goods were wool and cloth; madder and woad for dyeing, and alum, used as a mordant in cloth-making; oil and wine, including Cretan and Rhenish; wood-ash needed in glass- and soap-making; iron and the high-grade Swedish ore called osmund, timber for ship-building (cogholts), for house-building (clapholts), from Riga (righolts), deals, and Norwegian planks and spars for ship-building; wheat, rye, malt, garlic, onions, herrings, stockfish, saltfish; bow-staves; spices including ginger and pepper; salt and soap; turves (peat), firewood and kidds; lampreys; oxen, sheep and pork; tunny, almonds and rice; ermine, miniver, Cordovan and basil (sheepskin) leather and mercers' goods.[15]

At the end of April 1401 six Hull ships arrived with 200 tuns of wine, three having no other cargo. Between the beginning of April and the middle of July 6080 bow-staves, almost enough for an army, came in thirteen lots, and about 500 tons of Spanish iron (1,114,000 one-pound bars) in thirty-one lots. Much of the salt imported in the same period came with the wine; and there were also corks, canvas, alum, mica, oars, wax, wainscots (Baltic oak), tonholts (wood for barrels), flax, leather, wood-ash, yarn, oil and seed-oil, shuttles for wool and flax, woad, madder, saffron, painted cloths, crape, wooden combs, gloves, daggers, osmund, copper, resin, masts and spars, kettles, flax, leather, dog-skins and dogfish-skins (used in much the same way as sand-paper), one elk-skin, the fur of squirrels, martens and beavers, 2000 patten-clogs, 180 white and 400 black hats, cuttle-bone for smoothing; and a ship was ballasted with 40,000 paving stones and another with 16,000 which were sold. This was quite the most convenient way of getting rid of ballast, which could not be left in the haven or in the roadstead.[16]

In these seventeen weeks of 1401 only thirty-nine merchants trading in the port can definitely be identified as aliens, but so many names were Anglicised that probably more than sixty arrived. Eight were the masters of their ships, but most foreign ship-masters did not bring their own goods. Sixteen of the ships which arrived with cargoes belonged to Hull, and there were twenty-seven others, two of which made two voyages. Three English vessels belonged to Newhaven and one each to York, Beverley and Newcastle. Ten of the foreign ships were from such Netherlands ports as Dordrecht, Skidam, Kampen and Amsterdam. One German ship belonged to Bremen and three others to Dantzig. Twenty-seven ships which discharged also took on board cargoes at Hull — textiles, hides, and sixty quarters of oats.[17]

The dates of arrivals and departures show the effect of contrary winds, and some vessels may have been kept in convoy until they were clear of the dangerous area near the Humber mouth. The forty-five arrivals in the port were confined to twenty-two days, and the twenty-seven departures to twenty-one days. The approaches to the Humber were often infested with pirates. In 1316 a French merchant, coming to Hull in an Ipswich ship with his wine from Bordeaux, was taken at the mouth of the Humber. When Philip de Hedon, Adam the warrener of Cottingham, Robert de Malton and other merchants were sailing from Hull to Flanders they were captured by pirates and taken to Dunkirk, but this piracy may have happened on the other side of the North Sea. This was certainly the case with the Hull ship homeward bound with ashes, boards, flax, pitch and tar which was taken by a pirate of Kampen near Hamburg. Nicholas de Hamburg in 1322 sailing to Hull from the eastern Baltic was captured by pirates off Blakeney; but generally speaking Hull men were more frequently pirates than victims.[18]

Pirates rarely needed to go far to sea since they could make their best captures in or near ports or landfalls. John de Bedford of Hull lost his ship *la Godier* worth £40 carrying £60 worth of goods to Newcastle because she was blown so far north that she reached a Norwegian port, possibly in the Orkneys, and was there plundered by a knight and his men. Sometimes Hull pirates worked far from home. The *Eleyne* of Hull, based on Portsmouth, in 1342 was working with ships from Yarmouth, Ipswich, Blakeney and Sandwich in acts of piracy against foreign ships off the coast of the Isle of Wight. The *Michel* of Hull was in the same waters in 1369. About sunset on the last Friday in July a Breton ship anchored at a haven, no longer identifiable, called Hameloke. A barge from the *Michel* was rowed to her, and the mariners invited William Grysele to come on board. While he was drinking from a cup offered to him, one of the Bretons struck him between the shoulders with an axe. His comrades then boarded the vessel, killed all the Bretons and took away goods on one inquest found to be worth £86 but which another found to be no more than £12. The second inquest was a day later than the first and there may have been suggestions from the Hull men that it would be prudent to name a lower sum; and their advice would be hard to ignore since they had armour for twenty men and sixty bows and arrows. With an armament like this they can have been nothing but pirates.[19]

But all started from and most eventually returned to the haven, which had probably existed before the town, and for more than six centuries was its most important asset. In the earliest times goods must have been sold in the ships which bought them and unloaded over the side into keels and boats from York and Beverley. In 1280, however, the Sheriff of Yorkshire was ordered to proclaim at Hull that heavy penalties would be exacted from anyone offering his goods for sale before they had been landed. The aim was no doubt to defeat the archbishop's claims to tolls in the water of Hull, but for centuries it remained part of the fundamental law of trading in the town — everything must be landed before sale. The King's bailiff, Richard Oysel, was directed in 1297 to make a new quay for loading, discharging and weighing. It may be assumed that this was the quay at King's Stathe. The fourteenth-century rentals, however, show that there were numerous stathes in addition to this, each with its own quay which was rarely called a quay but almost always a stathe, so that the word came to mean both the narrow paved road leading to the river bank and the jetty of stone and timber at the eastern end of it. As long as the town remained under the rule of a keeper, the Crown undertook the repair of the Humber banks and those of the haven, spending £40 in 1313. There was a proclamation in 1321 directing that ships should not drop their ballast into the haven, causing obstacles to navigation, and this also remained a permanent part of town law. At first offenders were merely to remove it at their own expense, but since it often was irremovable, when, for instance, it consisted of gravel, increasingly heavy fines were imposed.[20]

The maintenance of the haven was made harder by the fact that the town had no control over its eastern side, and as Sir John de Sutton had lost his ferry over the Hull he can hardly have been disposed to grant any. In the reign of Edward III, however, he or a later Sir John de Sutton was alleged to have built a fort at the entrance of the haven, blocking the entrance to the port, but this turned out to be no more than a guard-house, built when there was a danger of foreign invasion, sixty feet long and twenty-five broad, with walls of plaster and a tiled roof. In 1377, as Sir Thomas de

Sutton of Holderness, he granted to the town a strip of land on the east bank of the Hull in Drypool, ten yards from north to south, and a hundred from east to west, on a ten-year lease for a nominal rent of one rose a year 'for a tower for the safety and defence of the town.' This was immediately north of the quay which served the ferry across the Hull.[21]

The trade and shipping of the fourteenth century as we have seen them, required a substantial town for their support — for wharves, shipbuilding and repairing, warehouses and houses for the customs' officials. The town had to exist in a very inconvenient situation, with a supply of water sometimes insufficient, and with frequent risk of floods from the Humber. The site was not entirely exposed to floods, since the earliest rentals show perhaps as much as 200 acres of ploughed land for corn existing in Wyke and *Suthwyk*, before building began. Floods not only did damage to property in the town. They also destroyed the banks of the Humber and carried dry land away; and they interrupted the water-supply, which from the late thirteenth-century or earlier had been coming from Anlaby and the land of John, Lord Wake (1292) along *Dernynghamdyke*. In March 1355 the Humber broke its banks and flooded the corn and grasslands of Myton and Hull. It seems likely that in the neighbourhood of Hull the flood water was not less than five feet deep since it was found that the road to Anlaby could only be made passable in a flood if its level was raised by six feet. On this occasion the town itself must have been inundated, as it has been so often since, and it was recommended that within the boundaries a sewer should be made from the end of *Oldehull* to the Humber. For the proper prevention of flooding it was also necessary to have a sewer from *Woldegate* up to the *Fourches* and so to the Humber, with a sluice, the cost being shared between Hull, Hessle, Ferriby, Swanland, *Braythwayt*, Westella, Willerby, Wolfreton, Anlaby, the priors of Ferriby and Haltemprice and Sir William de la Pole.[22*]

From the beginning there was a ditch round the town, but the actual boundaries were beyond the ditch. It was not until 1321 that a wall was contemplated, with battlements for defence. A year later the town was given the right to collect murage (a toll for the making or repair of a wall) for five years. In 1322 it seems more than probable that the people could see the fires of the Scots camped at High Hunsley after their victory over Edward II at

Byland, but the town was strong enough, or the Scots felt themselves already too far from home, to make it unnecessary to pay them the blackmail paid by Pickering, Driffield, Beverley and Bridlington. Possibly nothing much was done since again in 1327 the town was given permission to build a wall with battlements and also to fortify houses inside the wall, using stone or brick. Later illustrations and recent excavation show the walls to have been of such enormous size that it is surprising that there is no clear evidence of their existence until 1339 when Robert de Lichfield was given leave to build his house on part of the wall facing the Humber, the town retaining the right to take it over in time of war or during a siege. The circuit of the wall was incomplete when the pestilence of 1349 killed a great part of the inhabitants. In 1353, with the work still incomplete, it was claimed that most of them had died. The possibility that this may be true is not discounted by the fact that no indication of any falling off in trade can be detected, and it may be worth noting that in a similar, smaller, enclosed community a few miles away there were forty-nine monks and lay brethren at Meaux before the pestilence and only ten when it had ceased; and that immediately opposite Hull on the other side of the Humber, Barrow needed three new vicars in one year. By 1356 the whole circuit was probably complete. In that year the town leased building plots outside the wall from the west postern (the west end of the present-day Posterngate) to the new tilery and the Humber — with a clause requiring the tenants to maintain the banks of the river. By 1377 repairs were needed — a French invasion was feared — and the King ordered that everyone with property in Hull, whether he lived there or not, should pay his share towards the upkeep of the defences. But fear of an invasion did not deter people from living outside the walls. Richard Upsall, chaplain (1389), had a house and garden which had encroached on the common way round the walls on the west side, and he had to agree to give up twenty feet.[23]

From the earlier fourteenth century, if not earlier, the town had its own special code of law, written in French, which was still probably the language spoken by most of the burgesses. The procedure was expeditious. What would seem most peculiar to us about it was that in many cases a burgess could, instead of accepting trial by jury, produce a number of oath-helpers, whose oath, if properly made, could acquit him. This was probably no more likely to lead to injustice than trial by a jury of his peers and was the practice in many towns and in all church courts. The Hull code does not specify the number of oath-helpers required, but it probably ranged from twelve to thirty-six, according to the seriousness of the case.

The code, in Latin, not in French, which regulated the sale of corn, bread, ale and wine, looks very early, but from a reference to the mayor may date from 1331 or later. For the ordinary inhabitant the price and supply of bread was probably the most important thing of all. The price was regulated by the assize of bread, which the town was to change from time to time according to directions received from the King's marshal. The assize would be altered only when the price of corn changed by sixpence a quarter. A baker was allowed to make a profit of three pence on a quarter of corn and also have the bran and two loaves for himself, after charging for three servants at one-and-a-half pence each, two lads at a ha'penny each, a ha'penny for yeast, a ha'penny for his bushel measure and a ha'penny for salt. He was to bake bread of three qualities, as well as wastel, which was made only from the finest flour. For selling bread underweight he could be fined thirty pence or more and for the third offence be put in the pillory, a penalty which he could not escape by paying a much larger fine. The pillory or the thew must always be ready so that offenders could suffer punishment at the peril of their bodies.

So long as the farmer of the mill provided all things necessary, the miller must take only his proper toll. This was to be one-twentieth, taken by the level measure.

The assize of ale could be altered by a quarter-of-a-penny a gallon when the price of corn changed by twelve pence a quarter. The brewer is assumed to be a woman. For the first three breaches of the assize she would be fined, but for a third would be put in the tumbrel and drawn round the town. Wine was to be sold at the very high price of twelve pence a pint, and if the assize was broken the mayor and bailiffs would close the tavern, which could not be re-opened until the offender had made his peace with the King.[24*]

The commercial law was in part governed by statute and in part by local custom. The charter of 1334 granted Hull the status of a town in which the special seal was to be provided under the statute of Acton Burnel (1283) and the Statute of Merchants (1285). The mayor would have one-half of the seal and a clerk appointed by the Crown the other. Any loan granted under a bond with this seal would result in the immediate imprisonment of the debtor if he defaulted. If he still failed to settle, the creditor could take his chattels and hold his land until the debt had been paid out of the revenues. The effect of this was to make it possible for knights, squires and feudal magnates to raise money from such millionaires as the de la Poles and John Swanland, farmer of the customs in Hull, who may have been the person of that name who in 1348 with Walter de Chiriton farmed all the customs of England.[25]

It may be supposed that in these circumstances a considerable disparity appeared between the ordinary merchants and burgesses and the great men; but in most boroughs custom tended to favour, but not to establish, an equality, and though the Hull customs were less rigid than those of such old-established boroughs as Scarborough and Grimsby, there was at times a strong current of opinion in favour of greater equality. Ordinances of 1355 required, as was the case elsewhere, that alien merchants coming to Hull should find a host to sponsor them; but a host must not use his position to obtain more than his proper share of foreign merchandise. Proper shares were then defined in such a way as to make it clear that the aim was to establish equal opportunities for all merchants, not for all inhabitants. The shares which could be bought from foreigners, and the implication is that no smaller shares could normally be bought from them, were too large for any but merchants. No ordinary person would be interested in half a hundred (which may mean sixty) bundles of garlic, twenty barrels of onions, two tons of tar, or two-and-a-half hundred (probably 280) boards. But the ordinary townsmen were not forgotten. Anyone buying coal, saltfish or oysters at the haven was to allow anyone belonging to the town to have his share at cost price. In some cases buying must take place in the common tavern, and no sale was to take place after dark, or in secret at any time.

These ordinances reiterated the prohibition against forestalling which the Crown had already forbidden in much stronger terms. The makers of the 1355 laws were simply concerned that no one should forestall wine; that is, that he should not go out into the Humber to buy it before the ship had come to land, and that in particular he should not buy the wine which belonged to the mariners as distinct from that belonging to the merchants, which, when they were Hull men who had been to Gascony with the ship, would not be for sale except retail. The royal ordinance against forestallers, not exactly dateable but earlier than this, had called them public enemies and oppressors of the poor, intercepting before they reached the market such articles as corn, fish or herrings, pretending to the vendors that they would give them a higher price than they could get in the open market place. Heavy penalties were prescribed, with perpetual expulsion from the town for a fourth offence. Similar penalties were prescribed for anyone adulterating flour.[26*]

It seems probable that these local laws were still effective ten years later when they were modified in a manner which could only make for greater equality. There was now other merchandise to which the ordinary inhabitants could claim a share — herrings, boards, tar, pitch, garlic, onions and bow-staves. Herrings were a principal source of protein, and garlic and onions offered the cheapest way of making rotten or salty food palatable. Hull was full of people with boats who would need boards, pitch and tar, and a man who went to sea without a bow and arrows expected too much of Providence. No burgess could sell any of these things for his own profit until he had openly offered them to the inhabitants in the common tavern, and he had to wait a fortnight before he could send any of them away from the town.[27]

The royal ordinances against forestalling had been delivered with the standard bushel, gallon, yard and pound to the mayor and six lawful men, and it seems likely that Hull was governed for most of the time up to 1835 by a small and sometimes a very small oligarchy. In 1379, however, an attempt was made to devise a constitution, possibly short-lived, for an almost democratic system of government through annual free elections by the 177 burgesses, a number likely to increase continually through new arrivals in the town and in any case probably outnumbering the men who were not burgesses. They all met on 29 September, the day on which the election of officers was always held. Each year they agreed that they were to elect a new mayor with eight burgesses to share the government with him, and also two bailiffs and two chamberlains. Those elected to this body of thirteen would not be eligible for re-election until three years had elapsed, and in this way the government of the town would never be shared between fewer than thirty-nine burgesses elected by their fellows. There is no evidence that this populism lasted for long, and many indications that at all other known times the town was controlled by a body of burgesses, elected by their fellows, but elected for life, and only if they were nominated as one of the two put forward by the other twelve. The burgesses at large had virtually no freedom of choice, and if the bench was representative, this was never by design.[28]

Sources

1. Carus-Wilson, *England's Export Trade, 1275-1547.*, 36-48, 122.
2. *CPR* 1266-72, 47; *CPR* 1301-7, 548; *CPR* 1272-81, 50; *CPR* 1292-1301, 322; *CIM*, ii, Nos. 1728, 1628, 1341, 1772.
3. *CIM*, iii, No. 675; *CPR* 1343-5, 213.
4. *CCR* 1343-6, 93; *CPR* 1361-4, 288.
5. BB3, f.23.
6. *DNB*, s.v. POLE de la, MICHAEL, RICHARD, SIR WILLIAM and WILLIAM; A.S. Harvey, *The de la Pole Family of Kingston Upon Hull.*, M. McKisack, *The Fourteenth Century*, 156-7; *CCR* 1343-6, 138, 145.
7. *CPR* 1321-4, 217; BB2, f.169, undated; *CCR* 1302-7, 25.
8. *CCR* 1307-13, 172; *CPR* 1327-30, 236; *CIM*, ii, No. 703.
9. *CPR* 1364-7, 231; *CCR* 1339-41, 29, 324; *CPR* 1340-3, 345.
10. *CPR* 1313-17, 169; *CCR* 1296-1302, 248; *CPR* 1307-13, 235; *CCR* 1323-7, 567; *CPR* 1334-8, 566; *CPR* 1364-7, 15-17.
11. E. Power, *Studies in English Trade in the Fifteenth Century*, 341-2; Chamb. 19 Hen. VI.
12. *CPR* 1334-8, 414; *CPR* 1331-4, 414, 423; *CPR* 1340-3, 306; *CPR* 1343-6, 205; BB2, Rental of 22 Edw. III.
13.* *CPR* 1354-8, 43, 94, 285, 467, 472, 477, 518, 346; *CPR* 1358-61, 6. The tentative calculation of the small proportion of the harvest *known* to have been exported rests on the assumption that 300 acres would produce 1000 quarters then as against about 32,000 quarters in 1979 on average to poor East Riding land. The total acreage under the plough before the Pestilence of 1349 is assumed to be less than the 380,000 acres of ploughed land in the East Riding in 1918 — say 300,000 acres. Much of the best land was too far from Hull or from a navigable stream to transport corn,but a large acreage in Lincolnshire and the rest of Yorkshire had access to Hull by water. It is therefore thought reasonable to put the acreage from which any surplus could be conveyed to Hull at 300,000. The surplus shipped coastwise to London and the north must have been far larger. In one year the ninth Abbot of Meaux (*Chronicon de Melsa*, ii, 109) had 400 quarters in store in one single grange at Skerne, from which there was access by river to Hull.
14. Carus-Wilson, op.cit., 81-6.
15. BB2, f.169; BB3, f.19; C. Singer and Others, *A History of Technology*, ii, 354-6 (potash) and 366-9 (alum).
16. Frost, *Notices Relative to . . . Hull.*, Appendix, 1-18.
17. Ibid.
18. *CPR* 1313-17, 580; *CCR* 1302-7, 29; *CPR* 1307-13, 211; *CPR* 1321-4, 159.
19. *CCR* 1318-21, 52; *CCR* 1340-3, 594; *CIM*, iii, No. 732.

20. Frost, op.cit., citing BB2, f.75; *CCR* 1313-18, 29, 291.
21. YASRS, *Yorkshire Inquisitions*, iv, 147, footnote 'b'. BB3, f.44.
22.* BB2, f.130; BB3, f.40; BB2, f.79 (1347 Rental). *Oldehull*, also written as *Holdehull*, was 79 feet from Dagger Lane at the south end of the lane. The mill-race, assumed to be on or connected with the Old Hull was 764 feet north of the common way outside the town ditch, probably at a point now marked by High Flags, Wincolmlee. I am indebted to Mr W. Foot Walker for drawing my attention to the significance of High Flags.
23. BB3, f.40; G. Poulson, *Beverlac*, 92 ff; *Chronicon de Melsa*, ii, 246; *Gesta Edwardi de Carnarvon Auctore Bridlingtoniensi (Rolls Series)*, 79-81; BB2, f.196; *CPR 1350-4*, 417; BB2, f.236.
24.* The beginning of Bench Book I is not foliated. The French code of law is followed by the royal ordinances on bakers, brewers, vintners and forestallers.
25. T.T.F. Plucknett, *A Concise History of the Common Law* (5th edition) 392-3.
26.* *CCR 1346-9*, 446. The 'long hundred' of 120 remained in use until the nineteenth century in many parts of England which had come under Viking influence. BB2, f.147; BB1, unfoliated.
27. BB2, f.147, f.161.
28. BB2, f.210.

3

Houses, Walls and Water

It would be easy to collect from the records of the fourteenth and fifteenth centuries a repertory of extracts which would depict medieval Hull as an inhabited dunghill beside an open sewer. At the sheriffs' courts several persons were usually fined for the nuisance caused by their manure heaps, and in 1488 the church-wardens had a dunghill which encroached beyond the church gate. In the same year two men paid trivial fines for having dead mares in the sewer, and another man was fined twopence for washing skins in it.[1] Further, a sewer ran through the centre of the town from the churchyard of Holy Trinity to the north walls. But a picture of squalor would have as little relation to medieval reality as the *Morte d'Arthur*. Dunghills were an essential feature of an economy so closely related to agriculture and dependent on the use of horses. The town may well have smelt better than many villages, and a dunghill in the wrong place was the medieval equivalent of a car causing an obstruction. And sewer had a meaning then very different from that which it has now. A sewer was an open ditch, usually with flowing water, not ordinarily contaminated with dead horses. Indeed this particular sewer ran through a pond against the churchyard of Holy Trinity and fresh water was taken from it both for the church and for the almshouse of thirteen people in the churchyard.[2] It was the duty of the chamberlains to pay for the regular cleansing of the common sewer, and in the part against the moot-hall, which the guildhall or common hall was sometimes called, about six man-days a year were spent in keeping it clean. In 1450 William Chanon was fined for stopping the ditch at the southwest corner of the churchyard and John Andelot, merchant, for not keeping the gutter opposite his house clear.[3]

The pond against Holy Trinity was an important piece of town property about which there was a dispute with the Prior of Guisborough to whom the church belonged. In 1455 the common bell was rung to bring all the burgesses to the guildhall to consider the case of John Costard who had rented it from the prior and allowed it to become obstructed. Anyone who rented it from the prior in the future would be very heavily fined, and, if he was a burgess, would also be disfranchised.[4] The water in the town ditches was so fresh that in 1422 an order was made that no one was to fish in them except with the permission, or in the presence, of the mayor.[5] Reeds grew in the ditches, probably here identical with the moat, and there were swans. An order to get rid of them was made in 1472, but they were still there sixteen years later.[6]

Dead horses do from time to time occur in connection with the water supply, but they were almost certainly put in maliciously. The proper place for them was ground set aside for their burial outside the walls and known as *Dede Horssekirkgarth*.[7] Stable and household refuse was put, or should have been put, into the muck-cart which went around the town three times a week and then tipped its load outside the *Mamhole* at the south end of the town, to be carried away by the tide.[8] There must have been occasional lapses, when householders simply dumped their refuse in the street if the cart had not arrived, but all surviving financial accounts show that there always was a muck-cart, and it is to be assumed that the streets were not allowed to become really insanitary. The accumulation of debris revealed by excavation may be accounted for by the continual repair of the road surface, then always called the pavement, and probably also by the tipping of ashes into the mud on the road. If the town stank in the eighteenth century, when the growth of population had overfilled the space inside the walls, it is not to be assumed that it was worse in the Middle Ages. On the contrary, there is every reason to suppose that it was much better and that the ancient system of borough administration was adequate to deal with most of the purely physical problems which arose from the presence of 2000 or so people inside a fortified area, much of which was open ground without buildings.

There were seasons in which the town was virtually an island in a sea of flood water. It was found in 1365 that on the Holderness side the banks of the Humber had not been kept in repair at a place called the *Stelle* which pertained to Hull as well as to Southcoates, and in January and February there were huge floods.[9] Nothing on the Holderness side actually belonged to Hull, but it was in the interests of the town to keep roads from Holderness clear of flood water, and it may have been about this time that Hull took part in the construction of a waterway which in the following century appears on the Drypool side of the *Were*. It must have been of considerable importance to the town since in 1444 more than £53, which was about one-third of the total corporate expenditure in that year, was spent on it.[10]

Elsewhere there was frequent flooding, almost certainly with fresh water and not by the tide, since it was necessary to maintain a raised causeway for access to the Bushdike, the main source of fresh water at Beverley Gate. This causeway was called the *Wayour* and almost every year repairs were needed — in 1426-7 fifty-six cartloads of stones and twenty of sand requiring forty-five man-days, in 1447-8 twenty tons of cobbles, and in 1456-7 1000 bricks and 90 long kidds brought from Cottingham in three cart-loads as a revetment for the bank. A windmill was in the same vicinity and probably could not be approached except by the *Wayour*, or later, by a bridge.[11]*

The maintenance of roads in the town was less expensive, partly because the site was naturally drier, or the town would never have been there, and partly because wheeled traffic was rare. Sleds, probably rarely bearing more than five hundredweights, were the usual form of goods transport. In 1467-8 the toll on carts coming to the town shod with iron yielded only sixpence, and this had increased to no more than twenty pence by the end of the century.[12] Apart from the scale of charges which their owners could take, the only restriction on sleds seems to have been that they could not enter the ropery. All were horse-drawn, and horses were almost certainly used as pack-animals. For some reason, possibly connected with the fact that they would use any grass-land they had for beasts ready for slaughter, butchers had a bad name as early as 1409 for keeping their horses tethered day and night outside their shops, obstructing traffic, and, in particular, priests bearing the sacrament.[13]

Though the surface could not be kept free from horse-dung with mud in rainy and dust in dry weather, it was probably well main-tained. In a typical year street repairs required fourteen man-days to lay ketch-loads of stone in a ketch-load of sand.[14] Chapel Staithe in High Street in 1448, because it carried heavier traffic to and from the quay which was also called a staithe, needed twenty-four tons of stone laid in thirty tons of sand. Probably clay, already there, was rammed between the stones, as it certainly was in Horse Staithe where two cartloads of clay were used along with the stones. A post was set at the end of Chapel Staithe, most probably to prevent the entry of sleds or carts, since most goods would simply be carried by porters.[15] Probably most of the goods imported and exported never came into the town streets at all but passed along the riverside staithes into warehouses. Only the very small quantities of goods needed in the town by the inhabitants and perhaps about as much needed by people in nearby villages would ever leave the banks of the Hull and be carried by road. This would account for the absence of any evidence whatever of really bad roads in the town in spite of the fact that road maintenance was clearly very little of a burden. When Thomas Whyte was appointed bellman in 1477 he also became the official paver, gravedigger and sexton of both churches, with leave to be away from the town up to eight weeks a year so long as he found a substitute. Because he could make something out of his private practice as a bellman, although he was given a house rent free, he got nothing for repairing any length of road less than sixteen-and-a-half feet. For more extensive repairs he got sixteen pence for each additional sixteen-and-a-half feet, which suggests that this would keep him employed between three and four days, and in all cases the town provided the materials and paid his labourer.[16] There was still a bellman in Victorian times.

All the information we have on secular buildings suggests a high and improving standard, but all our sources deal with town property, and it may be that there were older buildings less solidly constructed. The collapse of buildings of this type may account for some of the plots referred to as waste. This must have been the case with two in the flesh-market once occupied by Ralph Barton, on which in 1455 it was decided to build.[17] But next to the moot-hall there was a waste plot never built on in the Middle Ages, a fair indication of how little the town was congested, and by 1457 it had become a pinfold.[18]

Everything seems to indicate that the buildings owned by the town were well built. Outside the walls, near Mytongate bridge

1. Early fourteenth-century timber revetment, River Hull. View from east of early fourteenth- century revetment at 28 High Street forming part of the medieval waterfront some 60 metres west of present bank of the River Hull. This feature continues to a full height of 3.47 metres.

2. Holy Trinity Church: pew-end of St George and
the dragon. One of a pair.

and Buttecroft dike, there was the tilery, which long produced most of the bricks used in Hull. It was surrounded by a dike over which there was a wooden bridge.[19] In 1423-4 100,000 bricks or tiles were made there for just over £23 and sold for £25.[20] Each clamp could be used only for a single firing, with turf as the fuel. The brick-clay seems to have been dug on the site. In that year it was moved by two men with wheelbarrows, who then moulded it. Five men loaded the clamp and tended it while the bricks were burned. In the course of the year three clamps were made. The clay was tempered with one ketch-load of sand. When necessary, as water transport cost little, bricks could also be obtained from Beverley. In 1456-7 1000 were bought for 3*s* 4*d*, and 1000 tiles for 7*s*.[21]

Though brick was widely used, many buildings, including some of the most important, were of post-and-truss construction with the spaces between the timbers filled by a mixture of mud, sand, lime and cow-dung over laths. Repairs to the weigh-house, once known as the wool-house, needed no bricks in a year when nine cartloads of sand and lime were used.[22] In 1447-8 much timber was used in repairing it, with seventy-four cartloads of mud. The roof was part lead and part tiled. In 1467-8 much of it was re-roofed by craftsmen surnamed *Sclater* with their labourers, using 7500 tiles, 3000 laths and 17,000 nails of various kinds; but under the laths and tiles the rafters and principals were still sound as no fresh timber was used.[23] Reeds kept the earth of the ground floor slightly damp to prevent dust.

There were still thatched roofs, but none are found in houses belonging to the corporation. The flesh-market, however, at the end of Denton Lane,[24] had a timber penthouse roof protected by a composition of pitch, tar and tallow.[25] The house where John Aldwyk lived was larger than most. He had been mayor in 1439-40 and died in 1444.[26] Repairs in one year needed 69 ridge-tiles, 1260 roof-tiles and 2000 brodnails.[27] In the same year, 1447-8, the house of Seman Burton, twice mayor, was repaired for £8, a sum nearly big enough to buy a small house. It had a counting-house roofed with fifty-two stones of lead, and windows, probably glazed, in a room called the *somer-hall*, which had probably been added to the original hall. Repairs to this newer hall were done with 2000 bricks. A tiler and his mate — the work actually being shared between four men — worked ten days on the roof and used 24 ridge-tiles and 3000 roof tiles. The gutters were of lead. The brickwork of the house may simply have been the nogging between timber posts, since much timber was used in the repairs and a wright and his mate worked for seven-and-a-half days. There was at least one central hearth without a chimney.[28]

There were still central hearths all over the town with the smoke rising through a vent in the roof covered by a slatted louvre. In the same year many louvres were repaired, and two houses, one of them certainly tiled, had five louvres. But two chimneys were also repaired.[29] With a chimney there was less risk of fire, and more were built in the course of the fifteenth century. In 1482-3 three chimneys were repaired, but no louvres.[30] In 1498-9 no louvres appear in the accounts, but at least six chimneys were repaired in various parts of the town.[31] Some louvres were enormous. In 1457 one house needed fifty *fyvefotebords* and it may therefore have had an octagonal louvre of more than eight feet diameter.[32]

Though windows were often repaired, the work done was with brick or wood, not with glass. Where there was glass it would still be regarded as part of the tenant's furniture which he could take with him when he left the house. One of the few indications of the use of glass was the construction in 1467-8 of a window over the dais in the council chamber at the Guildhall. It must have been quite large as a glazier worked on it for five days and used glass costing seven pence.[33] Some houses had an internal water supply. Wells have been uncovered in the course of excavations, but they could supply only poor though drinkable water, most probably used for washing. Henry Halibrand had a pump in his solar, and some houses had the fresh water from Anlaby piped in.[34]

When the town built houses as an investment it did not supply either glass or lead water pipes. In 1454-5 the complete rebuilding of John Aldwyk's house in Lowgate cost £42.[35] The cost of building a smaller house in 1439-40 was no more than £12, and it is most unlikely that it was jerry-built.[36] It was simply described as being in the southern part of the town, and therefore possibly not on any known street, or even on land recently reclaimed. A house costing slightly less than this, wholly timber-framed, with a tiled roof, was started on 6 October 1498 and completed on 25 November. At times more than twenty men were working on it. There was another, probably of about seventeen by twenty feet, started on 13 April 1499 and finished on 24 June. It was partly of brick and was roofed with 3500 tiles. The total cost was £15 16s.[37]

In the later Middle Ages much of the corporation revenue came from house rents and houses like these were built as an investment; but as new houses became available, some of the old ones decayed. By 1499, when £113 might have been collected in rents only £65 was actually received.[38] In 1423-4 before any expansion of this kind had been undertaken the rental was £47 and £45 was received, with no more than six properties vacant.[39] By the end of the century nine houses in Kirklane were falling down, nine had no tenant, and 63 could be let only at reduced rents. Even in 1456 the house at the corner of Scale Lane where John Bedford, twice mayor, had lived, had to be let to Margaret Yonker who left without paying any rent, and the tenant of another large house was equally unprofitable. Helward Place in High Street, perhaps dating from the earliest days of the town, was so substantial that the rent was £4 a year; but in 1498 one tenant had part of it for £3 3s 4d a year and the rest was let to three different people, one of whom used his room to store 200 boards.[40]

By far the most impressive secular building in the town was the manor house of the de la Poles, on the site corresponding approximately to that now occupied by the central post office and Manor Street. The seventeenth-century plans of Speed and Hollar show it with a tower hardly smaller than that of Holy Trinity. The house was not a palace, but simply the kind of large manor house which every nobleman expected to have on each of his big estates; and the de la Pole Hull estate was worth £425 a year when Michael, Earl of Suffolk, a favourite of Richard II and immensely wealthy, died in exile in 1389 in Paris.[41] The house stood in three gardens, each with a pond, and there were two dovecotes. The roof was so large that 4000 tiles were kept for repairs. Inside, there was a hall and a summer hall, eighteen chambers, one being above the chapel, two wine cellars, a pantry, a buttery, a kitchen and a bakehouse. Spoons and other silver were worth £95. It will be seen how large a quantity of plate this was when it is realised that his ship, the *Philip*, lying in the haven, was valued at £80 and thus was worth at least twice as much as any ordinary ship. In Hull and Myton he had seventeen bovates of arable land and his rents from town property brought him £77 a year. By far the greater part of his Hull income accrued from royal grants out of the customs and the fee-farm rent.[42] The King's final favour to him was to connive at his escape to the Continent when he sailed from Hull, probably to Dordrecht.

The town walls with their gates and interval towers were so enormous that they may perhaps have cost as much as all the other buildings in Hull taken together. In addition to more than twenty rectangular interval towers, there was a tower over the Mamhole where a gate gave access to the Humber, and barbicans spanning the moat, with inner and outer gates at Hessle Gate against the Humber and at North Gate near the ferry over the Hull at the north end of the High Street.[43] [These, and Beverley Gate, were referred to in the plural only, almost until the time when the walls and gates had ceased to exist.] There was a barbican at Beverley Gate also, but this was wholly inside the moat.[44]

The Mamhole, sometimes written without 'the', meant the ground outside against the river as well as the gate. The year 1466 was exceptional in that the town had a surplus in its revenue, so it was decided to drive fresh piles at Mamhole to prevent damage by the Humber.[45] There was a jetty, damaged in 1472-3 by a ship laden with timber, and the owners were made to repair it. Porters were not allowed to enter the town there, or they would have used the jetty for discharging cargo, and a keeper of the Mamhole was appointed.[46] There was also a refuse pit, which may explain why the living accommodation in the tower did not always have a tenant. In 1437 tilers worked on the roof there for fifty-six days, which indicates that the whole area of the barbican, and not simply the towers at Mamhole, may have been roofed.[47] The jetty was partly of stone, and occasionally a ketch-load of stones had to be brought for repairs, with kidds for the revetment of the Humber bank. In one year 660 of them were used, and the piles were reinforced with two hundredweights of iron.[48]

At Beverley Gate there was a chain repaired in 1468 with a whole hundredweight of iron.[49] When the roofs of the interval towers needed repairing lead was used — in 1498-9 eighty stones — and it seems that most of these roofs must have been of lead.[50] Stone from Ellerker as well as brick was used in maintaining the walls themselves.[51] In addition to the gates there were at least three posterns wide enough for only one or two people on foot, and over each there was a tower. From time to time one of the posterns was blocked up or reopened. The thickness of the walls made the construction of a new postern difficult. When one was made in

1423-4, 10,500 new bricks were needed in addition to old ones re-used.[52] Each postern needed a keeper, though in normal times it was left open in daylight hours. When John Gower was absent in 1454 it was arranged that John Wright should keep the key of the postern to the Charterhouse.[53] When the Duke of Suffolk was expected with his wife and mother in 1465 he needed a new postern so that he could reach the Charterhouse without having to go through any part of the town. The bench decided to make one if his receiver provided the materials so long as this was not taken as a precedent. The Duke was to have a tun of wine if he came.[54]

The inhabitants treated the walls quite casually except when the town was in danger. Robert Brygge was caught stealing stones from part of the wall in 1488. Either he worked hard at it, or this was a part of the wall so neglected that the stones were loose.[55] In 1486 Robert Boutham was fined two pence because his pigs damaged the walls, which also suggests a good deal of loose masonry, but Henry Fisher had to pay threepence because his pigs committed the more serious offence of walking in the streets.[56] Some people found it convenient to live in towers on the walls, and the inner side of the north walls, with a good southern exposure, was used in 1483 by two walkers who paid 6*s* 8*d* for the right to hang their cloth to dry after dyeing between the North Gate and Beverley Gate,[57] making good any damage they caused, while on the same terms shearmen had another part of the walls for the tenters on which they stretched their cloth. The privilege of making cloth was restricted to masters. Under heavy penalties journeyman weavers and fullers were forbidden to make cloth in their own houses.[58]

The walls extended along the north, west, and south sides of the town, so close to the Humber that it was only at Mamhole that any land was left outside. In the fourteenth century much land outside the town ditch fell into the Humber, and the place where *Mylkestrete* had been in 1347 no longer existed.[59] On the eastern side, against the haven, there were no walls, and there could be none without the demolition of the riverside end of all the houses on that side of High Street, the most important part of the town; but the haven served as so wide and so deep a moat that there could be little danger from that side until the use of guns became general. The staithes from High Street to the quays were so narrow that from the Holderness side the line of merchants' houses must have looked like a continuous wall until it thinned out towards the northern end of the town. This was where Hull was most vulnerable; and in 1470 when there was civil war in Yorkshire it was decided to take up the jetty on the Drypool side so that there could be no place outside the control of the town where an assault force could embark. Each burgess agreed to contribute to the cost according to his means.[60] It was probably the jetty opposite Horsestaithe which was taken up. Horsestaithe was near the south end of High Street.[61] The other jetty, for the ferry over the Hull, could be dominated by firing from the top of the North Gate.

Most of the quays by the side of the haven were private property but some belonged to the corporation. In 1426-7 the chamberlains paid for 300 pounds of iron needed for the quay at Horsestaithe,[62] and eight ketch-loads of stone were used with four bundles of litter on Hurystaithe, the Humber bank, and the jetty at the entrance of the haven.[63] The rebuilding of the quay at Chapelstaithe in 1451-2 cost £6 14s 2d. The jetty at the haven mouth could be used by ships arriving to moor for no more than one tide, and this restriction applied to all vessels moored or anchored anywhere south of the post at Grimsbystaithe.[64] Making fast a vessel under sail in a strong tide led to occasional collisions which damaged the jetty. When the *Gregory* collided with it in 1452 one of her owners, Thomas Hawton, agreed to provide a ketch-load of stone for repairs.[65]* A ship on fire in the haven was a much greater danger, but no orders against this contingency are recorded until much later when it had become less easy, with more congestion and ships of greater tonnage, to move a burning ship to the east side where the fire could not spread. Nevertheless the bench thought it prudent to record that a ship of Zeeland, of which William Stayes was master, caught fire in the haven on 15 August 1453 and was burned with a cargo belonging to York and Hull merchants.[66]

The staithes leading from High Street to the quays were kept in repair by the corporation. The re-making of Chapelstaithe cost £6 14s 2d, and Horse-, Rotenheryng-, Hornse- and Danyelstaithes were repaired at the same time. The word was used both for the quay and for the road in most cases and it is not always clear which kind of staithe was being repaired. The latrine at Kingstaithe made in 1442 was probably on the quay, and it was a structure with which some care was taken as it cost more than £5.[67] The fourteen tons of stone used at Rotenheryngstaithe were certainly for the road as a paver laid it in clay. A lock was provided at the end of this staithe, and there were gates at the end of every staithe locked at night.[68]

Frequent changes in the shoals of the Humber and the example of what was happening at Grimsby and Hedon aroused fears that the haven might be silted up. With many sections of the Humber bank very weak and much of the surrounding country waterlogged there was always the possibility that a season of heavy rain which normally would scour the haven might instead cause floods as disastrous as those of 1253 in which the main stream of the Hull would shift into a fresh channel, leaving the town stranded against a re-born and shallow Sayer creek. Everything possible had to be done to save the haven. There were strong fears of silting in 1453, and thereafter there were frequent orders against putting anything into it which might make the silting worse.[69] Edward IV granted a toll for the maintenance of the haven 'the weal whereof is treasure to all the realm of England'. Keels passing through without discharging, and the smallest ships, were to pay a toll of only four pence, but the largest, of a hundred tons and more, had to pay 3*s*.[70] In 1482-3 just over £9 was raised in this way, and ships arriving and departing from the haven paid nearly £3.[71]

The banks of the haven could be damaged by shipmasters casting their anchor on the green shore instead of anchoring or mooring properly. It was a device which entirely eliminated the risk of losing an anchor, but it was prohibited by an order of 1435-6.[72] The greatest preventable danger came from the deposition of ballast and town refuse. The haven had been damaged by floods and erosion which left the eroded soil as mudbanks, and the old order against using the haven for refuse disposal was renewed. This was the main reason for having the two-wheeled muck-cart;[73] and in 1481 the man who went round with it became the top salaried official of the corporation, though certainly not the first in precedence, with a salary of £6 13*s* 4*d* a year and the herbage of the tilery for his horse. At the same time it was ordered that all the holes in the quays through which refuse had been dropped should be stopped up.[74]

Another ancient order against discharging ballast into the haven was renewed in 1453. The seriousness of the offence was emphasised by the unusually heavy fine of 13*s* 4*d* imposed on Richard Fille of Dunwich for putting his ballast over the side.[75]

The bell was rung in August 1461 to bring the commons to the Guildhall, and it was agreed that those who owned ships unfit to sail must remove them from the haven to a *dok* on dry land;[76] and a year later everyone was given liberty to keep any wreckage, timber, broken anchors or cables which he could dredge up from the bottom of the haven.[77] But probably the most effective measure was the 1474 order that the men who had the monopoly of ballasting ships from their ketches should take all ballast for colliers, including those of Beverley, from mud-banks which had formed in the haven, and as far as possible should ballast all vessels in the same way.[78] In all states of the tide the Hull is now as muddy brown as the Humber, but it was not so then. The Humber was fresh enough for salmon to swim in such enormous numbers up-river that near York the Bishop of Durham could find nothing better to do with the immature fish caught in his weirs than feed them to pigs, and sturgeon of eleven stones or more could get at least as far as Tadcaster. At low water the haven itself was fairly clear and the water just drinkable.[79*]

But water from the haven was so poor that by 1401 every summer fresh water was being brought in boats. It may be that the boats had to go no further than about a quarter of a mile up the river to the end of Derringham dike where it discharged into the Hull and that this was done because the land route was too difficult. It was from this point that water was obtained in the earliest days of the town, but it may be that repeated flooding and the fact that the dike was completely outside the control of the corporation had made it necessary to find water elsewhere. Whatever the reason, water from boats was too expensive for the poor, and they were having to leave the town. The Crown appointed Sir Henry Percy the younger, Sir John Hotham, Sir Robert de Hilton and Sir John Scrope as commissioners to inquire with other justices what could be done and put their findings into effect.[80*]

In May 1401 they decided that a ditch twelve feet wide at the top, five feet deep and five feet wide at the bottom should be dug to bring water from Julian well at Anlaby, through the *Waldkerr* of Swanland, on the north side of Myton carr, up to a new ditch beside the Hull-Beverley road, and thence to Hull. The town would have to pay for various embankments to keep out salt water, and the cut was to be called Julian dike. It would also bring water from *Dernynghamenges* in Anlaby, which once belonged to Peter of Anlaby, and from a third spring in the northwest ings of Haltemprice field.[81] At the manor house where Peter de Anlaby had lived the channel entered the north end of a lake joined to the outer moat, not far away from the spring, and continued towards Hull from the south end, with various channels on its south side running to the Humber.[82]

Very soon there was a fairly constant supply of water discharging into the Bushdike but almost immediately a conflict of interest appeared between Hull and its neighbours. At Middleton-on-the-Wolds in 1409 a country jury reported to the Sheriff of Yorkshire that there were floods in the meadow and pasture of Gerard de Usflet, and of Anlaby, Swanland, Hessle and Ferriby, because Hull did not keep its watercourse clear from *Spryngheved* through *Darlynghamdyk* to the town gates. This led to a lawsuit in Westminster Hall in the Michaelmas term of 1413.[83]

But it was the flatness of the land and not neglect by the people of Hull which caused the flooding. The old watercourse had served to drain the land as well as to take the overflow from the springs. Julian dike was no more than the same watercourse widened and straightened. To keep a good flow of water up to the Bushdike it had to be kept as full as possible, and to keep out salt water from the Humber some other ditches had to be closed. A sluice at Sculcoates could be, and sometimes was, used to release any excess of water, but if Hull was not to go short of water the area of common pasture extending up to the boundaries of Hull and Myton shared by eleven or more places was bound to be exposed to the risk of flooding. Only a survey of the height of the land above mean sea-level, more accurate than was then possible, and careful control of flood-gates against the Humber, could have lessened the risk of flooding, and even then salt water would have got into the Hull supply whenever there were exceptionally high tides in the Humber.

Indeed, it did get in. The three *bushmen* whose horses pulled water from the Bushdike on sleds into the town appeared at the Guildhall in 1440 to answer a charge of supplying salt water instead of fresh; and they cleared themselves by undertaking that each of them would now pay 10*s* every year towards the maintenance of the dike from the town gate to Julian well.[84] In most years the cost of keeping it clear was less than this. A miller, probably with experience gained from the management of his own dam, undertook in 1492 for 20*s* a year to dredge and cleanse the fresh-water dike and Bushdike, repair the banks, and remove all straw, refuse or carrion.[85] In 1456-7 a dead body had to be removed from the water supply outside the town boundaries and two more in September 1457.[86] They may have been human, but the body taken out in June 1457 was that of a horse.[87] This may have been an exceptional year. To keep the water as clean as possible it was ordered in 1464 that all trees near the Bushdike should be cut down and that no pigs should graze there.[88]

Most of the friction with the villages which shared the common through which the fresh-water dike ran would have ceased if the water could have been carried in pipes laid underground instead of in an open ditch. The corporation did acquire power in 1447 to lay pipes in the ground as well as to acquire other springs.[89] Some lengths of pipe, usually called the *cundyth* (conduit) were laid outside the town. By April 1449 at least £36 had been spent on this project.[90] At Anlaby, Julian well, Glepwell and another well without a name were structures which in 1467-8 were repaired with brick after the mayor had been to Anlaby several times, and John Welles had allowed his land to be dug up for the conduit.[91] This was done merely to dismantle it. The only way which the town had been able to find of paying the £119 which it owed to the chamberlains in August 1461 had been to decide to dig up the lead pipes inside the town and sell them. Other creditors, instead of money, were given lead, valued at £4 for each fother of nineteen-and-a-half hundredweights.[92] The pipes were still under Whitefriargate five years later when the bench and the burgesses agreed to have them dug up and pave the road.[93] In 1476 part of it still existed, or was being re-laid, since John Adam gave four fothers of lead for the conduit and in return was exempted for life from liability to serve in any office of the corporation.[94]

Before Hull in effect acquired its monopoly in the fresh-water dike — it was called this far more often than Julian dike — villagers had taken water from it and watered their animals in it and saw no reason why they should not still do so. William Sturton, pinder, in 1450 took fresh water between Anlaby carr and Wold carr. Richard Bocher of Cottingham took water from two places opposite *Hynercroftes*, and from *Howndille-gote*, where a Sculcoates man also took it. This was done where the Sheriff of

Hull now had jurisdiction, but he probably had no power to prevent them from exercising a customary right not extinguished by any of the grants in favour of Hull.[95]

Now that the town had its own sheriff it was his duty to see to the execution of felons; but the way to the gallows passed through the *dedehorssekyrkgarth*, and Henry Myndram, who occupied the ground, in January 1480 would not allow the procession to pass. As the sheriff had with him a mace-bearer and a man with a pole-axe he should have had no difficulty in getting through. Possibly he feared the slightest taint of illegality, or he may have been in danger of being lynched himself if he used force. Whatever reason, he turned back and laid the matter before the mayor. Henry Myndram was brought before the bench and in the presence of the recorder and most of the burgesses raised such doubts about the existence of a right of way over his land that he was merely required to try to get the Duke of Suffolk's council to make a common highway to the gallows.[96] For those who had not qualified themselves for the gallows there was the pillory over a substantial shop in Marketgate belonging to the corporation.[97] From 1427 they had a roof to keep them dry and to protect them from the plunging fire of such missiles as were then available.

Sources

1. BB3A, ff.137b-47.
2. Ibid., f.85.
3. Ibid., f.19.
4. Ibid., f.85.
5. Ibid., f.17.
6. Ibid., f.116.
7. Ibid., f.214.
8. Ibid., f.86, f.130.
9. *CPR* 1304-7, 42.
10. Chamb., 6 and 22 Hen. VI.
11.* Chamb., 5, 26 and 35 Hen. VI. The *Wayour* at the Bushdike may sometimes have served as a causeway in a ford, but there is evidence of a brick bridge, and the most likely reason for the paving of the *Wayour* was to enable people to draw fresh water without making a muddy track from the Bushdike.
12. BB3, f.166.
13. BB2, f.260.
14. Chamb., 5 Hen. VI.
15. Chamb., 26 Hen. VI.

16. BB3A, f.123.
17. Ibid., f.75.
18. Chamb., 15 and 36 Hen. VI.
19. Chamb., 26 Hen. VI
20. Chamb., 2 Hen. VI.
21. Chamb., 35 Hen. VI, F. W. Brooks, 'A Medieval Brick-yard at Hull', *Journal of the British Archaeological Association* 3rd series, vol. 4, 1939, 156-74.
22. Chamb., 15 Hen. VI.
23. Chamb., 26 Hen. VI.
24. Chamb., 35 Hen. VI.
25. Chamb., 26 Hen. VI.
26. Ibid.
27. Ibid.
28. Ibid.
29. Ibid.
30. Chamb., 35 Hen. VI.
31. Ibid.
32. Ibid.
33. Chamb., 36 Hen. VI.
34. Chamb., 35 Hen. VI.
35. Chamb., 26 Hen. VI.
36. Ibid.
37. Ibid.
38. Ibid.
39. Ibid.
40. Ibid.
41. Ibid.
42. *Testamenta Eboracensia* (Surtees Society), ii. 105.
43. BB2, f.3; BB3A, f.4 and *passim*. Hollar's map.
44. BB3A, f.108b.
45. Ibid., f.116b.
46. Chamb., 5 Hen. VI.
47. Chamb., 15 Hen. VI.
48. Chamb., 35 Hen. VI.
49. Chamb., 7 Edw. IV.
50. Chamb., 14 Hen. VIII.
51. BB3A, f.69.
52. Chamb., 2 Hen. VI.
53. Ibid., f.98.
54. Ibid., f.144b.
55. Ibid., f.140.
56. Ibid.
57. BB2, Rental of 1347.
58. Chamb., 22 Edw. IV; BB3 f.98b.
59. BB3A, f.114.
60. Chamb., 38 Hen. VI.
61. Chamb., 7 Edw. IV.
62. Chamb., 2 Hen. VI.
63. BB3, f.18.
64. BB3A, f.34.
65.* Ibid., f.54. Zeeland in the Netherlands is most probable, but the name is usually spelled as *Sealand* and could therefore mean the Danish island of that name.
66. Chamb., 20 Hen. VI.

67. *CPR* 1436-41, 181.
68. Chamb., 35 Hen. VI.
69. BB3, f.95b.
70. Ibid., f.16b.
71. Chamb., 22 Edw. IV.
72. BB3A, f.52b.
73. Ibid., f.310.
74. Ibid., f.51.
75. Ibid., f.79b.
76. Ibid., f.81b.
77. Ibid., f.81b.
78. *Public Works in Medieval Law* (Selden Society), ii, 253-5; YASRS, *Selby Coucher Book*, ii, 342-4.
79*. 'The Life of Master John Shaw', *Surtees Society*, lxv, 1875, 134. [Referred to on his epitaph as The Reverend John Shawe.]
80.* *CIM*, vi, No. 191. Percy was probably of Leconfield, Hilston of Swine, Hotham of Scorborough; and the Scropes had a grant out of the fee-farm rent of Hull. *Derringham* was then called *Dernyngham*.
81. Ibid.
82. *YAJ*, xxxi, 339 ff.
83. BB2, f.289.
84. BB3, f.16.
85. Ibid., f.27.
86. BB3A, f.148b.
87. Chamb., 35 Hen. VI.
88. Ibid.
89. *CPR* 1446-52, 43.
90. BB3A, f.9.
91. Chamb., 26 Hen. VI.
92. BB3A, f.79, f.81.
93. Ibid., f.108b.
94. Ibid., f.121.
95. Ibid., f.25.
96. Ibid., f.124.
97. Ibid. f.101b.

4

Violence and Crime

After her visit to Bridlington in 1417, the King's Lynn mystic, Margery Kempe, was in Hull, Hessle and Beverley. In the autobiography which she related to a priest, using the third person, she said:

> And so she went to Hull on a day when they had a procession and a big woman treated her with great contempt . . . Many others said she ought to be put in prison, and they made great threats, but in spite of their malice a good man came and invited her to a meal, with right good cheer. Then the malicious people who had despised her came to the good man and said he must not help her as she was no good woman. On the next day in the morning her host led her out at the town's end, for he dared keep her no longer; and so she went to Hessle.

She would have taken the Barton ferry, but she was seized, and women came running out of the houses, shouting that she ought to be burned. The use of the gallows and the pillory seem to us deplorable barbarism, but the medieval town had no shortage of deplorable barbarians. In 1401 a ship-man named William Asselby and a leach from Barnard Castle named John Sharp, and a dozen others humbly submitted to the mayor, John Byrkyn, and the bailiffs 'because of great and horrible trespass done to the mayor, bailiffs and commonalty'. On 8 September they were to stand through the service in Holy Trinity, 'naked of body', without hats or shoes, each with a three-pound candle, which he was to give to the church. They were then to surrender the weapons they had used and return to prison until they had found sureties for the large sum of £55.[1]

They found their sureties, provided themselves with new arms, and resumed the practice of their trade. On 5 June 1402 they broke into the town gaol with battle axes and swords, yelling 'Fire! Fire!' (a cry bound to cause some confusion) and tried to kill the mayor, William Chery, and did wound him and his sergeant, crying 'Down with the mayor! Down with him!' Their object was not political assassination but the release of Stephen Richardson who was awaiting trial for felony, with the prospect of being hanged, and other prisoners who were held there in stocks, cheaper and more effective than irons. This second and more serious offence would be quite unknown if they had not had some highly-placed protector who within eight weeks had obtained a royal pardon for them.[2] They belonged to that class then regarded as a valuable element in the crews of ships taken for the King's service, and may be loosely described as unemployed pirates.

Naval service, diversified with piracy, was a taste shared by some of the wealthiest people in the town. John Tutbury and William Terry were Hull merchants interested in piracy and it was therefore only natural that in 1400 both were licensed to make war against Scots and Friesians, the King's enemies — Tutbury with two balingers and his ships *Petre* and *Gabriel* and Terry with one balinger and the *George*. Both had fresh licences in 1402.[3] What they did for the Crown is not apparent, but what they did for themselves is. Tutbury, who was nevertheless to serve as mayor, with an armed crew in the *Petre* and Terry in the *George* took the ship and cargo of Martin Garschowe of Lübeck, worth £178.[4] The names of the pirates are known only because English ambassadors had heard complaints in Prussia in 1406, where their victims had been able to identify them. Laurence Tutbury, perhaps a brother of John, had to appear before the King and his council at Westminster. John Herry of Hull, possibly confused with William Terry, captured the *Julyan* of Dantzig with a cargo of beer, then unknown in Britain except as an import, a hundred gold nobles, and £200 in the form of a bill of exchange for the Duke of Holland.

One of the few other Hull pirates known by name was William Burton who in 1400 took a Breton ship sailing in the Channel to Flanders with wine and lampreys.[5] Most piracy involved no more than a short passage to the mouth of the Humber and a good understanding with Grimsby. Men of both ports in 1434 took a

ship of Dantzig belonging to Andrew Egarot, although the
Dantzig merchants on board called out that they were not
enemies.[6] A year later they took the *Marie Knight* of Stettin.[7] Men
of Hessle and Beverley, having captured the ship of Isbrande
Harmonson, or having acquired her from other sea-dogs, in 1446
sensibly brought her to Hull.[8]

Usually the Humber and its approaches were the busiest places
for persons of this class. A ship of Kampen, at anchor in the
mouth of the Humber on passage to Prussia with a cargo of salt
from the Bay of Biscay in 1453 was taken from a balinger and the
owner, Isbrande Keyser with part of the crew were held to ransom
probably in Hull.[9] Occasionally Hull adventurers worked far from
home. During a truce with France in 1448 a crayer of Hull
captured the *Goodaventure* bound for London with wine taken on
board at Rouen. The pirates took her to Harwich, where they were
imprisoned, probably because they had made the mistake of
attacking a vessel which belonged to the lieutenant of Harfleur.[10]
Even so, it is unlikely they were treated severely. In Hull the
penalty for piracy against the King's subjects — nothing was said
about aliens — was 40*s* and disfranchisement if the offender was a
burgess. Piracy was therefore regarded as about equally criminal
with the adulteration of flour.[11] When in 1472, Robert Laverok, in
the *Trynyte* of Hull, captured the *Margaret* of Lowestoft as she
left her home port for Holland, it was in Lowestoft only that this
seemed outrageous.[12]

Merchants were on the whole less tolerant than mariners who, if
they suffered the effects of piracy, had the alternative of seeing
whether they too could make a profit out of this occupation.
Merchants did not really have this alternative. William Thorne in
1434 was homeward bound from Lisbon with sweet wine and oil in
the *Trinity* of Hull when he was attacked by 400 men from St Malo
and Mont-St-Michel. Four of her crew were killed and ten were
held to ransom with the prospect of being put to death if the
money, 260 marks, did not arrive by Whitsun. It was probably
unusual for the game to become as dangerous as this, but it was
bad for trade.[13] Even a ship of the largest size was unsafe. A
300-ton hulk of Dantzig sailing to Hull from the Baltic in 1453
with a cargo belonging to William Gaunt of York and Prussian
merchants established in London was already in the Humber off
Grimsby when she was captured by John Marchall of Newcastle

and the oarsmen of his barge, and taken to Berwick.[14] Robert Auncell, mayor in 1454-5, and other Hull owners lost their ship, the *Lyon*, to pirates, but had every prospect of recovering her, without her cargo, when she appeared in Hull in 1446.[15] Robert Spofford and W. Bald may have stopped their raids on shipping in the Humber when two balingers — fast whale-boats much used by pirates — were fitted out at Hull, provided always that the crews did not themselves turn to piracy.[16]

There was also a feudal vested interest in piracy. The operations of Lord Tailboys and Sir John Neville from Grimsby were not easily distinguishable from piracy.[17] Sir William Ryder in 1458 was owner of the *Giles* of Hull which captured a Spanish vessel, bound for England, the property of the Marquis de Vyleyne, with a cargo of wine and iron.[18] Henry Percy, Earl of Northumberland (1342-1408) owned a barge at Hull, probably for those purposes which it could serve as well as a balinger.[19]

With persons of this turbulent class taking to the sea the independence of the town was threatened. Some time prior to 1435 a lease of the Admiralty of the Humber had been obtained from the Duke of Exeter, and was several times renewed.[20] Henry Holland, the fourth duke (*c.* 1430-75) was an ally of Lord Egremont and had supported him in his northern rebellion of 1454.[21] It was possibly with the backing of Exeter that Egremont, a younger son of the Percys of Leconfield, came to Hull in April 1460 with a small army, determined to exercise admiralty jurisdiction which almost certainly belonged to the town.[22*]

His men came down the River Hull as well as by land. The gates were shut against them, and they thought it too dangerous to make an opposed landing at any of the quays. On 27 April the bench sent an appeal to the King's Council, with two tuns of wine to follow the messenger as soon as possible. They also sent profound apologies to Egremont regarding their inability to admit him to the town, and he, with the conditioned reflexes of a hardened feudalist, threatened to kill the men of Hull, so that none of them dared to go about their business outside the walls, while he expressed his determination to force his way in, so that guard had to be kept day and night.

It was more than a fortnight before the Council's reply arrived under the privy seal, with instructions that Egremont should not be allowed to enter with any substantial body of armed men. The bell was rung to bring the commons to the Guildhall, where it was decided to let him in but only with the strictest precautions. He would not be allowed to hold any Admiralty session, and would be told that no discussion of Hull Admiralty privileges was possible as most of the documents were in London. His retinue must not be armed. He would be honourably received at his inn by the mayor and 200 men of the greatest esteem. While he remained no more of his men were to be let in and there was to be a permanent guard of sixty townsmen, each ward providing ten men and an alderman. Twenty would guard Beverley Gate, twenty would be at the north ferry landing and twenty would be at the south end near the Humber jetty. On the following day Egremont decided to accept defeat gracefully, remembering that once he had tried to use force in York and had found armed citizens too much for him. He would come into the town with sixty horsemen, which was no more than the proper retinue for a nobleman and after that he seems to have troubled Hull no more before his predestined liquidation.[23]

On the whole Hull may be judged to have got the better of Egremont; but his enemy, John Neville, created Lord Montague in 1460, was altogether too big an opponent to be met on equal terms. He was brother of Warwick 'the king-maker', and warden of the East March against Scotland. It was for this reason that he too had a balinger at Hull. One night towards the end of March 1464 her crew robbed a keel, the *Peton*, of York, and the *Gertrude*, a Dutch ship, wounding one of her mariners. They endangered ships in the haven by cutting her cable, and then broke into a house called the *Whythors*, where they stole cloth. They were arrested and put in prison; but the bench, realising whose men they were, would have released them if only they would have sworn to keep the peace against the Dutchmen; but this they refused to do.

Montague chose to regard this as an act of lese-majesty against himself, and the messenger, Banks, who brought his letter from Wressel, openly said that if John Green, the mayor, came anywhere near Wressel 'either he should lose his head, or else he should be chopped as small as flesh to pot'. In reply to the humble explanation of the bench that it was only such threats as this which prevented them from coming to Wressel, Montague answered arrogantly that as Wressel was so near he should have been left to deal with the misdeeds of his men. The fact that he had no shadow of a claim to jurisdiction in the borough never seems to have crossed his mind. Indeed he said the bench must not be misled by the malicious folly of the mayor and they would find him their friend; and on the next day his men, having sworn to keep the peace, were let out of gaol.[24] The mayor never completed his year of office. On 13 July his widow came to the council chamber and delivered 'two maces of gilt with other ungilt, a sword with a black scabbard of velvet, one short sword with a scabbard, two scabbards of cloth of gold, two hats, one standing furred with grey, the other of beaver'.[25] Probably he had been murdered.

Hull had always been in the position of having to fight off the encroachments of feudal magnates, and it was not only in the semi-anarchy of the mid-fifteenth century that such men were dangerous. John Lound in 1351 forcibly released servants of Sir John Salvayn from the town gaol, and in consequence of the arrest the knight and others rode day and night in the vicinity of the town, making such threats that neither the mayor nor anyone else dared go outside the walls to see to the assembling of ships for the King's army, or to work in the fields.[26]

Although the town was strong enough to resist all attacks and its inhabitants were not pacifists, the hostility of persons of high rank, or not very high rank, could have awkward consequences. The power of the town, even after the creation of a separate county, never extended effectively beyond its walls. Minor feudalists served as justices of the peace and on commissions which could arrive at decisions detrimental to Hull; and the greater men had more influence in the governance of England than any mere parliamentary borough. The bench therefore differed in no way from a hundred or so similar bodies throughout the country in keeping up a constant stream of gifts and courtesies to men, and the servants of the men, whose friendship might be useful and whose enmity it was best to avoid. When there was a meeting of a commission of sewers at Hedon in 1436-7 it was prudent to give its members two gallons of wine before they considered a complaint affecting the town and heard the recorder in its defence. At about the same time the clerk of the castle at York was given his annual 'reward' of 6*s* 8*d*, and even his clerk had 20*d*.[27]

Sometimes the protection of a great lord could be invoked against smaller fry. In 1426-7 William Babthorpe, as the King's commissioner, summoned twenty-four burgesses to appear before

him at Beverley. A messenger rode to tell Lord Scrope, who had a
vested interest in Hull, at Faxfleet, and a barrel of wine costing £6
13*s* 4*d* was sent to remind him of the devotion of the borough to all
the Scropes. Sending the twenty-four men to Beverley cost 26*s* 8*d*.
Either then or some other time during the year, when six gallons of
wine and four capons were sent to John Ellerker, one of the
justices of the peace, the journey to Beverley must have been
smooth and comfortable, as 20*d* was spent on hiring a boat.[28]

Every messenger bringing the King's commands had to have his
reward. In 1456-7 the man who brought a letter from the Lord
Chancellor got no more than 16*d*, but the man who brought the
King's letter — it seems unlikely that Henry VI knew anything
about it — for preparing ships against the French got 6*s* 8*d*.
William Grymesby, of Grimsby, as a courtier and esquire to the
King himself, was given 40*s*.[29] Even the King's attorney had to be
given breakfast, a very large one, and then wine at noon with
pears, dates, marmalade and green ginger, the whole day's
peculiar entertainment costing 9*s* 3*d*.[30]

The town could recognise blue blood from some distance. In
1402-3 the men of Prince Henry, arriving from Barton, were given
beer. Sir John Bukton got a whole pipe of wine. Hugh Cliderowe
was sent to the Earls of Salisbury and Suffolk at Southwell. A
messenger from John, the King's son, then warden of the East
March and later Duke of Bedford was given 13*s* 4*d*, and a King's
messenger bringing news of a truce was rewarded with 20*s*.[31] This
crude diplomacy could be effective. Egremont, a raging lion in
1460, in 1456-7 merely came with a warrant for the arrest of the
Mariyonger and left no record of his coming other than the fact
that the mayor sent to ask Hugh Cliderowe to come home and
advise him and presented four gallons of wine to Egremont, eight
to the Countess of Northumberland, his sister-in-law, three to
Lord Graistok and two to Sir John Heron.[32]

Four of the fifteenth-century de la Poles died violent deaths, an
indication not so much of failure as of political eminence. The
bench even thought it worth while to note the names of the
feoffees of the Hull, Myton, Drypool, Newland, Cottingham,
Anlaby, Bewholme and Rimswell — lands of Michael, the second
Earl of Suffolk, who died in the siege of Harfleur in 1415.[33]

When the postern to the Charterhouse was made for the second
Duke of Suffolk the better-informed men in the town must have

known of the marvellous political acumen which he had shown in transferring his support, at exactly the right time, from Henry VI, who had restored him to his dukedom, to Edward IV, who gave him his sister as a bride. A protector of this calibre was worth having; and the 25*s* laid out on a banquet for the first duke's receiver was probably not wasted.[34]

The Bishop of Durham, with his manor at Howden and his Howdenshire estates, was then a person of national importance. J. Lauton was sent to Howden in 1447-8 in the hope of an audience with him. But the local power of the new Archbishop of York, George Neville (1433?-1476), was far greater; and as brother of Montague and Warwick he wielded power which extended far beyond his diocese. When some time in 1467-8 he made his first appearance at Beverley the whole bench thought it wise to wait on him with a pipe of wine, a barrel of sturgeon and a dozen lampreys, not forgetting 2*s* 8*d* for his guest-master who was responsible for their entertainment. In the same year they gave a pike and a gallon of wine to the great Lord Cromwell, and nine gallons of wine to Sir John Harrington.[35]. Gifts to the corporation from magnates were a rarity, but in 1436-7 Humphrey Lord Stafford (1402-60) presented a couple of bucks, probably from one of the Burstwick deer-parks, then held by his mother with the lordship of Holderness, and the servant who brought them was rewarded with 3*s* 4*d*.[36]

When the Duke of Gloucester was rising to the eminence that was to turn him into Richard III, he was often in York or at his castle of Sheriff Hutton. In 1482, when the town and its county raised soldiers at his command, two of the aldermen rode to York for an audience with him, apparently remaining for some time. Wine was presented to his steward, Sir Marmaduke Constable, a man whose local power was greatly inflated by this office; but the Earl of Northumberland, one of the great by birth, got eight gallons.[37]

In 1498-9 Sir Roger Cholmley,, a North Riding knight but for the time being of great importance to Hull because he was Sheriff of Yorkshire, had gifts of ten gallons of wine or more. The Earl of Surrey, Thomas Howard (1443-1524), Henry VII's lieutenant in the north, cost nothing át all in gifts, but Thomas Gayton was sent to him twice, without, apparently, the need to sweeten any of his servants with gifts. And the corporation spent 5*s* 4*d* purely as an act of piety on transport of materials for the crosses erected under the will of the Duchess of York who had died in 1495.[38]

Because of the absence of any detailed records of day-to-day proceedings in the borough court it is not clear whether men of rank interfered, as they certainly did at Grimsby, in town affairs by taking the side of one burgess against another; but there are fairly clear indications that they did. In 1443 the bench made an order that no burgess was to accept any fee or livery from a gentleman not living within the liberty. If he did so he could not hold any office or be in the mayor's council. It was found that the acceptance of liveries of great magnates had caused dissension in the town, and an order came from the King's Council requiring the sheriff and the bench to make a return of all Hull men who had offended in this way.[39] But even without a livery protection by members of a great family could be valuable. During the mayoralty of William Baron, William Constable so intimidated him that he released a Prussian from the borough gaol, where he had been held for failure to pay a debt of 13s 4d. Like all aliens visiting the town, the Prussian, named Pypersek, had to have a 'host' or guarantor. His host, William Goldsmith, induced Constable to intervene so that he would not have to meet the debt himself, which the law of the borough required him to do. But the next mayor for some reason had no fear of the Constables, and he had no sooner assumed office than, on 1 October 1483, he made Goldsmith pay.[40]

But sometimes a magnate had to be accorded all the respect he felt himself entitled to. There was a minor ferry over the Humber to Goxhill belonging to the corporation and for 20s this was leased to William Assby of Goxhill for one year; but the Lord Abbot of Thornton, immediately next to Goxhill, was a man of baronial standing and his wishes could not be ignored. He preferred Thomas Smith, and accordingly, only a month after the lease had been granted, it was easily cancelled in November 1457 on the ground that it had been made 'falsely', and a new lease was made for Smith.[41]

A debt of 13s 4d and a 20s lease are unimportant matters by comparison with some of those with which the bench had to deal and for that reason are all the more significant. If magnates concerned themselves with minor matters, they are not likely to have ignored cases in which more vital interests were involved.

Diplomacy was the only means by which the borough could maintain a partial independence, and as diplomatic advisers the bench always retained counsel who not only advised in strictly legal matters but also, through their access to the jungle-telegraph of all fifteenth-century lawyers of any standing, were able to keep the bench to some extent informed about the affairs of the noble and the great shedders of blood. And usually they were lawyers of great eminence. In a lawsuit with the Abbot of Thornton in 1397 one of the counsel for the town was William Gascoigne, who in 1400 became chief justice of the King's Bench.[42] John Ellerker, while he still had his annual retainer as counsel for the corporation, also sat as a justice of assize and was in the commission of the peace in five counties. He was given a pipe of red wine for his services in obtaining the confirmation of the charters in 1431.[43] Peter Ardern, retained at 40*s* a year from 1444 until 1449 sat as a justice of assize in 1443 at Hull, York and Newcastle, and only gave up his retainer when, as a sergeant-at-law, he became chief baron of the Exchequer and a justice of the King's Bench.[44] His place as counsel was taken by Robert Danby another sergeant-at-law who was in the commission of the peace for five counties including the North and West Ridings but not the East. He rode to York on the town's business in 1451-2.[45] John Portyngton, retained as counsel until 1441, or his father of the same name, became a justice of the Common Bench in 1443, and must have been of the same family as the gentleman named Portyngton to whom the bench sent three separate gifts of wine.[46] William Eland of Gray's Inn was living in Beverley in 1452-3 and may have been the archbishop's man as he was in the commission of the peace for Ripon and Beverley as well as for the three Ridings, but in other respects was more closely identified with Hull than any of the other counsel, and was the founder of a Hull family, served as sheriff, and was four times one of the Hull burgesses returned to parliament.[47]

The creation of the greatly enlarged county of Hull in 1447, though it brought the whole course of the fresh-water dike within the jurisdiction of the bench, made local diplomacy more difficult.[48] It is hard to see how the bench could establish its jurisdiction over the estate of Sir William Taylboys, one of the most violent of feudalists, or how it could manage Sir Robert Constable of Flamborough when he succeeded to the estate after the beheading of Taylboys in 1464.[49] Edward Scott of Hessle, with John Welles of Anlaby and a certain Whetley, also of Anlaby and also a gentleman as his sureties, submitted to the arbitration of two of the aldermen when he was indicted for felony in 1449; but this records a victory for the gentry rather than submission to the authority of the corporation.[50] An indictment for felony could be settled only by a criminal trial with the penalty of death as the price of failure, though gentlemen rarely suffered death except for political errors. The bench must have been equally uncomfortable when in 1458 it had to record that the feoffees of the estate of John Acclom of Hull, esquire, consisting of property at Newark, Calais, Hull and its county were Sir Ralph Bygot of Settrington E.R., Sir John Conyers and his father, Christopher Conyers of Hornby N.R. None of them could be described as a peacemaker and the Conyers were associated with Robin of Redesdale and Robert Hildyard who in 1469 raised a rebellion in Holderness and the north.[51]

Occasionally even ordinary crime was connected with the great. In 1467-8 a jury convicted William Broughton and his accomplice, unnamed, and both were drawn to the gallows on stakes and hanged; but Broughton was a priest and therefore could not be hanged except for treason. His treason may simply have been counterfeiting the King's coinage, but priests had been known to escape the worst consequences of this indiscretion and it must be concluded that he had no effective protector or was involved in real political treason. Fifteenth-century treason could mean no more than openly expressed opposition or continued loyalty to a lost cause. This kind of political activity did exist in Hull when shortly after the accession of Edward IV three women and seven married couples were ordered on pain of death to leave the town within twenty-four hours 'for their misrule against our sovereign lord king', and three other men were kept in prison.[52]

Those pursued for crime always had the chance of taking sanctuary for forty days in the two churches and churchyards at the Austin friars in Blackfriargate, the Carmelites in Whitefriargate, or at the Charterhouse; but a fugitive who reached Beverley was safe for life. One of the very few who got there was a woman from Pollington accused of killing an infant in Hull.[53] If a killer survived a few years service in war he might qualify himself for a pardon, as Stephen Barnysone did in 1303 by soldiering in

Scotland after he had killed John Iveson, also a Hull man; and at the same time another Hull soldier in Scotland, William Kembald, was pardoned for homicide.[54] In the Poitiers' campaign Richard del Kerre was pardoned for killing Hugh de Hanely, both being men belonging to Hull.[55]

So long as they avoided treason, clergy were virtually exempt from all possible penalties of crime, a consideration probably not absent from the minds of the vicar of Hessle and of Holy Trinity, and of a chaplain accused with him by the Prior of Watton (1352) of having robbed him of £100 at Hull. Edmund Quarel of Hull probably thought himself fairly safe in joining the Prior of the Pontefract Dominicans in an assault at York.[56] When the night watch reported (1450) that they found Friar Brown in the streets at unlawful hours there was nothing further they could do to him. They were merely recording social history.[57]

Petty criminals and suspects could be disposed of with very little trouble. For his many offences (1455) Nicholas Rogerson, a weaver, agreed to leave the town but was allowed like any other servant to return at any time for two days. His cup may have over-flowed as a result of participation in disturbances at the mayoral election of the previous day.[58*] More serious offenders could be treated similarly. For indecent assault on a girl of seven, William Rispyn, aged 60, was exiled for five years, a period equal to what was then accepted as his probable expectation of life in the ancient tables still in use.[59] Though even foreign sailors were allowed to come into the town wearing their daggers, John Weston, a man of uncertain temper was told (1470) that he would be expelled if he was found even with a knife.[60] Minor offenders did not suffer cruel or unusual punishments. Nicholas Rogersons was imprisoned (1453) but only in order to give the bench time to consider what to do about his secret fishing for tench at night; this was not strict incarceration, as he was found simply to have left the prison.[61] Fines, however, could be heavy. Those called 'night-stalkers' were often fined the equivalent of several days' wages, either by the bench or by the sheriff in his court. William Marsh and Robert Belton each had to pay 1s for continually being out at night in suspicious circumstances.[62] Emot Baxster (1488) was fined 6d for being a usurer; and Margaret Mason fined 4d for harbouring thieves was probably the Lowgate bawd, 'Big Margaret' (1485) fined 2s for receiving stolen goods.[63]

The town actually assisted whores to earn their living by letting to them the piece of land against the Humber called the *Foreland* with the adjacent three arches under the walls for £3 6*s* 8*d* a year.[64] At the same time it showed its disapproval of immoral conduct by fining them. Joan Frensshewoman (1450) was fined 4*d* for keeping a brothel in Whitefriargate, but Margaret Shipman, one of her staff, seems to have had her fine cancelled. Bawds, on the other hand, stood at an ill-defined point in the social scale which exposed them to moderate fines, sometimes with their husbands. They may have tended to become concentrated in one part of the town. In 1484 five of them lived in the flesh-market.[65] One of these had a status clearly marked by her surname of *Frerespowte*.[66*] There was at least one other in Lowgate, and another simply styled *Trowlop in Trypett*.[67]

Perhaps the bench was not always so tolerant. Margaret Yole (1453) for her many and notorious offences, was told in March that she must leave the town forever by November.[68] Alison Godewyn had been expelled for adultery and misrule (1461) but 'entered the town and occupied more misrule than she did before'. Two days later, therefore, she was set upon the common thew, a kind of light, portable pillory, and led out of Beverley Gate.[69]

Sources

1. *The Book of Margery Kempe*, (Early English Text Society, Original Series, No. 212) 129. BB3, f.242.
2. *CPR* 1401-4, 2.
3. *CPR* 1399-1401, 353; *CPR* 1401-5, 55.
4. *CPR* 1405-8, 236, 302.
5. *CPR* 1399-1401, 352.
6. *CPR* 1429-36, 357.
7. Ibid., 470.
8. *CPR* 1446-52, 41.
9. *CPR* 1452-61, 118.
10. Ibid., 237.
11. BB3A, f.68.
12. *CPR* 1467-77, 353.
13. *CPR* 1429-36, 355.
14. *CPR* 1452-61, 174.
15. *CPR* 1446-52, 41.
16. Chamb., 26 Hen. VI.
17. E. Gillett, *A History of Grimsby*, 48-50.
18. *CPR* 1452-61, 439.
19. *CPR* 1405-8, 58.

20. BB3, f.24b.
21. *Complete Peerage*, v. 212.
22.* BB3A, f.70. The charter of 1447 gave the borough Admiralty jurisdiction in the Humber on the death of Henry, Duke of Exeter, which did not take place until 1475.
23. BB3, f.71.
24. Ibid., f.90, f.91.
25. Ibid., f.96b.
26. *CPR* 1350-3, 153.
27. Chamb., 15 Hen. VI.
28. Chamb., 6 Hen. VI.
29. Chamb., 36 Hen. VI.
30. Chamb., 14 Hen. VII.
31. Chamb., 4 Hen. IV.
32. Chamb., 35 Hen. VI.
33. Chamb., 15 Hen. VII.
34. Chamb., 18 Hen. VI.
35. *CPR* 1441-6, 181.
36. Chamb., 35 Hen. VI.
37. Chamb., 14 Hen. VII.
38. Chamb., 18 Hen. VI.
39. BB3A, f.136b.
40. Ibid., f.60.
41. BB2, f.242; *DNB*, s.v. GASCOIGNE.
42. Chamb. 2 and 15 Hen. VI.
43. Chamb., 23 and 32 Hen. VI.
44. Chamb., 30 Hen. VI.
45. Ibid.
46. Ibid.
47. Boyle, 54-6.
48. *CPR* 1461-7, 367.
49. Ibid.
50. BB3A, f.9.
51. Ibid., f.63b; Chamb., 7 Edw. IV.
52. *Sanctuarium Dunelmense* . . . (Surtees Society) xlvii.
53. *CPR* 1301-7, 170.
54. BB3A, f.71.
55. *CPR* 1313-21, 477.
56. BB3A, f.19.
57. Ibid., f.89.
58.* Ibid., f.53. The life-table then in use, dating back to the third century, was attributed to Ulpian.
59. Ibid., f.51.
60. Ibid., f.137.
61. Ibid., f.140.
62. Ibid.
63. Ibid., f.137, f.138b.
64. Chamb., 14 Hen. VII.
65. Ibid., f.45.
66.* *'Frerespowte'* — a whore popular with friars.
67. Ibid., f.137b.
68. Ibid., f.45.
69. Ibid., f.78.

5

War

The port experienced both the hazards and the profits of the almost continuous wars of the later Middle Ages. The advantages which its position offered as a supply base against the Scots may have decided Edward I to acquire it from the monks of Meaux, and both in the Scottish and the French wars Hull provided men and ships as well as supplies. The potential of a port so far from Scotland as a base for a campaign in Scotland appear most clearly in the expedition of Edward Balliol in 1332.[1] His baronial allies, styled the *Disinherited*, in spite of their Scottish titles, were for the most part English magnates such as Gilbert de Umfraville, styled Earl of Angus, but with his principal seat at South Kyme, in the middle of Lincolnshire. Henry de Beaumont, Earl of Buchan, had most of his lands equally distant from Scotland; and for men like these it was convenient to cover more than half of the distance to Scotland by sea, with the advantages of speed and surprise. They embarked, most at Hull but a few at Barton, in eighty-eight ships, the largest number ever mentioned in connection with Hull, and within a week were all in Fife. Until the disastrous campaign of 1322 had brought the Scots deep into Yorkshire there had not seemed to be the need for anything more than a ditch to defend the town; and even then the half-flooded delta on which it stood and the Holderness marshes, through which Edward II in his retreat could not pass without a guide, guaranteed almost complete security.

At first the contribution of Hull to the Scottish campaigns was modest. In 1301 Hull was classed with Hedon and Grimsby in being required to provide only a single ship, whereas two were called for from Scarborough. These were ships equipped for war, sent to Berwick,[2] but other ships transported corn, meat, fish, wine and other provisions for the army, and several were wrecked (1332) at Hartlepool.[3] By 1317 the services which the men of the borough had rendered in this war gave them exemption from the payment of £118 arrears of taxation.[4] This was probably not so much an expression of royal gratitude as indirect payment for supplies, shipping and wages. Nicholas Putfra (1319) in his ship the *Nicholas* of Hull operated against the Scots at sea with an armed crew under three constables,[5] while Hull vessels were carrying timber for the construction of a peel-tower in the north.[6] The clerk with the responsibility for providing and transporting the timber was given power to conscript mariners for this voyage, which offered to them much less chance of profit than service in a ship of war.

Nevertheless supply and ordinary mariners rather than men for war were what the King usually wanted, and the knowledge that he had power to requisition supplies on his own terms could be sufficient to keep merchants away from his line of march. In 1332, therefore, after reaching Doncaster, Edward III ordered the bailiffs of Hull to proclaim that all merchandise would be paid for both there and at York.[7] There were occasions when troops had to be raised for war. In 1333 Hull had to provide 60 men for service against the Scots, when Beverley had to send 80 and York 100.[8] Springalds (1324) made in Yorkshire, Lincolnshire and Nottinghamshire, with 3000 quarrels, better weapons for sentries than the long-bow, were delivered to Richard de la Pole at Hull.[9] In 1331 it was impossible to provide the two ships ready for war which Edward III needed because Hull ships were fully occupied in transporting supplies to the north, and William de la Pole, then mayor, could send only Peter Tunnok in the *Trinity*, with a large armed crew.[10] Two years later two ships were prepared for war.[11] When the King was at Perth in 1336 orders were sent that in spite of the need for warships a vessel was to be sent immediately with arms and provisions,[12] and a few weeks later the *Mariol* and the *Lightfot* took barrels of flour to the English troops besieging Berwick.[13]

Both in peace and in war Hull had the advantage of being in the middle of an area where except in a famine year there was a corn surplus which may be conservatively estimated at 25,000 quarters,

or enough for a body of more than 20,000 troops for a year.[14]*
Even for the French campaigns of the fourteenth century supplies
were drawn from Hull. For the 1346 campaign when Portsmouth
was the port of embarkation,[15] corn, bacon and other provisions
requisitioned in Yorkshire, Nottinghamshire and Derbyshire were
brought to Hull from Tadcaster, Doncaster, York, Selby,
Wansford and Beverley. Warehouses were hired for twelve weeks
and as there was too much corn to be ground at the Hull mills
some was sent to Wawne, and some across the Humber to Skitter
before it was packed in barrels and loaded into ships in the haven.
Though the impressment of mariners may have been an economic
loss to the town, activities such as this were part of its livelihood.
The *Charite* (1354) a King's ship under a sergeant-at-arms had its
crew impressed in Hull before it sailed for London, but even so
some of their wages would eventually be spent in the town.[16]
Fitting-out and repairing ships was pure gain, and a year later
twelve carpenters with other workmen were employed in repairing
three of the King's ships.[17]

To see war as profit or loss to the community oversimplifies the
situation. War was simply a fact of medieval society to which it
was necessary to adjust, and in so far as the adjustment was made
successfully the town was able to prosper. But adjustment always
involved difficulties which were bound to affect some sections of
the community adversely while to others they caused perhaps only
minor discomfort. When ships were required for war in 1351, too
soon after the Black Death, there were serious riots.[18] There were
also occasions when the sudden need to raise large sums of money
for the Crown must have caused serious tension. Between 1397
and 1400 no less than £400 had to be provided for Richard II and
Henry IV,[19] and this probably helped to produce the riots referred
to at the beginning of the previous chapter. This money was in the
form of loans which might possibly be repaid, but the difficulty
experienced in raising it can be appreciated by comparison with the
normal annual expenditure of the town, which was less than £200,
and with the sums which had to be raised for war in 1481 and 1482,
which scarcely exceeded £60.[20]

The civil conflicts of the fifteenth century at times put Hull in
immediate danger of suffering the fate of Ludlow or Stamford —
a complete sack by an army of mercenaries; and guarding the walls
and gates was as important a duty as meeting the demands of the

Crown, which continued to be what they always had been — the provision of ships, men and money. In May 1454 there was an order for all ships of fifty tons and above to be taken for the King's service, and the impressment of men for the crews.[21] Two years later five men were sent to serve against the Scots. The chamberlains had to find nearly £10 for their pay; and as another ship was requisitioned they sent a man to Hessle to see whether it would be cheaper to victual her there, presumably at a time when corn was scarce and prices had risen.[22] Two royal officers who appeared in 1457 to arrest ships for the King's service were satisfied with taking the *Giles*. Her master, William Sutton, was given authority to press men for her crew, and within six months she was active in piracy, never clearly distinguishable from war at sea against the King's enemies.[23] Hugh Cliderowe, several times mayor, as a kind of elder statesman, was summoned by the mayor, John Scales, to appear before the King's Council in London and put the case for the town concerning the vessels fighting the French, an errand of some importance as it cost 53*s* 4*d*.[24]

This journey to London was almost certainly concerned with Admiralty matters, since in the same year the fees of an Admiralty lawyer in London cost £4. The bench first took a lease of Admiralty rights in the Humber in 1435, when the decisions to be taken were felt to be of such importance that the bell was rung to bring all the commons to meet the mayor and burgesses in the Guildhall.[25] It was then confirmed that the corporation should take a lease of these rights for the next four years, paying a rent of eight marks a year. This was closely connected with the impressment of seamen. The alderman serving as Admiralty commissioner exacted 6*s* 8*d* from each man taking the King's wages; and the rights to flotsam, lagan, deodands, grampuses and all fish with blubber were comparatively unimportant, and the dues taken from men serving the King probably gave the Hull Admiralty commissioner considerable influence in deciding who should serve and on what terms. As each lease expired it was renewed and in 1454 the mayor himself, Richard Anson,[26] went to London to try to get a longer lease which was still in force when the *Giles* sailed against the French in 1457 and Lord Egremont showed himself disagreeably concerned with Admiralty matters entirely outside his jurisdiction. It was probably fortunate that the Admiralty prison had just been repaired.[27]

In 1449 the night watch was increased to eighteen — two men and the constable of each ward sworn in by the alderman. They remained on duty from the closing of all the gates at nine in the evening in summer until they were reopened at four the next morning.[28] In the disturbances which accompanied the civil war of 1459 the bench behaved as if a siege might be expected. It ordered that no corn should be taken out of the town, that every man was to have the arms appropriate to his rank, and that there should be twenty-four men in the night watch, half of whom were to be on the walls.[29] This was in October, a month after the battle of Blore Heath. The crisis was over by early November and the watch was reduced to the normal number of eight.

On 5 July 1460 the bell was rung, the commons came to the Guildhall, and it was agreed to send thirteen soldiers to Henry VI, but they probably did not reach him in time for his defeat and capture at Northampton five days later.[30] Hull was again in danger and in September the strictest precautions were taken against a sudden assault. No less than a quarter of the men in the town were put on watch each night. Every gate except one was kept barred day and night, but Beverley Gate was open during the day with a man to supervise it.[31] With open, level ground and only one possible line of approach this was enough to provide warning of any possibly hostile force. In October an order was made forbidding anyone to leave the town without the mayor's consent — a fairly clear indication of divided loyalties in the town. All staithes opening on to the haven were to be blocked by gates or bars, and at the south end Mamhole was to be blocked 'by casting down muck', everyone working at this task on alternate days or providing a substitute. At Northgates the defences were strengthened by digging a ditch inside the walls.[32] The order forbidding the removal of corn was reissued in November, though this time, in order to hamper trade as little as possible, shipments with the approval of both the bench and a majority of the burgesses were allowed. No stranger was to remain more than one night unless he swore to be of good behaviour and his host undertook responsibility for him.[33] By 24 November the vulnerability of the town on the unwalled side against the haven had become so apparent that it was decided to order Claus Ortson's ship, presumably with guns, to lie at the jetty for the safeguard of the town.[34] An archer was stationed at each common staithe, and

Bishop Lane was blocked with large barrels filled with stones to reduce the chances of a successful attack against the northeastern part of the town where the houses in High Street did not form a continuous row and the ground was too soft for any satisfactory wall between North Gate and the Hull. All who could afford it, and especially those living on the staithes, were to provide themselves with guns and each one would support any person threatened because of the arrest of the young Irishman found on Claus Ortson's ship. Aldermen were authorised to search any house for strangers; and every man was to join in digging defences in front of the three barbicans which spanned the moat at North Gate, Myton Gate and Hessle Gate. A week later there were further precautions. About one hundred persons subscribed for a chain, for which a windlass was later provided, across the haven mouth, and no ship would be allowed into the haven until the master, the purser and the captains of armed men were examined by the bench. No more than one hundred men could be on shore unless the mayor gave permission, and none must have with him any weapon other than his dagger.[35]

During this critical time, which probably lasted until the battle of Towton on 29 March 1461, Henry Percy, Earl of Northumberland, visited the town. Seman Burton spent £4 on wine for him.[36] He was by far the greatest of the magnates within a day's journey or more of the town, and his ravaging of estates in Yorkshire,[37] a mainly Lancastrian county, must have been a powerful reason for the town's expensive subscription to aid Queen Margaret.[38]

According to tradition Richard Anson, as mayor, was killed at the battle of Wakefield on 30 December 1460, but it seems much more likely that if he was a casualty of war he died at Towton. It is unlikely that the bench would be willing to continue for three months with no mayor and only twelve aldermen, but they did not choose a new mayor, John Spenser, until 4 April, 'because Richard Anson, late mayor, died during the year'.[39] This was immediately after the receipt of a letter from Edward IV, then at York after his decisive victory, commanding them to elect a mayor. John Grene was elected to fill Anson's place as alderman; and at the same time John Worlaby asked to be relieved of his place as alderman, and John Swan was elected. With a new town clerk, and a new sword-bearer for the mayor, the balance between the factions in the town changed considerably and was soon followed by the expulsion from the town of the dissidents previously described.[40] Immediately after this purge three tuns of wine were sent to the new King, and the mayor rode to York with nine others in the hope of being admitted to an audience.[41]

Edward IV now required six ships with forecastles to serve him at sea, but there were delays caused by difficulty in getting a priest to join them, the slow delivery of victuals from York, and difficulty in checking the 250 quarters of corn which they were to transport;[42] which at least gave the town time to do something about its finances which the change of dynasty had almost ruined. In the year ending on 29 September 1461 the chamberlains had somehow to find or borrow over £200 more than their revenues provided.[43] The accounts were not made up and audited until Edward had long been firmly on the throne and it was therefore prudent to leave unrecorded the large sum which the town had provided for Queen Margaret. By January 1462 the partly new bench felt it prudent to sit with the recorder and summon Thomas Pateryngton for his refusal to contribute with the rest of the commons to this unprofitable expenditure. He was left in prison until he could pay ten marks.[44]

Loyalty to Edward IV proved to be the best policy, but it was expensive. The *Mary Bedford* had to be fitted out for him in 1462 at a total cost of £35. Some who had to contribute gave provisions instead of cash. The Prior of Ferriby gave six quarters of malt, a quantity far in excess of the needs of a single ship.[45] Peter and Laurens Berbruer, resident aliens, gave three tuns of beer, and other persons gave beer, fish, 170 stockfish, salt, and meat, while a miller did grinding of corn, this service being valued at 6s 8d. In the spring of 1464 the northern rising of the adherents of Henry VI brought more demands. The town and its county had to provide and equip thirty armed men to join the army of Montague which dispersed the Lancastrians at Hedgely Moor and Hexham.[46] The Hull troops cannot have taken part in both battles as they were not with him for more than nineteen days and may have remained in the Newcastle garrison, paid at the usual high rate of a shilling a day,[47] which largely explains why it was always easy to recruit soldiers for these short campaigns, and on their return they were given an extra 3s each 'in so much that the said soldiers shall have better will to serve the commons in time coming'. Though thirty had been called for, the pay of five only is recorded, but the town had already been rewarded. To compensate the men of the town for their losses of goods to the rebels[48] for ten years they were granted the privilege of shipping, free of custom, merchandise, other than wool, on which the duty would have amounted to £40 in the year. To spread the benefit the corporation levied the duty itself, and in several years an additional £40 was assigned to the chamberlains,[49] but in some years the duty on exports fell below £40, and they got less.[50] In 1468-9 the mayor took the £40 and spent the whole of it on the walls.

There was a rising in 1469 by Robert Hillyard (or Hildyard), known as Robin of Holderness, crushed by Montague before the rebels could reach York. In September an assembly in the common hall agreed to send twenty men to aid the King,[51] when Edward IV himself was engaged in the suppression of rebellion in Yorkshire. Another twelve went from the county, one burgess protesting, until he was threatened with imprisonment, that his assessment for the necessary tax was excessive. Feeling its insecurity on the side of the haven once more, the bench removed a jetty on the Drypool side to make an assault more difficult.[52]

In addition to the distractions of civil war, there was the constant attrition of war at sea. The *James* of Hull, under Robert Michelson, was captured in a sharp engagement with the French, and in February 1473 he was allowed £60 out of the customs to ransom himself, the seamen, and the merchants who had been taken, so this was evidently not a warship.[53]

The Earl of Northumberland, in September 1481, as warden of the East March, ordered that soldiers should be raised, and thirteen men in white jackets with another eight from the county were sent to him to serve under the Duke of Albany against the Scots.[54] They were paid at the usual rate of about a shilling a day for thirty-four days. There was then a short respite until men arrayed for war were summoned by proclamation to join the Duke of Gloucester, Lord Protector, at Pontefract on 25 June 1483.[55] By October, as Richard III, he ordered that as many as possible should be sent to him at Leicester to put down Buckingham's rebellion.[56] Fourteen were sent from Hull, four from Hessle, three from Ferriby with Swanland, two from Kirkella with Westella and Willerby and one from Anlaby with Wolfreton.

The cost of these recurring demands was too much for Hull to meet without assistance. The bench spent heavily in 1483 in sending its counsel with the town clerk and three aldermen to petition for a grant of £70 a year out of the customs.[57] They had some hope of success, since Hull, with York and the northern counties, had already been exempted from the payment of the tenth and fifteenth granted by Parliament, because of the expenses they had incurred in the wars with Scotland.[58] A year later in February 1484 and the customs grant was made, but for £60 a year, not for the £70 hoped for, for twenty years.[59] The difference of £10 hardly mattered since Hull trade had declined and in some years the exports of Hull merchants were not dutiable to that amount. The bench at first interpreted the grant as giving them the right to levy the duty for the benefit of the town, and in March to September 1484 the chamberlains received £36 from this source, but in their next surviving account no more than £11.[60] After that nothing appeared in their accounts as received from this grant which must therefore have been used for the purpose clearly intended, to assist trade, by allowing merchants to ship goods free of customs, rather than as a means of helping the chamberlains to balance their accounts.

With war so frequent aliens in the towns were sometimes felt to be dangerous. There were sixteen of them permanently resident in 1481, nine being Scots; and in addition there were seamen and merchants from foreign ships, who might occasionally add another hundred.[61] One, Henry Bailly, born at Stolpe in Pomerania, had lived so long in Hull and other places in the realm that in 1451 he was in effect naturalised by the grant of a patent enabling him to live peaceably in England.[62] In what looks like a temporary emergency an order of 1450 prohibited men from Scotland, Orkney, or Iceland from carrying any dagger, sword, or stick in the town, contrary to the mayor's proclamation.[63] The normal, less drastic precautions against the foreignness of aliens remained in force for a century at least. They must not walk in the town after dark without a light or at any time carry bows and arrows for shooting, walk on the walls, or cause any assembly in the town or fields.[64]

Sources

1. *Chronicles of the Reigns of Edward I and Edward II*, ii, 103.
2. *CPR* 1299-1301, 583.
3. *CPR* 1301-7, 108.
4. BB2, 15 March 1317.
5. *CPR* 1321-2, 351.
6. Ibid., 366.
7. *CPR* 1321-4, 86.
8. *CPR* 1333-7, 90, 91.
9. *CPR* 1318-25, 246-7.
10. *CPR* 1331-4, 418, 102.
11. *CCR* 1333-7, 22.
12. Ibid., 690.
13. *CIM*, ii, No. 496.
14.* *Chronicon de Melsa*, iii, 152; a cautious estimate based on the surplus which Meaux had in store, over 5000 quarters, before all the 1367 harvest was in. The probable surplus of the five other large monasteries within easy reach of Hull (York, Kirkham, Selby, Bridlington and Thornton) are estimated as being proportionate to their value; but York, because of the wide dispersal of its lands, is estimated at only half its value.
15. H.J. Hewitt, *The Organisation of War under Edward III*, 54-7.
16. *CPR* 1354-8, 106.
17. Ibid., 243.
18. Ibid., 102.
19. *CPR* 1396-9, 181; 1399-1401, 209, 353.
20. BB3A, f.129, f.130b.
21. *CPR* 1452-61, 172.
22. Chamb., 34 Hen. VI.
23. *CPR* 1452-61, 404, 405, 439.
24. Chamb., 35 Hen. VI.
25. BB3, f.24b.
26. BB3A, f.62.
27. Chamb., 34 Hen. VI.
28. BB3A, f.11.
29. Ibid., f.66b.
30. Ibid., f.71b.
31. Ibid., f.72.
32. Ibid., f.73.
33. Ibid., f.73b.
34. Ibid., f.74.
35. Ibid., f.74b.
36. Ibid., f.85b.
37. *DNB*, s.v. PERCY, HENRY, 1421-61.
38. BB3A, f.81b.
39. Ibid., f.47b.
40. Ibid., f.77.
41. Ibid., f.76b.
42. Ibid., f.77b.
43. Chamb., 39 Hen. VI, and 1 Edw. IV.
44. BB3A, f.81b.
45. Ibid., f.84.
46.* There was a sixteenth-century rhyme 'Hops, Reformation, Bibles and Beer came

into England all in one year.' Hull had the new drink much earlier. Today ale and beer are the same thing. Then beer was ale brewed with hops as well as with malt. Once imported from Germany, in the fifteenth century it was being made in Hull by Germans. It probably kept better than ale.

47.   Ibid., f.94.
48.   *CPR* 1461-7, 289.
49.   Chamb., 4 and 9 Edw. IV.
50.   Chamb., 8 Edw. IV.
51.   BB3A, f.112.
52.   Ibid., f.114.
53.   *CPR* 1467-77, 368.
54.   BB3A, f.129, f.130b.
55.   Ibid., f.133b.
56.   Ibid., f.135b.
57.   Chamb., 22 Edw. IV.
58.   *CPR* 1476-85, 339.
59.   Ibid., 455.
60.   Chamb., 1 Rich. III; 1 Hen. VII.
61.*   BB3A, f.129. In 1444 there were 22 resident Scots. Achlek was the only specifically Scots surname in the list.
62.   *CPR* 1452-61, 204.
63.   BB3A, f.25.
64.   Ibid., f.97.

6

The Market, the Ferries and Foreign Trade

The market, regulated in great detail, was vital to the lives of the inhabitants in that it was there that they obtained most of their food and household needs, and shops were few. The market served no other purpose. It had nothing to do with the general trading activities of merchants, and practically nothing sold in it could be used for any purpose other than the ordinary needs of the purchaser and his family. In many parts of the country up to the thirteenth century, Sunday markets had been common. The Hull markets were on Tuesdays and Fridays, but from 1 August to 29 September, the harvest season, the bench allowed trading on Sundays.[1]

The market bell cost 6s 8d to replace and must therefore have been something much heavier than a handbell. It hung on the Guildhall at the south end of Marketgate, just to the south of where the King William statue now stands.[2] Until the bell was rung at nine in the morning no corn could be sold, and it was not even lawful to open a corn-sack. Since no one could buy except for his household needs, cooks and victuallers could not buy meat in the market, though they probably could buy corn, but were to make their purchases more than two miles from Hull. No fish could be sold before six in the summer or seven in the winter. Because of the extreme difficulty of fishermen bringing their own catch to the market, there was an exception made to the normal rule that no one must sell in the market goods which he had bought with that intention. Instead, the limit imposed on fish-trading was that the seller must not merely be a salesman for those who caught fish. He had instead to sell his own fish 'bought at the sea or in the

Humber'.[3]

The corn market was supervised by an alderman until one in the afternoon, by which time householders and victuallers would have bought all they needed and others, such as shipmen and maltsters, could buy; though this was not expressly stated until the sixteenth century. Anyone caught forestalling the market was heavily fined. John Buck of Snaith paid 6s 8d for this offence, or considerably more than he was likely to earn in a fortnight, and Henry Hobson was found buying corn at the north ferry and sending it to Newcastle (1484); while another offender sold corn he had bought in the market to men from Newcastle and another took corn to York.[4]

Butchers, bakers and brewers were also subject to strict regulations. Butchers who lived in Hull (1440) were to have no shop or stall except in the Flesh-Market at the end of Denton Lane. If they appeared with country butchers in the ordinary market they were fined 3s 4d, and to make sure that no one escaped this penalty, a chamberlain who failed to exact it had to pay it himself. The country butchers could trade only in the New Butchery[5] but we are not told where this was, and by 1468 the rule was that they were to have their stalls on both sides of Marketgate from the end of Scale Lane and Whitefriargate southwards. Hull butchers could not join them, but had the advantage of being able to sell from their shops on any day of the week. The price of sheep heads and hearts was at the same time fixed at a halfpenny.[6] All butchers (*c.* 1470) had to be prepared to sell in halfpennyworths, pennyworths and twopennyworths, the implication being that although they could sell a smaller quantity by barter or credit they were not required to do so.[7] In 1440 it had been found that they were persistently obstructing the highway, to the particular inconvenience of priests with the sacrament, by tethering their horses outside their shops day and night, presumably because they wanted to reserve their grass closes for livestock and feed their horses from nosebags. Only burgesses paying their share of the fee-farm rent could be butchers and kill beasts. By 1492 they were not strictly confined to the Flesh-Market. There was a large butcher's shop under the Guildhall.[8]

Bakers no longer needed to fear infringing the assize of bread as much as they had to in the earliest days of the borough, probably because they were now fully assimilated into the community and not thought to be particularly prone to cheating. Perhaps most of their offences arose from the great difficulty of baking loaves of the correct weight. Hull bakers, like those almost everywhere, were fined with such regularity, and all at the same time, that the fine seems to have become a kind of licence-fee based on the assumption that any baker must have broken the assize, and that only notorious offenders need be heavily fined. In 1452 eleven of them paid fines, mostly of 2*s*, but one as much as 21*s* 4*d* — a sum equivalent to a fine imposed for causing death by dangerous driving in the week when this item in 1976 was extracted from the city archives.[9] This means that about two out of three bakers were fined for offences against the assize of bread, since in 1454 there were eighteen bakers, of whom eight were women, sworn to observe the assize.[10] Established bakers were protected from competition. The only persons allowed to bake were those sworn by the mayor in the previous year, and innkeepers were not allowed to bake even horse-bread.[11]

Brewers were also tipplers, that is, sellers of ale. They were obliged to sell at the price fixed by the bench, in sealed and approved measures, by pennyworths and halfpennyworths; and their barrels had to hold exactly 28 gallons and bear their mark.[12] A person brewing for his own household could buy malt in the market, but ordinary brewers could not.[13] Any keeper of an inn or alehouse giving lodging to any person for more than a day and a night was answerable (1470) 'for him and his deeds', and must close when the curfew was rung at eight or nine.[14]

Many of those coming to the market came by one or other of the ferries. Often the ferry from Barton was leased with the boat. In 1452 two partners took a lease of the south ferry-boat for three years at a rent of £20 a year,[15] while in 1459 William Eland, gentleman, possibly the lawyer of the same name, leased it for three years at a rent of £24, acting through a deputy and maintaining the boat in good condition.[16] By the 1490s it was usually impossible to lease it for more than seven or eight pounds, which must be taken as a fairly clear proof of a decline in traffic. The south ferry-boat was a vessel fit for seagoing, but even so, some time in 1423-4, it was lost. Hessle men who salvaged the wreck were paid 11*s* 1*d* and another 11*d* for finding the landing-bridge and bringing it to Hull. A place was made for her in the northern part of the haven until she was fit to be moved to Selby Staithe to have her painted sail bent. This salvage and refitting cost over £13, which indicates a vessel comparable in size with most of those arriving from overseas.[17] Though she carried two large sweeps, it is most unlikely that these were used except with the tide in a flat calm. As she had a bowsprit she also had the simple fore-and-aft rig which alone would enable her to sail fairly close to the wind, and a ship of her size would be useless as a ferry unless she could do so. She carried an anchor and cable, a fifty-fathom warp, a windlass, two boats and a bridge lowered to land passengers.[18] A contract for the making of a new Humber ferry-boat in 1541 was let for £26 13s 4d to Robert Wilson, who was to make the hull carvel-built, to decrease the friction in the water, below the water line, and clinker-built, for strength, above.[19] She was fitted (1447) with a pump for the bilges.[20]

The north ferry-boat was a smaller and less substantial vessel propelled by long sculls tipped with iron and with the shafts bound with iron where they passed through the rowlocks. When a new boat was made in 1436-7 her keel was about thirty feet long and she was between eight and ten feet in beam. The hull required 300 pounds of iron or more and 325 feet of timber went into the ribs. Sixty wainscots and twelve balks of Riga timber were also used, with two barrels of pitch and tar. She was half-decked, carrying four iron boat-hooks and three spare shafts. There was no rudder, but instead two steering oars. The old boat was sold for the ferry over the Derwent, at Kexby near York, for more than £6.[21*] As she was worked by two men only and was too wide to be rowed by one, the help of the passengers must have been needed.

Since Hull was a port with little industry, trade outside the market went on in far greater volume. There were still occasions when there was some communal enterprise of the type we have seen existed in the fourteenth century, but it was rare.[22] There is an entry in the chamberlains' roll for 1441-2 which reads: 'Profits of merchandise coming from the collector. Of merchandise bought by the community and sold by the collector nothing was received this year because such merchandise was not bought;' but in the following year R. Broggour, as collector or *corrector* bought Rhenish wine for £23 and made a clear profit of £28 to be shared among the burgesses. By this time it was a condition of such trading that no burgess had to contribute more than 13s 4d for his share in the year's ventures. Since so much garlic was used, a supply was bought in 1460 to be re-sold to the inhabitants at the original low-cost price when prices rose; but instead they fell and the bench ruled that this 'common garlic' must be shared among the commons, every man paying for his share.[23]

The position of Hull as a port was unique in that for several centuries it was the sole outlet for the foreign trade of a place of much greater importance — York, and for the trade of Beverley, which throughout the Middle Ages was bigger than Hull. At first, except when the de la Poles were merchants, there was little merchant capital in the town, and what there was had no difficulty in accommodating itself to the existence of larger capitalists from York and Beverley. By the second half of the fifteenth century, however, with merchants a majority, or largely represented, on the bench, the corporation began to assert its prior claims in virtually all foreign trade and to enforce ordinances intended to give Hull merchants a distinct advantage over all others. About 1470 an order was made to the effect that no one irrespective of whether he was a burgess must sell the goods of any alien as if they were his own.[24] The purpose of preventing Hull burgesses from acting as agents for foreigners was to make it easier to enforce the custom known as 'foreign bought and foreign sold' which finally gained status equal to that of a statute by Henry VIII's patent of 1532.[25]

It was in connection with Prussians, and the Hanse merchants of Dantzig, that the effects of this attempt to create special privileges for Hull merchants first appeared. At the end of 1454 various Prussians were warned that if they continued to sell their goods from their ships in the haven before they were landed, the goods would be forfeited. This was one of the ordinances made by the Crown when the borough was first created, but the intention now was to change its effect. William Pepir of Norwich was forced to pay a fine because he was in the habit of buying and selling in the town merchandise coming from Prussia. This was treated as forestalling, which was a considerable extension of the meaning of the word. As a specific charge was needed, he was indicted for buying two 'scokkes' of bast and re-selling it to Thomas Etton.[26] The Prussians were warned that they must not sell linseed except in bulk or pitch or tar in quantities of less than a ton, the obvious intention being to confine their selling to large merchants to the exclusion of all others.

The bench had apparently used its Admiralty rights in some way in its effort to monopolise Prussian trade. In February 1453 two Prussian Hanse merchants appeared with a royal writ which appeared to put their case outside the local Admiralty jurisdiction, but the bench decided not to give in without consulting their counsel, Adam Copendale, who, as soon as he arrived in Hull, told them that they certainly could not use their Admiralty rights in this case. Later another Prussian, Hans Croft of Dantzig, in St Mary's and in the presence of the mayor appointed another Copendale, Edmund, to act as his attorney. Apparently the 1456 agreement with Dantzig was not reached without conflict.[27] They could now sell their merchandise to any stranger, such as a man of York or Amsterdam, provided that they sold in bulk, but to burgesses only they could sell in smaller quantities. Every ship usually had a number of mariners owning cargo, and they were free to sell as they pleased to burgesses so long as they did not sell any of their goods to merchants who had sailed with them. The final conflict which produced this agreement had been brought about by the selling of a quantity of oars contrary to custom, and it was now agreed that this should be overlooked.

At the end of October 1463 three Prussian merchants not of Dantzig arrived in the haven and did not land their goods, almost certainly intended for York citizens. There was bitter feeling in York about the Hull trading customs and the mayor of York wrote a letter of protest to John Grene, mayor of Hull, about new 'ordinances to let (i.e. prevent) the citizens to buy and sell with merchants strangers', contrary to the King's laws. Grene replied that this was the custom, confirmed by law, and that there was no intention of hindering York men; though *they* had offended. He continued: 'Divers of the citizens as it is openly here known have here, within this port, contrary to the king's statutes ingrossed and bought great substance of merchandise of merchants strangers or (i.e. before) the said merchandises were landed, by which the said goods be forfeitable, as I report me to your wisdom. Yet, for to have continue of good neighbourhood I and my said conburgesses have forebeared to forfeit the same or to show any manner of cause of unkindness, as God knows, who have you in his grace and mercy'.[28*]

Disputes of this kind with York were to continue into the reign of Charles I. Having waited long enough for their York consignee, and possibly having heard of the exchange of letters, the three

Prussemen, now landed their goods at Bowerstathe; but the bench promptly ordered that for the next fortnight they could sell to men of Hull only. Further, two aldermen were to search the ship and compare the cargo with the original bill of lading in the mayor's possession, and in this way it would be known whether they had been illegally selling goods not landed. To close the last visible loophole, an order was made shortly afterwards that no burgess was to sell the goods of any alien under the pretence that they were his, a device which gave aliens the privilege of burgesses, which the bench was determined to deny them.[29]

But even in those days of fairly simple transactions it was found impossible to make regulations for the disadvantage of York and other boroughs which, if strictly interpreted, would not injure Hull trade. The bench was fortunate in having provided itself with its own discretionary loophole at least as long ago as 1445. From that year a new item under the head *Fines of strangers* appears in each annual roll of the chamberlains with the explanation added, in 1455 'for licences granted to them by the mayor for selling various merchandise'. In that year the amount so received did not reach £4 and was little more than one-and-a-half per cent of the town revenue. It lay entirely within the discretion of the bench, rather than of the mayor alone, whether to grant such licences, and in some years the revenue from this source was a few shillings only. The aim was not to raise money but to regulate foreign trade to the advantage of Hull merchants. In 1474 it was possible to collect over £16 or more than eight per cent of the total revenue in this way.[30]

A healthy dispute could be very long-lived, particularly where contact with the enemy was not very frequent. In the fledgeling days of Hull all disputes with Scarborough were ended by the sealing of a composition under which the authorities of each town agreed that their people should be free of all tolls and exactions in both. This was in 1305.[31] By 1455 good feeling no longer existed, and it was reported that at Scarborough Hull men were being made to pay a toll of 4*s* on each last (twelve barrels) of herrings. If any Scarborough men appeared in Hull the bench would be informed and would decide what to do with them. Clearly neither borough was keeping its compact which had also required that each should recognise all the privileges of the other.[32] It was decided in 1471 that no Scarborough man would be allowed to have a shop in Hull to sell his goods;[33] and as an additional deterrent it was ordered in 1473 that no Scarborough man coming to Hull could sell by retail. He could therefore sell only in bulk to Hull merchants, and at a price fixed by the mayor. If he was not satisfied with the price, he could not remove his goods for another forty days, and in that time could buy whatever he needed from burgesses only.[34] One Scarborough man, John Robynson, was also a Hull burgess and had (1480) to pay the very large fine of five marks for buying Scarborough herrings brought to Hull.[35] Even a citizen of London could be treated roughly where it seemed safe enough. A Dartmouth man in 1464 had appeared with a certificate showing that he was a citizen of London, but as he did not live there the bench refused to recognise his freedom from toll.[36]

It is more reasonable to regard this kind of friction with other towns and with aliens as incidental to the commerce of Hull rather than characteristic of it. Everyone in trade and shipping knew perfectly well that wherever he went he would find different customs which nevertheless would not be so wholly different everywhere that there was no family resemblance among them. In Hull, as in most other places, it was the rule that a stranger who had come to trade, whether he was English or alien, must find a host who would be responsible for him, advise him on local usages and perform all the functions of an agent except most of those which were economically crucial. In making bargains the stranger was expected to look after his own interests. A note in a fifteenth-century bench book about hosts and aliens was made not because hostage was unusual but because the strangers being accommodated were new. One was so new (*c.* 1449) that he was known only as 'the little sprot man'. He was not selling the little sprats but was small in build and had come with *sprods*, which were immature salmon. He had to pay only 20*d* for his right to trade, and he needed no host as he was selling just one commodity. At the same time John Northeby who had just served as sheriff was registered as host for Gilmyn Claisson who paid 16*s* 8*d*, and William Stove, who paid 10*s*; and the common tavern was let to Gilmyn Ducheman for 2*s* a week while he was selling his wine, and thereafter for 16*d* a week.

By the fifteenth century there were always aliens settled and established in Hull. In 1481 the majority consisted of nine thoroughly Anglicised Scots. Three of the others were named

Berbruer, which shows that beer as distinct from ale without hops may already have been brewed in the town. There was another alien called Henry Hattmaker, and next in the list there is a man with no surname, simply called 'the straw-hat maker'.[37]

In 1482 a final solution of the custom of *foreign bought and foreign sold* was almost reached with all Hanse merchants, and not simply those of Dantzig; and it is only a slight imperfection in the manuscript which prevents us from concluding that it was frustrated, over the manner in which whale-oil could be sold, by Richard Doughty, the town clerk, who was also a merchant and probably anxious that train-oil should be sold only in large quantities, and never in the small amounts which it was suggested should be saleable in special cases.[38] The merchants of the Hanse had obtained writs from the King which would probably have frustrated any regulation of their trade, and in London were represented by the counsel. Richard Doughty rode to London and acted jointly with the counsel then retained for the corporation.

The legal shipment of wool from Hull overseas was on a smaller scale than it had been in the fourteenth century, but the decline did not become marked until the middle of the century. By the last decade the trade recorded had shrunk to less than a tenth of what it had been in 1401-10.[39] This decline was largely the result of the growth of a large English cloth industry, and from the 1380s the export of cloth from Hull continued on a very large scale. In good years several thousand cloths were shipped, almost 3200 in 1424-5, over 6500 in 1428-9, and over 5000 in 1437-8. But decline was imminent as London began almost to monopolise the export of cloth. In the 1450s the number of cloths leaving Hull was over 3000 in one year only, and over 2000 in five. As the London exports soared towards 20,000 cloths a year Hull usually exported not more than 1000. There was a recovery in the 1470s with frequent totals in excess of 2000 cloths. By 1519 when London exported over 66,000, Hull did not quite reach 1000. But although first wool and then cloth were the most important of English exports, Hull also exported lead and corn, and imported a great variety of foreign and particularly of Baltic merchandise. Hanseatic merchants were involved in the Hull cloth export to the extent of between about twenty-five per cent in an average and sixty per cent in an exceptional year; but everything indicates that they were far more involved in importing their own goods at Hull. The trade of the port, if customs returns can be trusted, stagnated in the middle of the fifteenth century, but by the end was of much the same volume as it had been at the beginning.[40]

Denmark controlled the entrance to the Baltic, and for this reason alone would have been important to Hull. In 1447-8 the chamberlains paid T. Chapman 13*s* 4*d* for taking a letter to Denmark and 20*s* to Hugh Hurlok for producing a record of certain proceedings there.[41] In 1450 a knight named Beelz had transacted business for the town in Denmark, where he presumably must have gone for some other purpose, and the mayor and nineteen others each contributed 3*s* 4*d* to recompense him for his services. This amounted to £3 6*s* 8*d* a good sum, but quite insufficient if Hull business had been his sole employment.[42] The incompleteness of the records would leave us in the dark as to what this business was; but it is safe to assume that on both occasions it was Iceland.

Since the Iceland trade was forbidden by the King of Denmark, Norway and Sweden, it had peculiar attractions for the Robin Hood element in Hull and must have been viewed with horror by the more solid merchants and shipmen who feared that the Baltic could be closed to them in retaliation for the misdeeds of Hull and other semi-pirates. These included the kidnapping of the governor of Iceland and his deputy in 1425, for which it was not all Hull men alone who were responsible; but in his long catalogue of English misdeeds which the governor drew up after his arrival in a civilised nation he had a great deal to say about the violent law-breaking of John Percy and other Hull mariners.[43] As a consequence of this the English government forbade all Iceland trade except through Bergen. From the petition to Parliament drawn up by the English traders we learn that officials of the King of Denmark, Norway and Sweden in Iceland had confiscated English goods worth £25,000.[44] Of this amount £5000 was accounted for by goods from York and Hull. The safer historical conclusion to be drawn from this is that York merchants were supplying capital for ventures to Iceland from Hull, and that this amounted to about a fifth of the total English trade there. Bristol and Lynn were more prominent, but not in malfeasance.

A royal prohibition was quite insufficient in itself to stop this trade. Hull ships, and some from Scarborough, were among those seized in Iceland with cargoes worth between £200 and £300.

Iceland stockfish were what the English merchants wanted, and as there is no reason to suppose that Hull was any different from Grimsby and Cromer, a ship having arrived and discharged its cargo, then employed its people in line fishing and salting the catch on shore.[45] Officious interference with so profitable a venture was still violently resisted, in spite of which the English government continued to grant licences to trade with Iceland. Hull contacts were so regular that when John Blockwich was made a bishop in Iceland he arranged to maintain all his contracts with his diocese through a merchant of Hull.[46] This trade was so important that under Edward IV there was something of a revival of communal trading from the town. Year after year, probably to spread the risk as well as the profit, the bench regularly sent three or four ships to Iceland in the name of the corporation.[47] There is no record of the sharing of the profits; but these contacts were so reliable that London fishmongers, instead of setting up their own venture, preferred to trade through Hull.

The Iceland connection was throughout marked by violence, but the nature of the records are in part responsible for this impression. Men from Dantzig, Hull, Beverley and Lynn (1439) in the *James* of Hull plundered the *Mariknight* of Amsterdam in an Irish harbour where she had arrived with stockfish from Iceland.[48] It may have been this piratical aspect of Iceland ventures that made it inadvisable for Sir Henry Brounflete, an East Riding knight, to deny (1439) that he had sent the *Katerin* of Hull to Iceland, without the formality of customs' duty and clearance, with cloth, linen, beer, iron, sweet wine and other goods to a total value of £393. In the 1450s there were frequent inquiries into Hull trade, as well as that of other ports principally interested in Iceland and Finmark, the most northern part of Norway, since unless these voyages were first licensed, they were contrary to statute.[49] The trade between Bergen and Iceland was largely in the hands of Hanse merchants, and it was only through Bergen that English trade with Iceland could be legally carried on. Merchants of Hull and Bristol would have regarded it as a gross neglect of commercial fundamentals if they had not committed piracy against ships of Hamburg and Dantzig. But there still was a legal trade, of sorts. For his services to the cause of Edward IV, Montague was temporarily transformed into the Earl of Northumberland and further rewarded by a grant of the *Antony* of Hull, forfeited for unlawful trade with Iceland, where he was now licensed to send her.[50] Her former owners included a London stockfishmonger and Thomas Patrington of Hull, sheriff in 1452-3.[51]

Sources

1. BB3, f.17b.
2. Chamb. 15 Hen. VI.
3. BB3, f.96.
4. BB3A, f.132b.
5. BB3, f.19; Chamb. 26 Hen. VI.
6. BB3, f.98b.
7. Ibid., f.96b.
8. BB3A, f.148.
9. Ibid., f.41.
10. Ibid., f.71.
11. Ibid., f.132, f.197.
12. Ibid., f.19.
13. Ibid., f.94.
14. Ibid., f.96.
15. Ibid., f.39.
16. Ibid., f.66b.
17. Chamb. 2 Hen. VI.
18. BB3A, f.68.
19. Ibid., f.231b.
20. Chamb. 26 Hen. VI.
21.* The two *handrothers* of the north ferry-boat may have been rudders, not steering-oars. Chamb. 2, 11, 15 Hen. VI.
22. Chamb., 19,20 Hen. VI.
23. BB3A, f.73b.
24. Ibid., f.96b.
25. Boyle, *Charters and Letters Patent* . . ., 64-5.
26. BB3A, f.74b.
27. Ibid. (unfoliated).
28.* Ibid., f.89, f.89b. Here this passage is slightly abridged, without alteration

of meaning and the spelling is modernised as it will be in all English passages quoted.
29. Ibid., f.96b.
30. Chamb. 24 Hen. VI, 33 Hen VI; 13 Edw. IV.
31. BB3, f.44.
32. BB3A, f.76.
33. Ibid., f.114.
34. Ibid. f.117.
35. Ibid., f.96b.
36.* Ibid., f.15, f.16.
37. f.17. Some were master-craftsmen.
38. Ibid., f.129, f.130b.
39. Carus-Wilson, *England's Export Trade 1275-1547*, 36-119.
40. *VCH*, Hull, 89.
41. Chamb. 28 Hen. VI.
42. BB3A, f.22.
43. E. M. Carus-Wilson, 'The Iceland Trade', 164-5 (in E. Power, *Studies in English Trade in the Fifteenth Century*).
44. Ibid., 167.
45. E. Gillett, *A History of Grimsby*, 35-6.
46. Carus-Wilson, 'Iceland Trade', 170.
47. Ibid., 174.
48. *CPR* 1436-41, 270.
49. *CPR* 1446-52, 430, 479; 1452-61, 172, 176.
50. Carus-Wilson, 'Iceland Trade', 181.
51. Ibid., 177; *CPR* 1461-7, 378.

7

Charters and Town Government

The people of Hull, in their little world, were governed by thirteen aldermen under a set of rules defined by local custom and law and the interpretation of royal charters. After the 1331 charter which granted the borough in fee-farm and in effect made it a self-perpetuating, autonomous community, the charter of the greatest importance was that of 1440. A century of legal and administrative change had limited the autonomy of the borough, and in particular the growth of the importance of the county justices of the peace—as yet there were none for the borough—had nullified the virtual independence guaranteed by the previous charters. Their jurisdiction extended into all parts of the East Riding, including the boroughs, their powers were extensive, and their outlook was that of landed feudalists guided, but seldom rigidly bound, by a knowledge of common and statute law and with almost complete indifference to the opinions of shipowners and merchants. No new charter could abolish for Hull the awkward and anarchic aristocrats of the fifteenth century, but the 1440 charter did completely withdraw the town from the jurisdiction of these justices by making it a separate county in which the mayor the aldermen were the justices of the peace.[1]

A further royal grant in the same year added to the dignity of the bench by giving the mayor the privilege of having a sword carried erect before him, since he was the representative of the King, and the aldermen liberty to have robes and hoods in the same manner as those of London.[2] In an age in which differences of dress indicated status this was not meaningless, as it has now become; but what was of greater significance was the enlargement of the county by the charter of 1447 which made the fresh-water dike the northern boundary and brought Hessle, North Ferriby, Swanland, Westella, Kirkella, Tranby, Willerby, Wolfreton, Anlaby and Haltemprice into the new county. This grant was significant in extending the area in which the bench exercised their authority as justices of the peace, but it did not explicitly exclude the county justices from the extended county.[3]

The sheriff was not an alderman and in the nature of things most sheriffs, since there was a different one every year, could never become anything more exalted. He and his wife both wore crimson gowns, and like the mayor, he was not allowed to go out of the realm during his tenure of office.[4]. Having acquired a sheriff, the corporation immediately restricted as far as it could his power and dignity. He could not put an alderman on a jury unless he was ordered to do so by a judge or commissioner of the Crown presiding over a session in the Guildhall.[5] He was obliged to have a mace-bearer, and a mace was frequently used as a blunt instrument, but normally in daylight he could not be followed by any officer carrying an axe or a *wisell,* a kind of pole-axe. The pole-axe could accompany him in an emergency, when a sergeant needed help to prevent the 'rescue' of a prisoner, when there was a great affray or rising, or when a great crowd of strangers was assembled to watch any shooting, wrestling or game.[6] He had his own occasional court or *tourn* which dealt with such small matters as unlawful games in taverns, loitering in the streets at night, at staithe-ends, encroachments on highways or commons, the wrongful digging of ditches and offences affecting the fresh-water supply.[7]

The 1447 charter sanctioned the manner in which officers of the town had long been elected. In such elections all the burgesses voted, but they were limited to candidates, known as *lites* nominated by the bench. In a mayoral election the two *lites* were aldermen; in the election of a sheriff they were two burgesses; in the election of the chamberlains, four burgesses. Aldermen held office for life, and when there was a vacancy it was filled by the nomination of two *lites* from among the burgesses by the remainder of the bench. The burgesses then elected one of these.[8] In 1456, immediately after the election of the year's officers, an order was made that in the election of chamberlains no burgess must use his two votes maliciously or fraudulently. Malice and fraud were involved since the office of chamberlain was something to be avoided. In the election of all officers no one should hinder the counting by the clerk by moving from where he was sitting or standing, and except in a mayoral election each *lite* could have a scrutineer who went round with the clerk recording the votes.[9] At all elections (1459) it was ordered that every alderman must vote audibly and not secretly.[10] Since 1434 the burgesses also had been obliged to vote audibly.[11] If the election of the mayor resulted in a tie, the candidate for whom the out-going mayor had already voted was the winner.[12]

The mayor (1440) was fairly strictly controlled by the other aldermen. If any townsmen complained of any injustice done to him by the mayor, the latter was to be 'reconciled and reformed' by his brother-aldermen. They could fine him if in any important matter he acted against their advice, and if he made any stranger a burgess without their consent they could fine him £100. This order, made by the bench when John Aldwick was mayor, was confirmed by the commons when they were summoned to the Guildhall.[13] Like the sheriff and the chamberlains, in his year of office he could not go out of the realm at all, or be absent for more than a month.[14] Nevertheless the office of mayor could give great power to its holder. Three of the burgesses, at the 1455 election in the Guildhall, with the probable support of at least one alderman, riotously tried to prevent the election of Nicholas Elys.[15] Contempt of the mayor was treated as a most serious offence. When John Swan was mayor in 1466 his award in an arbitration displeased Robert Gilliott who said that he 'gave a false award and judgement as a false churl should', and for this he was left in the town gaol until he paid the large fine of £5, with the possibility that he might also lose his position as a burgess.[16] All elections, and all the business of the bench, were transacted in the Guildhall, which lay across the south end of the market place. There was a prison in the common hall there, with a pair of manacles, used for a chaplain in 1426-7 and for a madman called Nicholas thirty years later.[17] There appears to have been a separate prison for offenders of higher status, which in course of time was to become the debtors' prison. The sheriff and the bench (1455) agreed that the highest chamber in the Guildhall tower should be a prison for keeping and punishing persons who had offended against the mayor or the alderman who acted as Admiralty commissioner.[18]

The bench was no more immune than any other governing body from aspirations of Utopianism. They decided in 1441 that the aldermen were to refrain from all quarrels with one another and that each was to 'bear good love and true heart to other'. As far as possible each must avoid giving support to any stranger having a dispute with an alderman. If aldermen disagreed they were to notify the mayor, and he would arrange arbitration by their brethren, to which they were to submit. An alderman who failed to do this would be fined £10 for a first offence and for a second permanently excluded from the bench. Every alderman was obliged to attend all meetings so long as he had been summoned on the previous night and did not make any reasonable excuse for his absence.[19]

All of this, except the aspiration that the entire bench should live in harmony, was quite straightforward, in that it was not too difficult to enforce. The order (1440) that the sword-bearer was to be in the household of the mayor, who was to pay half his stipend of four marks, bore the same mark of thrift and realism.[20] Everywhere within the precincts of the town the mayor had to have the sword carried before him, and the sheriff his mace, and neither they nor any alderman could sell ale or wine from their houses.[21]

The powers of the corporation over the ordinary burgesses far exceeded those of any modern local authority; yet, except at a fairly low level, no one was employed full-time by the corporation. The sword-bearer could be nothing but a full-time but honoured household servant of each mayor. At the annual elections, after the important officers had been chosen, the burgesses elected six wool-porters, four turf-porters and three salt-meters and wine-porters from the four who were turf-porters. They were not paid by the corporation, but were nevertheless elected to positions which must have given them all or the greater part of their earnings.[22] The keepers of the north ferry were elected at the same time.

Normally the corporation spent more than a quarter of its revenues on its officers. In 1467-8 the mayor, John Darrys, had his 'pension' of £20 and his sergeant 13s 4d. His sword-bearer had 53s 4d, now entirely paid from the common purse. Richard Doughty, as common clerk, had 53s 4d, a substantial addition to his income. The sergeant of the gilt mace had 40s, and the common sergeant, almost a full-time minor official, 53s. The keepers of the north ferry were paid 60s between them. Usually there were two waits or minstrels, but now there was only one, paid 26s 8d. In the same year a good deal was spent on their liveries—40s on the expensive grey cloth known as *musterdevelers,* and 58s on cheaper cloth. The common clerk was supplied with his new livery costing12s, and Philip Douland, one of the counsel, was presented with a robe costing 10s.[23] The north ferryman also received gowns.

At the end of the century payments and liveries of much the same kind as these continued; but in addition Robert Merwyn, formerly a chamberlain, and now the broker, had 53s 4d. Richard Alan was paid 13s 4d. for looking after the wool-house, and a keeper of the fresh-water dike had 20s. Walter Calverley was paid 6s 8d for looking after the new hall—an indication of an extension of the Guildhall, not of the replacement of the old one. A man, not named, had 6s 8d for looking after the new land, which was probably land regained from the Humber at the southeast corner of the town.[24]

In 1453 Thomas Lorymer was appointed common messenger with no definite salary as he would be paid for each message he carried. If he had to be absent from Hull he was obliged to provide a substitute. As the rewards for carrying messages would not give him a real living he was at the same time made a wool-porter.[25] There were also town minstrels, not usually required to stand for re-election as their skill was a rare one. In 1402 each had a stipend of 13s 4d. The chamberlains provided them with new gowns, each costing 4s at the same time as they provided the boy-bishop with a new cope.[26] Each of the minstrels or waits had a silver collar belonging to the corporation, for which he had to provide a surety.[27] In 1454 both were dismissed.[28] The minute of their dismissal calls them *histriones,* actors, and as the name of one of them was given it must be recorded that John Wardlaw was the first Hull actor whose name is known. They may have had no successors until in 1459 William Butler and Robert Speke, the waits, provided sureties for their collars.[29]

The master of the grammar school may be ranked with these supernumeraries since in 1454 it was decided to provide him with a new gown as often as necessary. His scale of fees was drawn up a few weeks later. He instructed little children gratis but had 6d a quarter from each to whom he taught reading and 8d a quarter from those learning Latin.[30]

The bench, as we have seen them, governed the town. In the country, where they had the support of their sheriff, they exercised only the powers of justices, but since usually none of them was of the same standing as the greater landowners, in the county they can have had nothing like the same authority as they were able to exercise in the borough, where their powers were practically unlimited. They were in no sense an autocracy. On occasion they would have their orders confirmed by all those who had been chamberlains or sheriffs, and even more often all the burgesses would be summoned to the Guildhall for the making of a new order. This was probably as much in order to ensure that everyone knew of the order as to guarantee that everyone was in agreement with it. If they expected that the commons would object they were always at liberty to make their orders without them.

Quite apart from their judicial authority, they conducted the court of the borough through which virtually all lawsuits between burgesses were decided. No burgess could bring an action against another, for any matter determinable within the borough court, in any other court, without the consent of the mayor;[31] and in 1445 William Ripplingham lost his rights as a burgess for doing so.[32] About half-a-dozen attornies were sworn to act for those who did not want to conduct their own cases, and no other lawyer could practise in the court. From the things they were warned *not* to do it is to be assumed that the standard of professional conduct was low. They were not to foment lawsuits; not to trick the court into considering matters outside its jurisdiction, not to take any fee from the party against whom they were acting but to be true to their clients, not to urge any client to take elsewhere a case within the jurisdiction of the court, and not to retain money due to clients for their own profit but to pay it to them immediately.[33]

The proceedings of the bench were so secret that any alderman revealing them might lose his place for ever. As it had cost him a good deal to get it in the first place, this must have been a considerable deterrent. All the evidence points to the fact that by the fifteenth century no one could become an alderman unless he had first served his year as a chamberlain, and most chamberlains, though qualified, never became aldermen, though some became sheriffs. Their office was costly and burdensome. They had to collect virtually all the revenues due to the borough in the year, including fines. For some revenues, such as the water toll, a collector was appointed. Usually the expenditure of the corporation exceeded its income, and they had to supply whatever money was lacking, though they were eventually repaid by their successors. Hugh Cliderowe and Ralph Forne, elected in 1426, were among the lucky minority in that their revenue exceeded their expenditure, but even so, as the money came in at irregular intervals, they found themselves acting as bankers for the town. Richard Byll and Richard Flynton, elected in 1447 and never rewarded with any higher office, had to provide the town with £80. Thomas Etton, subsequently mayor, and Thomas Brygge, never anything more than chamberlain, who succeeded them, were even less lucky and had to find £110. From 1434, within eight days of his election, each chamberlain had to pay his predecessor £20. which he would eventually recover from his successor, or pay a fine of five marks to have someone else elected in his place.[34] This second alternative may have been slightly less expensive, but few took advantage of it.

So much was owed to the chamberlains of 1460-1 that their successors, unable to pay them, were imprisoned. The bench, with the ex-chamberlains still continuing, and the ex-sheriffs, decided that they must stay there until they could pay their predecessors £80 each and the mayor £15 for the confirmation of the charters by Edward IV. They stayed in prison as they could not pay and others were elected to take their place. None of these unfortunate men was ever elected to any higher office.[35]

Every burgess was obliged to attend at the common hall when the bell was rung for an assembly.[36] If this was a burden, there were advantages to outweigh it, apart from the rights guaranteed under the charters, and their participation in the elections. Parliamentary elections are not at all prominent in the records. Normally those elected as members had been burgesses settled in the town for some time, and there is no indication that anyone was ambitious to serve as a burgess in Parliament. Usually, except for aliens paying a suitable fine, a craftsman wishing to become a master and employ others had to pay 40*d* a year or become a burgess. When this order was made in 1421-2 the crafts which had their guilds in Hull were goldsmiths, who probably were that in name only, cobblers, barbers, chandlers, skinners; and weavers, shearmen and fullers.[37] The existence of this last group shows that

Hull had a fully developed, but probably small, cloth industry. No guild of tailors is yet mentioned, but since 1378 it had been the law that no alien or stranger could open his shop in Hull as a master tailor until he became a burgess.[38*]

Arrest in civil actions, especially for debt, was then the rule; but no arrest in a civil action could be made in the house of a burgess. In 1462 custom was outraged by the sergeant of the sheriff when he went so far as to make an arrest in the house of Thomas Etton, an alderman.[39] For this the bench decided to imprison him until it saw fit to release him. After he had been there for more than four months he simply walked out of his own accord and would have been disfranchised if Thomas Etton had not interceded for him when he made his humble submission.

In other respects sanctuary should have been solely under ecclesiastical control, but the bench, though far from anti-clerical, kept the clergy much more strictly in their places than they were entitled to do. They ordered in 1462 that no officer could make an arrest except for treason, felony, or breach of the peace, in the houses of either order of friars, in churches or churchyards, or in the houses of burgesses.[40] This was a clear infringement of the rights of the church; and in 1482 they infringed still further by ordering that anyone who had escaped from custody could be removed from any ecclesiastical sanctuary.[41] The question of whether any person was in sanctuary or not was complicated by the fact that in 1435 much of the churchyard of Holy Trinity lay open. Horses could get in, for which the fine was 4*d*, and carts were driven across it, and for this the fine was 12*d*, the money in each case going to the church.[42] The churchyard of St Mary's may have been similarly open, but by the end of the century that of Holy Trinity must have been properly walled, as there was a stile at the southwest corner.[43] The churchyard was treated as town property. Two wrights were imprisoned in 1462 for felling a tree there without the consent of the bench or the churchwardens. The vicar humbly asked that they should be released and that he himself should have the tree. His requests were granted on condition that he planted six trees.[44]

The bench was able to intervene outrageously in purely ecclesiastical matters. In November 1463 they decreed that no priest in the town should serve under the archbishop as rural dean and that if William Hundeslay did not resign his office before

Christmas he would no longer have the stipend paid to him by the corporation.[45] At the same time, in the sheriff's court Richard Mason, a priest, was fined a shilling for holding a temporal court, which no doubt meant that he had dealt with secular matters in a church court.[46] If any priest had informed the archbishop of these Erastian proceedings he would have deprived himself of any chance of benefiting from the ecclesiastical patronage dispensed by the corporation. An order was made in 1459-60 that if any chantry or similar office in the gift of the bench fell vacant it should be filled by the election of an able priest who had been in the church for many years. Votes given to any other would not be counted. The same procedure applied in both churches.[47] By 1483 the bench was paying the stipends of five priests, four being from foundations established by the pious and affluent deceased—John Greg, John Tutbury, John Bedford and John Aldwick. The stipend of the fifth came from town revenues.[48] There was also an endowment of £3 0s 8d for an almshouse attached to the Greg chantry.

The most important of the pre-reformation almshouses was that of the Charterhouse, outside the north walls, established by Sir Michael de la Pole in 1384, shortly before he became Earl of Suffolk,[49] on the site and with the endowments which his father had, in 1354, set aside for a hospital and convent of poor Clares.[50] There was a dispute in 1454 between the town and the Carthusians over a right of way, and the bench appointed keepers of the postern leading to the Charterhouse. This was referred to arbitration.[51] With the earls of Suffolk as founders it is not likely that the Carthusians would need to fear any adverse verdict very greatly.

For the rest, the bench, apart from attendance at church for which there is no direct medieval evidence but which may be assumed from the customs of the next century, confined its attention to rogation days and church clocks. The rogation day processions through the fields round the town, apart from their religious aspect, defined and commemorated boundaries, and every year bridges were made over ditches so that the procession could pass freely; and then, since the annual cost was only 12d, they were removed and stored until the next year.[52]

The parish clerk was paid 13s 4d in 1423-4 for looking after the clock in Holy Trinity and a clock-keeper at St Mary's was paid

6*s* 8*d*. After about 1460 only a clock in Holy Trinity was maintained at the expense of the town.[53] This was a large clock, possibly with a dial in the tower. Five wainscots were needed to repair it in 1426-7 and two men worked on it for nine days.[54] Ten years later John Clokmaker came from Beverley to repair it. He was paid 12*s* and used a shilling's worth of coal, which suggests the work of a blacksmith rather than that of an horologist.[55]

Sources

1. Boyle, *Charters and Letters Patent* . . . 41-2.
2. Ibid., 46.
3. Ibid., 54-6.
4. BB3A, f.56.
5. Ibid., f.31b.
6. Ibid., f.23.
7. Ibid., f.25.
8. Boyle, op. cit., 51-2.
9. BB3A, f.55.
10. Ibid., f.65.
11. BB2, f.64.
12. BB3, f.88.
13. Ibid., f.13.
14. Ibid., f.19.
15. BB3A, f.89.
16. Ibid., f.106.
17. Chamb., 5 and 35 Hen. VI.
18. BB3A, f.28.
19. BB3, f.21b.
20. Ibid., f.13.
21. Ibid., f.21.
22. BB3A, f.23.
23. Chamb., 7 Edw. IV.
24. Chamb., 14 Hen. VII.
25. BB3A, f.47.
26. Chamb., 2 Hen. VI.
27. BB3A, f.40.
28. Ibid., f.69.
29. Ibid., f.68b.
30. Ibid., f.71, f.92.
31. BB3, f.19.
32. BB3A, f.84.
33. Ibid., f.55b.
34. BB2, f.164.
35. BB3A, f.81.
36. BB3, f.23.
37. Ibid., f.17.
38.* BB2, f.99. (BB3, f.98b further illustrates the nature of the Hull cloth industry. For the third offence any weaver or fuller making cloth in his house could be banished.)
39. BB3A, f.83.
40. Ibid., f.83b.
41. Ibid., f.87.
42. BB3, f.16b.
43. Chamb., 17 Hen. VII.
44. BB3, f.94b.
45. Ibid., f.88b.
46. Ibid., f.146b.
47. Ibid., f.93.
48. Chamb., 22 Edw. IV.
49. J. Cook, *A History of the Charter-house* (Hull), 2.
50. *CPR*, 1354-8, 158.
51. BB3A, f.69.
52. Chamb., 2 and 35 Hen. VI.
53. Chamb., 7 Edw. IV.
54. Chamb., 5 Hen. V.
55. Chamb., 15 Hen. VI.

8

Hull in the Early Sixteenth Century

The greatest change in the sixteenth century in the affairs of Hull did not come about until the construction of the massive fortification on the east side of the haven in consequence of the northern rising against the Reformation and the awareness of the Crown that unless special measures were taken the town could be captured in a foreign invasion. In the first half of the century, except for this, there was no great change. The cloth trade continued to decline, until by 1540 it was only one-hundreth of the size of the London cloth trade,[1] and the corn surplus of much of Yorkshire and Lincolnshire continued to be shipped from the haven. In some years, probably following a poor harvest, the trade was small. In Richard Huntingdon's year as mayor (1518-19) no more than about 900 quarters of corn were moved coastwise, to London, Newcastle, Brightlingsea in Essex and to Walberswick and Southwold, both in Suffolk.[2] In 1530-1 the quantity moved exceeded 2224 quarters, or one-fifth more if they counted by the long hundred. One vessel sailed direct from Beverley and another from Stoneferry.[3] It is not at all clear whether any or all of this larger quantity went to the Continent. Certainly it corresponds with the amounts sent to Europe in the mid-fourteenth century. Throughout the sixteenth century there are indications of an increase in this trade.

Corn was not the only commodity shipped direct from Beverley through the haven, and from Beverley some ships probably went in ballast to Newcastle for coal. All had to pay haven tolls, which in the fifteenth century had realised from £10 to £20 a year, though only about £12 towards the end of the century.[4] By 1533 traffic had increased to such an extent that the governors of Beverley, the equivalent of aldermen, were claiming toll-free passage at Hull—with no knowledge that it was as a kind of out-port of Beverley· that Hull may have originated. The bench chose, to negotiate with Beverley, Robert Kemsey and Sir Edward Madyson, a Hull merchant who had come from County Durham and who had now built up a large estate in Lincolnshire, to which he was soon to retire.[5] It was agreed to submit the dispute to the arbitration of Richard, Abbot of Meaux. He gave a verdict which, though impartial in appearance, was entirely in favour of Hull. Between Sculcoates sluice and the Humber all Beverley vessels were to pay a toll of $1d$ a quarter on corn, Hull vessels paying the same if they passed through the bridge over the Hull at Beverley.[6]

Another dispute which was settled by arbitration, an increasingly common device at this time, was with John Nandych, Prior of Haltemprice, about the fresh-water dike. The award, in 1517, gave the town its existing rights in the dike and the east well at Anlaby, and the Prior his rights as lord of the manor of Willerby and Newton. Hessle and Anlaby would be able to take their water from the dike, as they had always done, and were to scour the spring head at Easter and Michaelmas. Every year eight men of Hull, Hessle and Anlaby were to view the dike. One of the Hessle men was to be the officer of Sir George Tailboys, who was to keep the salt water out of his precinct.[7]

Unless it was a holy day, the bench assembled at nine every Thursday morning, to deal with such routine matters as these, in the Guildhall.[8] Occasionally their business was sensational. In 1503 they had to consider a royal letter ordering the arrest of John Bampton of Hull and John Watson, a monk of the Charterhouse. There was no difficulty about Bampton, but Watson was protected by his status as a priest, though the Carthusians already had him under arrest. The mayor's lieutenant and the deputy sheriff therefore went to the Charterhouse to confer with the proctor, apparently a person who served as a sub-prior, and with the vicar, who, after consultation with the brethren, surrendered John Watson. Both prisoners were dispatched to face the King's justices.[9] It seems probable that there was suspicion of treason.

But whatever Bampton had done was not serious enough to remove him permanently from his environment—a partly criminal one since in 1510, on the receipt of another royal letter he was arrested with other *promotours*—informers who were themselves suspected of being involved in crime. John Bampton was displayed to the public, first in the stocks, then in the pillory. Robert Womersley was also pilloried, and then both were forwarded to London, where Womersley died in prison. The third *promotour,* Thomas Bank, a barber, was first carted round the town in the common thew and then banished from Hull.[10]

Occasionally the bench was faced with a serious problem for which it had no solution. One winter day early in 1524 a vessel, simply described as the black barque, sank at and blocked the mouth of the haven. The bell-man went round to announce the news but no one claimed her. The market-keeper was then sent to York to see a man called Norman who was said to be the owner and turned out not to be. It was then said that she was the property of Sir Robert Constable of Flamborough, who could not be found as he was in London, but his son, Sir Marmaduke, assured the bench that his father did not own her.[11] The tide, the mud and a few collisions probably dispersed the wreck quite soon.

There were other times when corporation affairs aroused interest in all the town. The Crown appointed a special commission in 1510 to decide a case almost certainly involving violence. The commissioners sat at the Guildhall, presided over by the Earl of Northumberland, with Sir Humphrey Coningsby, a newly appointed justice of the King's Bench.[12] As always when dealing with great men or courtiers, the aldermen had to behave with particular care and courtesy. For them a complicating factor was the attainder of the last of the de la Pole Dukes of Suffolk, and the grant in 1514 of the lordship of Hull and Myton to the distinguished soldier, Sir William Sidney. His steward (1523) compelled Thomas Wardal, a burgess, to find with the rest of the Myton jurors that an affray had taken place in Myton, when on a Hull jury he had already found that it was in Hull.[13]

And there were some deaths which provided public entertainment. The master of the *Christopher* of Brightlingsea (1518) brought ashore a dead man for burial in Holy Trinity churchyard; but the mayor had not viewed the body. It was therefore dug up again, and the mayor satisfied himself that Thomas Meake, aged 70, had suffered no wound and had died naturally.[14] The death of Thomas Lard was, at the time, much more interesting (1524) because of a rumour that he had been killed by castration, the scandalous implication seeming to be that someone had caused this to be done to him as an act of revenge. He had lived in Hull for many years, enjoying a good reputation, and in fairness to his memory it was recorded in the bench book that his body had been disinterred and found to be in no way mutilated.[15]

The living also could provide innocent enjoyment, though unwillingly. When there was war with Scotland (1524) the rumour spread that one of the aldermen, Robert Parker, was actually a Scot. To prove his innocence he brought a canon of Newsham and several other witnesses over from Lincolnshire to show that 56 years previously he had been baptised at Killingholme. The fact that he had two husbandmen for godfathers indicates that he came from a humble family and was a self-made man.[16]

Everyone in the town could know all its laws, without being able to guess how the aldermen would interpret them. They were publicly proclaimed every year in the Guildhall, probably in the full version which was not recorded until 1566, though the proclamations had been made since the 1430s.[17] By far the most important part of the Hull laws dealt with commerce, and since decisions and orders were often written down imprecisely it seems reasonable at this point to imitate the more exact sciences by constructing a 'model'—a hypothetical reconstruction of what a Hull burgess would have regarded as the best of all possible worlds. Ideally, a Hull merchant who was a burgess ought to have been able to work with very little capital. Ships came to Hull with their cargoes, and if only Hull burgesses could buy the goods, they ought also to be able to perform the transaction as a matter of book-keeping only, with no money changing hands until the Hull man had made his profit. All the capital needed would be provided by merchants of such towns as York and Beverley which could only satisfy their needs through Hull. So long as no one except a Hull merchant could buy imported goods, having sold them, the Hull man could pay off the foreign merchants and leave himself with a discreet margin of profit. Only two things stood in the way of Utopia: human nature, for the richer merchants had no need to buy on credit and therefore were most unlikely to join the rest in banning cash transactions in the purchase of imports; and the laws of England, since even after Hull aspirations had been largely embodied in the charter of 1532 it was often far from clear what was a lawful and what an unlawful deal.

Nevertheless the bench never abandoned its aspirations of making York and Beverley provide most of the capital for Hull overseas and coastwise trade. From time to time it was necessary to remake some of the necessarily complicated orders which governed trade. No stranger or alien was to sell to any other (1503) in the town unless the other either took the goods away with him or sold them to a Hull burgess; and in these dealings no stranger or alien was to act as agent for any other. The fines for infringements could be fixed at the mayor's discretion. The order was re-issued in almost exactly the same form in 1527.[18]

Even without the embodiment of any of these aspirations in a charter there was a great deal that the town could do for itself. To encourage importers to sell as quickly as possible and at as low a price as possible, they were forbidden to store their goods anywhere except in the house of the Hull burgess who acted as their host. The fine of 3*s* 4*d* for illegally storing the goods of aliens and strangers was quite large enough to discourage the practice—though any person, moved by charity, could store them free of charge if he was so far demented.[19]

The wording of the town laws was so imprecise that in this order the storage of merchandise in the wool-house, which was perfectly legal and a source of common profit, was overlooked—because everyone knew about it. To ensure that all dealings could be traced and infringements penalised it was ordered at the same time that the keeper of the wool-house was to keep a record of all goods which he received or released, noting the name of the owner. The chamberlains were to see his account quarterly, but he was to be ready at all times to show his books to three burgesses appointed by the mayor: and every Saturday night these three were also to see the records of the keeper of the cloth hall and of the water-bailiff.[20]

To keep down the price of red herrings and sprats no one was allowed to store them in his house, shop or cellar.[21] This order was made in 1524. It could only be evaded by risking detection in the breaking of an older law—that everything must be landed before sale. In the same year John Dobs of Lowestoft was fined 20*s* for selling six barrels of white herrings and a quantity of red herrings to a man from Fishlake, and a Yarmouth man had to pay almost as much for the same kind of offence.[22]

The export of lead to the Continent was becoming an important element in Hull trade. To turn this traffic to the maximum advantage of Hull ships an order of 1532 required persons shipping lead to Holland, Zeeland, Brabant, or Flanders to bring back a ton of other merchandise for every 'great piece' of lead. The freight was to be 14*d* for the great piece and 8*d* a ton for the goods brought back.[23] As far as possible all trade was to be kept for Hull ships. In Hull itself there could be no serious difficulty about the enforcement of this rule—but the boundaries of the port extended to Grimsby and beyond Scarborough. There was always, therefore, a danger of surreptitious loading of merchandise in some creek or haven. An order was made in 1532 that anyone who loaded goods into any other ship, if a Hull ship was available, could be fined up to £20. Any English ship could be used if there was no Hull ship.[24] This must have been difficult to enforce—the size of the penalty being some measure of the difficulty.

At last, in 1532, the corporation got the charter which it needed for the full validity of its restrictive trading. Edward Madison, as the alderman most likely to succeed, was away for forty days, mostly in London. Part of his business, in addition to consultation with lawyers, consisted of distributing to the right persons, often in humble positions, various sums of money which would now be regarded as bribes but which were then entirely regular. He was rowed to Greenwich four times in the hope of seeing Thomas Cromwell, then no more than one of the lords of the council and master of the Court of Wards, but already a principal adviser of Henry VIII. Small bribes had to be given to the servants who kept the doors of his chamber before Madison could get in to make his case, in writing, and offer him a purse with twenty gold angels which had cost £7 10*s* in ordinary money.[25] The whole business cost just under £32 before the charter was safely home in its new box.

The preamble depicted the distress of Hull in pathetic but not necessarily untrue terms:

> The haven of our town of Kingston upon Hull has fallen into great decay by the rage of the sea dashing against the sea walls and embankments erected there to defend it so that the mayor and burgesses are not able to repair the damage done to the haven without help from us.

And the help was to consist of something which could be

granted at no expense to the Crown:

> We have granted . . . that no stranger or foreigner to the liberty of
> the borough shall henceforth buy from any stranger or foreigner
> within that borough any merchandise or anything else, or sell the
> same to him, except only in the time when the markets and fairs are
> held, under pain of forfeiting the merchandise.[26]

The town had almost achieved its aim of making York and
Beverley provide a great deal of the capital needed for its sea trade.
There was a clause reserving the present and future treaty rights of
foreigners, notwithstanding the charter, but this took very little of
the virtue out of it. The whole charter goes far towards explaining
the economic recovery of the town in the sixteenth century. The
bench was to complain repeatedly of losses at sea, which may well
have been more serious now that every enemy ship encountered
was likely to be much more heavily gunned than a merchantman;
but without war the strategic value of the port would not have
existed—and the Crown was much more interested in strategy than
in trade.

With the renewal of war with Scotland in 1524, an arbitration
award settled that, whenever soldiers were needed for the King, the
county of Hull outside the borough should provide no more than a
dozen men; Willerby joined with Wolfreton to raise two of them.[27]
For the war in the North Sea the flagship was the *William* of York,
but as she was of 240 tons the citizens of York can never have seen
her except at Hull. She had a crew of 179, of whom more than 150
must have been fighting men.[28] Twenty-four Dutch gunners were
sent from London to join her at Hull. Both the Hull ships
employed were of 120 tons carrying eighty-nine men—the *Thomas*
under Thomas Ellerker (probably one of the Ellerkers of Risby
who at this time were gaining great distinction in war) and the
Edmund under Thomas Clere. A prize, the *Yenett Purwyn,* of
sixteen guns, was delivered to the mayor.[29] A few years later the
sixth Earl of Northumberland, not normally a very effective
person, was indignant when the mayor, relying on his admiralty
rights, refused to give up a Scots ship driven into the Humber by
storms.[30]

Hull seafarers could not fail to know something of the
continental Reformation, and five of them can be identified as
having attended Lutheran services at Bremen in 1527 or 1528—
Roger Danyell, Robert Clarcke, Nicholas Bayly, Robert Robynson

and an apprentice named William. With Henry Burnet of Barrow they were in the crew of a Dutch ship of Amsterdam which was at Bremen for nearly six weeks. Robynson, as a suspected Lollard, had already had to do penance in the market place and in Holy Trinity.[31] Danyell brought back at least one copy of Tindale's translation of the New Testament and faced proceedings by the Dean of York. Among mariners in particular, therefore, the general drift of Henry VIII's ecclesiastical policy was understood. One shipman, on a visit to Grimsby in September 1536, boasted that at Hull they had taken the precaution of selling the church plate to keep it out of the King's hands.[32] The order which the bench had made a few days previously was worded with caution. All plate belonging to the corporation was to be sold to pay the wages of members of Parliament, for repairs to town property and to Holy Trinity, and for the maintenance of the chantry priests there.[33] Probably most of the bench were not really surprised by the Pilgrimage of Grace—the rising against the King in Lincolnshire and Yorkshire.

The news of the Lincolnshire rising led to an insurrection at Beverley on Sunday, 8 October, one week later. In Hull there was no rising, but on the 13th four representatives came from Hull to confer with the Beverley rebels and William Stapleton their conscripted leader, about the terms on which they would be allowed to enter Hull. It was important for them to do so, since it was only through the ports that the King's captains could bring artillery quickly enough to cow the rebels. Stapleton met Sir Robert Constable in Holy Trinity, where Constable declared his intention of holding the town for the King, which did not save him from execution for treason in 1537. On the 15th, therefore, the rebels began an ineffective blockade of the town. On the east side of the River Hull Stapleton's men were at Sculcoates, next to 200 Holderness men. The west side of the river was held by the men of Thomas Ellerker of Risby and the Cottingham men, Ombler's 100 men at Hull hermitage, and the men of Hull-shire under Sir Christopher Hildyard.[34] Men of the hamlets on the banks of the Hull proposed to Stapleton that they should set fire to ships in the haven by floating barrels of burning pitch on the ebb tide. He would not allow them to do this, but could not prevent them from pulling down the windmills at Beverleygates.

By 20 October, though the rebellion was spreading all over the north, much of the original enthusiasm had leaked out of the local insurgents; but on that date three aldermen, Ellaunde, Knollys and John Thornton, the first two soon to be knighted, arranged for them to enter Hull peaceably, just as they had been informed by Robert Hornclyff of Grimsby that the Lincolnshire rebels were dispersing.[35] This so displeased the Hull and Yorkshire men that they imprisoned him at Hull, which a month later was still regarded as being in a state of rebellion.[36] After the King had made his vaguely generous proposals for peace at the Doncaster colloquy, the Yorkshire rebellion also ended with no further acts of violence and Hull, if it had ever left it, now returned to its allegiance.

There was, however, at least one person involved in the rebellion, at first reluctantly, Sir Francis Bygod of Settrington E. R. and Mulgrave Castle N. R., who believed that the King had a plan for a more complete pacification of the north with troops supported by artillery landed at Hull and Scarborough. He won over a few other determined men to his way of thinking, including John Hallam of Cawkell Farm, Watton; and with Hallam he arranged that while he took Scarborough, Hallam should quietly infiltrate Hull on a market day and seize the town. Those of Hallam's men who had joined him only through fear, arranged during their journey to send a message to the mayor to warn him. After a short tussle at the gates Hallam was taken by Ellaunde and Knollys. The Hull plot was as complete a failure as that at Scarborough.[37] The rebels had done hardly the slightest harm to the town, though as late as 1541 the bench gave permission to Richard Saull, merchant, to prosecute the country-men who had entered his house in his absence 'in the time of the last disturbance'.[38]

While Hull was technically in a state of rebellion it was alleged that the rebels had captured ships at sea. A letter under the signet from Richmond required that the vessels should be restored to their owners. On investigation it was found that no ship had been captured, but that during the rebellion some had been unable to start their voyages.[39] After the capture of Hallam, the mayor, with Sir Ralph Ellerker the younger and others, was directed, by another letter under the signet from Greenwich, to examine him under torture. A commission would be sent down for his trial, and after his conviction he was to be hanged in chains over the walls, where the largest number of people would be able to see him.[40] The chains probably caused him to die very slowly, and this would ensure that the maximum value to the government would accrue, as many people as had a taste for such things would be able to spend a long time watching him die. Hull was duly thanked for its services, and there were no Hull men excepted from the general pardon.[41]

During Henry VIII's brief visits to Hull in September and October 1541, at his command Sir William Ellaunde was made mayor, though John Johnson, who willingly stood down, had just been elected to that office.[42] The King had plans for making Hull more secure against attack. The de la Pole house, now the King's, was to become a citadel, the moat was to be scoured, Scots and vagabonds turned out, the ramparts repaired, the gates provided with portcullises and guns of iron, not of brass, were to be set up. Further, the sluices were to be so modified that the Humber could be let in to flood the surrounding country, and the fresh-water dike was to be diverted to supply the new citadel. And for the first time there was to be a bridge over the River Hull, at the north end, to be kept in repair, and in the first instance partly provided, with cash and labour contributed by Hull and Holderness.[43]

It was about this time that John Leland wrote his description of Hull. He knew about the de la Poles and believed, incorrectly, that the town owed its rise to the Iceland fishery. Because cargoes of stockfish were so light, it was necessary to ballast the ships with Iceland cobbles, with which the whole town was now paved. The walls, dating from the 14th century, and most of the houses were brick. In the walls he counted twenty-two towers—twelve between North Gate and Beverley Gate, then another five up to Mytongate and five between there and the Humber. Outside the walls there were no suburbs. Leland noted that the de la Pole manor house, opposite St Mary's, all of brick, was more like a palace. All the brick had been made at the tilery. He was impressed by the great central tower of Holy Trinity and four 'notable' chantry chapels on the south side against the free school erected by Bishop Alcock. On the west side of the Market Place, and next to Gregg's hospital, there was a row of priests' houses, and Selby's hospital was on the north side of the church. The dissolved house of the White friars was next to Beverley Gate and that of the Austin friars near Holy Trinity, near the town hall with its prison in a brick tower; and outside the north walls there was the Charterhouse, then serving only as a hospital[44*]

By February 1542 Henry VIII had decided that a more complete fortification of Hull was necessary. He informed the bench of his decision and of his appointment of Michael Stanhope as his lieutenant, not to take away any of the privileges, but rather for their benefit.[45] Hull was to have a 'notable fortress'. At first Stanhope commanded a garrison and was himself expected to live in the King's manor house, but the rooms there were so large that he could not furnish even one of them. Instead he bought a house at the south end with the King's guns in front of the door, pointed at the entrance to the haven. At the end of May 1542 the garrison was dismissed, and there was no one under his command to man the guns either there or five miles down the Humber at Paull. He needed twelve gunners at least. Further, he would soon find it impossible to obtain supplies as the Archbishop of York would not allow the King's officers to exercise their right of fixing the price for the goods they bought in Beverley market. If this went on country victuallers would take their wares to Beverley instead of to Hull. Here Stanhope was also concerned with his own interests as he was acquiring an estate in Beverley, but even so the men employed on building the Hull fortress would have to be supplied with food, preferably at prices fixed by royal officers.

By May 1543 he had spent almost the whole of the £18,000 which the King had provided for the fortress;[46] but by the end of the year the work was completed for rather more than £23,000. Stone from Meaux Abbey, which could have provided a great deal, and from the church of St Mary's in Hull, which can hardly have provided much, was used, and bricks in great quantity were made on the site. The principal fort, with outer walls nineteen feet thick, lay opposite Church Lane staithe, about midway between smaller but massive blockhouses, the northern one lying very slightly to the south of the new bridge over the Hull, and the south blockhouse on the Humber bank. Walls fifteen feet wide connected the blockhouses with the central fort. In Hollar's view, the central fort looks impressive; but the view was designed to impress. It was built as low as possible with walls as thick as possible so that ships firing on it from the Humber could do little damage; it was a tremendous fortification.[47]

Notwithstanding the King's assurances that Michael Stanhope

had not been set up as a governor to abridge their liberties the Privy Council found that the townsmen showed hostility to him in 1546. A royal letter was sent to the bench indicating the King's displeasure. They were to send such of their number as Stanhope selected to appear before the Council, and Stanhope was to send two representatives of his own who could put his case against them.[48] After the fortifications had been entrusted to the town in 1552 there was no further direct cause of friction, but the £50 a year received from the Crown proved quite insufficient to maintain so great a work so hastily put together, and on marshy ground.

Both houses of friars were dissolved in 1539. There were only about eight of the White friars and probably the same number of the Black. They possessed so very little that there can hardly be the slightest doubt of their having kept their vow of poverty with great rigidity.[49] The dissolution of the chantries followed in 1547. The best endowed was Alcock's chantry in Holy Trinity, where the incumbent had £10 a year and the school-house rent free and was master of the free grammar school. He had been a monk of St Mary's, York, and so also enjoyed a pension of £5 a year. There were also seven other chantries, one founded quite recently, and three certainly dating from the fourteenth century. Their total value, excluding Alcock's, was £34 9s 0d. There were also two chantries in St Mary's, each worth rather less than those in Holy Trinity.[50]

The dissolution of the chantries made less difference to the appearance of the interior than the destruction of images. On a pedestal against the clock-house in Holy Trinity there was a huge, three-headed representation of the Trinity. This, and images blackened with the smoke of votive candles were all burned on a bonfire outside, and the pictures painted on the walls were covered with whitewash, not without some complaints from the people.[51]

All 'monuments of popish superstition' had to go, including perhaps some masterpieces of art from the Netherlands. Thomas Dalton, twice mayor, left £8 in 1497 for a religious painting 'bought beyond seas', and perhaps as much for one other.[52] Robert Herryson, a Hull merchant from Skidbrooke, in Lindsey, in his will made in 1520 stipulated that his executors were to place before the Corpus Christi altar 'a table of oversea work price £10 and the story to be of Corpus Christi'.[53] Holy Trinity also had certain tapestries which were now probably disposed of. Thomas Wood, draper and alderman, had bequeathed his tapestry coverlet of Arras work, to be laid on his grave-slab in the church yearly on the anniversary of his death, and on St George's day to be hung in the church 'with other worshipful beds'.[54] In 1461 a priest made a similar bequest of his best blue bed made with JHC'.[55] There was also an apparatus, made in imitation of that which Alderman William Goisman had seen at King's Lynn, for which in 1502 he left £10. It had images of angels descending from the ceiling of St Katherine's chapel at the elevation of the host, and rising again when the priest reached the words 'Ne inducas nos in tentationem' — 'And lead us not into temptation'.[56]

The *maison dieu* or hospital for the aged, attached to the Charterhouse survived the dissolution. Though better endowed than most of the Hull hospitals and built for twenty-six persons, in 1539 it contained a dozen or fewer.[57] The Edward VI charter which gave Hull the new fortifications also transferred the Charterhouse hospital to the corporation.[58] Gregg's hospital also survived. If these two and all the other pre-Reformation foundations had survived to the 1530s there would have been provision for more than 100 and probably up to 150 persons; but it seems unlikely whether in many cases they lasted long enough to be dissolved by Henry or Edward VI.[59]

Sources

1. Carus-Wilson, *England's Export Trade 1275-1547*, 116-18.
2. BB3A, f.180.
3. BB3, f.176b.
4. Chamb., *passim*.
5. BB3, f.178.
6. Ibid., f.180.
7. Ibid., f.104.
8. Ibid., f.109.
9. BB3A, f.162.
10. Ibid., f.170.
11. Ibid., unfoliated, last entry.
12. Ibid., f.171, and *DNB*, s.v. CONINGSBY HUMPHREY.
13. BB3A, f.208b; *DNB*, s.v. SIDNEY, WILLIAM.
14. BB3A, f.197b.
15. Ibid., f.234.
16. Ibid., f.206.
17. BB3, f.88.
18. Ibid., f.99.
19. Ibid., f.99.
20. Ibid., f.100.
21. BB3A, f.21.
22. BB3, f.172.
23. Ibid., f.176b.
24. Ibid., f.176b.
25. Ibid., f.29.

26. Boyle, *Charters and Letters Patent . . .*, 64-5 [taken from Letters Patent of 24 Henry VIII]
27. BB3, f.172b.
28. *LPH* VIII, iv. part 1, No. 691.
29. Ibid., No. 83.
30. *LPH* VIII, v, No. 1559.
31. *Archaeologia* Vol. 48, ii, 257.
32. A. G. Dickens., *Lollards and Protestants in the Diocese of York*, 28-9.
33. *LPH* VIII, xii, part 1, No. 481.
34. BB3, f.180b.
35. E. Riding Antiquarian Society, x, 82-106.
36. *LPH* VIII, xi, No. 1103.
37. *LPH* VIII, xii, No. 201.
38. BB3, f.182b.
39. A. G. Dickens in *YAJ*, xxxiii, 300.
40. Ibid., 302-5.
41. Ibid., 411-14.
42. *LPH* VIII, xvi, No. 1227.
43. Ibid., No. 1232.

44.* L. Toulmin-Smith, *Leland's Itinerary*, i, 48. Where these or similar cobbles survive Mr A. Royle has found that old inhabitants unkindly call them 'Irishmen's kidneys'.
45. *LPH* VIII, xvii, No. 30.
46. Ibid., No. 358.
47. *VCH*, Hull, 414-15.
48. *APC* 1542-7, 533.
49. *VCH*, Yorkshire, iii, 269-70.
50. Surtees Society, *Yorkshire Chantry Surveys*, 340-7.
51. G. Hadley, *A History of Hull*, 88-9.
52. Surtees Society, *Testamenta Eboracensia*, iv, 127.
53. Ibid., 22.
54. Ibid., 60.
55. Ibid., 60-1.
56. Ibid., 209.
57. *VCH*, Yorkshire. iii, 311.
58. Boyle, op. cit., 70.
59. *VCH*, Hull, 334-5.

9

The Tudor Town

In a town as old as Hull now had become it was inevitable that social changes should produce signs of decay which might lead one to suppose that decay was general. In High Street, many of the houses beyond the wool-house, towards the north, were in disrepair and 'disbeautified'. The remedy for this was to oblige all Scots trading with Hull to resort to that part of the town. It was there that they were required to find their hosts, and if they did not store their merchandise in the wool-house, it had to go in some cellar or warehouse in the same northern quarter.[1] This remedy, first applied in 1562, produced no permanent cure. In 1586 it was found that some inhabitants thought it to their advantage, if their houses were on the east side of High Street, to sell the rear part with the staithes. Consequently buildings near the water-side which had beautified and defended the town were being demolished. This was now forbidden, and all such structures were to be maintained.[2] But while part of the town was being demolished, much was being rebuilt. The fifteenth-century rentals indicate that there may have been courts with tunnel-entries, but it is not until 1576 that we have any direct reference to them. James Smith, provided he let them only to honest persons who had lived in Hull for eight years, was given permission to build houses on his plot in Scale Lane. There were to be ten houses in all—four on the street with the entry in the middle and six behind in the court.[3]

A minor but significant indication of prosperity was the size of the mayor's chain of office. By 1554 he was wearing a gold chain of almost five ounces given by a former mayor, Sir William Knollys, and immediately displayed to the people in the

Guildhall.[4] By 1571, through gifts from Knollys's widow and others it had more than doubled in size, with 317 links weighing 11.375 ounces.[5] When in 1595 it was recommended to Burleigh that William Gee should be deputy-secretary of the Council of the North, it was said that he had come from Leicestershire fifty years previously and established himself as a merchant. 'The town being very populous', he had spent £300 on the rebuilding of the grammar school (where his merchant's mark is still to be seen), £150 on Holy Trinity, £200 on a covered corn market, £1000 on a hospital for ten poor people to whom he made a weekly allowance, and he had offered £200 towards the cost of bringing water from the wells in lead pipes instead of in open ditches.[6] He had been three times mayor, and his gifts included twelve silver apostle spoons, a silver salt and other plate weighing 157 ounces in all. For the mayoress he had provided a gold chain to be worn on Sundays and holy days, and his gifts of gold came to twenty ounces.[7]

The appearance of the town did not match the mayor's finery. When a royal visit, which never happened, was expected in 1575, it was ordered that all the houses were to be newly painted and the gable ends either repaired or taken down.[8] In 1601 the walls were 'pestered with such filth and ordure' that an order was given for the postern near the tilery to be re-opened so that refuse could be taken along Posterngate to the tilery.[9] But if any improvement was made, it was not permanent. For the visit of Charles I in 1639 it was necessary to make another order 'that the ramparts along the walls be forthwith made level throughout by taking down hills and filling up holes with earth, and the ordure and filth to be dressed, cleansed and carried away'.[10] This would explain why Hollar's plan showed such a neat-looking place if it were not for the fact that he is known to have omitted such features as the Bushdike, But none of this is a sign of decay. It is much more reasonable to see it as the first sign of the inability of the old system of government to accommodate itself to a society no longer almost static. The principal instrument for the preservation of the walls was the annual proclamation that any person who took stone or brick from them could be pilloried and fined 40s—almost the heaviest penalty that could be legally inflicted.[11]

The corporation had enough money to be able to make loans, for we know that Richard Beseley of York had borrowed £140. When he asked for extra time to repay, the bench met in its council house in Holy Trinity,[12] a place where evidently they frequently met, for in 1561 their meeting place was also described as 'in the chapel in the Trinity church of this town'.[13] Meetings at the Guildhall still continued, and there is nothing to distinguish matters discussed in the church from those discussed in the Guildhall. In 1595 they again met 'in their council house in the Trinity church'.[14] The explanation of their needing to meet there seems to be that the proper council house was being repaired.

By 1633 patching up would no longer do, though the old common hall was not so decrepit as to need demolition. Instead it was decided to join a new one of the same height to it, and John Catlyn, bricklayer, undertook the contract. The new council house was to stand on brick arches, adjoining the old house on the south. Externally it was to be forty-four feet from east to west, and internally twenty-one feet from north to south, the walls being four bricks thick. Above this there was to be an upper room twelve feet in height up to the tie-beams of the low-pitched roof of lead, insulated with lime and hair. Externally the roof was hidden by decorative battlements. The contractor was also to provide windows of freestone, a chimney, stone quoins and all necessary piling. For his work he would receive £120 out of Mr Ferries's legacy. The corporation would provide piles, timber, woodwork, iron work, would pay the wrights, supply lead and glass and pay the plumbers and glaziers.[15]

Though the officers of the town comported themselves with humble civility in the presence of noblemen and officers of the Crown, they were no longer at their mercy, and their humility must often have concealed considerable pride in their wealth. By 1577 the bench felt that it was no longer necessary to keep a special barge 'to fetch noblemen and such like' from Barton, and as it badly needed repair it was sold for 33s 4d.[16] Sir Thomas Gargrave, the recorder, who is most unlikely to have acted in person since he was also vice-president of the Council of the North, because of the smallness of his salary was presented with a hogshead of Gascon wine.[17] In 1592 the mayor and two aldermen went to York to present a half-tun of Gascon wine to the new lord-lieutenant and to welcome him to the north.[18] The bench in 1600 provided transport for the deer which Lord Sheffield of Normanby (near Scunthorpe) had presented to Sir Robert Cecil.[19] An assize judge was treated with particular ceremony. In 1630 as Baron Trevor was

expected to arrive late at Barton four persons, two being
aldermen, were sent to meet him with provisions for a banquet.
His ship, hired for the occasion, was to fire three guns on casting
off from Barton, and on his arrival four would be fired from the
fort at the south end and three from the blockhouse. When he left
the town for Meaux, chambers, the smallest possible guns, would
be fired, and three guns at the blockhouse.[20] He was honoured as a
representative of the Crown, but guns were occasionally fired in
honour of a private person. Because of the favour which the
Hildyard family had shown to Hull, when Mr Henry Hildyard of
Winestead arrived with his bride and her father, Lord Deyncourt,
a salute of three guns was fired from the south blockhouse.[21]

As population increased, the place looked, and smelled, less
rural. The fine for anyone who kept a pig within the walls for more
than six days was exceptionally heavy.[22] In the same year, 1559, a
heavy penalty was threatened for anyone having a haystack inside
the town, and this was later (1576) doubled to £2.[23] Those who
lived in High Street with houses backing on to the river were not
allowed (1579) to keep either a horse or a cow. Master mariners
had told the bench that a 'ness' was growing at the east side of the
haven mouth caused by the tipping of refuse. If there were no
stables near the river the risk would be less, and there was a fine of
20*d* for putting ashes, cinders, moulds, refuse, horse or cow dung
into the Hull.[24] Stables, however, were to be found in all other
parts of the town—enough to produce a commission to dig in the
town for saltpetre issued by the Crown in 1595 to Richard Heyton.
The bench had to give him £6 13*s* 4*d* to take his tubs and
implements away without digging.[25*]

If a building was destroyed by fire the tendency was to put
something safer in its place. This, and orders made by the bench
gradually produced a town built almost entirely of brick and tiles.
There was as yet no general prohibition of thatch, but it was
banned in particular instances when a house was being re-roofed.
James Halsey lived in the market place and was fined 40*s* because
he ignored the mayor's command not to thatch the rear part of the
house.[26] When in the same year (1576) permission was given to
build the new court in Scale Lane the owner was required to
remove the thatch from his other houses and to tile them.[27] A year
later Mr John Gregory, one of the aldermen, was required to
replace the thatch of his house in Vicar Lane with tiles and a glover

was given until Mayday 1578 to tile his thatched house in Mytongate or pull it down.[28]

The ready availability of water from the river, the town dike, and open sewers made fire-fighting easier than in many towns, and the existence of so much building in brick and stone from very early times saved Hull from any really disastrous fire; but the danger was always there. To lessen it, no one was allowed to take any light, except one enclosed in a lantern, into any stable or other place with inflammable materials.[29] Brewers and bakers (1585) could not light their fires before two in the morning and had to extinguish them by ten at night. The bench ordered two dozen leather buckets, four ladders and long poles with iron hooks on the end for fire-fighting—and all were kept securely locked to prevent their being stolen. Every householder was required to have a shovel and a spade ready, and all chamberlains and ex-chamberlains were in addition to have a pick.[30] But it was in the haven that the strictest precautions were taken against fire. As soon as he boarded an incoming vessel and told her master that she could not anchor south of the hand or beacon standing in the garrison[31] or drop ballast or refuse, the pilot had to warn him not to heat any pitch or tar on board, to have no fire or candle burning except during the hours of daylight, not to remove barnacles with a lighted torch, and to see that all his gunpowder was removed to some place on shore within twenty-four hours.[32] The first order for fire precautions in ships was made in 1564 when through the carelessness of the crew the *Dragon* caught fire, moored in a position from which she endangered the town as well as everything else in the haven.

The bench frequently made new orders regarding matters affecting public health. In 1565 'places of easement for the common people called jakes' were re-built—which put Hull three centuries ahead of Hardy's Casterbridge. From 1576 no one living within the walled part of the town could keep more than two cows, and the fine for infringement, 20s, was really heavy.[33] Three men had upstairs privies on the east side of their houses projecting over the jetty at the Horsestaithe, and under the same penalty had to get rid of them 'for that the same privies are very noisome to the passengers in the ferry-boat'.[34] It was felt (1606) that danger of infection was caused by the keeping and 'burning' of the fish-livers called blubbers, and this activity could not be carried on within half a mile of the town.[35]

The connection between water-supply and disease was well known, though it was never understood until the latter part of the nineteenth century. Some common-sense measures must really have been beneficial to public health. No woman-servants were to wash clothes near the Bushdike or the town dike, and dung or dung-tubs could not be left near the North Gate, on the town walls, near the town ditch or near sewers.[36] Water was conveyed into the town from the Bushdike in carts called *bushes*, and the bushmen's charge was fixed at ½*d* a load in 1565.[37] Every bushman or sled-man had to pay 3*s* 4*d* a year to the corporation. Brewers and others could have their own bushes free of charge, but they too had to pay 3*s* 4*d* if they supplied others.[38]

The whole course of the fresh-water dike was scoured annually to prevent blockages by vegetation. In some years the cost was exceptionally heavy. In 1575 £41 was spent on scouring Darningham-dike which extended 8100 feet from Julian-dike to the Bushdike against the town walls; and at first it was thought it would be necessary to levy a rate, then a very rare expedient, to meet the cost.[39]

James Blaides of Hull, in the summer of 1595, with two men of Sculcoates, asked that for two days and one night the fresh water should be allowed to run through the stone bridge at Sculcoates, so that they could water their cattle, and this was allowed, as it would not lessen the supply of water to the town;[40] but in the following summer water was less plentiful, and Mr John Aldred illicitly employed two masons from Cottingham to use a pick on the great stone at the bridge to let spring water into Sculcoates. The bench decided that an action for trespass should be started in London.[41]

The bush-men carried on their trade long after a partnership had set up waterworks to supply the town in or before 1612, presumably using a horse-mill to work its pumps in what came to be Waterworks Street, outside the walls. Those paying for the company's water had to agree not to give away or sell any, but there were those who in some ways were contriving to steal it.[42]

Every householder each Saturday had to clean the road against his house up to the middle,[43] and in the greater part of the town he was responsible for the repair of the same portion of the road. In the market place, however, and along Whitefriargate and the walls of the manor there were gutters at each side of the road, and not a single gutter down the middle, and on these roads the frontagers had no responsibility for the part between the gutters, which was probably cambered.[44]

No means were then known of preventing the plague, but it is more than probable that the measures taken by the bench limited its spread. Hull was infected in the autumn of 1575 and the economic effects had reduced many to poverty. If they continued to go round begging they might spread the infection. It was announced in the churches that they were to stay at home to receive aid from a poor-rate, to be paid by all householders as long as the plague remained. Blackfriargate was the worst infected street and was therefore 'impaled' and enclosed at each end and at the lane joining it on the south side. A man was appointed to watch, ready from daylight until five to open the gate at the west end for persons from houses not infected, and also the gate from High Street when they needed to move such heavy things as hops or beer. He was also to warn those living there not to go to church or to the market. Twice a week between six and seven in the evening they were to bring all their refuse to a sled appointed by the common officer to tip it into the Humber.[45]

By February 1576 infected persons had been removed to pest-houses in Myton carr, and a man was appointed by the common officer, at this time the *factotum* of the bench, to see that none of them came outside of the houses to talk with one another, and to prevent them from coming into the town. As soon as he went home for the night he told the keeper of the town gates, who then kept them closed.[46] The plague lasted right through the summer, and it was impossible to hold the usual midsummer feast provided by the mayor as the large crowd would add to the danger of infection, but as some kind of compensation £5 was to be shared among the poor.[47] By the following summer the plague had gone. A pest-house was being cleansed, probably by singeing the walls with a torch, when it caught fire. A mariner was paid 40s to rebuild it.[48] The existence of plague in the town earlier in the year seems the likeliest explanation of accusations of witchcraft in 1604. In September Baron Saville held a session of gaol-delivery. Mary Holland, Jennet Wressell (also called Beaumont) and Jennet Butler were hanged with Roger Beadneys and John Willerby, the last named 'confessing many things at his death, accusing divers of witchcraft'.[49]

In 1552 the Edward VI charter for the first time extended the area of the town—the 1447 county was hardly more than a legal fiction—by granting to the corporation the manor of Myton, and one sixth of that of Sutton; and for the first time the bench found itself involved in non-urban problems. No problems arose concerning Sutton, which was, in the Hull portion, mainly marsh and cow-pasture; but Myton-with-Tupcoates was at least a real hamlet. John Herryson, an alderman, owned a sheep-cote in Myton, and this gave him common rights for 200 sheep. After his death it was found by the manor jury that he had demolished the sheep-cote and that, as it was copyhold, his widow was obliged to rebuild it; but on further inquiry the bench with the aid of another jury found that it was freehold and there was no obligation to rebuild.[50] The charter had not given the corporation any *property,* but simply the lordship of the manors.

By 1594 some of the aldermen no longer lived in Hull. A hundred years previously residence outside the walls would have been far too dangerous and potentially fatal. But the time had not yet come when the majority of the bench wished to acquire country seats, and it was inconvenient not to have everyone immediately available, so it was decided that a non-resident alderman could be displaced and a successor elected.[51] For a quite different reason non-resident burgesses could be displaced. One of the indications of the importance of Hull to West Riding textiles was the order of 1559 that a burgess who lived in Halifax and another who was in Wakefield must return and live in Hull or be disfranchised.[52] John Barker, on the other hand, was given permission in 1563 to reside in Antwerp for three years and remain a burgess.[53] Whereas the two former were West Riding men or migrants disguising themselves as burgesses for the sake of the trading privileges they enjoyed, the latter was a loyal burgess whose absence abroad was likely to promote Hull's sea-borne trade. Burgesses were beginning to feel that anyone desiring to join their number was an interloper. It was thought in 1575 that by allowing their numbers to increase they were acting against their own interests, and it was therefore ordered that for the next three years there should be no new admissions except of those qualified by paternity or apprenticeship: no one was to be able in that period to buy his freedom of the borough.[54]

Burgesses lost one important privilege. Until 1575 no arrest in a civil action could be made in the house of a burgess even if the person whom the sergeant had come to arrest was standing at the door. This is where Robert Grimsby was when the sheriff's men took him, and he complained to the bench of this undoubted breach of his privilege; but the bench decided that the custom of the town had encouraged debtors to defraud their creditors and abolished it forthwith, leaving the unlucky burgess a prisoner for debt and a victim of instant legislation. But the house of a burgess still remained a civil sanctuary for anyone inside it, and not simply for the burgess himself. It was the extension of the right to the area within the eavesdrop—the overhang of the roof—which was considered to encourage frauds at the expense of merchants, who were not unrepresented on the bench.[55] Ordinary criminal sanctuary had been abolished everywhere in 1540. An inquest in 1542 found that William Orrell, gentleman, had murdered John Lownd, merchant, by stabbing him in the throat. He took sanctuary in St Mary's but under the new Act was allowed to go to Westminster for trial, where he would be in a much better position to purchase a pardon.[56]

Until almost the beginning of the present century no employee had the right to a pension from the corporation: but an officer of the white mace, being too old to perform his duties, was given a pension of 40s a year in 1581,[57] a notable illustration of the inprovement in borough finance. Because of his poverty John Whelpdale, who had been sheriff, was given a 40s pension in 1595; but he had to earn it by viewing the town's works whenever necessary and the fresh-water dikes weekly.[58]

Sources

1. BB4, f.41.
2. Ibid., f.243.
3. Ibid., f.47.
4. BB3, f.61.
5. BB4, f.80.
6. *CSPD* 1595-7, 49.
7. BB4, f.309b.
8. Ibid., f.124.
9. Ibid., f.341b.
10. BB5, f.240.
11. BB4, f.68b, No. 25.
12. Ibid., f.26.
13. Ibid., f.42.
14. Ibid., f.292, f.318b, f.347b.
15. BB5, f.156.
16. BB4, f.167b.
17. Ibid., f.123b.
18. BB4, f.270.

19. HMC, Salisbury, x, 124.
20. BB5, f.69.
21. Ibid., f.189.
22. Ibid., f.22, f.47.
23. Ibid., f.22.
24. BB4, f.108.
25.* Ibid., f.286. C. Singer, *History of Technology,* ii, 370. The floors of stables, and scrapings fron the walls, provided the material for the making of saltpetre.
26. BB4, f.149b.
27. Ibid., f.47.
28. Ibid., f.168.
29. Ibid., f.70, No. 52.
30. Ibid., f.237b-39.
31. Ibid., f.68, Nos. 21-3.
32. Ibid., f.51.
33. Ibid., f.56.
34. Ibid., f.166.
35. Ibid., f.376b.
36. Ibid., f.69b. Nos. 42-3.
37. Ibid., f.23.
38. Ibid., f.56.
39. Ibid., f.128b.
40. Ibid., f.292b.
41. Ibid., f.303.
42. BB5, f.25.
43. BB4, f.69, No. 41.
44. Ibid., f.29.
45. Ibid., f.139b.
46. Ibid., f.144.
47. Ibid., f.147b.
48. Ibid., f.168.
49. Ibid., f.359.
50. Boyle, *Charters and Letters Patent* . . ., 69.
51. Ibid., f.288.
52. Ibid., f.21.
53. Ibid., f.145.
54. Ibid., f.129b.
55. Ibid., f.125.
56. 32 Hen. VIII, cap. 12; BB3A, f.225b.
57. BB4, f.221b.
58. Ibid., f.294b.

10

Pure and Protestant Hull

In the Middle Ages the guild of Holy Trinity had simply been one of many. By 1464, however, it was the guild of the ship-masters and mariners, to whom Edward IV granted the dues called lowage and stowage, for which, along with the Vicar of Holy Trinity, they had supplicated, so that they could build an almshouse with a chapel for thirteen poor people impoverished by 'infortune of the sea'. Their petition also had the support of the bench.[1] Some forty years previously, though the guild was well established, it was not mentioned in connection with the ten-year grant to Hull of tolls in aid of the Spurn beacon being constructed (1427) by the hermit Richard Reedbarowe.[2] Some time between then and the middle of the century it had become the mariners' guild. It survived the reformation unimpaired.[3] By 1560 the master and assistants were of much the same Puritan outlook as the aldermen, whom they met in the council house 'adjoining to the Trinity church', in order to offer them £6 a year towards the stipend of an additional preacher.[4]

Melchior Smith, Vicar of Hessle and Holy Trinity, was so Puritan in outlook that some of his parishioners made their complaints against him to the archbishop. They represented him as having preached against vestments, against bishops, against the nobility, holding that all men were equal, as a person who wore his hat in church even in service time and as a husband so ungentle to his wife that on one occasion she had jumped either into the haven or into the mud. He had satisfactory answers to all these charges, but they reveal him as definitely Puritan. It is clear that he considered that some of his parishioners were still Catholics, as they probably were. He had once rebuked them for receiving communion in the papist manner, and he constantly preached against papacy, heresy and vice, probably attaching much more importance to the sermon than they did. Matters had come to a head when on All Saints' night they had kept on ringing the bells, contrary to the repeated orders of the mayor and himself. In the uproar in the dark when he arrived in the church with the mayor and his officers someone bumped into a mariner who bled from the nose and mouth, and it was believed that the vicar had punched him.[5]

From the case made against William Steade, the parish clerk, in 1570, it seems that he was considered insufficiently Protestant. He was blamed for bell-ringing on All Saints' night, for being too popular with well-connected Catholics, and for cutting short the sermon at the grave-side by bell-ringing and in services by manipulating the clock and playing the organ too long. He denied all these charges, but in a manner which suggests that there was probably some substance in them and that his real enemy was the curate, Simon Pynder, who preached the two-hour sermons which were then popular.[6]

Every order made by the bench with any bearing on morals shows their proper hatred of sin, which they too often equated with poverty though their stern Puritanism was often savoured with real humanity. One of their earliest orders against sin will illustrate their attitude.

> Forasmuch as in every well-ordered commonwealth most principally is sought out the heinous offencers or insensible persons which be delighted in drunkenness, excess, riot, whoredom, wantonness, lightness and scolding with such like, that by reasonable and politic laws and ordinances may be corrected, made sensible, and brought to good order: we, therefore, the said mayor, aldermen and burgesses, knowing nothing more convenient, needful nor requisite than to redress, supplant or pluck up these great infections and enormities most especially at this present time rearing in this town do with one assent, consent and agreement enact, order and agree that from this present 18th day of December [1563] no manner of person or persons within this town be so hardy as to commit any whoredom, fornication or adultery, nor use nor exercise himself in excessive drinking, riot, dispending his or their time in idleness, wantonness, lightness, scolding, or maliciously blaspheming the name of God, to the great provocation of God's wrath against this town, upon pain that everyone offending be punished and made an example of to

warn others, whether it be by cart, tumbril, cuckstool, thew, stocks, pillory or otherwise by imprisonment at the discretion of the mayor and the most part of the aldermen.[7]

This attitude was combined with greater moderation than might have been expected. James Graie spent three days in prison because his wife was a common scold and sold ale without licence. When he was released the common thew was put outside his door as a warning to his wife.[8] The next year (1560) the wife of an apothecary was a notorious scold and in a fight broke the head of Nicholas Maungye. The thew was therefore put outside the door as a rebuke and a warning to her. She came out in a furious rage and chopped it to pieces, but even so was only imprisoned for two days and on the intervention of a gentleman and a merchant was released on condition that she paid for a new thew.[9] But attitudes hardened when it was found that a whole half-century of righteous orders failed to produce a reformation of manners. Margaret, wife of Richard Bell (1612) was imprisoned until she could find sureties for her good behaviour because it was suspected that she was 'a housekeeper of bawdry'. At two in the morning and again at eight there were Dutchmen in the house and mutton roasting on the fire.[10]

Real crime attracted much more severe penalties. In 1565 an ingenious couple of blackmailers were discovered. By arrangement with her husband, Thomas, Isabel West entertained young men and did not confine her services to Hull. When the client was assured that the husband, a tailor, was safely absent, and both were in bed, the tailor came out from behind the hangings with a dagger. In this way they collected £3 4s from a London merchant. When they were detected the husband was disfranchised, both were carted round the town 'with papers on their heads declaring their offences', and they were then permanently banished from Hull.[11] Thomas Garmon and his wife (1567) contrary to the statute professed to be able to find lost or stolen goods by magic, and on conviction in March were both ordered to leave the town by May.[12] But quite serious offences sometimes attracted only the mildest of penalties. Richard Moore, a Shropshire man (1601) pretended that he had come with authority from the Lord Treasurer to inquire who could best afford to lend money to the Crown. The bench thought it advisable to refer the matter to the Council of the North, which directed that he was to be stood on a scaffold in the market place from ten to noon, with a paper pinned to him inscribed in capitals, FOR SPREADING SEDITIOUS AND SLANDEROUS RUMOURS. He was then brought before the mayor and Sir Christopher Hildyard in the Guildhall and was dismissed after humbly reading out a confession in his own writing.[13] But a man who was not a gentleman could not avoid death. Thomas Emerson (1595), condemned at York, was hanged at Hull. With the aid of soldiers sailing with him he had taken passage in a Dutch ship sailing from Berwick to Hull and robbed and murdered the master, throwing his body overboard.[14]

The bench was convinced that public morals would improve if ale was weaker and less was drunk. In 1560 George Shaw, a mariner who had been sheriff, was imprisoned for three days and fined 20*s* for keeping an unlicensed alehouse, his offence being graver in that keeping an alehouse was entirely unfitting for an ex-sheriff.[15] Such places were necessary evils. In the code of town laws read annually from 1566 it was laid down that all strangers were to have good lodging for their money. The inns were for horsemen and the taverns for those coming on foot. If necessary those on foot could apply to a constable who would conduct them to an alehouse which must accommodate them. No inn or alehouse must have less than two beds for travellers, and they could accommodate as many as could sleep there. After the eight o'clock bell rang they were to close except for those lodging there. They must have a sign at the door. They must not serve drinks except at meals and could brew beer, but not ale, which they were to get from the *tonners* if the guests wanted it. Servants were not to be admitted except when they came on their master's business.[16] So long as they had four gallons in stock, alehouses both in the town and the county were required to sell to all comers.[17] They offended also if they refused to provide accommodation. Anthony Winter (1603) forfeited half his recognisance of £4 because he had refused lodging to poor maimed soldiers. He might have got off more lightly if he had not allowed backgammon to be played.[18]

In 1574 there were twenty-one brewers, ten inns and twenty-nine alehouses. The bench agreed with the clergy:

> The learned, zealous and godly preachers of the most holy name of God within Kingston upon Hull do with one consent most earnestly and vehemently exclaim and cry out against the blasphemy of the most holy name of God, drunkenness, disorder, and infinite other

abominable and detestable sins which do abound by reason of the great number of alehouses, the unreasonable and excessive strong ale by brewers there brewed and the continual and disorderly repair of people to these lewd houses. They also do thunder out the manifold, grievous and terrible plagues of God hanging over this town if a speedy reformation be not had.

This was in 1574, when the bench ordered that all the rules already laid down should be strictly kept, observing that this was sound economy as well as theologically correct as over a thousand quarters of malt and much fuel would be saved if such unreasonably strong ale were no longer brewed.[19] To check 'that terrible vice of drunkenness' innkeepers and victuallers had been forbidden to brew, but in 1567 as this had not produced the effect hoped for the order was withdrawn.[20]

Each generation of aldermen took up the fight. It was ordered in 1593 that they should inspect each ward, and those persons found least suitable to keep an alehouse, or able to live by an honest trade, were to lose their licences. Disorders had arisen, it was said, because there were too many alehouses, and some had given up their trades to live idly as alehouse keepers. Many were sinking into poverty through play and drink.[21] In 1612 the bench noted that there were many statutes against frequenting alehouses 'and little good hath ensued but still the number of ale-houses do increase by the continual resort thereunto of unthrifty persons, labourers, and others of the poorer sort for the most part'.[22] By 1630 in Hull there were forty-two keepers of alehouses, five at Hessle, two at Anlaby, two at Ferriby and one at Kirkella. The bench had been trying to reduce the number; but the interruption of shipping by Dunkirk privateers had caused so much distress that some persons could support themselves only by brewing and keeping an alehouse. All, therefore, who had been in the trade at Michaelmas 1629 could continue so long as they paid 10s for their licence.[23]

Brewers were never allowed to buy their corn for malting in the market but were obliged to go to the country for it.[24] After a bad harvest the rule was stricter. At the beginning of 1597 alehouses were closed except for the reception of travellers. As long as the dearth of corn lasted any inhabitant going to an alehouse to drink ale or beer had the choice between a fine of 3s 4d or a week in prison.[25] Alehouses also had a bad name for such unlawful games as bowls, dice, cards and backgammon prohibited in the annual proclamation of laws, along with filthy jests and ribald songs.[26]

The range of lawful pleasure was limited. As early as 1534 the bench unanimously decided that if any mayor gave anything to minstrels, players, jugglers or bearwards it should be at his own expense.[27] Christmas revels came under suspicion, and early in 1573 it was noted that 'of late by sinister persuasion of some lewd and ill-disposed persons some prentices of this town be prime mummers and displayers' and it was ordered 'that henceforth no person shall go a-mumming or disguised in any masquing apparel' and that under pain of imprisonment no one should lend such stage properties.[28] Plainly these were amateurs, but by 1599 it was necessary to make an order against professionals: 'Because the players are for the most part strangers and therefore not so conveniently restrained from playing as the inhabitants from hearing such frivolous and vain exercises' for the future, anyone who attended a play would be fined half a crown and anyone letting a house to players one pound.[29]

On an August Sunday in 1601 Thomas, second Lord Burleigh, then President of the Council of the North, Lord Evers of Malton and other knights and gentlemen of the Council dined with the mayor. Their tastes were not those of the bench, so, in spite of the day, a firework show was arranged for their entertainment in the market place, under the direction of a Hull gunner. When he planted a chamber in the ground, charged with gunpowder and wildfire, it exploded, killing four persons and wounding many others 'to the great grief of the said lords, mayor and burgesses'. The entry in the bench-book seems to suggest that nothing less could have been expected.[30]

But there were times when a majority of aldermen were in favour of the continuance of moderate and proper pleasures. In 1573 they resolved:'That from time out of memory of man Mr Mayor had yearly, upon the even of St John the Baptist commonly called midsummer (23 June) coming to his house all the inhabitants both poor and rich and there hath bestowed upon the poorer sort cakes and drink upon the richer sort such victuals as to his discretion was thought convenient, whereby not only the poor had relief, but also mutual society and good neighbourhood among the rest nourished and maintained.'[31] A player came to the mayor's house with a licence from the master of the revels. The mayor consulted with Mr Ferries and two other aldermen, and,

3. i. Richard Bylt, a
fifteenth-century
merchant.

3. ii. Richard or
William de la Pole.

4. i. Thomas Whincup
(1550-1624)

4. ii. Sir Samuel
Standidge (1725-1801).
Whaler,
Nonconformist and
Squire of
Thorngumbald.

finding that the player's name was not in the licence refused him permission to stage any play.[32]But there could be no real objection to pleasure which was both honest and Protestant. The celebration on 5 November 1634 by the firing of guns to 'commemorate God's great deliverance from the gunpowder treason' was entirely in order;[33] and John Simpson, who came as H.M. servant with a licence from the office of the revels in 1636 was allowed ten days to display the portrait of the Protestant hero, the Elector Palatine, with his family.[34] Augustine Harrison had restored the town's portrait of Queen Elizabeth which hung in the Guildhall. The banquet provided by every new alderman after he was elected was a lawful pleasure. It was not simply for the bench, but for all the townsmen, and in 1631 the order that he must give this banquet within forty days of his election, under a penalty of £20, was renewed. Two defaulting aldermen were given warning, and Alderman Chambers was fined £10 for his failure in spite of his excuse that the ship bringing the provisions from London had capsized in the roadstead.[35]

The bench gave powerful reinforcement to the statutes regarding church attendance. In 1566 it was ordered that in addition to being in church on Sundays, at least one person from each household must be present at the services on Wednesdays, Fridays and holy days.[36] No one must speak ill of anything done by magistrates or the ministers of God's word in the performance of their duties.[37] This was part of the annually proclaimed code. The twelfth order was that keepers of inns and alehouses were to sell nothing on Sundays before the end of morning service, and were to close during the service. The next order was that bush-men and sled-men were not to go round with water on Sundays, but butchers and others with shops need keep them closed only in service time. In 1606 the Sunday rules about the town gates were made more explicit.[38] The keeper of the town gates, who was paid 40*s* a year and had two rooms rent-free, over Beverley Gates, one having a chamber, each Sunday was to lock the gates and posterns except North Gate where he was to wait for the lecturer, Mr Whincup, and after locking those gates follow him to Holy Trinity and deliver the keys to the mayor, standing near him during the service. No one could then either be let into or out of the town without the consent of the mayor. The parents of any child (1577) which cried during the service were fined 1*d*.[39]

There was a dispute among the gentlewomen about the places which they should occupy in Holy Trinity. This came to the notice of Matthew Hutton, Archbishop of York and President of the Council of the North, in 1600. He and his fellow members of the northern Court of High Commission directed that it should be settled by the mayor, Mr Gee, and Mr Briskin, the lecturer. The wives of the mayor and aldermen were not, in this re-arrangement, to lose their places.[40]

The current climate of opinion, and the distance of Hull from the seat of ecclesiastical authority in York meant that in addition to its busy concern with moral improvement, the bench had certain ecclesiastical authority delegated to it. Because so many mariners were guilty of fornication and adultery the archbishop noted that they had often gone to sea by the time the churchwardens were ready to deal with them. He therefore authorised the bench to deal with such offenders, as was already done in London and other well-governed places.[41] Richard Nixon, a tiler who kept an alehouse, was put in the burgess prison for two days and two nights in 1576 because he had allowed a young unmarried couple to lodge for the night in his house and commit fornication.[42] Mr Briskin gave the bench such active support that Jane Smith, angry at the treatment given to her son, possibly for selling water on Sunday, said: 'They went about to punish the town with water, and punished her son. She wished and trusted to see as great plague come to the town as ever there was. Briskin, who was the preacher, was the cause of it—the devil brisk him out of the town as she doubted not he would shortly.' They dealt with her with surprising moderation, sitting her in the stocks with a paper on her head declaring her offence and gave her four months to leave the house which she rented from the town.[43]

In 1599 the archbishop found that because their poverty prevented them from travelling to the church court at York some offenders were not being prosecuted for drunkenness and sexual offences, 'poverty or misery being a thing most incident to persons of such bad qualities'. So that they no longer escaped punishment he delegated his authority to any of the aldermen, sitting with Theophilus Smith, the vicar, or Thomas Whincup, the lecturer, and arranged for their proceedings to be recorded by John Spence of Hull, who was learned in canon law.[44]

This happy union against sin was rarely broken by the slightest disharmony; but in 1608 Theophilus Smith, as vicar, and many others, pulled up and burned two posts and rails which were part of a fence in Vicar Lane. A few weeks elapsed in which tempers might have cooled, but feeling against the vicar was so high that an alderman was sent off to London to start a Star Chamber action against him.[45] By 1614 all was harmony again, and the salaries of the clergy were increased at their request. Mr Whincup, as town preacher, was given an extra £10 a year, and Mr Smith, the vicar, had the same increase for his fortnightly preaching—he was also responsible for Hessle—and 'for his edifying the poor'. If Mr Whincup were sick he could be requested to perform his Sunday duty.[46]

The conduct of the poor was the main concern of the authorities—there were more of them and they were not altogether to be trusted—but the well-connected and the virtuous also came under scrutiny. Notices were read in the churches in May 1577 that those who allowed their wives to wear velvet in their gowns, capes, or kirtles would have to turn out with a light horse, a more expensive token of rank, at the musters.[47] Nevertheless the Queen's proclamation against excess in apparel, read in both churches in 1578, went unheeded. Many were still wearing clothing too expensive and ostentatious for their station in life; and all householders were ordered by the bench to show strict obedience to the proclamation, and to see that their servants, particularly the women, obeyed it also.[48]

Moral offenders, however, are usually found in humbler stations. Alderman Ferries (1620) reported that a drunken sail-maker spoke abusively against the town authorities; for which he was imprisoned until he could find sureties for his good behaviour and then pay 5*s* or sit in the stocks.[49] In the same summer a list was compiled of all those who had been 'faulty for bastards', and who were then to be carted round the town and ducked.[50] And one Sunday (1620) James Atkinson was found in bed with the wife of Arthur Wilkes by his wife and competent witnesses, who were examined by the mayor. Both delinquents were carted round the town and the husband was left in prison until he could find sureties that he would stop beating his wife.[51] And in 1629 a young woman, the daughter of James Jefferson, shipwright, was put into the house of correction to earn her living on the complaint of her mother that she was undutiful to her parents, idle and 'would not work but gadd abroad'.[52]

The bench took what measures it could to prevent the migration of the poor into the town, where their chances of keeping alive were notoriously better than in the country. The code proclaimed annually (1566) required that no one was to harbour vagabonds or those without means of subsistence.[53] Poverty was too easily mistaken for immorality. In 1563, after a ferocious denunciation of drunkenness and immorality the bench saw an easy way to the uprooting of sin in issuing an order that no one was to lodge vagabonds, evil livers and 'persons not having whereby and wherewith honestly to live', without first telling the mayor.[54] Fortunately they were also able to view the situation objectively. In 1556 they had a list made, which does not survive, of all the inhabitants and their occupations. Significantly, on the day they made the order, John Gospell came before them and said that because of his poverty he wanted to leave Hull, and he was given 20*s*.[55] They still believed, however, that able-bodied persons without work were merely idle and in 1559 ordered that in each ward the aldermen should list the impotent and deserving poor who ought to be relieved, and those capable of working, so that they could be made to work or be banished, since by their begging they were taking the alms which ought to have gone to those physically incapable of work.[56]

However, they were aware of the fact that some people could not get work. They made an order in 1577 that inquiry was to be made at Doncaster how the poor were employed in knitting, so that the poor could be employed, instead of begging from door to door.[57] The money for the project was to be raised by selling licences to buy and transport corn. Within six weeks two women had been found who were prepared to come from Doncaster to teach the poor how to knit, an art still unknown in Hull, for £8 a year, with a house rent-free and a bed without bedding.[58] By the late autumn a storehouse in Holy Trinity had been repaired and a chimney added for the knitters.[59] In 1583 William Lyon of Yarmouth was given £10 to come to Hull with his family 'and use only the trade of fishing in the sea here', each year training some of the inhabitants to be fishermen. On his arrival he was to be made a burgess, and his children already born would also become burgesses when they reached the right age.[60] When Edward Dalton's lease of the lime kiln was renewed (1591), so that the kiln could be kept in good order and work provided for the poor it was ordered that no one was to buy lime except from him—'good stuff and at as reasonable a price as before'.[61] By this time it was thought that the provision made for the poor was better than in other places and that this was drawing them to Hull. Unless, therefore, the aldermen of the ward thought that a newcomer was 'not likely to become chargeable to the body politic', no house-room must be provided for him in Hull or Myton.[62]

For children who would not otherwise be able to live except by begging there was Charity Hall, where, under Richard Coggishall, master and overseer, they spun yarn for the knitting of stockings. All the burgesses, including the mayor either paid money to maintain them or took their turn to feed them in their own houses. Some began to refuse this obligation (1594). The mayor and eight of the aldermen therefore ordered that a rate should be levied on those who were refusing to contribute, with imprisonment for defaulters.[63] On the departure of the overseer about a year later the scheme had to be abandoned. A collection was made for the children. Twelve were provided with clothing and in addition another four boys and a girl were placed as apprentices.[64] Fortunately it was soon found possible to revive Charity Hall. In 1631 the master, Peter Whitaker, was feeding the children and for the three months in which corn prices were high, had 12*d* a week for each child irrespective of whether or not the child could work. As the price remained high the bench agreed to supply them with corn until Michaelmas, half rye and half beans, and would do so whenever the price rose above 26*s* 8*d* a quarter.[65]

New trades were appearing to provide work. In 1596 Thomas Woodhouse, servant to Mr Gilby, was allowed to open a shop to sell books and to carry on his trade as a book-binder;[66] but the authorities continued to help when necessary. Thomas Rogers (1592) was a weaver of poldavy, a course canvas used for sails. He was lent £4 to get a stock of hemp.[67] In 1597 Joshua Smith was lent £40 free of interest to assist him in his weaving of fustians, which he had started and which it was hoped would provide work for the poor, 'who now surcease through idleness and seeking to live through begging'.[68] The meaning of this is different from what it appears to be. It simply says that the poor were perishing from unemployment. *Idle* for another seventy years was the normal word for *unemployed*. The plight of the poor when corn was dear was recognised. In December 1595 the price of corn was so high that the poor could not provide themselves with bread, and high prices soon after harvest meant that much worse was to come. The bench therefore decided to buy a stock of corn, before prices rose any higher, to sell a peck at a time to them at cost price, and William Gee immediately contributed £100.[69] In his will he bequeathed £160 to provide a stock of food for the poor.[70] The price of corn was again rising in 1597, and the bench now acted more drastically, taking a quantity of white rye from every corn ship from abroad at a price which would give the owner a reasonable profit, but which would be below the market price. This was sold at the cost price to the poor by mets, bushels and pecks.[71]

In another important respect provision for the poor either improved or matched the growth of the town. The Reformation did not result in the abolition of any important almshouses in Hull. By 1640 there was also Brotherick's hospital (1579), Harrison and Fox's hospital (1550), Ratcliffe's hospital (1572), Gee's hospital (1595), Ferries's hospital (1625) and Lister's hospital (1640); together providing for forty or more inmates.[72] Further, William Walthall of Hull, formerly a London alderman, in 1608 left £100 to be lent in portions of £25 at four per cent interest to set up poor young men in trade.[73] Edward Stanhope was born when his father was governor of Hull, in 1546, knighted in 1603, and left £200 for material to provide work for the poor. By agreement with the executors in 1609 it was decided to use the capital to make similar £20 loans at eight per cent to young men who could provide sureties.[74] His brother John, also born in Hull, created first Baron Stanhope in 1608, as Mr John Stanhope of Bilton in Holderness in 1580, was heavily in debt to Hull merchants and aldermen, and persuaded Burleigh to press the bench to give him extra time for repayment.[75] He had married the daughter of Sir William Knollys of Hull and was a member of the Council of the North.

For Catholics this was not a happy time. The northern rising of 1569 was their last chance, and the Council of the North believed that the seizure of Hull was one of their objectives. Though the actual rebellion never came within forty miles, years later the town was proud of its loyalty and the troops it had assembled in the crisis. Sussex, as President of the Council, ranked Hull in importance with York, Pontefract and Knaresborough.[76] Some thought it far more important. It might have been seized by a Spanish invasion from the Netherlands, and Alderman John Thornton anxiously wrote to the Council of his news of Alva's preparations at Antwerp, and persons connected with the rebels had recently gone overseas from the port.[77]

Thereafter the Hull Catholics can be seen only as victims. In 1577, in sending an account of northern recusants to the Privy Council, Archbishop Sandys said that there were twenty-two prisoners at Hull, of whom only three were gentlemen—members of a class whose delinquency stood the best chance of being overlooked. There was also a graduate in divinity, five priests, three schoolmasters, a yeoman, a labourer, a blacksmith, a saddler, a tiler, a carpenter and a weaver. Yet year after year they were still feared. As late as 1595 the Privy Council instructed Huntingdon, President of the Council of the North, to remove all recusants from Hull. He assured their lordships that he had done this, and that there were now none in the blockhouse, where, if they were not completely secured, they could be potentially dangerous.[78] At that time Anthony Atkinson, customs searcher at Hull, was a fanatical enemy of all recusants, seeing all his numerous enemies as crypto-Catholics, which they may well have been. In 1597 he proposed that he should recruit Hull men for a raid on Twigmoor, south of Scunthorpe, reputed to be a Catholic stronghold.[79]

Yet the general inefficiency of government, their own perseverance and the disputes among their enemies enabled Catholics to survive, even retaining something of their former status. Hull had at least one recusant shipowner, John Chapman, whose ship *Hopewell* in 1608 sailed for the Netherlands and Spain, with a recusant passenger, Boulton, who intended to remain there until he had learned the language.[80]

Sources

1. BB3A, f.97b.
2. *CPR* 1422-9, 457.
3. *VCH,* Hull, 399.
4. Ibid. 401.
5. J. C. Purvis, *Tudor Parish Documents in the Diocese of York,* 210.
6. Ibid., 227-31.
7. BB4, f.50.
8. Ibid., f.23.
9. Ibid., f.30.
10. BB5, f.13.
11. BB4, f.55.
12. Ibid., f.71.
13. Ibid., f.340b.
14. Ibid., f.238b.
15. Ibid., f.35.
16. Ibid., f.67 ff. Nos. 14, 16, 57, 59-61.
17. Ibid., No. 17.
18. Ibid., f.347.
19. Ibid., f.117b.
20. Ibid., f.73.
21. Ibid., f.283.
22. BB5, f.10.
23. Ibid., f.106.
24. BB4. f.71, No. 32.
25. Ibid., f.304.
26. Ibid.. f.67b, No. 7.
27. BB3A, f.230b.
28. BB4, f.67.
29. Ibid., f.235b.
30. Ibid., f.339.
31. Ibid., f.109.
32. BB5, f.101.
33. Ibid., f.176.
34. Ibid., f.208.
35. Ibid., f.129.
36. BB4, f.66b, No. 1.
37. Ibid., No. 6.
38. Ibid., f.366b.
39. Ibid., f.144.
40. Ibid., f.326.
41. Ibid., f.112b.
42. Ibid., f.154.
43. Ibid., f.226b.
44. Ibid., f.326.
45. Ibid., f.373b, f.375.
46. BB5, f.18.
47. BB4, f.164b.
48. Ibid., f.157.
49. BB5, f.35.
50. Ibid., f.41.
51. Ibid., f.35.
52. Ibid., f.105.
53. BB4, f.67b, No. 11.
54. Ibid., f.50.
55. Ibid., f.5.
56. Ibid., f.25.
57. Ibid., f.167.
58. Ibid., f.168.
59. Ibid., f.174b.
60. Ibid., f.230.
61. Ibid., f.257b.
62. Ibid., f.268.
63. Ibid., f.287.
64. Ibid., f.299.
65. BB5, f.129.
66. Ibid., f.300.
67. Ibid., f.274.
68. Ibid., f.305b.
69. Ibid., f.8.
70. Ibid., f.296b.
71. BB4, f.305b.
72. *VCH,* Hull, 341-6.
73. BB5 f.7.
74. Ibid., f.2, f.5.
75. BB4, f.219, *DNB* s.v. STANHOPE, JOHN.
76. *CSPD* Add. 1566-79, 85.
77. J.J.Cartwright, *Chapters in the History of Yorkshire,* 147.
78. *CSPD* Add. 1566-79, 179.
79. HMC Salisbury, vii, 300.
80. Ibid., xx, 42.

11

The Tudor Economy of Hull

The craft guilds were so prominent in the economic life of the town that one might see a symbolic significance in the twenty-one-year lease granted in 1607 of a chamber over Beverley Gate to serve as a Guildhall for the weavers, shoemakers, goldsmiths and bakers.[1] In 1598 the bench had undertaken a thorough reform of the system and had either created new guilds or revised the constitution of existing guilds of the glovers, joiners, carpenters, bricklayers, coopers, bakers and goldsmiths.[2] The guild of the goldsmiths shows the determination of the bench that each craft should have its guild organisation, since it consisted not only of five goldsmiths, but also of eleven smiths, two pewterers, four plumbers who were also glaziers, four painters, four cutlers, three musicians, two stationers and bookbinders, and two basket-makers. In every one of the 1598 guilds it was the bench and not the members who appointed the first wardens and searchers. Thereafter in most cases it seems that the freedom of election was limited, the members choosing between two candidates for the new warden, one of whom was nominated by the retiring warden; and in some crafts they chose one only of the searchers since the retiring warden himself became a searcher, though in others they could choose two of four persons standing for election. From 1490 at the latest only masters had votes at elections in the weavers' company, but this restriction does not appear in the ordinances of any of the other guilds. Since, however, apart from any other power he might have, any master could delay the payment of a journeyman's wages for a week, and orders against enticement made it difficult for a journeyman to change his employer, it is clear that the power of masters in elections must normally have predominated.

But it would be a mistake to see craft-guild organisation as a tyranny of masters over men. Most workshops were small, with two apprentices at the most. Virtually all masters had served seven-year apprenticeships and many must have commenced as journeymen. Nevertheless conscious class-antagonism may not have been altogether absent. In the 1599 ordinances of the bricklayers their clerk, Thomas Burie, wrote in the preamble:

> Plato. All men are by nature equal, made all by one workman of like mire; and howsoever we deceive ourselves, as dear unto God is the poorest beggar as the most pompous prince living in the world.[3]

It is possible that the clerk was speaking for more than himself, since the second and fourteenth ordinances are emphatic about the need for secrecy.

The powers of guild officers were greater than any community would now tolerate. Any house could be searched to ascertain whether a tailor was being illegally employed there, and the searchers of the cordwainers could prevent any leather worked by curriers being sent out of the town if they judged it unfit; and the curriers had no voice in the cordwainers' elections, and apparently no guild of their own.[4] The ordinances of several of the companies, therefore, included a rule that the searchers must not practise extortion, and it was not usual to make rules against what never happened. Any person employing a joiner or wright to do carpenter's work could be fined $21d$,[5] for each day he employed him. Anyone employing a bricklayer who was not a member of the bricklayers' company could similarly be fined a shilling for each day;[6] and those taking on a cooper who was not in the coopers' company had to pay a single fine of $3s\ 4d$.[7] These rules may not have been felt as burdens since they were probably long established and well known. Other restrictions were comparable to modern demarcation agreements. Cobblers must not work as shoemakers and shoemakers must not be cobblers.[8] Keepers of inns or alehouses were not to bake for those lodging with them.[9]

In most of the companies it was the rule that no apprentice must be taken without the consent of the bench, and that at the time of their apprenticeship the youths must be inhabitants of Hull, and in some cases they were required to be natives of Hull. The people still saw the town as a closed community which as far as possible must provide their children with a trade. No cobbler could employ a stranger without the mayor's consent:[10] members of the bricklayers' company, which also included tilers, wallers, plasterers and pavers, ingeniously kept their wages up by imposing a fine of sixpence a day on any townsman who employed a building labourer who did not belong to Hull;[11] and no master glover could employ a man who had a wife and children living outside the town.[12] The cordwainers in 1624 went much further and ruled that in future no master must take on any servant known to have a wife or children and that a master having an employee who showed signs of any intention to marry must report him to the mayor and dismiss him, after which he could not be employed by any member of the company.[13] Surely it is reasonable to see a petty tyrant at work here.

Though each company aimed at maintaining a monopoly, it was not impossible for an outsider or even an alien to set up as a master, and in some of the companies it was not necessary for a master to be a burgess. Occasionally the ordinances reveal the particular way in which the craft was connected with the life of the town. One of the best-paid jobs done by coopers was packing herrings, salmon and other fish; and the weavers probably produced more sailcloth than anything else, each cloth being between 23 and 25 yards in length and 9 yards and 9 inches wide. The Puritanism of the town also appears. Bricklayers bound themselves to teach good behaviour to their apprentices and to bring them to church on Sundays, and at times when he ought to be working no bricklayer would go off to an alehouse, or play at dice, cards, or other 'unthrifty' game. Some of the companies also still required that all should attend the burial of any member, and the bricklayers also undertook to be at the burial of the wife, child, or servant of any brother of the company.

At the fair and the market the companies temporarily lost their right of keeping out all strangers; and the market was still the place where most of the inhabitants made their household purchases. The annually proclaimed code of laws included most of those made in the Middle Ages, but more had been added to these, or put into writing. No one with a house or shop in the market was allowed to obstruct the footway by setting up his stall between his door and the gutter, an offence serious enough to merit imprisonment.[14] After one o'clock brewers and bakers were now permitted to buy any corn left in the market. No corn or meat brought to the market could be taken out of the town or stored, which meant that the basic foodstuffs in the market had to be sold, however low the price had become; but these restrictions did not apply except to those who came from the country, thus giving townsmen a distinct advantage. Butchers and cooks were forbidden to sell corrupt meat, and no meat offered for sale was to have its appearance improved by blowing up the veins or choking the animal; and butchers must sell to all poor persons who could pay.[15] In 1574 the price of butter had risen excessively because Hull dealers had accumulated stocks for the London and overseas trades. In October, therefore, a search of all houses was ordered and all butter in excess of household needs was seized. As a result of this search about two tons was taken to the Guildhall and sold to the poor on market days, the money received being passed back to the owners of the hoarded butter.[16] Much of the fish offered for sale in the market (1585) was brought by Flemings, and the market-keeper was required to see that it was wholesome.[17] Fish was also still being brought from villages on the Holderness coast and the Humber.

The livestock market was for the butchers, though not solely for them since horses also were sold, rather than for the ordinary people. Because of the state of the roads in the bad months it was open for little more than half the year. In 1598 an order was made that the market for oxen, horses, cows and other animals should begin on the first Friday after Easter and continue until the second Friday after Michaelmas.[18]

There was a 'reformation' of the market in 1623, which included the building of a new market cross paved with free-stone. Because they were likely to spoil or monopolise it butchers were not allowed to use it.[19]

For most of the people, since they had to buy corn and get their flour from the mill, mills were almost as important as the market. It had long been the custom that no miller in Hull could take multure (a share of the corn to be ground) but must instead charge a fixed toll, which in 1555 was fixed at $1\frac{1}{2}d$ a bushel for the next three months of the winter only.[20] The ordinary charge, proclaimed each year, was a penny a bushel.[21] Millers preferred multure if they could get it, and in 1587 it was necessary to re-enact the order.[22] In famine years millers tried to override the law, and this brought an alderman, Robert Dalton, to grief in 1595. He had acquired most of the mills in or near the town. He was taking multure for corn, and at his horse-mill charging 6*d* instead of 4*d* a quarter for malt. His millers were not re-delivering proper quantites even after taking multure. At the session's a jury of honest and substantial burgesses made these charges against him, and to intimidate them Dalton threatened a Star Chamber action for perjury; while his wife wrote an unseemly letter to the mayor, accusing him of harshness and injustice. But the bench could not be bullied in this way, especially with William Gee still active. At nine on a Wednesday morning the mayor held a session with seven aldermen, Mr Smith, the vicar, and Mr Briskin, the preacher. Leaving his place as alderman Dalton expressed his humble repentance 'that he had so long persevered in so bad a cause'. He asked that they should judge him 'as if they themselves were in like case'. Surprisingly they did no more than order him to cease his malpractices. He knew nothing of the letter which his wife had written, and she was sent for. She showed herself equally penitent and said that it was she alone who was guilty in respect of the horse-mill.[23]

They were much luckier than Thomas Hewitt *alias* Borehouse who on a market day in 1599 was whipped along with his carrier for taking multure from peas and rye brought to his mill.[24*] But by this time Robert Dalton was no longer penitent and had again quarrelled with the corporation and ceased to be an alderman. In 1603, reduced to poverty, he appeared before the bench in tears and promised to abandon all the lawsuits he had started against them. In view of his poverty and his pitiful submission he was awarded a pension of £10 a year to support himself and his family, on the clear understanding that the pension would cease if he again became troublesome or went to law with the corporation.[25] One suspects an element of blackmail.

Most of the corn for local consumption came to the town on packhorses. By the end of 1577 the state of the roads was so bad, especially in Holderness, that very few packhorses were coming in. It was therefore decided to raise money to buy corn, particularly wheat and rye, to supply the market, but because of plague relief and law costs the corporation had no money. Those burgesses who could afford it were therefore required to make loans to the town, with a promise of repayment by Whitsun.[26]

For those who had to pay them, market-tolls were regarded as a serious burden, and the great majority of country people coming into Hull had to pay. A few places on the Humber-Ouse network had managed to prove that they were ancient demesne of the Crown and therefore toll-free. These were Barton and Barrow, Rawcliffe, Temple-Hirst and Tickhill. Other places were free because of their borough charters. These in 1595 were London, York, Lincoln, Nottingham, Chesterfield, Beverley, Grimsby, Boston, Leeds and Hedon. It is unlikely that the inhabitants of the more distant places—Newcastle was another—normally appeared in the market, but they are likely to have been at the fair, where freedom from toll was also of value. Newcastle men were so often in Hull in their coal ships that it is possible they also frequented the market with other goods.[27]

The 1598 charter granted a fair of sixteen days beginning each year on 16 September. The bench then made new regulations, which as regards livestock were much the same as they long had been. The horse fair was outside North Gate along the walls, where the horses could be put through their paces. Oxen and cows were to stand 'all alongst the manor and walls, from sewer-side along Denton Lane to Bishop Lane and so to the postern northwards'. Persons selling mercery ware, groceries, goldsmiths, 'and such like' stood in High Street from North Gate to the end of Chapel Lane. Salthouse Lane was for pewterers, pedlars, shoemakers, glovers, linen drapers and sellers of wooden ware and hardware, etc.[28] Each fair opened with a proclamation of a free fair with freedom from arrest by the sheriff except for those outlawed or excommunicated, and a court of *pie-powder,* for the quick settlement of disputes.[29] Even with their own fair, Hull people sometimes could not buy what they wanted except outside the town. The master of the grammar school (1575) with 40*s* allowed him by the bench for a 'great dictionary' and Cooper's *Latin Dictionary* had to go to Beverley Cross-fair to buy them.[30*]

Goods sold in the fair or market were not generally subject to the fixing of prices by the corporation except in the case of bread and beer. One necessity, wood for fuel, was not sold in the market only. Firewood and turves were sold at the haven, where the mayor fixed the price of all fuel brought by strangers but not that brought by burgesses. Some burgesses had taken advantage of this by passing off the wood of strangers as their own and selling it at a higher price, to the detriment of the poor in particular. In 1569, therefore, it was ordered that for the future the mayor would fix the price of all such fuel, and that the poor, buying bundles of firewood brought by water, were to have one extra bundle for each half-hundred they bought.[31]

Just as the possession of a market and fair was seen as a great advantage, so, conversely, the appearance of any new market was regarded as a threat. Hull was fortunate in still enjoying some degree of government patronage. After Gainsborough, on the Trent, had restored its market, the Privy Council in 1592 ordered that it was not to be used to the detriment of Hull and that no foreigners were to go up the Trent other than those already accustomed to do so.[32] The bench also made a new order intended to limit the economic range of Gainsborough. Formerly, when goods could not be obtained in the markets of Bawtry and Gainsborough people had come to Hull for them. Now Londoners were sending hops, pitch, tar, flax and other goods to Hull where they were put into keels and barges and sent to Gainsborough, 'to the great decay and utter overthrow of trading within this town'. To stop this competition in merchandise commonly imported by Hull merchants, every owner, master, or purser of a ship sailing to London had to give a bond for £20 which he would forfeit if he brought such commodities from London or places near with which London merchants could continue their 'late extraordinary and bad dealings'.[33] Gainsborough was still seen as a threat in 1594 because of its new fair. A London merchant named Pulson sent iron to Hull to be forwarded to Gainsborough, and the bench caused it to be detained in the Weigh-house. Pulson started a Star-Chamber action, and the court issued its decree against him in June 1594 to the effect that Gainsborough fairs should not take the accustomed trade from Hull, 'and that no foreigners shall resort up that river in other sort than in former times they have done'.[34] On the strength of this decree and the grant expected in the new charter, in 1598 the bench arrested more goods of Londoners, others belonging to a partnership of two Londoners with a man of Newark, soap and iron for Gainsborough men, soap, iron and hops for a Doncaster man, flax and vinegar for a Mansfield man, and iron and flax for a Nottingham man.[35] The charter of August 1598 did in fact contain a clause, with an exception in favour of the customary trade of York, that all goods brought by water should be discharged at Hull.[36]

The 1566 code of bye-laws made it illegal for any Englishman not belonging to Hull to sell any merchandise in a house instead of in the market or at the haven, or for any householder to let him do so.[37] A few years earlier it had been necessary to insist on the strict enforcement of the rule that all cloth sold by any alien or stranger should be sold in the cloth hall and nowhere else as this custom was being widely disregarded.[38] It was only by restricting all trade to places where it could be kept under observation that the town was still able to maintain its privileges. To any individual burgess, however, it could be an advantage to share them with outsiders. Some burgesses were living in towns overseas and were forming partnerships with strangers. In 1575, as it was thought that this might cause the ruin of the town, except in shipowning, all such partnerships were forbidden.[39] Hull men were also acting as agents (1581) for Londoners, and as this also was thought damaging to the prosperity of the town it was ordered that London goods were to be received only by Hull men who had really bought them and who were not acting as agents.[40] Further, in 1585, it was found that some 'evil disposed persons' were profiting by avoiding the use of Hull ships and making bargains with aliens to bring salt-fish and other goods to Hull in their ships; and as this was detrimental to Hull fishing and shipping this also was forbidden.[41] It was only rarely that the bench could see any advantage in greater freedom of trade. It had long been the custom to take fines from strangers before allowing them to trade, and in 1499-1500 these fines had produced about six per cent of the town's revenue. In 1592 it was at last realised that this was harmful to trade and it was decided to take no more such fines.[42]

Monopolies enjoyed by others were easily seen as harmful. Thomas Wilkes, clerk to the Privy Council, had a monopoly of the trade in salt, and in 1587 Hull made known its grievances, since salt was a raw material necessary to so much local trade.[43] In 1589 Yorkshire knights and burgesses concluded an agreement with him on the shipping of salt to Hull. In 1591, with the advice of the leading burgesses, the bench agreed to buy a licence from his deputy for £700 for three years, and thereafter for £200 a year. Two aldermen and two burgesses went to London to sign the agreement under which the corporation obtained its licence for the sale of salt in the port and its members.[44] Formerly much of the salt used in Hull had come from Scotland. An order was made in 1575 forbidding any inhabitant to buy Scots salt anywhere in England except at the haven.[45]

Hull in 1592 came very near to obtaining a monopoly of the entire coastal trade of northeast England. London merchants had illicitly brought iron and other goods to Grimsby, included within the port of Hull area, and because Hull was 'a port of the greatest worth and importance in the north parts' the Privy Council ordered that no one other than Hull burgesses was to convey by sea any goods except corn or millstones to any place between Boston and Hartlepool. Very soon their lordships realised that they had misdirected themselves and referred their decision to the law officers.[46] None of the ports affected by this prohibition was or could be a serious rival, but the prohibition, if it ever came into force, did not last long.

It was with the corn trade that there was the most evident conflict between merchants and ordinary inhabitants, the former wanting to ship as much as possible, especially when the price was high, and the latter needing to do whatever was possible to keep prices down. Generally speaking the East Riding produced a surplus of corn, shipped mainly from Hull, but in famine years corn had to be obtained from the Continent. In 1565 the Council of the North, after the East Riding justices had complained of excessively low prices of corn, had permitted the movement of corn from Hull and Bridlington—2500 quarters, of which nearly half was peas and beans and only a fifth wheat. Shipments could continue only as long as wheat stayed below 10*s* a quarter and barley or malt below 6*s* 8*d*. By June prices had risen above this level and an order went out for shipments to cease, though it by no means follows that they did cease,[47] since there was a great deal of corruption among the officers of the port. In 1569 they were preventing the sailing of a crayer with corn for the garrison at Berwick during a prohibition on exports; but according to the agent of the Treasurer of Berwick the customer of Hull had been bribed to allow the shipment of 7000 quarters to Hamburg, Flanders and Newcastle.[48] The President of the Council of the North in 1572 reported to Burleigh that Hull men complained that the price of corn was rising because so much was evading the payment of customs duty by being shipped in the vessels of strangers from creeks in the Humber.[49]

The quality of port officers at this time and long after is exemplified by John Hewett. At the end of 1585 Patrick Hogg reported to Archibald Douglas, Earl of Angus, that he had found that Hewett was an excellent man to deal with. He was a dealer in corn at Hull and would arrange to send to Scotland 4000 quarters of beans from convenient ports in the Humber at 10*s* to 11*s* a quarter, a famine price, with 6*d* a quarter commission for himself.[50] He was excellently placed to arrange the deal, since he was customs searcher at Hull, responsible for preventing precisely the kind of activity in which he was himself engaging. It is possible that he was also helping recusants to go abroad illegally.[51]

Perhaps the law was more strictly enforced when Anthony Atkinson replaced Hewett as searcher. He got the job through the influence of a female relative, Jane Jobson of Brantingham, who was a niece of Burleigh, who appointed him at her request. Atkinson showed his gratitude to her by giving her £100;[52] and it seems that his standards, although probably higher than Hewett's, may not have been impeccable.[53] According to the account which Atkinson gave of himself to Sir Robert Cecil in 1596, Hewett had long been his enemy and had been making £1500 a year or more out of customs frauds, and since 1586-7 he himself had increased the customs receipts from £1200 to £2800 a year.[54] In doing this he had lost £900 of his own, and was in some danger from influential recusants. Later in the year he appealed to the Earl of Essex, giving him a full account of bribery as practised in the port and his own proposals for checking smuggling. In spite of all his efforts the corn shipped from Hull in 1595 for Newcastle and Holy Island mostly went to Scotland. Since the death of the Earl of Huntingdon (1595) he had no one to protect him and would be in great danger if his communication with Essex became known to the customs authorities of the Exchequer.[55] It is unlikely that he had many supporters in Hull since his favourite plan for checking the evasion of customs was to end the ancient privileges of the private staithes on the banks of the Hull and limit all shipping to two quays, which the bench claimed would ruin the town and especially the houses in High Street which depended on the profits made by their cranes.[56]

The authorities of the medieval borough seem to have ignored, as far as they could, the illegal export of wool.[57] In this sense the privileges of the staithes were certainly ancient, and under the statue of 1 Eliz. cap.11, they had become part of the law of the land. Hull was the only port in which the Crown recognised the extent of its impotence. The act explicitly said that no goods could be either discharged from or loaded on to a ship except at a quay to which officers of the customs had access. It was equally explicit that this condition did not apply to the port of Hull.[58] To adopt Anthony Atkinson's scheme for the evasion of customs would therefore have involved ignoring a statute. The Crown was quite capable of doing this when it could find agents to enforce its policy, but neither the Hull aldermen, nor the landowners who were so prominent in the Council of the North would be likely to show much energy in enforcing a policy contrary to their own interests. Hull, therefore, had to be given a much greater latitude than any other port; and since the illicit export of wool went on in less privileged places,[59] it may be assumed that the almost free export of wool remained one of the pillars of local prosperity for two centuries or more. There were, of course, limits beyond which illicit trade could not prudently be taken. Customs officers were not altogether prevented from performing their duties, but the Hull privileges made it easy to obstruct them. If any over-zealous officer of the Crown was eager to end smuggling, recollection of the treatment which Atkinson received was enough to stop him.

Atkinson kept his position as searcher until 1599, continually harassed, he claimed, by Hewett and his friends. The Privy Council thought it necessary to instruct the East Riding justices to inquire whether his life really was being threatened by John Aldred, himself a justice, as well as by Hewett.[60] Though the corporation may have disliked him, it also disapproved of *some* smuggling. The bench was instructed at the end of 1598 by the Privy Council to prevent the smuggling of corn out of the country in vessels which were supposed to be carrying it to other English ports.[61] In February 1599 they earned the approval of the lords of the Council by arresting a fly-boat of Enkhuizen attempting to take barley to Holland.[62] They had often complained to the Privy Council that coal-ships were taking coal, cloth and other goods, nominally for conveyance up the Ouse and Trent, but actually for export, thus avoiding prohibitions and the payment of duty. The Privy Council remedy for this was that a substantial bond must be taken from every shipmaster to be forfeited if he failed to produce a certificate showing that the merchandise had been delivered at an English port.[63] Atkinson had already explained in some detail to Essex how bonds were rendered ineffective by the dishonesty of officers of the port, and by the summer of 1600 the bench was again complaining to the Council of the North that in spite of a Privy Council warrant for the restraint of exports the officers of the customs and the searcher were still allowing ships to sail with corn.[64]

There seems little doubt that the movement of corn through Hull increased considerably in the sixteenth century. Nearly all the quantities mentioned at various times are much larger than formerly. In 1577 the finances of the town were assisted by the grant of a licence to ship 20,000 quarters in the next twenty years.[65] This the bench interpreted as giving them the power to sell licences to export at a lower rate, to meet the price paid for the licence. Their decision to spend £30 granted by the Crown a year later with £20 of their own on the improvement of the road into Holderness was not prompted solely by the fact that the disrepair of the sluice on the north side of the blockhouse was preventing people from reaching the market.[66] They needed to ensure that the corn trade was not interrupted by foul roads. For the engineering work necessary they were granted thirty trees from the royal woods at Rise and Cottingham.

Though there were times when the interests of the merchants conflicted with those of the people, usually they overlapped. In famine years it paid merchants to import corn from the Baltic, and with so much passing through the port the poorest were less likely to perish of starvation than elsewhere. Acts of 1532 and 1540 severely limited the use of foreign shipping for imports, but as in the summer of 1615, it seemed likely that drought would cause a poor harvest, Hull merchants were allowed to bring timber as well as corn from the Baltic in foreign as well as in English bottoms.[67] 1623 was another famine year. In response to a circular from the Privy Council the mayor reported that in the town and its county there was only sufficient corn for seed and for current needs. There was no corn trade or buying of corn in the ground. Hull merchants had imported corn from Europe, chiefly rye, to the amount of 2000 quarters or more, and it was being sold daily for 32s a quarter for white rye and 24s for beans, with the very little wheat available going at £3 a quarter. It was the belief of York merchants had imported corn from Europe, chiefly rye, to the amount of 2000 quarters or more, and it was being sold daily for 32*s* a quarter for white rye and 24*s* for beans, with the very little wheat available going at £3 a quarter. It was the belief of York merchants, probably well founded, that there were actually 30,000 quarters hoarded in Hull, and that at these very high famine prices profits of 3*s* to 5*s* a quarter were being made as it was sold to country chapmen.[68] Hull people at any rate would pay somewhat less ruinous prices than outsiders; and much more ground was coming under cultivation. The harvest of 1639 produced such a surplus in the newly drained Hatfield Chase that low prices would leave farmers unable to pay their rents unless they were allowed to export 8000 quarters of oats, barley and rye through Hull.[69]

Sources

1. BB4, f.372b.
2. J. Malet Lambert, *Two Thousand Years of Gild Life,* 217, 251, 259, 263, 272, 276, 285, 306.
3. Ibid., 276.
4. Ibid., 320, No. 16.
5. Ibid., 260, No. 5.
6. Ibid., 273, No. 3.
7. Ibid., 287, No. 8.
8. Ibid., 312, No. 2.
9. Ibid., 307, No. 4.
10. Ibid., 312, No. 5.
11. Ibid., 278, No. 18.
12. Ibid., 219, No. 7.
13. Ibid., 322-3, Nos. 1-2.
14. BB4, f.66b.
15. Ibid., f.69, Nos. 34-5, 37.
16. Ibid., f.115b-16.
17. Ibid., f.237.
18. Ibid., f.237.
19. BB5, f.60.
20. BB4, f.11.
21. Ibid., f.69b, No. 48.
22. Ibid., f.250.
23. Ibid., f.288b.
24.* Ibid., f.320; at this time there was nothing sinister in an *alias.*
25. Ibid., f.355b.

26. Ibid., f.178.
27. Ibid., f.128.
28. Ibid., f.322b.
29. Ibid., f.333.
30.* Ibid., f,128b *DNB* s.v. COOPER, THOMAS, Bishop of Winchester. He published his *Dictionary,* an enlargement of Eliot's, in 1548.
31. BB4, f.69.
32. *APC* 1591-2, 531.
33. BB4, f.270.
34. Ibid., f.271.
35. Ibid., f.212b.
36. Boyle, *Charters and Letters Patent* . . ., 128.
37. BB4, f.68, Nos. 19, 20.
38. Ibid., f.79 (1555).
39. Ibid., f.129b.
40. Ibid., f.223b.
41. Ibid., f.239.
42. Ibid., f.269: Chamb. 14 Hen. VII.
43. *CSPD* 1581-90, 413.
44. HMC Salisbury, x, 402.
45. BB4, f.131.
46. *APC* 1592, 385.
47 *CSPD* Add. 1566-79, 559, 565.
48. Ibid., 77.
49. Ibid., 436.

50. HMC Salisbury, x, 115.
51. *CSPD* 1581-90, 413.
52. *VCH,* Hull, 131.
53. HMC Salisbury, xx, 148.
54. Ibid., x, 67.
55. Ibid., 378.
56. Ibid., vii, 202-3, W. Woolley, *Hull Statutes,* 237.
57. BB3A, 79.
58. Woolley, op. cit, 238.
59. J. H. Clapham, *Concise Economic History of Britain to 1750,* 237, 282.
60. *CSPD* 1595-7, 166.
61. *APC* 1598-9, 405.
62. Ibid., 569.
63. Ibid., 677.
64. HMC Salisbury, x, 187.
65. *CSPD* 1547-80. 574.
66. BB4, f.190b.
67. 23 Hen. VIII, cap. 7; Hen. VIII, cap. 14; *APC* 1615-16, 262.
68. J. J. Cartwright, *Chapters in the History of Yorkshire* 282, citing State Papers (Domestic) James I, 182.
69. *CSPD* 1639-40, 428.

12

Mariners and Warfare

Hull was always a port, or nothing, and the £4 raised in 1576 for the ransom of prisoners taken by the Turks from London ships is an indication of widening activity.[1] Hull seamen may well have been among them, but the first one identifiable was Thomas Fisher of Drypool for whom in 1644 a collection was made in both churches towards his ransom. He had then been a slave in Algiers for six-and-a-half-years.[2] In the list of tolls taken at the haven, however, the range of goods was much the same as in the later Middle Ages, but wider, including such fabrics as velvet, damask, silk and chamlets as well as fustians, buckrams and canvas; and walnuts and fruit were now being imported.[3]

Hull ships had ceased for a time to sail to Iceland, but whale-oil was imported both from Normandy and the Baltic, and Hull men were now engaged in whaling in northern Norway, far north of the Arctic Circle and round the North Cape to Wardhouse (Vardö). A Russian ambassador seems to have passed through Hull in 1577, possibly in consequence of this trade.[4] In 1574 the trade had already been established for several years and the customers of Hull were exacting duty on whale-oil and gutted fish brought from Wardhouse. John Logan, the merchant probably most active in this venture, made his complaint known to Burleigh, who granted him the exemption he desired because it was 'a new invented trade and seemeth to tend to the increase of navigation, in which respect it deserves more favour'. Because of the extreme cold of the north his mariners and fishermen were infected with various diseases. Some died and some were lamed, and consequently he and his partners sometimes made a loss on a voyage. He had, therefore, taken with him only the ship's crew and men to catch, split, handle and salt the cod. The whales were taken by Norwegians.[5] It looks very much as if, as in so many early Arctic voyages, his men suffered from scurvy, and that with a smaller ship's company fresh provisions would last longer and so delay the onset of the disease.

Certainly the obstacles to northern whaling were so far overcome as to allow the continuance of Wardhouse voyages, often with great danger. The records of Trinity House show that the *Ann Gallant* was there in 1581,[6] and that ten of the crew of the *Lion* were lost before she had caught half her intended number of whales. This was in 1585 when the *Marie Rose* also lost six men.[7] The *White Bear* was there in 1592 and in addition to whales came back with cod.[8] The trade was large enough to make the Muscovy Company fear for its monopoly. It petitioned in 1621 for the prohibition of Hull whaling in Norway, Greenland and Tartary, and Hull submitted a counter-petition.[9] In 1623 Hull whaling was prohibited, and the bench informed the Privy Council that though it would be ruinous to the town and country adjacent they had ordered Thomas Anderson, Richard Warner and others not to sail.[10] Anderson appears to have been an Arctic mariner of some standing since in 1621 he had undertaken to try to discover the northeast passage for Sir Clement Edmonds, a courtier, diplomat and Privy Councillor. He now asked to be released from his bargain.[11]

The earnings of men in these ships could be high. In 1605 Jeremiah Gaskin, apparently an ordinary seaman, earned £9 10s and in 1626 Mr Richard Raikes owed John Maunsey £18 for a Greenland voyage.[12] As two Hull whalers approached the Greenland ice in 1631 they sighted the hut of eight of the crew of the Muscovy Company's *Salutation* who had been forced to winter there, and rescued them.[13] The Trinity House records indicate that there must have been whaling voyages every year. In 1632 Hull and York merchants were partners in a Greenland venture.[14] The warden and assistants frequently adjudicated in disputes about wages for whaling voyages—the £7 and the 'benefit of his oar' claimed by Thomas Oates (1635), the £6 15s and oar money claimed by a cook (1638), and the case of a man who was alleged to have stolen a fin, for which the owner tried, unsuccessfully, to withhold his wages.[15] The ships which went to Greenland could also be engaged in other trades in the same year. In 1642 Lancelot

Anderson was master of Mr Percival Levitt's *Whale* for one voyage to Spain and another to Greenland, for both of which the crew had to claim their wages.[16]

From Logan's account it would appear that the actual pursuit of whales was left to the natives of Finmark. References to oar money due for Greenland voyages indicate that Hull men had now learned the art of pursuing the whale. They had to, since they were no longer safe at Wardhouse. In the 1599 season the King of Denmark seized five vessels, including those from Hull, threatening to drown some of his prisoners. He was even rumoured to have beaten some of them himself; and all English vessels were warned to keep out of his seas.[17] The bench sent William Tayler, master of one of the vessels which had been seized, to give Sir Robert Cecil an account of their losses and the cruelty of the King.[18] He was instructed to hold himself prepared, with Thomas Hardwick, to accompany the reluctant and incompetent Lord Eure on his mission to Denmark in 1602, which achieved nothing.[19*]

By 1639 whaling was feeling the adverse effects of the monopoly granted by Charles I to the London company of soap-boilers. Whale-oil and potash were the materials from which soap was made and the merchants of Hull and York, rarely in agreement, jointly petitioned for a relaxation of the monopoly. It was not only injuring trade, but because drought, floods, or frost could stop the navigation of the Ouse for a good part of the year, York was having difficulty in keeping itself supplied with soap.[20]

York was normally in conflict with Hull over the question of foreign bought and foreign sold. One example of this ancient custom is that in 1541 the bench prohibited the sale of victuals in the town by one stranger to any other except a Hull man.[21] In 1577, because of the alleged decay of the town, and as a reward for loyal services, a further grant not materially different from that of Henry VIII was made.[22] This time salt and fish were exempted from the grant, but matters were made much worse by the concession in the same patent to the Hull company of merchants of the legal status of a corporation with a virtual monopoly of overseas trade in the town. Within less than a year feeling ran so high in York that the citizens refused to allow Hull keels into the city or to have any York cargo in Hull ships; and the bench retaliated by imposing a fine of £4 on any person who took York goods into his house or landed them at his staithe.[23]

It required the intervention of the President of the Council of the North, the Earl of Huntingdon, to compose these differences, and a 'composition' was drawn up under his guidance in 1578. As far as York merchants were concerned, most of the sting was taken out of Hull's trading customs. In the first ten days after the arrival of any ship York citizens could buy up to half the cargo, and thereafter any amount they desired. If York had supplied the money for the greater part of the venture, York men could also *sell* the cargo at Hull, up to a value of £150 if the goods were Spanish, or £110 if they came from Bordeaux. If, however, the cargo was mainly a Hull venture, York men could buy but could not sell in Hull. They could store the goods they had bought anywhere in the town, but in the case of those they were free to sell they must be in a separate warehouse, the mayor being notified in either case. All their goods, and lead in particular, weighing more than twelve hundredweights had to be unloaded by the crane at the Weigh-house, but if they could not be landed without unreasonable delay, they could be discharged at any staithe where its owner agreed. The bench would not order the people not to buy from York men, and would not take any coal brought for trans-shipment to York in keels, which could ride at the mouth of the haven to 'save their tide'. A York keel which was delayed might have to wait a fortnight or more to get up the Ouse. All reprisals between Hull and York would cease, and York merchants in choosing a ship for their overseas trade would give preference to any well-found Hull vessel with a competent master. If at any time Hull's patent of foreign bought and foreign sold were cancelled, the composition also would cease to have any force, and York undertook not to work for the cancellation of Hull privileges. All differences as to its interpretation were to be settled by arbitration.[24]

Relations with York now became much more harmonious. The cloth merchants of the two towns appear to have worked together in 1611 to persuade the Privy Council to stop trading by Robert Kay, merchant, which was prejudicial to them.[25] Discord reappeared temporarily during the dearth of corn in 1623 when York alleged that 30,000 quarters were hoarded in Hull and that as soon as Hull men knew of the arrival of any ship in the river with corn they sent pilots to buy it for them, so that all corn reaching Hull was already sold and York men were unable to exercise their right under the 1578 composition of buying one half.[26] York feeling was especially bitter because in the past year its merchants had exported nearly 50,000 kersies through Hull. Further, for ten years Hull men had bought all the herrings coming to the town, sometimes five or six shiploads at a time; and they had broken the composition with regard to Newcastle coal, allowing no York man to buy until they had taken all they wanted, so that sometimes keels missed their spring tides to York.

For Hull shipowners avoidance of disputes with York was always desirable. A survey of 1572 shows Hull as having more ships capable of keeping the sea than any port except London, Bristol and Southampton, with four vessels of over 100 tons, twenty-one between fifty and 100 tons, and another twenty between twenty-five and fifty tons. If the smallest craft of six tons were counted Hull was only twelfth in the list, and it is probable that for this reason such towns as Yarmouth may have had a larger population of mariners; but nothing of less than twenty-five tons was much use in naval warfare, and this was what mainly interested the Crown surveyor.[27] Moreover, shipbuilding had become a most important activity. In 1567 John Hodgkinson, mariner, took a twenty-one-year lease of land in the Trippett for his 'dock', which was more probably a slipway, as it was so far to the north, than a place for discharging cargo.[28] Joseph Blades, shipwright, in 1607 had forty yards of ground in a similar situation—measured from the mud wall outside North Gate and not coming any nearer than five feet to the causeway leading to the bridge.[29] When warrants for guns were being issued by the London Trinity House in 1626 there were nineteen Hull-built ships in the list, one of 200 tons and none of less than 80 tons; and it is safe to assume that the total number of Hull-built craft was much greater than this.[30]

The mud wall between North Gate and the haven, where the ground was not solid enough to bear a brick wall, was built or rebuilt in 1585 to make the town more defensible.[31] With guns at the south end commanding the entrance to the haven and the guns of the north blockhouse overlooking the only bridge, and a complete circuit of walls interrupted only by the haven, the town could be made safe from any attack.

The corporation had had the custody of the new and massive fortifications on the east bank since 1552. The guns there remained

Crown property, and some seem to have been removed in 1558 for the defence of Bridlington and Flamborough.[32] Thomas Foxley, the town's common officer, was responsible for the guns, powder, shot and timber (1563) and was allowed to graze his horse (1571) 'in the garrison'.[33] In the ordinary sense of the word there was no garrison. The fortifications were without soldiers to defend them, except in an emergency. When attempts were being made in 1576 to persuade the Crown to give further assistance towards their maintenance, the town's representatives were instructed not to give them up for a garrison of soldiers.[34] Two months earlier the Privy Council, as a result of complaints from Hull, sent Sir Henry Gate, who lived nearby, with Thomas Boynton and others to survey the works.[35] With the aid of Mr Pelham of Brocklesby who had served in various campaigns in Ireland and in Europe, and a former marshal of Berwick, they made their report in April 1577. They found that many repairs were needed, that the ditch on the east side was almost completely silted up and that in the central castle and the blockhouses the timber was too weak to carry guns of any size.[36] The Crown immediately decided to provide 300 trees from the West Riding, each capable of giving good timber sixteen inches square and twenty-four feet long for the repair of the fort, the blockhouses and a new jetty to protect the south blockhouse from the Humber.[37] For the town's share, the bench ordered 120 spades, 120 shovels and sixty pickaxes for clearing the ditch on the east side, with a good store of saltpetre for making gunpowder.[38]

It is more likely that the condition of the fortifications was a result of hasty construction on bad ground, than of neglect by the town. Six years later Sir Henry Gate and others reported that another £669 would be needed for repairs, but that Hull since 1576 had spent more than twice as much as its revenue from the Crown for repair and maintenance.[39] If, as seems probable, the population[40] was now about 5000, a good many men were avoiding their obligation to be trained in the use of arms, since in 1584 no more than 714 could be mustered.[41] Of these, 252 had firearms, and there were still eighteen archers who might be very effective on the battlements against an enemy arquebusier taking aim. These amateurs would probably have been useless in the open field against Spanish mercenaries, but fighting from the walls, with no need for complicated manoeuvres they might well have held the town.

In February 1588 the town increased its precautions against an invasion from the Netherlands. As early as 1572 the bench supported the popular sympathy for the revolt against Spain in the Netherlands. Two small ships, probably two of William the Silent's 'Sea-beggars' put in to revictual which they were allowed to do and 'to pass from hence to Camphire, for it appeareth the town is revolted against the Duke de Alvay'.[42] Now, since towns and fortresses were more frequently captured through treachery than by direct assault, every night innkeepers had to let the aldermen of their wards know whether they had any guests who were strangers to them. All the gates except Beverley Gate and North Gate were closed day and night, and each of these two had two warders. At the posterns the planks over the moat were removed. Ten men were on watch every night, four being in the guardhouse at the south end, newly provided with a chimney. There was a watch-house at the north end also, and in both houses an hour glass so that each hour the bell could ring for the changing of the guard, all of whom had loaded calivers. The gates at the staithe ends were secured with iron bolts, and each night the chain was drawn across the haven.[43] Edmund Gorrel was employed from the beginning of 1588 on refurbishing the town's corselets and other armour, and on repairing calivers.[44] When it seemed certain that the Armada would sail, Hull was required to provide two ships and a pinnace for the fleet, the order being sent on 7 April. The mayor replied that this was not possible as so many mariners had been taken for H.M. service, but before the end of the month ships had returned from Newcastle and the order was complied with.[45] It therefore seems likely that they would have to remain at sea for three months or more, or long enough for the scurvy, far more deadly than the enemy, to break out. Some 200 Hull seamen served.

Hull ships had transported men for service in the Netherlands in 1585[46] under John Burgh, who led the men from Lincolnshire, and Captains Yorke and Vavasour.[47] They performed a similar service in 1591, conveying 400 Yorkshire men and 450 others to reinforce Henry of Navarre against the Spaniards in Normandy. If the ships needed guns, the Privy Council ordered the mayor to remove them from the town defences;[48] and it is probable that some of the best guns were needed for the ship which Hull was at the same time required to provide for the expedition against the Azores.[49] Trinity House entertained Sir Martin Frobisher before his expedition sailed to Brest in Hull ships in 1593.[50]

In 1596 the archbishop, as President of the Council of the North, reported to Burleigh on the defences of Hull, which were better than had been thought. The forts or blockhouses were kept in good repair and watch and ward kept in them when necessary. They were well furnished with powder and weapons though many were old and rusty. Recently brass guns had been removed for H.M. service and iron pieces substituted. The bench wanted more brass guns than before as the danger was greater. They had spent £400 on a gun platform at the south end, the most vulnerable point. Every householder was ready with his weapons and forty or fifty men were on watch every night.[51] Shortly afterwards the bench ordered 'that some honest men be placed in the castle to dwell there', and that the chain across the haven should be made more effective by being floated on fir logs until it could be replaced with a boom.[52]

In 1595 Hull was ordered to provide a ship against an expected invasion to be ready by the end of March 1596.[53] The *Elizabeth Jonas* was prepared, some burgesses being required to pay up to £50 towards the cost, to which York would also contribute, and to give her her full armament, guns of up to twenty-one hundredweights as well as smaller pieces had been taken from the *Hopewell,* the *Mary Rose* and the *Griffin.* She sailed in the successful expedition against Cadiz.[54]

On the death of the old keeper of the south blockhouse in 1598, Edward Brown, mariner, was employed in his place for £13 6*s* 8*d* a year. To make sure that no enemy vessel entered the haven, it was his duty to search all vessels of strangers before they were allowed to enter. If they did not anchor in the roadstead when he signalled to them with a flag, he was instructed to fire a great piece, overshooting her, and then to keep shooting nearer until she anchored. The vessel was to pay for all the shot used.[55] William Biggins was hired as a full-time gunner, presumably for the maintenance of the guns, in 1626.[56] There were guns in the castle and blockhouses weighing between twenty-three and twenty-six hundredweights, and in 1630 the Crown promised twelve more. The bench agreed to pay for their shipment in the first convenient vessel, and also to buy a ton of shot and a dozen barrels of powder.[57]

Guns had greatly increased in weight since the eastern forts were built and it was necessary for the town to repair some of the floors with deal planks. Some of the floors were of plaster laid on timber and the partitions underneath of plaster and hair. All were renewed when necessary, and all floors were screwed up with jacks and underpropped with balks of timber. Some guns had been removed into the town, but with the completion of the repairs they were brought back and Mr Ramsden was to inquire about a bronze falcon and a bronze falconet in London.[58] In the town there were also arms in the artillery house at the exchange, and these were now removed to the castle and blockhouses. These weapons were muskets and calivers. Arrangements were also made for the repair of corselets and the renewal of firearms with crooked stocks.[59] On the town side of the haven, facing the Humber, the gun platform had been reconstructed in 1629, with a new and broader outer wall, and the platform itself had been raised to a level at which it could not be flooded.[60]

Hull was ordered in 1626 to provide ships to take 1600 men to assist the King of Denmark, the uncle of Charles I, in the war in Germany, landing them at Stade in the Elbe estuary. Only 1169 men arrived and while they were being assembled were billetted in Beverley, Cottingham and Newland, and not in the town until the week in which they were embarked.[61] In September of the same year, on instructions from the Privy Council, the bench fitted out the *Merchant Bonadventure* and the *Mayflower* for war at sea.[62] In 1627 another order was received for four or five ships to take another 1400 men to reinforce the King of Denmark in Germany.[63]

The transport of troops and the provision of ships for the fleet were not the only services rendered by the ships of the port. An act of 1581 would have interrupted the Hull trade in herrings brought from Marstrand in the Kattegat. The trade was to continue uninterrupted for seven years, notwithstanding the act, in order to keep ships and mariners employed. The preamble put the number of seamen so employed, perhaps with some exaggeration, at 300. A condition attached to this exemption was that for every twelve barrels of herrings brought from Marstrand a ton of shipping should be employed either in Iceland or in the herring fishery.[64]

The increase of navigation and seamen was a constant objective of Tudor policy not simply for national security but also because piracy and privateering were rampant in the absence of any permanent navy to police the seas. When Sir Michael Stanhope was governor of Hull he gave the Privy Council an account of the measures he had taken (1545) against privateers. Two French pinnaces and two Scottish warships of sixty and a hundred tons chased ships off Flamborough Head, capturing the Hull collier, *Antony,* of eighty tons. The rest took refuge in Scarborough Road where they were protected by the guns from Hull which he had put in the castle. While this was happening two small vessels from Hull sailed out of the Humber and captured one of the pinnaces with twenty-four men and her armament. She became part of a force of Hull ships, consisting of two small crayers, a ship of a hundred tons, and two others of eighty tons sent out against the enemy.[65]

Some pirates were English with useful friends along the coast. In August 1577, with a commission from the Lord High Admiral, the bench prepared the *White Hind* and the *Salamon* to operate against pirates. After little more than a week, off Ingoldmells in Lincolnshire, they captured the *Elizabeth* of Chichester commanded by Lancelot Greenwell and owned by Mr George Veyner of Chichester.[66] They had some assistance from a Newcastle ship, the *George of Beuricke,*[67] and the commendation of the Privy Council for the capture of a notorious pirate.[68] She was well found, with a crew of eighteen and gear worth £214, or considerably more than the total value of most ships. The Earl of Huntingdon came to Hull with others of his Council and with the mayor tried and condemned the pirates, of whom three were pardoned and fifteen died in what was probably the largest festival of hanging ever staged in the town.[69] There was another Hull expedition against pirates in 1581, and as a reward for his services as a ship's surgeon John Kydd was made a burgess.[70]

In December 1598 the appearance of five eighty-ton ships of Dunkirk, heavily manned, off the Holderness coast caused such panic that country people began to flee to Beverley. From Winestead Sir Christopher Hildyard complained that ships from Hull arrived too late to be of any service.[71] The Privy Council, however, was satisfied that the ships had been fitted out with proper dispatch.[72] Another eight Dunkirkers appeared off the coast in April 1599. In the summer of 1600 the bench advised the Privy Council that the coal trade was interrupted to such an extent by Dunkirkers that there would be a shortage of fuel in the villages in the winter, since it was only during the summer that the roads were fit for the conveyance of coal. There was a Dunkirk fly-boat of eighty tons in Bridlington Bay which in May took the crayer *Ann* of Hull, bound for Newcastle with goods worth £26, off Hornsea, and another Hull vessel, threatening to behead one of the owners until he yielded to their demands. The *Catherine* of Hull, captured off Scarborough, was ransomed for £40 borrowed there.[73]

There were few deaths in these encounters, but many Hull seamen were held as prisoners until they could be ransomed. Francis Mitchell was taken by Dunkirkers when bound for Elbing. Five of the crew remained with him, which suggests that the rest joined Dunkirk ships. He managed to ransom the cargo, and the five loyalists returned with him in 1632 after six months as prisoners.[74] Hugh Ross, a Scottish gentleman, claimed to have ransomed Hull prisoners in Dunkirk in 1626, but did not make his claim for another thirteen years.[75]

Dunkirkers sailed under the Spanish flag and Dutchmen, the principal enemies of Spain, were on that account welcomed in Hull. In 1635 two Dutch officers were sent as prisoners to Hull. They would never have been taken but for a Dutch invasion of Scarborough harbour to deal with Dunkirkers seeking shelter. They were therefore not seen in Hull as enemies and seem to have been confined in comfortable conditions in the Guildhall prison. This became known when an officious watchman found one of them in Ann Peacock's alehouse at eleven at night in the purely nominal custody of the sheriff's sergeant, and another lounging at the door of the Guildhall. These encounters produced such tempestuous language that many persons got out of their beds and came into the street to watch. The offending sheriff's mace-sergeant was bailed to appear at the quarter sessions.[76]

For English prisoners, collections were sometimes taken in the churches. When the *Darling* and the *Mary Bonaventure* on passage from Hamburg to the Baltic were taken in 1627 the crews were imprisoned at Dunkirk and Ostend. The collections in both churches produced £54 towards their ransom.[77] The losses of Hull were substantial. In stating its case for financial assistance from the county towards the provision of ships in 1598, when the Dunkirkers had been off Tunstall, the bench reminded the Privy Council of its services since Hull had provided eighty men against the 1569 rebellion, and estimated the recent losses to privateers at £6000. The Mayor hoped that their lordships would not be moved by the arguments of Sir Christopher Hildyard to rescind their order that the county should share the cost incurred with Hull.[78] All three Ridings contributed to the cost of the Hull ships sent against the Armada,[79] and York, Leeds, Wakefield and Halifax all bore their share of the £1400 to be met after the return of the *Elizabeth Jonas* from Cadiz in 1596.[80] The justices of the West Riding had to be pressed by the Privy Council to make the 'rich clothing towns', as Hull called them, pay their share. According to the bench the total cost of the Cadiz expedition met by Hull was £2145. The value of the *Elizabeth Jonas* with her guns was £600, as she was a vessel of 200 tons. Normally Hull would meet three-sevenths of the cost and York four-sevenths. It was only fair, according to the bench, that Leeds, Wakefield and Halifax should pay £400 or £500 as they shipped much of their cloth from Hull and obtained most of their alum, oils, brasill, woad and madder there.[81]

They were made to pay, and the Privy Council also issued an order that they should contribute to the cost of driving off the five Dunkirkers in 1598. York had first had its contribution raised to four-sevenths at the time of the 1591 Azores expedition and continued to pay without any further protest until 1619 when another ship was required for the suppression of pirates.[82] As late as about 1630, however, Leeds and Halifax complained about the contribution required from them for three ships of 200 tons each provided by Hull.[83] Their dependence on Hull was negligible—'no more than any other the remotest place in the kingdom'. Their cloth went to London, Newcastle, Chester and other ports as well as to Hull. Lancashire clothiers and the lead-miners of Derbyshire were more commercially involved in Hull than they were.[84]

Sources

1. BB4, f.144.
2. BB5, f.313.
3. BB4, f.216.
4. Sheahan, 96.
5. BB3, f.303b.
6. YASRS *Miscellanea*, v, 1, F. W. Brooks, *Early Judgements of Trinity House*, 1.
7. Ibid., 4.
8. Ibid., 5.
9. CSPD 1611-18, 503.
10. CSPD 1619-23, 559.

11. Ibid., 328.
12. F. W. Brooks, op. cit., 19, 43.
13. *Methodist Magazine*, xxix, 129.
14. YASRS. F. W. Brooks, *Order Book of Trinity House*, 8.
15. Ibid., 18, 32, 2.
16. Ibid., 56.
17. PRO State Papers, Domestic, 271; 106.
18. HMC Salisbury, ix, 349.
19* Ibid., x, 62, 296, 363. Lord Eure of Malton was also known as Lord Evers.
20. *CSPD* 1639, 45.
21. BB3, f.175.
22. BB4, f.165b.
23. Ibid., f.194b.
24. Ibid., f.188.
25. *CSPD* 1611-18, 19.
26. J. J. Cartwright, *Chapters in the History of Yorkshire*, 282.
27. *CSPD* 1566-79, 440.
28. BB4, f.75.
29. Ibid., f.369b.
30. *CSPD* 1625-6, 530.
31. BB4, f.273b.
32. *APC* 1556-8, 84.
33. BB4, f.47, f.85.
34. Ibid., f.150b.
35. *CSPD* Add. 1566-79, 503.
36. Ibid., 514; *DNB* s.v. PELHAM, SIR WILLIAM.
37. BB3, f.304b.
38. BB4, f.168b.
39. *CSPD* Add. 1580-1625, 101.
40. F. W. Brooks in *Miscellanea*, v, 101-2 (YASRS).
41. *VCH,* Hull, 157.
42. BB4, f.88.
43. Ibid., f.245b.
44. Ibid., f.250b.
45. *CSPD* 1581-90, 474, 478.
46. HMC Salisbury, ix, 165; *DNB* s.v. BURGH, JOHN.
47. Ibid., 262.
48. *APC* 1591, 26.
49. HMC Salisbury, x, 302.
50. Ibid., ix, 165; *VCH,* Hull, 401.
51. HMC Salisbury, x, 302.
52. BB4, f.302.
53. Ibid., f.297.
54. Ibid., f.299b, f.300.
55. Ibid., f.311, f.318.
56. BB5, f.72.
57. Ibid., f.109, f.110.
58. Ibid., f.163.
59. Ibid., f.171.
60. Ibid., f.95.
61. Ibid., f.80.
62. Ibid., f.72.
63. Ibid., f.82.
64. Boyle, *Statutes and Letters Patent* . . ., 99-100.
65. *LPH* VIII, xx, part 1, No. 9.
66. BB4, f.169.
67. Ibid., f.170b.
68. *APC* 1577-8, 71.
69. BB4, f.180b.
70. Ibid., f.221b.
71. HMC Salisbury, x, 494; ix, 141.
72. Ibid., ix, 165.
73. Ibid., x, 187.
74. F. W. Brooks, *Order Book of Trinity House*, 3.
75. BB5, f.258.
76. Ibid., f.205.
77. Ibid., f.85, f.89.
78. HMC Salisbury, ix, 142.
79. BB4, f.297.
80. Ibid., f.299b, f.300b.
81. HMC Salisbury, x, 58, 278, 424.
82. Ibid., 122.
83. *CSPD* 1619-23, 21.
84. Cartwright, op. cit., 296.

13

Before the Civil War

Elizabeth died on 24 March 1603. At six in the morning on the 27th Lord Clinton with a retinue of ten men arrived at the mayor's house with the news, and asked that James I should be proclaimed. The mayor consulted with the bench and the recorder in the council house in Holy Trinity and decided that there could be no proclamation without orders from the Council of the North. The order arrived on the next day, and the Lord President commended the bench for their discretion. He recommended that when the King was proclaimed bonfires should be lit 'and such other as hath already been used in London upon his proclamation'. The bench book says nothing of bonfires; but three trumpets were sounded three times, and after three solemn *Oyes* from the crier the town clerk read the proclamation, 'to the great joy and comfort' of all. Mr Barnard, who was then mayor, with William Gee, esquire, soon to be a knight, and the recorder rode to York to present themselves to James, and the recorder read a loyal address.[1]

Apart from what was left of the Charterhouse, and the hamlet of Drypool at the southeast corner of the defences, there were few buildings outside the walls, and visitors were impressed by the suddenness of the transition from 'a great flatt' of almost deserted country to the now thickly-populated town. Coming from Beverley in 1680, Baskerville noted that 'the way thither seems for the most part to be a deserted country'.[2] As yet, however, most of the buildings of Hull, as appears in Hollar's map, were confined to the eastern half of the town, with the gable ends fronting the street. West of Lowgate and Marketgate much of the town was open, with buildings nowhere touching the walls, though some had done in the Middle Ages, and there was a house in the tower over Broger's house as late as the 1580s, perhaps still inhabited.[3] There was little building near the south walls, arched on the inner side, and much of the area was occupied by the ropery. This section of the walls ran from Hessle Gate in the west to Horse-stairs at the mouth of the Hull. Near the centre was Mally tower, outside which lay the South End. This was the nucleus of the foreshore reclamation on which Wellington, Pier and Nelson streets were later to be laid out, but as yet it was still a dumping ground known sometimes as Mucky South End. From Marketgate to Beverley Gate the main east-to-west highway, of which the eastern end is now Silver Street, was then all known as Whitefriargate, much of it without buildings. The principal mainly-empty area was the site of the former Carmelite friary, soon to be given to Trinity House by Thomas Ferries.[4] The great landmarks were still Holy Trinity with its huge tower, and the manor house, with a still more massive but lower tower. Almost directly opposite, on the east side of Lowgate, was St Mary's, then towerless since the fall of the newly-built western tower in 1518.[5]

The cobbled streets seen by Leland were seen by John Ray, the naturalist, who noted in 1661 that Hull was 'paved handsomely'.[6] Many of the cobbles probably came from Holderness beaches rather than Iceland. This solid road surface usually made the streets less offensive, and the town healthier than the low-lying site would otherwise have been. It should be noted that in spite of the plague the parish registers up to *c*. 1625 show more baptisms than burials.[7] The health of the town was probably further improved by the new waterworks, where Ray and Evelyn were impressed by the ingenuity of the pump worked by a horse-engine. Chain pumps were well known, and what they saw must have been the improved kind of square-pallet chain-pump which gave a more continuous flow. This was a device long used in China and coming to be known in Europe about that time.[8] In 1612 and 1613 John Revell, an 'engyner', of Whitgift with two Londoners and John Cater of Nether Langton, Lincs, took a hundred-year lease of land near the Bushdike for their works.[9] Pipes must have been laid almost immediately, since in 1615 William Popple, a master-mariner, had water supplied to his house in High Street for 13*s* 4*d* a year.[10]

But, as we now know, moderately clean streets and a good

supply of water could not prevent the plague. The bench did what it could, ordering in August 1603 that as long as the infection lasted there, no London goods, except soap, oil, iron, or steel were to be brought into the town until they had been aired in the Groves, now mentioned for the first time, for at least twenty-four hours.[11] But the plague was already in Hull. There had been 223 deaths in 1602, about 80 or 100 more than usual, 167 in 1603, and 171 in 1604.[12] An order was made in May 1604 for moving people from infected houses to cottages in Myton, even without the consent of the owner.[13] Drinking in alehouses had been forbidden, to reduce the risk of infection, in 1603.[14] When plague was believed to have broken out in Scarborough in 1624 watch was kept to see that neither men nor ships from Scarborough were allowed to enter.[15]

There were 300 burials in 1635 as against the more usual figure of 186 in the previous year. In the first half of 1635 burials were fewer than usual, but plague appeared on 15 July 1637, and the town suffered by far its worst recorded visitation since the pestilences of the Middle Ages.[16] Between July and December 1637 the registers record a total of 762 deaths, of which 626 were from the plague, which killed not less than one person in every ten in the town. The mayor himself died and the elder Andrew Marvell, master of the Charterhouse and lecturer in Holy Trinity, who had remained with his flock, preached the funeral sermon. The bench now met in the castle instead of in the Guildhall, and the markets were removed to Drypool.[17]

The economic life of Hull was virtually suspended and those no longer earning enough to keep themselves had to be supported by charity. From Durham, Thomas Alured, who had interests in Hull, sent £100 for the poor, and gifts of food were sent by others,[18] including the York Merchant Adventurers.[19] By December the bench petitioned the Privy Council for aid, and the Council sent letters to the Council of the North and the justices of the three Ridings. In February 1638 James Watkinson, the mayor, with nine others, again appealed to the Privy Council. Including those in the pest-houses at Myton, the town was having to provide relief for 2500 persons at the rate of 1s 6d each. The North and West Ridings had contributed £263, but the East Riding had now stopped its weekly contribution of £60. As long as the commerce of the town remained under a prohibition it would be ruined without speedy relief from the rest of Yorkshire, which would itself be endangered if the poor could find no other way of living except breaking out of the town to beg.[20] The view of the East Riding magistrates was that since they had contributed £700 and the bench distributed relief too lavishly, they could be expected to do no more, particularly as there had only been twenty-five plague deaths in the first three months of 1638.[21] The officers responsible for the impressment of men for the navy also reported the great diminution of plague deaths in Hull, but they had only been able to recruit seven men from Hull and twenty others.[22]

Hull was almost entirely Puritan. On the bench, only the Dalton and Ellerker families had recusant connections. In 1637 Dr James Primrose, a physician best known for his opposition to Harvey's proofs of the circulation of the blood, was in trouble for his recusancy with several members of his family.[23] The blockhouse usually held a few Catholic prisoners. From 1601 until 1603 when he was buried in Drypool churchyard, Thomas Cletheray, brother-in-law of St Margaret Clitheroe of York, was a prisoner there.[24] Nevertheless it is now known that conditions in the blockhouses were less stringent than was once supposed.[25]

In spite of the Star Chamber action started against Theophilus Smith, settled by the mediation of the archbishop,[26] the views of the clergy did not clash with those of the corporation until Smith was succeeded as Vicar of Hessle and Holy Trinity by Richard Perrot, so little of a Puritan that he actually wanted to re-install an organ in the latter church in 1623. The archbishop warmly supported him and recommended John Roper to do the work; but the bench disliked the whole project, and no more than £36 was raised for it.[27] It was difficult for a vicar of this complexion to work with the lecturer, the elder Andrew Marvell who was appointed in 1624. According to Fuller 'Marvell was well beloved, most facetious in his discourse, yet grave in carriage, a most excellent preacher'.[28] He was a moderate Puritan and engaged in a profound theological exchange of letters with the Revd Richard Harrington of Marfleet, who accused him 'of a proud and haughty spirit'. In Archbishop Neile's 1632 visitation there was no sign of nonconformity, but in 1633 five men were named as wearing their hats in service time. Later in the same year directions were given for minor alterations in both churches according with the emphatically anti-Puritan views of William Laud, Archbishop of

Canterbury.[29] The morning service prayers of the Book of Common Prayer had been omitted with the cessation of services during the plague and were not resumed; Perrot's curate, Gouge, having little taste for the Prayer Book and rapidly lapsing into nonconformity. Pressure was put on him by the official of the archdeacon. Perrot, on the other hand, moved so far in the other direction that he was impeached by the Long Parliament for a sermon preached on New Year's Day, 1639.[30]

In the Middle Ages Hull's obligation to return two burgesses to every Parliament was often very expensive, as almost invariably they were paid, though sometimes they also attended to corporation business in London.[31] By now, however, there were influential outsiders anxious for a seat in Parliament, and the bench appreciated the letters on political affairs which some of its representatives, including Andrew Marvell, regularly sent.[32] John Edmondes (1604) and Sir John Bourchier (1614) were strangers to the borough which they represented. Maurice Abbot, elected in 1621, was brother of the high steward of Hull, George Abbot, Archbishop of Canterbury. Though he may have owed his election to the archbishop's influence, the commercial interest in Hull must have been glad to have a member of the Levant company, and governor of the East India Company, as one of their representatives.[33]

Throughout this period one of the borough members was always a Hull merchant. The most outstanding of them was the younger Alderman John Lister, knighted in 1639. It was at his house in High Street, rebuilt after the Restoration as the present Wilberforce house, that Charles I stayed in the same year.[34] On the death of Lister in 1640 his place was taken by Alderman Peregrine Pelham, a signatory in 1649 of the death warrant of Charles I.[35] Pelham's colleague was the younger Sir Henry Vane who owed his seat to the influence of the Lord High Admiral. The corporation had at first been reluctant to accept him, but the elder Sir Henry, his father, had helped the corporation in an action (in which it is not difficult to see an element of blackmail) about the castle and blockhouses which had dragged on expensively for six years. He had been governor of Massachusetts, was active in the impeachment of Strafford, and throughout the civil war was treasurer of the navy, and was judicially murdered for high treason in 1662.[36] His high office in the administration of the navy was probably one of the factors which saved Hull in the civil war.

To have men in high positions politically connected with Hull was useful when it came to obtaining the patents of 1610 and 1611 which together confirmed the privileges of the borough. The second patent also gave the corporation the right to collect toll on all Derbyshire lead even if it was not unloaded (but lead coming from York was exempt), the right to appoint the master of the grammar school, and the five acres and six cottages in the Trippett which had previously been Crown property. It also gave the corporation the offices of tronor and peisor (the weighing of wool) and of the gauger of wine and other 'liquors'. The latter office was obtained for a rent of 20*s* a year,[37] and the former by buying out Mr Rande who had bought it from the Crown for £15.[38] Having Robert Cecil, Earl of Salisbury, Secretary of State and Lord Treasurer as High Steward of Hull probably helped a good deal.[39]

The one guild in the town over which the bench certainly exercised little or no control was Trinity House to which almost all matters connected with the movement of shipping were left. The bench had interfered in 1572 to control certain pilotage dues. Alien fishermen bringing fresh fish to Hull disputed the pilotage rights of Trinity House, and the bench ordered that their vessels were to pay no more than 12*d* each for pilotage 'considering that by their frequenting this port with fresh fish from the seas much pleasure and profit cometh'.[40] Since so many of the elder brethren of the house were aldermen there was no real conflict of interests.[41] When in 1577 the warden and assistants complained of dangers to ships caused by poor-quality rope, the bench readily made an order that summer and winter hemp should not be laid together in one rope, that the rope should not be exposed to rain when being made, and that ropers should no longer employ unskilled persons who could not 'make their thread all in like round without knots'. For the future all rope and the materials for making it were to be passed or rejected by two qualified searchers.[42]

Under its charter of 1581 Trinity House licensed pilots and appointed a haven-master to regulate the use of the haven, now sometimes congested in times when trade was brisk. He carried an axe as the symbol of his authority and could in the last resort use it to cut the headrope and sternrope of any ship improperly moored. The commonest infringement of mooring rules was to make a vessel fast to two already moored abreast, thus making it impossible to work the middle ship. William Wilkinson was fined 10s in 1638 (and such incidents were common) for laying his ship, the *Isabell*, in a position which made it impossible for Henry Coward to discharge. He was also ordered to move the *Isabell* on the next tide.[43]

All the quays were on the west side of the haven, and to make better use of limited space vessels were now often berthing 'stern on', discharging over the stern. But with the tide running a ship could easily swing, and as this method of berthing also narrowed the navigable channel, Trinity House had to deal with numerous disputes arising from collisions in the haven, and in 1611 fined its haven-master for using abusive language in dealing with one such incident.[44] There was a dolphin in the Humber at the mouth of the haven to assist ships in warping into or out of the haven. Francis Tennant rammed it in 1632 with the *Indeavour* of Newcastle, and was fined 20s.[45] Even before 1600 Trinity House had positioned beacons and buoys to facilitate the navigation of the Humber and was making a profit on the dues it charged; but it opposed the 1618 plan for a Spurn lighthouse and in 1637 would not support proposals for a light on Flamborough Head,[46] though in 1614 it supported Newcastle in an application for tolls to maintain Scarborough pier.[47]

In 1639 Captain William Legge told Sir Francis Windebanke, Secretary of State, that Hull was mainly inhabited by 'sailors, lightermen and porters', and that the merchants were mainly at York, Leeds, Halifax and other places.[48] Though there were York merchants associated with Hull, his information was sadly out of date. When a trading company was formed in 1609 in an abortive attempt to monopolise the French trade there were thirty-five York merchants who joined and thirty from Hull; and the town had such prominent resident merchants as Thomas Swann, Thomas Ferries, John Ramsden and Robert Dalton.[49] The development of the West Riding towns tended to leave York stranded up the largely unnavigable upper reaches of the Ouse. A few years later the corporation of the city declared: 'Trade is decayed, the river here unnavigable by reason of shelves, Leeds is nearer the manufacturers and Hull more commodious for vending of them'.[50]

Lead came to Hull in great quantites from the high Peak of Derbyshire and the Yorkshire dales. Much of it went to London—

in 1628 almost 5400 out of approximately 6000 tons.[51] In course of time the coastal trade in lead for London was reduced by the growth of exports to the Continent and to Holland in particular. The 1611 charter largely removed Hull control from Yorkshire lead but not from that of Derbyshire, where lead-merchants had their grievances against knavery and delay at Hull. In 1640 they asked the corporation to appoint a new master of the Weigh-house who would deal with them fairly and punctually.

Much of the Hull sea trade with London was in dairy produce and other food, and increased with the continuous growth of the capital. London took seven times as much food from the northeast in 1638 as it had done in 1624. The return trade to Hull consisted of a great range of commodities including soap, hops, madder, groceries, oak planks and barrel-hoops.

In 1621 the Privy Council ordered twenty ports to appoint delegates to a conference to consider 'the true causes of the decay of trade and scarcity of coin within the kingdom'. For Hull John Ramsden submitted a statement of his views. The trade of the town overseas was the export of cloth to the lands of the eastern Baltic, cloth and lead to Germany and Holland and the importing of wine from France. Both the value and the volume of these trades had declined. Much of the market was now taken by foreign cloth, and the trade in English cloth was impeded by heavy export and import duties, and by tolls imposed by the King of Denmark, the King of Poland and the Duke of Prussia. The King's revenue would grow if the lead trade were stimulated by the reduction of export duties. Since the renewal of the long war with Spain, Holland and the Low Countries were buying cheaper Polish lead from Dantzig. Formerly all lead exported through the Humber came to Hull to be weighed officially, and the merchants came fortnightly, to the considerable benefit of Hull traders, since they also bought provisions for their houses. Now there was a beam at Bawtry to weigh lead, and much lead for other English ports now went direct from there. Hull was further handicapped by the new Gainsborough fair, and another fair, and Londoners frequenting them sold many of the commodities which formerly Hull had provided for Yorkshire, Derbyshire and parts of Leicestershire.

Formerly seven or eight great ships went to Wardhouse every year, and to Lappia, for fishing, and used to bring back 200,000 fish. 100,000 lings were imported from Holland and Yarmouth men brought up to 3,000,000 herrings, but (surely an enormous exaggeration) the fish trade was not one-sixteenth of what it had been. It would help if the Newfoundland and Virginia fisheries were open to all. Appealing to the well-known prejudice of James I who had no vices except sodomy he noted: 'The immoderate use of tobacco to be qualified.' He could think of no reason for the decline of the fish trade—'except it be the poverty of the husbandmen which for want of money are forced to live off butter and cheese'.

Hull trade, he continued, was suffering from the privileges enjoyed by the chartered companies, and especially the Muscovy and Eastland companies: 'We did seek to revive our trade by securing and finding out the land now called Greenland, where we were the first that found the country and the first to kill the whale.' Hull ships were continuing to go there, instead of restricting themselves to Spitzbergen, which the award of the Privy Council required them to do. The Muscovy Company complained that when their nine ships arrived at Whale Head in 1626 they found six ships of Hull and York owners which had demolished the fort and the other shore establishments.[52] During the civil war the Dutch took over the northern whale fishery almost entirely, and even before the war Dutch ships were bringing into Hull an increasing proportion of such commodities as iron, formerly carried in English bottoms.

Hull, like every other town, suffered from the demands of the early Stuarts for money. When money was asked for in 1622 to enable James I to subsidise the Protestant cause in Germany the bench pleaded poverty, decay of trade and losses at sea, and asked the Privy Council to be content with £132 6s 2d. John Ramsden, with Thomas Swanne and Thomas Ferries, appeared as the wealthiest merchants when a later assessment for a forced loan was made. Forced loans, billeting of troops, the depredations of Dunkirkers and insufficient help from the Crown for the maintenance of the castle and blockhouses go far to explain why, in the civil war, Hull took the side of Parliament. On 23 April 1642 Sir John Hotham was to offer Charles I 'the most signal and solemn affront which could be put on a king by sealing the gates of the city [*sic*] against him'.

Sources

1. BB5, f.347b, f.352.
2. C. Morris, *The Journeys of Celia Fiennes*, 87.
3. BB4, f.3b.
4. Borthwick Institute: York Dioc. Reg. Probate Reg. xli, f.351.
5. *VCH*, Hull, 296, footnote 68.
6. E. Lankester, *The Itinerary of John Ray*, 157.
7. *VCH*, Hull, 157.
8. J. Needham, *Science and Civilisation in China*, iv, part ii, 339 ff; part iv, 666-7, 698.
9. KHRO, D.796A, D.797A.
10. BB4, f.349b.
11. Hull University Archives, DX, 5/3; 5/4.
12. BB4, f.358, f.349.
13. Ibid., f.349.
14. BB5, f.62.
15. *CSPD* 1637, 439.
16. Hull University Archives, DX, 5/3, 4, 5.
17. KHRO, L.267.
18. BB5, f.477.
19. *CSPD* 1637-8, 225-6.
20. Ibid., 71.
21. Ibid., 374.
22. Ibid., 323.
23. H. Aveling, *Post-reformation Catholicism in E. Yorkshire*, 65.
24. Ibid., 23-4.
25. Ibid., 27, *DNB*, PRIMROSE, JAMES.
26. PRO Star Chamber: 8/79/5; 4/268.373.375.5.9.
27. KHRO, L.192, 202.
28. T. Fuller, *Church History*.
29. A. Marvell, *Complaints Against the Perverse Behaviour of the Inhabitants of Hull*.
30. *VCH*, Hull, 97-8.
31. Chamb. *passim*.
32. KHRO, BRL 2758.
33. KHRO, L.166-7, 198, 204. *DNB* s.v. ABBOT, SIR MAURICE.
34. BB4, f.122, f.123.
35. *Commons Journals*, II, 59.
36. *CSPD* 1639-40, 568; BB5, f.522; L.230. *DNB* s.v. VANE, SIR HENRY (1613-62).
37. Boyle, *Charters and Letters Patent . . .*, 131-51.
38. BB4, f.250, f.253; D/790A.
39. *CSPD* 1635-6, 12.
40. BB4, f.88.
41. F. W. Brooks in YASRS Misc. v, 111-12.
42. F. W. Brooks, *Order Book of Trinity House*, 30. (YASRS).
43. BB4, f.131b.
44. Brooks, *Order Book*, op. cit.
45. BB5, f.55, 68, 208-9, 227, 305: BB6, f.251.
46. Brooks. op cit., 3.
47. Ibid., 24.
48. *APC* 1613-14, 217.
49. *CSPD* 1638-9, 333.
50. *CSPD* 1625-6, 421.
51. T. S. Willan, *The English Coasting Trade 1600-1750*, 72, 119.
52. *APC* 1621-3, 40.

14

The Civil War and After

When the enthusiasm of Charles I for the Book of Common Prayer had made war with the Scots inevitable, military supplies were built up in Hull and York. In 1638, to the chagrin of Sir John Hotham, governor of Hull, Captain William Legge, master of the King's armouries, was sent to see that the town was adequately defended.[1] The manor house, formerly of the de la Poles but now owned by Henry Hildyard of Winestead, was taken over as the town's magazine.[2] The ditch was cleaned and dressed and entrance restricted to the 'three ordinary gates'. The bench arranged for a night-watch of six men for the magazine because of the great quantity of gunpowder there.[3]

In January 1639, preparing for the invasion of Scotland, Sir Jacob Astley visited Hull where he found two ships arrrived from the Netherlands with arms. In a siege 1000 men could hold the place, he reported, and provisions could be brought in from Lincolnshire. Troops could be drawn from Holderness and from Sir John Hotham's regiment at Beverley.[4]

With only three days' notice to the mayor the King arrived to inspect the fortifications and the arsenal on Thursday, 4 April. William Dobson, then sheriff, met him at the boundary of the county of Hull and escorted him to the Beverley Gate where he was met by the mayor (William Popple), the recorder, the aldermen and other notables. He was presented with a purse of a hundred guineas and treated to a fulsome and sycophantic speech from Francis Thorpe, the recorder, who was to be a commissioner at his trial in 1649.[5] The King spent the night at Sir John Lister's house in High Street, soon to be rebuilt as the Wilberforce house of today.[6] The next day he inspected the store of arms and ammunition, and the fortifications, heard the guns fired, and returned through Beverley to York, apparently well satisfied.[7] By June he had discovered that his forces were virtually useless and made peace with the Scots.

In the spring of 1640 preparations for a second attempt against Scotland were being made. Troops mustered in the south were marched to Hull in batches of sixty cuirassiers or forty carabineers to receive their arms. They were not quartered in the town but in the unhappy villages where quartermasters immediately began to practise extortion.[8] Some were in the end billeted in Hull.[9] War no sooner started than the Scots were over the Tweed, and by September had crossed the Tees and there were fears for the safety of Hull, where Sir Thomas Glemham was governor, with impeccable loyalty, a regiment of foot and 3000 firkins of rotten butter in the magazine.[10] The bench put twenty men on guard-duty every day and eighty at night, of whom twenty-four were in the castle and blockhouse.[11]

Jealous of their independence, the corporation had already refused to have any more guns in the town, and Robert Morton, as mayor, incurred the displeasure of Parliament itself.[12] Nevertheless he strongly objected to a military governor as an infringement of the patent which in 1552 had granted the castle and blockhouses to the town. Strafford told him that Glemham's appointment arose from His Majesty's princely care for the town's safety; and from the court at York Sir William Lister, brother of Sir John, wrote that it was the King's intention to visit Hull with many lords.[13] To avoid this embarrassment the bench gave Glemham the keys, and the royal visit was deferred. Glemham's appointment ended when his regiment was disbanded in July 1641.

As the breach between the King and Parliament grew, war began to seem a possibility and to both sides Hull, as a port, a fortress and a place commanding the approaches to the Ouse and the Trent, seemed, and was, an invaluable prize. There was undoubtedly a royalist party in the town, and Hotham later expressed the opinion that five out of every seven were for the King, though many were persuaded by Sir Henry Vane and Peregrine Pelham, the borough members, who were both strongly for Parliament.[14] When Parliament in November 1641 decided to remove 'superfluous' arms and ammunition from Hull to the Tower it did so because of the possibility that the town might yet declare for the King.[15] Early in January 1642 the King sent the Earl of Newcastle and Captain Legge to secure Hull for him;[16] but Parliament nominated Sir John Hotham as governor with instructions that he should 'not deliver up the town of Hull or magazine there without the King's authority signified unto him by the Lords and Common House of Parliament'.[17] The mayor, Henry Barnard, protested, in vain, that *he* should be governor as of right.[18]

Hotham was in London and for several weeks his son, Captain John Hotham, acted for him, arousing some hostility by his tactless bearing.[19] This made the problem of billeting troops all the more difficult and early in February Barnard was summoned to the bar of the House and told by the speaker that Parliament 'did require him to comply with Mr Hotham . . . in the execution of such orders . . . as they will receive from this house by Mr Hotham'.[20] The King, arriving at Doncaster on his way to York in March 1642, raised with Sir Thomas Glemham the possibility of taking Hull by cutting off the freshwater supply if he were shut out. Glemham replied that the inhabitants, in an emergency, could do without their supply from the springs. At low tide, the water in the haven was good enough and

> every man can dig water at his door; and they cannot bury a corpse there but the grave first drowns him ere it burys him.[21]

With the King at York preparing his forces it was necessary for Parliament to make sure of Hull. The garrison was reinforced with 1000 men, the troops were regularly paid, and the master of the ordnance was directed to send men to service their equipment.[22] There were rumours of a possible naval attack being organised at Elsinore by Lord George Digby; but in April there were more plans to remove powder and guns to the Tower. This meant that the King would have to obtain possession of the magazine immediately or not at all.

On Friday, 22 April, a market day, a party of about fifty, including the King's eight-year-old son James with his nephew, Karl Ludwig (the exiled Elector-Palatine), Lord Newport, Lord Willoughby de Eresby and Sir Thomas Glemham arrived and were welcomed by the mayor who, when an alderman, had been at York and recognised them. They assured Hotham that they were leaving the next day for York. The next morning they were inspecting the area of the south blockhouse when Sir Lewis Dyve came with the news that His Majesty intended to dine in Hull that day. Hotham immediately convened a meeting of some of the aldermen and Peregrine Pelham, one of the town members, and in view of the explicit orders of Parliament they decided not to admit the King and sent a messenger to meet him on the road from Beverley. The drawbridges were raised, the gates barred and a house curfew imposed for the day to prevent any popular disturbance. And so, a little before noon on Saturday, 23 April 1642, a rainy day, Charles I found himself shut out with his retinue at Beverley Gate, while the young James, Duke of York, and his party were at a banquet given in their honour by Trinity House.[23] At four in the afternoon, after a long parley, the King delivered his ultimatum giving Hotham an hour to change his mind. He did not, and at five two heralds proclaimed him guilty of high treason, and the whole royal party returned crestfallen to Beverley followed by the Duke of York and his attendants. The heralds returned on Sunday to see whether Hotham 'having slept on it and better considered of it', now intended to admit his sovereign. Hotham courteously refused. Two days later Henry Barnard, the royalist mayor, received a letter from the King demanding entrance and exhorting the soldiers and inhabitants to overthrow the traitor, Hotham. Matthias Barry made a fast ride to Westminster and on the 26th Parliament learned that the rumour that Charles was in Hull was false. The royal proclamation of Hotham as a traitor was declared to be a high breach of privilege, the thanks of the House were voted to Hotham, two ships were sent to defend Hull and the Humber, and the sheriffs of Yorkshire and Lincolnshire were directed to suppress any moves to raise forces against the town.[24]

Though the beginning of the civil war is usually dated from the raising of the royal standard at Nottingham in August 1642, and though no blows were struck, it was at the Beverley Gate in April that the Parliamentary opposition to the Crown was 'stripped of sophistries and reduced to the sword's point'. Hotham had reason to fear for his safety if he had admitted Charles, who in 1640 had threatened him and Sir Hugh Cholmley with hanging when they protested against the conduct of his troops in Yorkshire.[25] A Mr Egglestone later told the House of Commons that the King had intended to hang him in 1642;[26] and he could have done so if his entrance into the town had produced a royalist demonstration.

Hotham had committed himself. He expelled all those who refused to profess their loyalty to Parliament which, while seeing that Hull was prepared for defence, continued to withdraw munitions from the magazine to the Tower in case it was not.[27]

To gain possession of the town for the King, Thomas Beckwith of Woodhall near Beverley tried to suborn his son-in-law, Lieutenant Fowkes, then serving in one of the Parliament's ships in the Humber. The plot was discovered and could have resulted in the slaughter of royalist infiltrators,[28] but Hotham, to prevent bloodshed, informed the King that all the details were known and that 'he might spare himself the trouble of carrying on the contrivance'. There was next a badly organised plot for royalists to come in in disguise and seize Hotham himself, but the drunken talk of some of them gave them away and 'some were taken, others suspected, most fled'.[29]

A third attempt grew from the resourceful optimism of George, Lord Digby. Pretending to be a sea-sick Frenchman he secured an interview with Hotham and then told him who he really was. According to Clarendon he persuaded him to surrender Hull if the King appeared and, to satisfy honour, fired a single shot. Hotham's account, when on trial for his life two years later, was that he had taken him to be merely a French spy who brought him good intelligence, though he afterwards learned that the spy was Digby.[30]

On 3 July 1642 Charles I moved his court to Beverley, with some hope that Hull might surrender without a siege. Holderness was largely royalist, and the Queen sent from Holland an advance consignment of supplies in the 300-ton *Providence*. This vessel was chased by the Parliament ship *Mayflower* and took refuge in Keyingham creek, and, with local help, landed its supplies. A force sent out, perhaps half-heartedly, by Hotham, was beaten off, and soon after the siege began the King visited Keyingham from Beverley and received a petition from the people of Holderness who bitterly complained of raids by the Hull garrison and flooding caused by the cutting of the Humber banks.

It was this flooding which in both sieges made it almost impossible to capture Hull as long as Parliament controlled the sea. If a royalist force tried any of the usual stratagems of siege warfare, almost every trench they dug to get their artillery in position to destroy the walls was full of water before it could be used. If, without these precautions, they advanced through the flood waters they were at once under fire from the walls and without protection. Hessle and Myton Gates, which might have been approached along the Humber bank. were blocked up, and the defenders constructed half-moon batteries in front of Beverley, North and Myton Gates. The town was not wholly united and Henry Barnard proved so unco-operative as mayor that Hotham had him arrested. The brethren of Trinity House, in case the worst happened, divided their silver and money among the individual brethren for safe keeping, retaining only one beer-bowl and one wine-bowl.[31]

In response to Hotham's request for reinforcements Parliament sent 500 men commanded by Sir John Meldrum, a tough veteran who was to be killed besieging Scarborough: and another 1500 men arrived a few days later, while two more warships, *Rainbow* and *Unicorn,* patrolled the Humber. The royalists commanded by the Earl of Lindsey were ill-armed, of uncertain quality and badly supplied. In an attempt to command the river approaches Lindsey put batteries at Paull, Hessle and Barton.

This force had set out from York on 3 July 1642. After some unsuccessful attempts by Hotham to destroy their gun-sites, on the 10th, Sir Thomas Metham destroyed some of the windmills outside the walls and the long-range bombardment began. There was heavy gunfire at night from the 10th to the 13th, though on the 12th a sortie of 500 men under Meldrum destroyed one of the royalist positions. A week later the Earl of Warwick, Parliament's commander-in-chief of the navy, was able to report the destruction of all the royalist forts. On the 27th a force under Captains Lowinger and Legard attacked the headquarters at Anlaby, half the troops marching along the raised but flooded causeway and the other half approaching on rafts. The King's magazine was destroyed, losses were light, many prisoners were taken; and the royalists were so demoralised that the siege was raised.[32]

The Hull garrison was now able to make raids across the Humber and as far west as Cawood; but the danger from within still remained. A number of royalists, pretending that they were stranded Danish sailors, were enlisted in the garrison, but were closely watched. Their plan was to blow up one of the gates with a petard to admit an attacking force, but they were caught red-handed on 27 November, and the royalists coming to join them from York were dealt with by Sir Thomas Fairfax and Captain John Hotham.

With the landing of the Queen at Bridlington in February 1643 with munitions from Holland, the loyalty of both Hothams to Parliament wavered, and Sir John was already in correspondence with the Earl of Newcastle. Hotham junior made contact with the Queen, ostensibly about the exchange of prisoners, and the royalists were soon convinced that both Hothams were ready to change sides. In the correspondence which followed, and which was partly known to Parliament, this became more and more clear. Sir John's pride was injured by the appointment of Ferdinando Lord Fairfax as parliamentary commander-in-chief in the north. In late March or early April Digby was sent secretly to Hotham with captured parliamentary papers to show Hotham that he was now under suspicion. The Puritan John Saltmarsh, a relative of Hotham, was sent to him by Parliament, and as an *agent-provocateur* got him to speak of his intention of changing sides as soon as he could. Saltmarsh then informed Parliament, through Captain Moyer of *Hercules,* one of the ships in the Humber.

Captain Hotham was detached for duty against Newark where the indiscipline of his troops led to his arrest; but he escaped and was back in Hull by 28 June, where his father made a bitter protest to Parliament. Their disloyalty was known to Captain Moyer and a few others, including the mayor, Robert Raikes, and Sir Matthew Boynton, who had secret orders to raise the town against its governor if necessary. Late on the 28th this group, with the aldermen and other friends of Parliament, met to concert their measures. The next morning 100 men from the *Hercules* took the castle and blockhouses without bloodshed. A party of soldiers and townsmen took the walls and gates, with the magazine, and arrested Captain Hotham. Sir John escaped through Beverley Gate, but found he could not cross the river at Stoneferry to reach his fortified house at Scorborough without passing through Beverley, where he was arrested and brought back. Soon afterwards the *Hercules* sailed for London with both prisoners.[33]

The day after the arrest of the Hothams Newcastle routed Lord Fairfax and his son, Sir Thomas, at Adwalton Moor, near Bradford. Sir Thomas made a fighting retreat to Hull with his cavalry where he joined his father; and very soon Wressel castle and Hull were the only places of any importance in Yorkshire not held by the King's troops.[34] Parliament made an appointment agreeable to the town, where events had now greatly strengthened anti-royalist sentiment, by naming Lord Fairfax as governor; though the bench still held that the existence of a governor was an infringement of the liberties of the corporation.

Hull was left in peace throughout July and most of August as Newcastle was busy occupying Lincolnshire; but a raid of Sir Thomas Fairfax as far as Stamford Bridge convinced him that a garrison in Hull was a threat to York itself and he began to retire from Lincolnshire at the end of the month. The younger Fairfax, with a greatly inferior force, held him for a while west of Beverley and then again made a fighting retreat. The royalist pillaging of Beverley was a cruel warning of what could happen to Hull, now besieged for the second time on 2 September 1643.

There was now practically no chance of any betrayal from within, and the defensive earthworks outside the walls had been greatly strengthened, and a battery just east of the south blockhouse provided enfilading fire for the eastern walls and covered the entrance to the haven. Newcastle's forces were based on Beverley, Cottingham and Newland. The freshwater dyke was cut, but water from wells, and from the Hull at low tide would suffice for a long time.

To meet the threat from the north, Lord Fairfax demolished the Charterhouse and built an earthen rampart on the site, countered by the royalist *Fort Royal* to the north of it, but so distant from the town that its fire, even with red-hot balls, did little damage. In expectation of this, Fairfax had ordered the removal of anything which could burn from the upper part of all the houses, and every householder was to be ready to help in the putting out of any fire. *Fort Royal,* under constant fire from the Charterhouse site, was captured, but on 9 September an attack on Newcastle's position at Anlaby was defeated; but four days later Fairfax opened the sluices and cut the river banks, so that no further approaches to the walls could be made without very heavy losses.

On 16 September a gunner carelessly entered the magazine in the north blockhouse with a lighted match (the slow-burning fuse applied to the touch-hole of guns), and an explosion partly destroyed it; but twelve days later a royalist magazine at Hull

Bank, Cottingham also exploded, and the ships *Lion* and *Employment* destroyed the fort at Paull.

Colonel Oliver Cromwell crossed the river with the Lincolnshire commander, Lord Willoughby of Parham, and they were so confident of the defensibility of Hull that they withdrew Sir Thomas Fairfax with his twenty troops of horses which were soon to perform invaluable service at Winceby near Horncastle. Relations between the town and the governor were far better than they had been under Hotham, and when the time came for the mayoral election Lord Fairfax overcame the reluctance of Thomas Raikes to continue in office for a second year.

There was continuous fighting outside the defences. The garrison destroyed the battery sites at Sculcoates and Derringham bank; and the royalists overran the defences at Hessle Gate near the west jetty and at the Charterhouse, but were under such heavy fire from the walls that they had to withdraw. Their misery was made worse by heavy rain in September and deeper floods brought by the October spring tides. Sir Philip Warwick who visited Newcastle about this time thought that 'those without seemed likelier to rot than those within to starve'.[35]

On 5 October the garrison was reinforced by Sir John Meldrum with 400 men and a little later Sir William Constable joined him with another 250. On 11 October 1500 men were assembled for the final attempt to drive off the royalists. Vice-Admiral Rainsborough came ashore from the *Lion* to serve as a colonel and with Meldrum and Colonel John Lambert commanded a mixed force of soldiers, sailors, townsmen and four troops of horse. They paraded at first light. They drew the attention of the enemy to the north by making a thrust from the North Gate and then made their real attack west of the town. There was a battle lasting seven hours, ending with the capture of all the royalist positions and their two greatest guns Gog and Magog, which were turned on them. At the end of the day refreshment was provided for the victors; 'The inhabitants of Hull sent great store of bread and meat, and many gallons of sack and strong beer to the west jetty, which came very seasonably for them that had been fighting all day.'

'*Memorandum imperpetuum*', the bench declared, 'to the praise and glory of God that the 11th of October 1643 the siege was raised which had been continued by the Earl of Newcastle's great

army for the space of   weeks.'[36]* This victory alone might
not have ended the danger but for the fact that on the same day
Manchester and Cromwell, with the cavalry withdrawn from Hull,
defeated a royalist army, twice as large as their own, at Winceby.
The younger Fairfax long remembered that the cannonade at Hull
could be heard when the firing at Winceby had ceased. Until the
Restoration the deliverance of Hull was celebrated by a public
holiday on 12 October, with the peculiar consequence that in 1658
the shooting-off of blank ammunition and the beating of drums
was heard because of exceptional atmospheric conditions for
twenty-five miles around and was thought by some to be a warning
from heaven and by others was heard as a real battle, so that many
ran home in terror.[37]

Hull had made an important contribution to the eventual
victory of Parliament and had suffered little. Trinity House
recorded that only eight men were killed in the final battle.[38] The
Puritan John Shawe saw divine providence in the fact that so few
of the righteous in the town were killed in the bombardments.[39]
The Holy Trinity Registers, however, show that there was a high
death rate in 1643, perhaps from overcrowding and
unemployment caused by the war. Burials exceeded baptisms by
fourteen per cent. The same causes, whatever they were, continued
into 1644, an even worse year - and Holy Trinity accounted for
most of the town - with 373 burials, 75.9 per cent more than the
baptisms. Even so, by 1652 the population of the parish cannot
have been less than about 6500, forty per cent more than it had
been *c*.1620.

Hull ships were still involved in the war. John Lawson of
Scarborough, later knighted and an admiral, made coasting
voyages from Hull. He afterwards wrote to Sir Henry Vane:
'During part of the first war I served in a small ship of my own at
sea, my livelihood being by trade in that way . . . my wife and
children being banished two years to Hull.'[40] In the *Covenant* of
Hull he took ten guns from an enemy ship off Scarborough in
1644.[41] The *Hector* of Hull, provisioned by William Peck and
William Raikes, continued in the service of Parliament.[42] But
when in 1645 seamen were required to assist in the siege of
Scarborough castle, Roger Wattes, one of the Trinity House
assistants, spoke in such a manner as to dissuade them, for which
the House made him pay 6*s* 8*d* to the poor.[43]

Towards the end of the war the economy of the town was badly affected and yet the people were called on to continue heavy financial contributions for the siege of Pontefract and like purposes.[44] Most of the inhabitants were seamen. boatmen, labourers, or sledge-men. According to the bench about half the trade by sea was for merchants of London, York, Leeds, Derby and other places which bore no share of the cost when men were lost or captured at sea and their families had to be maintained. Since the beginning of the war Londoners had agents in Hull to buy cloth and much lead was going directly overseas without touching Hull. Since the beginning of the war Londoners were setting up in wholesale and retail trade, to the detriment of Hull grocers, mercers and others. As well as supplying ships for war, the town paid heavy assessments for the army. It was costing £40 a month to keep the fortifications in repair, and watch and ward cost another £40. It would cost £2000 to repair the blockhouse damaged in the explosion of the magazine and the bridge over the haven, which had taken some of the blast.[45]

For individuals who had sided with the King, life was difficult. Leonard Scott, a merchant with property in Hull worth £40 a year, was fined £74 for serving under Newcastle. In 1645 he was in France.[46] Sir Henry Hildyard of Hull, with estates in three counties, had been a colonel of the trained bands and was originally fined £14,742, estimated to be two years' income, but in 1648 this was reduced by more than half because the Hull manor house, his property, had been given to the corporation for its services.[47] James Watkinson, merchant, was fined £43 10*s* or one-tenth of his capital because he had worked in the King's magazine at York.[48] Matthew Topham was a Hull merchant with a partner, Christopher Topham, in Dantzig. He himself had gone to York, and after its surrender, to Holland. He was unable to appear personally to pay his delinquency fine of £90 because the river at Rotterdam was frozen.[49] Robert Cartwright of Hull was a draper who served as a captain under Newcastle in the siege and had gone to Holland to obtain munitions for the King. He was a prisoner at the Ouse bridge in York when he paid his delinquency fine of £47 on his estate of £20 a year value.[50]. Edward Dobson was another Hull draper who claimed that he had been expelled by Hotham and had taken no part in the war. When his fine was fixed at £65 13*s* 4*d* he was in prison at Dantzig.[51]

In 1646 Parliament decided to continue the Hull garrison. The bench bitterly protested that loans, still outstanding and totalling £90,000, had been made to Hotham, Fairfax and Meldrum and losses at sea amounted to £30,000.[52] Parliament replied that 'in time of public calamity particular suffering could not be attended to'.[53] And in the summer of 1645 when there was plague in the West Riding there was fear that trade might bring it again to Hull.[54] There was the possibility that there might even yet be a royalist *coup* supported by invasion from abroad, and naval mutinies added greatly to the danger in 1648.[55] In June 1648 the committee of both Houses reminded Fairfax 'how much the kingdom is concerned in the security of Hull, as you know'. And it was not only individual royalists who suffered heavy financial losses through having joined the losing side: William Sykes, merchant, had sacrificed his whole estate for Parliament, for 'which he had great affection', and, in his petition for compensation, he added that he had suffered greatly as a prisoner of war.

In both the churches there was unedifying clerical strife, and, because of the general adoption of religious toleration, much sectarian rivalry. At the beginning of the war the Vicar of Hessle and Holy Trinity was William Styles, zealous in the cause of Parliament, who, when Hotham refused to admit the King, told him 'honour would sit on his shoulders for that day's work'. The Puritan John Shawe fled from his parish of Rotherham in 1642 and was welcomed by the bench but expelled by Hotham.[56] He had been a contemporary of Milton at Christ's College, Cambridge, and under the same tutor, and was regarded as a preacher of notable eloquence. In 1644 he was able to return as lecturer at Holy Trinity.[57]

In August 1645 Parliament ordered the election of elders, on the Presbyterian model, in every church; and at Holy Trinity Shawe set up a strict Presbyterian church discipline, not without strong opposition. He quarrelled with Styles over which of them should preach in Holy Trinity on Sunday mornings before the governor and corporation; and the bench, on the whole favourable to Shawe, effected a compromise; but soon he was complaining that his stipend was in arrears.[58]

In 1649 Parliament decided that all office-holders, including the clergy, must take the 'Engagement', an oath of loyalty to a Commonwealth without a King or House of Lords. Neither

A History of Hull

William Styles at Holy Trinity nor John Boatman at St Mary's could stomach this.[59] It was not until the end of 1650 that the oath was tendered to them, and when both refused to take it, they were given twenty days to leave the town, though the bench and their parishioners had interceded for them.[60] There is little doubt that Styles was implicated in the conspiracy of Presbyterians to join with the royalists in a counter-revolution.[61] While he was preaching in Holy Trinity on a Sunday it was assumed that most of the troops would be there to hear him, 'he being a person much followed in the town', and Hull plotters were then to seize the gates and let their collaborators in.[62] But there was insufficient evidence to incriminate him and he eventually became Vicar of Leeds, though at the Restoration he tried to recover his Hessle and Hull benefice. Boatman died as Vicar of St Peter Mancroft at Norwich in 1658.

Even before the departure of Styles, Shawe and his party were involved in a conflict with John Canne, an Independent who, under the patronage of Colonel Robert Overton, the governor, became chaplain to the garrison.[63] Shawe in his memoirs treated Canne as a rancorous clerk of small intellect; but he was actually a man of some considerable learning who had long been pastor to the English congregation in Amsterdam. The Council of State pressed the corporation to pay Shawe's stipend, but in other matters he had insufficient support to prevail over Canne and the Independents of the garrison. The rift between the two Puritan factions was such that early in 1651 the troops built a brick wall in Holy Trinity to separate the nave from the chancel, which they occupied with Overton while Shawe and his presumably larger congregation had the nave.[64]

It was necessary to find a successor to Styles as Vicar of Holy Trinity. Some wanted Canne, but the Council of State used some influence for Shawe 'a person well affected who had preached at Hull a year and a half without any pay'.[65] Shawe would have liked to be vicar but the Council of State agreed to the corporation's choice of Henry Hibbert, with Shawe continuing as lecturer.[66] He had some compensation for his disappointment as he now became master of the Charterhouse; and it was reported that he 'expects an equal interest in the ministry if not a superior power with Mr Hibbert's'. With Overton already in the Tower for his involvement in Fifth Monarchy conspiracies, Canne, whose opinions were now equally extreme, was banished from Hull in 1657.[67*]

There is no reason to believe that either Holy Trinity or St Mary's suffered much from Puritan iconoclasm. Perhaps the only sign of this era still visible is that in Holy Trinity, with one exception, only the matrices of memorial brasses remain. The brass of Richard Bylt (1451) does survive in the south aisle of the choir, with a Latin inscription not actually repugnant to even the most extreme Puritan. The bench, wishing to separate Holy Trinity from Hessle parish, in 1652 obtained an order from Durand Hotham and two other commissioners appointed to settle various disputes. They undertook to solicit the Council of State to have both churches made parochial.[68] Much of the old order continued at Holy Trinity with little change. When it was known that anyone had died, the bellman was to ring, and to cry that the burial would be 'at three o'clock this present day in the High Church.'[69] Two aldermen were detailed to arrange with Mr Gabriel Fenby to have the chimes repaired.[70] Though much that was traditional survived, there was virtually complete religious liberty for all Protestants. Soon there were a few who felt the weight of too much liberty. One of these was George Carr, from South Shields, who went about the town 'declaring himself to be Christ, and that the Holy Ghost was in him.'[71]

From time to time gifts of ale which had now simply become an alternative name for beer, were sent to various friends of Hull in London. In November 1651 the town's officer was ordered to send two barrels each to the Speaker, Sir Henry Vane and Peregrine Pelham (still the borough members) and Mr Thorpe, now a judge as a Baron of the Exchequer.[72] The beer-trade was strictly controlled. Joshua Foster spent a month in the House of Correction for his second offence of unlicenced brewing; but Ann Readman, Margaret Haburne and John Jenkinson, probably first offenders, were 'committed to prison, to stay there three days, for each of them keeping a common alehouse, not being thereto lawfully licenced.'[73] Ale was probably part of the offence of two old men, Ellerker Potts and Joshua North, who for a time lost their places in God's House Hospital when they married without permission.[74] For the first time the bench now made orders concerning East Hull. They regulated grazing in the east and west fields of Southcoates, and also in the South Ings and Humber Field. In 1651 they agreed to have Southcoates Wood surveyed and divided.[75]

Assizes again began to be held for Hull and the mayor was allowed £12 for the entertainment of the judges.[76] The mayor and aldermen decided that they ought to present themselves to 'Lt Gen. Lambert's wife, Col Deane's wife and other gentlewomen who are come from Scotland in the *Speaker* frigate', perhaps the first time such honour had been paid to women who were not of noble birth.[77]

Under Cromwell the Levellers had high hopes of Overton. He was a friend of Milton, and much more of an intellectual than most squires. At the other extreme, Prince Charles corresponded with him, hoping that he might turn royalist. His position in Hull, with its magazine, made him of great importance to the army. He was made one of the seven commissioners exercising the office of commander-in-chief. In 1660 he showed himself sternly republican. He opposed Monck, the commander principally responsible for the Restoration, but finding his position untenable, he peaceably surrendered the Hull garrison to Col Charles Fairfax.[78]

Since the Restoration would have been impossible without the support of moderate Puritans of the pattern of Shawe, he was made a chaplain to Charles II in 1660, and was at the coronation in 1661. Even after he was inhibited from preaching in Holy Trinity he was able to have an interview with the King: 'I spoke with his majesty and he gave me good words.' He may have owed something to his connection by marriage with Lord Bellasis, the new royalist governor, and for a while he had an enthusiastic congregation at the Charterhouse until he was forced to resign in 1662.

Sources

1. KHRO, L. 271.
2. L. 273.
3. BB5, f.263.
4. *CSPD* 1638-9, 310.
5. The full speech is printed in the Hull histories of Tickell and Hadley; *DNB*
   s.v. THORPE, FRANCIS.
6. N. Pevsner, *Yorkshire: York and the E. Riding,* 276.
7. KHRO, L. 288.
8. *CSPD* 1639-40, 529; 1640, 43, 47.
9. KHRO, L. 292, 294-304.

10. *CSPD* 1640-1, 34, 38, 61, 424; KHRO, L. 305.
11. BB5, f.263.
12. *Commons Journals* II (i) 224, 226.
13. KHRO, L. 305A.
14. E. Clarendon, *The History of the Rebellion*, ii, V. 236ff.
15. *Commons Journals* II (i) 304.
16. *CSPD* 1641-3, 253.
17. *Commons Journals* II (i) 371-2.
18. KHRO, L. 265.
19. De la Pryme, f.239.
20. *Commons Journals* II (i) 415.
21. 'The Life of Master John Shawe, *Surtees Society*, lxv, 134.
22. *Commons Journals* II, (i), 468, 480, 497.
23. Tickell, 716; F. W. Brooks, *The First Order Book of Trinity House,* (YASRS), 55; *DNB* s.v. PRIMROSE, JAMES.
24. *Commons Journals* II (i) 551.
25. *DNB* s.v. CHOLMLEY, SIR HUGH.
26. *Commons Journals* II (i) 551.
27. Ibid., 561, 562, 578, 584, 594-5, 637.
28. Ibid., 287-9.
29. Anon., *A Happy Discovery of the Strange and Fearfull Plots layde by our Cavaliers for invading of Hull* (London, 1642).
30. Clarendon op. cit., ii, V. 432ff; G. Poulson, *Beverlac,* 356; Anon., *Sad News from Beverley and Yorkshire.*
31. F. W. Brooks, op. cit., 55.
32. B. Reckitt. *Charles I and Hull,* 95-6.
33. Ibid., 84; BB5, f.295; *DNB* s.v. SALTMARSH, JOHN.
34. *VCH,* Yorkshire, ii, 423.
35. B. Reckitt, op. cit., 95ff.; *YAJ*, viii, 214-18; E. Broxap, 'The Sieges of Hull during the Great Civil War, *English Historical Review*, xx, 457-73 [includes reference to Sir T. Fairfax's *Short Memorials of the Civil War.*]
36.* BB5, f.296. The blank space is in the original.
37. J. Horsfall Turner, *Yorkshire Folklore,* 88 (a broadsheet of 1658).
38. F. W. Brooks, op, cit., 63.
39. J. Shawe, *Memoirs of Master John Shawe,* 164.
40. *Notes and Queries,* VI, viii, 3.
41. *CSPD* 1644-5, 223.
42. *CSPD* 1644, 528.
43. F. W. Brooks, op, cit., 70.
44. KHRO, L. 385-6, 392.
45. BB5, f.331.
46. *Yorkshire Royalist Composition Papers,* (YASRS, vol. 15) i, 64.
47. Ibid., 97.
48. Ibid., 109.
49. Ibid., 143.
50. Ibid., ii, 5.
51. Ibid., 145.
52. Tickell, 492.
53. Ibid., 490; Hadley, 196.
54. KHRO, L.388, 357, 363, 367 and *passim.*
55. *CSPD* 1648-9, 88, 90.
56. J. Shawe, op. cit., 35-6, 140.
57. Ibid., 38.
58. Ibid., 37; *CSPD* 1650, 323.
59. *CSPD* 1651-2, 9.
60. KHRO, L. 511, 512, 513.
61. W. Cobbett and T. B. Howell, *State Trials,* i, 406ff.
62. S. R. Gardiner, *History of the Commonwealth and Protectorate,* i, 406ff.; HMC Portland I, 579-85.
63. *CSPD* 1651-2, 211.
64. KHRO, L. 514-16; J. Shawe, op, cit., 47.
65. *CSPD* 1650, 399.
66. *CSPD* 1651-2, 211.
67.* DNB s.v. OVERTON, ROBERT, and CANNE, JOHN; J. Canne, *The Time of the End* (London, 1657). Overton was born at and had an estate at Easington, East Riding.
68. *DNB* s.v. HOTHAM, DURAND; BB6, 8 Jan. 1652.
69. Ibid., 4 Dec. 1651.
70. Ibid., 13 Jan. 1652.
71. Ibid., 12 Dec. 1650.
72. Ibid., 5 Nov. 1651.
73. Ibid., 8 and 20 Dec. 1651.
74. Ibid., 28 Mar. and 9 Oct. 1651.
75. Ibid., 12 Feb. 1651.
76. Ibid., 18 Sept. 1651.
77. Ibid., 4 Sept. 1651.
78. *Calendar of Clarendon State Papers,* OUP ed. iv, pp. 525-6 and *passim.*

15

Hull under Charles II and James II

At the Restoration various people expected rewards for their loyalty. Capt. Luke Whittington was given an appointment in Hull to compensate him for the loss of his estate of £5000 when Hotham expelled him in 1642 and as a reward for his exploits at sea in the years 1649-53 leading the royalist squadron which he formed at Dunkirk.[1] The Hildyards wanted to regain the Hull manor house, and it was from Hull that Sir Robert wrote about a dangerous conspiracy of Quakers which he thought he had found in Holderness. The bench lent him £160, and complimented the other Hildyard, Sir Henry - 'Yourself and your noble family have merited all honour and esteem.'[2] Much courtesy was shown to John, Lord Bellasis of Worlaby near Brigg, a Catholic royalist, soon to be governor of Hull and later of Tangier. A ship was sent to bring him over the Humber. On his arrival he was met by the mayor and aldermen who gave a banquet in honour of him and of Capt. Charles Fairfax.[3] Bellasis wanted the town to raise two infantry companies. The bench asked him to let them name two captains, two lieutenants and two ensigns. The climax of prudent loyalty came with the coronation - 'God by his wonderful Providence having returned our lawful King to his people.' For a public feast £45 was taken from the iron chest.[4]

Relations between the Crown and such chartered boroughs as Hull centred on the determination of the restored Stuarts to ensure that well-disposed members were returned to Parliament. Since the result of the election could be so greatly influenced by the borough officers, there was a thorough purge of all who were repugnant to the Crown under the power conferred by the act 'for the well-being and regulation of corporations' of 1661. Orders came for the deposition of three aldermen - Dewick, Rogers and Wood - 'brought in by the Usurper'. These three 'did willingly give obedience', but John Shawe, 'a person of unsound principles' tried unavailingly to resist.[5]

To show its loyalty Hull returned to the Crown the fee-farm rents purchased in 1649-50, presented £100 to the commissioners 'for a free and voluntary offering from H.M. good subjects', and burned Milton's 'book against the portraiture of his sacred Majesty'. As early as the spring of 1661 the town began to negotiate for the confirmation of its charters.[6] A new charter was granted at the end of the year and substantially re-modelled the membership of the corporation, naming several new aldermen, the mayor, the high steward, sheriff, recorder and town clerk.[7] The powers of the oligarchy of thirteen aldermen and the custom of restricting the freemen to voting for *lites*[8]* nominated by them was more precisely defined. Except for a short time under James II this was the governing charter until 1835.

After the Restoration contested parliamentary elections became more common. In 1661 there were four candidates. With the backing of Lord Bellasis, the governor, his deputy, Anthony Gylby headed the poll. He was a thorough royalist; but Andrew Marvell was elected with him despite his republican associations. He had represented Hull in Richard Cromwell's Parliament but it was Sir Henry Vane the younger who sat as sole member for Hull in the restored Rump.[9] Marvell had again been elected to Monck's Convention Parliament, and from then until his death in 1678 sat as a member for Hull. The popularity of Marvell came partly from his connection with the influential Blaydes and Popple families through his sisters' marriages. He quarrelled with Gylby about some matter arising from the election and was censured in the Commons by the Speaker for a tussle with Thomas Clifford MP.[10] In 1662 he went abroad for almost a year in the embassy of the Earl of Carlisle to Russia and the northern powers, and in March 1663 Lord Bellasis clumsily tried to persuade the corporation to have him unseated because of his neglect of his parliamentary duties; but the bench was well-disposed to Marvell and warned him of the move being prepared against him, so that on 2 April he was able to write to them informing them that he had resumed his seat in the Commons.[11]

When he died in 1678 the court party made a determined effort to secure the election of their candidate in a town where there was now strong anti-royalist feeling once more. The Duke of Monmouth, as high steward, strongly recommended Capt. John Shales, a protégé of James, Duke of York; but Shales was so disheartened by lack of support in Hull that he withdrew, and Alderman William Ramsden was elected.[12] At the general election of 1679, however, Monmouth secured the election of Lemuel Kingdon, paymaster to the forces. He told the burgesses that 'he must judge to the reality of their affections to him by their readiness to gratify him in acceptance of a person that he so earnestly concerns himself for.'[13] Ramsden was re-elected with him. William Gee, the third candidate, with no success, petitioned against the return on the grounds of menaces and compulsion, but in the second election of 1679 he was returned with Sir Michael Warton of Beverley. All Kingdon could do was to express his regrets to the mayor and aldermen that he had not been chosen, and to pay for the building of a new market cross in the hope of improving his chances another time.[14]

The second and third Dutch wars (1665-7 and 1672-4) weakened local enthusiasm for a King so manifestly less Puritan than Hull and hardly capable of protecting its sea-borne trade. In July 1666 when Lord Bellasis arrived from Lord Dunbar's house at Burton Constable there was such fear of a Dutch attack that preparations were made to block the haven by sinking three ships. In November Whittington reported that the Hull convoy and the colliers dared not leave the Humber because of three great Dutch warships in Bridlington Bay. People were saying that things were better-managed under Cromwell.[15]

In both wars France was the ally, and in 1672, with seamen fleeing into the country from the press-gang, Lord Dunbar had little success in recruiting men in Hull to fight for Louis XIV. Ships again delayed their sailing for fear of the Dutch. In May 1672 no vessel dared leave the Humber without a convoy. It was the same in June, when a Dutch privateer came into the mouth of the Humber, and Col Gylby heard that for greater security ships were anchoring off Paull. When Trinity House pilots were wanted for the navy most were not at home. Some may have been with the fleet in August when the Duke of York anchored off Bridlington and Hornsea to put sick men on shore and for re-victualling. A few weeks later fear of the Dutch again halted all sea-going ships, so that by November it was feared that the town and the garrison would run out of coal before Christmas. The crew released from a ship which the Dutch had taken arrived in Hull with an account of nine great Dutch men-of-war off Holderness. Few had been willing to enlist for France, but with the Dutch still at war after Britain made peace in 1674, two ships sailed from Hull, in spite of a royal proclamation against enlisting troops for Holland, with a hundred or more men recruited in several counties for the forces of William of Orange.[16]

The 1679 election marked the growth of local opposition to royal policy, though, as the case of Daniel Hoare showed, the bench was split, with a third of the aldermen supporting him, when, under the Test Act, he was deposed from the bench as a Nonconformist.[17] In 1681 they voted four to three with six abstentions to declare their loyal opposition to the Exclusion Bill then being promoted by the Whigs to prevent any Catholic from ever becoming King: but in 1682 they decided by seven to four not to send any address to the Crown expressing abhorrence of this attempt to exclude the Duke of York from the succession.[18]

The uncontested election of Gee and Warton in 1681 showed growing feeling against the Stuarts.[19] The Crown was able to counter this for a while through the Tory Earl of Plymouth, governor, high steward and eventually recorder also. Though he had taken the almost royal surname of Windsor his original name was Hickman. On the death of Charles II the corporation declared its loyalty to James II and their intention to secure the election of men loyal to H.M. person 'and abhorrers of the late votes for exclusion'.[20] Consequently, in the election of March 1685 Gee and Warton were soundly defeated by John Ramsden, a local merchant, but no Whig, and Sir Willoughby Hickman of Gainsborough, a relative of Plymouth who, within a week of the election informed the mayor, John Field of the pleasure the result gave to His Majesty.[21]

Soon, however, Hickman and Ramsden were noted as being among those who were alienated by James's granting of army commissions to Catholics and his proposals for repealing the Test Act. The bench, divided in other matters, was solidly Protestant. The feeling of the town was shown at the assizes by the refusal of the sheriff to attend Mr Justice Allybone at the service in the

Catholic chapel while the aldermen were with Mr Justice Powell in Holy Trinity.[22] In all other ways the judges had been accorded every respect. A yacht had been hired from the customs officers of the port. They were met at Barton by several members of the corporation and they were entertained on the crossing of the river with wine and other refreshments.

As parliamentary opposition to the Crown increased Charles II had responded with an attack on the charters of corporate boroughs. On 11 July 1684 Lord Chief Justice Jeffreys and Mr Justice Holloway came to press the bench to surrender the charter, and they agreed to do so; but in August the mayor and the rest were still considering who should go to London to make the formal surrender.[23] It was not until after the accession of James that new letters patent were issued displacing three aldermen, and with a provision that the King could remove any of the town's officers.[24]

After the Restoration it was important for the bench to be kept informed as one crisis in national politics followed another. Gilbert Mabbot, as agent and correspondent, wrote to them regularly about politics and London gossip, and was followed by Robert Stockdale who as the corporation's London agent sent no less than 422 news-letters between 1633 and 1680, usefully supplementing those of such MP's as Andrew Marvell and Anthony Gylby. When Parliament was sitting Marvell was an assiduous correspondent, and it is probable that he wrote more than the 294 letters of his which survive. The politically dangerous ones may have been destroyed; and he also gave much help to Trinity House. On the whole his letters are coldly factual, and the man who was both a poet and joint Latin-secretary to the Commonwealth with Milton, his friend, could placidly record the digging-up and hanging of the bodies of Cromwell, Bradshaw, Ireton and Pride at Tyburn. In the crises of the 1680s Edward Haslam, who was town clerk, and James Kinvin, sent useful information and comments, receiving in return their instructions from the bench.[25]

Thomas Baskerville wrote an account of his visit to Hull about the year 1684. At his inn he had 'good stale beer and good claret' but apparently none of the famous Hull ale. He thought the women and girls had 'Dutch faces, being not so clear-complexioned as those living further inland'. Like Defoe, who may have had his information second-hand, he described Hull as now compactly built and populous.[26] The prosperity was a consequence of the renewed increase in the Baltic trade after the third Dutch war. It is doubtful, however, whether the population was much more than 7000 by the end of the century. Rigorous quarantine had kept the plague out in 1665, though it came as near as Garthorpe, not far from Scunthorpe, but there were serious epidemics.

The increasing wealth of Hull merchants is indicated by frequent references to building, in the town records. Some of the houses of that time are known from sketches, mostly made in the nineteenth century. There were many pleasant gable-ended houses in High Street, such as Crowle hospital (1664) and Etherington House (pulled down *c.* 1870 and 1974). Some were characterised by the style which Sir John Summerson has called 'artisan mannerism' and of these Wilberforce house is the last intact survivor. In the latter half of the seventeenth century much of the medieval manor-house of the de la Poles with its out-buildings was demolished and the site built on; but there was still a forlorn fragment standing in 1884 when the historian-artist Tindall Wildridge drew it.[27]

The haven was continually becoming more congested. Some Nottingham merchants were again coming to Hull having found that the Trent was too difficult for vessels built to sail in the North Sea. Even with a Hull pilot the *Adam and Eve* capsized. With spring tides and deeper water, the *Black Dog* took several days to cover eight miles.[28] Nicholas Stone and other Nottingham merchants again began to bring their lead to Hull. In 1661 Mr Daniel Sully and Mr Bunting asked the bench to let them land their lead on the same terms.[29] Other trade, especially in cloth from the West Riding was growing. In 1637 34,355 kersies were exported. By 1700 the number had grown to 53,868. The export of 'northern dozens' rose from 21,493 to 27,335; and in 1700 17,175 bays also were shipped overseas. Charles Whittington, collector of customs, in 1668 optimistically told Sir J. Williamson that two ships had arrived from Bordeaux wholly laden with 'prunes, rosin and vinegar, a thing never known in this port before'.[30] In 1671 he wrote that 'there never was more exportation of cloth, lead and butter'; but the trade in rapeseed had fallen off.[31] Six ships, in which York also had an interest, went to Virginia in 1674, but this trade turned out to be disappointing. The growth of trade, still mainly in Baltic flax, iron, hemp, pitch and tar led to the port having a customs revenue smaller only than that of Bristol and London. Though colonial development was shifting the economic centre of gravity of Europe to the west, Hull shipping was helped by the Navigation Acts which aimed to limit Dutch shipping in English ports. But it was from Baltic trade that the wealth of the Maister, Crowle and Mowld families grew. Hull also had a reputation for very strong ale. Sir Joseph Williamson, now MP and clerk to the Privy Council, was told by the Revd Dr Henry Hascard that his friends had drunk his health 'in your Hull ale so powerful as to make us use the proverb *from Hell, Halifax and Hull deliver us*'.[33]

The growth of trade brought benefits to the builders and repairers of ships. The Admiralty ordered three frigates from Hull yards in 1670, and in 1671 two third-rates were planned, costing £21,700.[34] The Blaydes family, with their own yard since 1607, prospered on shipbuilding and repairing. Government contracts would have been even better for them if they had been paid on time. In December 1665 William Blaydes reminded Samuel Pepys that the Navy Board owed him £40. He would, however, repair the pink, *Wivenhoe*, a vessel later in the Hudson Bay trade. When he had done the work he was still owed £111 and asked that the treasurer of the Hull prize office should be authorised to pay him. Three months later he had not been paid, and he was reluctant to repair the *Lizard* unless he could be paid out of the Hull customs. His timber came from Sherwood Forest - floated from Bawtry to Stockwith and then brought to him in boats. Waiting for payment did not ruin them and the connection with the Navy Board was useful. Joseph Blaydes expected certificates to protect six of his shipwrights from the press-gang.[35]

In 1682 the composition between the company of shipwrights and the corporation listed forty members. Benjamin Blaydes was the first warden of the company and Joseph Blaydes the first-named of the assistants, who all held office for life. The voting rights of the rest were restricted to choosing between the *lites* nominated by the warden and assistants. Every month the warden with two or more of the assistants inspected work in progress and then made the mark of the company on all vessels which they approved. This was a company controlled by the owners of yards. If a journeyman-shipwright broke his contract of service he could be fined 40*s*, but a master who dismissed a shipwright unfairly was fined 10*s* only; and no member of the company could sail as a shipwright without permission.[36]

Economic growth and victory over the Hull company of merchants greatly strengthened Trinity House. Basing their claims on the 1577 charter, the merchant-adventurers made a last effort to prevent anyone not of their society from engaging in overseas trade. Thomas Weeton, a freeman and master of his ship, was fined £4 for bringing in seventy bars of iron. Jervase Wearinge had been going to sea for four years without interference from the company, but they summoned him to their hall over the grammar school and fined him 5*s* for bringing in a few barrels of whale-oil from Holland. This was too much for Trinity House. The warden and brethren brought a case against the merchant adventurers and after the decision made by the attorney-general and solicitor-general they gave up all attempt to monopolise foreign trade. Their grasp on the real world diminished with their power. When Sir William St Quintin asked them to support his promotion of the Aire and Calder Navigation bill they answered 'That passing such a bill will be injurious to this town and may in time ruin the trade thereof'.[37] This was a ludicrously false prophecy.

Trinity House grew and prospered. In 1667, during the second Dutch war, at the request of Lord Bellasis, governor of Hull, they undertook responsibility for putting buoys in the Humber.[38] In the same year the navy commissioners rebuked them for putting an allegedly blind pilot on board a Dutch prize, the *Stadthaus*, of Haarlem. Their answer was that Capt. Thorpe was aged but not blind. 'He had as much sight and judgment as not to carry down the ship in the night when the wind failed and the tide was against him'; the prize was 'unruly in her working'.[39] On the whole Trinity House had been opposed to a lighthouse at Spurn. They said it would be useful to Dunkirkers, which was true and could also be said openly. What they did not say was that the fewer the aids to navigation the greater the need for the skills of pilots. Nevertheless in 1677 Justinian Angell, a private speculator, obtained his patent to build the first of the modern lighthouses at Spurn Point.[40]

The Civil War and a century of exposure to wind and water had done no good to the fortifications on the east bank of the Hull, though they served to confine such political prisoners as Sir Henry

Slingsby and Col Robert Brandling.[41] It was government policy that the Hull garrison should be kept 'defensible and secure', but a survey made in 1657 had shown that repairs would cost £5000.[42] In 1670 storm-damage threatened the stability of the south blockhouse. Eleven years later the Ordnance Commissioners were ordered to 'cause the fortifications and repairs at Tilbury, Sheerness, Portsmouth and Hull to be set forward with all expedition according to proposals already presented'.[43] What from this time was called the Citadel was the work of a Swedish artillery officer, Martin Beckman, who had already worked on the fortress at Tangier and other defence works. From 1685, with a knighthood, he was 'chief engineer of Great Britain'.[44]

His plans took in some additional ground to make an equilateral fort with a wide moat, excluding the old north blockhouse and the line of wall between it and the central 'castle'.[45] The 'castle' and south blockhouse were re-modelled and formed two angles of a roughly triangular fort, including a magazine, three barracks and the governor's house. On the south side there was no moat, but a quay along the Humber; and the whole embodied the latest ideas about fortification. The first instalment of money for the work, in 1683, consisted of £4000 from a loan secured on timber to be felled in Sherwood Forest.[46] Under James II the work was continued, still under Sir Martin Beckman, partly financed by 'the very rich lading of gold, silver and other treasures,' salvaged by the *James and Mary* from a treasure-ship wrecked on the coast of Hispaniola.[47]

In 1651 the bench had petitioned Parliament for the separation of Holy Trinity from Hessle and St Mary's from Ferriby.[48] St Mary's was never legally separated from Ferriby, though in fact it became a separate parish church. At the Restoration William Styles, from Leeds, made his legal claim to Holy Trinity and the bench restored his benefice to him on 1 November 1660. He stayed in Leeds and Alderman William Foxley went with three parishioners of Holy Trinity to purchase his renunciation of his rights in the benefice.[49] At the end of the year the act turning Holy Trinity into a parish separate from Hessle received the royal assent.[50] The corporation got the advowson and the vicar's stipend of £100 a year, very much larger than the average stipend enjoyed by clergy, was to be raised by a rate. He also had his tithes, but in Hull, as in most towns, these were negligible. The parishioners had to keep the whole of the church in repair.[51] Nicholas Anderson became vicar in 1662 and remained for twenty-seven years.

In his time necessary repair work was done and in accordance with the act £200 was raised for the repair of the chancel; but the spirit of the parish was still Puritan and the scheme for an organ, in 1678, came to nothing. The pews in the chancel, nave, galleries and lofts were so arranged as to yield the highest possible rents. It became necessary to lock the doors of pews and watch particular sittings to stop the wives of garrison officers from taking those allotted to aldermen's families. In May 1679 it was ordered 'That Ensign Garlick's wife, Ensign Johnson's wife, Lieut Wharton's daughter and Mrs Margaret Stow be not permitted to sit in the middle pew appointed for the alderwomen: and the sexton shall take care of this.' They were doing no more than following the example of officers who, with careless abandon, took seats reserved for the corporation with complete disregard for the dignities of the aldermen.

Though all nonconformity was virtually outlawed at the Restoration, resistance continued at Hull. John Ryther, the ejected Vicar of Frodingham (now part of Scunthorpe) served an Independent (Congregationalist) group of worshippers from his home in Brough.[52] It was reported in 1663 that 'Mr Rider [*sic*] a grand fanatic priest has come into the town and preached at Mr Lockwood's house to a great concourse of people. The governor has secured some of the heads'.[53] On the evidence of Col Gylby, one of the Hull MP's and deputy-governor, there was good reason to think that the bench disliked the laws against nonconformists. He informed Sir Joseph Williamson that seditious meetings were being held in the garrison, and he had spies to keep him informed of conventicles in the town, After evensong, on 22 May 1670, when Mr Anderson left the church to conduct a funeral in the Holy Trinity burial ground, the mayor, aldermen and most of the people stayed in their pews. Then, with the mayor's connivance, George Acklam, as a nonconformist, mounted into the pulpit to preach a sermon but Alderman George Crowle forced him out with the help of Capt. Bennet, acting-commander of the garrison. Crowle's colleagues greatly resented his action.[54]

Anderson's last years as vicar were marred by differences with the corporation about lectures. They wanted more of them, and there were also differences about his stipend. The act of 1661 made it clear that his £100 a year was to be raised by a rate of no more than eightpence in the pound paid by the inhabitants of the parish, and non-residents with property in the parish were not rated. By 1683 his stipend was so far in arrears that he employed a local scrivener, Benjamin Graves, to distrain on the property of those who had not paid their rates, and in 1683 he again threatened legal action.[57] Under the 1661 act he could have recovered the arrears from the corporation but neither he nor any of his successors ever used this remedy.

The one outstanding clergyman connected with Holy Trinity was the young Abraham de la Pryme. He was born at Hatfield, near Doncaster, in 1671, and buried there in 1704. His ancestors were Huguenots. After graduating at Cambridge, he was curate at Broughton near Brigg, and he came to Holy Trinity as curate and reader in 1698. In March 1700 he asked the bench to let him 'look over and view the ancient charters and other records and antiquities in order to compose a catalogue thereof and revive the ancient rights and privileges' of the borough. He completed the task, and two-and-a-half years later he was presented with eight guineas for making an index. During this time he wrote the first surviving history of Hull, never printed, but freely used by several later historians. He came from a wealthy family and though he died young the name has been perpetuated in Pryme Street since the eighteenth century.

The Quakers were among the early sufferers from the laws against nonconformists. They were then regarded as turbulent and dangerous sectaries. Few had the quietism of later members of the Society of Friends. William Garbutt, John Holmes and Thomas Wilson were amongst the earliest of the Hull members,[58] and the Sutton meeting (embracing east Hull) included a lawyer, William Ellerker, Thomas Brown and several Richardsons.[59] Persecution actually began under the Commonwealth. In 1659, because they refused to pay the parish rate for what they called 'the steeple house', William Ellerker and several other Sutton Quakers had their goods distrained; and legal distraint was often brutal. In one instance Richard Bishop, the parish constable, was described as hitting a Quaker on the back with a cudgel violently enough to have felled a tree.[60]

Other sects had their teachers and followers of whom the authorities were particularly suspicious after the attempted rising at Farnley Wood near Pontefract in 1663.[61] A minister named Anderson, 'a dangerous man and a concealed Presbyterian', was reported to be in Hull in 1664.[62] Richard Astley, who had connections with Canne and Col Overton and may have been a Fifth Monarchyman, had an Independent congregation of fifty-five persons in Hull in 1669.[63] A meeting gathered to hear 'an illiterate Scot' was in that year stopped by the acting-governor, Capt. Carteret;[64] and the official view was that the Hull magistrates virtually ignored meetings of the 'disaffected'.[65] It was thought that the town was two-thirds Presbyterian, with active encouragement from London Presbyterians.[66]

The royal Declaration of Indulgence of 15 March 1672 gave religious toleration to licenced preachers and congregations provided that they and the places where they met were notified to the authorities. The Independent minister, Richard Astley, was licenced to preach in John Robinson's house in Hull and Joseph Wilson, of Newland near Hull, was licenced to preach in Richard Barnes's house.[67] Wilson was the Vicar of Hessle ejected in 1660. In 1662 his followers riotously tried to open the doors of Beverley Minster so that he could preach there. As happened with several nonconformist families of this period, his son subsequently took Anglican orders.[68] In July 1672 a licence was issued for 'a new meeting-house built by the Presbyterians at Blackfriargate', one of the first in northern England.[69] But Anglican intolerance of nonconformity, and fear in the Commons that the royal Declaration was really intended to promote Roman Catholicism, forced Charles II to cancel his Declaration of Indulgence, and nonconformists were once more forced into secrecy until the Toleration Act of 1689.

In Hull, however, the fact that the Protestants' hero, Monmouth, was governor, meant that the laws were not rigorously enforced. On the death of Joseph Wilson in 1679 he was succeeded by the Revd Samuel Charles at the meeting-house in Bowlalley Lane, and, according to Calamy, 'his carriage in that place procured him much respect from the magistrates of the town.' Formerly he had been Vicar of Mickleover in Derbyshire.[70] When Monmouth became too deeply involved in plots to procure his succession to his father, Charles II, he lost his post as governor and the Earl of Plymouth took his place, and put an end to the calm of relative toleration. When the Earl arrived at the end of

1682 he 'did intimate formally to the bench that two conventicles were commonly reported to be held in the town'. Astley and Samuel Charles could not then be found, but two of their followers, Michael Bielby and John Graves, were admonished 'to forbear to meet any more at unlawful assemblies.' When arrested on 2 February 1883 Samuel Charles had the best of the argument with the alderman before whom he was charged. Under the Five Mile Act, because he was an ejected minister, he could not reside in any corporate town, but the fact of his disqualification had to be proved, and it was not proved. The argument, as recorded by Calamy, was as follows.—

Mr C.   Where are the two witnesses? Let me see them face to face according to the manner of England, that . . . will swear that I did refuse to give my assent to the Act of Uniformity.

Ald.   It is no matter.

Mr C.   There must needs be proof that I am such a person as the act describes, for there are more preachers in Hull than Mr Astley and I. If you have not proof you may as well send for the man that goes next in the street and execute the Five Mile Act on him.

Ald.   Do you think we sit here like a company of fools? Will you take the oath according to the act?

Mr C.   Let me see according to the act that I am concerned in it, and then I will tell you more of my mind.

Ald.   You do preach. You do baptise. You do administer the sacrament.

Mr C.   Did you see me?

Ald.   No, but we did hear so.

Mr C.   And you would deprive a man of his liberty by hearsay?[71]

On the evidence of a single witness, the constable of Austin ward, he was imprisoned for six months for unlawful preaching. He then retired to Welton but still sent his written sermons to his congregation. Richard Astley escaped, but the persecution of lay nonconformists still went on.[72] In 1686 three nonconformists were fined £20 each and one of the three had to pay the additional penalty of £20 for each month for not attending the parish church. Michael Bielby, who had been imprisoned during the Monmouth rebellion, was harassed in the same way.[73]

Plymouth denounced Alderman Johnson for not joining his fellow-magistrates in imprisoning those charged with attending conventicles.[74] James II was determined to have a more compliant corporation. In February 1688 the bench had to decide whether to contest *Quo Warranto* proceedings;[75] but almost immediately, with a dignified declaration of their chartered rights, they gave in.[76] Hull was too independent for a Stuart. At the time of the Monmouth rebellion in 1685, many suspected persons, including Daniel Hoare, were imprisoned in the new Citadel, and there was some popular support for the rebellion. There was a rumour that Monmouth had captured the King's artillery and was four days' march from London.[77] Even after the rebellion was crushed, John Hay of Heckmondwike, in a Hull ale-house, declared that he would be a soldier for Monmouth, and Mary Lee, who was with him, said she too would enlist as a man and lie with him.[78] It was significant that in the new corporation nominated by James II all but one of the aldermen had to be removed, and in an effort to gain nonconformist support Daniel Hoare was named as mayor without the requirement that he or other officers of the corporation should take any of the tests previously enacted to exclude both Catholics and nonconformists.[79] Within less than a month fear of the invasion by William of Orange made James issue a 'proclamation for restoring corporations to their ancient charters, liberties, rights and franchises', and on 6 November the old bench, so recently put down, met again with all their powers and no enthusiasm for James II.

Marmaduke Langdale, of Holme-on-Spalding-Moor, a Catholic, became governor in 1687 on the death of Plymouth, and was received with respect; but he got little satisfaction when, in pursuance of a circular to all governors and lords lieutenants, he tried to ascertain whether in the next election Hull would return members willing to comply with the King's wishes. Robert Carlisle, as mayor, told him the bench would not commit themselves to support members who approved of the Declaration of Indulgence. Langdale proposed Sir John Bradshaw of Risby (a deserted village on the Wolds east of Little Weighton) as a suitable member, in a highly minatory letter, to which the bench made a dignified reply. The election would be 'fair and free according to the laws of the land', and they could not guarantee the return of anyone in advance. As governor, Langdale was in a position to use the troops of the garrison. Charles II had so distrusted Hull that he would not put arms into the hands of the inhabitants, and so there was no militia such as existed in the East Riding.[80] The Citadel garrison was becoming tame. When Monmouth was governor he found in 1685 that although part of the garrison could be marched anywhere, his own company and his deputy's could not be taken from Hull.[81] Many of the soldiers were married. He would let them keep their wives, but no more were to marry. Plymouth found that one company had only thirty-eight men and that they were made up to fifty for his inspection by putting substitutes into uniform. He suspected the other five companies were no better. An officer desiring real military experience could learn little in the Citadel. The life was too tedious for Lieut Thomas Legard. In 1687 he left the Citadel to serve with the Venetians against the Turks in the Morea.[82]

Since 1686 there had been difficulties about billetting and payment for quarters. It is possible that Abraham de la Pryme was correct that Langdale, to punish the town, turned the troops loose; though it may be that the contemporaries, who gave him the information a few years later, tended to exaggerate. It was firmly believed that if the Revolution had not come in 1688 the town would have been ruined.[83]

When William of Orange sailed from Holland it was thought he would land in the north. Langdale prepared for a siege, hung the chain across the mouth of the haven, and opened the sluices to flood the countryside. He was reinforced by troops of the Duke of Newcastle, Lord Lieutenant of Yorkshire, and secretly prepared to arrest his Protestant officers. His plans became known to them. They approached the mayor and aldermen, probably knowing already that the nobles and gentry assembled at York had declared for William, with a plan to sieze Langdale. Late that night, with the help of the magistrates, the townspeople were silently armed to defend the Protestant faith. Langdale and his Catholic officers were taken without bloodshed and the next morning Capt. Copley, the vice-governor, secured the rest of the Catholics in the garrison.[84] The *coup* produced a temporary breakdown in law and order in Hull, in which some violence seems to have been done to Catholics and royalists. The bench issued a warning to those who 'go to several houses in the town and violently take away and spoil their goods and break and spoil their houses, contrary to law and justice', and had the bellman proclaim it; while Copley summoned his troops by beat of drum to warn them.[85]

These events guaranteed the north for William of Orange, and for more than a century were celebrated as 'town taking day'.[86] The formal address from the bench, noting that the safe arrival of the Prince of Orange had 'miraculously delivered the nation from those eminent dangers which threatened the perversion of religion and the introduction of tyranny and arbitrary government', was probably more sincere than earlier addresses on a change of regime. Sir John Hotham became the new governor and by February 1689 those in the town who had billetted troops had received much of the money owed to them. Six months later Col Beveridge's regiment marched to Scotland, and the town was again left to keep the Citadel and fortifications. Men of the town had to do guard duty with an inadequate stock of forty-seven muskets, forty-six iron caps and forty-two swords, previously 'lodged in the Exchange'.[87] Towards the end of 1689 an army of 12,000 or more Danish mercenaries landed at Hull on their way to William's war in Ireland. They were warned that no excesses would be tolerated, and de la Pryme, who saw them, thought them very well-behaved. Only the plaque on the south side of St Mary's, Beverley records the death of two who were not.

The Revolution stopped religious persecution of Protestants and nonconformists could attend worship publicly. The Presbyterian chapel was built in Bowlalley Lane in 1691-2, and the new chapel of the Independents in Dagger Lane was completed in 1698 when, as the law required, Joseph Watson applied for a certificate from the bench.[88] There were few Catholics, and they tried to be inconspicuous. As late as 1743 the churchwardens reported to Archbishop Herring that there were no Catholics in Hull. They were probably just outside the jurisdiction of the bench, in Sculcoates.

During the seventeenth century various small charities were set up, some being lost subsequently, or merged with others. The Charterhouse was the oldest of the almshouses still in being, much improved by John Shaw. The Trinity House hospital (almshouse) was of much the same standing. It is probable that by 1700 Ferries's hospital (1625), Lister's (1640), Crowle's (1661), Robinson's (1682), Ellis's (1683) and Weaver's (1693) provided for about thirty of the aged.[89] Some who were favoured were helped by the bench when they were in want. They were probably known personally to various aldermen. In 1682 Mrs Burton was allowed sixpence a week for help in the house while she was ill; 14*d* was allowed to Sarah Mattam 'until her husband comes home', and Susan Popplewell, in consideration of her 'low condition' was to pay only a shilling a year for her house provided she kept it in good repair. In 1661 something of the old spirit of benevolence to the poor appeared in the resolution to take £40 from the iron chest to buy clothes for the children of Charity Hall.[90] The population of the town was maintained in spite of a large death rate by the arrival of many newcomers, and when any of them needed assistance from the parish the six annually elected overseers of the poor had the difficult task of deciding whether it would be better to give relief or to remove them to the town from which they had come. Overseers were unpaid conscripts doing arduous parish duty for a year while still looking after their own business. When it came to the turn of Ambrose Metcalfe to be overseer of Whitefriar's ward he 'refused peremptorily' and the bench decided to hire a substitute for £15.[91]

To vagrants and the nameless poor the law was applied in all its harshness. It was believed that many people, for profit, were letting some still poorer share their houses with them, and by this means strangers were claiming a poor-law settlement in Hull and the right to relief. An order was made in 1690 for a general inspection of all houses so that those harbouring 'inmates' could be dealt with according to the law, and the 'inmates' legally removed from the town.

In 1697 the corporation obtained 'An Act for erecting Workhouses and Houses of Correction in the town of Kingston-upon-Hull for the Imployment and Maintenance of the Poor there'.[92] A most significant thing about the act was the deliberate linking of the treatment of poverty with the punishment of petty offences in the House of Correction. The mayor, recorder and aldermen, with twenty-four guardians, became the Corporation of the Poor which, with few changes, lasted until 1929. The guardians were elected by inhabitants rated at twopence a week for the poor. Charity Hall, on the north side of Whitefriargate at what later became the west corner of Parliament Street, was taken over for the new establishment, with particular provision for orphans and the destitute.[93] In 1743 it was reported to Archbishop Herring that half of the inmates were children and that the total consisted of forty-three males, ninety females, and eleven babies 'at nurse'.

For most of the people the Revolution of 1688, however glorious, made little difference. Guild ordinances show further restrictions of the rights of journeymen. The tailors lost the right they had enjoyed of electing their officers, now chosen by an inner circle of elder brethren.[94] Laws of the weavers, a company long under the masters' control, made in 1673, now included a clause for strike-breaking, which suggests there had been strikes. The masters were allowed to have work done outside the town if the journeymen would 'not work well, and at reasonable rates, and in reasonable time'. The significance of this was veiled by the next clause - 'That the warden and his brethren shall be loving, friendly and gentle to one another'.[95] In that company it was no longer possible to limit the number of apprentices as a means of ensuring that there was never a surplus of labour. The master could have one apprentice for every three journeymen as allowed by the statute;[96] but in other companies, in defiance of statute law, the number of apprentices was still limited. The Company of Bricklayers, one apparently dominated by workers, by 1753 was so far under the masters' control that there was provision for what was in effect a blacklist of refractory workers.[97] The Shipwrights' Company, from 1682, ingeniously maintained its charity for indigent brethren by a levy of twopence in the pound on the earnings of every brother who worked at sea as a ship's carpenter, which he could not do without the warden's consent, and another levy of twopence for every ton of new shipping constructed.[98] Whoever dominated Hull after 1688, quite clearly it was not the mob. For the inhabitants death was a more fearful enemy. Year after year, in the nine-tenths or more of Hull covered by the Holy Trinity registers, there were far more deaths than births—forty-one per cent in 1689, fourteen per cent in 1709 and a terrible hundred-and-six per cent in 1729.[99] There was no plague but the diseases of poverty and bad drainage were, in the long run, even more deadly.

Sources

1. *CSPD*, 1660-1, 187.
2. Ibid., 21; BB6, 13 Dec. 1660.
3. BB6, 9 Aug. 1660, 8 Jan. 1661.
4. Ibid., 6 June 1660, 18 May 1661.
5. KHRO, L.654; BB7, ff.369-70; Tickell, 518-19; J. Shawe, *Memoirs of Master John Shawe*, 66.
6.* KHRO, L. 649; the book *Eikonoklastes* was Milton's answer to *Eikon Basilike*, then a sacred text of royalists but now recognised as a forgery.
7. *VCH*, Hull, 118.
8.* BB8, f.71. 'Lites' is from the medieval French 'Elites' - chosen.
9. C. H. Firth (ed.), *Memoirs of Edmund Ludlow* (1894).
10. *DNB* s.v. MARVELL, ANDREW (1621-78); Leg., 27.
11. BB6, f.386; Leg., 34-5.
12. *CSPD*, xx (1678), 375, 561; BB7, 598; KHRO, L.893-4.
13. KHRO, L. 925-6; *CSPD*, xxi (1679-80) 53, 96.
14. BB7, ff.607-10, 614-16; KHRO, L. 929-30, 936, 943, 955.
15. *CSPD*, 1665-6, 534; Carleton Monckton MS, 30.
16. *CSPD*, 1671-2, 189: *CSPD*, 1672, 15, 169, 54, 470, 562; *CSPD*, 1672-3, 141, 180; *CSPD Addenda*, 1660-85, 442, 445.
17. Tickell, 550-5; *CSPD*, xxi, 530; BB7, ff. 633-7, 672, 675-6, 684, 692.
18. BB7, ff.346, 770.
19. *CSPD*, xxii (1682) 189, 192.
20. KHRO, L. 1068.
21. BB8, ff.164, 185.
22. Tickell, 573.
23. BB8, ff.100, 103.
24. Boyle, *Charters and Letters Patent . . .*, 190 ff.
25. KHRO, L. 892-7.
26. British Museum, *Rowlands*, A 189, f.192.
27. T. T. Wildridge, *Old and New Hull*, 93-6.
28. *CSPD*, 1665-6, 533, 399.
29. BB6, 31 May 1661.
30. *CSPD*, 1668-9, 17.
31. *CSPD*, 1671, 406, 471.
32. *CSPD*, 1673-6, 1 Nov. 1674.
33. *CSPD*, 1671-2, 82.
34. *CSPD Addenda*, 1660-71 233; *CSPD*, 1671, 278.
35. *CSPD*, 1665-6, 87, 119, 318; P.C. Newman, *The Company of Adventurers*, 109.
36. J. M. Lambert, *Two Thousand Years of Gild Life*, 341-8.
37. Ibid., 179.
38. *CSPD*, 1667-8, 41.
39. Ibid., 66, 85, 80.
40 BB6, f.183.
41. Ibid., f.192b.
42. *CSPD Addenda*, 1660-71, 298.
43. Ibid., 253.
44. *DNB*, s.v. BECKMAN, SIR MARTIN (d. 1702).
45. BB6, f.241.
46. *CTB*, viii, part iii, 1399; part iv, 2039, 2098, 2110.
47. *CSPD*, 1670, 144.
48. BB6, f.27.
49. Ibid., 89; KHRO, L. 642-3, 645.
50. K. A. MacMahon, *Acts of Parliament . . . relating to the E. Riding . . . and Kingston upon Hull 1529-1800*, 26, No. 57.
51. C. Hill, *Economic Problems of the Church*, 92-3; 2 and 3 Edw. VI, cap. 13.
52. *CSPD*, 1661-2, 359, 371.
53. *DNB* s.v. RYTHER, JOHN; A. G. Matthews, *Calamy Revised*, 421.
54. *CSPD Addenda*, 1670, 233, 249, 289, 240 and *passim*.
55. BB8, ff.39, 70, 81, 140, 177, 179; BB8, f.210.
56. Ibid., f.37.
57. Ibid., ff.81, 152, 250.
58. Surtees Society, *Depositions from York Castle*, 21.
59. *Journal of the Friends' Historical Asssociation*, ii, 103.
60. T. Blashill, *History of East Hull*, 178.
61. *YAJ*, xxi; *VCH*, Yorkshire, ii, 430.
62. *CSPD*, 1663-4, 637.
63. A. G. Matthews, op. cit., 17.
64. *CSPD*, 1668-9, 396.
65. Ibid., 623.
66. *CSPD*, 1670, 309.

67. *CSPD*, 1672, 398.
68. A. G. Matthews, op. cit., 537.
69. W. Whitaker, *Bowl Alley Lane Chapel*, 41, 99 ff.; *CSPD*, 1672, 398.
70. A. G. Matthews, op. cit., 110-11.
71. Ibid.
72. BB8, ff.100, 116.
73. Carleton Monckton MS, 35.
74. BB8, ff.42, 114; KHRO, L. 1029, 1039; *VCH*, Hull, 312.
75. BB8, f.207.
76. Ibid., f.209.
77. Surtees Society, *Depositions from York Castle*, 283.
78. Ibid., 278.
79. Boyle, op. cit., 226-7, 251.
80. *CSPD*, Feb.-Dec. 1685, No. 212.
81. *CSPD*, 1675-6, 164.
82. *CSPD*, Jan. 1686-May 1687, No. 1597.
83. Carleton Monckton MS, 36.
84. *CSPD*, Jan.-May 1687. No. 1284; BB8, f.231.
85. Ibid., f.232; Hadley, 276.
86. Tickell, 583.
87. *CSPD*, 1689-90, 322.
88. BB8, f.430.
89. *VCH*, Hull, 342-6.
90. BB6, 17 Jan. 1661.
91. Ibid., 13 May 1661.
92. K. A. MacMahon, op. cit., 27, No. 67.
93. Tickell, 595.
94. J. M. Lambert, op cit., 210, No. 5, 211, No. 6.
95. Ibid., 241, No. 2.
96. Ibid., 211, No. 10.
97. Ibid., 282.
98. Ibid., 244, No. 10; 345, No. 22.
99. F. M. Eden, *The State of the Poor*, iii, 839.

16

The Beginnings of Change

Between the reigns of Anne and Victoria the town changed more rapidly than it had ever done before. By 1700 it was just beginning to grow beyond its medieval and Tudor defences. Hollar's view of c.1640 still shows much open ground inside the walls. Baskerville in the 1680s and Defoe, or his informant, noted how congested building had become.[1]* In High Street merchants still lived at their counting-houses, but soon they began to move out to the healthier areas to the north and west, especially after the building of the ring of docks round the old town; and by 1833 none of the thirteen aldermen-merchants lived in old Hull, though four were in Sculcoates, then its northern suburb.[2]

This growth was the consequence of economic expansion as the industrialisation of the West Riding and the Midlands increased the demand for shipping to the markets of the Continent. The three docks which accommodated this shipping, as they were constructed between 1774 and 1829 destroyed the last relics of the medieval walls and the civil war earthworks outside them. The western half of these earthworks was still there when Thew made his map in 1787, but it was only the citadel which was of any military importance.

Soon after its foundation in 1792 the Hull Society for Literary Information carried out a local census because of public curiosity about the size of Hull. It was then estimated that Hull with Sculcoates had a population of 22,286.[3] Using the parish registers and estimating an average of 4.5 persons in a family the society put the population at 12,964 in 1767, and 15,678 in 1777; and modern estimates give the Hull and Sculcoates population in 1700 as about

7,512.[4] In the eighteenth century in most years there were more deaths than births. It was through the arrival of newcomers that the town grew so rapidly. In the whole town in 1783, one of several exceptional years, there were sixty-three per cent more deaths than births; but there were other bad years. In 1789 deaths exceeded births by thirty per cent, and in 1794 they exceeded births by sixty-nine per cent. Holy Trinity parish, in the later eighteenth century (1752-95) actually had three per cent more births than deaths, but St Mary's parish, now rapidly growing, was much less healthy, with a total of fifteen per cent more deaths than births in the period 1754-95; and in that parish females were much less likely to survive than males.[5] There was an almost fourfold increase in population in the eighteenth century; and by 1831 it was over six times larger than in 1700.

Growth made it increasingly difficult for the bench to deal with problems arising from building and rebuilding, traffic, street repairs, sanitation, watching and lighting. To deal with these matters it was necessary to obtain the passage of local acts which would provide authority to raise rates and do whatever was necessary to effect improvement. Proposals made in 1734-5 for an Improvement Act got no further than preliminary planning.[6] In 1750 the corporation sponsored a bill for street-cleaning, lighting and repair; but this was defeated by the objections of Trinity House and the ordinary burgesses. The opposition, led by a merchant, John Collings, objected that if the bill became law it would be burdensome to the 'middling classes', and that the income of the corporation from rents, tolls and dues had doubled in recent years, making it unnecessary to burden the townsmen with a rate. Those opposing the corporation were irritated that after a draft of the bill had been made public, amendments were added without any opportunity for those outside the corporation to see them. Trinity House objected that the bill in some respects was an attempted infringement of its chartered rights, as, for example, in a clause forbidding lights on ships in the haven at night.[7]

Nevertheless, within five years, as conditions grew worse, several of the leading inhabitants met the corporation to consider the possibility of promoting an improvement bill; but all that was done was to embody a few proposals in a bill to amend three earlier acts for the relief of the poor, and the first Improvement

Act was passed in March 1755.[8]

This was the first of no less than seven Improvement Acts passed in the next sixty years, each usually intended to 'supply the deficiencies' of earlier acts. In 1762 a comprehensive local act laid down stringent regulations affecting the streets and introduced certain rates on property; and two years later a further act, with other provisions, altered the basis on which rates were assessed.[9] During the committee proceedings on this second bill the town clerk, Carleton Monckton said that 'it would make the act more effectual if certain powers were taken out of the corporation and vested in the inhabitants at large'. He was not advocating local democracy but the device of a body of improvement commissioners, drawn from a wider circle than the aldermen, but this change was not made until the 1810 act.[10]

With their extended powers the bench had to deal with a variety of problems, though they had contrived to deal with some without the need for legislation. As in most other towns, domestic and industrial activity obtruded on the street. In 1683 the inhabitants of Church Lane had been warned to 'forbear to wash or rench their cloathes in the streets'.[11] In 1702 Benjamin Blaydes was ordered to appear and explain how it was that some four months previously he had allowed the 'boltspright' of a ship in his yard to lie so far across North Bridge as to make it impossible for carts to pass.[12] In 1682 and 1694 the coopers were cautioned, not so much because they made their casks in the streets as because their fires 'lit in the public streets at unseasonable time' created a risk of conflagration.[13] Three houses were burned down in 1694 as a result of flax-dressing by candle-light in a shop in Grimsby Lane, and an order was made that no one was to dress flax by candle-light or when smoking a pipe.[14]

Small shopkeepers trespassed on the street by putting up posts and signboards, and by erecting stalls outside the shops. By long custom the owners had come to think it their right to make these encroachments. Action against 'posts at doors' was taken as early as 1699,[15] and in the 1740s a token payment of a shilling a year was demanded for such street trespasses.[16] In 1750 offenders were given fourteen days' notice to get rid of their 'bulks' — projections from their shops, under threat of having them removed. The 1755 Improvement Act gave statutory power to deal with them.

New building in the town involved the possibility of permanent encroachments, though official permission was needed for all new buildings. With streets sometimes flooded by the tide, it was tempting to have steps outside the house, even though this encumbered the street. After 1770 many references to encroachments suggest bow-windows. In November 1771 John Baker, who had a shop on the east side of Lowgate, was given a fortnight's warning about his window, but no action was taken for fully eight months.[17] Under the 1783 Improvement Act a projection into the street of up to twenty-two inches was permitted for any portico, steps, or similar addition,and action was taken in 1784 against Colonel Maister because of his railings and against the elder Charles Frost for steps projecting from his new building in Scale Lane.[18] In 1793 the builder and architect George Pycock was employed by the corporation to supervise the removal of all encroachments.[19]

There could be other and much more offensive encroachments. Before the committee of the Commons, hearing evidence on the abortive Improvement Bill of 1750, the town's husband, Robert Taylor (the officer chiefly responsible for corporation property) referred to 'dirt and other annoyances' frequently laid in the streets at night 'in such a private manner as renders it extremely difficult to detect the offenders'.[20] The traffic in Hull nightsoil had probably already begun, and Arthur Young in 1770 wrote that it was in great demand in the country, 'extraordinary good stuff' being sold for 5s a load.[21]

Sometimes street improvement could only be brought about by the removal of a house, and there were occasions when an owner was paid compensation for undertaking not to rebuild on his site. John Cox in 1746 was promised £35, after he had demolished an old building over Grimsby Lane, on condition that he did not rebuild but would 'leave the lane end open'.[22]

As traffic grew the roads needed more frequent repair. It was felt that much damage was caused by 'iron-shod' carts and narrow wheels. In 1682 the streets had been 'much torn and wrought up' and an order was re-issued which in 1677 had prohibited the use of the streets by carts with iron-bound wheels carrying lime, bricks, or tiles.[23] In 1718 the bench prohibited the use of all carts with iron-bound wheels under a penalty of 5s. Sometimes posts were set up across the street to keep all vehicles out, as was done with Sewer Lane in 1706 and South End in 1739. In 1718 it was reported that

John Cooper had pulled up the post at the east end of Posterngate and 'employed carts and carriages there to the damnifying of the pavement of the said street and the common sewer therein'. As in modern American usage, *pavement* then meant the road surface, not the side-walk. The post was replaced and Cooper reprimanded.[25]

Under the local act of 1755 no more than three draught animals could be harnessed to any vehicle in the town, all wheels were to be nine inches wide in the felloe and none was to be iron-bound except under specified conditions. In 1764 carts or waggons carrying corn, hay or straw within two miles of the town could have iron tyres.[26] In 1783 the town's husband was instructed to obtain plans or models of goods carts permitted in other towns, and in 1793 Alderman Benjamin Blaydes was asked to make a model of a truck for use in the town which would be quieter and less damaging than those then being used.[27] He produced a model of a wheel for inspection, and it was then ordered that all wheels must be at least 2 ft 2 in. in diameter and not less than six inches in the felloe. This did not apply except to vehicles for the carriage of goods and some consideration was given to truck-men who had bought new five-inch wheels within the previous twelve months.[28]

Until about 1760 much of the gravel and cobbles needed for the streets was obtained from the Holderness foreshore, over which the Constables of Burton Constable, as hereditary lords of Holderness, exercised control. The best cobbles came from Spurn but in 1761 there was a quarrel over a 'large fish' stranded on Cherry Cobb sands, between William Constable (a friend of Rousseau) and the mayor in his capacity of Admiral of the Humber. William Constable was grievously affronted and refused all further dealings with the corporation. William Taylor, the town's husband, was then told to buy ballast cobbles from ships when he could get them for the usual Spurn price of 3s a ton.[29] No further attempt was made to get Spurn cobbles. It was partly because so much road surface consisted of these hard, rounded, glacial cobbles that until the second half of the eighteenth century sleds performed better on them than anything on wheels, and were much quieter.

Another consequence of the increase of road traffic was the gradual disappearance of the central gutter. In 1691 it was ordered that the street from Market Place to Beverley Gate should be repaved with side gutters and a central camber.[30] In 1718 Carleton Monckton noted that Church Lane was 'new paved which before had a channel in the middle, as also had the High Street which was new paved from North End to South End'.[31] No particular attention was given to side-walks until after 1760. An order was made in 1766 for the paving of the north side of Bowlalley Lane with flags,[32] and in 1761 the east side of the market place also was flagged.[33] Trinity House flagged their own side of Whitefriargate and the corporation did the north side. From 1786 there are frequent references to 'flag-curbs' and 'kirbstones' at the side of the road, dividing the pedestrian area from wheeled traffic.[34]

More streets were laid out to the north of the town after the opening of the first dock in 1778. The town's surveyor, John Fox, or possibly his son of the same name, was sent to London in 1824 to 'make himself completely acquainted with Mr Macadam's plan of repairing roads'. After his report had been received Wellington Street was the first to be macadamised.[35] And as the town grew it became necessary to have the streets identified by name. It was ordered in 1779 that the name should be 'affixed' at the corners, and in 1784 the order was repeated. Names were to be painted on the walls at street ends or on boards.[36]

The usual practice was that the householders in a street would petition for the surfacing of a street with cobbles. The corporation provided the materials, and the occupiers paid for the labour, each being responsible for his own frontage up to the middle of the street. The 1755 Improvement Act included clauses for the compulsion of those who did not comply. In 1730, when it was decided to pave Salthouse Lane and Lowgate, three aldermen appointed as supervisors had to undertake to pay the workmen if the householders refused to meet the labour costs.[37] It had been necessary in 1738 for the corporation to stipulate that it would only repair Grimsby and Trinity Lanes when the inhabitants had undertaken to meet the cost of the pavers, who were then charging $2\frac{1}{2}d$ a square yard.[38] Even with the powers conferred by the 1755 act the bench found it convenient to have a promissory note from the principal inhabitants before work began on a street. Under the act the market place, the fish shambles and the common staithes were the main places for which the corporation was solely responsible.

As the town grew it spread into Myton, which was part of it, and

Sculcoates, which was not; but in both places the repair of roads was a charge on the parish under the supervision of the annually elected overseers of the highways. There was an Improvement Act for Sculcoates in 1801 and for Trippett, Myton and the reclaimed land south of Humber Street in 1810. For Sculcoates the act named thirty-nine improvement commissioners, and for Trippett and Myton there were 113; and it was the responsibility of the commissioners to apply the provisions of the acts for lighting, watching, flagging and paving.

Some water was still being carted as late as 1816. By 1701 the corporation owned a one-third interest in the waterworks which supplied piped water.[39] In 1765 they got the rest by paying Alderman William Wilberforce £50 and four per cent interest on £3000, the remainder of the purchase money.[40] Water was distributed through elm pipes from the water-house at the end of Waterhouse Lane. The water-house was improved in 1735 and new pipes were laid in Whitefriargate, Silver Street, Scale Lane and High Street. Wilberforce obtained 'awme' trees from London for pipe-making.[41] From these wooden mains lead 'strings' were linked with pumps in the houses. Four years later new pipes were ordered to be laid in Blackfriargate and the Butchery and from Scale Lane through Lowgate to the end of Salthouse Lane; and in 1777 another main was laid from the water-house to High Street.[42] Bored elms were used as pipes to the end of the century, but by 1819 iron water pipes were being laid in Story Street.[43]

The supply was found inadequate by 1770, when horses were still working the pumps. In 1773 Mayson Wright took the works on a twenty-one-year lease, paying the corporation £250 a year.[44] At first he used an engine of the Newcomen type, no doubt as improved by Smeaton, but in 1778 replaced this with a new Boulton and Watt engine, with a substantial subsidy from the corporation.[45]

Even as early as 1621 aldermen and others who could afford it were obliged to have candle-lanterns at their doors each evening, except in moonlight, from mid-November to 1 March.[46] This order was renewed from time to time, and in 1672 required that all who were rated at 3*d* a week or more for poor-relief to have 'lanterns and lighted candles therein in dark winter's nights at their foredoors till nine o'clock daily', and this order was renewed in 1699.[47] In 1682 inquiries had been made about London street lighting but it was not until 1713 that Alderman Sir William St Quintin was requested to obtain lights from London, and in the following year the aldermen of each ward were to collect subscriptions towards the cost of maintaining the lamps.[48] The weakness of this scheme was that subscriptions were not compulsory and it was not until the Improvement Act of 1762 that a lighting rate was introduced. The third Improvement Act put the responsibility on the parishes with power to levy a rate of up to 8*d* in the pound and keep lamps burning from sunset to first light on the next day from 1 October to 1 May and also during the assizes. Whale oil was much used until after 1820 when coal-gas began to be used. Lights did not merely make the streets more visible. They also increased public security, and in 1795, a bad year, the bench subscribed £20 towards street lamps for the prevention of riots; and the popularity of the theatre and of assemblies owed something to these improvements.[49]

The turnpiking of local roads after 1744 brought more traffic to the market where already in 1722 it had been necessary to order that all vehicles and horses must be out of the market area after a reasonable time for taking up and setting down.[50] It was not until 1904 that market stalls were excluded from the original market place, making the movement of traffic possible at all times.[51] The south end of the market place, except for an arch leading to the butchery, was blocked by the Guildhall, the old gaol and the guardhouse. The market cross, rebuilt in 1682, was a little to the north. In 1734 the statue of William III further congested the market area. It had originally been intended for Bristol. Under 1 October 1734 George Vertue wrote in his diary that 'the equestrian statue of King William made, modelled and cast by Mr Scheemaker at Westminster, being of a composite hard metal, lead, pewter etc. now finished to be set up at Hull in Yorkshire'. The subscriptions list headed by Lords Micklethwaite and Cholmondeley, each of whom gave 100 guineas, raised £824 5*s*. This was barely enough, and in 1737 the corporation provided another £13 9*s* 10*d*.[52] The statue was unveiled on 4 December 1734 when, according to Carleton Monckton, the town clerk, 'the houses that night were much illuminated'. All this Whig enthusiasm was satirised by a local versifier, who necessarily remained anonymous, hinting at hidden scandals:

To William's memory, lo! a statue rear'd!
Strange that till now it should have been deferr'd:
Just now's the time, the Humbrian zealots cry.
And who may give an alderman the lie?
But, by their leave, methinks they should have stay'd
Till stable-room and horse-hire had been paid.
But let their squabbles, blunders, and what-not,
Inscription, pedestal, be now forgot,
Since on this day their loyalty was shown
To drink his memory till they lost their own.

Rails were put round the statue to protect it in 1735, removed and put back on an octagonal plan because they had inconvenienced coaches and carriages, and then removed altogether in 1744. By 1750 the statue of King William was in danger of falling and was rescued at a cost of £30.[54] Though removal to a different site was considered, it stayed where it was, protected once more by railings, and regularly painted and re-guilded.[55] In the second world war, because of the danger that it might be destroyed by bombing, the statue was moved to Houghton Hall, near Sancton, the seat of Colonel Philip Langdale whose ancestor, Marmaduke Langdale, was governor of Hull in 1688, turned out by the arrival of the Protestant hero, William of Orange, at Torbay. Through the endeavours of Mr William Broady rather than of the corporation, William and his horse were replaced on their plinth in 1949; and the town is still fortunate in having this happy imitation of the ancient equestrian figure of Marcus Aurelius in Rome.

There were seditious speeches by a few Jacobites in 1745. Henry Hamelton, a Catholic, was a sugar boiler. His wife, speaking from an open window near the Sugar-House, damned all Protestants and said Hull ought to let the Pretender in, and two labourers said they would fight for him. Others said he should never enter while they had powder and shot.[56] In case the Jacobite army should approach, the bench borrowed twenty cannon from a frigate mounting them on the walls, and in the autumn they welcomed the Duke of Ancaster with his new militia regiment.[57]

To make more space in the market the butter cross was demolished in 1761 and public ceremonies which had previously been held there were now transferred to the gilded statue. A cleaning in 1784 left it in good condition for the celebration of the centenary of the Glorious Revolution in 1788.[58] When the official party left the service in Holy Trinity three volleys were fired by the troops on parade and the whole procession went three times round the statue.[59] That night there was a general illumination, and the bench supplied the Quakers with free candles to put in their windows so that the mob would have no excuse for breaking them.

After the market cross, the market house at the east end of Holy Trinity was the next to go, and with some adjacent tenements it was replaced with shambles for the butchers.[60] More space was made in the market by the removal in 1768 of a semi-permanent 'mountebank-stage' used by strolling players and showmen.[61] West of the church, Priest Row, which belonged to the corporation, was demolished and a new street, King Street, was laid out.[62] There had already been much demolition along the line of the butchery down to Harry Ogle's tower, and the surviving walls and shipyards on the Humber foreshore.[63] The old gaol at the south end of the market place was demolished in 1791, and the guardhouse in the following year. The 1783 Improvement Act provided for a new gaol, built in Castle Street, the westward continuation of Mytongate beyond the walls.[64]

In 1793 the demolition of the old town hall and the building of a new one on the same site was considered,[65] but because of the war it was not until 1801 that an act was secured for enlarging and improving the market place, the butchery and Queen Street, with power to make a dock and wharf for the ferry and market boats.[66] Considerable progress had been made by 1804. Then the last remains of the southern part of the wall along the Humber was pulled down, and on the artillery ground to the south and on land reclaimed from the Humber, Wellington Street, Nelson Street and Pier Street were laid out and named in 1813.[67]

It was decided in 1813 to demolish the seventeenth-century town hall and sell the materials, with the intention of building a new 'Guildhall' in Humber Street, 'at or near the site where Harry Ogle's tower formerly stood'.[68] William Jarratt, however, then mayor, offered to lease his house in Lowgate as a mansion-house and town hall, and it was used for these purposes until Cuthbert Brodrick's attractive Italianate building was erected on the eastern part of the site of the present-day Guildhall.

The new butcher's shambles on the east side of Queen Street, replacing those against Holy Trinity, cost £12,000 raised by a tontine.[69]* At the opening at the beginning of 1807 Mr Scatcherd brought a large vessel, carried by two men, which he had had made at the Hull pottery. This contained several gallons of punch, drunk by each of the butchers who had voted for W. J. Denison, an enormously wealthy banker of Leeds, elected in 1806.[70*] Between January 1800 and December 1805 another £33,000 was raised for improvement projects, mainly financed by ordinary annuities. As four of the aldermen were trustees of Cogan's charity, £5275 from its funds was converted into corporation stock and about £10,400 was raised by the sale of four of the corporation's £250 dock company shares.[71]

Some notable improvements, of which the main one was Parliament Street, came from private enterprise. The idea of linking Whitefriargate with Quay Street was started by Aistroppe Stovin of Bowlalley Lane, a Guisborough attorney who came to Hull in 1793. He offered £30 for the flagging and paving, and published his proposals with the approval of the corporation. The capital was to be raised by a tontine which had fifty-four original subscribers, including Sir Henry Etherington, Samuel Thornton and the builder, George Pycock. The corporation sacrificed the old house of correction and cleared slum property in Mughouse Entry; and the building of the Neptune Inn by Trinity House opposite the end of the proposed street provided an attractive vista. The whole scheme was expected to cost no more than £13,000.[72] The act was passed in April 1795.[73] The social exclusiveness of the scheme, partly an index of the prosperity of the town, contributed to its success. The houses were to be let for between £21 and £25 a year.[74] and an archway screened the northern end from the narrow and irregularly built Quay Street, which led to the dock-side. A suburb was also developing on the northern side of the dock as conditions in the congested old town deteriorated. The Dock Act of 1774 required the company to make a street forty feet wide from the site of Beverley Gate to the North Bridge, and on the completion of the dock all land not needed could be sold. This led to building in George Street, Charlotte Street, North Street and Bond Street.[75]

As Holy Trinity was next to the market place there was much misuse of the churchyard. Orders to check this were made in 1720, and also for a passage to the church on the north side from the market place;[76] but even in 1742 William Mason, the vicar, allowed sheds in the 'lesser graveyard' for corporation stores.[77]

Vestry meetings continued to be held in the chancel and as late as 1794 the volunteer infantry were drilled in the nave.[78] There was no organ after the Reformation until in 1711-12 a voluntary subscription was organised and raised about £600 of which £150 came from Sir William St Quintin, one of the borough members, and £50 from William Maister, the other. With this an organ, said to have been designed originally for St Paul's Cathedral, was bought, improved and repaired by John Snetzler in 1756.[79] Lofts and galleries had first been built in the nave between 1580 and 1615.[80]

A new loft was built at the west end in 1708 and the others were enlarged in 1727.[81] Pew rents in 1691 ranged from 2*s* a year in the lofts to £1 4*s* nearest to the mayor and the reading desk.[82] Places were allocated for the master and boys of the grammar school. A minute of 1728 indicates that churchwardens sometimes took bribes from persons wanting a better place. The locking and allocation of pews continued until 1846. The parish clerk of St Mary Lowgate in 1720 provided a fitting comment on the system. Of six customs officers requiring a whole loft for themselves he wrote: 'NB it will be as nigh heaven as they will come'.[83]

In Holy Trinity the great east window, probably damaged by rioters, was repaired towards the end of the reign of Elizabeth. Then, or when the Puritans removed the rest of the glass, it was bricked up from the base to the springers of the arch, and so remained until 1831. Early in the eighteenth century the altar was restored to its original position under this window and an altar-piece, a painting of the last supper, was obtained in 1711 from Jacques Parmentier for £50.[84] The painting, in a bad state, was removed in 1829, but sixty years later, reduced in size, was replaced on the walls of the north choir aisle.

The choir was for a long time unused except for communion services, and until the middle of the seventeenth century one of the disused chantry chapels on the south side of the chancel served as a council chamber for the bench. It was here that the parish library was housed.[85] What survived of this library, some 800 volumes of mainly theological works of the sixteenth and seventeenth centuries, came to the library of the then University College in 1938.

Because of non-payment of parish rates, the vicar's salary of £100 was often in arrears, and in 1762 the bench decided to distrain the goods of those failing to pay.[86] Because of rising prices the Revd J.H. Bromby asked for some increase in 1802 and the bench raised his stipend to £150 'during their pleasure' but between 1817 and 1824 he only had the lower sum.[87] When he abandoned his claim to Easter offerings ten years later the bench gave him no compensation.[88]

The growth of population and nonconformity made it desirable to have a chapel of ease for Holy Trinity and in 1788 the Revd Thomas Dykes submitted his plan. Though he was a friend of William Wilberforce and had the support of the vicar, the bench opposed his scheme, but changed its mind in 1789. He was an Evangelical who proposed to finance the scheme with money left to him by his father's sister, Rose Dykes, and to reimburse himself out of the sale of pews.[89] There was some difficulty in finding a suitable site until in 1790 William Osbourne offered to give up the land which he held from the corporation. It was thus that St John's, on the site now occupied by the Feren's Gallery, was consecrated, still unfinished, by the archbishop in 1791 and opened for services on 13 May 1792. As the site covered part of what had once been the town ditch there was difficulty with foundations when extensions were made in 1803. Galleries were added in 1823.[90]

All Hull freemen could vote in parliamentary elections whether they lived in the town or not. The parliamentary borough was far less corrupt than Grimsby, but in 1816 Thomas Oldfield commented that the Hull price was two guineas a vote and that each election was more corrupt than the one before.[91] The corporation liked to have a Hull man as one of the members. The Hull merchant, Sir William St Quintin, was a member continuously from 1695 until his death in 1723. When he was first returned his colleague was Charles, the brother of Thomas Osborne, Earl of Danby, but when Danby was impeached in 1695 and withdrew from public life in 1699, Osborne's place was taken at the 1701 election by another Hull merchant, William Maister.

On the first return of St Quintin with Osborne in 1695 Sir James Bradshaw of Risby, the defeated candidate, petitioned against the return on the grounds that under pressure from the bench the sheriff, Martin Raspin, had briskly held the election the day after the receipt of the writ. He further alleged that the aldermen had threatened some of his supporters and admitted twenty-seven new voters on the day of the election. His petition failed. He stood again in 1701, together with Charles Osborne, was defeated, and again petitioned unsuccessfully.

From 1701 for nearly a quarter of a century both members were Hull merchants. When Maister died in 1716 he was succeeded by his brother-in-law, Nathaniel Rogers. On the death of St Quintin in 1724 Sir Henry Houghton, the government candidate, had the support of the corporation which would normally have given him the seat, especially as many persons were newly admitted to their freedom. But George Crowle, a Hull man, was elected.[92] Crowle continued to sit until 1747 when his younger brother, Richard, was defeated by Lord Robert Manners and Thomas Carter, a Lincolnshire squire. Viscount Micklethwaite, who was returned with Crowle in 1727, died in 1734. The by-election was uncontested. Henry Maister, son of the former member William Maister, was returned. He was a man of very great wealth who had to pay £300 as a fine for non-acceptance of the office of alderman, but £50 was returned to him when his property in High Street had to be blown up to prevent the spread of a fire.

When Carter died in 1744 General Henry Pulteney was returned without a contest. Richard Crowle was elected in 1754, but from the election of Pulteney until that of Wilberforce in 1780 the borough was, with that one exception, represented by outsiders. Lord Robert Manners, eighth son of the Duke of Rutland, was returned in 1747 with government support and had the distinction of not making a single speech in the House in thirty-five years and five elections. He owed something to his position as lieutenant-governor of the garrison, and apparently dealt satisfactorily with the corporation's parliamentary business. Richard Crowle, a lawyer and a wit, being required to kneel before the Speaker for the use of caustic language in the Commons, on rising dusted his knees with the remark that 'it was the dirtiest house he had ever been in'.

On the death of Crowle his place was taken by Sir G. M. Metham of North Cave. On his resignation in 1766 the Marquess of Rockingham, then Prime Minister for the first time and High Steward of Hull, recommended William Weddell of Newby, his relative by marriage, and there was an unopposed return. The 1768 general election was preceded by the admission of many freemen and 850 burgesses voted with Weddell, at the top of the poll, returned with Manners, though the third man, Captain Thomas Lee, a native of Hull, claimed he could rely on the support of forty customs and excise men.[93] Rockingham himself was entertained by the corporation in the summer following the election, and Weddell's victory also was celebrated.[94] At the request of Hull merchants who disliked the 'great idleness and disorder of the races' Weddell stopped his contributions for prizes to be run for by horses at Hull, perhaps knowing already that he could sit for Malton, another of Rockingham's boroughs, as soon as he felt ready.

The egocentric and opinionated David Hartley, son of the philosopher of the same name, was elected in the place of Weddell in 1774. He was a friend and confidant of Sir George Saville, was well known to Rockingham, and on terms of close friendship with Benjamin Franklin. Probably with Rockingham's support, he became British plenipotentiary in Paris where in 1783, with Franklin, he drew up and signed the treaty which ended the American War of Independence.[95]

Captain Thomas Shirley, the defeated candidate in 1774, petitioned against the return, alleging partiality shown by the sheriff, Henry Horner, and complaining that qualified persons were not allowed to vote and that unqualified voters were counted for Hartley. He withdrew his petition, and greatly annoyed the corporation by not making full payment for clerical work which he had asked to be done for him.[96] On the war with America, Hartley differed radically from the stupid loyalists of the corporation. The mayor and aldermen published strong disclaimers in several newspapers.

This being his position, he stood no chance against William Wilberforce at the election of 1780.[97] Wilberforce, having spent £8000 to ensure his election, headed the poll and was returned with Manners. The family had grown wealthy in the Baltic trade; and though they were rivals it may well be that the enlightened Hartley (again a member for Hull from 1782, after the death of Manners, until 1784) influenced the thinking of the young Wilberforce on the question of slavery.[98] Hull had never in any one Parliament been represented by two such outstanding men.

But pearls are thrown before swine, and Hartley was a poor third when Wilberforce and his cousin, Samuel Thornton, were elected in 1784. Wilberforce, however, was elected for the county.

At Hull he then backed Walter Spencer Stanhope of Cannon Hall near Barnsley, and he had an unopposed return.[99]* Spencer Stanhope was never popular in Hull, and did not stand in 1790. Samuel Thornton was the eldest of the three merchant sons of the wealthy John Thornton. The father did not belong to Hull, but his mother, a relative of Wilberforce, was a Hull woman, and he himself became the leading Russia merchant in Hull. All the Thorntons, with Wilberforce, were Members of Parliament and members of the Clapham sect of Evangelicals. Samuel was continuously member for Hull for twenty-two years. His wealth and virtue were so great that on the eve of the 1790 election the bench formerly recorded its 'approbation and satisfaction' of his parliamentary conduct; and in 1802 they again testified to his value as a member, notified the town's officers that he was receiving their support, forwarded copies of their resolution to the Dock Company and to Trinity House and gave him a public dinner and his freedom in a gold box.[100] The fervour of official support was such that 389 new freemen were admitted in the fortnight before the election. William Bell, a Hull bookseller, stood as anti-corruption candidate and got only three votes to Thornton's 1266.[101]

An independent voter hated nothing more than an uncontested election, and as this hatred grew the deliberate introduction of a third man became more obvious. In 1796 neither the Earl of Burford nor Mark Sykes of Sledmere would stand. Sir Charles Turner then appeared and was elected with Thornton; but it cost him at least £8000 in a rather close contest. Despite his election, Turner seems to have been unwelcome and most of the corporation's parliamentary business was done by Thornton, which further enhanced his reputation. It was understandable that when, in 1799 Thornton wanted to buy a piece of ground in the 'growths or groves' of Sutton lordship, the corporation was pleasantly accommodating.[102]

In 1802 Lord Fitzwilliam, heir to the Rockingham interest, sponsored William Joseph Denison, and John Staniforth also intervened with ready money and was returned with Thornton; but at the 1806 election the magnitude of Denison's fortune was properly understood and he turned Thornton out at last, with the support of the Sykes family. But in 1807 things went badly wrong for the freemen. Denison decided not to stand. John Thornton, the son of Samuel, decided to come forward and to ensure a contest Lord Mahon, son of Earl Stanhope, was also persuaded to be a candidate; but to the horror of the voters Thornton refused to provide any money for bribes and withdrew, giving Lord Mahon an unopposed return.[103]

In 1807 the sitting members presented themselves for re-election and so many were eager to take part in the contest that 276 new freemen were admitted in four days; but as there were only two candidates it would be unnecessary for either to bribe anyone. Writing in 1816 Oldfield described what then happened: 'At the last general election in Hull in 1812, the freemen of Hull wanted a contest, but no candidate appearing to gratify their wishes, a great number of the lower order stopped a gentleman who was passing through the town of Beverley, who was a perfect stranger to them in name and character, and offered to support him if he would be their champion upon this occasion. The offer was accepted and the following day he was chosen their member by acclamation.' It would have been nearer the truth to say that there was a sham contest with the unknown gentleman, George W. Denys, getting 905 votes gratis and Staniforth and Mahon having to pay for their votes; and since everyone had two votes the 905 would give their second vote to one or other of his rivals and so be sure of something. He was returned with Staniforth.[104] Having got in for nothing in 1812, Denys had no desire to stand in 1818 and pay for his election.

The introduction of an essential third man was repeated with even greater success in 1826 when 700 or more freemen promised support for Augustus John O'Neill against Daniel Sykes of Raywell and Charles Pelham Villiers. It was a very necessary move since in 1820 two members had been returned without a contest. O'Neill came comfortably top and was returned with Sykes, all candidates having more than a thousand votes each.[105] He intended to stand again in 1830, but withdrew when he found that this time he would have to pay, and Sykes preferred to stand for Beverley. T. G. Burke had been brought forward as the necessary third man, Sykes backed W. B. Wrightson, and the freemen put forward Aderman George Schonswar. These two were elected. But Burke served his purpose, presumably at no cost to himself, by ensuring that his rivals would suffer the usual financial pressure of a contested election.

The willingness of the poorer burgesses to sell their votes is understandable. They needed the money, but preferred to disguise their motives. From Beverley a Hull voter wrote in 1826: 'It is a third man which teaches the other two candidates properly to appreciate our worth and rightly to value our elective franchise. Was it not for a third man our votes and interest would never be solicited.'[106] The *Rockingham* said 'they would have brought into parliament a chimney-sweep or walking broomstick possessed of the will and the way to make the usual compliment to his friends'.[107] More responsible burgesses objected in principle. The quality of a new man was unknown, and the system could result in the rejection of such a man as Thornton, in 1806, by, as the corporation put it, 'the wayward plaudits of a fickle and misguided populace'.[108]

After the general election of August 1818 the corporation took counsel's opinion on the admission of freemen. Between 9 and 17 June 487 new freemen had been admitted, and it had been difficult to check fraudulent claims in so short a time, particularly in the case of non-residents.[109] After considering Sergeant Hullock's opinion the bench decided that the claim and supporting documents had to be deposited with the town clerk and that there must be a fortnight's notice of all claims.[110] When John Mitchell and Daniel Sykes were returned without a contest in 1820 there was a marked decline in pre-election admissions to freedom; but the election of 1826 was contested and with the approach of polling day Tuesdays and Fridays had to be set aside for special meetings of the bench to swear freemen.[111]

Even without a contest Hull elections were expensive for the candidates, since from about 1760 poll money was given at the rate of two guineas a head. According to Robert Broadley of Ferriby, Weddell and Manners gave two guineas a head in 1768, the whole election costing Weddell about £5000 and Manners £6200. 'Plumpers', freemen who voted for one candidate only, were probably, as in other boroughs, paid more.[112] There was also the cost of official fees, committee rooms, treats, flags, banners and musicians. The travelling expenses and maintenance of non-resident voters was also costly. According to Broadley only ten or a dozen Hull freemen made the journey from London in 1768,[113] but in 1780 non-resident voters cost Wilberforce £10 each. And between elections any member intent on re-election had to spend freely on good causes in the constituency.

A Hull member was expected to introduce local bills and watch the progress of others which might affect the interests of the town. Sometimes he was asked to support bills, such as those for navigation schemes geographically distant from Hull, which might nevertheless benefit the port. In 1781 the corporation thanked Wilberforce for his attention to 'the bill regulating the importation of yarn in neutral bottoms' and his help in supplying information about the whaling-ship bounty when it was intended to present on behalf of the town a petition against a threatened decrease in that subsidy.[114] John Staniforth in 1814 kept a close watch on proposals for the re-building of the Ouse bridge at York, as there was strong resentment of the possibility that this might become a charge on the whole county.[115] If a borough member was politically unsuitable for the purpose the bench was quite willing to use another. In 1833, with a reformed House of Commons, a public petition reflecting on borough administration was being prepared. The defence of the corporation was not entrusted to borough members, who were reformers, but to Richard Bethell of Rise, one of the Conservative members for the new East Riding constituency.[116] Before the days of reform the corporation tended to regard the Hull members as its servants, not to be used by others without permission. Samuel Thornton and the Earl of Burford presented a petition to the Treasury in 1793 from the Hull Dock Company, and the bench expressed surprise that they had not been consulted first.[117]

Sources

1. D. Defoe, *A Tour through the Whole Island of Great Britain* (Everyman) ii, 242-5. He wrote that the bridge over the Hull had *fourteen* arches.
2. Gawtress, *The Corporation of Hull*, 71.
3. Tickell, 854.
4. *VCH*, Hull, 190.
5. F. M. Eden, *The State of the Poor*, iii, (1797) 839-41.
6. BB8, ff.797,799.
7. *Commons Journals*, xxv, 936, 969, 982; BB9, ff.136,145-6.
8. 28 Geo. II cap. 27; *Commons Journals*, xxvii, 95, 137 and *passim*; BB9, f.224.
9. 2 Geo. III cap. 70; 4 Geo. III, cap. 74.
10. 50 Geo. III cap. 41.
11. BB8, f.53.
12. Ibid., f.490.
13. Ibid., ff.38,366.
14. Hadley, 289.

15. BB8, f.455.
16. Ibid., ff.87, 89.
17. BB9, ff.409,420.
18. Ibid., ff.620,624.
19. BB10, f.192.
20. *Commons Journals*, xxix, 182.
21. A. Young, *A Six Months Tour through the North of England*, i, 163.
22. BB9, ff. 90, 96.
23. BB8, ff. 38, 423.
24. Ibid., ff. 559, 875.
25. Ibid., f. 681.
26. BB9, f. 352.
27. BB10, ff. 136-7.
28. Ibid., ff. 139-40, 145.
29. ERCRO DDCC 139/64 HUL. Ibid., 11 Dec. 1764; BB9,ff.325,351; Hadley, 337-8.
30. BB8, f.269.
31. Carleton Monckton, 41.
32. BB9, ff.365.
33. Ibid., f.465.
34. BB10, ff.29,103 and *passim*.
35. BB11, ff.333,335.
36. BB9, ff.488,619.
37. BB8, f.763.
38. Ibid., ff.280,307.
39. BB7, f. 732; BB8, ff. 465, 472, 486, 505, 527.
40. BB9, ff.357-9.
41. BB8, ff.803,808,814,820; Carleton Monckton, 42.
42. BB8, f.888; BB9, f.469.
43. BB10, f.230; BB11, f.194.
44. BB9, ff.396,400,425-7.
45. Ibid., ff.469,974; Tickell, 657.
46. BB5, ff.90,97.
47. BB8, f.451.
48. Ibid., ff.39, 41, 625, 641.
49. BB10, f. 235.
50. BB8, f.710.
51. Market Committee Minutes, 1904-5, 16.
52. Walpole Society, *The Diaries of George Vertue; Gentleman's Magazine*, 1734, p. 701.
53. BB8, ff.802,804; BB9, f.66.
54. Ibid., 160.
55. Ibid., ff. 264, 304, 384, 391.
56. ERCRO, Calendar CSF, Michaelmas 1745, file and certificates.
57. Tickell, 612-13.
58. [Hull] *Daily Mail*, 11 Oct. 1949.
59. Tickell, 640.
60. BB9, ff.332,337,342; Hadley, 343.
61. BB9, ff. 377, 408.
62. Ibid., f.399.
63. Cf. Bower's plan, 1791.
64. Tickell, plate opposite 849.
65. BB10, f.186.
66. Ibid., ff.308,313,323.
67. Ibid., ff.430, 447-8.
68. Ibid., f.462.
69.* Ibid., 464. In a tontine the subscribers received an annuity progressively increasing, until the last survivor took the whole of the income.
70.* *HA*, 7 Mar. 1807. His fortune founded the Londesborough peerage for his nephew.
71. BB9, f. 430.
72. *HA*, 18 Oct. and 1 Nov. 1794.
73. *Commons Journals*, vol. 50; 35 Geo. III cap. 46.
74. *HA*, 13 Sept. 1794.
75. *York Courant*, 11 Sept. 1781; 14 Geo III cap. 56.
76. BB8, f.693.
77. Ibid., ff.733-4.
78. *HA*, 13 Dec. 1794.
79. Holy Trinity parish officers' book, ii, 164.
80. A. de la Pryme, MS. History of Hull, 136.
81. (As 79), ii, 165.
82. G. J. Jordan, *The Story of Holy Trinity Parish Church, Hull*, 73, 78.
83. St Mary Lowgate, Churchwardens' accounts, 1720-73.
84. (As 79), ii, 85, 89; *HA*, 28 Oct. 1831.
85. (As 79), i, 148. A. de la Pryme: MS, 170-1.
86. BB9, ff.339,348.
87. BB10, f.362; BB11, ff.131,344.
88. BB12, f.193.
89. J. King, *Memoir of the Revd Thomas Dykes*; BB10, ff.61,68,71,76,80.
90. Ibid., ff.97,115,126; J. King, ibid., 144.
91. T. H. B. Oldfield, v, 276-7.
92. *Daily Post*, 29 Jan. 1724.
93. *VCH*, Hull, 203, footnote 86.
94. BB9, ff.377,379,381.
95. G. H. Guthridge, 'David Hartley M.P. an Advocate of Conciliation 1774-1783', in *University of*

California Publications in History vol. 14, no. 3 (1926) 301 ff.

96. T. H. B. Oldfield, v. 275; BB9, f. 439.
97. Ibid., f.483; L. Namier and J. Brooke, *History of Parliament*, i, 592-3.
98. Ibid., s.v. WILBERFORCE; R. S. Coupland, *William Wilberforce.*
99.*Namier and Brooke, op. cit., s.v. THORNTON, SAMUEL; *VCH*, Hull, 204. Through Marian Thornton much of this fortune descended to E. M. Forster.
100. Namier and Brooke s.v. SPENCER STANHOPE; BB10 f.369.
101. Ibid., ff.369,389; *HA*, 12, 19, 26 June 1802.
102. BB10, f.313.
103. *HA*, 18, 25 Oct. 1806; *VCH*, Hull, 205.
104. T. H. B. Oldfield, v, 278; *R*, 3, 10 Oct.

1812.
105. Ibid., 17 June 1826; *HA*, 26 May 1826.
106. ERCRO DDX/24/25.
107. *R*, 10 Oct. 1812.
108. *HA*, 13 Dec. 1806.
109. BB11, ff.184-5.
110. Ibid., ff.219-25.
111. Ibid., ff.428-30.
112. Journal and Account Book of Robert Broadley, Mar. 1768-Jan. 1773, Brynmor Jones Library, Archives, University of Hull, Ref. DP/146, 18 and 28 Mar. 1768.
113. Ibid., 18 Mar. 1768.
114. BB9, ff.546-7.
115. BB11 f.90.
116. BB12, f.116.
117. BB10, f.170.
110. Ibid., ff.219-25.

17

The Beginnings of the Modern Port

Increasing congestion of shipping in the haven, and pressure from the customs and excise for a legal quay where goods could be appraised (Hull was notorious for evasion of customs duties), at last made it necessary to have a real dock. Between 1716 and 1730 it is thought that the annual tonnage of foreign-going ships entering the port remained at about 11,000 tons; but by 1751 it had more than doubled to 24,000 tons.[1] Shipments of wool give an indication of the scale of Hull's coastwise trade about the middle of the eighteenth century. In 1749, 25,792 tons of wool were brought into Hull by sea from other parts of Britain, and in 1755 this had grown to 36,208 tons.[2]

Additional accommodation for shipping could not be provided on the east bank of the Hull. It was a minor matter that the east side was not in the county of Hull. Much more important was the fact that it was occupied by the Citadel, essential for the defence of the town and the Humber until long after the end of the Napoleonic war. A number of merchants joined with Trinity House in 1743 to petition for a bill for 'enlarging, cleansing and repairing' the haven; but the corporation was able to veto this by requesting the borough members not to present the petition.[3]

There was a vested interest in keeping things as they were. An Act of Elizabeth I, and another of 1662, laid down that all goods except fish must be landed or laden in daytime at open wharves in places where there were resident customs officers. In these statutes, however, Hull alone was expressly named as exempt from these provisions, and smuggling thrived. Officers of the customs were not excluded from the merchants' staithes and the common staithes at the ends of the narrow streets from High Street to the river, but the topography of Hull gave unrivalled opportunities for revenue evasion, and the dilatory habits of customs officers were also an incentive to fraud. Certain Hull merchants in 1756, including Thomas Broadley, Andrew Perrott and Edward Popple prepared plans for a harbour on the Humber bank westwards from the jetty at South End; but they made no provision for a legal quay. This, and the outbreak of war, frustrated the scheme.

There were more proposals between 1764 and 1772, with wrangling between merchants, the bench of aldermen, Trinity House and the customs and excise authorities who insisted that any new scheme must provide for a legal quay 'owing to the irregular manner of conducting business relating to the revenues'.[4] In February 1772 the bench noted the representations of Trinity House on the 'dreadful condition of the harbour dangerous to the town, and destructive to shipping'. Trinity House would support proposals for increased accommodation for shipping, and there were leading merchants anxious for a dock west of the river Hull, with a legal quay. There were others who insisted that a legal quay would 'retard trade to the extent of £6000 to £7000 per annum'. The bench was now ready to proceed with a bill for a dock.[5]

There was much further dispute before the bill took its final form. The contending interests were made to see reason by the threat of customs commissioners to 'establish a legal quay at some other place connected with the Humber'. This was not an empty threat. A petition was submitted to the House of Commons in 1772 from various mercantile interests in the Midlands for a port on the Trent at Gainsborough, which did not actually become a port until 1840.

There were 112 sections to the Dock Act of 1774. It created the Hull Dock Company which was authorised to raise £80,000 in £500 shares and if necessary by loans; and an additional £20,000 could be raised. All the walls, ditches and defences west of the river Hull were vested in the company and £15,000 allocated out of the customs revenues. From the end of 1774 the company had power to levy tonnage rates on shipping entering or leaving the port. Seven years were allowed for the building of the dock, which was to be dug along the line of the wall and ditch between the Hull near North bridge and Beverley Gate, and it was to be as deep as the river bed 'or within fifteen inches thereof'. Accordingly Beverley

Gate and the north walls were demolished in the first stage of port improvement. There were to be legal quays in the dock, and open 'sufferance' quays on newly constructed linked staithes lining the west side of the haven, into which they were not to project more than fifteen feet; and they were to be open to customs officers.[6]

One hundred of the 120 £500 shares were bought locally and the remainder largely by London concerns. Under the act neither the corporation nor Trinity House could take more than ten shares each, and the trustees of the Charterhouse could take two. These early shares were highly profitable. The ten per cent dividend declared in 1780 set the pattern.[7] Trade continued to grow and by 1805 shares had appreciated by about 300 per cent.[8] Some subscribers sold out early. The Hull merchant, William Hammond, in a pamphlet published in 1787, sarcastically listed the names of 'those subscribers who happened to be so TIMOROUS as to sell out, and whose apprehensions of danger to the undertaking happened to exceed their expectations of profit and induced them to sink the interest of the money they had advanced'.[9]

Though seven years were allowed, the completion of the dock within four years was a triumph of civil engineering. Most of the excavated spoil was deposited on ground north of the dock, and the land on which George Street and others were later built was therefore five feet above earlier levels. The dock walls were lined with bricks made near the site and were built on novel but inadequate piling. There was subsidence, particularly on the north side, and at various times some rebuilding was necessary. There was similar difficulty with the entrance lock, where the walls had to be rebuilt in 1785-6; and this lock was completely reconstructed in 1824. A balanced two-leaved drawbridge 'on the Dutch plan' was made over the lock gates which separated the lock from the dock basin. Each leaf could be raised or lowered in thirty seconds. Henry Berry, who had been appointed dock engineer at Liverpool in 1752, was the engineer in charge. The first stone was ceremonially laid by the mayor, Joseph Outram, on 19 October 1775. At the opening festivities in August 1778 the Hull whaler, *Manchester*, with the *Favourite*, 'in all the magnificence of naval triumph' were the first ships to enter.

When the provision of a dock was first considered it had been the intention of the bench that they themselves should undertake the work; but realising the magnitude of the task, they gladly delegated it to the Dock Company, in which their own participation was legally limited. The engineer who actually planned the dock was Henry Berry (1720-1812) the foremost man of his day. It was perhaps because his services were so much in demand elsewhere, and he was so hard a man to find and fix, that the work was formerly wrongly attributed to John Grundy. Much of the actual labour was performed by Irish navvies who flocked to the town. On the advice of Smeaton, a special cement was used for the dock walls, with pozzolana, particularly serviceable for use under water, specially imported from Italy. And it should be added that when they had thought of building the dock themselves the bench had failed to take into account the fact that they did not have the necessary capital.[10]

The ten-acre dock was for a time the biggest in England, but had no name until it became Queen's Dock in 1854. With the development of coastal trade and inland navigation most of the smaller craft berthed in the haven, leaving the improved amenities of the enclosed dock to the whalers and the larger foreign-going ships. The whalers were sometimes laid up in the dock for eight months in the year, and the haven was so overcrowded that it was difficult to pilot a ship to the dock entrance. By 1825 master mariners were complaining that it sometimes happened that the passage from St Petersburg took less time than the odyssey from the Humber between boats, keels and timber-rafts into the dock.[11] As early as 1781 there were proposals for some kind of canal from the dock into the Humber 'through Hessle gates'.[12] The location of the dock still left the town as a port on the river Hull rather than on the Humber estuary. In the 1774 act the clauses abolishing the customs privileges of Hull preceded those dealing with the dock. The primary purpose of the government was to put the port on the same footing as all the others. Some smuggling was still attempted. As near to Hull as made no commercial difference to him, Edmund Barker of Thorne, in 1787 was caught, and fined punitively, shipping more than three tons of wool from Goxhill,[13] on the south bank of the Humber. In 1788 three Swedish vessels in the dock were found with wool hidden among their cargoes, and a ship of one-hundred-and-fifty tons reached Dunkirk with a large cargo of wool from Hull. Interested parties denied that illicit export of wool from Hull was going on.[14]

The decade from the end of the American war and the outbreak of the French war in 1793 saw the fastest growth-rate the port had ever experienced. Customs revenue went up from £86,000 in 1783 to £200,000 in 1793, and in the last five years of this period shipping tonnage inwards rose from just under 140,000 to 200,000.[15] In 1788, 1058 ships, coastal and foreign-going, arrived in the port. Within four years the number had gone up by almost fifty per cent to 1522. Clearly, further dock space was needed and in 1786 the corporation subscribed 300 guineas in support of proposals for a second dock.[16] With the backing of Trinity House and mercantile interests in Lancashire, the West Riding and County Durham, a petition was presented to the House of Commons for a bill to authorise the Dock Company to enlarge its accommodation. The Dock Company, however, was satisfied to leave well alone and earn increasing profits with no further risk.[17] It was not until 1795 that the company was prepared to go ahead with plans for a new dock.[18] There was opposition from those who were anxious to keep the centre of gravity of the port as near as possible to High Street,[19] and the act for the second dock was not passed until the summer of 1802.[20]

This dock, between Hessle Gate and Mytongate, was to have a direct connection with the Humber, to have room for seventy ships, and be completed within seven years. This time half the cost was to be borne by the corporation and Trinity House. The Dock Company was empowered to raise new capital by borrowing and also by the sale of thirty new shares, which sold for an average of £1571 each. Additional powers, including the right to raise further capital by issuing another thirty shares, were given by another act in 1805.[21] The Dock Company was required, upon notice given by the corporation, to lay excavated earth, which it did not need, on the Humber foreshore.[22] This made it possible to reclaim the area south of Humber Street on which Nelson, Wellington and Pier Street were soon to be laid out.[23] Further, the 1802 Act defined the conditions under which the Dock Company would be required to make a *third* dock for sixty ships between Mytongate and Beverley Gate. This would be when the average tonnage of shipping for three years bore the same proportion to the area of the two docks as that for the years 1791-3 bore to the area of the first dock.

The eminent engineer John Rennie was responsible for the Humber Dock project, with William Chapman as resident engineer. A problem not encountered with the first dock was the great depth of soft mud, and silting by mud from the Humber. It would have been impossible to make proper foundations for the dock walls without mechanical dredging. The effectiveness of the steam bucket-dredger which Rennie designed was such that Samuel Smiles wrongly credited him with its invention. It raised 300 tons of mud a day from a depth of twenty-two feet, and when the dock was completed, removed 36,000 tons of mud each year. It is therefore not surprising that the Humber dock cost over £233,000 or about ten times the sum which had been thought necessary when the first proposals were made in the 1780s. The opening was early in the morning on 30 June 1809 with bands playing and cannon firing while the *Effort* was warped in with her yards manned by Trinity House boys.

Largely because of the reduction in continental trade caused by the war, fewer ships were using the port. The tonnage plunged from 210,000 in 1802 to 79,000 in 1809; but from 1810 many more continental ports were open and the tonnage rose to 173,000. By the end of the war in 1815 it was 265,000.[24] By 1825 dock dues were being paid on 449,000 tons and the criteria laid down for a third dock were now satisfied.

The military works between the former Beverley Gate and Mytongate had long been levelled. Immediately to the west and extending as far as Tanhouse Lane (Waterhouse Lane) was the new livestock market established in 1782. The corporation in 1818 decided to sell it to the Dock Company in preparation for the third dock and actually did sell it in 1821 for £10,000.[25] In 1819 the Dock Company made proposals for its third dock, and then almost immediately dropped them. There was a meeting of merchants and shipowners concerned about competition from Goole and Selby.[26] The rivalry of Selby had been noted in 1819 as a compelling reason for a new dock in 1823. The bench appointed three aldermen to confer with Trinity House and the Dock Company about the threat raised by the Goole and Knottingley canal.[27] The Act for the third dock was passed to the satisfaction of the majority of Hull interests in 1824.[28]

After Telford had reported on the project for the exchequer loan commissioners, work on the Junction Dock began in 1826 with James Walker as chief and Thomas Thornton resident engineer. It was opened on 1 June 1829 with the usual festivities

5. Humber Dock and the Mariners' Church, Dagger Lane, built 1834.

6. S.S. *Forfarshire* in the Humber c. 1839.

and the Trinity House yacht, dressed overall, sailed right round the whole site of the town through the docks and the haven. Though part of the town was now outside the ring of docks, access to its oldest and still most important part was over the bridge at the Whitefriargate lock, known after 1835 as Monument Bridge because of the monument to Wilberforce standing there. It took about five minutes to work a ship through, and this often closed the road to all traffic six to eight times in an hour.

The completion of the line of river-improvements and canals linking the Humber and Trent with the Mersey was roughly contemporary with the first of these three docks;[29] and by 1790 Hull was linked by canals and waterways with Birmingham, Liverpool, Bristol and London.[30] Lead from Derbyshire, Nottingham and Derbyshire hosiery, much in demand in northern Europe, the iron and brass products and general hardware from Birmingham and the Midlands, the pottery and light-metal products of Stoke and the Potteries came in barges and small boats to the Humber and Hull for local distribution or onward shipment coastwise or overseas. In return, groceries, foodstuffs, timber and Swedish iron made up keel cargoes for the widening Midlands. Improvements in the river Don between 1726 and 1740 assisted the movement of south Yorkshire iron and steel to the Humber, and by 1819 the canal had reached Sheffield itself. As well as iron and steel products and cutlery, building stone, plaster and the farm produce of the Doncaster area now came to Hull.

The eighteenth-century expansion of Hull was also connected with the huge growth of West Riding textiles. Up to the end of the seventeenth century cloth from Leeds usually travelled overland to York and then by the Ouse to Hull. It cost six shillings to get £100 of cloth from Leeds to York, but only eighteenpence to move it from York to Hull.[31] Between 1699 and 1828 four Aire and Calder Navigation Acts gave the West Riding effective communication with Hull by a cheap and direct route. By 1797 it cost a shilling to carry a hundredweight of goods from Wakefield to Hull, and 1*s* 6*d* to get them from Huddersfield. Even Lancashire textiles were involved. By 1810 Manchester merchants were describing Hull as 'the quay through which our manufacturers alone find a passsage for the markets of Germany, Switzerland and the borders of Italy'.

The local need for road improvements was urgent. In the middle of the eighteenth century travellers between Hull and Kirkella had to make a three-or four-mile detour because much of the road was impassable. The turnpike from Hull to Beverley[32] was opened in 1744, with toll bars at Newland and Woodmansey, and these remained in use until the tolls on the road were abolished in 1871. There was a proposal in 1764, not carried into effect, that Cottingham should be linked with the road as the farmers and gardeners found it impossible to use carts and had to bring their produce to Hull on horseback. The turnpike from Hull to Kirkella[33] was opened in 1745, and in the same year the corporation supported a Hedon proposal for a turnpike from there through Preston, Wyton and Bilton to the North Bridge at Hull.[34] Most of the East Riding was turnpiked before 1800.

Two turnpike Acts which came later gave Hull two new main roads. The pleasant Wold country to the west of Hull was attractive to those who could afford to live away from their place of business. As early as 1789, J. R. Pease, the banker and industrialist, had built his elegant mansion at Hesslewood. Charles Frost, a solicitor and historian, was similarly situated. To those who could come into Hull daily on horseback or by carriage a turnpike road was attractive. The corporation was unenthusiastic, and the Hull-Anlaby-Kirkella turnpike trustees were opposed to any road to the west which might compete with theirs, but the Act for the Hull-Hessle-Ferriby turnpike was passed in 1825.[35] This made Hessle Road, and tolls were collected until 1873. A scheme for turnpiking Dansom Lane to Ings Road to give better connection with Sutton failed to get enough support in 1826. There was no direct route to Hedon, but although the corporation gave little support Frost and the other promoters got their act in 1830 for a new road from Great Union Street in Hull to Hedon, and Hedon Road came into being in 1833.[36]

The original North Bridge had a lifting span in the centre to allow the passage of ships. It was re-built in 1676 and substantially repaired in 1719.[37] As the haven became more congested shipmasters were tempted to moor to the bridge, and the bridgemaster was therefore empowered to cut all such moorings and to see that no bowsprits hung over or rested on it.[38] A more substantial bridge was needed, and on the recommendation of Smeaton his former assistant, John Gwyn, was employed to supervise its building,[39] the old bridge remaining in use until it was completed. Gwyn's substantial stone bridge of four arches with a central drawbridge' was finished in 1787. By 1831 it was urgently necessary to reconstruct it. James Oldham was retained as the superintending engineer, and George Leather, who had worked on the Pocklington Canal and at Goole, as the man actually in charge.[40] While work was in progress the bridge could not be used, and a temporary bridge had to be erected to keep open the road to Holderness and the route by which much of the nightsoil was removed to fertilise the land. Partly because of the need for a temporary bridge, the work cost £4000 more than had been estimated.

The Humber ferries were the subject of numerous disputes, none of which produced any real improvement in the service; but in 1815 the corporation was in possession of all the ferry rights of any importance and in 1821 leased them to the proprietors of the Barton-London coach service. They used a steam packet instead of the usual hoy. Their paddle-steamer *Waterloo* made two daily crossings each way, and when she was replaced by the superior *Royal Charter* in 1826 there were four crossings each day.[41] The ferry-boat had for centuries started from the Horse Staithe, just inside the haven, until under an act of 1801 the corporation was empowered to make a ferry-boat dock.[42] This was not really a dock but a pier parallel to the Humber bank at the east end of Queen Street, acting as a breakwater giving some shelter in rough weather. Nevertheless, the municipal corporation's inquiry commissioners in 1833 noted that a superintendent was employed at £5 a year with duties which included opening and closing of the gates of a non-existent dock.[43]

By the 1660s the Dutch had entirely taken over the northern whale fishery, but soon the Americans, sailing from Nantucket, were also taking whales, and American whale-oil was coming to England. Such Hull merchants as Christopher Scott and James Hamilton were active importers. The demand for whale-oil lamps, for lubricating and for soap-making and the processing of leather and wool was increasing. The French and Indian wars greatly reduced American supplies from 1752 until 1762. The British government offered a subsidy of 2*s* a ton on whalers of 200 tons and above; and James Hamilton, therefore, in 1754 sent the *York* direct to Greenland. Three other ships were fitted out by the Hull Whale Fishery Company, and the venture was a success until

American imports were started again in 1762.

Tension with the American colonists brought the imposition of a duty on American oil and the continuance of the subsidy on whalers encouraged Samuel Standidge to send the *Berry* from Hull in 1766 to fish for whales. She brought back one whale and 300 seal-skins. One whale and no more might have ruined him, but the seal-skins provided him with the capital needed to make him a successful whale-ship owner. His innovation was to get country tanners to process seal-skins, which the Dutch had ignored and Hull tanners had refused to handle.[44] He sent a ship whaling in 1767, and another in 1768. Others followed his example. Seven Hull ships were whaling in 1770, nine in 1772 and twelve in 1775, when two were lost.[45]

The whale-ship bounty was reduced in 1777 to 30*s* a ton, but Hull and other ports petitioned for the restoration of the old rates 'having cause to fear that since the rupture between Great Britain and the United Provinces (i.e. Holland) the navigation to the Greenland seas and Davis's straits will be attended with more peril than heretofore'.[46] The old rate was restored in 1781. Nine of the eighty-nine ships engaged in whaling in 1784 came from Hull, and fourteen out of 140 in 1785. In spite of the impressment of seamen for the navy in the war with France after 1793 and occasional captures by French cruisers, the number of Hull whalers rose from twenty-four in 1790 to thirty-eight in 1805 and fifty-seven in 1815. There were good seasons and bad, irrespective of the number of ships fitted out. In 1790 each Hull ship on an average produced no more than thirty-six tons of oil. With some fluctuations, there was a steady increase in productivity, and each ship by the end of the war was producing sixty-six tons of oil. In 1805 and 1820 the amount was over 130 tons for each ship, and between 1814 and 1817 Hull was by far the biggest whaling port in Britain.[47]

The whale-ship subsidy was reduced in 1787, 1792 and 1795, when it was no more than £1 a ton. The corporation had petitioned in 1786 for a continuance of the higher rate, pointing out that 'the seamen bred in this nursery were the hardiest and most adventurous race always ready at the shortest notice to man H.M. ships of war in case of a sudden rupture with any foreign power'.[48] The latter part of the proposition was a prudent way of saying that the press-gangs were perhaps keener to catch whale-men, if they could, than any others. Expansion of Hull whaling went on in spite of the press-gang and the reduction of the subsidy, partly because there was now a good market for whale-bone as well as for oil. The whale-bone manufactory in South Street advertised sieves, gratings, ornamental blinds and chopping blocks, and Mr Samuel Crackles of Hull in 1808 was able to supply patent whale-bone brushes for cleaning roads, chimneys and ships. Further, the temporary suspension of tallow imports from Russia increased the demand for whale-oil to be used in street-lamps.

The life of a whaler was extremely dangerous, but the rewards were high. John Sanderson, surgeon, sailed for Greenland in the Hull whaler *Samuel* in March 1787. The ship was leaking badly and had to put in at Lerwick for repairs, but, Sanderson wrote, 'she still made a great deal of water. Her sides appeared to be very weak. The seams in her upper decks opened considerably and she was very weak in her upper joints.' He thought that it ought to be the responsibility of customs officers to examine whalers 'to see they are sound and proper for a voyage of this kind'. But in spite of these difficulties the *Samuel* was back in port with six whales before the end of July.[49]

In 1775 ten whalers left Hull. Six returned with no whales at all and two were lost; but in 1794 the *Egginton* caught fifteen whales, 3000 seals and five bears, all within a hundred days, and in the same year did two voyages to St Petersburg. The *Progress* in 1828 took fourteen whales in four days. In some years losses were unusually severe, though the crew of a whaler crushed in the ice usually had a good chance of being rescued. Five vessels out of thirty-three were lost in 1808, and nine out of sixty-one in 1821. Six of the thirty-three Hull whalers fitted out in 1830 were lost in Baffin Bay. The *Abram* brought the news to Hull. A subscription was made in aid of the distressed seamen and families as the pay of a crew ceased from the day the ship was lost. Danger had been greatly increased by the reduction of the number of whales east of Greenland and in the Davis Straits as a result of so many being killed. Whalers were venturing much further north into Baffin and Melville Bays.[50]

In 1835 five Hull ships were frozen in and only two of them escaped. The *Swan*, owned by Messrs Spyvee and Cooper, was given up for lost. The next year, according to tradition, a memorial service was being held for her crew on Dock Green and a collection of £47 had already been taken when the news came that she had entered the Humber.[51] Such escapes seemed miraculous. After four years in the Arctic, Commodore John Ross and his crew were rescued by William Humphreys, master of the Hull whaler *Isabella*, in which he had once sailed.[52]

The most famous of the Hull whale-ships was the *Truelove*. She was a three-masted barque built at Philadelphia in 1764, captured during the American War of Independence. Between 1784 and 1868 she made seventy-two voyages to Greenland, Davis Straits and Spitzbergen. In 1864 when she was a hundred years old she was the only Hull whaler sent to the Arctic and was feted on her return to Philadelphia in 1873. For several years she was then employed in bringing ice from Norway for Hull fishing smacks, and ended as a coal-hulk in the Thames.[53]

When the industry was at the height of its success whale-ships accounted for fifteen per cent of the inward (foreign-going) tonnage; and for many years the air was polluted with the smell of the Greenland yards where blubber was boiled and whale-bone cleansed. There was public rejoicing on the safe return of a whaler, especially if she had been 'nipped' and had been forced to winter in the ice. As she docked, Trinity House boys manned the yards, and as soon as the men were paid (the wages could be up to £60 after a successful voyage) there was a spending spree. And, as the unsympathetic poor-law commissioners observed, within a few weeks of a ship's return, the family of many a whaling man had to be relieved out of the rates.[54]

After 1820, as the number of northern whales decreased and voyages became less profitable, Hull merchants gradually ceased to be interested in whaling and looked at new commercial possibilities. Within twenty years the number of whaling ships declined from sixty-three to only twenty-seven in 1833. Scottish ports, which had a stronger interest in sealing, sent out whalers until as late as 1913;[55] but in 1861 only six whalers left Hull. In 1869 the *Diana*, then the only ship still sailing—she was actually a screw steamer with sails—was lost on Donna Nook, and Hull whaling came to an end.

Sources

1. G. Jackson, 'The Struggle for the First Hull Dock', *Transport History*, i, no. 1 (Mar. 1968) 27.
2. BB9, f.239.
3. Ibid., f. 40; W. G. East, 'The Port of Kingston-upon-Hull during the Industrial Revolution', *Economica*, xi (1931) 193.
4. BB9, ff.412-15; *Commons Journals*, xliii, 537.
5. I. S. Beckwith in *Lincolnshire History and Archaeology*, ii, 8 ff.
6. 14 Geo. III, cap. 56.
7. Hull Dock Company Minutes, 2 Feb. 1780.
8. BB10, ff.455-6.
9. W. Hammond; *Remarks on a Publication . . .*(1787).
10. *Transactions of the Institute of Civil Engineers*, i (1836), 1 ff; G. Jackson, *Hull in the Eighteenth Century*, 243-6.
11. *Commons Journals*, lxxiv, 140.
12. Ibid., xlix, 220; BB9, f.557.
13. J. Mayhall, *Annals of York, Leeds and the Surrounding District*, 167.
14. Hadley, 412-15.
15. Tickell, 870.
16. Hull Dock Company MSS 29/13-14.
17. *Commons Journals*, xlii, 51.
18. Ibid., vol. 50, p. 51.
19. Hull Dock Company MSS 29/156 and *passim*.
20. Hull Dock Company MSS 29/170; 42 Geo. III, cap. 91.
21. BB10, f.328; 45 Geo. III, cap. 42.
22. BB10, ff.333, 335, 338.
23. BB11, f.50.
24. J. M. Bellamy, *The Trade and Shipping of Nineteenth Century Hull*, 61; S. Watson, *The Reign of George III*, 515.
25. BB9, ff.562, 576; BB11, ff.187-8.
26. *HA*, 26 June 1819.
27. *HA*, 20 Sept., BB11, f.296.
28. 5 Geo. IV cap. 52.
29. J. Priestley, *Historical Account of the Navigable Rivers, Canals and Railways throughout Great Britain*, (1967 reprint), 418-30.
30. T. S. Ashton, *An Economic History of England: the 18th Century*, 89.
31. T. S. Willan, *River Navigation in England, 1600-1750*, 38.
32. K. A. MacMahon, *Acts of Parliament . . .*, op. cit., 31, No. 95.
33. Ibid., No. 96.
34. Ibid., No. 97.
35. 6 Geo. IV, cap. 152.
36. 11 Geo. IV, cap. 96.
37. BB8, ff. 36, 86-8, 693.
38. Ibid., ff.834, 848.
39. BB9, ff.621-2, 624.
40. BB12, ff.35, 43, 51, 55.
41. BB11, ff.248, 251, 259.
42. 41 Geo. III, cap. 65.
43. MC, 1554, 1561-2.
44. J. Craggs, *Guide to . . . Hull* (1817) 66.
45. H. Munroe, 'Statistics of the Northern Whale Fisheries from the year 1772 to 1852',

Journal of the Royal Statistical Society, xvii (1854); G. Jackson, *Hull in the Eighteenth Century*, 159.

46. Hadley, 362.
47. MC, 1573.
48. BB10, f.12.
49. J. Sanderson, *A Voyage from Hull to Greenland . . . in 1789*; W. Barron, *An Apprentice's Reminiscences of Whaling in the Davis Straits* (1890).
50. J. Leslie, R. Jameson, H. Murray, *Narrative of Discovery and Adventure in the Polar Seas and Regions* (1845); W. Scoresby, *Journal of a Voyage to the Northern Whale Fishery*, App. vi, 453.
51. S. Cooper-Scott, *Things that were* (1923) 11.
52. Sheahan, 205; *DNB* s.v. ROSS, SIR JOHN (1777-1856).
53. B. Lubbock, *Arctic Whaling* (1927).
54. Cooper-Scott, op. cit., 12.
55. S. G. E. Lythe in *Scottish Journal of Political Economy*, xi, 158-69.

18

Hull and the War, 1793—1815

There was war for most of the period in which the town was feeling the effects of the industrial revolution, and from 1793 until the final peace of 1815 the impact of war also was felt profoundly. The first refugee from the French Revolution was seen when the Marquis de la Sierre arrived from St Petersburg,[1] just as the infantry volunteers were being requested not to use Holy Trinity as their winter drill hall.[2] The *Hull Advertiser* wrote:'The vicar of Holy Trinity Church, for some reason we are yet unacquainted with, has signified to the different companies of volunteers his disapprobation of their assembling in the body of that Church to perform their exercise'. They were never more than amateurs who could afford uniforms. One summer Thursday in 1795 they had a field day with the Cottingham volunteers, at Cottingham, with one casualty from blank ammunition.[3] 'During the performance of the platoon exercise, one of the soldiers having left his ramrod in the firelock, on discharging the piece the ramrod entered and very nearly went through Captain Outram's leg, grazing the bone in its passage.' Patriotism made them volunteers, but it also ensured that their names would not be drawn in the militia ballot, which would put them on permanent duty for five years and under strict military discipline in some remote part of Britain or Ireland. They did serve a purpose in putting down riots and as a substitute police force. When there were too many burglaries in the dark nights of 1800 they patrolled the streets and arrested suspects.[4]

Before the war had caused distress there were fervent outbreaks of patriotism. July was the month for the parades of the friendly societies of which twenty-five had had their rules confirmed by the bench before the outbreak of war.[5]

> The utmost loyalty, good order and regularity was conspicous in their assemblies. Most of them after having heard divine service in the morning, paraded the streets of the town, preceded by a band of music and colours flying. The music played loyal and patrotic tunes, and the colours were ornamented with inscriptions significant of their attachment to the Constitution, and of the names of the respective Societies to which they belonged. Then they adjourned to dinner and spent the rest of the day in peaceable conviviality . . . a member of one of the societies having refused to drink a constitutional toast was immediately expelled.[6]

Some were real friendly societies, others merely social clubs and many also organisations for getting money and treats out of MPs and candidates. There were another twenty-six which had not yet been registered, including one named Church and King, which was probably safe, and another, the Revolution Society, which was not. But war with France had turned former revolutionaries into friends, and on Independence Day the masters of U.S. ships entertained their Hull friends on board.

This summer patriotism was entirely spoiled by the press-gang. Previously the authorities looked the other way when men were being caught for the navy. There had been no record of any friction with the naval officers responsible since 1741 when Captain Gascoign of the tender *Diligence* stationed in the Humber resisted the constables with a pistol after he had threatened an alderman, and several of his crew had assaulted an anchor-smith.[7] Captain O'Hara was presented with a silver box in 1777 'for his humane conduct and attention to the peace of this town in his station of regulating officer'.[8] But now, after the friendly societies had put their flags away, a Hull jury had found a verdict of wilful murder against Captain Essington for his attack on a Hull whaler at sea, and his chances of acquittal were so slight that the Admiralty immediately sent him to India. The case and the feeling against him were so strong that he was kept in continuous service until 1810 and so inevitably became a Vice-Admiral. He was then brought back to stand his trial at the Admiralty sessions in 1810, on the motion of Mr William Bell, of Hull, to the Attorney General, which may well have been a smart piece of deception.[9] When he apppeared for trial it was found that all the papers relating to his case had been lost.[10]

What happened in 1794 was this. The Hull whaler, *Sarah and Elizabeth*, was homeward bound from Davis Strait. She was intercepted by Captain Essington, anxious to press seamen for his frigate *Aurora*. On the approach of the frigate the crew battened themselves in the hold. Laying the *Aurora* beside the whaler the captain prepared to use hand grenades until the master of the whaler told him that the explosion would probably blow up both ships. He then put a party of marines on board, and, acting on his orders, they fired down the hatchway, killing Edward Bogg, carpenter's mate, and wounding the bosun and two others. Victorious so far, he took away most of the crew in irons.[11] On 22 July he was off Flamborough Head and sent a letter to the mayor, putting the whole of the blame on the whale-men. They had wounded his men, the master was no longer in control, and 'considered her in a state of piracy'. Her crew had said 'that before any of her men should be taken some blood should be spilt'. But he did not appear to tell any of this to the coroner's jury who returned a verdict against him of wilful murder. J. R. Pease, the Hull banker, and no fire-brand, was so indignant that he went to London to cause an investigation to be held and got fourteen of the crew, including harpooners, the carpenter and the second mate, released from the navy.[12]

Pease had already made his attitude plain in the courts. At the Hull assizes he had been on the grand jury with such magnates as Richard Tottie, the oil-miller, of Anlaby, Robert Schonswar, the timber merchant, Joshua Haworth and Henry Sykes of Westella. No case could go forward for trial by jury until they had agreed that it should. The one vital case they had to consider was that of Mark Bolt who had shot Charles Darley, a member of a press gang, in the chest. The press-gang wore no uniforms and it might be held, as the jurors at an inquest had held, that their cries that they were acting in the King's name did not make it clear that they were not really common criminals. They therefore considered that Mark Bolt had committed manslaughter in self-defence, and it was on this peculiar charge that he would be tried if the grand jury agreed. The judge told them that if they did anything else they would not be regarded as friends of the constitution and might be suspected of 'being encouragers of resistance in the common people'. Nevertheless, though the *Advertiser* described them as 'persons of unquestionable loyalty and steady friends of government' they threw out the indictment, a clear sign of the unanimous indignation caused by the encounter between the *Aurora* and the whaler.[13]

Even the aldermen showed an unusual sympathy with popular feeling. Captain Blackwood of the *Nonsuch*, the guardship to which pressed men were removed, asked the mayor, William Bolton, to help him in finding seamen. He was sharply told that 'the best and most expeditious way' would be to let men who had been pressed stay near home as part of the crew of his ship.[14] Formerly the bench had offered bounties to volunteers for the navy—in 1756 three guineas for an able—and two for an ordinary seaman; and in 1781 they had offered the same bounties.[15] Under the quota system Hull had to find 731 men for the navy, which itself offered, but did not always pay, bounties of £31 5s for an able-seaman, £23 10s for an ordinary seaman and £17 5s for an able-bodied landsman. There were too few volunteers and in Hull impressment went on until 1815.

The Hull mob, which often meant most of the poor, could not have been kept down without the militia, which never consisted of local men who might sympathise with them. The Earl of Euston's Suffolk Militia had put down the disgraceful anti-Catholic riots of 1780.[16] Food riots by people on the verge of starvation were a different matter. In 1795 it was hoped that corn bought by a relief committee would keep prices down, but at a Tuesday market in August there was a rise in the price of flour. Women and boys began breaking windows on the dock-side, and a party of the Surrey Militia was called out to disperse them. Since worse trouble was feared the well-affected were sworn in as special constables while the independent cavalry and the volunteers stood by to uphold the constitution.[17] Since it was inedible, the poor did not care whether it was upheld or not so long as they had the means of keeping body and soul together. Their plight was desperate, and may well have become worse as the war went on. In 1789 during a severe winter, nearly a third of the population was 'found to exist in this place almost without fire or food.'[18] In June 1796 nine-hundred families, thought to include one-eighth of the population, depended on the Hull Incorporation of the Poor, from which each family received just over a shilling a week, considerably less than a labourer earned in a single day.[19]

The riots of May 1796 were more serious.[20] Again the trouble was started by a rise in the price of flour. Women and boys chased a miller to his house and broke the windows until a detachment of the Nottinghamshire Militia arrived. The Revd Barnard Foord and another magistrate then read the Riot Act, and most of the mob went home. That was only the beginning.

> The next day being market day the mob again assembled in the market place and different parts of the town and compelled the butchers and country people to part with meat, butter, poultry, eggs etc. at prices of their own fixing, besides wasting great quantities by throwing them about the streets in the most wanton manner. They then went to the place where the market-boats land and there committed similar depredations on the property of people who bring provisions from Lincolnshire etc. Several of the ringleaders were apprehended.

If the writer felt any sympathy with the mob the fact that he had recently had to report the imprisonment of the editor of the *Sheffield Iris* would be enough to keep him quiet.

Those who could afford the price of a theatre-ticket, however, were still fervent patriots. When Prince William of Gloucester, the King's brother, 'attended the theatre the strongest expressions of loyalty repeatedly burst forth'.[21] He was the first member of the royal family to come to Hull since Charles I. He reviewed the Surrey Militia, a troop of the Hanoverian cavalry and the volunteers. He was received at the citadel with a royal salute of guns and at the *Nonsuch* with another. Samuel Standidge, then mayor, presented him with the freedom of the borough and he was made a brother of Trinity House and 'partook of an elegant entertainment provided by the mayor'.

There were festivities and a general illumination when the news of the victory at Camperdown arrived in October 1797. The captured Dutch ships were watched by crowds on the Holderness cliffs as they came along the coast. The *Vestal, Endymion, Isis* and *Ethalian* escorted the prizes *Jupiter*, a 74, and *De Vries*, a 68, to Hull and the sick and wounded were brought ashore to hospitals provided by Mr J. Kirkman. No such hostility was felt against these Dutch prisoners as against the French, and a subscription was opened for them.[22]

Earlier in the same year there had been the great naval mutinies. One of the Sheerness men had formerly been in the *Nonsuch* at

Hull;[23] and because of sympathy with the mutiny the *Circe*, frigate, and the *Hart*, brig-cutter, had to return to Hull. A bosun's mate had been urging the men to join the mutineers; and four men from the *Inspector* had been put in the Hull house of correction in Whitefriargate for mutinous talk.[24]

In 1798 the press-gang again roused great indignation. Lieutenant Loten of the impress-service as he was going home from the rendezvous (the headquarters of the press-gang) was attacked by a sailor with a large Greenland knife. He was rescued, slightly wounded, and the seaman was taken and put on board the *Nonsuch*. A mob assembled and broke the windows of the rendezvous and other houses. Three of the aldermen were unable to persuade them to go home, and the danger of a general uprising was such that the 4th and 5th West York Supplementary Militia were called out to patrol the streets for three hours with the armed association, the infantry volunteers and the yeomanry cavalry.[25]

At the end of July the whaler *Blenheim* arrived in the Humber from Greenland. The *Nonsuch* and the *Redoubt* fired several shots to bring her to, with the intention of taking most of her crew, but she held her course. Boats were then sent in pursuit, but the boarding parties were persuaded with harpoons and flensing knives not to leave their boats. The *Nautilus*, sloop of war, joined in the chase, but the *Blenheim* still held her course, the crew having locked the master and the pilot in the cabin. They got her as far as the mouth of the haven, where she grounded. Shots were fired from the boarding parties in the boats, and the *Blenheim* fired a swivel loaded with grape shot, which killed at least one man. Crowds of spectators stood at the garrison side, the shipyards in Humber Street, and the ferry-boat jetty to enjoy the contest in spite of the risk from bullets. All the whale-men got ashore.[26]

Resentment of the navy was more intense because French and Dutch privateers were far too numerous to be controlled. From time to time some were taken. Three Frenchmen taken from a Dutch vessel driven into Saltfleet by gales were almost the first prisoners to be brought to Hull, at the end of 1794. French prisoners brought to Scarborough after the capture of their lugger-privateer were marched to Hull by the Ayrshire Light Dragoons;[27] but Hull seamen were being captured in far greater numbers. News of them frequently arrived in letters from prisoners in France, or as a result of the privateers' friendly habit of sending prisoners home in some craft they did not want, as they were far more interested in commerce-raiding than in men. Two Hull crews in 1797 actually arrived home the day after sailing as a result of this custom. They belonged to the *Eagle* and the *Jupiter*, taken off the Humber by the *Intrepide*, then seven days out from Dunkirk with a total of ten prizes. The captain did not want either the prisoners or the *Eliza*, a Yarmouth brig, in which they sailed to Hull. One reason for this friendly feeling was that 'a great many of the seamen on board the privateer appeared to be Englishmen, for they spoke the language with the greatest fluency, and said the lugger-privateer was close inshore'.[28]

Most captures, as in earlier wars, were made near the English coast, but it was far out in the Atlantic that the *Expedition* of Hull was taken by a privateer of twelve guns a little to the windward of Barbados. Smith, the master and six of the crew had been removed on board the privateer when she sighted another prize and gave chase. The mate and the carpenter were still on board the *Expedition* with two boys, and decided to make their escape. They crowded on all sail. The privateer tried to disable her by firing at her masts and sails, but no shot took effect and on the following day she reached the island and was moored with the help of the navy.[29] And though the life of a seaman in the navy could be appalling, a very few had good luck. Thomas Branton of Preston in Holderness, taken by the press-gang, had engaged himself to marry Jane Watts of Hull, and in 1800 sent her a hundred guineas, his share of the prize money earned when the *Alcmene* captured a Spanish frigate.[30]

For most, 1800 was a terrible year, hardly enlivened by the visit of the Russian general, Arbeneff, and his inspection of the huge militia force which it was still thought necessary to keep in Hull—the third West York Militia, the East Sussex Militia and the Sussex Fencible Cavalry.[31] Famine was so near that Wednesday, 12 March was observed as a fast day. 'The churches and chapels were particularly well attended and the prayer for relief from the effects of the present scarcity was devoutly heard by all well-affected people.'[32] In spite of the increase in poverty the poor rates were 'lowered by one half and the imposters on the charity detected and exposed'.[33] To show their appreciation of this economic miracle the Grocers' Company, meeting at the Ball and Sun in Mytongate, resolved to present an inscribed silver plate costing £50 to Thomas Thompson Esquire 'governor of the poor of this town for his meritorious and valuable services rendered to the inhabitants by introducing a system of economy and industry into the workhouse'.[34]

The serious intestinal epidemic with a high mortality which prevailed in Hull that year as well as in many other places was probably connected with near-starvation. Almost three-quarters of the people were thought to have had it, often with dysentry, and it was particularly fatal to babies and the elderly.[35] The well-known reluctance of the poor to die without a protest resulted in combinations of workers to raise wages. This expedient was illegal under Acts of 1795 and 1799; and two shoemakers of Hull, Thompson and Smith, were tried at York assizes and sent to Newgate for nine months for trying to form a combination to raise wages to keep up with prices.[36] By 2 May eight vessels had arrived from Hamburg and two from Rostock, all with corn.[37] Wheat came down 5s a quarter, and then down to £5 10s, which was still a famine price, with corn arriving from Hamburg, Bremen, Emden, Rostock and Königsberg.[38] Other food was so dear that the ancient and illegal practice of forestalling the market was revived. The *Hull Advertiser* wrote in July: 'In this town the evil has reached that height that people are met coming from the country and their butter, eggs etc. almost forcibly taken from them at a high price, and several instances have occurred of things thus unfairly bought being instantly sold for a good profit.'[39]

As usual millers were blamed for high corn prices, and may not have been entirely innocent. In 1795 the Anti-mill was built by a consumers' co-operative. 1800 was thought to be a good year for printing 'a neat west view of the Anti-mill supposed to be the largest windmill in England'.[40] It was far from the town but this was no obstacle to its success. The mill tower stood in a yard between Balfour and Arundel Streets on the south side of Holderness Road until about fifty years ago. Because of its success another non-profit venture, the Subscription-mill had its foundation stone laid in 1800, rather nearer the inhabited part of the town, in Dansom Lane. William Osborne, who laid the stone, gave ten guineas, Sir Samuel Standidge five and Samuel Thornton MP fifty.[41] At the end of September all the mills had been stopped by several windless days and it was feared that a shortage of flour would start riots such as had happened in other parts of the country. When a wind came on a Saturday evening grinding went on all night and bread was immediately baked and sold on the Sunday, though a recent law required all bread to be twenty-four hours old.[42]

The short-lived peace of Amiens (1802-3) brought some changes, and left some matters as they were. Some of the seamen discharged from the navy drew up to £100 in wages 'from the collector of customs for this port, pursuant to the highly laudable regulations adopted by the lords of the Treasury for the payment at their own homes of this meritorious but too thoughtless and extravagant class of Britons'.[43] But the town was no longer full of troops to back up the authorities. At a Saturday market in July 1802 some hucksters tried to raise the price of peas from 4*d* to 6*d* a peck. The mob then wrecked all the market stalls and looted the butchers' shops, so that some families were seen carrying whole carcasses away. The magistrates appeared and read the Riot Act, but as there was no one to shoot at them the mob chased their masters into the town hall. Every window was broken, so that the magistrates, who were said to be armed with pistols, had to retreat into an inner room while the kitchen was wrecked and the utensils thrown into the street. This went on until the rioters had had enough.[44]

Before the peace was actually ratified the press-gang was no longer needed, and it was thought appropriate to present Captain William James with his freedom and a cup worth thirty guineas 'for his very humane and exemplary conduct during the time he was employed as regulating officer in the impress service at this port'.[45] As soon as the war restarted in 1803 Lieutenant W. H. Dillon, who lived to be a Vice-Admiral, was posted to Hull as an officer in the impress service under Commander Grey, who never rose any higher than post-captain. He had a letter of introduction from Lord Hawke to the collector of customs and to the mayor and aldermen, who received him cordially and hospitably. But he was made aware of his real situation from the moment of his arrival. Meeting a former shipmate (his own description), the sail-maker in the *Crescent*, he greeted him as a friend, only to find that the friend fled as soon as he learned what his employment was. One of the men he captured, a carpenter, was so valuable to his employers that they offered £300 for his release, and his wife tried to organise a rescue. He escaped by jumping through the closed window of an upper room to which he had been brought for medical examination. On one occasion Dillon was pelted with brickbats, and one evening as he was reading, a volley of shot was fired through his window. He soon had enough men for the frigate *Caroline* to be brought to receive them, marines being landed to prevent any attempt at a rescue. He was sad at leaving Hull when his posting came as he was in love, or at any rate thought that 'a very advantageous match would have been arranged'. He never wore uniform when out with his gang.[46]

This form of kidnapping, legal only because of long usage, went on year after year, and was so apt to rouse the mob that a large garrison was always needed. A sailor was impressed in 1808 just after he had reached home after a voyage prolonged by his ship being frozen in the Baltic. A man who lived near the gaol had his windows broken by a mob as he was believed to have betrayed him to the press-gang. Troops were called out to protect him.[47] In 1810 Captain Croft courted popularity, and gave his men a rest and opportunity for reconnaissance, by announcing that there would now be no impressment on a Sunday.[48] There was a riot as late as May 1815 when a mob rescued a man taken by the press and wrecked the pub used as their rendezvous.[49*]

Sailor-lads who had been apprenticed carried protections against impressment. Those belonging to whalers were thought to be particularly disorderly, and people who were completely safe from impressment suggested that the press should nevertheless take these boys because of their bad behaviour. 'On Sundays in particular it is scarcely possible for a woman to pass along the streets without suffering the grossest insults, particularly in Whitefriargate.'[50] But even the respectable had to take their chance of being balloted for the militia, and it was advisable to insure against this risk. Subscribers to Bell and Hendry's militia insurance for a premium of £2 18s received £20 if their name was drawn, but the cost of substitutes was so high that many were said to be paying double premiums in order to be sure of £40.[51]

The severity of militia discipline was visible to everyone. In 1804 a soldier of the North Lincoln Militia at Hull 'was being tied up to receive punishment agreeable to the sentence of a court-martial'.[52] The civilian spectators pelted stones at the adjutant and William Etherington and Thomas Meadley of Sculcoates and Christopher Gibson of Hornsea were sentenced, as inciters of the riot, to be imprisoned in York castle gaol for six, four and two months. Even before the law was altered to legalise the compulsory removal of men from the militia to the regulars, some were volunteering for the sake of the bounty. A private who in 1805 had volunteered for a line regiment was ordered to Beverley before he had time to spend his bounty-money. He therefore hired a post-chaise for the journey to arrive in style, but when he found he had to pay the toll at the Newland Bar, although he had already paid for his transport, he sent it back and continued on foot, in heavy rain.[53] Men of the Carlow Militia volunteering for the regulars in 1812 got drunk and there were fights with Hull men because of 'the shameful and opprobrious use of nicknames and national distinctions by lads of the town'.[54]

Militia officers had their own amusements, duelling being one of them. There was a duel in 1804 'in a field on the west side of Wold Carr near the Anlaby Road'.[55] Captain Dyer's bullet dangerously wounded an artillery surgeon named Kelly, and the captain and both seconds decided to disappear. A few weeks later there was another Wold Carr duel between a captain and a lieutenant of the Warwickshire Militia, but neither was hurt.[56]

All the time the war was going on, often within fifty miles of the port. While Earl St Vincent and Admiral Trowbridge were visiting Hull there was at least one heavily armed French privateer off Spurn. St Vincent and the admiral inspected the citadel and three warships which were on the stocks, and were then taken to the batteries at Paull and Spurn. On their departure the *Royalist* and *Osborne*, transports then being fitted with sixteen to eighteen thirty-two pound carronades, and the *Sheerness*, tender, manned their yards while the crews cheered loudly.[57] And at this time, though there was nothing the navy could do about it, a privateer of sixteen guns with a crew of 150 was making captures off the Yorkshire coast. Her captain released the master of a Sunderland brig, whom he had treated with great kindness, and told him 'that light vessels were not his object but that he had come to that part of the coast for the purpose of looking out for Hull traders'.[58]

Though French privateers occasionally came to grief, their commerce-raiding went on year after year. In 1807 Captain Gatecliffe of the *Amphitrite*, captured off Dungeness, reported from Arras that he had found Captain Oxtoby, of the *Jupiter,* there, and that the ship which had captured the *Amphitrite* had a few days earlier taken the *Henry and Mary*, homeward bound from Riga, off Spurn. All three were Hull ships. The whaler *Sarah and Elizabeth* in 1805 was intercepted off Flamborough Head by a privateer of ten or twelve guns, which before attempting to take her changed her course towards a brig. Captain Ewbank, realising that she could take both separately, deliberately put himself between the brig and the privateer. If the latter had then tried to make her capture the whaler could have crossed her stern, raking her from end to end, perhaps only with two guns but with probably devastating effect. It was too risky for the privateer, and both ships escaped harm.[59*] But in 1806 the Hull whaler *Molly*, while attempting to double the ice, and in fog, was taken by the French frigate *Syrene*;[60] and in 1812 while the whaler *Lynx* of Hull was on passage from Quebec to London—Greenland ships were often able to make a transatlantic or Baltic voyage in addition to their annual trip to the Arctic—she was captured by a French privateer. Her crew were released and put on board an English brig.[61]

In the same year the *Sampson*, bound for Lisbon, was taken by a French squadron;[62] but the *Richard and Anne* and the *Hope* were both safe at Gibraltar after being recaptured from privateers. Most of the *Richard and Anne*'s crew had been on board the privateer and had swum ashore when she was wrecked on the Barbary coast.[63] What was much worse news was that English sailors, this time Hull men, were being found on board privateers. When the *Pomona* of Hull, bound for London from Quebec, was stopped by a French privateer she escaped on the approach of H.M.S. *Goshawk*. Two Hull men were recognised in the crew;[64] and as soon as the U.S.A. was involved in the war many seamen saw much less objection to deserting to an English-speaking enemy. Several Hull ships were taken by Americans in 1812. The master of one of them recognized the coxswain as formerly a Hull apprentice. Two of his own apprentices and four of the seamen decided to join the Americans.[65] There was not much consolation in the arrival of two Danish prizes with barley and a hundred casks of gunpowder.[66]

At home the virtuous did their best to make everyone as good as themselves. The committee for the suppression of vice had a good year in 1810. The pollution of the Sabbath, as they called it, had been diminished by the prosecution of drovers for driving cattle (on a day largely free of traffic), of butchers for slaughtering (on a day when they did not need to be in their shops) and of connoisseurs of cock-fighting, duck-hunting and gambling, as well as hairdressers 'for allowing their ordinary occupation on the Lord's day' (when ordinary people could have their hair cut in daylight). Further 'the disorders which used to take place on Easter Sunday and Whit Sunday on the Humber bank and its adjacent fields as far as Hessle' were suppressed. Disorderly public houses had been dealt with. Seven people had been indicted for keeping brothels, and five were about to be prosecuted. 'One also fled and dismissed her girls through fear of the society.[67]

But Satan was so much at home in Hull that it now always needed regulars as well as militia to prevent him taking over completely. When General Vyse had to send a troop of Scots Greys to suppress Luddites at Huddersfield, they left at 11 p.m.; and by 9 a.m. a squadron of cavalry (their horses must have been almost dead with exhaustion) arrived from Sheffield—'it not being thought expedient to leave Hull without military'. They were reinforced the same day by a squadron of the second Dragoon Guards, who left for Huddersfield on Wednesday, the Scots Greys returning to Hull on the Thursday.[68] The danger must have been thought considerable, and not from invasion.

But there was some progress during the war. Small-pox vaccination began to replace the old and risky system of inoculation (though the new method was still called inoculation) in 1800. 'The female world will be infinitely indebted to Dr Jenner for his discovery—that genuine cow-pox produces no postules on the face.'[69*] Dr Byron, secretary and apothecary of the Hull General Infirmary wrote: 'To Dr Alderson, whose readiness to aid the progress of science has only been equalled by his humanity, we are indebted for the inoculation for cow-pox in this place.' To encourage others, he had his own child vaccinated, and free vaccination was offered to the poor at the infirmary.[70]

And the wealth of the town, except for the poor, was growing at such a rate that it was no longer only bankers who could afford a country estate. Gardner and Joseph Egginton had an oil-mill at Sculcoates and a whaler named after them. In 1802 they were able to buy Everthorpe manor with 500 acres of land, auctioned by Bell and Hendry, for £14,750, in the splendid Neptune Inn.[71]

There were now enough wealthy families to attract fashionable portrait painters from London. John Russell R.A., whose Hull connection originated with the Wilberforces, died of typhus at his lodging in Storey Street in 1806, 'No less eminent as a Christian than as an artist'.[72] William Chamberlain, formerly a pupil of Opie, may have come to fill the gap. He was in Hull with his family when he died in 1807.[73]

Russell, and probably Chamberlain, were buried in the new cemetery on the outskirts, on the south side of Mytongate. All the latest graves were there, except for the few buried in the detached churchyard of St Mary's, where grave-watchers were sometimes employed to see that the body was not stolen for the anatomy schools of Edinburgh or London. There were some, probably the very poor, who were not buried at all, but stacked against the east wall of Holy Trinity,

> Filling up the space between the buttresses (in) little penthouses, just to cover the dead, who are literally left exposed to *rot above ground* in the Market Place, and even, lest the filthy walls and tiles should not sufficiently suffer the effluvia to escape, holes have been made by leaving out a few bricks in the wall. just the height of a man's nose.[74]

There were other anomalies equally strange. It could be so difficult to light a fire or a lamp that sometimes gunpowder had to be mixed with the tinder. No shopkeeper was allowed to keep more than a few pounds of powder, which was thought absurd as there was so large an amount two or three hundred yards away in the Citadel. A Humber Street brewer, trying to get a light in the dark, used some gunpowder, failed to notice that he had left a trail of powder leading back to the flask, and blew the skylight out.[75] To us it seems strange that there was no such domestic convenience as a box of matches in the years when the liberating power of steam had already arrived. The Hull firm, Mead and Penrose, advertised their steam-engines which, needing a space of no more than ten feet square, could be set up and started in ten minutes. A small engine would grind flour for a family — surely a reflection of the contemporary attitude to millers. Engines of ten horsepower would pump water, turn a lathe, work cranes, pile-drivers or threshing machines, or 'be found useful in moving boats in rivers or navigable canals'.[76] This suggests that something was known about the steam packet reputed to have been built at Wincolmlee in 1796 and of Robert Fulton's steamboat on the Seine.[77]

It was well-known that at that time Britain led the world in machinery and invention, and the laws were enforced to prevent the emigration of those who knew the secrets. In 1809 the Hull magistrates ordered the arrest of two factory workers as they were embarking for America.[78] The export of machinery was illegal, and long after the war, as late as 1838, machinery for France was found hidden under a cargo of bricks being sent from Hull to Yarmouth.[79] There was, however, no restriction on the products of the machine age. In 1815 two Hull ships were 'taking on board the works of a large cast-iron bridge for erection in India'.[80]

War did not impede the rituals of polite society. Horse-racing, popular for many years, continued on the Wold Carr, in Newington, often with as many pickpockets as gentlemen.[81] About the time of the autumn meeting, there was a flying visit by Lord Milton (heir to the Fitzwilliam peerage), Daniel Sykes of Raywell, W. J. Denison, no longer a Hull MP, but High Sheriff of Yorkshire and, with his fortune of £2.3 millions, perhaps the richest man in the county. They did not come for the races but to encourage the Whig interest. The market place was illuminated by flaming barrels of tar so that several large barrels of beer could be enjoyed.[82]

There was a strong interest in music. Lord Stanley, and Lt Col Horton (probably his second-in-command) arranged a performance at the Neptune Inn of string quartets of Haydn, Mozart and Beethoven, starting at six, with an 'elegant supper' at half past nine, 'after which glees, madrigals etc. concluded the evening'.[83] The presence of commissioned officers was not always as decorous as this. At Tate Wilkinson's new theatre in 1809 (many years before the national anthem had become an unavoidable observance) a few naval officers insisted that 'God Save the King' should be played between the main piece and the farce:

> The cry of *Hats Off!* not being generally attended to, some of the naval officers threw themselves from the boxes and began to enforce compliance by rough methods. Their attempts were obstinately resisted, and the whole house was thrown into confusion and alarm. Several ladies were handed over the orchestra, and many persons jumped on the stage to get out of the fray.[84]

'Numerous persons of the frail sisterhood' regularly attended the theatre, but a censorious person who objected to their presence did not want them to be excluded altogether. No more was needed than that they should not be allowed into the lowest tier of boxes.

From the earliest times there were actresses whose morals were not above reproach. The lucky ones were connected with men of rank and fashion. This seems to have been the position of Anna Maria Plowden who, appearing in Hull, announced that but for the generosity of the Duke of Queensberry she would never have been able to arrive. It was 'dire necessity' rather than natural inclination which kept her on the stage, and she denied a rumour that she had an allowance of between £250 and £500 a year from her first cousin, Mrs Constable of Burton Constable. But for the help of the Duke, she continued, 'I know not what would have become of me, being left with my dear mother, totally destitute'.[85]

Like most who played leading roles in the provincial theatre, she is now quite unknown; but occasionally there were performances on the Hull stage by such great actresses as Mrs Jordan, mistress of the royal Duke of Clarence, and Mrs Siddons, more rigidly moral. In 1799 Sarah Siddons was in Hull for plays of Shakespeare, Rowe, Otway, Congreve and Kotzebue.[86] In 1808 she played in some of the same parts again during 'positively the last time of her appearance on this stage'.

To celebrate the final victory at Waterloo, there was a fireworks display by Mr Nervoni, 'engineer and artist in fireworks to their Royal Highnesses the Dukes of York and Clarence'. A military band played 'appropriate pieces' for the twenty-four items, which began with rockets, probably the only part of the entertainment visible to those who had not bought tickets from the newspaper offices, or from Sam's Coffee House, Church Side.[87]

Sources

1. *HP*, 9 Dec. 1794.
2. *HA*, 13 Dec. 1794.
3. *HP*, 6 July 1795.
4. *HA*, 1 Feb. 1800.
5. F. M. Eden, *The State of the Poor*, iii (1797) 843-4.
6. *HA*, 19 July 1794.
7. Hadley, 316.
8. Ibid., 348.
9. *R*, 23 June 1810.
10. *HA*, 9 July 1810.
11. Ibid., 26 July 1794.
12. A. A. R. Gill, 'Press Gang Times in the East Riding', *Trans of the East Riding Antiquarian Society* xxv, 154.
13. *HA*, 2 Aug. 1794.
14. BB10, f.234.
15. Hadley, 362.
16. Ibid., 358.
17. *HA*, 8 Aug. 1795.

18. Hadley, 424-5.
19. Eden, op. cit., iii, 837.
20. *HA*, 30 Apr. 1796.
21. *HP*, 10 Nov. 1795.
22. *HA*, 28 Oct. 1797.
23. Ibid., 10 June 1797.
24. Ibid., 17 June 1797.
25. Ibid., 21 July 1798.
26. Ibid., 4 Aug. 1798.
27. Ibid., 22 July 1797.
28. Ibid., 8 Apr. 1797.
29. Ibid., 3 Feb. 1798.
30. Ibid., 1 Mar. 1800.
31. Ibid., 4 Jan. 1800.
32. Ibid., 15 Mar. 1800.
33. Ibid., 25 Jan. 1800.
34. Ibid., 23 Aug. 1800.
35. Ibid., 18 Oct. 1800.
36. Ibid., 15 Feb. 1800.
37. Ibid., 3 May 1800.
38. Ibid., 17 May 1800.
39. Ibid., 26 July 1800.
40. Ibid., 3 May 1800; *VCH*, Hull, 256.
41. *HA*, 12 July 1800.
42. Ibid., 27 Sept. 1800.
43. Ibid., 1 May 1802.
44. Ibid., 24 July 1802.
45. Ibid., 9 Jan. 1802.
46. Navy Records Society; *Dillon's Narrative*, ii, 9-13.
47. *HA*, 4 July 1808.
48. Ibid., 24 Nov. 1810.
49.* Ibid., 30 Mar. 1816. (Assize report: Smith v. the inhabitants of Hull.)
50. Ibid., 21 Feb. 1807.
51. *R*, 15 Sept. 1810.
52. *YC*, 16 Apr. 1804.
53. Ibid., 27 May 1805.
54. *R*, 5 May 1812.
55. *YC*, 12 Mar. 1804.
56. Ibid., 9 Apr. 1804.
57. Ibid., 10 Sept. 1804.
58. Ibid., 26 Nov. 1804.
59. *YC*, 29 July 1805. The manoeuvre was called 'crossing the T'.
60. Ibid., 25 Aug. 1806.
61. *R*, 8 Feb. 1812.
62. Ibid., 30 May 1812.
63. Ibid., 25 Apr. 1812.
64. Ibid., 15 Dec. 1810.
65. Ibid., 24 Oct. 1812.
66. Ibid., 7 Mar. 1812.
67. Ibid., 19 May 1810.
68. Ibid., 12 Feb. 1812.
69. *HA*, 6 June 1800. But see P. Razzell, *The Conquest of Small Pox* (Caliban, 1977).
70. *HA*, 9 Aug. 1800.
71. Ibid., 21 Aug. 1802.
72. *YC*, 28 Apr. 1808; *DNB* s.v. RUSSELL, JOHN (1745-1806).
73. *HA*, 17 July 1807; *DNB* s.v. CHAMBERLAIN, WILLIAM (d. 1807).
74. *R*, 22 Oct. 1808.
75. *HA*, 19 Oct. 1811.
76. *R*, 29 Oct. 1808.
77. Sheahan, 368; *Chambers' Biographical Dictionary*, 505.
78. *R*, 26 Aug. 1809.
79. J. H. Clapham, *The Early Railway Age*, 485-6, 498; *R*, 3 Mar. 1838.
80. *HA*, 8 Apr. 1815.
81. *R*, 27 Oct. 1808.
82. *R*, 3 Sept. 1808; G. R. Park, *Parliamentary Representation of Yorkshire*, 105n.
83. *R*, 19 Nov. 1808.
84. *R*, 11 Mar. 1809.
85. *HA*, 16 Feb. 1811.
86. *HA*, 16 Nov. 1799.
87. *HA*, 15 July 1815.

19

Civic Rule and Borough Reform

Long after the first steamboats had crossed the North Sea, and in the year when the railway reached as far as Selby, Hull was still living under an unrepresentative system of local government hardly altered except in detail since it was set down in writing in 1440, and considerably less effective than it had been then. But the system was in its last days. The Municipal Corporations Act, the logical corollary of the 1832 Reform Act, standardised government by elected councils in corporate towns, and a system strongly resembling our own had its beginnings.

In law it was all the burgesses who constituted the corporation but it was the thirteen aldermen, elected for life, who exercised effective power. A man was a burgess if his father had been one at the time of his birth, even if he was born outside the borough. He could become a burgess through a seven-year apprenticeship; and he could also buy his freedom, though this was a less frequent and the most expensive mode of admission to the corporation. In 1698 Thomas Cobcroft became a burgess for £4, but James Clark, a surgeon and able to pay more, had to pay £10.[1] In 1766 his freedom as burgess cost William Keeling £21 and John Crompton twice as much;[2] and a month later two men paid thirty guineas each.[3] William Sharpe, master-mariner, paid 250 guineas and Captain Mallery Hasslewood paid the same sum in 1817, whereas in 1814 J. C. Fitchett and Joseph Lambert got in for £150 each.[4] John Brodrick and Thomas Ward did not take the chance to buy their freedom for £300 and 350 guineas respectively.[5]

Occasionally applicants were treated charitably. A tailor, with the approval of his company, was admitted on condition of making two coats for the beadles.[6] This was in 1699. Ten years earlier William Bradley got his freedom on taking a poor boy as his apprentice for eight years.[7] In 1694 a blacksmith who had served an eight-year apprenticeship at Pocklington got in for 10s, because he had a wife and four children.[8]

Occasionally, usually as an honour, freedom was granted without a fine John, son of Alderman Ramsden, and Thomas Stead, whose grandfather had twice been mayor, were given their freedoms out of respect for their families.[9] Captain Richard Pearson, R.N., formerly of the *Countess of Scarborough*, and Captain Thomas Piercy of the *Serapis*, who by their action against Paul Jones off Flamborough had saved a Baltic convoy with Hull ships sheltering at Scarborough, were honoured with their freedoms; and William Foster of Bridlington received the same honour for keeping Hull informed of the movements of Paul Jones.[10] Joseph Buttery in 1736 was made a freeman because at a fire in the market place and High Street he had 'tirelessly worked the water engines', and it was hoped that this would 'encourage others to be active on such unhappy occasions'.[11] Dr John Alderson was made a freeman in 1813 'for his twenty years' service to the sick and the poor'.[12]

For most freemen, their vote in parliamentary elections was what counted. In 1832 there were 1631 living in Hull or within seven miles of the town, and there may have been another 1200 non-resident freemen.[13] There were also real economic advantages for some, especially merchants. Toll exemption could in 1833 be worth as much as £100 a year.[14]

Though the aldermen controlled the corporation, a merchant could find that election to the bench interfered with his liberty to carry on his business; but a merchant could be virtually blackmailed into taking up his freedom by the threat of being put out of business. As happened with Joseph Fearnley in 1697, he could be assessed at the maximum for poor relief until he decided to become a freeman—though some were too rich for that to matter.[15] Fearnley was also allowed exemption from the offices of sheriff, chamberlain and alderman by paying a total of £170.

It was only with great difficulty that William Crowle, son of the founder of Crowle's hospital escaped being made an alderman in 1704. In the end the bench refused to accept his offer of £25 and sued him at York assizes. They got a verdict for £100, but because they had to pay nearly £34 in law costs were worse off than if they had accepted his proposal.[16] Richard Sykes, merchant, refusing to serve as alderman, was fined £300 in 1742.[17]

If a man became an alderman, it was difficult for him to get his resignation accepted unless he was aged, infirm and had friendly colleagues. In 1792-3 it cost Alderman Edmund Bramston 100 guineas to get his infirmity recognised. On the other hand, the corporation could be generous to an alderman who had become impoverished. Daniel Hoare was given financial help when he resigned in 1712 and was soon employed as town's husband, the equivalent of a borough treasurer.[18] Alderman William Cookson was given a pension of £40 a year when he resigned in 1775;[19] and for several years a pension was paid to the widow of Andrew Hollingsworth who had died as mayor in 1813.[20]

It was a common practice in the election of mayor that one of the lites should be the most junior alderman and the other the most senior whose turn had come round. It was then up to the burgesses to choose. As a result, in 1738, Andrew Perrott became mayor two days after he had been an ordinary freeman.[21] Once an alderman was elected mayor, he was for his year of office rather more than first among equals. Minutes of meetings could not be confirmed if he was not there,[22] and there could be no meeting of the bench without him or his deputy. In 1704 the meeting for the election of the new mayor and borough officers had to be held in his bedroom, since he was too ill to be moved, and even so, after a meeting in the Guildhall, the bench returned to his house for dinner.[23] When Sir William St Quintin was mayor in 1715 and had to go abroad, the aldermen took turns at performing the office, each serving for a fortnight.[24]

The accepted custom was that an alderman was not required to serve more than three times as mayor. When a mayor died in his year of office in 1768, it was decided that the period served by the substitute mayor should not count as one of his mayoralties;[25] but when in 1798-9 John Sykes had to serve for nine months in place of the deceased, the decision went the other way.[26]

In 1833 there was no salary, but in 1700 there is record of the mayor's salary being increased from £80 to £150.[27] This was twice raised,[28] at times when the mayor was frequently entertaining navy and army officers, but in 1797 his salary ceased and £500 was subscribed for national defence.[29]

The sheriff was usually an ex-chamberlain.[30] He was responsible for the gaol, empanelled grand and petty juries at quarter sessions and assizes, and was returning officer in parliamentary elections.[31] The office was expensive and when a burgess was to be one of the lites who might be chosen as sheriff it was sometimes worth while for him to pay a fine for exemption, if it was not too large. The usual sum was £80. J. T. Froggett in 1713 and 1714 was in danger of having to pay £200 for refusal of office.[32] James Houseman was threatened with election simply because his office as customs surveyor made him unpopular, but in the end he got off for £50.[33] In 1697 Bartholomew Towers, a Hull burgess but a member of Leeds corporation, refused to serve as sheriff and was sued for £200.[34] Elihu Jackson of Doncaster was caught in the same trap and at York assizes in 1715 had £200 awarded against him.[35] By 1833 such fines were rare. Samuel Wright in 1774 was not made a lite for sheriff when he pointed out that he had always been a dissenter and was therefore not qualified; but in 1805 the wealthy Gardiner Egginton, brother of the mayor, was fined £200 when he refused to be sheriff.

In the course of the eighteenth century the town's husband took over the functions which had been performed by the chamberlains. The chamberlains were still elected, and each of them had to pay him £6 16s 6d, but he was appointed by the bench, and they were not even allowed to see the accounts prepared in their name. The 1833 commissioners wrote: 'Everything connected with the control and auditing of accounts and the secrecy preserved in these matters occasions great and general dissatisfaction and distrust.'[36]

The office of High Steward was first held in 1590 by a privy councillor and Elizabeth's vice-chamberlain, Sir Thomas Heneage; but Sir Robert Cecil was the first to hold office under the charter of 1598.[37] In the eighteenth century for many years there was no High Steward, but in 1766, to increase his patronage in the borough, the Marquess of Rockingham accepted election.[38] The popular Earl Fitzwilliam was elected in 1801; but on his death in 1833 there was a tussle between the bench, who wanted Wellington, and the burgesses, who wanted the radical Durham.[39] Wellington then refused to be nominated. The office of recorder also carried a great deal of influence and a salary of £150 and was usually given to a barrister of some standing who could act as an emissary of the corporation. His opinion was taken on lawsuits and the drafting of bye-laws; but it was his deputy who usually presided at quarter-sessions.[40]

The appointment of the High Steward, recorder and town clerk needed the consent of the Crown. The town clerk was now the most important officer of the corporation. This could lead to difficulties, as the Crown could issue a warrant of appointment without the knowledge of the bench. This happened in 1736 on the death of Thomas Peacock, when the bench wanted his deputy, John Wilkinson, to succeed him.[41] Before they could present the petition for his appointment James Barry arrived with a warrant for his own appointment from Walpole. Barry was believed to have had the support of the borough members.[42] A compromise was attempted by the appointment of Barry while Wilkinson became council chamber clerk, the effective executive officer of the corporation.[43] Barry, however, insisted that he was entitled to both offices and it was not until 1746 that he gave up his claims on the payment of £80 costs.[44] The very same day the bench petitioned for the appointment of Carleton Monckton, who served until his death in 1788. In his leisure hours he compiled a highly informative set of notes on Hull as he knew it.[45]

Edward Codd, a Hull attorney who had served as his deputy since 1788, succeeded him and served as town clerk until he was presented with a piece of plate worth 100 guineas on his retirement in 1822.[46] He was succeeded by his son George who loyally served and ably defended the unreformed corporation in its last days. The new corporation of 1836 did not continue his appointment.

Many of the ancient minor offices under the corporation continued until the end. The last two waits, who as late as 1792 had been required to practise on the trumpet for ceremonial occasions, were released from all further duties in 1798 and ordered to give up the instruments belonging to the corporation.[47] Since 1823 there had been a house steward who served as butler and catering officer.[48]

Dr William Chambers speaking to Alderman Pool in 1778 'had used to him many indecent and opprobrious expressions highly reflecting upon this corporation', and was forced to apologise.[49] In 1802 'several false and illiberal reports for the purpose of raising the public clamour' were said to have been made against Alderman Wray, who in consequence was not, as he hoped, elected mayor, Alderman W. W. Bolton being chosen instead, apparently against his own wishes.[50] The following year radical burgesses joined with non-burgesses in trying to unseat the duly elected alderman after the occurrence of a vacancy through death, but they lost their case when they took it to the King's Bench.[51] As long as the war continued all criticism of authority was severely discouraged, and reformers made very little progress.

The Hull reformers were such men as Thomas Thompson, B. I. Johnson, Joseph Noble, J. M. Thistleton and the talented and energetic young solicitor, William Woolley, who in 1830 produced his *Statutes relating to Kingston upon Hull and Sculcoates*, which provided indispensable information for all local politicians. The most flamboyant figure among the reform party was James Acland (1799-1876) who came to Hull as a journalist from Bristol, after being an actor, a teacher in France and a lecturer on Shakespeare and phrenology.[52] He started his *Hull Portfolio* after the pattern of his *Bristolian*, which had brought about his imprisonment for libel. He began a campaign against the aldermen on such issues as the Humber ferry,[53] market tolls and pew rents in Holy Trinity. He dealt scathingly with Trinity House and published criticisms of each alderman in turn.

He was really a mob leader. George Codd, the town clerk, said of him: 'Abuse and reformation of the corporation were a passport to popularity.'[54] He was expert in publicity and advertisement. When he tried to break the Humber ferry monopoly he started his own boat, the *Aire*, renamed *Public Opinion*, with the corporation arms upside down on the flags and paddle boxes. In his campaign against market tolls he set up his own stall near King William's statue,[55] refused to pay tolls, flew flags marked *Free Trade* and *No Tolls*, selling ginger-bread figures of the mayor and aldermen and cards printed with devices applicable to the occasion. He was in prison for libel when the municipal corporation inquiry commissioners visited Hull in 1833. Later, from his 'anti-corporate Castle in Queen Street he sold 'anti-corporate tea', 'public opinion coffee' and 'radical tobacco'. After he had been elected church-warden he left in 1833, leaving no proper account of £27 of the Holy Trinity money.[56]

Acland was also active in the local agitation for parliamentary reform. At a meeting called in 1831 by 'local gentlemen of great respectability' Acland assembled 'a large concourse of the lower classes' and made a long speech about aristocrats—'the locusts of the state'—and bishops—'the agents of anti-Christ'. He then organised the Hull Political Union in association with John Jackson, T. B. Smith and J. Noble. The more respectable reformers founded the Hull Parliamentary Reform Association.[57]

The Reform Act of 1832 created the new parliamentary borough of Kingston upon Hull, embracing Sculcoates, Trippett, Myton and Garrison Side, in addition to the original town.[58] Though he was in gaol in Bury St Edmunds, Acland stood as a candidate at the first election for the new constituency and came at the bottom of the poll.[59] Nevertheless, the fact that 433 freemen voted for him, probably losing all chance of a bribe, showed that he did genuinely reflect the feelings of some.

In the first session of the reformed Parliament a select committee was appointed to inquire into the state of municipal corporations. One of its members was the Cottingham-born political economist George Pryme (1781-1868). Hull was one of the twenty boroughs chosen for investigation, and the committee visited the town on 23 and 24 April 1833. Pryme recommended that commissioners should be sent to every corporate borough, and a royal commission was appointed. Its assistant commissioners were young and mostly radical barristers. The two who investigated Hull were the Jamaican-born lawyer and dramatist F. W. L. Dwarris,[60] and S. A. Rumball. At a meeting of the bench a dignified protest was drawn up by George Codd and approved.[61] The inquiry lasted ten days in December 1833, fully reported in the local newspapers. The reports of William Gawtress of the *Hull Packet*, printed separately in 1834, were particularly valuable.

The report of the commissioners criticised the secrecy of the bench, the failure to publish accounts and notices of bye-laws, and the administration of justice by the aldermen in the petty sessions. The traditional bribe at the annual elections—half-a-crown and a jack of rum—was noted, and also strained relations between the aldermen and other commissioners of the court of requests, a local court for the collection of small debts, set up under the acts of 1761 and 1808.[62] In other places, though not all, there was a body of 'assistants' intermediate between the aldermen and the burgesses, which lessened friction, but at Hull there was no such buffer. Press-gang riots and the activities of Acland had shown that there was no effective policing. The bench refused its full co-operation in the investigation of finance, but enough emerged to show that expenditure was exceeding income and that the system was only maintained by raising loans and selling annuities. In thirty years 283 annuities were sold, and as proper annuity tables were used it is to be expected that this actually brought in a profit.[63] Between 1781 and 1835 £76,000 was borrowed at rates of 4½ to 5 per cent, mostly from individuals. But although most corporations were strongly criticised for their financial policies, the Hull bench deserved credit for its considerable expenditure on improvements and public works.

The old corporation was abolished, along with all other borough corporations, by the act of 1835, and the elections for the new council were held at the end of the year. Though the freemen kept their parliamentary vote, unless they were ratepayers they had no say in municipal elections; and the new corporation had no say in the administration of justice. Under the terms of the act, because its population exceeded 12,000, Hull was divided into wards. The town council consisted of fourteen aldermen and fourteen councillors, based on seven wards. Many of the new councillors were shopkeepers, and no member of the old corporation was elected. The only Conservative returned was Denis Peacock, a councillor for west Sculcoates. The Whig revolution was complete.[64]

Before its dissolution, an inventory was taken for the old corporation. In addition to plate, linen, china, and glass, there were 208 dozen bottles of port, thirty-six dozen of Madeira, twenty-nine dozen of sherry, twenty-three dozen of claret and two dozen of hock.[65] All this was sold at a three-day auction in March 1836. What the new men called the 'ostentatious frippery' of the ancient regalia narrowly escaped being 'put forthwith into the crucible and converted into grateful testimonials to Viscount Melbourne and Lord John Russell'. Fortunately nothing was done about this suggestion; but it was not until 1851 that, on the suggestion of Alderman Anthony Bannister, then mayor, the mace, the sword of state, and the cap of maintenance were again used for ceremonial occasions.

Civic reform should not be seen as the triumph of virtue, and Anthony Bannister himself will point out the moral for us. He was a complex individual capable of good, but now known to have committed an act of the sort of villainy which Wilkie Collins might have invented. About the time he was mayor a certain Henry Storrer owed him £60. Bannister sued him for debt, and obtained a verdict in his favour. The debtor could not pay and so suffered imprisonment until he could pay. The debt was very soon paid; but Bannister refused to sign a discharge or any document certifying that the debt was no longer owed. Henry Storrer remained in the abominable Hull gaol, not, as might be supposed, for a few weeks or months, but for six years. Some well-disposed lawyers then took an interest in his case which, as Storrer v. Bannister, was heard in the Queen's Bench in 1858. The judges were amazed that such an outrage had been possible, but with more regard for property than for liberty decided to make no judgment provided Bannister paid his victim, whose family and health had suffered considerably, £225 damages.[66]*

It was not until 1851 that the new corporation took over the powers of fire-prevention, lighting, paving and drainage until then exercised by the Sculcoates Improvement Commissioners and by the Hull and Myton Commissioners.[67] When the new poor law unions with their elected boards of guardians were set up locally in 1837, the united parishes of Holy Trinity and St Mary's remained under the old Hull Incorporation of the Poor. The parts of Hull to the west, north and east formed the civil parish of Sculcoates, containing a population of about 20,000 almost equal to that of the rest of the town. The new civil parish was the nucleus of the poor law union of the same name.

An assistant Poor Law Board commissioner at the beginning of 1837 met the overseers of the poor of the eighteen parishes which formed the new union,[68] and in the course of the year the ratepayers elected the Sculcoates Board of Guardians. Each parish kept its own old workhouse in use until the union workhouse was completed in 1844 on the site of the present Kingston General Hospital.[69] Even with the old workhouses, the guardians managed to economise, probably causing much suffering to the poor. In the three years ending on 25 March 1844 the amount levied in poor rates was 17.3 per cent less than it had been in the three years immediately before the formation of the union, and in Sculcoates parish the poor rates were actually 20 per cent smaller.[70]

Though in the hungry forties there were fewer deaths in the Sculcoates than in the Hull workhouse, this may have been because starving fugitives from Ireland were turned away at

Sculcoates and passed on to Hull, where, if they were refused admittance, they were able to show initiative, break a window in the presence of a policeman, and get themselves put in the town gaol, which in most respects was better than the workhouse which stood at the corner of Whitefriargate and Parliament Street. It had been a terrible place even in 1800 when Thomas Thompson the banker, taking his turn as Governor of the Poor, described the foul smell in the room where paupers picked oakum as quite unendurable.[71] There were then 150 paupers in the house: after 1840 there were often over 400. In 1844 a shabby expedient was tried to reduce the congestion. There were about fifty Irish inmates, most of whom had worked in Hull for years — and indeed they would not have been admitted unless they were known to have a legal settlement. Ignoring the law that no settled person could be removed, still less deported, the Governor of the Poor called in the police and had them all sent to Dublin by way of Liverpool. More would have been sent but for the fact that Fr Render protested, and there was a question in the Commons.[72] The great Irish famine brought still more, many of whom seem to have been taken into the workhouse to die, irrespective of their legal settlement. A quarter of the inmates of the Hull workhouse died in 1847. In Sculcoates the mortality was only 14 per cent.[73]

The Poor Law Commissioners wanted to end the separation of Hull from Sculcoates, and many of the upper classes in particular wanted a single workhouse for the town, demolishing the old one. Very often there were infectious diseases in the workhouse which the well-to-do householders of Parliament Street feared would spread to them. A servant girl did die of typhus, and twenty-four householders signed a protest against the continued existence of the house.[74] The guardians could build a new workhouse, but in many respects they were free from supervision by the Poor Law Commissioners. If two-thirds of them could be brought to agree to incorporate with Sculcoates, the old Incorporation of the Poor could be ended. A memorial in favour of a single poor law union for the whole town was signed by nine former Governors of the Poor, three bankers, Sir William Lowthrop, six of the Anglican clergy, and ten doctors: but nothing could move the members of the Incorporation.[75]

With people so often moving from one part of the town to another there were disputes between the two authorities about responsibility for the poor. One scandalous case in 1849 involved a sailor who broke his leg on board his ship in dock. He was born in Hull, but had lived in Sculcoates for two months. Both authorities disclaimed him and a magistrate's order was needed to settle the matter.[76] The law, for the whole country, was clarified by the act of 1865 (28 & 29 Vict. cap. 79) which gave all people a settlement in the last union in which they had lived for a year — a strong encouragement for poor villagers to move to Hull, since rural authorities normally refused all relief to the unemployed. In Hull and Sculcoates, with enormous unemployment in winter, relief was given on a very meagre scale to applicants who were required to do test work — six days a week of stone breaking, which was painfully difficult for clerks and shop-men in particular. This was still going on when the old poor law was abolished in 1929.

Until then Hull kept its two separate Boards of Guardians. The old Incorporation of the Poor moved the inmates to the new workhouse, where the Hull Royal Infirmary now stands, on Anlaby Road in the summer of 1852.[77] In 1847 a Governor of the Poor said it was impossible to describe the hardship the poor had to endure since the passing of the act.[78] He was referring to the legislation of 1834 which regulated the relief of the poor and aimed at denying all relief except in a workhouse, but everywhere it was found quite impossible to administer relief only to paupers in the workhouse. In 1848 the Hull Incorporation had to give outdoor relief, on a very scanty scale, to 6000 persons, not less than one seventh of the population of its area.[79] Outdoor relief taught the poor that hunger was preferable to actual starvation and could just be endured; and increasingly, as time passed, the poorer half of the population benefited from the workhouse infirmaries, which dealt with far more people than the Hull Royal Infirmary.

Sources

1. BB8, ff.424-5.
2. BB9, f.365.
3. BB9, f.366.
4. BB11, ff.58, 87, 91, 141, 147.
5. Gawtress, 5.
6. BB8, f.451.
7. BB8, f.240.
8. BB8, f.334.
9. BB8, ff.122, 687.
10. BB9, f.501; Hadley, 353.

11. BB8, f.827.
12. BB11, f.62.
13. *MC*, 1548; Gawtress, 42.
14. Report of the Select Committee on Municipal Corporations, 1833, *Minutes of Evidence*, Q.7193.
15. BB8, f.424.
16. BB8, ff.529-30.
17. BB9, ff.8, 9.
18. Hadley, 300; BB8, ff.618, 629.
19. BB9, f.444.
20. BB11, ff.44, 131.
21. BB8, ff.852-3.
22. BB8, f.457; MC, 1548.
23. BB8, f.352.
24. BB8, f.655.
25. BB8, f.62; MC, 1648.
26. BB8, ff.9, 378.
27. BB9, ff.241, 244.
28. BB10, ff.347, 708.
29. BB10, f.291.
30. *MC*, 1548; Gawtress, 47.
31. *MC*, 1552.
32. BB8, ff.623-3, 635-6, 641.
33. BB8, f.384.
34. BB8, ff.418-22, 450.
35. BB8, ff.622-5, 637, 645-6, 670; BB10 f. 451.
36. *MC*, 1552; Gawtress, 78-80.
37. BB4, f.258b.
38. BB9, f.363.
39. BB12, f.126.
40. *MC*, 1552.
41. BB8, f.821.
42. BB8, f.824.
43. BB8, f.828.
44. BB8, ff.835-6.
45. BB10, f.40; Carleton Monckton MS, Hull Central Library.
46. BB11, f.310.
47. BB10, ff.139, 151, 292.
48. BB11, ff.314-15; Gawtress, 92.
49. BB9, ff.274, 275.
50. BB10, ff.411, 423.
51. BB10, f.428.
52. *Hull Portfolio*, i, no. 13 *passim*.
53. K. A. MacMahon, 'James Acland and the Hull Ferry Monopolies', *Transport History*, ii, 168 ff.
54. BB12, f.210.
55. *R*, 5 Nov. 1831; *Hull Portfolio*, op. cit., p. 101; MC, 1560.
56. Holy Trinity parish order book, f. 368.
57. *R*, 15, 22 Oct., 5 Nov. 1831; 2 June 1832.
58. *Report of Commissioners upon Boundaries* 1837 XXVII, pt II, p. 137.
59. *R*, 15 Dec. 1832.
60. *DNB* s.v. DWARRIS, SIR F. W. L.
61. BB12 f.153.
62. 2 Geo. III, cap. 38; 48 Geo. III, cap. 109.
63. BB10, ff.359, 406.
64. Gawtress, 71; Sheahan, 289.
65. BB12, f.243.
66.* *HA*, 16 July 1858. This piece of villainy would not have been discovered but for the diligence of Mr Bernard Foster researching in 1976.
67. *VCH*, Hull, 231.
68. *HA*, 3 Feb. 1837.
69. B. Foster, 'Public Health in Hull in the Nineteenth Century' (Hull University M.Phil., 1979) 122.
70. *HA*, 24 Sept. 1841.
71. Foster, op. cit., 124.
72. Ibid., 127.
73. Ibid., 135.
74. Ibid., 133.
75. *HA*, 13 June 1849.
76. Ibid., 27 Apr. 1849.
77. Foster, op. cit., 147-8.
78. Ibid., 130.
79. Ibid., 132.

20

The Town: Improvement and Change

Problems of public health and sanitation in nineteenth-century Hull were certainly no worse than in, say, the large industrial towns of West Yorkshire and Lancashire, but the port had special difficulties of its own in providing essential services and basic amenities for a population which rose spectacularly from 22,161 in 1801 to 239,157 in 1901. The low-lying site inevitably brought problems of water supply and the provision of effective deep drainage. Furthermore, and reflecting the character of the port's developing trade, certain types of offensive occupations—among them soap manufacture, candle making, tanning, seed crushing, whale-oil boiling and, in due course, fish-manure works—were established. Such activities necessitated the treatment of offensive substances as well as the effective disposal of obnoxious waste; and, of course, with widening trading contacts in an age when international health controls as they are now understood had yet to develop, Hull, like any other port, was vulnerable to any ship-borne infection.

Two major types of epidemic disease in this period and the heavy mortality which followed provided a rude shock for authority and helped to bring about drastic appraisal of the conditions which nurtured them: first were the major outbreaks of cholera in 1832 and again, far more virulently, in 1849; second was the smallpox epidemic of 1881. As an epidemic disease, bubonic plague had died away in England in the second half of the seventeenth century, but Hull was probably hardly ever free of other types of infection. There were outbreaks of scarlet fever and smallpox in 1794 and again between 1814 and 1818, when typhus was also recorded: no doubt the introduction into Hull in 1800 of Jenner's system of vaccination helped to lessen future ravages of smallpox, particularly after 1805 when vaccination became freely available to the town's poor.[1]

In 1831 cholera, a water-borne disease endemic in India, was virtually unknown, but much feared on the basis of reports from eastern and central Europe. Following its arrival at Sunderland in October 1831 via Berlin and Hamburg, the local press, at the behest of the Central Board of Health, published a list of ten principles to be followed to combat the spread of the disease.[2] In November, at a meeting in the Mansion House, a Local Board of Health was formed, consisting largely of magistrates, clergy and local medical men, a measure suggested by Dr William Bodley of the Hull Infirmary some three months before, but turned down by the corporation.[3] Two doctors, Joseph Ayre and G.D. Longstaff, were dispatched to Sunderland and Newcastle to study its progress there.[4] Hull was so far clear, but by April 1832 the disease was reported to be virulent at Goole, and inevitably Hull soon had its own cases, the worst affected area at first being the Witham-Wincolmlee district.[5] Between early April and early September there were 270 deaths from cholera.[6] Subscriptions were called for to raise money for the cholera-stricken poor, provide food and clothing, and to take such measures as were necessary to prevent the situation worsening.[7] According to Dr James Alderson, the incidence of the disease was worst in the northwest suburbs of the town, which he described as having many lodging houses, tramps, Irish labourers and paupers. The death rate was particularly high in Bellamy Square, which on one side was bounded by pig sties.[8]

Doctors held different opinions about treatment. Joseph Ayre in 1832 published an essay *On the Pathology and Treatment of the Cholera*, advocating the use of calomel and opium.[9] Alderson did not agree. In a letter to the *Lancet*, Ayre somewhat unprofessionally specifically referred to one of Alderson's patients, with the result that at the next meeting of the Board of Health Alderson accused him of unprofessional conduct. It was said that both sides exchanged insults, that Alderson pulled Ayre's nose, and that there was a fight; but it does not appear to be possible to verify this story. Alderson was already F.R.C.P. and such behaviour, though not impossible, seems out of character. He was already thirty-six at the time of the quarrel and was to be president of the

College. He called calomel 'the sheet-anchor of the quack', and Ayre counter-attacked.[10*]

Such unprofessional capers were scarcely calculated to encourage public confidence, and no doubt some victims, potential and real, may well have been inclined to place their faith in such contemporary nostrums as Reinhardt's Anti-Cholera Mixture, Morison's Pills and Dr Fleischman's Cholera Drops.

Although the cholera visitation of 1832 was vicious in its effect, historically it can be regarded as a warning that, at a time of expanding population and intensifying industrial activity, urban environmental conditions were rapidly deteriorating, and official action could not be long delayed if worse was not to come. Such rationalisation of administrative control of essential public services was imperative. West of the River Hull the borough corporation was responsible for water supply while the two separate bodies of Improvement Commissioners (those of Sculcoates and Hull-Myton respectively) were charged *inter alia* with responsibility for drainage, lighting and street paving: east of the river, where industrial growth was quickening, no sanitary authority as such existed at all.

But a close and satisfactory assessment of social conditions in early Victorian Hull is not easy, inasmuch as the personal impressions of some observers would appear to belie the statistics. The somewhat favourable report of conditions prepared by James Riddell Wood for the Manchester Statistical Society and presented to the British Association in 1841, and the impressions of the town vouchsafed to the Royal Commission on Large Towns and Populous Districts by James Smith of the Central Board of Health, are chilled by official figures. Overcrowding evoked particular comment, and referring to these conditions Wood remarked on the 'courts'—'there are courts and courts of a very peculiar construction, a court within a court and then another court within that', and gave an example of as many as fifty people 'generally of a very questionable character' living in the one house.[11*] For the three years 1840, 1841 and 1842 Hull's mortality rate was 3 per cent—not so serious when measured against Liverpool's 3.5 per cent or Manchester's 3.2 per cent, but well above York's 2.4 per cent and the national average of 2.2 per cent. In 1841, of 1206 registered deaths in a population of 41,130, 515, or 42.7 per cent, were of children under the age of five: in that year

236 of Hull's population over the age of five died from fever and epidemic disease and 164 from consumption.[12]

The overall statistical impact of such figures is hardly vitiated by the possibility of mistaken diagnosis in individual cases. But a local assessment of urban conditions is provided in nauseating meticulousness by the Sanitary Committee of the thirty-three-strong Medical Society of Hull in November 1847. The Report, which virtually coincided with news of cholera in Russia, was signed on behalf of the Society by twenty physicians and surgeons, including leading figures like Henry Cooper, Humphry Sandwith, Henry Monroe and Robert Craven. The survey pulled no punches and its mass of scarifying detail testifies to its accuracy as a word picture of conditions in Hull and its developing industrial suburbs. Dividing the town into districts for the purpose of the survey, it recorded, for example, 'lazy streams of filth', overcrowded living conditions, stinking dunghills, muck garths and midden stands, ubiquitous pigs and their evil-smelling sties, and the overbursting graveyard of St Mary's Lowgate, where one burial could mean the enforced removal of three or four coffins. But Hull's public health problems were not unique.[13*]

The publicity given to this and other social questions in these middle years of the century owed much to the influential local newspaper, the *Hull Advertiser*, which under new ownership in the thirties changed its political spots from Tory to Radical Reformer, coming under the editorial control in 1841 of Edward Francis Collins, erstwhile secretary to Joseph Hume, the parliamentary 'philosophic radical' and indefatigable reformer. By detailed reporting and compelling leader article alike, Collins continued and extended the influence of 'true reform principles', and up to his death in 1866 exerted an unusual influence on the Hull of his time.

By the middle of 1848 Hamburg as well as Berlin was in the grip of a cholera epidemic, the incidence of the disease being particularly severe in the German port, where some 800 British seamen were affected:[14] indeed, there was an outbreak among a Prussian crew in Hull from a ship which had passed through Hamburg *en route* from an unaffected Baltic port. With York and Beverley, Hull petitioned to adopt the provisions of the Public Health Act of 1848—powers which otherwise could only have been obtained by securing a local act, although the Public Health Act could be imposed on an area if the death rate exceeded twenty-three per thousand.[15]

After the first recorded case in July 1849 cholera struck early in August with a terrifying intensity, and it was not until 19 October that the town could be declared clear of infection. According to Henry Cooper,[16] who read two papers to the British Association at its Hull Meeting in 1853, no less than 1860 (the majority of them in the prime of life) died in the epidemic, a figure representing one in forty-three of the population. The disease reached a climax in the second week in September, when over 500 people perished, the death rate being the highest of any other town in the country. The following table covering the middle of September and based solely on the Registrar's returns of mortality, is some measure of its intensity at the height of the infection.

Mortality 31 August-4 October 1849

	*Premonitory cases**	*Cholera*	*Total*	*Daily average*
7 days ending:				
6 Sept.	35	363	398	56.9
13 Sept.	58	449	507	72.4
20 Sept.	51	273	324	46.3
27 Sept.	27	144	171	24.4
4 Oct.	21	91	112	16.0
35 days ending:				
4 Oct.	192	1320	1512	43.2

* i.e. those with preliminary symptoms of the cholera disease but at the time of death not yet diagnosed as being cases of true cholera.

In pious prose the Revd James Sibree, the Minister of Salem Congregational Church and chaplain to the Hull General Cemetery Company, recorded his recollections of these grim days and unwittingly provided due evidence of his own devoted labours. In his journal he recorded Sunday, 9 September as 'An Awful Day' when he 'preached twice, visited the graves twice and interred forty-three bodies' of cholera-stricken victims.[17] It was a time when barrels of tar were fired in the streets as a prophylactic, and 'the sun seldom shone brightly'. Collins of the *Hull*

Advertiser, not prepared to paper over cracks, published detailed mortality rates for the various areas, streets, alleys and courts. The public had to be made aware that the disease originated in dirt, bad drainage, overcrowding, personal profligacy and the burial of the dead among the living. No one was exempt from infection, and as the death of Dr R. Firth, temperance advocate and respected schoolmaster, illustrated, abstinence and virtue were no safeguards against the pestilence. If authority in Hull, said Collins, had only been able to compel leading figures like Henry Broadley and George Liddell to cover up their foul drains three years before the crisis came, lesser men could have been similarly coerced and many lives saved.[18]

On the evidence it is not easy to acquit the responsible authorities of impotence and dilatoriness—particularly so in the case of the two Boards of Guardians for the Sculcoates Union and the united parishes of Holy Trinity and St Mary's, who had statutory responsibilities for the removal of nuisances. Dr John Sutherland of the General Board of Health somewhat scathingly remarked on local authority's too-philosophical acceptance of the view that the cholera visitation was a manifestation of the 'hand of Almighty God' and implied at the same time that the hands of the local Boards of Guardians could have been better employed at getting to grips with a rapidly worsening crisis. He put his finger on the basic administrative weakness when commenting that 'the experience of Hull when contrasted with Sheffield . . . affords evidence of the great saving of human life which would have been effected had the recommendations of the General Board of Health been adopted when they were first given: while it ought to raise the question of resorting to other means for protecting the public than trusting implicitly to the management of Boards of Guardians.'[19]*

Appalling though they were, the grim realities of the 1849 epidemic could have been worse had it not been for the fortuitous opening of the General Cemetery on Spring Bank in 1847. The problem of the 'overcrowding of the dead' in the rapidly growing towns of the early nineteenth century was an insufferable scandal. Hull was no exception, and the problem had become obvious before a local Improvement Act of 1783 had made practicable the purchase of a burial ground in Castle Street for the parish of Holy Trinity. The acquisition of a twenty-acre site along Spring Bank was the result of a joint stock venture by leading townspeople and was financed by the issue of one thousand £10 shares: a further addition to the site was made in 1862 at the instance of the Local Board of Health. So an attempt was made to fulfil a desperate public need, and the decent disposal of the dead at the same time afforded some financial return for the living. Because the whole area was attractively laid out—and not least because of its peculiarly tragic associations—it acquired something of the nature of a quiet park before parks came to be regarded as essential public amenities. The Revd James Sibree engagingly confessed to the fact that some of the best hours of his life were spent in its shady walks and amongst the tombs; and amid the rank overgrowth of more recent years the poet has not always sought the Muse in vain.[20]

Although in these crisis years, 1830-50, urban filth and substandard living conditions were considered by contemporaries to be the main reason for the two major outbreaks of cholera, the town's wholly inadequate water supply must have been highly suspect, although, surprisingly, proportionately small comment is made on the fact at the time. Polluted water was the sole cause of cholera.

Until 1845 the supply from Springhead via the Spring Ditch was adequate, but *c.* 1750 became less so as population grew and suburban sprawl developed. As early as 1785 a survey was ordered to be carried out to see how far the rapidly developing Sculcoates' demands could be met.[21] Five years later the corporation could make the momentous decision that, at the parish of Sculcoates' expense and for an acknowledgment of five shillings per annum, a channel could be cut from the Spring Ditch and water taken weekly between Saturday night and Monday morning on the understanding that on fourteen days' notice from the corporation, supply would cease.[22] Urban expansion west-wards obviously heightened the risk of contamination of the Spring Ditch and the possibilities of illegal abstraction of water. Therefore in 1790 the £188 estimate of a builder, George Jackson, was accepted for its arching over 'from the bridge leading into West Street to the Infirmary bridge'. Further modifications were carried out in the vicinity of the West Street bridge. The section of the Spring Ditch fronting the Infirmary was, as yet, left uncovered but posts and palings were ordered to be fixed on the opposite side to prevent unauthorised access to the water.[23] It was not until 1799 that plans were implemented for covering the line of the stream opposite the Infirmary:[24] these included the excavation of a pond or ornamental pool, the spoil from which was offered for the raising of the level of Prospect Street, provided the pool could be supplied from the Spring Ditch. A quarter of a century later, for reasons which will be apparent, this pool was filled in, and from 1833 Sir Richard Westmacott's statue of Dr John Alderson embellished the site.[25] The protective culverting of the all-important Spring Ditch lagged on suburban development: the significance of this cannot go unnoticed within the context of public health.

Attempts to improve supply and meet increasing demands brought lengthy crises, but ultimate success. In 1794 Julian Springs at Anlaby were bought outright by the corporation for £150 and in 1825, a year of drought conditions, further springs in the immediate vicinity were leased from trustees acting for Sir Thomas Legard.[26] In 1830, following the opening of the Junction Dock the previous year, the corporation decided to make a new street (St John Street) linking Junction Dock Bridge with Carr Lane. This scheme necessitated the demolition of the existing waterworks on the east side of Engine Street. New works, which cost the corporation £7500, were built 'near the Willows' immediately to the south of what is today Spring Bank, Spring Bank West and Princes Avenue.[27] It was at this time that several 'respectable inhabitants' with Charles Frost, the solicitor-historian, as their spokesman, besought the corporation to lay out a walk or promenade along the line of the Spring Ditch. Their immediate hopes went unfulfilled: the line of the old watercourse as far as the new waterworks was progressively filled in, and on financial grounds the aldermen found it impracticable to accede to the request.[28]

These changes coincided with extension of the town's boundaries and the growing importance of Sculcoates as a residential area led to the charge that, over matters of water supply, the town itself was being neglected to the advantage of the more affluent residents of Sculcoates.[29] Requests for extending supply to Sutton, Drypool, Southcoates and Garrison Side had to be refused and efforts to boost supply to meet ever increasing demands resulted in the leasing of another spring at Springhead and a decision to lead water to the waterworks from the Cottingham Drain along Newland Tofts Lane (Newland

Avenue).[30] But it was clear that inadequacy of provision would soon demand a drastic re-appraisal of the whole situation. The deliberations of a corporation water committee set up in 1838 resulted in an invitation being extended to Thomas Wicksteed of London, a hydraulics engineer of some reputation, to act in a consultative capacity. The results of the tests which Wicksteed carried out to assess the capacity of the springs at Springhead provided glimpses of the obvious in the opinion of Dr James Alderson and others, who considered that the real potential of Springhead needed to be more fully investigated—a theme reflected in the press at the time. As was so often the case, public controversy tended to develop on party lines. The majority of the members of the corporation supported Wicksteed's recommendation that the answer to the problem was that water should be taken from the River Hull: the opposition minority, supported by doctors like Alderson and Fewster Horner, and activists outside the corporation like J.J. Matthewson, tended to be lumped together as Tory diehards. Wicksteed's plan was accepted, the necessary Act of Parliament obtained in 1843, and on 24 August 1845 the first complete supply of water was obtained from the new corporation waterworks built on the banks of the River Hull immediately to the north of Stoneferry. Wicksteed considered that, unless population increased 'in a greater ratio' than anticipated, there would be a supply of 101 gallons per day for every house in Hull until 1880.[31]

This switch in 1849 to a dependence on river water was the sole cause of the cholera epidemic in 1849. The opponents of the scheme were not convinced that the water had any degree of purity, although after extraction from the river it went into two large settling reservoirs at low tide ('the great Salt Lake at Stoneferry') and then was filtered. They commented on the industrial and organic pollution contributed by Beverley and Driffield: there were complaints that the water was both muddy and salty, and Matthewson, in an intolerably prosy lecture to the Mechanics Institute in 1861, added flavour to public disquietude by asserting that 'the drainage of the cemeteries finds its way into the water we drink', and commented that 'you may filter pea soup until it is as fine as sherry but it will still be pea soup'.[32*]

After the epidemic of 1849 growing dissatisfaction resulted in the calling in, as consultant, of a second engineer, James Simpson, and attention was re-directed to Springhead as being an obviously purer source of supply. Simpson's views confirmed those of Wicksteed as well as that of Robert Aspland Marillier, the waterworks engineer, who, in an attempt to improve the position, investigated the possibility of the corporation extracting river water north of Wawne.[33]

It was William Warden, a plumber and glazier of Hessle, who ultimately confounded and surprised the experts. Warden considered from his own knowledge and experience that Springhead could be made to yield a more than sufficient supply of water if bores were sunk in the chalk, and in January 1858 he addressed a letter on the subject to Alderman J. W. Mayfield, chairman of the waterworks committee. Three months later he pressed the point and offered to procure five million gallons a day for a fee of £500 or nothing if he failed. Warden's confidence in a time of growing crisis had its own appeal, and an agreement was reached. Despite some delays two bores were sunk, and in 1860 a test revealed that water was being raised at the rate of four-and-a-quarter million gallons a day—far in excess of normal requirements. During the building of the Springhead pumping station by Thomas Dale, who succeeded Marillier as Engineer in 1861, a partial supply of Springhead water was made available to the town in 1862, piped to the Stoneferry Works, and distributed from there. Three years later, the river was for a time abandoned as a source, and soon afterwards the rest of the Spring Ditch was filled in. By July 1865 nearly six-and-a-half million gallons a day were being pumped at Springhead, more than justifying Warden's most optimistic claims, and providing assurance that, additional to domestic and industrial requirements, water was available for the fire service.[34*] Warden hardly received the recognition which was his due, but within the context of public health in Victorian Hull he must be numbered among the foremost of the town's benefactors.

The two decades following the epidemic of 1849 saw the real beginnings of improvement in other matters of public health. Government pressure, the ravages of the cholera (and a reminder again in 1854 when another outbreak claimed a further twenty-four victims) helped to persuade public opinion that there was much to be done.[35] But improvements had to be paid for, and the edge of local politics could become sharp, when it had to be tempered on the anvil of finance. It would require a close analysis of town politics in this period to identify all those directly concerned with improvement and those who for one reason or another were in opposition to change: few were prepared wholly to discount the cost, and, to use Lord Palmerston's expression, a 'war of the clean and the dirty parties' was fought out in Hull, as in many other towns. Inevitably doctors such as Alderman Sir Henry Cooper and Dr Boulter were in the ranks of the reformers. With them were such men as the youthful Councillor John Middleton, who became Chairman of Hull's Board of Works, and thus was largely responsible for some major street improvements. Ranged against them were those whom the militant Collins sweepingly designated 'the muck interest'. Among these could be numbered Aldermen Thomas Jackson and John Tall, Councillor Newton, 'the pet champion of the great garth interest' and Councillor Glossop, the brewer whose strange innate conservatism on virtually all matters of public health included an active defence of the individual's unrestricted right to keep pigs,[36] and earned him the title of 'Glossop the guardian angel of the grunters'. The improvement of the whole urban environment, whether expressed in terms of sanitation, housing regulations, or sewerage, necessarily involved interference with private property and 'private rights': in political terms the issues could run deep, and not least of all there was an understandable opposition to schemes which seemingly made 'the pockets of the people of Hull subservient to the pet experiments of the General Board of Health'.

A provisional order of 1851 constituted the borough council the Local Board of Health. Among the Board's first schemes was the optimistic promotion of an improvement bill in 1854, the draft of which, by the time it was introduced, had been severely mauled by local opposition interests: nevertheless, it had its importance and in addition to the Local Board of Health being empowered to provide municipal cemeteries, the resulting act laid down stringent building regulations. As the historian, Sheahan, with his personal experience of contemporary conditions, put it, 'The Improvement Act totally altered the existing state of things here as well as the character of the buildings'. Back-to-back housing was prohibited, outer walls had to be a minimum of nine-inch brick and minimal spatial requirements in terms of courts and yards were laid down. The Sanitary Committee organised more efficiently the removal of nightsoil and the cleansing of the streets and, under the Nuisances Removal Act of 1855, an inspector of nuisances began effectively to deal with the importation and exposure for sale of foodstuffs unfit for human consumption.

The elimination of open drains and the implementation of extensive drainage schemes was essential if the risk of cholera and typhoid was to be avoided. In 1853 much needed work began in the district east of the river, but in a low-lying area and without the aid of pumping engines, a fall of four feet per mile of necessity had a low effectiveness.

A sewerage scheme for the town west of the river was not begun until 1863, when on 25 September, before a substantial gathering of interested townspeople, Councillor Robert Waller manfully descended twenty-six feet below the surface of Neptune Street, off the developing Hessle Road, in order to lay the foundation stone of new drainage works. He received the inevitable silver trowel for his pains and then with local worthies adjourned to a tent for the even more inevitable luncheon and speechifying which such an occasion demanded. Anti-climax came early in 1864 when the contractors found themselves unable to proceed on the agreed contract price, and a delay of some months occurred before the work was resumed. But a whole decade of controversy had preceded the jollifications of September 1863, the basis of much of which was whether to 'pump' or 'gravitate': that is, whether to secure the discharge of sewers into the Humber by steam pumps or by natural fall. As a contemporary expressed it, 'the words "pumping" and "gravitation" were on every tongue'.[37] But the energetic and economic Henry Lambert and his 'gravitationists', on a plan produced by Constantine Butler, the assistant surveyor (who got £250 for his pains), won the day, and the Secretary of State was induced to authorise the necessary loan of £21,000.

But continuing population expansion (numbers topped two hundred thousand by the last decade of the century), industrial growth, and the constant threat of a sudden epidemic infection presented by large numbers of transient emigrants from Europe *en route* via Liverpool to the Americas and elsewhere, provided increasing health hazards to the town community. There was a vicious outbreak of scarlet fever in the autumn of 1881, which reached epidemic proportions with high infant mortality: in fact there were no less that 689 deaths from the disease in Hull and

Sculcoates, mainly of children under five.[38] Immediate public reaction forced a government inquiry in 1882. There was a growing concern, too, over high infant mortality from other types of infection, which would be even more directly related to an inadequate sanitary system. Action and counter-measures were more briskly practical than those of a generation before at the time of the cholera. In 1884 a Hull Sanitary Association came into being, the activities of which owed much to the exertions of William Hunt, the Editor of the *Eastern Morning News*,[39] and the Revd J. Malet Lambert, the Vicar of Newland, and which, for some ten years, helped to educate the public and concentrate attention on matters of sanitary reform. Official action resulted in a hospital for infectious diseases being opened in Hedon Road in 1885, improvement in refuse and nightsoil collection, the provision of a refuse destructor in Chapman Street in 1882, and, most vital of all, in due course the building of pumping stations at the sewerage outfalls to make discharge possible at high tides and so quicken clearance. But until after the first world war no real progress was made with plans for conversion of houses to a system of water-borne sanitation.

In the ten years following its formation in 1852 the Local Board of Health carried out an unusual degree of street improvement, widening and resurfacing, earning at the time the commendation of the astringent and critical Collins.[40] A substantial amount of credit for this must be given to Councillor John Middleton who, in 1852, when in his early twenties, was elected by the ratepayers of Market Place Ward on the Board of Health ticket and quickly became Chairman of the Committee of Works which carried out major improvements in the Market Place, Lowgate and Nelson Street, and laid out Park Street which at first was called Elm Tree Avenue. Footpaths were widened and granite sets replaced cobbled surfaces. Middleton's short spell in public life did not go wholly uncriticised, but the illness which obliged an early retirement from public affairs and brought about his premature death in 1863 at the early age of forty-four, deprived Hull of an unusually able civic leader and active reformer.

In 1863 the Local Board of Health received new powers under an act confirming certain provisional orders relating to Hull and certain other towns, particularly in respect of acquisition of land and property for street improvement. In fact, by then and under plans which were prepared by the Board's surveyor, T. F. Sharpe in 1862, much had already been done, and yet more was to be achieved. In the old town, Lowgate was widened opposite St Mary's Church. This coincided with the restoration of that fabric by George Gilbert Scott and the threatened demolition of the tower was avoided by providing a 'walk through' at ground level. Improvements were also carried out at the north end of Lowgate in order to improve access to the new Town Hall, then being built to the plans of Cuthbert Brodrick. The Victorians were scarcely conservationists, and to widen corners, for example, property was demolished at the junctions of Scale Lane and Salthouse Lane with High Street. Outside the old town Great Passage Street was widened, and the improvement of access southwards to the Western (Albert) Dock was effected by laying out Commercial Road, which, skirting the Holy Trinity Burial Ground, linked Castle Street and Kingston Street: the widening of Waterhouse Lane eased traffic flow northwards from the new dock towards Sculcoates.

Reinforcing the view of Charles Frost and his associates in 1831, that a 'promenade' be laid out along the Spring Ditch, a project had been mooted as early as 1837 for an avenue or walk girdling the town from Humber bank to Humber bank. At the time such a scheme was little more than a pipe dream, but it indicated in an age of rapid growth and suburban overspill a growing awareness of a need for recreational amenities, which probably owed something to the Linnaeus Street Botanic Gardens being opened to the public in 1821 and the laying out of the Spring Bank Zoological Gardens in 1840.[41] In 1845 plans were revived and the Grand Victoria Promenade Company was registered with the object of implementing such a scheme, and constructing a wide tree-lined avenue.[42] Hull regrettably did not get its 'Victoria Promenade', and the scheme which, in essence, would have had to have been a form of turnpike or toll road to secure appropriate financial return to investors, failed to get off the drawing-board. Nevertheless, Frost lived long enough to see a Spring Bank scheme coming to fruition after 1855 with the filling-in of the Spring Ditch. But one official and far-sighted scheme did prove abortive, unfortunately: following legal action, the failure of the corporation in 1863 to secure part of the Citadel site, when it was sold off by the Commissioners of Woods and Forests, meant the end of plans to develop the area as a park.

In 1860 the growing public demand for a park was met by the combined efforts of the Mayor and the Local Board. Early that year the Board appointed a Committee to consider the 'practicability' of providing a 'people's park'. The Committee advertised for offers of land, but the Mayor, Zachariah Pearson, a well-to-do shipowner, with philanthropic ideas spiced by business acumen, offered, under certain conditions, twenty-seven acres of land on the west side of Beverley Road. The area was to be planned by the Board of Health as a park, with trees and shrubs, and gas-lighted roads were to give access to the properties on the ten acres on three sides of the proposed park, which Pearson had reserved for building purposes: with the religious susceptibilities of the well-heeled middle class who were to reside there well in mind, no music was to be allowed on Sundays. Thus Hull got its first public park and the area which otherwise could have succumbed to industrial development was preserved for prosperity.[43]

Pearson's tragedy of personal bankruptcy, which came two years afterwards, as the result of his buying ships to attempt to run arms through the Federal blockade during the American Civil War, was pathetically heightened by his decision to present a statue of the Queen, which had been commissioned from the sculptor Thomas Earle, in commemoration of the royal visit of 1854. With a tact and delicacy which was universally admired, William Moss, who was Mayor in 1862, bought the statue from the bankrupt's assigns and so was enabled to implement Pearson's original plan.[44]

In spite of the triumphs of iron, coal and steam, Hull remained poor and squalid, but with a superior kind of poverty, and a longer life in which to enjoy it. Between 1851 and 1854 the town spent more than £108,000 on improved streets and drains. Deaths per thousand of the population fell from 30.5 in 1852 to 22 in 1864,[45] never rising again above a peak of 27 (1875) and falling as low as 16 in 1889 and 1894. In some years the birth rate was 41 per thousand and up to 71 in the wards with the younger population.[46]

Illness and mortality were connected with sewage-disposal, with whole streets of houses having nothing but earth closets until as late as the 1920s, with nauseous smells, especially on warm days. The wooden seats of the shared privies in Victorian slum courts were soon chopped up for firewood, and the iron rail which replaced them, as was the case in a court in Mill Street, was often too high for children, who had to defecate on the floor.[47] In 1899 there were about 59,000 houses, and to 36,000 there was no access except through the front door, but as only 10,000 had their own closet this was not as inconvenient as it might seem, though in most of the 10,000 the night-soil collectors had to carry their baskets through the house.[48] This often happened when the inhabitants were at breakfast. As their name implies, the nightsoil men were intended to work at night, but as in most cases there was no one to let them in, they had to choose a time which enabled them to collect the ash and excrement and, as the law required, have their carts off the streets by ten in the morning.[49] When their carts were too full it was not ash only that fell on to the pavement, so that in a wet season in the streets there were 'stagnant channels of a lightish brown syrup', and the dust which blew about in dry weather consisted of road grit and horse-dung pickled in this liquid. Nevertheless a guest at the dustmen's annual dinner noted that 'their occupation did not interfere with their appetite'.[50]

At first the muckgarths to which the nightsoil was taken were outside the town, but as the built up area grew some by *c.* 1865 were in thickly inhabited districts. There was one, warm, wet and stinking in the August rain near the splendid Ionic portico of Kingston Wesleyan chapel in Witham, to the indignation of the middle-class householders who published a protest.[51] Several sites became famous. There was one on Hedon Road which in the hot summer of 1881 began to ferment so dangerously inside its protective cover of clay that it was decided that there might be an explosion if its contents were disturbed, and it was left until cooler weather made it possible to take the contents out to sea.[52] Near the slums of the Groves, on the east bank of the river, there were muckgarths draining into the water of the tidal Sutton drain, which at low water was 'lined with black, putrid matter'.[53] Once a butcher was fined because he used his backyard privy as a slaughterhouse, and another came to grief not because his slaughterhouse was in a muckgarth (some were intersected by lanes) but because his meat was rotten.[54] Even at the end of the century bad meat was carried round the poorest streets by hawkers with their dirty handcarts.[55]

As late as the 1930s there were stables with dunghills in the town attracting such clouds of flies that no food or drink could be left uncovered. In the nineteenth century there were far more stables. but the connection between flies and disease was not understood. Some doctors suspected that it was the clouds of flies which caused the summer epidemics of diarrhoea. One of them, Dr Holder, wrote that in his experience deaths from diarrhoea were ten times commoner with bottle-fed babies than with those who were breast-fed, and he must have seen that it was flies that contaminated the bottles.[56] He was exceptional in his understanding, and even twenty years later a journalist could write 'It is somewhat strange that medical authorities are in some doubt respecting the precise cause'.[57] It was a very fine summer when ice for refrigerators as well as for trawlers was coming into the Hull docks from Norway at the rate of three thousand tons a week, and in a single month there were more than sixty deaths of babies dehydrated by diarrhoea.

Typhus, especially in the poorer parts of the town, was still common in the 1860s. The cause was not then known to be the rickettsia transferred by bites of the body louse. It was a dangerous disease, with a twelve per cent mortality.[58] Prague Terrace, Beverley Road, was known as Plague Terrace even after the eccentric change of name to Kottingham Close. There were three cases of typhus there, one fatal, in October 1865. Privies and pigsties soaked the ground, and there was a wall 'covered with an excretion of nightsoil which has worked its way through'.[59] It was the whitish efflorescence which had once been the raw material of the saltpetre-man.

The least unsavory smells were those from urban cowsheds, one of which still stood at the corner of Craven Street in 1920. The Hull Cowkeepers' and Farmers' Association often complained about the regulations of the Local Board of Health. A cowkeeper and milkman in Alexandra Road came to public notice not so much because of the flies from his dunghill as because of the 'black froth' oozing from the soil where cattle, killed under a foot-and-mouth disease order, had been buried in a shallow grave.[60] Naturally there were complaints about the smell. The stipendiary magistrate, incensed by the dreadful odour of rotten linseed at a kiln in Beeton Street, imposed a fine of ten shillings for each day for which it still continued.[61] A man living in Blanket Row complained of the smell from the cattle, slaughterhouses and sawmills there, and the painful bites from swarms of little black flies. Just before the great diarrhoea epidemic of 1885 the authorities were asked to do something about a muckgarth near Beverley Road: 'The stench of this fetid matter is quite sufficient to cause a fever'.[62] It was not until it was almost ended that the visitation was shown to have been caused by pollution of the water-supply. A traveller from Leeds wondered whether the cause might be the very bad smell from a tannery near Paragon Station which gave his wife 'a violent fit of vomiting' as soon as they arrived at their hotel.[63] He was not altogether mistaken. If all the causes of smells had been removed most of the causes of epidemics, though not of this one, would have been removed also. Smells were to some extent masked by smoke from coal fires and the 250 industrial chimneys which even in 1894 had only sixteen 'smoke-preventers in use'.[64]

There was one disease, smallpox, which was almost completely overcome, by vaccination, but the method of vaccination which had to be used for ninety years sometimes, though rarely, brought other diseases. Full protection against smallpox was possible only if there was a second vaccination, so in any epidemic there were always some smallpox victims who had received a single vaccination in childhood. Opposition to vaccination was especially strong in Hull and was long based on the defects of the old method - the injection into the arm of matter from a patient who had already been successfully vaccinated. In 1877 a Mr Henry James Rumming expressed his conscientious objection:

> He *would* have it done directly from the animal. Medical testimony was to the effect that ninety per cent of the blood of Hull's population was poisoned with syphilis. He had a moral right to protest against his child's blood being poisoned through the sins of others'.[65]

The danger which was the grounds for his opposition to compulsory vaccination was real. The press occasionally printed horrifying accounts of babies dying through the effects of vaccination: but the risk was small and his belief in the almost universal prevalence of syphilis was ridiculous. Even in the insane asylum only one death in twenty was from tertiary syphilis,[66] though a sensible man might sometimes distrust official pronouncements in a town where the Medical Officer of Health certified houses as fit for habitation, in a narrow court of sixty houses, with the two upper rooms unusable from rotten floors and falling ceilings, and the other rooms measuring only twelve feet by nine feet nine inches.[67]

The Anti-Vaccination League had many members in Hull. At one of their open-air meetings, on Hessle Road, addressed by a Dr Atkinson from Leeds, the vote against the compulsory-vaccination law was unanimous.[68] To be known as an opponent of vaccination could be a political asset. In a council by-election in 1885 in the middle-class Coltman Ward (where Sir Tatton Sykes II was believed to keep a mistress) the leftish James Wilson defeated a mainly Conservative candidate. Wilson was almost a Socialist, but it was his opposition to vaccination which brought him victory.[69]

By that time it was becoming possible to avoid the arm-to-arm method. The secretary of the Hull Anti-Vaccination League would not have his child vaccinated unless it was done with pure calf-lymph and the doctor took full responsibility. He was offered a tube labelled 'Animal Lymph from Calf Number 22', but the doctor would not accept sole responsibility. The man was able to maintain his status as a martyr for conscience by refusing vaccination for the child on these conditions. He was fined,[70] and it is quite possible that he was not prosecuted again. Certainly the lay magistrates were believed to deal gently with objections such as this until compulsory vaccination was abolished in 1898. Experience showed that vaccination really was very effective. When smallpox appeared in a lodging-house in 1884 none of the inmates who had been vaccinated twice was infected and the two who died had never been vaccinated at all.[71] About that time it was believed that a child had died from erysipelas caused by vaccination; but in the last serious epidemic of smallpox in Hull those who had received two vaccinations remained immune. Those vaccinated once only, if they caught the disease, were found to have one chance in ten of dying from it, but those never vaccinated had only a fifty per cent chance of surviving.[72]

From 1865 there was an excellent supply of spring-water from the pumps at Springhead. Newland took Hull water while it was still part of Cottingham because of the decision of the local board to let the overflow from the settling tanks go into Newland beck, from which all the domestic supply of the hamlet had been taken, and also because the water-closet of the former snuff-mill flushed into the beck. The vicar and other influential inhabitants of

Cottingham protested that one part of the parish was being allowed to poison another.[73] After a Local Government Board inquiry in 1885 Newland and St John's Wood were allowed to take their water at a cheaper rate from Garbutt's private water-works in Newington, which he had set up for his Avenues estate.[74]

When the Hull supply was so fatally taken from the river, polluted with the cholera vibrio, the pumps were at Stoneferry, in Reservoir Road, and when the Springhead works were opened the same pumps were still used. There was one strange consequence of this. Immature eels make their way up river and wriggle over wet grass into fresh water. The route from the river Hull to the reservoirs was ideal for them, though many were found in Queen's Dock also. From the reservoirs the little eels were drawn into the water-mains, and many years after the danger was gone, boys were warned not to put their mouth to the tap to drink, since they could swallow a 'worm'. Sometimes an accumulation of eels blocked pipes as far away as Coltman Street, where many of the most affluent families lived. A plumber named Cherny charged much less than the corporation for restoring the supply. He simply blasted them out 'by applying his powerful force-pump'.[75] Once back in the mains they might block other domestic pipes and provide him with more work. In 1879 half the water from the springs went through the Stoneferry engines, but soon only one quarter went that way.[76] The Springhead water was hard and pure, but Dr Kelburn King suggested that the main cause of typhoid was probably that when the pressure was dropped at night sewage from the soil entered joints and cracks in the mains.[77] With iron pipes the maintenance of a constant pressure involved the loss of part of the supply into the ground. It was realised that other springs must be tapped. The Sand Beck water-works were constructed at Cottingham and connected with the Hull system. The water was pure, but the mud on the navvies' boots was not, and this led to the great diarrhoea epidemic of 1885. There were more than 20,000 cases, but no one who drank only Newington water was affected.[78]

In many places where new houses were built there was good brick-clay which was dug out and made into bricks by clamp-burning. Brickponds multiplied and soon became foul with all kinds of refuse. One on the east side of Beverley Road gave off a smell 'highly dangerous to public health'.[79] Often when the pond was overflowing the ground was consolidated with still more rubbish, and houses were built in the middle of what soon became a swamp. The Improvement Act of 1882 did not provide a real cure, since it only required that before a site could be built on, it had to be filled to within two feet of the surface and then covered with four inches of concrete. This still left twenty inches for a kind of moat. Even this imperfect arrangement was too much for the corrupt Newington local board. When the area was about to be brought into Hull not less than 6000 house-plans were rushed through and approved so that jerry-builders would not be inconvenienced by Hull by-laws; and when in 1893 sanitary reformers eventually persuaded the Hull council to make stricter building regulations, the friends of builders on the planning committee quickly passed 7000 plans for houses which would have to conform to the old rules only.[80]

Disabling intestinal griping was for a long time called 'summer cholera', caused, it was thought, by fruit and especially by bad fruit. Probably the actual cause was the contamination of fruit and other food by flies. Some immunity was acquired. One winter children were seen sucking ice from 'one of Nature's icecream saloons', a ditch in which sewage could be seen. Dealers used to throw rotten plums to hungry children, and children ate fruit and crab claws from land against the Sculcoates Lane muckgarth.[81] In the packed classrooms of the new Board Schools it was soon realised that many children were half-starved. Some came to school hungry. Others were absent because mothers, with no food in the house, kept them in bed all day. The Radical Club wanted the School Board to follow the Grimsby example and provide penny-dinners, and free dinners would be better still.[82] It was Dr Evan Fraser who drew attention to the children who had to stay in bed, and he too wanted free dinners for them.[83] Shortly afterwards a charitable free-breakfast scheme was started, and in one district alone it was found that two hundred children had been coming to school without any breakfast.[84] In 1892-3 the School Children's Help Society gave 320 free dinners a day between December and May, but a year later could only afford half as many.[85] Compulsory school attendance also demonstrated the seriousness of the ailments of children which were then called 'zymotic' diseases. In January 1882, after consulting Birmingham and Leicester, the Medical Officer of Health asked for an extension of the Christmas holiday to check a bad outbreak of scarlet fever.[86] It was found that parents, for fear of prosecution, often sent children back to school before they had recovered properly, and when for this reason the Board started fewer prosecutions, there was an alarming rise in the number of absentees.[87]

All this was connected with poverty. Not all absentees had been ill. A child not a school might earn a few pennies. Many people thought that drink was the real cause of poverty. Though much Victorian temperance propaganda displayed in schools as well as for adults now seems bizarre, it did have its effect, and the Victorian poor probably could never have escaped from poverty unless they had ceased to spend so much on drink. There was long a tendency for all increases in wealth to become transformed into the fortunes of brewers and distillers. At the end of Victoria's reign, with the national income rising more slowly than now, in the years 1892-1901, English spending on drink rose by 81 per cent, and though Hull was poor, the people are not likely to have drunk much less than others.[88]

Drunkenness was readily recognised, but drug-taking was much less visible, since it usually led to no disorderly conduct, and it may just possibly have done more good than harm. To keep babies asleep for most of the day while mothers were away at work for wages without which the children might have starved, they drugged them with such opium-based patent medicines as Godfrey's Cordial. Even the children of the rich—Wilberforce was one—were often dosed by nurses ignorant of the fact that this could lead to a lifelong addiction. Enormous amounts of laudanum were taken by adults who had acquired the habit. One old woman took up to six ounces a day,[89] and a Hull druggist in a small way of business sold a gallon a week.[90] The drug chest of Lofthouse and Saltmer, wholesale grocers, in 1879 contained thirty-one pounds of opium.[91]

Alcohol, far more noticeable, was the drug chosen by most in its various forms of beer, rum, gin and the like. They felt the need to drink in outlandish places. In a storm off Cape Horn the mate of the *Prince Charlie*, bound from Callao to Hull, had such an unquenchable thirst that he assaulted the stewardess to get the keys of her store of cordials, and was heavily fined by a Hull magistrate.[92] A man who had been drinking with soldiers from the garrison woke up in a privy at the South End, surprised to find that he was in military uniform.[93] A pauper, refreshed on his day out from the Sculcoates workhouse, was not penalised for returning drunk as he was a freeman, politically drunk because he had just voted in the 1867 general election;[94] but three men who came back drunk after one of their days out from the Hull work-house in 1875 lost all leave for three months as they had merely been treated in the ordinary way.[95] There was a tendency to see all who had suffered misfortune as deserving a drink. No penalty was imposed on a man found trying to take rum illegally to his father, a prisoner for debt, and another man was let off for smuggling liquor to a debtor, though he was unrelated to him.[96]

Nevertheless Hull opinion was Puritan and strongly opposed to drink, and for a long time the only Conservatives who could stand in a Hull election were teetotallers, though the outlook of the mob was different. Bruce's 1872 Licensing Act led to three riots in a week. The worst started outside the Artillery Barracks in Park Street, where the Liberals had intended to celebrate the glory of Bruce, Gladstone, and shorter drinking hours. The mob then went to Anlaby Road, to Market Place, and to Holderness Road, smashing lamps and assaulting policemen. A few of them were arrested and gaoled.[97] There were less dangerous ways of demonstrating liberty. The Bricklayers' Arms, North Street, had a removable brick so that, especially on Sundays, customers could be served through a hole in the wall, in the house next door.[98]

After the passage of Bruce's Act public houses opened at five in the morning and closed at midnight, remaining open for nineteen hours a day, except on Saturdays, when they had to close at eleven and not open again until noon on Sunday. Those whom the law recognised as *bona fide* travellers, however, could be served on Sunday mornings, and to become *bona fide* drinkers walked into the country, or hired cabs to take them on excursions to the inns of Welton, Elloughton, Cottingham and Anlaby. Some were inclined to get out and fight on the way home and extra police were needed to deal with them on Anlaby Road especially.[99] It was thought that some of those who had never seen the sea did actually arrive at Hornsea or Withernsea, drinking on the train and spending all day in a public house. The electric trams of 1899 took passengers to the edge of the city at eight miles an hour, so that they were able to spend much of Sunday drinking in the country, 'a nuisance to most of the neighbouring villages and a disgrace to the city'.[100]

Though drinkers survived, many were ruined, but a few made a fortune out of drink. Sir Hew Crawfurd-Pollock, Bart (1843-86) after serving in the U.S.Cavalry married a barmaid who lived with her mother in Dock Street. They separated because of his violence and Lady Pollock, with an income from the estate equivalent to £15,000 a year tax-free in 1988, withdrew to Withernsea.[101] The husband was perhaps more typical of Victorian drinking habits than the wife, and the work of temperance societies probably confirmed many in their determination not to drink even beer and persuaded some to become teetotallers. The lapse of a century has made the celebrations of these societies look strange. On Good Friday 1865 (very few could be persuaded to observe the day as the most solemn in the Christian year) supporters of the Hull Temperance League heard an oration by Thomas Worsnop, 'the Yorkshire Garibaldi', and then listened to 'temperance melodies', such as 'My drink is water clear'.[102]

Some results of the movement lasted into the present century. In 1875:

> Mr Charles Wilson MP, with a view to discouraging the drinking habits of the working class, resolved to try the experiment of converting his old office in Railway Street into a refreshment room where a cheap and good meal and non-intoxicating drink could be obtained'.[103]

He was following a plan which had been tried successfully in Liverpool, and his refreshment room eventually became one of those conducted by the People's Public Houses Company. Their first house was opened in 1877 opposite Coltman Street, on Hessle Road, in 1877,[104] with the support of Wilson, Francis Reckitt and Thomas Stratten. A capital of £10,000 was subscribed and within two years, when the annual meeting was held at the Prospect Street Cocoa House, there were seven other houses providing temperate refreshment, and two more were projected. In winter meat-pies and soup were offered as well as cocoa (the favourite drink because it was also a food) tea and coffee. The company paid a dividend of ten per cent and was still able to put money into reserve. In 1881 there was a new venture, now that some of the needs of the temperate working class had been met, ' a place where middle-class ladies and gentlemen can go and procure refreshment of a superior quality at moderate prices'.[105] This, the Wilberforce Café, at the corner of St John Street and Queen's Road, is now the

St John's public house. The company was declining by 1920, with eleven refreshment rooms, when it had once had twenty, and was soon to be dissolved.[106] These refreshment rooms were the most permanent outcome of the efforts of Charles H. Wilson. As one of the two Hull MPs he promoted bills in Parliament to close all public houses on Sundays. He had much enthusiastic local support and aroused furious opposition, even among the Radicals. Some were for Wilson, before he fomented the great dock strike, but their most articulate member, N. B. Billany, was against him, since Sunday was the day when a working man could drink without losing time at work; but Billany had no objection to closing public houses at all other times.[107]

Many Anglican clergy and virtually all Nonconformist ministers were strong supporters of the temperance movement. May festivities, once entirely pagan,[108] were revived in the cause of temperance, mainly by Nonconformists. The Revd G. T. Coster, pastor of the Fish Street Congregational Church, in 1867 started May-day early morning breakfasts for children, and ten years later the Campbell Street Free Methodists and the Beverley Congregationalists also were giving free breakfasts. At Fish Street, at first light on May morning, more children turned up than the classroom could hold, and there was a large crowd waiting outside.[109]

Sources

1.   *HA*, 18 Oct. 1794, 22 Nov. 1794, 7 June 1800, 21 Sept. 1805, 10 Feb. 1816, 3 Jan. 1818.
2.   Ibid., 28 Oct. 1831.
3.   BB10 f.57.
4.   S. Middlebrook, *Newcastle upon Tyne: its growth and achievement* (1950) 204-6.
5.   *HA*, 6, 20 Apr. 1832.
6.   *HA*, 14 Sept. 1832, which reported no more cases in the town.
7.   KHRO, WM 31.
8.   J. Alderson, *A Brief Outline of the History and Progress of the Cholera at Hull* (1832).
9.   See the *Lancet*, 28 Apr. 1832.
10.*   J. Ayre, *A Reply to Certain Statements . . . Board of Health* (1832); Some members of the Board of Health, *Statement of Facts . . . Observations made by Dr Ayre* (1832). From information supplied from the research work of Mr Bernard Foster;

DNB s.v. ALDERSON, SIR JAMES.

11.* Rep. Select Cttee on the Health of Towns (1840) *Minutes of Evidence* Qs 2324, 2350-62. Mr Foster has demonstrated that the report for the Manchester Statistical Society contains inconsistencies.

12. *HA*, 27 Aug. 1841: App. 1st Rep. Comm. State of Large Towns 1844, Vol. XVII. Session 1844. p. 2: 2nd Rep. 1845, Vol XVIII 308 ff.

13.* The report is printed *in extenso* in *HA*, 26 Nov. 1847. Cf. Canon Cooper Smith in *Things that were* (1923). Mr MacMahon wrote this before Mr S. Bryant's republication of the report of the Medical Society (1977).

14. *Report by General Board of Health . . . 1849*, p. 6.

15. Ibid., 46.

16. H. Cooper, 'On the Mortality of Hull in the Autumn of 1849' and 'On the Prevalence of Diseases in Hull', *Report of the 23rd meeting of the British Association for the Advancement of Science*, pp. 102-3.

17. J. Sibree, *Fifty Years' Recollections of Hull; or Half-a-Century of Public Life and Ministry* (1884) 84.

18. *HA*, 28 Sept. 1849, 21, 28 Dec. 1849; 1 Jan., 1 Feb. 1850.

19.* *Rep. to the General Board of Health on the Epidemic Cholera of 1848-9* (1850), App. A 101-6 (Report by Dr Sutherland on Cholera in Hull). Both Boards of Guardians claimed that they had lost letters from Dr Sutherland and from the General Board of Health.

20. Sibree, op. cit., 77.

21. BB10 f.19.

22. BB10 f.95; KHRO, D. 941b.

23. BB10 ff.102-3.

24. BB10 f.310.

25. BB10 f.310; H. Simpson, *History of the Hull Royal Infirmary* (1888) p. 11; *Dict. Br. Sculptors*.

26. BB10 f.211; KHRO, L. 1364; BB11 f. 370.

27. BB11 f.541; Gawtress, 225.

28. BB12 ff.52, 87.

29. Gawtress, 226.

30. BB12 ff.84, 199, 206.

31. Sheahan, 705-7; KHRO, Report Water Ctte, 1842; Letter Wicksteed-Thompson, 1 May 1843; J. W. Mayfield, *History of the Springhead Waterworks . . .* (1909); J. Matthewman, *A Lecture on the Water we drink* (1861) pp. 16-17.

32.* Matthewman, op. cit., 6-7. The water taken from the river came from a point close to the Hull sewage outfall.

33. Mayfield, op. cit., p. 25 ff. Matthewman, op. cit., p. 10 ff.

34.* Sheahan, 708; Mayfield, op. cit. In dry summers water was still taken from the river, and consequently some household pipes were blocked by eels.

35. C. Creighton, *A History of Epidemics in Britain* (1965) 852.

36. *Portraits of Public Men*, 4, 95, 100, 158; *Hull Free Press*, 1853.

37. Sheahan, 423.

38. Mins. Sanitary Ctte.

39. *EMN*, 7 July, 2 Nov. 1883; i Feb. 1884; 7-12 July 1884.

40. *HA*, 23 Sept. 1863.

41. Sheahan, 697-8; *HA*, 27 July 1841.

42. Sheahan, 694; Mayfield, 55.

43. Mins Local Board of Health, 19 Jan., 18 Feb. 1860; Mayfield, op. cit.; J. Smith, *Proceedings relative to Pearson's Park*, (1860).

44. Mayfield, op. cit.: Sheahan, 274, 694; S. T. Xenos, *Depredations, or Overend Gurney and Co. and the Greek and Oriental Steam Navigation Company* (London,

1869).
45.   *EMN*, 3 May 1865.
46.   Medical Officer of Health, *Report, 1901*, 11.
47.   *EMN*, 4 Aug. 1865.
48.   B. Foster, 'Public Health in Hull in the Nineteenth Century', (Hull University, M.Phil., 1979) 121a.
49.   *EMN*, 22 Aug. 1878.
50.   *Hull Critic*, 10 Jan. 1885, 7.
51.   *EMN*, 15 Apr. 8 Aug. 1865.
52.   *HN*, 25 June 1881.
53.   Ibid., 20 Sept. 1879.
54.   *HA*, 4 June 1841.
55.   *EMN*, 15 July 1899.
56.   Ibid., 21 Aug. 1878.
57.   Ibid., 4 Aug. 1899.
58.   H. Zinsser, *Rats, Lice and History*, 235.
59.   *EMN*, 20 Oct. 1865.
60.   Ibid., 24 Oct. 1885.
61.   Ibid., 2 Sept. 1885.
62.   Ibid., 24 Feb. 1885.
63.   Ibid., 28 Mar. 1885.
64.   Ibid., 31 Jan. 1894.
65.   Ibid., 17 Nov. 1877.
66.   Ibid., 11 Mar. 1885.
67.   Ibid., 12 Jan. 1885.
68.   Ibid., 15 June 1882.
69.   Ibid., 24 Apr. 1885.
70.   Ibid., 11 May 1882.
71.   *Hull Critic*, 5 July 1884, 5.
72.   *EMN*, 1 July 1899.
73.   Ibid., 16 Apr. 1865.
74.   Ibid., 17 Mar. 1885.
75.   Ibid., 11 May 1865.
76.   Ibid., 27 Sept. 1875.
77.   Ibid., 23 Jan. 1875.
78.   Ibid., 14 Apr. 5 May 1885.
79.   B. Foster, *Living and Dying: a picture of nineteenth century Hull*, 66; *EMN*, 3 Apr. 1875.
80.   Foster, M.Phil. thesis on Public Health, op. cit., 117, 121a.
81.   *EMN*, 19 and 25 Aug. 1878.
82.   Ibid., 23 Feb. 1885.
83.   Ibid., 3 Nov. 1885.
84.   Ibid., 12 Jan. 1886.
85.   Ibid., 3 Feb. 1894.
86.   Ibid., 7 Jan. 1882.
87.   Ibid., 1 Jan. 1894.
88.   R. C. K. Ensor, *England 1870-1914*, 204, 320.
89.   Foster, *Living and Dying*, op. cit., 131-5.
90.   *HA*, 10 Feb. 1843.
91.   *HN*, 18 Jan. 1879.
92.   *EMN*, 9 June 1867.
93.   *HA*, 7 May 1841.
94.   *EMN*, 19 July 1867.

95. Ibid., 18 Mar. 1875.
96. *HA*, 11 Dec. 1840, 7 May 1841.
97. *HN*, 4 Jan. 1873.
98. Ibid., 12 Feb. 1881.
99. *EMN*, 7 June 1882.
100. Ibid., 1 Sept. 1899.
101. J. Bateman, *The Great Landowners of Great Britain and Ireland*, 362; *EMN*, 6 Jan. 1886.
102. *EMN*, 15 Apr. 1865.
103. Ibid., 14 Jan. 1875.
104. *HN*, 9 Sept. 1877.
105. Ibid., 11 June 1881.
106. Kelly's *Directory* (1920) 576 (Cocoa and Coffee Rooms).
107. *HN*, 6 June 1881.
108. J. G. Frazer, *The Golden Bough* (Abridged Edition) 119-35.
109. *HN*, 5 May 1877.

21

Railways

In August 1824 4000 or more people bought tickets to the Citadel to watch the filling of a balloon with gas and the ascent of W. W. Sadler—one of his last, since he was killed a few weeks later. Many thousands in the town and nearby villages saw him go up, with one passenger, Mr Rees Davis, and come down at Preston, a few miles to the east.[1]

The arrival of steamboats on the Humber, ten years before this, was of far greater importance than this spectacle. The first was the *Caledonia*, built in Scotland, which came to Hull in 1814, soon joined by the *John Bull* and several other boats plying from Hull to Grimsby, Gainsborough, Selby and Thorne.[2] The capital came mainly from farmers and landowners in the neighbourhood of Thorne, one of whom, Pearson, had a shipyard at Thorne. It was there that the *Kingston*, the first Hull sea-going steamer was built, with engines from Overton's, a Hull firm.[3] She was timber built, nearly 106 ft long and with her 60 horsepower engines, just able to go to London and return within the week. In the early days of steam, boiler pressures were low, but there were occasional explosions, some serious. In 1826 the *Graham*, with passengers for Hull from Grimsby, blew up in the Humber, killing four men and injuring many.[4] The explosion on the *Union*, at the Ferryboat Dock in 1837, as she was ready to sail for Gainsborough, was worse. Twelve passengers and a man standing on the pier were killed.[5] Nevertheless every year there were more steam packets on the river, providing services which the railways were soon to offer. In 1834 it was possible to leave Hull at seven or eight in the morning, according to the tide, take the train at Selby, and be in

Leeds by one. On Tuesdays and Thursdays, though the line over the Pennines was unfinished, Hull people could reach Liverpool in the evening.[6] There were seven boats a day for Grimsby, several to Barton and New Holland, and, except on Sundays, one a day for Gainsborough, Thorne, Selby, Goole and York.[7] Many of the steamers towed lines of barges with horses and livestock. All this led to a great increase in traffic since the little steamers were quite the most economic form of transport yet developed. The pack horses, once congesting parts of Hull on market days, had been able to carry rather more than one hundredweight, and on a turnpike a horse could draw a cart with one ton. River boats moved fifty tons per nominal horsepower, though for the sake of speed they actually carried much less.[8] With passengers and cargo the *Vivid* went to London at ten knots.[9]

Just before the first railway line reached Hull, as well as the services across the North Sea, there were two packets a week to Yarmouth, weekly packets to Hartlepool, Newcastle, Leith and Aberdeen and a packet which sailed for Newcastle on Sundays with arrangements for passengers for Whitby, Hartlepool, Sunderland and Shields to leave by boat.[10] Because of their wide paddle-boxes these early steamers could not get into the Humber dock and often obstructed other shipping by berthing in the Humber dock basin.

For a long time, because of their being independent of the wind at most times, steamers were sometimes handled with too little caution. The *Forfarshire* (the Grace Darling ship) was wrecked on the Farne Islands with the loss of 35 lives simply because she left Hull with one boiler not working.[11] The magnificently furnished *Victoria* had two separate explosions, both after her arrival in the Thames. The first, in March 1838, killed three of the crew.[12] Repaired and back in service she reached London in twenty-one hours. A collision with a collier in the Pool of London stopped her engines and when the boiler exploded four of the crew were killed.[12]

Neither this nor the arrival of the railway ended her career. In 1843 it was worthwhile to fit her with Napier's patent paddles which provided great power with less breadth, so that with her reduced beam she was able to enter the dock.[13] At the end of the century it was still possible to get a return ticket for Aberdeen by sea for fifteen shillings, with the usual attendance of stewards and stewardesses who would provide provisions and liquors at moderate rates. There was electric light throughout.[14]

The iron-built *Edina*, of Leith, until the outbreak of war in 1939, provided a service to the Firth of Forth for passengers, who could be put off at Newcastle. She sank in Princes Dock when hit by a bomb in 1941.

Wednesday, 1 July 1840, the day the Hull and Selby railway line was opened, is a milestone date in the history of modern Hull, for with the port's first railway—in effect an eastwards extension of the Leeds-Selby line which had been opened six years earlier—a new form of communications link, supplementing waterways and roads, was established with the industrialised West Riding. But though it was inevitable that Hull should become the eastern terminal of an east-west belt of railways, town enthusiasm for such a project was far from being evident. As early as 1825, the year of the opening of the Stockton and Darlington Railway, George Stephenson had surveyed a proposed line of railway between Leeds and Selby on behalf of Benjamin Gott, the Leeds cloth manufacturer. 'Rocket' had yet to prove its worth at the Rainhill trials, and at the time Gott and his associates were not satisfied with Stephenson's proposals for using inclined planes and stationary engines for nearly half the distance between Leeds and Selby. James Walker of London was invited to carry out a new survey, also sponsored by Gott. Walker varied the direction of Stephenson's proposed line, and advocated the use of locomotives throughout.[15] Despite some active opposition by the Aire and Calder Navigation and landowners, the Leeds and Selby Railway Company came into being, but at a difficult stage in the bill's progress the Hull aldermen decided not to give petitionary support.[16] The act was obtained in June 1830 and the railway was opened in September 1834.

The failure to construct a Leeds-Selby-Hull railway—for such a project had been canvassed in the local press as early as 1825—may be explained by the opposition of the proprietors of steam packets which ran up the Ouse to Selby,[17] shipping interests in Selby which saw the economic advantages of Selby being a river-port terminal, the opposition of country landowners east of Hull, and—probably as much as any other factor—by natural circumspection over investment in a new form of transport, which had yet to prove its worth. Such cautiousness was later reflected in the slowness with which capital was ultimately obtained for a Hull-Selby railway project.

At the same time, however, there were those in Hull who were alive to the potential dangers of a developing regional economic situation, inimical to the town's interest. The Goole and Knottingley canal had been opened in 1826 and therefore Goole, with the possibility of its soon having a rail link with the Barnsley coalfield, was increasingly feared as a competitor: such a railway project had been mooted as early as 1830. Furthermore, in the early 1830s, certain interests in Scarborough and Bridlington were actively concerned with a scheme for an east coast-West Riding railway, which, if implemented, would link up Bridlington with Driffield, Pocklington and York, thence onwards to Leeds via a York-Leeds line, which was under active consideration. Such a railway, if built, would not only serve the agricultural interests of the Wold country and the Plain of York, but would give a marked fillip to the development of Bridlington as a fishing port by providing easy access to a rapidly expanding West Riding market.

John Exley, a Hull Customs officer, who later had the honour of having one of the Hull and Selby Company's locomotives named after him, was in the van of a local campaign to direct public attention to the necessity of obtaining a Hull-Selby railway line. In a letter to the Hull *Rockingham* in December 1833 and addressed to 'the Bankers, Merchants and others of Hull . . . on the necessity for, utility of and benefit to be derived from a rail road from this town to Selby', he discussed the material advantages which would follow. On the basis of contemporary trade figures he considered that there would be an annual income of £26,690 on a railway estimated to cost £170,000. Deducting organisational and administrative cost he dangled the sizeable carrot of a ten per cent dividend before the noses of the local banker and merchant.[18] The Hull press supported the project, duly raised the bogey of Goole as Hull's competitor, and reminded readers of the advantages which Liverpool was deriving from the Liverpool and Manchester Railway. In February 1834 the Hull Guardian Society for the Protection of Trade actively took up the matter, and suggested that 'if immediate steps are taken to bring about so desirable an object, it will probably put an end to the projected railways from Scarborough and Bridlington which, if carried into effect, will no doubt prove highly injurious to the port'.[19]

George Liddell and James Henwood, the Hull bankers, took the initiative in raising the £20,000 to satisfy the requirement of the parliamentary standing order preparatory to a bill being sponsored. It is significant that, although most of the directors of the Hull and Selby Railway Company had close local connections, two of the biggest shareholders were Benjamin Gott and John Marshall, the Leeds flax spinner.[20] An impoverished Hull Corporation subscribed £30 towards the expenses of the necessary survey and agreed to take up forty shares.[21] Before the end of 1834, £100,000 had been raised, and preparations for introducing a bill into the House of Commons went ahead.[22] Some four months later (February 1835) a deputation of the Provisional Committee sought to persuade the corporation to take up additional shares: but the economic outlook was bleak, and the aldermen of the unreformed corporation, soon to face their corporative demise, regretted that they were unable to help and 'declined to accede to the proposition'.[23]

Other difficulties were Sabbatarian in character or arose from the objections of landowners or the company's realisation of the necessity of wooing the banker-merchant-gentry when capital investment was being sought. The prospectus, for example, issued in 1835, noted that 'the line had been kept to the south and also on the shore (of the Humber) under Mr Pease's seat at Hesslewood with a view to avoiding injury and opposition as much as possible'.[24] Robert Raikes of Welton was opposed to the plan for a railway which passed through his estate, and complained that it would be 'a very real nuisance and eyesore' to it, 'wholly and for-ever destroying all its present advantages of scenery and rural and picturesque privacy'. Raikes opposed the bill both in the Commons and the Lords, and ultimately received substantial financial compensation, coupled with an assurance that there would be no station on his estate.[25] Hence a railway scheme originally intended to link Welton, North and South Cave, was abandoned in favour of a foreshore route through Brough, straight as an arrow for some eighteen miles.[26] There were other objections to the Hull and Selby Company's plans, including one from the Hull magistrates, clergy, merchants and others, who petitioned for a clause prohibiting Sunday travel, except in special circumstances—a petition which was rejected in the House by 101 votes to 14.[27]

The act was secured in June 1836 and four years later, on 1 July 1840, the line was opened. The Hull terminal was in Kingston Street west of Humber Dock. Despite the rain which resulted in the cancellation of an intended procession through the streets, the spirits of many remained undaunted, and members of the Manchester Unity of Oddfellows, for instance, 'paraded the principal streets accompanied by several bands of music'. The opening of Hull's first railway was celebrated with characteristic Victorian capacity for jollification and junketing.[28] Understandably, the new railway was well patronised, and a total of 4526 passengers was carried in the first week, to the detriment of the river steamers.[29] Its progress was reported regularly in the local press, until, some five weeks after the opening day, a derailment at Wressel caused five deaths: rather naively the Company attributed the fall in the number of travellers immediately thereafter to the partial suppression of Sunday travel.[30]

Soon after the through connection from Hull to Leeds had thus been secured, the directors began to make plans for a line from Hull to Bridlington. It was estimated in 1842 that every week 5500 persons travelled between Hull and Beverley, through which the line would go. It was expected that the number would be much greater if there was a railway. The Hull-Selby line had been expected to carry about six hundred passengers a week. It was actually soon carrying more than 6000. Further, a railway to Bridlington would be able to bring the 2000 tons of fish caught by Flamborough boats each year.[31] In part the reason (for the project) was strategic, for the building of such a railway would prevent the resurgence of any schemes by locally interested parties to connect Bridlington with the West Riding. The Act of Parliament was obtained early in 1845 but, by the end of June that year, the Hull and Selby Company had been leased to the York and North Midland Railway, and therefore immediately came under the control of the Railway King, George Hudson.[32] Hudson therefore became intimately concerned with the Hull-Bridlington project, which, in its own regional setting, accorded with his grand master plan of linking Derby and the Midlands with the Tyne, and developing the east coast ports and watering places. In particular, such a railway integrated with his own East Yorkshire plans for a line from York to Scarborough, connecting via Seamer with Filey and Bridlington. The York-Scarborough line was opened in the summer of 1845, and in October the following year the Seamer-Filey and the Hull-Bridlington railway links.[33] The opening of the Hull-Bridlington line was made the occasion of a truly 'royal progress' by 'King' Hudson: the three locomotives, *Aerial, Antelope* and *Hudson*, drew a motley train of some sixty-six carriages, conveying a horde of influential courtiers through to Bridlington and a sumptuous lunch in the station goods shed there, where 'Royal' George held temporary court, and where a whole series of monotonously laudatory speeches was made to the liquid accompaniment of twenty-one toasts.[34]

Up to 1848 all Hull's railway traffic was dealt with at the Kingston Street station, but the opening of the Hull-Bridlington line, coupled with the north and northwesterly growth of the town, emphasized the desirability of having a more centrally placed terminal to deal with the increasing traffic. The result was that Paragon Station—so named after Paragon Street, and not because of its magnificence or any intrinsically superlative qualities as a building—was opened on 8 May 1848 'without any particular éclat' as the nineteenth-century historian, Sheahan, put it.[35] The Station Hotel, completed in 1849, but not officially opened until November 1851, was an integral part of the whole scheme for a grandiose Hull terminal.[36] Both buildings were to the design of George Townshend Andrews, whose personal wagon by now was well and truly hitched to the Hudsonian star. This hotel-station project of 1848-9, condemned by contemporaries as a 'Hudson's Folly', uselessly extravagant, both in conception and plan, despite later alterations, remains George Hudson's chief memorial in Hull. In a very real sense too, it is Andrew's monument, for it was the last great railway design of the comparatively young architect, who died impoverished in 1853 following Hudson's fall from grace four years earlier.

Andrew's three-spanned railway section, which covers some two-and-a-half acres and had architectural affinities with his York station of 1841, was linked up in a broad sweep of track with the Hull-Selby and Hull-Bridlington lines.[37] The old Kingston Street station was relegated to the status of a goods station and was rebuilt in 1858: an interesting reminder of Hull's early railway

7. i. Joseph Rank (d.
1943). Methodist, flour
miller and philanthropist.

7. ii. Sir James Reckitt
(1833-1924). Quaker,
manufacturer and founder
of Garden Village.

8. i. Anthony Bannister
(1817-1878). Businessman and
railway pioneer.

8. ii. Sir Alfred Gelder
(1855-1941). The City's first
town planner.

history ended with its demolition in 1961.[38]

'Railway Mouse' (presumably of Hull) was not the only critic who, as early as 1846, was voicing his criticism of the 'Spooney Railway Monarch', 'his ill-managed dominions', and the 'petulant and servile sycophants' who surrounded him:[39] such comments were but the preliminary rumblings of the collapse to come. As one wit, Bernal Osbourne, MP, put it, Midas kept everything but his accounts, and 'King' Hudson's empire crumbled to ruin in 1849.[40] Later railways in the Hull area were to be the work of less well-known men. Working with Hudsonian drive and energy, it was Anthony Bannister of Hull who was the leading figure in promoting the building of a railway to Withernsea in Holderness.

Within fifteen years of the fall of George Hudson, two railway schemes of local significance—the Hull and Holderness and the Hull and Hornsea—had been carried out. Both had importance insofar as 'commuter' residential development in Hull's suburbs and at Hornsea and Withernsea was concerned, and both provided increased opportunity for the day excursionist. Yet both had only a limited economic value for the agricultural Holderness they served. Because of their small size it was inevitable that neither could survive as viable economic units, and after a short period of independence they became victims of 'take-overs' by the rapidly expanding North-Eastern Railway Company.

The Hull-Holderness Railway Company was essentially the brain child of Alderman Anthony Bannister of High Paull House, a formidable figure in mid-Victorian Hull. His energy and drive as well as his penchant for colourful phraseology 'culled from the coal yard and the fishing smack' were admired by his contemporaries. Bannister, who had done much preparatory work, outlined his plans at a meeting convened at the railway office in Paragon Street in August 1852, the year of his first mayoralty. Such a railway he considered had long been deemed desirable: Patrington Haven was rapidly silting up and the trade in corn it once had (and on which Sir George Head had remarked in 1835) would come to the railway; the countryside was level and railway building therefore would not be expensive; the York and North Midland Railway, while not prepared to take a proprietary interest in the scheme, was paternally favourable and would give assistance; socially, Bannister maintained, there would be the convenience of a nearby watering place to Hull.[41]

In fact an essential and integral part of Bannister's scheme was the development of some place on the Holderness coast in the same way as Hudson had justified the building of his lines, by helping to develop Scarborough and Whitby West Cliff. Withernsea was not immediately selected and, in fact, the Holderness coast from Easington to Tunstall was surveyed for an appropriate coastal terminal. In 1851 Withernsea was a village of 109 people—'a handful of houses with a single shop and a very apocryphal public'—as a contemporary described it three years later.[42] But Withernsea was to be organised for the visitor, the vocation of landlady encouraged, and a scheme for a dignified Station Hotel (later the Queen's Hotel) was to be part of the whole project. Local support was forthcoming and Sir Thomas Chichester-Constable of Burton Constable, J. G. B. T. Hildyard of Winestead, Joseph Pease of Hesslewood and Samuel Preston of Sutton, among others, became directors. But the project had its difficulties. The corporation of Hedon refused to relinquish its right to tolls, and the line had therefore to be altered in order that Hedon station should be outside the parish boundary.[43] The Revd Charles Barker of Hollym complained of damage to the church at Withernsea (already in a ruinous condition) and alleged that church glebe had been intersected in a way he had not anticipated.[44] The project went ahead, Cuthbert Brodrick (to acquire fame as the designer of the Town Halls of Leeds and Hull, the Grand Hotel at Scarborough and the Hull Royal Institution) prepared plans for Withernsea's Station Hotel and the railway station there:[45] Withernsea was soon on the way to being Brightonised. It was Bannister's boast that the railway line was opened within eleven months of the bill receiving the royal assent.

The Hull and Holderness Railway was opened on 26 June 1854. The Hull terminal was the Victoria Station on the Victoria Dock Railway, which had been constructed a year before, ringing the town in a three-and-a-quarter miles sweep of track. By crossing the main radial roads on the level, the railway company helped to sow the seeds of later urban traffic problems.

The Hull and Holderness Company did its best to make Withernsea attractive to the visitor and not only registered concern at the 'dilapidated state' of Withernsea church and offered help (which was refused), but invested in bathing machines (including two old ones from Scarborough), and paid staff to 'work them'.[46]

But Anthony Bannister's schemes for a flourishing Brighton on the east coast were not achieved. Despite the encouraging start the railway could not exist as an independent unit and in 1860 the line was leased to the North Eastern Railway: in 1862 the company itself was dissolved. Later, the Queen's Hotel was purchased by Sir James Reckitt and presented to Hull Royal Infirmary for use as a convalescent home. Killed by the motor car, the railway line was closed in 1964/5. Bannister died in 1878; his only tangible memorials today are his statue in Hull Guildhall and his name which has been given to a Withernsea street.

The relative failure of the Hull and Holderness Railway did not deter a second Bannister in the person of Joseph Armytage Wade, Hornsea resident and Hull timber merchant, from being the enthusiastic instigator of a railway line from Hull to Hornsea. There is little doubt that if George Hudson's reign had been longer a railway from Beverley to Hornsea, sanctioned in 1846, would have been built.[47] Had this come about a Hull-Hornsea railway would never have got beyond the preliminary planning stage. Wade and his associates were convinced that compared with Withernsea, Hornsea could offer superior residential amenities. The necessary act was secured in 1862 and early in October that year, amid the usual scenes of jollity, Wade, having been presented with an elegant wheelbarrow of Italian walnut, and a polished electro-plated shovel (implements now part of Hull's Transport Museum exhibits) 'turned the first sod and filled his barrow with a truly workmanlike manner amidst prolonged and vociferous cheering'.[48] But before the line was opened in March 1864 the Company ran into serious difficulties—unsound ground at Hornsea, expensive embankment at Hornsea Bridge and, on the eve of the opening of the line, an ugly attack on Wade by certain shareholders, including Bannister, with allegations that the chairman had bought up land and materials and then resold them to the company.[49] The government inspection carried out before the line could be opened was both rigorous and revealing. Captain Rich, the inspector, found crossing-gates below the standard, the junction with the Victoria Dock branch line (of the North-Eastern Railway) had been made west of the Stoneferry Road, instead of east thereof, as specified in the act, the platforms at Marton (re-named Ellerby from 1 Jan 1922) were substandard, and most regrettably, during the course of the inspection of a bridge,

Captain Rich fell in the Sutton Cross Drain. Government consent to the opening of the line was only received on the eve of Easter, and hasty celebrations were organised to mark the occasion.[50]

But the report at the half-yearly meeting of the Hull and Hornsea Company in August that year was depressing. Although with the use of Paragon Station as terminal instead of Wilmington, passenger receipts had risen, goods and mineral traffic were well below expectations. Hornsea, too, was reluctant to be conditioned to receive visitors, despite admonitory appeals by the company. Like the Hull and Holderness Railway, the Hull and Hornsea line was too small for effective independent working: independence lasted only two years and in 1866 the company was merged with the North Eastern Railway. In 1964/5, like its neighbour, it was 'axed,' (passenger traffic ceased on 19 October 1964 and the goods service on 3 May 1965) and as these words are written the grass grows over the ribbon of former track.

By reason of the nature of the area served, these two railways had more of a social than an economic value, when compared with, say, the Hull and Selby and the later Hull-Doncaster and Hull and Barnsley railways. Their regional contribution was essentially to the residential development of Hornsea and Withernsea, and as Hull spread, and before the age of the motor car, the lines had an important local commuter value. Furthermore, before the coming of the horse-drawn, steam and electric trams, both railways, with their stations such as Botanic, Wilmington, Southcoates and Sutton, performed the function of suburban 'feeders', and in this sense made a definite contribution to urban development, but statistically impossible to assess. The days of Bannister and Wade were short, but within mid-Victorian Hull's social setting they were by no means either inglorious or unimportant.

The North Eastern Railway was dominant and from time to time there were proposals to break its monopoly. It was felt that if there were an independent line to the south Yorkshire collieries a much greater amount of coal would come to the port. To bring this about was the aim of the Hull and Barnsley Railway Company, set up in 1879 under the chairmanship of Lt Col Gerard Smith, Liberal MP first for Midhurst and then for High Wycombe. He was head of the Hull bank of Samuel Smith Bros & Co., and great-grandson of its founder, Abel Smith. The bank had held the account of the Hull Dock Company which, threatened by the new project, removed it; and Gerard Smith resigned his seat on the board of the Dock Company.[51]

A new dock was to form the eastern terminus of the railway and it was to be the largest on the Humber. When Col Smith cut the first sod, though it was winter, there were public rejoicings and processions with decorations and illuminated pictures, called transparencies, sold by Edwin Davis of Market Place. The artillery barracks in Park Street had the only hall big enough for the great banquet which was held.[52] With the excavation of land for the dock and the local building of the railway line and embankments, the town soon had more navvies than had ever been seen before.

By June 1881 they were carried by train at six miles an hour along the line they had made from Springhead to Willerby, to work on the cuttings between Kirkella and Eppleworth.[53] Sometimes there were fights at Newington and Springhead, mainly because the English believed the contractors favoured the Irish navvies. In a battle at Springhead the Irish finally fled across the fields.[54] The Easter weekend passed peacefully and all were taken on again.

The works at the Hull end were managed by a local man, George Bohn, son of the aged publisher. His staff of forty draughtsmen in the summer of 1841 were working on engineering drawings into the small hours.[55] It was not only the dock which accounted for the scale of the works: there were no level-crossings, the line being carried on embankments, still part of the Hull scene, with sixty bridges crossing the roads and land-drains.

In 1885 the work was complete, though the line stopped at Cudworth, just short of Barnsley, with junctions to other lines. The official opening of the dock and railway was on Thursday, 16 July. It might have been expected that a royal personage would preside, but none was available. The *Eastern Morning News* commented

> The day was one of unmitigated rejoicing. Even if royalty was absent ... we were spared the formality and convention which are the invariable accompaniments of a royal visit.

Princess Alexandra, however, gave her name to the dock, and nearly 200,000 medals were struck to commemorate the opening and the prosperity which it was expected would ensue.[57] Already, to meet the competition, the Hull Dock Company had constructed a new graving-dock, big enough for the largest ships using the port which had previously been forced to dry-dock at Goole or Grimsby.[58] The Alexandra began with two graving-docks of even greater size. With the new facilities, the shipments of coal increased as had been expected (though the company was on the whole unprofitable to its shareholders). In 1880 coal had accounted for only 1.6 per cent of the value of Hull exports. Five years after the completion of the dock, the figure rose, in 1890 to 3.4 per cent, and soared to 10.1 per cent in 1900.[59]

The Hull Dock Company had long used hydraulic transmission of power generated by steam-engines. At Alexandra Dock the coal-hoists, cranes, and lock-gates were all hydraulic. The Hull Hydraulic Company had been formed in 1877, with its steam engines and hydraulic accumulator in Machell Street, Wincolmlee, and continued into the present century, with high pressure pipes working the machinery of its subscribers, and some of the fire hydrants of the corporation. It was the first public power system in Britain:-

> The installation at Hull differs little from the numerous private plants at work in the docks and railways of the United Kingdom . . . The large public hydraulic works established since are to be directly attributed to the Hull undertaking.[60]

Internal combustion engines, perhaps more convenient, were soon being used also, and manufactured in Hull. In 1885 Crossley's, of Manchester, were making gas-powered engines of up to 40 horsepower, and one of the smaller type was used to print the *Hull and East Riding Critic*.[61] Priestmans of Williamson Street also began to produce engines of the same type using petrol. Engines made by boths firms were illustrated in the 1902 *Encyclopaedia Britannica*.[62] No one foresaw that petrol engines were to alter the town very much more drastically than the railways had done and that within a hundred years three of the lines would no longer exist.

Sources

1. DNB s.v. SADLER, W. W. (1796-1824); *HA*, 13 Aug. 1824.
2. F. H. Pearson, *The Early History of Hull Steam Shipping*, 2.
3. Ibid., 3.
4. *SM*, 10 Nov. 1826.
5. Sheahan, 208-9.
6. *R*, 3 Oct. 1834.
7. *HA*, 9 Nov. 1838.
8. C. Singer (Ed.), *The History of Technology*, iii, 438.
9. *R*, 6 Jan. 1838.
10. Ibid., 9 Nov. 1838.
11. Pearson, op. cit., 46; *R*, 21 Sept. 1838.
12. *R*, 24 Mar. 1838.
13. *HA*, 27 Jan., 3 Feb. 1843.
14. *EMN*, 6 July 1899.
15. For Walker's report see G. G. McTurk, *A History of Hull Railways* (1879) pp. 18-32.
16. BB11., f.543. There is a copy of the Bill in the Morrell MSS York City Library.
17. The Corporation invested £1000 in this venture in 1828, BB 11 f.503.
18. *R*, 28 Dec. 1833.
19. Ibid., 8 Feb. 1834.
20. W. W. Tomlinson, *The North Eastern Railway*, 291.
21. BB12, ff.166, 193.
22. Tomlinson, op. cit., 233.
23. BB12, f.207.
24. Report to Subscribers . . . McTurk, op. cit., 41.
25. *Commons Journals*, 91 (1836) 12, 22, 28 and *passim*.
26. For prospectus see McTurk, op. cit., 42-6.
27. *Commons Journals* (1836) 228; see D. Brooke, 'The Opposition to Sunday Travel in North-Eastern England 1834-1914', *JTH* VI (1963) 95.
28. *HA*, 3 July 1840: K. A. MacMahon, *Beginnings of the East Yorkshire Railways* (EYLHS Series No. 3, 1953) 8-9.
29. *HA*, 10 July 1840.
30. Ibid., 14, 21 Aug. 1840; BTC (York), HSE/1-2 *passim*.
31. *HA*, 21 Sept. 1842.
32. McTurk, op. cit., 80 ff. R. S. Lambert, *The Railway King* (1934) 143.
33. Tomlinson, op. cit., 473; MacMahon, op. cit., 12-13.
34. *HA*, 9 Oct. 1846.
35. Sheahan, 679; Tomlinson, op. cit., 489-90; *VCH*, Hull, 393.
36. *HA*, 21 Sept. 1849.
37. G. H. Hutton, 'An Early Victorian Railway Station; being an architectural and historical survey of the new station of Hull, now called The Paragon, with reference to the life and times of its architect, Andrews' (Hull Dip. Arch. thesis, 1953) *passim*. [Copy in Hull Local Studies Library .]
38. TGSEY, v, pt II, 57; *HDM*, 30 Nov. 1961.
39. *HA*, 16 Oct. 1846.
40. Lambert, op. cit., 244 ff.
41. BTC HUH 1/2/1.
42. *ECH*, 29 June 1854.
43. BTC HUH 1/3/15-17.
44. BTC 1/3/55-72.

45. MacMahon, op. cit., 15-16.
46. BTC HUH 1/3, 66, 136, 138, 140-1.
47. Tomlinson, op. cit., 472.
48. Sheahan (1864 ed.) 573; BTC HUH 1 *passim*.
49. *ECH*, 3 Mar. 1864.
50. Ibid,. 17, 24 Mar. 1864.
51. *EMN*, 29 Oct. 1885.
52. *HN*, 8, 15, 22 Jan. 1881.
53. Ibid., 18 June 1881.
54. *EMN*, 5 Apr. 1882.
55. *DNB* s.v. BOHN, HENRY GEORGE (1796-1884); *EMN*, 18 June 1881.
56. *EMN*, 17 July 1885.
57. Ibid., 28 June 1881.
58. *HN*, 18 June 1881.
59. J. M. Bellamy, *The Trade and Shipping of Nineteenth Century Hull*, Table IV (A).
60. Kelly's *Directory* (Hull) 1921, 330; *Encyclopaedia Britannica* (10th ed.) vol. xxxi, 893.
61. *EMN*, 14 Aug. 1885.
62. *Encyclopaedia Britannica*, op. cit., vol. xxviii, 184-5, 189b.

22

Mid-Century

In the early and middle years of Victoria's reign there were several men who were important in the development of Hull. Very few now know anything about them. Their lives overlapped with those of Ferens and Rank, whose names are still familiar thanks to the enterprises and institutions which bear their names.

Family circumstances and alliances could be of great importance. Ferens himself seems to have had no advantage except those conferred by his talents until he married a Miss Field, a rich young lady of rather masculine appearance. They do not seem to have been able to have any children; but it may well have been her generous temperament and the support she gave him which launched Ferens on his charitable career.

Thomas Thompson (1782-1865) owed a great deal to his connections. He came from a poor family of Long Boughton, near Alnwick, but his mother had an uncle, Thomas Nesbitt, who was a Hull merchant, and the manager, Marshall, was an uncle of Thomas Thompson. After only two years in the village school he was sent to Hull in a sloop which plied between Selby and the Tyne. That was in 1797, when he might well have been taken by the press-gang, but as at other junctures in his life, he was lucky. He worked under his uncle, and three years later when Nesbitt died, the uncle took over the firm and later provided capital to set Thomas up in his own business. In 1817 he had sold corn to a miller of Kirbymoorside. The miller failed. There had never been any means by which corn could be taken from Hull to that part of the world. Thompson must have been speculating by buying within a few miles of the miller.[1] This failure cost Thompson £500 but he was well enough established to refuse the offer of a loan from a generous merchant usually unsympathetic to his Liberal stand in politics. He was successful in the Hamburg fruit trade and then began to import hides.[2] This turned his attention to India. He chartered the *William Lee*, now well known from John Ward's painting of her first arrival from Calcutta in January 1839. She sailed again in March and continued in this trade year after year.[3] She had been a whaler. This, and her main cargo of hides, partly spoiled the rice which she carried, but the hides were Thompson's main concern, they sold well, and on her second sailing she fired a two-gun salute. On one Calcutta voyage he made £3000, equivalent to something over £40,000 in 1988, and for a small merchant this was a very large profit. He also chartered other ships for his Indian trade.

He was one of the owners of the *Lion*, reputed to be the first iron ship from a Hull yard, and though he was not primarily a shipowner he was often in conflict with the Hull Dock Company, which in due course made him a director. He was active in politics as a Reformer, supporting Col Thompson, who was not related to him, and the Anti-Corn Law League. He was elected to the new town council, served as mayor, and for several years was Governor of the Poor. He failed to realise that it would be dangerous to take town water from the river Hull and laid the foundation stone at the Stoneferry waterworks, where one of the engines was named after him.

For a time he was associated in business with William Batchelor Brownlow, who may well have been an illegitimate son of one of the noble Brownlows of Belton, near Grantham. His obituary referred to his being born somewhere near Louth and his being brought up by 'his friends'.[4] They were able to give him a fairly expensive education in Hull, first under Mr Symons in King's Court, High Street, and then in Mr Passman's commercial school in Bond Street. About 1808 he was articled as a shipping clerk to William Laverack, agent for the Hull and London Union Contract after which he became the junior partner in Weddle & Brownlow, shipping agents. They acted as one of the agents of Pearson's, the Thorne shipowners, and when Weddle emigrated to America the firm became Brownlow and Pearson. Their first steamer was the *Duke of Wellington*, bought from Dublin owners, and with her they started a Goole service. The *Kingston*, possibly the first steamer to sail regularly in the North Sea, was built for them by Pearson's of Thorne in 1821, and with her they began a weekly London service. The *Yorkshireman*, from the same firm, was doing two London voyages a week by 1823, but for several years there were no sailings in winter.[5] It is possible that they were not the sole owners of the *Yorkshireman*, but they were certainly her agents. She was their largest vessel registered at about 400 tons, which made her about the same size as the *Lincoln Castle*, and her two sister ships, the last steam ferries on the Humber in the present century. With the *London*, built at Gainsborough, with engines installed at Selby, in 1828 they began the first Hull-Hamburg steam service.[6] On a site now covered by the Albert Dock, they set up their own shipyard in 1847. They launched the paddle-steamer *Lion* and then began to build screw steamers, the first being the *British Queen*, launched in 1849. In that year they showed a robust attitude to their workers. Having dismissed two whom they judged to be too old for their work, they faced a strike and were unable to break it by bringing in skilled men, first from Goole and then from Belgium.[7] Brownlow himself was generous, though he enjoyed speculation in corn. He was a guarantor for the building of the new church of St James, at the end of Lister Street, and was reputed to set aside £300 a year for charity.

When steam-tugs became common, making sailing craft arriving in the Humber independent of wind and tide, Samuel Talbot Hassell (1809-82) and a few others connected with shipping realised that it would be a good thing to have a semaphore telegraph system between Spurn and the Pilot Office at the South End,[8] where a small window in the south-east angle still shows where the signals were received. Subscribers were given flags and a code-book and could be kept informed of arrivals and departures. Thomas Wilson joined when the signals office told him that one of his sailing ships was aground on the Stony Binks, and could be saved if a tug was sent. In the winter months of 1839-40 bad light stopped signals on only one day in six.[9]

Hassell was perhaps more closely connected with the Scandinavian trades than anyone except such shipowners as Thomas Wilson Sons and Co. He married the sister of Clements Good, the Danish consul general, a knight of the Dannebrog, the highest of the Danish orders of chivalry. As a youth Hassell spent a year with a merchant in Riga. Then he made a tour of the French ports and visited St Petersburg, Stockholm, and the ports of the Gulfs of Bothnia and Finland. His firm had most of the Humber trade in Baltic tar. They imported up to 25,000 barrels a year, sending it first to Grimsby, to avoid the high charges of the Hull Dock Company, and then putting it into barges which discharged at the Old Harbour at his wharf. This resulted in his becoming the leader of the Old Harbour interest against the claims of the Company. For a time he was chairman of the Hull Flax and Cotton Mills. He also invested in several seed-crushing concerns and exhibited seeds and oil at the Great Exhibition in 1851. Earlier, it was through his initiative that the Public Rooms (now the New Theatre) were built in Jarratt Street.

Joseph Sanderson (1793/4-1877) was another of those who from their first appearance realised the advantages of steamers on the Humber.[10] He claimed that he had been before Brownlow in chartering them; and he joined with others to build steam-tugs to tow sloops to Hull from Goole and the canals. The partners sold out when they found that no one wanted a tug when there was a favourable wind. Some credited him with having drawn the attention of the Hull Dock Company to the advantages of the position in which the Victoria Dock was built - the first to be opened east of the Old Harbour. He thought it 'one of the best docks and obtained at the smallest cost of any in the company's possession'. He was also interested in road transport, introducing from York the first hansom cabs (with six-foot wheels) which soon took the place of the old six-passenger coaches, and he was one of the promoters of the act for the turnpike to Hedon, which became Hedon Road.

Sanderson was interested in the Hamburg trade, much of which was brought to Hull by Carl Christian Bröchner, son of a Lutheran pastor of Assens in Denmark. At that time the Danish frontier touched Hamburg, which was an important depot for Danish trade. After an apprenticeship, Bröchner set himself up in Hamburg, where he continued after the great fire of 1841. After the Prusso-Danish war of 1848-9, which caused such devastating unemployment in the Humber ports, he brought his business to Hull, where he already had connections with Messrs M. & R. Keighley. He rose to such eminence that he was made a knight of the Dannebrog. This was in part a reward for his prominent share in building the Danish church of St Nicholas, visited by thousands of Danish emigrants passing through Hull. He died in 1882 at his residence, Sutton Hall, only a few miles from the borough.

When, in old age, Brownlow moved into the country, he went no further than Ellerker, but John Henry Atkinson, born in Hull in 1828, on his second marriage became a grandee, living at the splendid Palladian house at Gunnersbury, Middlesex, though his business remained in Hull with the shipowning firm of Brown, Atkinson & Company.[11] Like many Wesleyans, he was a Conservative and a teetotaller. He stood with the coal-owner, John Buckingham Pope, in the general election of 1880, when both were defeated by the Hull Liberals.[12] In 1885 he was returned for the Brigg division of north Lincolnshire. Because of his business connections with Russia the Associated Chambers of Commerce sent him there in 1867 with an address to the Czar, and on his return to Hull he commented on what he regarded as the outstanding feature of Russian industrial relations:

> It is especially worthy of remark, when one of the greatest difficulties which employers have to contend with in our own country is the determined effort of employees to rule by strikes and other combinations, how stringently the mill-hands in Russia are under the rule of their masters.[13]

He was twice mayor and in 1890 was made an honorary freeman.

Charles Morgan Norwood, shipowner and a Liberal member for Hull from 1868 until 1885, came from Derbyshire in 1839 to gain experience in the Hull firm of James T. Hill, a Russia merchant. Next he was manager for another shipowner, John Beadle, chairman of the Hull Dock Company. When Beadle retired the firm became C. M. Norwood & Co, but he still found time to be a town councillor, a supporter of Samuel Plimsoll's proposals for a load-line on all ships, and an enthusiast for the Suez Canal project. In connection with this Ferdinand de Lesseps visited Hull to confer with him. Norwood was so far to the right in the Liberal party that he unwisely expressed his contempt for the Hull Radicals, the most active party workers. This caused the Radical Club to put up its own candidate, Nils Boynton Billany, and the split vote let in a Conservative for the new Central division.[14]

By the middle of the century much of the town had assumed the appearance of a gigantic slum, which was to remain with little change for the next fifty years. In addition to its natural increase, the town had received newcomers from Yorkshire and Lincolnshire, and it was noted that most of the new arrivals, and especially those from Ireland, would work for wages lower than those which had been customary.[15] There were some occupations little affected. Few newcomers were in a position to compete for jobs with the 486 Hull shipwrights, the 300 or more engineers and fitters, the 108 boiler-makers or the 2268 seamen; but they must have been in competition with the 2100 labourers, and with the 3200 domestic servants and charwomen.[16] One group consisted almost entirely of new arrivals—the 2188 persons who described themselves as cotton operatives. More than half were women, and in spite of the rapid growth of the Hull cotton industry, many must have been casual workers. Since 1838 the Hull Flax and Cotton Mill Company had started four factories, and there was the still larger factory of the Kingston Cotton Mills in Wincolmlee.

On a contemporary estimate, in 1849 the cotton mills were contributing £1100 a week to the wages of Hull workers. Many of the workers had come from the neighbourhood of Ashton and Wigan—'as low in civilisation as anywhere'. Preference was given to those male workers who could bring their wives and daughters to work with them; but some, unable to get work, remained at home and were supported by the females of the family. It was feared that the moral consequences would be deplorable and that these people showed 'mental grossness and darkness as to spiritual things'.[17] According to the Revd H. Ward, of St Mark's:

> As a natural consequence of an experiment so unwholesome in its character as the establishment of large factories you must look for a great proportion of reckless and improvident characters. This has been realised in the Groves, but it is only fair to add that the worst and most degraded of the factory people come from their wretched homes in different parts of the town—Mill Street, New Garden Street, Wincolmlee and High Street each contributing some of their stores of squalid degradation to pass twice daily down the Groves.

Population flowed into Hull because wages were high in comparison with those obtainable in the country. When few rural families in the East Riding had as much as £1 a week, Ward knew of a man with a wife and two children. Between them they earned £1 15s a week: 'These people never prepared any food whatever at home but bought everything ready prepared—slices of pie for dinner, hot cakes for breakfast, soup all hot, penny pies, plum tarts etc.' Plainly this horrified him, but it was a far better diet than that of the families of most farm labourers. For a working-class family £1 15s a week looked like opulence. A seed-crusher working in one of the Wincolmlee oilmills earned about £1 4s a week and could keep his family on £1 or even 15s a week. Few, however, felt any inclination to save, and it must be remembered that quite apart from the temptations of drink, savings banks were as yet hardly regarded as safe. In 1850, after the secretary of the Scarborough savings bank was found to have stolen part of the deposits, there was some alarm about the state of the Hull and Beverley savings bank, not lessened by the very sudden emigration of the secretary: but in fact he had taken nothing and the savings bank was intact.[18] Still, the habit of saving was rare. One seed-crusher who had earned £1 10s a week was found to have furniture worth no more than 17s when the bailiffs were in—and he had been in regular employment for two years. Another who had worked for twelve years at £1 8s a week had to send his family to the Sculcoates workhouse as soon as he lost his job.

Because so few of the workers were savers, most families depended on a system of weekly credit from the shopkeeper. This was thought to cost them up to twenty per cent more than cash payments would have done. For a family without work credit was essential, but for many, shopkeepers included, it was ruinous. The shopkeepers were men of small capital, and if they were unlucky in their customers they could be ruined. A shopkeeper in Wincolmlee, through being too liberal with credit, lost the whole of the £500 he had put into his business and had to become a labourer.

As a consequence of the transition to iron ships, shipwrights of the old kind, formerly among the best of craftsmen, by 1849 were found to be receiving lower rates of pay than they had had in 1812, which was probably a good year, or in 1822 which had been an exceptionally bad one. One of their exceptional hardships was that when they were working in a wet dock they often lost their tools overboard and might have to renew two-thirds of them in a year; and many had no more than three months work in a year.[19]

The number of engineers and boiler-makers was increasing. Though 1849 was a slack year, the most prosperous of the shipyards had fifty engineers, engine-smiths and mill-wrights, 160 boiler-makers, forty carpenters and nine moulders. The thirty apprentices earned from 3*s* to 10*s* a week, the labourers from 12*s* to 17*s*, and the rest between £1 and £1 12*s*. Few of them were unemployed. They worked a twelve-hour day except on Saturdays, when they were paid and finished two hours earlier.[20]

Seed-crushing was mostly done in east Sculcoates and the men earned between £1 and £2 a week, the average being about £1 4*s*. Labour relations were said to be excellent and many of the men were teetotallers:

> Some of the proprietors of establishments have occasionally entertained the whole of their workmen and wives and sweethearts to a social cup of tea, which always brings back in return the most grateful feelings.[21]

Joiners complained that they were always hounded by the master-builder or his foreman and the breach between employers and employed was said to be constantly widening, the men complaining that their lives were a burden. Because of the large numbers of apprentices in the trade earnings were down to 16*s* or 18*s* a week. But their morals were of a very low tone and their conversation debased. The bricklayers, of whom there were about 250 were rather better off, but 100 of them might be unemployed at any one time. Wages were £1 1*s* in winter and £1 4*s* in summer. Standards were being lowered by sub-contracting, the whole of the bricklaying for one house being done for £1 10*s*. Builders' labourers—'the most immoral characters that can be imagined'—earned from 16*s* in the winter to 18*s* in the summer.[22]

Though not the highest paid, boot-and shoe-makers were the most independent of workers with a strong union and working entirely at home. They still celebrated St Crispin's Day and 'St Monday'— i.e. they spent every Monday drinking and were often unfit for work on Tuesday, and in a Sabbatarian town the fact that they worked on Sundays instead, now that there was no law to prevent them, did not improve the opinion which the respectable held concerning them. They were mostly radicals:

> The majority style themselves political reformers and fancy if they had the affairs of state to manage they would soon set all right, and they would have no objection to assist in running the church.[23]

They were probably Chartists. For ten years or more after

Henry Vincent revisited Hull, [24] except for a few absorbed into the Anti-Corn League, most Hull Radicals were Chartists. Vincent (1813-78) born in London was a printer's apprentice in Hull before he became active in politics. He addressed many crowded meetings in the autumn of 1838, preaching a 'political sermon' one Sunday to a crowd of 3000 on Dock Green, on universal suffrage and 'the blackest treachery' of the Whigs who had enacted the new poor law.[25] He was probably the first to try to arouse the political consciousness of Hull women. He spoke to women's meetings at the Freemasons' Lodge, Mytongate,[26] and when he was about to return to London the Hull Female Patriotic Association held a meeting to honour him.[27]

In response to the resolution of the national Chartist Convention for a national holiday, which would have been a general strike, there was a demonstration, beginning with a procession from Salthouse Lane. The mayor asked all peaceable persons to go home, and a strong line of police confronted the speakers. These speakers were Mr Jackson, Dawson (a stonemason) Lundy (an ironmonger) and Mead (a tailor).[28] At the municipal election in November 1840 there was a Chartist candidate in the Marketplace Ward. The 77 who voted for him outnumbered the 53 Tories, and there may have been Chartists among the Reformers, who were in the great majority.[29]

The *Hull Advertiser* sometimes ridiculed the Chartists, and at other times urged them to support the Reformers. At the time of the 'National Holiday', when it was Chartist policy to try to start a financial panic by withdrawing deposits from the savings banks, the *Advertiser* warned them that they were far less likely to succeed than to be robbed of their savings.[30] Subsequently it was known that in Hull 'the funds of the bank were very considerably reduced'.[31] It printed a sympathetic report of a Chartist meeting broken up with some violence during the general election of 1841.[32] There was also an objective account of the misfortunes of a Hull 'socialist missionary', R. Cooper, who walked to Keyingham for a debate in a barn with the Revd Seth Cooper of Patrington. Most of the 500 who attended this gathering supported a resolution rejecting socialism as 'irrational, atheistic, contradictory and blasphemous'.[33]

The mayor did not attend but in December 1841 allowed the Town Hall to be used for a crowded meeting 'to consider the defective state of the representation of the people in Parliament'. Though it was in an afternoon and few working men could attend, it became a Chartist demonstration, with speeches by Ernest Jones and other orators.[34]

Because of the 'inflammatory' speech of West, 'A Chartist lecturer from the Emerald Isle', the police broke up an evening meeting at the King William statue in 1843.[35] This led to another meeting, advertised by green posters, at the Freemasons' Lodge, to call for a parliamentary investigation into the conduct of the magistrates and the police. About 300 persons attended. They were not the sort of Chartists who could be won for the Reformers. The *Advertiser* consequently ridiculed the Hull accent of John Lundy, who spoke of how poor workers were exploited by 'the rich drones.'[36]

In February 1846 at a meeting of landowners and farmers at the Beverley Sessions House a Hull working man, John Hargreave Atkinson, insisted on being heard on the subject of the corn laws;[37] and in April 1848 a Chartist named Webster from Hull stood for an hour at Driffield in the rain addressing a group of workers on the People's Charter.[38]

Dockers, then called lumpers, were regarded as among the most depressed and degraded of workers—'treated more like brute beasts than rational beings'. It was almost impossible for those who were not heavy drinkers to obtain work. The master-lumpers who employed them were publicans, or had an arrangement with some publican that their men should be paid in his house. In 1849 very few were in regular work, and even in the busiest times were unlikely to work more than three days a week. The summer pay was 3*d* an hour and the winter pay 4*d*. Working in winter from 9 a.m. to 4 p.m. they earned 2*s* 4*d* or just over 11p a day. Among the dockers, however, there were the deal-carriers, who were in a much happier position since they were employed directly by timber merchants and were consequently free from the extortions of publicans. Their wages were somewhat higher, and when there was no dock work for them many were able to work for the same employers as lath-renders. Newcomers to the town often got work as lath-renders and some found themselves obliged to patronise the shop kept by the foreman as a condition of employment.[39]

The seamen in the Baltic timber trade enjoyed the best conditions, probably because men of high quality were needed to handle a ship which might be in danger of being frozen in. Those who brought timber from North America had to put up with a great deal of salted food, and with the storage of lath-wood and deal ends in the forecastle. Hull seamen demanded higher wages than those of most ports since the Baltic trade was usually closed for four months of the year; and whereas London men were paid £2 2s to £2 5s a month, Hull seamen would not sign articles for less than £3 to £3 5s. But although the change had not yet reflected itself in rates of pay, nearly the whole of the Hull coasting trade was now done in steam vessels, and since hands of less skill could be shipped the conditions of seamen generally was soon to suffer. In 1851 the seamen of Hull went on strike in a dispute arising out of the new Merchant Shipping Act and at a tea-meeting attended by 500 persons at the Sailors' Institute a Mrs Oliver, the widow of a sailor, urged the women of Hull to 'rise in a body' to obtain the repeal of Labouchere's infamous act.[40]

By 1860-1 the losses of Hull steam vessels in the North Sea were becoming notorious among underwriters.[41] C. M. Norwood, a Hull shipowner and soon to be one of the Hull MPs, as president of the Chamber of Commerce in February 1861 warned his colleagues that there might be government interference if they did not themselves devise standards of safety. He advised them to appoint a committee of owners, captains and engineers, and expressed his own opinion that vessels should be built in such a way as to prevent water from reaching the boiler room and putting out the fires (in many ships no deck covered the engines and boilers). In discussion members of the chamber complained of the attitude of underwriters. Z. C. Pearson, now at the height of his glory as owner of the largest Hull steamer, the *Circassian*, a vessel of 943 tons but already involved in the dealings with Overend and Gurney which were to ruin him,[42] like most of the other shipowners was strongly against any regulation by law. It must have been his experience of seafaring from cabin-boy to shipmaster which made him advocate the improvement of freeing-ports and his hubris which made him declare 'that the carrying of a moderate deck-cargo was rather a benefit than a disadvantage'.

But in 1849 much of the older traditions of seafaring survived:

> The *bona fide* Hull man is domestic in his habits and gladly returns to his wife and family on the expiration of the voyage. Very many instances might be quoted where the majority of a ship's crew have

sailed voyage after voyage and year after year in the same vessel and
with the same captain, a fact creditable alike to both parties.[43]

The highest qualities of seamanship were still found in the now
vanishing whalers, and there the still more ancient tradition
survived that the ship's master was less of a despot than the
chairman of a committee of senior mariners who would ignore his
orders if they disagreed with them.[44] Nevertheless, academic
knowledge of navigation was deficient in Hull, and though
apprentices ground their way through *Norrie's Epitome* at one of
the two night schools or in the superior Trinity House School, at
sea their opportunities of shooting the sun and using the
chronometer were so rare in the northern trade routes still
followed by the majority of Hull vessels that they had to learn to
find their way by the utmost refinements of dead-reckoning.[45]

The seafaring population supported a considerable number of
'sharks'—brothel keepers, low publicans and the like; but it was
thought that the victims of these parasites were men belonging to
other ports who after signing off in Hull soon found that they had
no more than their rail-fare to London and Liverpool. A
comfortable sailors' home—none yet existed—was suggested as
the best means of protecting them.[46]

Few of the homes of the workers of Hull could be called
comfortable. The Revd R. Kemp Bailey, Vicar of Sculcoates, did
not regard the St Paul's district in his parish as the worst in the
town. Most of the parishioners belonged to the 'industrious
labouring classes', and had little regard for cleanliness. Many,
especially of the poorest, had only a single room for a whole
family. In Flagged Square there were seventy people in four small
houses. Outside his district, in the courts and alleys off Witham
most of the houses were damp, dark, low and below the level of
the street—in an area which was itself below the level of high tides.
In Howard's Row on Sutton Bank there were twenty four-roomed
houses with nearly 300 persons living in them—'chiefly the low
Irish'.[47] In the large houses of Mill Street with six or seven rooms
in a house up to twelve persons in three families occupied a single
room. Dirt could be scraped off the walls, which were almost
black and the smells on the landing were described as unbearable
to anyone first coming there.

The streets, the pavements, and the interior of courts and alleys
contained such accumulations of mud and filth that it was almost

impossible for anyone to keep clean.[48] Yet many and perhaps a majority wanted to be clean. Great numbers walked two miles to the experimental penny baths at the Stoneferry waterworks. Several contemporary observers speak of the great difference which could be seen in those houses where the wife was a careful and industrious woman; but even the effort to keep clean could be self-defeating as it meant that more often than not the men returned from work to a home made uncomfortable by the constant washing and drying of clothes.[49]

Many young persons left home at sixteen or eighteen and lived in lodgings with others of their own age, which was thought to involve moral dangers. The women who supported themselves by letting such lodgings let the accommodation for 1s 6d a week and gave the lodgers a week's credit for their food, which she in turn obtained on credit from a shopkeeper. If any of her lodgers fell into arrears she was afraid to press them to pay in case they decamped and left her in debt, which all too often they did in any case.[50]

It was not surprising that so many young persons left home. The incumbent of St Mark's noted: 'Mobs of little dirty children may be met with daily who attend no school, and considering whom the greatest marvel seems that they should have any place called home.' He also knew of sixty or seventy women deserted by their husbands, living in the utmost poverty, and rapidly losing all control over their children; and though he had a National School, people were so migratory that the average child who did go to school—and most did not—remained there for six months only. Another person[51] reported that among the working classes only one child in three went to school. The master of the Vicar's School, Vicar Lane said that most boys came at the age of seven and on an average remained for a year only.[52] In another well-established school only a quarter of the children on the register had attended for two years—and the average boy there left school at the age of nine after sixteen months of schooling. Out of 194 boys who left one school there was not one who went to an apprenticeship. Parents sending their children to school had to pay small fees and the temptation to let a boy leave so that he could become an errand-boy for a shopkeeper and earn 3s a week was for most irresistible. Some earned twice this amount and would never return to school after experience of independence.[53] The incumbent of St James's had a lay assistant who was unable to run a night school for youths of 15 to 20, who presumably wanted to learn, for he was 'frustrated by the disturbances intentionally occasioned by the mates of the pupils'. But by 1863-4 the St Stephen's night school established several years previously had twenty or more voluntary men and women teachers, opened on thirty-four nights in the winter, and had an average attendance of 113 men and 24 women.[54] Some were probably there for want of a better and warmer place to go. Certainly they had long ago decided that they would not go to the Mechanics' Institute where 'the real mechanic was ousted by the clerk and shop-man and nothing was done by the committee to develop the latent talents of the workman'.

It was just possible that an errand-lad might become a shop-man and so eventually reach the Mechanics' Institute; but it was generally thought more likely that he would go to gaol. The tasks of errand-boys were not simply limited to the delivery of goods. It was possible for them to steal money from the till, and since they often had to collect payment from the customers they could cheat here also. Shopkeepers did not normally prosecute delinquents, who simply moved on to a similar job, but after several dismissals it was impossible for some boys to obtain employment with shopkeepers and so they would take to rope-stealing or pocket-picking. At this point there were two alternative courses. A boy might join the lowest class of criminals known as *cranchers* and *fraggers*; or to save him his parents might send him to sea. The moral influence of salt water was felt to be so strong that in 1868 the old fifty-gun *Southampton* arrived at Hull and for more than forty years served as a reformatory in which seamanship was taught.[55] She was welcomed by the mayors of Hull, Beverley, Grantham, Lincoln, Middlesbrough, Wakefield, Bradford and Sheffield, by Admiral Duncombe, MP, and by Lord Wenlock, Lord Lieutenant of the East Riding.

By one mode of initiation or other in 1849, 3700 persons in Hull, of whom 1080 were under twenty-five, were charged with crime. Most of the female offenders were much older than the males, and only one person in five charged was a woman or girl. There were 627 prostitutes. And there were Fagin type schools:

> There are known at present moment to the detective police constables a number of houses to which these young thieves resort

and which serve not only as hiding places and as depositories for stolen goods but also as schools of mutual instruction in the varied artifices of shop robberies pocket-picking and burglaries . . . Some of these juvenile offenders have been imprisoned from 12 to 15 times prior to their transportation.[56]

It was thought that the criminal statistics had been distorted by a recent marked increase in the number of vagrants, especially from Ireland.[57] If they could not be let into the workhouse they immediately committed some offence which would admit them to a gaol which had the marked advantage of being less terrible than Ireland in the forties. The 1851 census showed that in the Hull and Sculcoates union areas just over 3000 persons, in a population of 95,000, had been born in Ireland. The union areas included a number of villages, but the population was largely concentrated in Hull. Twenty years later the Irish-born population had declined to 2600 in 119,000, but there must have been a great many second and third generation Irish in Hull. What is surprising is that a number of them were Orangemen and in 1883 the vicar and curate of St Andrew's, Holderness Road, preached in their Orange regalia against ritualism and the Salvation Army to a congregation of Orangemen. It is possible that these were not descendants of the early arrivals but men employed on the construction of the new Alexandra Dock.[58]

Hull had no Catholic church in 1851, but the church was in Jarratt Street, Sculcoates, which in everything but name was part of Hull. When the religious census was taken on the last Sunday in March 1851, 1260 Catholics attended Mass, though there were sittings for only just over 800. The Catholics, the majority being undoubtedly Irish, were distinguished from all other denominations in that their attendances considerably exceeded the seating capacity[59] of their churches; but they were ecumenical in that, as in other denominations, more stayed at home than went to church. Nevertheless, they were more faithful church attenders than the others, who on the Sunday of the census left half the places unfilled.

In the worst parts of the town, containing many recent arrivals from Ireland—though even here the Irish were only a minority—Sunday was the worst day of the week:

The streets are full of the lodgers lounging about and going backwards and forwards for drink, the children running almost wild, and very frequently fights and thorough *Irish* rows occurring, apparently to the delight of crowds of spectators from the windows and the ends of the alleys.[60]

On any day of the week even young women could be seen in the streets smoking pipes; and it was regretted that the reading of low fiction was so prevalent. In Mill Street alone there were about 500 people who could not read, and they would listen to one who could. And for those for whom imagination offered no escape, opium was the opium of the people. The Revd R. Kemp Bailey thought there were not many opium addicts in his parish, but Mr Watson, the lay assistant in Christ Church district, simply said 'opium and laudanum-taking prevails to a great extent, especially among the female part of the population'. A slightly healthier diversion was dog-fighting. It was illegal to hold dog-fights for betting and the spectators, like those at prize fights, had to take a walk into the country. For a fight scheduled to come off at Beer Houses another name for Dunswell in August 1850 for £5-a-side a crowd of men left Hull at midnight on Saturday and the dogs fought for nearly an hour before the police arrived.[61]

One of the spectators who was fined complained that he was an innocent butcher looking for moribund cows to supply his trade. A dog-fight, perhaps one of many, was held in Mill Street, in 1840, but on a winter night, in the darkness of the small hours.[62] A dog used in a fight on the Humber Bank was found by the R.S.P.C.A. in a house in Blackfriargate, 'torn nearly all to pieces', and its antagonist, found in a beer-shop at the corner of Grimsby Lane, was 'literally torn into ribbons.'[63]

There was a prize fight at Aldborough in 1834 in which a Hull butcher named Brown was killed. The other boxer, William Hackney, made for Hull and then went, probably by packet-boat, to Tom Spring's house in London. Brown's second surrendered to the Hull police in Witham.[64] One way of frustrating the authorities was to arrange two matches. In 1867 the police of Hessle and Hull dogged a crowd of two hundred which set off at four in the morning from Neptune Street until they were finally dispersed in the afternoon at the Sportsman's Rest, Hedon Road. Meanwhile, though the police followed another crowd and two carts from Hull to Hessle, Willerby, Cottingham Castle, Walkington and Beverley, the real fight came off in a ring pitched in Beverley Parks.[65] A few weeks later, possibly those who had been decoys for the April event were taken by steam tug from Hull to Stallingborough to witness a fight.[66]

The pious deplored the way in which men and boys played the game called 'dab-and-trigger' even on Sundays on a piece of ground near Dock Green.[67] The Pottery was in the same district and had its annual feast as if, like Drypool, it had once been a separate village. In 1843 there was 'low dancing' in a booth in which a 'bloody tragedy', a comic song, and a farce, were all done in the course of twenty minutes. There was less drunkenness than usual.[68] How much drunkenness was permissible was entirely a matter of individual opinion. One moralist deplored the fact that the county members, Christopher Sykes and Henry Broadley, were patrons of the Hedon races run in March 1875, when:

> The company was composed principally of the very lowest class of both sexes, whose aim was, apparently, to get drunk, which they did to perfection.[69]

Some were probably also smoking the cigars, containing only twelve per cent of tobacco, made by a man in St James Street. The other contents were paper, dried leaves, and four per cent gunpowder.[70]

If the pleasures of the people were brutish, it must be remembered that Hull was still a Puritan town, perhaps now with a good deal of hypocrisy, and some legitimate pleasures were condemned. The Nonconformist conscience was a thing to be feared. Even as early as 1810 the Whig *Rockingham*, while accepting theatre advertisements, had found it prudent to print hostile reviews of almost every play and a Hull Methodist told his congregation repeatedly that no player could go to heaven and that theatre-goers too would be damned. This did not kill the theatre. It was in 1810 that Mrs Jordan made several appearances at a new theatre[71] and Hull produced one minor dramatist—Benjamin Thompson (1776?-1816) the translator of Kotzebue's *Stranger* and himself the author of two plays. But the Nonconformist view of the theatre took a powerful hold on the ignorant as well as on the pious conscience. The Revd Parkinson Milson (1825-92), an influential Primitive Methodist, held this view in all its virulence. In 1855 at Hull he made a convert, a woman who, when she first went to the theatre 'had to get some drink during the performance to stifle her conscience'. And on her the theatre had taken so strong a hold that she insisted on seeing *Jack Shepherd sic* before she was converted.[72] When laying the foundation stone of a new Hull theatre in 1865 even Lord Londesborough found it prudent to admit that in recent years the theatre had declined (perhaps the godly saw something providential in the burning of the Theatre Royal in 1859) and to insist 'that the legitimate drama must have a tendency to elevate and purify the tastes of the people'. Significantly, although he was accompanied by the sheriff and ex-sheriff, the mayor was absent. And when Jenny Lind had made her second appearance in 1848, singing in *La Somnambula* at the old Theatre Royal, much was made of patronage by the aristocracy, and of the Nightingale's patronage of the Hull German Lutheran church.[73] What else could be done in a town where the Nonconformists were clearly in the majority? At the time of the 1851 religious census more than 13,000 of the worshippers were Nonconformists. There were fewer than 9000 Anglicans, who at that time were probably much closer to the Nonconformists in matters of public policy than they were to the 1260 Catholics.

In 1858/9 John Middleton Hare, one of H.M. school inspectors, reported on Hull-with-Sculcoates. Hull had 27 schools attended by 4396 children, boys considerably outnumbering girls, as they did in Sculcoates also which had 35 schools with 3669 children. He called all these schools 'public' to distinguish them from the many small private schools which catered for a much smaller number.[74] If schooling had been needed for all children between three and fifteen, there would have been a deficiency of 13,000 places or more. In Hull the average school life of the boys was 33 months. Girls had only 21 months at school in Hull, but in Sculcoates, probably the more prosperous part of the town, they were at school for 43 months, or six months longer than the boys.[75]

Teachers believed that parents removed their children from school more than was strictly necessary. The fishermen kept their sons away from April to November and took them to sea. Hull Fair interfered with school attendance as there was a two-day holiday, and parents would not pay the two-pence fee for a 'broken week'. There were times, however, when dire necessity reduced school attendance. When the Crimean War closed the Baltic and there was so much less dock work 356 children started school and then left within the year.[76] Most people of the town, with the probable exceptions of the destitute and casual labourers, were not illiterate.[77]

The only schools which charged parents no fees were the two ragged schools, the Trinity House School, the orphan school, and the Cogan Charity school for girls. The Cogan school prepared girls for domestic service and even as late as 1882 the trustees believed that a very limited education would be enough for them.[79]

There was one part of the town where parents showed some enthusiasm for education. Fathers of families, by putting in extra time at work, raised £280 towards a new National School in St Paul's parish, which cost about £2000.[80] Though some families were too poor to be able to afford any education for their children, teachers thought that free schooling would not help much. Some children of poor parents had their fees paid by the Boards of Guardians. Their attendance was very poor. Mr Hare overlooked the fact that they were probably the hungriest and least healthy children in the town. Methodists arranged to pay the fees of 40 children at the Dock Green School, but their attendance was so patchy that the scheme had to be abandoned.[81]

Those who had missed school often tried to make up for lost time when they were older and could attend an evening school. There were ten of them, as against only one in 1851. Males outnumbered females by five to one. Half were over sixteen, and 49 men and boys were studying mechanics.[82] One 'night-school' which was particularly popular was St Stephens, entirely staffed, as most of them were, by volunteers. It was open only in the winter and for many must have been a refuge from the darkness and the cold outside.[83]

Mr Blundell required all his apprentices to attend an evening school.[84] Few of the employers shared his enthusiasm. The secretary of the Hull Dock Company was prepared to concede that skilled workers were 'greatly improved in mind and habits.' Labourers were not. Brownlow regretted that education did nothing to reduce 'in-temperance, the great curse'. The Kingston Cotton Mills ran a library.[85] Mr Holmes, an engineer found working men 'vastly amended'.[86]

The inspector was greatly impressed by the Jewish school conducted by Mr Philip Bender 'the officiating minister of the synagogue'. Though he was a foreigner he taught English as well in addition to the instruction in Hebrew.[87] Though the town was strongly Protestant, there were Catholic children in non-Catholic schools and prejudice did not prevent 'Protestant children from finding their way into schools managed by Roman Catholic priests and the Sisters of Mercy.'[88]

In 1869 this tolerant spirit was damaged by the *cause célèbre* of the year, *Saurin* v. *Star and Kennedy*, tried in Westminster Hall before the Lord Chief Justice, who thought it the longest civil action ever prosecuted there. Mary Saurin, in religion Sister Mary Scholastica Joseph, a nun, of Irish extraction, brought an action against the Prioress, described as Mrs Star, and her deputy, described as Mrs Kennedy, for wrongful expulsion from the convent on Anlaby Road. She was awarded £500 damages, only a tenth of what she had claimed.[89] In Hull it was quite forgotton that she had been expelled. She was believed to have been kidnapped for her fortune, and parents encouraged their children to run past the convent, even as late as *c.*1912, in case they too might be kidnapped. The convent flourished. There were fourteen nuns in 1869, with four hundred children in their school. In 1876 they had increased to forty, and were teaching 2500 children.[90]

Though all the denominations, except the Catholics, had been able to provide far more accommodation than they could use, Holy Trinity, the oldest surviving place of worship, was near to ruin. At a meeting at the town hall in 1868 to raise a fund for its restoration, the Archbishop of York said:

> Its pavement was so damp that there was already a vegetable growth upon it, and a suggestion which he had made to warm the edifice could not be carried out, because as one of the churchwardens had said, to attempt to warm the church would be like attempting to warm the firmament of heaven, so free was the intercourse between the inner and the outer air.[91]

To the unknown writer (probably Collins) who in 1849 collected much of the material on which this chapter is based it seemed that industrial society too was on the verge of final dissolution, and on the whole less likely to survive than the fabric of Holy Trinity. For him the evils of the slums and courts which he described at great length, and the extent of unemployment and of the unfair exploitation of workers, were symptoms portending revolution. He does not mention the *Communist Manifesto* but the following passage would seem to suggest that he had read it.

> The employers will act upon right principles in the considerable majority; but the minority who do not are generally the persons carrying on the most extensive business. I have often been appalled by the statements made to me by workmen of the feelings entertained by them towards their masters. The tone in which these statements were made convinced me of the terrible earnestness of their meaning. They complain that they are regarded as machinery for the production of their master's fortune, that as their masters become richer and richer they become poorer and poorer; that there is nothing which ingenuity can devise which is not practised to minimise the wages they receive; that nothing is left untried to break their spirits and reduce them to servility; that in fact they are becoming *helots* and retain the name of freemen but as a mockery and a provocation. I am here interpreting to the upper and middle classes of Hull languages which if they choose they may hear in many of their own workshops and at many of their own back doors.

He nowhere attempts to show that this point of view was mistaken and must have felt that a crisis was near.[92] He seems to have had no notion that workers might defend and improve their position by collective action or that even an apparently unsuccessful strike might act as a disincentive to greater exploitation. In May 1864[93] the bricklayers gave notice of their intention to strike if they did not receive an increase of wages from 4s to 5s a day with an advance for the labourers from 18s to £1 1s a week. The employers refused, though trade was brisk, 'several public buildings and a large number of first class houses and manufactories being in the course of erection'. They had strike pay of 5s a week and several hundred men came out. As the master-builders resisted many building workers left for Manchester.[94] The strike was partly successful and in June 1866 the men belonging to the operative plasterers' society resolved to strike for an advance from 5s a day to 5s 6d with a Saturday half-holiday. At the same time the builders' labourers came out for an increase of 1s a week.[95]

The 1864 builders' strike coincided with a strike of labourers at Earle's shipyard who wanted an advance of 6d a day. Several were arrested on a charge of going to the house of a man who refused to strike and threatening him. None of these strikes was undertaken without notice of at least a week, and in some cases of several months, being given to the employers. In 1865 the Hull painters struck, after ample notice of their demand for another 6*d* a day which would bring their wages to £1 7*s* a week.[96] The association of master-painters expressed its determination to resist to the last and to bring in men from other towns. But it was noted: 'the men have chosen a good time to ask for an advance as many of the masters have large contracts on hand, and the trade generally is tolerably good.'

In 1866 the Hull members of the Amalgamated Society of Engineers sent a circular to the employers asking for an advance of 3*s* a week. No kind of reply or acknowledgement was received. A week's notice of an intention to strike was therefore given, and success seemed so likely that non-union men also joined the strike until about 2000 men were out. At the beginning of March, after less than a fortnight Earle's decided to go more than half-way to meet the men and offered 2*s* a week. The union recommended acceptance, the other employers could not afford to lag behind Earle's and the engineers returned to work.[97]

These men were certainly not 'helots'. They belonged, of course, to the more skilled and privileged groups of workers, but the size of these groups was increasing. In 1851 there were certainly fewer than 1000 engineers. In 1864 there were 2000 or more, and by 1891 they numbered more than 3000. If our unknown writer continued to believe in his diagnosis arrived at in 1849 it must nevertheless have seemed to him at times that there were signs of impending disaster for the system. He had referred to the Hull Flax and Cotton Mills Co. as 'a Behemoth'. In 1857 the chairman was charged with forgery and the company failed with liabilities of over half a million.[98] In 1856 there had been twenty-one bankruptcies, a not exceptional number; but in 1857 there were thirty-four with liabilities almost ten times as great, amounting to a million. Four of the bankrupts had fled and one was doing four and another ten years' penal servitude. And in 1861 Raikes Bank failed with liabilities of about £70,000.[99]

But in Hull, as elsewhere, the Victorian economy was resilient. In 1864 both cotton mill companies were struggling to survive the American cotton famine. The Hull Flax and Cotton Mill Co. had been closed down for a year and the Kingston Cotton Mill Co. had done no work since 1861 but the latter was hoping for cotton from Egypt in 1864 to enable it to recommence spinning operations.[100] Some of the workers went to the flax mills at Leeds but found they could not tolerate the damp and cold atmosphere needed in such mills. Thirty others went into the Sculcoates workhouse.[101] Except for three, they stayed only for a day or two. This may have been their response to the principle of 'less eligibility' but the guardianssaid: 'Of those who went in a majority had done so only for a freak in order to see what sort of place it was'. The authorities of the mills wished to keep their hands together and wanted the parish to help them.

The Hull guardians who looked after the half of the town not in Sculcoates also had difficulties arising from the American war and the cotton famine.[102] The number of vagrants admitted to their workhouse rose from 489 in 1860 to 706 in 1861, 1294 in 1862 and 1398 in 1863. A minor consequence of the war was the arrival in Hull, in March 1864, of 150 German recruits, some wearing the Solferino medal, for the U.S. Federal Army.[103] Brownlow and Lumsden's steamship *Leopard* brought them from Hamburg. Others came in the *Harlequin*, landed at the corporation pier and were marched through the town to various German lodging houses until they could be sent to Liverpool by rail.

At this time the fame of Samuelson's works was so great that to this day the land at the southeast corner of the Hull bank and the Humber is known as Sammy's Point. In ten years Martin Samuelson built ninety-five iron ships[104] and was able to turn his works into the Humber Ironworks and Shipbuilding Co. On a single day in 1864 they launched two iron barques and a steamer, with a banquet attended by the directors, the mayor and both the borough members, one of whom was a large shareholder in the firm.[105] But financial collapse came in the same year, almost certainly as a consequence of a company with insufficient capital undertaking too much work—a 'cash-flow' problem. In this situation the firm had to pay wages and for materials before it had received full payment from those for whom it was building ships. Samuelson was forced out of his position as managing-director, and in January 1865 the other directors reported that they trusted that the company would prosper 'now that the hindrances to the progress of this business which have hitherto existed have been removed'.[106] They vainly tried in 1865 to raise more capital and in February 1866 they decided that liquidation was the only course open to them.[107] The ensuing liquidation lasted for many years. Samuelson himself continued to be regarded as one of the principal men of Hull.

Samuelson's was soon to be surpassed by Earle's whose gantry-crane was a landmark visible for miles around until its removal to a Japanese yard in Hong Kong fifty years ago. With eight slipways, by 1878 they had built 200 ships. They had constructed ships of the then enormous size of 3000 tons (for the North German Lloyd), five ships for the Navy, the *Valparaiso* and the *Almirante Cochrane*, ironclads, for the Chilean Navy, and a brace of steam yachts for the Czarewitch.[108]

The opening up of Russia, comparable in scale to that of the American mid-west, contributed to the prosperity of Hull. In 1825 it was felt to be something of a triumph when a Hull gentleman made the journey from Moscow via St Petersburg in eighteen days. He was at sea for twelve days.[109] By 1846 the steamer *Rob Roy* commanded by Lieut. Knocker, R. N.[110] was making the passage from St Petersburg in half the time, bringing an average of £100,000 a month in gold from recently-opened Russian mines. When she sailed on an August night in 1846 in addition to manufactured goods she carried twenty to thirty passengers, mostly engineers intending to work in Russia.[111] There was always a demand for skill there. The increase in Hull Baltic trade in 1868 was held to be largely attributable to the great quantities of iron rails and machinery shipped to Russia; but according to a contemporary, Sir D. M. Wallace, a man in sympathy with the Russian Government, much of the machinery soon ceased to be used and was left to rust.[112]

A Humber bridge from Hessle to Barton was designed by C. S. Todd, not himself an engineer, to provide Hull with an alternative railway route to London and Sheffield. The project was revived in 1867 and on subsequent occasions, chiefly because of hostility to the rail monopoly enjoyed by the North Eastern Railway; but nothing came of it.[113] This reflected the optimism of Hull business men. In 1860 they were prepared to pay £160 for a single Dock Company share which five years earlier would have been worth no more than £80.[114] The Dock Company seemed to justify the confidence of investors by its enterprise in constructing the Albert Dock[115] between 1863 and 1869. In 1866 the contractor, J. M'Cormick, MP, was employing 1000 men and 120 horses with several steam engines, when in September heavy rains and the gushing-up of a spring from the chalk under the clay completely flooded the works and destroyed part of the embankment between the dock and the Humber.[116] The whole scheme cost about £1m. The dock was 3000 feet long, varying in width from 180 feet to 430 feet, with one of the largest entrance locks in the country, and a cold-storage warehouse on the south side.[117] Edward, Prince of Wales, opened the dock on 22 July, arriving at Paragon Station with Princess Alexandra, from Brantinghamthorpe, where the ill-starred Christopher Sykes must, as so often, have been the victim of the Prince's cruel practical jokes.[118] Royal salutes were fired from H.M.S. *Dauntless* in the Humber and 5000 school-children burst into 'God Bless the Prince of Wales'. It may be pertinent here to observe that in spite of his lack of redeeming qualities this oafish man was as much worshipped in Hull as elsewhere. When in 1871 he appeared to be dying of typhoid the Revd Parkinson Milson noted:

> My soul felt unutterably for Albert Edward, Prince of Wales. I was returning from Mr Humphrey's at nearly midnight and asked a policeman if he had heard anything of the Prince, (and was told) 'Nothing new'. In Dansom Lane I overtook a man in conversation with another policeman. Their conversation was the illness of the Prince. I spoke to them. As we walked along a woman opened her door and enquired of the policeman concerning the Prince. His danger seemed to be an absorbing subject with all.[119]

But there was no gloom on 22 July 1869. The royal couple were accompanied by the Duke of Sutherland, by far the richest of all peers, whose widow was afterwards to marry Sir A. K. Rollit, the most profusely decorated of all Hull solicitors.[120] With him there was also another Duke and Duchess, assorted peers, four Members of Parliament, ten mayors and as many town councillors as could get invitations, and the whole party went in procession in their carriages through cheering crowds and triumphal arches in the old town, with the benefit of a prayer from the Archbishop of York. The splendour of this occasion was not unique. There were other princely visits, the historical importance of which lies in the holiday atmosphere which they brought to the town, with all the people, at any rate for a day, joining in a common experience in a way which would have seemed impossible to the unnamed chronicler of 1849.

The celebrations were a little muted when the new offices of the Dock Company, still standing with their triple domes,[121] were opened in the presence of the Lord Lieutenant, the mayor and corporation and the Lord Mayor of London. The most fantastic celebration of a temporarily-felt social unity[122] was probably on the occasion of the planting of the first tree in the park given to the people by Z. C. Pearson, in August 1860, when the procession was three miles long, so that half of it must still have been at the town hall when the head of the procession finished its march. There was more celebration in 1868 when the statue of Prince Albert, by Earle, a native of Hull, was unveiled, with a public holiday, a banquet at the town hall, fireworks in the park, and a balcony for 1000 of the more privileged spectators.[123]

On such occasions as this politicians were present in force, but much of the popular interest in them, at any rate before the Ballot Act, came from their potential as distributors of bribes; and grass-roots political activity consisted mainly of looking after the business of bribery to see that it was done as prudently and as economically as possible. There was occasionally an overlap between the traditional politics of corruption and an emerging democracy. Ingram Eskdale Moat,[124] who in 1852 had been employed to organise the bribeable among the temperance voters, had a brother Francis who was a trade union secretary, and had worked with Hart, a Chartist organiser: but usually bribery was the main consideration, once the voters had been registered. Some dexterity, not always available, was needed to ensure that voters remained loyal to the party which registered them. For the 1841 election the Orange party registered nearly 300 new voters but the Blues succeeded in buying over 100 of these to their side. Col. T. P. Thompson, son of a Hull banker and successively a midshipman, a soldier, a mathematician and a radical MP spent over £1100 at this election and though the money was said to have had a wonderful effect, he was defeated. Some daring voters took money from one side and voted for the other. There was a block-maker who had 7s 6d and free drinks from the Blue party and voted Orange after receiving £1 10s from them.[125] On that occasion the Blues had a committee room with a hole in the door through which the voters were paid. At the election of 1852 the corruption was so notorious that both members were unseated and for a while Hull was left without representation. Yet everything had been organised with loving care. The Orange party had seventy men to keep the committee informed as to the state of the poll. 'Steady, sober men, men that had their heart in the right cause, that would work without getting drunk. We have had men that got drunk and lost the returns, and we have been left in a state of uncertainty.' For any emergency which might occur during the poll, at least one party of voters was 'bottled' by the Blues at the Mile House on Holderness Road. These were shock troops, kept drunk but sufficiently awake to be taken to the poll, and spies from the other side, including a former Bow Street runner, were employed to keep them under observation.[126] Some committees were in reality no more than parties of 'bottled' voters, wearing long smocks for disguises. The commission of inquiry asked an eating-house proprietor from St John Street:[127]

> What did the committee do? Did they do anything except eat and drink? Yes, I believe they were working very hard all one night. I cannot tell what they were doing. The night before the election they were up all night.—The night before the election they were very hard at work? Yes, very hard.

Some voters understood the advantages of combination. On the night of the nomination twenty of them met at the Albert Inn in Adelaide Street to try to get up to £2 10s for their votes. One of them, a sail-maker, gave a transparently simple explanation: We had been there well into a month as a poor man's committee, to endeavour what we could do for the two parties, but not for any benefit to ourselves whatever. More convincing expositions of the two-party system have been given: but the conventions of Victorian politics were that no man was disgraced by losing his seat as Clay and Goderich did in 1853 after fifty-seven days of inquiry. Clay was again elected in 1857 and Goderich, Viceroy of India and Marquess of Ripon became High Steward of Hull.[128]

It is possible that many of those who might have been militant in politics had emigrated, and certainly the letters of some emigrants do show an obsession with freedom. In 1830 more than 4000 applications were made in Hull for a passage across the Atlantic[129] and fifteen ships were ready to sail with passengers, mostly for Quebec. In April 1842 alone the *Llan Rumney* with 180 passengers, the *Andrew Marvell* with eighty and the *Lord Wenlock* with 108 sailed for Quebec, and the *Sir Edward Hamilton* with 131 for New York: and within a few days three more ships were ready to sail for Canada.[130] The majority of the passengers were probably from villages near Hull, but some Hull people undoubtedly did emigrate. A William Newton who was born in Hull and made his will in Virginia in 1784, leaving property in Hull and Campbell's Forth, must have been one of many who left in the eighteenth century.[131] The Revd G. C. Cookman, the son of a Hull alderman, became chaplain to the U.S. Senate and in 1850 his son visited Hull from Philadelphia.[132] The fifty persons who on 13 May 1850 left by the 6.10 for Liverpool on their way to Iowa included Hull tradesmen and their families.[133]

A great many of the emigrants who appeared at Hull were from Europe on their way to America. This was one of the trades which built up the firm of Brownlow and Pearson. Their steamer, *Victoria*, in a single trip in May 1846 brought 134 Belgian and German emigrants from Hamburg and within a week they sailed for Quebec in the *Sir Edward Hamilton* with ten English emigrants and some Russians and Poles.[134] This traffic increased year by year, some of the intending emigrants getting no further than Hull, where several of their descendants have gained distinction.

In this chapter much has been said of the unpleasantness of the town in mid-Victorian times, but it also had its attractive side. From Scarborough[135] 2500 people made a summer excursion to see the Zoological Gardens, though their pleasure was spoiled when the grate dropped out of the engine on the way home. Though the theatre was wicked, Dickens was highly moral and the music hall was packed[136] for his farewell visit in 1869 when he gave readings from *Martin Chuzzlewit*, and the highly dramatic reading from *Oliver Twist*, the too frequent performances of which were thought to have helped to cause his death. No part of the town was very far from the country and the view along the Holderness Road from Holderness House showed seven windmills in the town—and there were many more.[137] And by 1869 'the more enterprising of our townsmen engaged in the ironmongery trade were able to supply one of the most delightful and humane inventions ever made—already by then called the bicycle but more usually a velocipede, and by us the 'penny-farthing'. In June 1868 Mr F. Hall of the Flowerpot Vaults, Whitefriargate, took the New Holland ferry and reached London by bicycle in three days, the machine being manufactured by the Beverley Iron and Waggon Company; and after five weeks' practice a young gentleman employed by the British Gas Company rode to York on Saturday and returned on Sunday, pedalling for a total of thirteen hours. Soon there were bicycle clubs and excursions into the country every weekend; and by the time the modern type of bicycle had appeared in the nineties they would occasionally see even a farm labourer on a second-hand cycle.

Sources

1. J. H. Clapham, *An Economic History of Modern Britain* vol. ii: *The Early Railway Age 1820-1850*, 231.
2. *EMN*, 13 Sept. 1865 Obituary .
3. *R*, 8 Feb. 1839, 22 Mar. 1839.
4. *EMN*, 29 Aug. 1865.
5. F. H. Pearson, *The Early History of Hull Steam Shipping*, 4-5.
6. Ibid., 11; *EMN*, 29 Aug. 1865.
7. *HA*, 13 Apr. 1849.
8. *EMN*, 7 Apr. 1882 Obituary .
9. *HA*, 27 Mar. 1840.
10. *EMN*, 20 June 1877.
11. Ibid., 13 July 1885.
12. G. R. Park, *The Parliamentary Representation of Yorkshire* (1886) 111.
13. *EMN*, 4 Feb. 1867.
14. Ibid., 14 Oct. 1885; Park, op. cit., 110, 279.
15. *HA*, 1 Feb. 1850.
16. BPP, Population vol. ix, pp 721-3 (Census of 1851).
17. *HA*, 11 Jan. 1850.
18. Ibid., 1 Feb. 1850.
19. Ibid.
20. Ibid.
21. Ibid.
22. Ibid.
23. Ibid.
24. *HA*, 14 Sept. 1838.
25. Ibid., 2 Nov. 1838.
26. Ibid.
27. *HA*, 16 Nov. 1838.
28. M. Hovell, *The Chartist Movement*, 159; *HA*, 16 Aug. 1839.
29. *HA*, 16 Nov. 1840.
30. Ibid., 16 Aug. 1839.
31. *Hull Critic*, 9 Aug. 1884, 5.
32. *HA*, 18 June 1841.
33. Ibid., 14 June 1841.
34. Ibid., 10 Dec 1841; *DNB*, s.v. JONES, ERNEST CHARLES (1819-69).
35. *HA*, 14 Apr. 1843.
36. Ibid., 28 Apr. 1843.
37. Ibid., 13 Feb. 1846.
38. Ibid., 28 Apr. 1848.
39. Ibid., 11 Jan. 1850.
40. *The Times*, 7 Apr. 1851, 3c.
41. Ibid., 11 Feb. 1861, 10e.
42. *TC*, 114; *HA*, 30 Apr. 1864.
43. *HA*, 11 Jan. 1850.
44. Ibid.
45. Ibid.
46. Ibid.
47. Ibid., 21 Dec. 1849.
48. Ibid.
49. Ibid., 1 Feb. 1850.
50. Ibid., 21 Dec. 1849.
51. Ibid., 28 Dec. 1849.
52. Ibid., 3 July 1840.
53. Ibid., 14 Dec. 1849.
54. Ibid., 19 Mar. 1864.
55. *The Times*, 3 July 1868, 12b.
56. *HA*, 21 Dec. 1849.
57. Ibid., 1 Dec. 1848.
58. *Hull Critic*, 30 June 1883, 4.
59. BPP, Population, vol. x, 107.
60. *HA*, 21 Dec. 1849.
61. Ibid., 10 Aug. 1850.
62. *HA*, 17 Jan. 1840.
63. *EMN*, 1 Aug. 1865.
64. *R*, 14 Feb. 1834.
65. *EMN*, 27 Apr. and 6 May 1867.
66. Ibid., 12 June 1867.
67. *HA*, 3 Feb. 1840.

68. Ibid., 21 Apr. 1843.
69. *EMN*, 23 Mar. 1875.
70. Ibid., 31 Mar. 1875.
71. *R*, 30 June 1810, 13 Oct. 1810.
72. *DNB*, s.v. THOMPSON, BENJAMIN (1776?-1816).
73. *HA*, 15 Sept. 1848.
74. BPP, Education, vol. v, Report of John Middleton Hare, 217.
75. Ibid., 229.
76. Ibid., 235.
77. Ibid., 251.
78. Ibid., 238.
79. *EMN*, 7 Jan. 1882.
80. BPP, Education, vol. v, 244.
81. Ibid., 249.
82. Ibid., 226.
83. *EMN*, 17 Jan. 1867.
84. BPP, Education, vol. v, 263.
85. Ibid., 310.
86. Ibid., 310-11.
87. Ibid., 249.
88. Ibid., 243.
89. W. L. Arnstein, *Protestant versus Catholic in Mid-Victorian England*, 108-22.
90. Mother Austin Carroll, *Leaves from the Annals of the Sisters of Mercy*, 479-91.
91. *The Times*, 7 Feb. 1868, 10f.
92. *HA*, 1 Feb. 1850.
93. *The Times*, 6 May 1864, 11b.
94. Ibid., 9 May 1864, 8b.
95. Ibid., 4 June 1866, 10f.
96. Ibid., 6 Apr. 1865, 8f.
97. Ibid., 15 Feb. 1866, 8f.; 5 Mar. 1866, 12c.
98. Ibid., 30 Oct 1857, 5a; 13 Jan. 1858, 7b.
99. Ibid., 4 June 1861, 7c; 6 June 1861, 7c; 10 June 1861, 6a.
100. *HN*, 12 Mar. 1864.
101. Ibid., 30 Apr. 1864.
102. Ibid., 5 and 12 Mar. 1864.
103. Ibid., 9 Jan. 1864.
104. *TC*, 14.
105. *The Times*, 20 Oct. 1864, 8a.
106. Ibid., 31 Jan. 1865, 5a.
107. Ibid., 31 Mar. 1865, 12a.
108. *TC*, Appendix, p. ix.
109. *R*, 10 Dec. 1825.
110. *HA*, 14 Aug. 1846. Lt Knocker returned to the Navy with the rank of commander and was lost on the coast of West Africa.
111. Ibid., 21 Aug. 1846.
112. *The Times*, 4 Jan. 1869, 7c; Sir D. M. Wallace, *Russia on the Eve of War and Revolution* (Random House, 1961 reprint) abridged version of the author's *Russia* first published in 1877.
113. *The Times*, 24 Oct. 1867, 11d.
114. Ibid., 26 Nov. 1860, 8c.
115. Ibid., 22 July 1869, 9f.
116. Ibid., 16 Sept. 1866, 12e; 20 Sept. 1866, 9d.
117. Ibid., 23 July 1869, 9f.
118. C. H. Sykes, *Four Studies in Loyalty* (1946) 27ff.
119. G. Shaw, *Life of Parkinson Milson*, 272.
120. *DNB*, s.v. LEVESON-GOWER, GEORGE GRANVILLE WILLIAM SUTHERLAND; *Who Was Who* (1916-28) s.v. ROLLIT, Sir A. K.
121. *The Times*, 12 OCt. 1871, 5f.
122. Ibid., 26 Aug. 1860, 10d.
123. Ibid., 15 Oct. 1868, 5f.
124. *Report of the Commissioners to Inquire into the Existence of Corrupt Practices in the Borough of Kingston-upon-Hull* 1854 XXII, Qs 14561 ff.
125. Ibid., Qs 133, 620 ff.
126. Ibid., Qs 7133 ff.
127. Ibid., Qs 3157-60 ff.
128. G. R. Park, op. cit., 108.
129. *R*, 10 Apr. 1830.
130. *HA*, 29 Apr. 1842.
131. *The Times*, 20 Sept. 1867, 8b.
132. *HA*, 2 Aug. 1850.
133. Ibid., 17 May 1850.
134. Ibid., 22, 29 May 1846.
135. Ibid., 9 Aug. 1850.
136. *ECH*, 4 Mar. 1869.
137. T. Sheppard, *The Evolution of Kingston-upon-Hull*, 151.

23

Fishing

The fishing industry altered the character of the southwestern end of the town, which was so socially separate from the rest—its inhabitants having arrived either from Devonshire, Ramsgate, or some workhouse—that few people seemed to notice what was happening. The arrival of the new type of fishing smacks cannot be dated exactly because smacks had been coming to Hull for so long. Fishing boats could reach the town along the Humber (in which they could also fish) and the appearance of some fishing boats was simply part of the general scene. In 1796 for example, a Hull fishmonger agreed with certain proper persons at Gainsborough to supply that town with fish weekly: 'By this means a seasonable relief, particularly to the poor, will be afforded and a stop put to the shameful monopoly by which the poor have been too long injured'.[1] In 1834 about 2000 tons of fish were caught each year at Flamborough and sent to Hull by road and thence to Leeds and Wakefield, where it was much too expensive for the poor and not in very good condition.[2]

It seems to have been the taste of the upper classes for fish which brought the smacks to Hull. The men of Brixham were naturally secretive about their invention of the weighted beam-trawl which enabled them to catch sole and turbot in great quantities for the London market. In the early nineteenth century they had found they could often best supply London by transferring their boats to Ramsgate; and since part of London high society migrated annually to Scarborough, in 1831 two or three Ramsgate smacks followed them[3] and were so successful that during the Spa season of 1832 eight more smacks arrived complete with the households of the crew;[4] and it was this movement to Scarborough which brought them to Hull also. William Isaac Markcrow, in 1863 a Hull smack-owner, had come to Hull from Ramsgate about 1843 when others were going to Scarborough. He came with about forty other vessels, and at that time there was only one trawling smack at Hull.[5] Gregory Windsor was a native of Brixham who moved to Ramsgate and then in 1853 to Hull.[6] He had gone to Ramsgate so that he could get his fish to London more cheaply and then came to Hull because there was better fishing with access to more markets, and after a few years at Hull had prospered to such an extent that he no longer went to sea himself. By 1878 he was the owner of three smacks.[7] Thomas Halfyard went to Scarborough first of all in the days when the smacks used to return to Ramsgate after fishing from Scarborough. Brixham and Scarborough smacks found the Scarborough market so good that the owners moved them to the north. He started as an apprentice, rose to be a skipper owning half a smack and made so much money fishing the ground off Flamborough called 'California' that by 1863 he owned several smacks free of all debt.[8] Joseph Potter had served his time at Brixham from the age of eleven until he was twenty-one, but came to Hull about 1854 to fish the Dogger Bank, where he could catch five or six tons in forty-eight hours.[9] The two smacks which he owned in 1863 had become eight by 1878 when he was the third largest of the Hull owners. An owner named Vivian had come from Ramsgate to Hull because of the Silver Pits, along with many others.[10] The general pattern appears to have been that because of the Scarborough market smacks from Brixham and Ramsgate found rich fishing grounds in the North Sea, taking much bigger catches with their beam-trawls than the local line-fishermen could get, and many of them moved to Hull because of the better facilities offered there—while some were leaving Hull for the still better facilities at Grimsby. Until the 1860s at least as much fish was landed at Scarborough as at Hull.

It was not until 1846 that Hull people seem to have noticed the increase in fishing. In March 1846 ten smacks arrived one Sunday, and the demand from the industrial West Riding was so great that fish was more expensive than meat.[11] It was perhaps for this reason that as early as 1848 cod-fishing in Davis Strait was tried. This appears to have been an enterprise quite separate from that of the new trawling smacks. The vessels were bigger, and the entrepreneur, Mr John Bowlby, was a local man. He had bought the *Bee*, of 70 tons, formerly a revenue cutter, and a schooner of 190 tons, the *Seaflower*, in which a number of Orkney men experienced in cod-fishing were shipped.[12] They sailed in June and the *Seaflower* returned in October with 12,000 cod, three tons of halibut and about four tons of cod-liver oil. The fish were landed in a yard at Stoneferry for the completion of the curing.[13] There is no indication of Hull fishermen returning to the west coast of Greenland in the folllowing half-century.

In 1850 two of the almost permanent characteristics of the industry made their first appearance in Hull—extreme danger and sadism. In January six vessels were lost in a gale. They had left on Christmas Eve, should have been back by 4 January and were given up for lost on the 18th. It had at first been thought that seven smacks had foundered, but one turned up later at Scarborough. A public meeting was called to consider the means of providing for the thirteen widows and twenty-five children left by the thirty or more men who had been lost.[14]

Why fishing produced so much cruelty is not clear. Later, attempts were made to deny that there was any cruelty at all, but the record is quite certain: there was a great deal;. and unless they committed murder, which was not unknown, the perpetrators usually got off lightly.[15] In 1850 the skipper and two of the crew of a smack were found to have treated the ship's boy, Isaac Nill, with extreme cruelty. Indeed, the constable who brought him ashore said that he was called to the smack because 'he heard there was a boy almost dead on board'. He found him 'laid out on deck shaking like a dog'. He had been seized by the hair and dragged about the deck until he fell into the hold, wounded in the scalp with a knife, revived by having water thrown over him, hung over the windlass and allowed to fall on deck, and kicked in the ribs. He was examined by a surgeon and was found to be dirty, starving and emaciated. The skipper had already been bound over for ill-treating an apprentice. He was fined £5 and the others £2 each.

Cases of this kind at Grimsby and Hull had become so frequent by 1882 that a parliamentary select committee was appointed to look into this and kindred matters. By then, of course, the industry had grown to enormous proportions, entirely dominating Grimsby, and providing a living for more than a quarter of the people of Hull. From the beginning the members of the committee intended to produce a report favourable to skippers and owners and their partisanship was quite blatant. They refused to hear the evidence of one lad who could give details of extreme cruelty to another on board the *Rising Sun* although the mercantile marine superintendent, not a tender-hearted man, told them it looked like a serious case, and they justified their refusal on the grounds that they had not come to look into particular cases and the lad had too little experience for his evidence to have any weight. It was an entirely different case on board the *Rising Sun* which had led to the public indignation which made some kind of public inquiry unavoidable. An apprentice had told the wife of the skipper, in the presence of the skipper, that there was an improper intimacy between him and the lad's sister. The skipper had said he would murder him when they got to sea, had done so, and had been hanged. Henry Toozes, the smack-owner who gave this particular piece of evidence to the committee, denied that there was much cruelty, and as to skippers in general, there were not better or kinder men going, a sentiment which in general the report of the select committee endorsed.[16] But the public wondered whether murders committed at sea were always discovered, and a scrutiny of the minutes of evidence seems to show that there was reason to wonder. The death of an apprentice, Richard Richer, for example, was classed as suicide, when in fact he had jumped overboard from the *C. M. Norwood* to escape being beaten by the skipper. To adduce evidence of the general beneficence of the system and the extreme rarity of cruelty one carefully coached apprentice was asked a series of leading questions by members of the committee and was given full marks.[17] In his four years at sea he had seen only one casualty—an apprentice carried away by a sea at night when reefing a sail—through his own carelessness. He had seen no cruelty, and had worked under a dozen masters, who were all humane.

Throughout the second half of the nineteenth century, fishing from Hull increased tremendously. In 1845 there were at Hull only twenty-nine smacks with an average tonnage of nineteen tons and an average value of £225.[18] In 1854, 1586 tons of fish had been landed; in 1864 6293 tons and over 19,000 tons in 1886.[19] The size of the smacks also increased. In 1878 there were 386 averaging fifty-six tons each. By 1863 the cost of a smack ready for fishing was between £700 and £900, but by 1882 a smack with a steam capstan cost up to £1600.

Ice had first been used to preserve salmon sent from Berwick to London, *c.* 1800. At Grimsby ice was first taken from local ponds, and then within a year or so brought over from Norway. The older-established Hull smacks almost immediately followed the Grimsby example, some owners moving to Grimsby because their crews objected. By 1864 it was coming to Hull from Norway at the rate of almost 3000 tons a year, and it became possible to stop the landing of fish on Sunday, which was as pleasing to the town as it was to the numerous skippers and owners who were strict Nonconformists.[20] The use of ice was combined with the practice of grouping some of the smacks into fleets which in the summer remained at sea for twelve weeks or more, sending their catch back daily in a faster sailing smack, known as a cutter and receiving fish boxes and fresh ice from a returning cutter.[21] The smacks which in April 1869 left Hull in two fleets were provisioned to stay at sea until August:

> One of the most animated scenes ever witnessed on the Humber was presented on Thursday afternoon when two or three partnership fleets of Hull smacks left the port for their summer fishing grounds. In that single tide no fewer than seventy smacks were towed out of the Humber Dock, all decked with flags. Some time before high water the vessels were hauled up on each side of the Humber Dock ready to be taken out as soon as the dock gates could be opened lying in tiers three deep, each fleet being headed by the admiral's flagship with the distinguishing flag of the admiral. Each vessel displayed her burgee at her mast-head, and having been re-fitted and newly painted the smacks made a very gay appearance. Not a single man was the worse for liquor.

Some fleeting seems to have been done before the smacks came to Hull, but now they were larger. William Isaac Markcrow in 1863 said that, with crews no larger, smacks were of seventy to eighty tons, and since they were faster, they were able to haul a forty-two foot beam-trawl, which actually was illegal, instead of the old thirty-six foot trawl. At that time they were remaining at sea for a month or five weeks only, and cutters took their catch to Hull or London daily. Thomas Halfyard owned three cutters, which he called ice-cutters. The fish, gutted and packed, was sent to Hull if possible, since their agents were there, or to Lowestoft or London if the wind was from the north.

Richard Thomas Vivian, one of the Hull witnesses who supplied evidence to J. Caird, MP and T. H. Huxley, FRS when they were making their 1863 inquiry into the effects of trawling on traditional inshore fishing, was the son of one of the pioneers and never went to sea except for pleasure. He must have been one of the first to be purely a fish-merchant, salesman and smack-owner. He told them that each cutter carried 8-10 tons of ice, which was very dear. As the fish could be got to London in better condition if it went direct in cutters instead of being put in railway vans at Hull, the owners had decided to fit up twenty cutters and use them solely for this purpose. They reached London in three days, or, much more rarely, in five. If necessary they were towed by tugs from the mouth of the Humber to the Thames.

For the first thirty-five to forty years after the arrival of the smacks at Hull, fish was so plentiful that it was not necessary for most vessels to go fleeting. Instead they went single-boating, which meant that they sailed alone, returning after a fortnight at the most and putting out again within forty-eight hours. Markcrow said that 'California' was beginning to be less profitable, but the Dogger Bank was so prolific that if they wished they could glut the market every day, and they therefore kept away from it. They took fish in such quantities that when the railway companies were charging 12s a basket, haddock and plaice had to be thrown overboard. Thomas Ramster who had trawled out of Hull since 1843 said that even now, if they were at sea for a month, they threw away most of the small fish.

Much less fish was wasted when the owners came to terms with the railways. Markcrow had gone to Derby to see George Hudson to try to get the charges for carrying fish reduced and it then became possible to send *offal fish*—plaice and haddock—to market, and lower prices brought it within reach of the poorer classes:

> For the last 17 years I have been travelling all over England, Scotland and Ireland at the expense of the North Eastern Railway Company to open markets. In many of the towns I went to there was not a fishmonger's shop, and never had been, and it was just a chance to have a few fish brought in by a hawker travelling with a donkey. There are now four, six or seven fishmongers in such towns, all of them getting a living and all of them taking their fish from Hull.[22]

R. T. Vivian dated the change as taking place about 1856-7, and since then it had not been necessary to throw anything back into the sea, and the poorer classes were able to buy plaice and haddock.

Because fish was plentiful and the industry was expanding, during the whole of the period in which sailing smacks predominated the Hull smack-owners, with few exceptions, consisted of men who had begun as apprentices, often from very poor families. When Samuel Decent met Huxley and Caird he said that in the twenty years in which he had been in Hull business had increased five-fold, and that in the room he could scarcely see anyone who had not started as a fisherman, borrowed money to become an owner and then paid off the loan.[23] He owned two smacks himself. It was common for a steady sailor, not a drunkard, to save and then borrow money from a friend in order to buy his first boat. John Tims was another who had done this and now owned a smack, and he explained, 'That is what we may term coming in at the hawse-hole and coming out at the taffrail'.[24] This career pattern was so well established that during strikes, when boats were tied up at Hull, the men on strike did not interfere with the sailing of any boat whose skipper was 'working her out'—paying off his mortgage on his first smack. In 1863 it was said that there were no large capitalists in the industry and that a man could get a loan at 5 per cent from his friends to buy a boat second hand. In this pattern the apprentices also had their place. As long as the expansion of fishing kept pace with the increase in their own numbers they could reasonably expect to become skippers and then owners. It was only when the numbers of apprentices became so great that a large depressed group of apprentices became an exploited class, still enabling the others to realise their ambitions. In 1863 this point had not yet been reached. The typical smack was manned by a skipper, a mate who was called the second hand, and three apprentices. The skipper and mate were share-men, paid not by wages but by fixed shares of the profits, and some of them were part-owners of the vessels in which they sailed.

At first the smacks lay in the Humber, as the Hull Dock Company demanded dues of 6*d* per ton. As they reduced the dues some of the vessels came into the Humber Dock, and with a second reduction by 1851 all were using the dock. In addressing the Hull Trawl Fishermen's society in 1888 C. H. Wilson, MP, the shipping magnate said:

> I can remember when the fishermen were put into a corner of the
> Humber Dock and it was there that they held their Billingsgate.
> Those who did business with the larger craft thought the fishermen a
> great nuisance there and wanted to get rid of them. The fishermen
> did not want to be moved as they thought they had very comfortable
> quarters from which they could easily get into the town. Still, the
> business outgrew the accommodation provided in the Humber Dock
> and the fishermen were moved to the Albert Dock (1869). It was not
> very long before the same thing happened there when the fishermen
> were again looked upon as a great nuisance. The large ships and
> fishing boats interfered with each other and the end of it was that the
> latter removed to the St Andrew's Dock, which had been built
> for them as a permanent home (1883). I hope it will be your own
> place of business.[25]

The effect of this was to keep the fishing community
permanently at the western end of the town. Before St Andrew's
Dock was built it had been thought that one of the Victoria Dock
timber ponds could be deepened and provided with a lock into the
Humber[26] to accommodate the smacks; but all those concerned
with fishing, except for a few of the most prosperous smack-
owners, already lived within a few hundred yards of Hessle Road,
west of the River Hull and near to the fish dock, and any move to
the eastern side of the river had become impossible. As the smacks
moved further west, the centre of gravity of the merchant shipping
interest moved continually further east. With the isolation of their
homes at one end of the town, and with the very special conditions
under which those connected with the trade worked, for a whole
century the fishing community was almost completely severed
socially and geographically from the rest of Hull.

There were only slight interruptions in the growth of prosperity.
The cotton famine for a while reduced the demand for fish. S.
Decent said: 'They have no money inland now to buy fish'; but
this simply meant that fish had to be diverted to London where
there were much better prices,[27] and one of the owners, H.
Toozes, who complained of the effects of the depression, was to
become mayor and one of the richest of steam-trawler owners.
Usually the only people who suffered financially were those who
invested in smacks without having acquired any experience of
fishing at sea. Fishing families were so much better off than others
that on Saturdays Hessle Road looked like a fair:

That important industry, the fishing interest, remains to the advantage of the neighbourhood at the west end of the town, and that vast, populous and growing locality, has for its main artery the Hessle Road which is 'going' to be widened . . . on Saturday nights especially, when the moving mass of people may be described as being like unto a fair for numbers, such persons as desire to progress quickly had better avoid the main thoroughfare.[28]

And this large population was considerably younger than that of the rest of the town. The 1887 birthrate of the Newington district was fifty-four per thousand and by far the highest in the town.

Those who worked on shore in connection with fishing were far more than those who went to sea. By 1878 there were fifty smoke-houses in which fish was cured, the first having been started by a man named Self in 1849 and the yards in which smacks were built and repaired employed fifty blacksmiths as well as a far greater number of shipwrights and riggers.[29] One of the leading owners estimated in 1882 that the capital of the industry was £500,000 and that 20,000 persons were directly or indirectly dependent on it.[30]

At that time the industry was thought to be undergoing a crisis. A change in the law had resulted in the disappearance of almost all the Hull apprentices, and no skipper was any use unless he had served his time in smacks. The fisher-lads had got to know of certain provisions in the Merchant Shipping Act of 1880 and simply refused to go to sea. The stipendiary magistrate, E. C. Twiss, had explained to the owners that a lad would be committing an offence only if he was actually on board when he refused duty; and, as to this, Henry Toozes said, 'Our difficulty was to get them on board'.[31] His own apprenticeship in Devonshire, served when the system was far more paternalistic, was far behind him and he was already a fishing magnate. In 1880 he had had eighteen apprentices. Most of them had run away, and now he had 'not three'. He had been lucky in having good lads, he said, and did not think he had had more than two in prison for desertion. But although he felt that the disappearance of apprenticeship might bring ruin, the accounts of his smack *Progress* which he produced showed that a voyage of eight weeks earned him £50 profit—and this would mean that his profit was of the order of ten per cent on his investment assuming the vessel cost £1600 new and depreciation at fifty per cent in ten years.

Most owners considered that the apprenticeship system was

essential and that imprisonment must if necessary be re-introduced in order to make apprentices go to sea; but the Hull stipendiary would not imprison deserters. In 1881 and 1882 he imprisoned no more than sixteen, for offences other than desertion—and all but three were imprisoned in 1881 because by 1882 the apprentices had simply gone away. At Grimsby, on the other hand, corrupt magistrates and their servile clerks in the same period imprisoned 279, most of them in the Hull Hedon Road gaol. The trick was to use the police to make an arrest on shore of any apprentice thought likely to desert. There was no shadow of legality in this, but no apprentice had the resources which might have enabled him to sue the authorities and recover damages. As soon as a policeman brought the apprentice on board, he was asked to be ready to sail. His refusal could then legally be regarded as desertion, and after trial he could be sent to prison. Passengers on the New Holland ferry-boats greatly resented the sight of these lads chained together on their way to Hedon Road. Hull smackowners, though they and skippers were almost unanimous in their clamour for stern penalties for 'deserters', could not use this device because of the vigilance of the stipendiary magistrate who fully understood the law.[32*] The system was not wholly evil. Henry Toozes said that some who were apprenticed before they were thirteen were without homes, and many were what he called gutter lads, and if they survived there was nothing to prevent them from becoming skippers. Examples were known of workhouse apprentices who had become owners.[33]

The necessity for imprisonment, however, showed what the lads thought of the system and of the extent to which it had degenerated into brutal exploitation. Even as early as the election of 1865, an angry father asked one of the candidates, James Clay, what he was going to do about the system which had ruined the son, apprenticed at eleven without the father's knowledge or consent and imprisoned three times for desertion.[34] The treatment of fishing apprentices was becoming notorious. 'Index' thought there was 'a touch of heroism' in the 'passive resistance' of the lad who, on coming out of gaol, returned again for three months rather than sail in a smack again.[35] 'Index' suspected that at sea there was much neglect and cruelty. Two years later he wrote, concerning the 1200 Hull fishing apprentices:

The treatment they receive is very harsh and no better than the accommodation for washing and sleeping. They are often five or six weeks out, perhaps all the time without having their clothes off, their only bed being the cabin floor. The cooking is done by one of themselves, who also has to work among the fish.[36]

In 1878 the Hull stipendiary magistrate, T. H. Travis, dismissed the case against three apprentices, arrested for desertion, as they claimed that the smack was not seaworthy,[37] and an apprentice surrendered himself as a deserter from the 21st Hussars rather than return to sea.[38]

The life was a hard one, and sometimes cruelty made it unbearable. George Gilchrist was fined 40s for making his apprentice drink sea-water in a 'revolting liquid' mixed with sugar.[39] A few days later a coroner's jury found that in December 1864, on the smack *Comet*, Jacob Kessler died of cold, exposure, insufficient food, and ill-treatment.[40] T. H. Travis, dealing with a lad charged with desertion, after hearing his defence cancelled his indentures and fined his master £5 for cruelty to him.[41] The minds of so many were warped by the cruelties of apprenticeship that even after Hull apprentices were free to desert if they chose to do so, sadism and fishing often sailed together. A Finn was found to have had his face horribly abraded by scrubbing with the skin of a dogfish, and Jakob Meitty, on the *George Peabody*, was treated with such murderous cruelty that when she docked he was taken to the Infirmary half-dead.[42]

When a deputation of Hull and Grimsby owners went to the Board of Trade to ask for legislation to restore fishing apprenticeship, Joseph Chamberlain said:

Surely such a state of things does not exist in any trade or business. Either the men do not like your bargains, or they must be the very worst class of men to be found. What you say is that you cannot get men to work except under threats of imprisonment. That would be reducing matters to a state of serfdom. As to the apprenticeship system we hear of the most cruel treatment of apprentices being common amongst smack-owners in Hull and Grimsby.[43]

Alderman Robert Waller, chairman of the Sculcoates Poor Law Union, though he had sent forty lads as fishing apprentices, of whom twenty-six had done well, spoke with intense bitterness about his vain attempts as mayor to secure the release from apprenticeship of a widow's son who was soon afterwards drowned, and of 'the parties who got hold of that lad and had him bound apprentice'. As a visiting justice he had found that it was rare to see apprentices from any other trade in prison, where some of them, from the company they were forced to keep on and off the treadmill, became hardened criminals. Henry Webster, governor of the prison, was of the same opinion, and added that lads sent to prison frequently complained of ill-treatment by the hands but did not complain to their masters when they returned on shore.[44]

Those who ran away were nevertheless often going out into the cold. A youth of nineteen, with no relatives, had come to Hull from Reading and served in the smacks. He ran away and turned up in Howden workhouse, where he refused to do task work because he was too ill. Medical attention was refused and he was sentenced to fourteen days' imprisonment. At Hedon Road he was immediately put in the prison infirmary where he died of pneumonia ten days later.[45]

The Commons select committee was appointed as the only concrete result of the owners' deputation to Chamberlain; and they were provided with evidence from industrious apprentices. One of Mr Ansell's apprentices did not know how old he was, but knew that he had served six years and nine months of his apprenticeship. He began as an indoor apprentice, which meant that he lived in his master's house, and was well fed and cared for, but he was now an outdoor apprentice—living in lodgings. He liked the life, though it was hard in winter, but he was well clad and put up with it. Thomas H. Smith was either very good or knew how to put on a show.[46] On shore he lived at home with his parents and did not associate with other fisher-boys. It was the lads with money in their pockets who were enticed to the bad parts of the town. He went to the music hall and had been to the theatre once, but on Sundays ashore he went to the Walton Street Sunday School. He had pocket money of 1s a week. Even a not-entirely-industrious apprentice could give evidence which was music to the committee's ears. One such was a deck-hand aged eighteen who had been at sea for five years.[47] Shortly after he was apprenticed he deserted for eighteen months. He had been in prison three times—'It only cured my conduct. It did not improve me'. In winter it was better at sea than in gaol as the food was good. Some of the lads could not help going to prison. He assured the committee that cruelty was not the cause of desertion and that he intended to remain at sea and become a skipper.

More independent witnesses had a rougher passage.[48] A deck-hand of twenty-three said he had run away from York and had apprenticed himself when he was fourteen. At sea he was often kicked and knocked about for not doing his work as he was too small. He was not cheeky or unwilling. Later there was less ill-treatment. When he was afraid of his master he deserted and was imprisoned without any chance to defend himself—'The gaffer had all the talk'. Now he was out of his time he had plenty of good clothes and did not think it worth trying to save. He was asked: 'If you have always been ill-treated have you never thought of getting another occupation?' and he answered, 'They have got it all out of me now'. Now he preferred the sea, but if he were still an apprentice he would prefer prison. He was asked why, if a man could become a third hand in three years it had taken him nine and there was the following exchange:

> 'I was not fit for it. They never learned me.'
> 'Do you mean you never learned yourself? You were brooding over
> your grievances instead of attending to your work?'
> 'I always attend to my work.'

If cruelty was not the cause of all the apprentices going away some other explanation had to be found; and since the dangers of fishing, especially in winter, were well known, this was given an airing, but no more. Henry Toozes admitted that in recent years casualties had increased, but no one asked him why. They had not increased any more among lads than among men, but a lad in his early voyages, before he had got his sea-legs, was not aware of the dangers and could soon be over the rail. He held that there were few cases of lads being set to do tasks beyond their capacity.[49] The transfer of fish from smacks to cutters in rowing boats, or boxing as it was called, was a cause of loss of life, but boats selling liquor at sea were much worse. The position of a boy was deplorable with the crew under the influence of fiery spirits. On one occasion a liquor boat had come out to the fleet from Bremerhaven and the three men had been drowned. Cases had been known of the entire crew being drunk and the vessel being left under the care of a boy.

For Victorian Hull the most satisfactory explanation of the break-up of the system was that the woman tempted him and he fell. It was said that after the passage of the 1880 Act many of the lads from the smacks could be found in the back-street slums of Hull. Toozes, who had an extremely friendly hearing from the committee, said that girls met the smacks and lured the lads to disreputable lodging-houses—and this was the main cause of desertion.[50] 'When the girls have got a lad's money then the owner sees no more of him.' The docks were infested with young wenches. Lads as young as sixteen came home with £3-£5. They coaxed them home to their parents, and half their money was spent in brothels. James Mason, the borough medical officer, had been with Mr Gray, an assistant secretary at the Board of Trade, to visit several places frequented by the lads in Trundle Street and Union Court—south of Osborne Street, off Waterhouse Lane.[51] They saw half-drunk lads with girls who were not decent. Some of the lads were apprentices, but they were ragged and their clothing was not of that character you would expect to find on lads engaged in fishing. He had not seen their overalls or waterproof clothing, and as these are not garments ordinarily worn in the pursuit of love we must assume he meant that they had pawned them. Some of the girls he saw with Mr Gray were rather under-clad than over-clad. Some were bare-shouldered and in their bare feet. He had no official knowledge of the state of health of the girls or of their expectation of life. Neither of them thought that the lads looked as if their physique was well kept up.

Smack-owners protested about the Merchant Shipping Act of 1880 as if they had been robbed—and indeed they had been robbed of their apprentices whom both they and members of the select committee regarded as their property. All concerned must have known that in law no person can be the property of another, but their words betrayed their true feelings. Toozes was asked, 'No man should own an apprentice who does not own a smack or part of one?' and he replied, 'I quite agree with that'. He was also asked 'Is there any difference between those who own a large number of apprentices and those who own a small number?' To this he said there was little difference and that small owners had as much trouble with bad lodging-houses and desertions as large owners did.[52]

The members of the Hull Trawl Fishermen's Society completely agreed with the owners that apprenticeship was essential and that apprentices must be kept to their indentures by imprisonment if necessary.[53] But imprisonment for simple desertion on shore was not restored and almost immediately the issue was forgotton in the clash between the men—and it must be remembered that most of the men were skippers or mates—as to the continuation of sending fleets of smacks to sea to remain fishing for long periods in the winter months, a very different matter from summer fleeting, and far more dangerous.

In the March gales of 1883, 180 Hull fishermen were lost.[54] Though this loss was heavier than usual, the occupation was quite exceptionally dangerous, the loss of life per 11,000 men employed being about ten times as great as in coal-mining. But whereas mining disasters tended to produce large numbers of casualties in a single explosion, much more life was lost in fishing by the merciless attrition of the sea—a man taken overboard by a wave, a rowing boat upset when carrying fish to a steam-cutter, or an apprentice dragged over the rail by a bucket; and those who were lost were relatively young. Most of the Hull men known to have been drowned in fishing between 1878 and 1882 were in their twenties.[55] The oldest was forty-four. A fund was opened for the dependants of the men lost in 1883, and the smack-owners immediately subscribed £900 for the 60 widows and 200 orphans. Some, no doubt, owning one or two boats, could give little; but by now many men had become rich through fishing: 'It would doubtless astonish the general public if they were informed of the total amount they have put by in the savings bank, or invested in building societies.[56] And it was men of this class who between them parsimoniously raised £900, just over half the cost of a smack, towards the relief of 260 persons.

The origin of trawl-fishing from Hull was so recent that in 1883 some of the pioneers were still active. Councillor Ansell, when he met the trawl fishery commission under Lord Dalhousie, could remember the discovery of the Silver Pits in 1837 and the establishment of the trade in 1844. In the early days it had been realised that the Dogger Bank could not be fished from Hull without the use of ice to preserve the catch.[57] It was then believed that ice in sufficient quantities could only be obtained in the Arctic and it was thought that the cost would make any such venture impossible; but by 1845 ice cut from the lake at Wenham, Massachussetts, was being taken to India, and if ice could be sold at a profit with a double crossing of the equator, it could obviously be brought to the Humber from lakes in Norway.[58] So much ice was imported that the opinion was expressed that the quantity should have been included in the statistical account of Hull trade in 1864.[59] It was still taken from local ponds and carted along the main roads from the villages to the docks, and in the cold winter of 1867 sold for 10s a ton.[60] Properly insulated stores were needed to reduce melting. There was a very large brick-built ice-house in Cambridge Street, Anlaby Road, insulated by packing nine inches of sawdust behind boards. Since there was no real town planning the maltkiln of Messrs Gleadow, Dibb and Co. was next door and sparks or fire from the chimney ignited the slate roof of the ice-house. The slates were fire resistant, but the hundred tons of sawdust packed immediately underneath were not. The fire destroyed half of the building, but a strong partition-wall saved the other half, which eventually became the Icehouse Citadel of the Salvation Army.[61]

The use of ice virtually began the change from small owners who had been fishermen to capitalists on a larger scale, who in the nineteenth century had usually started as fishermen, but who like Councillors Toozes and Ansell, became essentially business men. It was quite possible for the small owner to use ice, but it was much more profitable for a large limited company, especially if it was able to operate with fleets of smacks. By 1880 two such fleets, linked to the selling of ice, dominated the fishing of Hull—the Red Cross, and the Great Northern. This did not necessarily increase the earnings of owners at the expense of the fishermen's shares, but it certainly increased the power of the owners and left the fishermen feeling that they could be cheated in the now very complicated settlement transactions. This alone would not have led to a rupture. It was the gales of March which started the fishermen's strike of October-November 1883. The men were convinced that fewer lives would have been lost if the smacks had not been crowded in fleets with too little sea-room to avoid collisions, and they objected to the greater dangers of boating and boxing in the winter months.

Some of the smacks which came to Hull in the 1840s were already used to fleeting, but it was limited to the summer; for the rest of the year they were single-boating. The cutters which took the daily catch to Hull or London were used in ordinary trawling in the winter. In 1863 it was thought that the use of steam-cutters would be impossible. Even if it were possible to keep the fish and the ice far enough away from the heat of the boilers, a steam-cutter would be far too big. Twenty would be needed, and it would be uneconomic to use them to carry the usual twenty tons per day. But by 1880 improvements in insulation and the development of triple- expansion engines had changed all this, quite apart from the fact that there was more fish to be carried. Six steam-cutters costing £6000 each were able to serve the two fleets which totalled 120 smacks. The owners were anxious to use their cutters all the year round; and their anxiety was increased by the first signs of over-fishing. Although Councillor Ansell was able to repeat the shibboleth of smack-owners—'He thought that trawling improved the fishing grounds rather than injured them'—some of his colleagues told the trawl fishery commission of 1883 that although more vessels were fishing the amount of fish caught had not increased proportionately and that within the last few years there had been a great falling off in catches.[62]

Winter fleeting appears to have started in 1880. Most skippers were still single-boating and it took the loss of 180 men to bring about a real crisis. This, then, was the background of the strike in which the skippers and mates made a last effort to put an end to winter fleeting. There is no trace of what other fishermen thought about it. Nearly all the apprentices had freed themselves and their places had been taken by hands paid by the week, some of whom were probably ex-apprentices, but during the strike nothing was heard from them. It was a strike with a single and simple purpose, the end of fleeting and boxing in winter. During the summer the Hull Trawl Fishermen's Society gave notice to the owners that all sailings would cease from Monday, 1 October 1883 if this demand was not met: 'The impending strike was made known at Billingsgate on Saturday by the town crier whose intimation created no inconsiderable interest.'[63]

There were 800 members of the society, or enough to tie up some 400 boats, and at first it was not clear how many would actually strike. Some small owners spoke of the men with contempt:

> Why, when we came down to Hull first we had nothing but boarding. There was no ice then. It was work boarding fish then and no mistake. We used to have to handle great baskets of a couple of hundredweight and get them in and out of the boat.[64]

Before the end of the first week of the strike there was a meeting between the two sides. The owners protested that the abandonment of winter fleeting would cause them heavy losses, and suggested that the men should decide just how far north the fleets should go. The men raised the question of why there were so many unemployed fishermen, and although there was apparently no animosity shown, there could be no agreement.[65] They had their own separate meeting in the evening, attended by some men who were not members of their society, and a general feeling was expressed that it was proper to strike as it was a question of life, not of money; and ten days later one member said, if the strike was on a question of money he would wash his hands of it.[66]

At the end of the second week the strikers held a public meeting which was attended by some women, and by members of the Trades Council. Here feeling was much stronger. Mr Mullineaux, president of the Trades Council, said:

> The people will give liberally when widows and orphans are made by the fleeting system, but they are backward in giving help to put an end to a system which makes the widows and orphans. Vested interests are the cause of any amount of cruelty to the working men, and it is vested interests which are banding the owners together to compel them to go fleeting in winter.[67]

Others referred to the long absences from home which fleeting involved, tending to reduce the crews 'to the condition of savages', to the dangers of fleeting and to the fact that some of the smacks were so bad that the crew had to spend half the time at the pumps. Yet another skipper said he would not strike for money, but that this was a question of life and death. The secretary of the society told them that after the March gales a third of their funds had gone in funeral expenses. They must avoid all violence, and because they were in the right, God would defend their cause. The outcome was to show that he was misinformed.

Inevitably there was some intimidation of the few who were willing to go to sea, but during the whole strike no more than twenty members of the society lapsed. Sixty owners who among them owned 300 smacks met to protest that they were not receiving the help from the police to which as large ratepayers they were entitled. They had interviewed the secretary of the Dock Company, the town clerk and the chief constable.[68] What they wanted was liberty of property. Left to themselves two-thirds of the men would be willing to start boxing again; and as to the dangers of fleeting, a court of inquiry had found not only that this was the best method of supplying the market but also that the loss of vessels was mainly due to the negligence of crews.

The police seem to have decided to help.[69] Three days after the meeting of the owners, six constables and an inspector were in Neptune Street to see a man safely to his ship. A threatening crowd assembled, and police evidence—there was no other—showed that they had refused to disperse. Four men, including James Carrick, president of the Fishermen's Society, were arrested. The trial before the stipendiary lasted two days. Many defence witnesses were called, and the case was dismissed—though the concluding remarks of the magistrate seemed to show his belief that the defendants were lucky. Mr Carrick was carried in triumph round the town, and one skipper went so far as to declare it was now a struggle between capital and labour.

During the strike owners repeatedly pointed to the injustice of the strikers in stopping single-boating as well as fleeting. Their answer was that they did not stop those skippers who were working off a mortgage on their boats and would not stop any owner who cared to go out in his own boat. As for single-boating, many owners of smacks employed in this way, as the majority had been, were shareholders in the Great Northern or the Red Cross Company which did the fleeting and creamed off the profits. Further, at any rate with Toozes' vessels, if a skipper had a bad trip he was ordered to go fleeting.[70]

The strike was ended on 12 November by the mediation of the Trades Council—though this mediation did little more than hide the virtually complete victory of the owners. There was a meeting on the 8th. Mr Mullineaux told them that they felt it their duty to try and end the strike. Councillor Ansell, the largest owner, admitted that the dangers of fleeting might be limited if there were fewer vessels in a fleet.[71] Three days later the men decided to resume single-boating, and the following day ended the strike altogether.[72] The owners had professed to be willing to allow the men to appoint the admirals in charge of the two fleets, but then found that they could not make this concession as the steam-carrying companies—themselves in a different capacity—made these appointments; but they did concede that no more than fifty vessels should be actually fishing in any one fleet. Mr Mullineaux thanked them for the kind manner in which they had received his deputation and was pleased that both parties had discussed the question as men of business; and his colleague, Mr Jennings, hoped that in future they would realise that trades-unionists did not organise to make war on capital but endeavoured to give strength and confidence to it. Councillor Ansell tactfully said that but for their intercession the dispute might have lasted much longer, and they had done a great deal for the fishing trade and port.

The dangers of fleet-fishing are apparent in an almost jocular account of 'boxing' as seen from a boat of the Mission to Seamen, rolling heavily and shipping seas:

> The uproar culminated round the mouth of the hold where were being heaped up, upside down or on their ends or anyhow, the boxes which arrived faster than they could be stowed away. When a great mass of water lifted a boat to the level of the steamer's bulwarks, one of the inmates scrambled aboard. A brief struggle, then he was established on deck, and now received the boxes from his mate in the boat, the moment for doing this being selected with the same judgment. The man on the carrier threw it on the deck. Now it was dragged or kicked as near the mouth of the hold as the blockade would permit.[73]

The 'blockade' was the crowd of men and lads from other boats struggling to get rid of their boxes. The system did produce fish of very high quality and continued, with steam trawlers, until the 1930s.[74]

The Hull Trawl Fishermen's Society carried a quite innocuous resolution at the Hull meeting of the TUC in 1886.[75] It was a union with few militants. Skippers were still bemused with the idea of becoming owners, and many of them probably succeeded in doing so as the richer and more enterprising owners were anxious to transfer their capital to steam-trawlers. As early as 1878 there was said to be one steam-smack in Hull, in all probability one of the steam-cutters or carriers which, it was realised during the strike, could be used independently for fishing. In the rush to get into steam-trawling, which must have ruined many recent purchasers of smacks, Mr C. Pickering sold his sailing-smacks in Portugal, Belgium Holland and Germany;[76] though with his partner, Haldane, he had had a new smack launched at Goole as late as 1886.[77] Already by 1885 Earles' had built five steam-trawlers, all with triple expansion engines for Grimsby owners and were to build more.[78] Grimsby owners were in advance of Hull, but by

1893 the number of Hull smacks had shrunk to 300 and there were 150 Hull steam-trawlers.[79] One company alone, the Humber Steam Trawling Company, had twenty-seven of the new trawlers,[80] and Sir A. K. Rollit, MP, the Hull solicitor, and C. H. Wilson, MP, the shipowner, were among those Hull grandees who without any experience of fishing were nevertheless investing successfully in steam-trawlers;[81] while fried-fish shops were using the often under-sized fish which these vessels caught in vast quantities. At the end of 1892 it was found that 170 steam-trawlers had been built at Hull, 62 at Beverley and only 13 at Grimsby. There was no port on the Humber other than Hull where the new compound or triple-expansion engines could be produced and fitted.[82] More than a million must have been invested in Hull fishing, but when in January 1895, 106 Hull fishermen were lost, no more than £2400, considerably less than half the cost of one trawler, was all that could be raised for immediate assistance for their 200 or more dependants. Yet ordinary fishermen, with little hope of becoming rich, though they did occasionally earn something from salvage, every year risked their lives to rescue men in distress at sea, and lost earnings because of the time spent in bringing them into port when they could have been fishing. At the other end of the scale, Sir A. K. Rollit, in spite of the Married Women's Property Act, had £100,000 or more a year from his wife's estate, probably for twenty years. And every year the number of trawlers grew. In 1895 there were 5513 arrivals of trawlers at St Andrew's Dock, 5896 in 1896 and 6134 in 1897.[83] By 1899 all that remained of the hundreds of sailing-smacks were a few left in St Andrew's Dock extension and a few used as 'mark' boats by the boxing fleets.

Reuben Manton, probably the man of that name, an unusual one, who later became head of the first Hull Nautical College, gave evidence to the Royal Commission on Labour in November 1891. Replying to Lord Hartington, he said that boys of eleven, totally unfit for the work expected of them, were at sea in the fishing-fleets.[84] Moreover, a trawler was often short-handed when one of the crew was injured and had to be put on board the Mission to Seamen boat, where there was a sick-bay. The Mission-boats did carry spare hands, but too few, and a crew might be short-handed for several weeks. The trawler-owners ought to provide a remedy. Owners still used various devices to cheat the share-fishermen out of a percentage of their earnings. Often an owner would undertake to act as fish-saleman and for his services would take five per cent of the proceeds of a voyage, when in fact the work was really being done by someone else, paid at the rate of two-and-a-half per cent only.[85] Much of the fish caught by Hull and Grimsby trawlers went straight to London in the steam-carriers.

Although fishermen bought their own provisions they were not signed on unless they did so at stores in which the owners had shares. There was also sharp practice with the charge made for ice supplied for the voyage.[86] This had almost led to a strike.

There was no easy work in fishing-vessels:

> I myself, the last time I was at sea, which was 18 months ago, have worked for six consecutive months, 15 hours a day, seven days a week, with three Sundays at home.[87]

Others worked even longer. A man who went to sea one Monday worked fourteen hours, thirteen on Tuesday, then eighty-four hours in the next ninety-six, after which it was Sunday, and he worked only eleven hours. On Monday he was landing fish for seventeen hours.[88] Men ought to be properly rested before they went back to sea again, but they were not.[89] The time they spent on watch was actually counted as 'free' time. The change from sail to steam had put many men out of work.[90] For those on watch sailing at speed was a severe mental strain, and a good many trawlers were not really seaworthy, with pumps out of order, sails (then still used with steam) not repaired, and defects in the hull and rigging.[91] The owners' mutual insurance arrangements made the annual survey an empty absurdity. On some ships the drinking water was bad. The cast-iron ballast was not clean, and the fish-slime which leaked on to it made a dreadful smell. In summer the crew's quarters were overheated by the engines and boilers, which were not properly lagged. In summer the men were 'nearly broiled.'[92]

There were great dangers in fleet-fishing and no claim could be made under the Employers' Liability Act. If trawlers were well-found, there would be fewer accidents. There was no proper survey of the ship's boats used in rowing boxes to the fleet-carrier. In a single voyage men might have to ferry boxes fifty or sixty times.[93] Trawlers went back to port in rotation at intervals of eight or ten weeks, and every morning fish had to be rowed to the carrier.[94] Trawlers ran far greater risks in a storm if they were crowded in a fleet than if they were sailing alone. In the March gales of 1883 twenty-seven were lost with all hands.[95] If they had been free to choose, some skippers might have 'run up to southward of the Dogger Bank, or hauled the vessel round.' Fewer would have been lost, but the owners maintained that as in coal-mining dangers had to be faced.

Manton agreed with Lord Hartington that steam-trawlers were safer than fishing-smacks. 'There are not as many men lost now.'[96] Unfortunately there was a surplus of skilled fishermen and to get work they often had to sail not as share-fishermen, but as paid weekly-hands, with loss of status and respect. With steam-trawlers, training in seamanship was less necessary than it had been, and for men who had gone through a long apprenticeship in sail, the change to steam was not wholly beneficial. He made these points in his answers to the great Cambridge economist, Alfred Marshall, adding, with considerable emphasis:

> It is through our industry, our skill and our pluck that the concern
> pays at all, and we are the people who make the concern pay.[97]

The total earnings of share-fishermen were very much greater than earnings in other occupations, but they worked very much longer, and often in great danger. The Board of Trade, about a year later investigated profit-sharing, and so took account of share-fishermen, but not of those who had been reduced to sailing as weekly hands. On a carrier the skipper had 30s a week and a share of not less than a shilling in the pound on the net proceeds of the voyage. Even the third hand did not earn much less.[98] The first engineer had three guineas a week and three-pence in the pound.

The gales of February 1900 took another sixty men.[99] Summarising the events of the year the *Eastern Morning News* said: 'At no previous period in its history has the fishing trade of Hull been under such a dark cloud as overshadowed it during 1900.' But it was the high price of coal, £1 1s a ton, which formed the cloud. Under the share-system many skippers and hands found themselves settling in debt, only the two largest companies had a profitable year, and the shares of some of the new trawling companies which had been formed fell alarmingly. Yet catches had been good. The next year was much better. The price of coal fell and there was a long strike at Grimsby which quickened the demand for Hull fish,[100] and when the trawler engineers and trimmers (stokers) refused to accept a reduction of 2*s* 6*d* a week, the owners felt it prudent not to press them. But there was still no permanent relief fund for the dependants of men lost at sea; and so many trawlers had been built in the rush to get into steam that in spite of the launching of several vessels intended for fishing off Iceland, some Hull trawlers were sold to other ports. The London and Yorkshire Steam Trawling Company[101] was liquidated and its vessels sold to French firms, but in 1902 many new vessels were being built in Hull, a new ice factory was producing fifty tons a day, and a new fish-manure and oil works was set up with American plant.

Perhaps the best remembered event in the history of Hull fishing happened on the Dogger Bank on 21 October 1904 when the imperial Russian fleet, on its way to destruction at Tsushima, fired on the *Gamecock* fleet to protect itself from Japanese torpedo boats which by some miracle were thought to have reached the North Sea.[102] The trawler *Crane* was sunk, her crew wounded and the skipper and the third hand killed. The error was inexcusable, but there is irony in the existence of a monument to commemorate this encounter when no monument stands to record the deaths of the several thousands of fishermen who in a hundred and thirty years have been drowned in the course of the most dangerous of all occupations.

At this period much was heard of the vessels of Charles Hellyer. He or his forebears had had four sailing-smacks in 1878. In 1905-6 he had fifty trawlers for use in fleeting built within nine years[103] and he probably had an investment exceeding half a million in the Hull industry which by the time he had completed his plans had a capital exceeding £2 millions. About a quarter of all the Hull trawlers belonged to his fleet. In 1905 he complained that because of the high cost of sending fish by rail, over 50,000 tons,—half the Hull total—went to London by his and other carriers.[104] In the following year he decided to have two fast steam-cutters to bring fish direct to Hull to be sent to inland markets without handling, providing jobs for over 600 men; but in 1907, although the railway had provided many new wagons specially for fish, he decided that though his trawlers would sail from Hull, all his cutters would go to London.[105]

Though the rich had not been sent away empty, the fishing boats of Hull had filled the hungry with good things, and all too soon it was to be realised in 1914 that without trawlers converted to mine-sweeping, the Grand Fleet would not have been able to move a cable's length out of Scapa, while Hull and Grimsby skippers, mostly with far more sea-time than even an Admiral of the Fleet, trawled for a different harvest.

Sources

1. *HP*, 29 Mar. 1796.
2. *R*, 21 Mar. 1834.
3. Ibid., 6 Aug. 1831.
4. Ibid., 29 June 1832.
5. Fisheries, 1863, 154-61.
6. Ibid., 161.
7. *TC*, 142.
8. Fisheries, 1863, 170-3.
9. Ibid., 173-4.
10. Ibid., 177-9.
11. *HA*, 14 Mar. 1846.
12. Ibid., 2 June 1848.
13. Ibid., 20 Oct 1848.
14. Ibid., 18 Jan. 1850.
15. Ibid., 22 Mar. 1850.
16. Apprentices, 1883, 67 ff.
17. Ibid., Appendix 7.
18. *TC*, 133.
19. Fisheries, 1863, 112; *VCH*, Hull, 255.
20. *HN*, 30 Apr. 1864.
21. Ibid., 15 Apr. 1869.
22. Fisheries, 1863, 166-7.
23. Ibid., 168-9.
24. Ibid., 175.
25. *EMN*, 3 Jan. 1888.
26. *TC*, 134.
27. Fisheries, 1863, 169-70.
28. *Hull Critic*, 23 June 1883, 4.
29. *TC*, 136-7.
30. Apprentices, 1883, 15.
31. Ibid., 152.
32.* D. Boswell, *Sea Fishing Apprentices of Grimsby*, 70-1 and *passim*; does not mention that the procedure was illegal; E. Gillett, *A History of Grimsby*, 247-73.
33. Apprentices, 1883, 152.
34. *EMN*, 1 July 1865.
35. Ibid., 8 May 1865.
36. Ibid., 8 Mar. 1867.
37. Ibid., 31 Jan. 1878.
38. Ibid., 14 Feb. 1878.
39. Ibid., 5 Jan. 1865.
40. Ibid., 18 Jan. 1865.
41. Ibid.
42. Ibid., 8 June 1885.
43. *Grimsby News*, 7 July 1882.
44. Apprentices 1883, 397.
45. *EMN*, 31 Mar. 1886.
46. Apprentices, 1883, 273.
47. Ibid., 277.
48. Ibid., 276.
49. Ibid., 169.
50. Ibid., 175.
51. Ibid., 193.
52. Ibid., 158, 175.
53. Ibid., 393.
54. *The Times*, 29 Mar. 1883, 4a.
55. Apprentices, 1883, Appendix 7.
56. *TC*, 135.
57. *EMN*, 14 Dec. 1883.
58. *Encyclopaedia Britannica*, ninth ed., xii, 614.
59. *EMN*, 6 Jan. 1865.
60. Ibid., 3 Jan. 1867.
61. Ibid., 23 Jan. 1875.
62. Ibid., 14 Dec. 1883.
63. Ibid., 1 Oct. 1883.
64. Ibid.
65. Ibid., 6 Oct. 1883.
66. Ibid., 16 Oct. 1883.
67. Ibid.

68. Ibid., 18 Oct. 1883.
69. Ibid., 24 Nov. 1883.
70. Ibid.
71. Ibid., 12 Nov. 1883.
72. Ibid., 13 Nov. 1883.
73. Ibid., 28 Sept. 1885.
74. G. Pearson, *Hull and East Coast Fishing: a commentary on the Fisheries Galleries*, Town Docks Museum Kingston-upon-Hull (1976) 8-9.
75. *The Times*, 11 Sept. 1886, 10c.
76. Fisheries, 1893, 37-40.
77. *EMN*, 5 Feb. 1886.;
78. *Hull Critic*, 21 Mar. 1885, 22.
79. Fisheries, 1893, 23-8.
80. Ibid., 34-7.
81. *The Times*, 19 Jan. 1895, 5f.
82. *EMN*, 20 Jan. 1894.
83. Ibid., 11 Jan. 1900.
84. BPP, Royal Commission on Labour, *Minutes of Evidence*, Qs 11154ff.
85. Ibid., Qs 11169ff.

86. Ibid., Qs 11175ff.
87. Ibid., Qs 11188.
88. Ibid.
89. Ibid., Q. 11193.
90. Ibid., Q. 11196.
91. Ibid., Q. 11197.
92. Ibid., Qs 11203ff.
93. Ibid., Q. 11211.
94. Ibid., Q. 11220.
95. Ibid., Q. 11223.
96. Ibid.
97. Ibid., Q. 11239.
98. Board of Trade (Labour Department), *Report by Mr D. F. Schloss on Profit-Sharing*, HMSO (1894) 10.
99. *EMN*, 1 Jan. 1901.
100. Ibid., 1 Jan. 1902.
101. Ibid., 2 Jan. 1903.
102. Ibid., 31 Dec.. 1904.
103. *The Times*, 13 Feb. 1906, 8c.
104. Ibid., 23 Jan. 1905, 10d.
105. *EMN*, 1 Jan. 1907.

24

An Age of Improvement

Hull became one of the new county boroughs in 1888 and a city in 1897. For some it was the golden age, before things fell apart in 1914, and even the majority, far from well-off, in old age looked back on the late Victorian and Edwardian years as the best of their lives. It was the time when some schools, still in use, were built, such as Southcoates Lane and Sidmouth Street,[1] with the City Hall, several swimming baths and thousands of houses still useful, though originally they had only cold water and earth-closets. There were still court-houses, and some dreadful slums, but there was continual pressure for improvement.

Advances in technology helped to mitigate the ancient squalor—advances best known in shipbuilding and engineering, though for so large a place Hull was still very poor. Bradford, then only a little larger, had been able to afford a public investment on works and amenities twenty times greater.[2] Shipyards and engineering works were too vulnerable to the ebb and flow of the trade cycle, though in bad years some far-sighted firms took advantage of reduced prices to place orders at Hull. At Earle's, Edward James Reed, formerly chief constructor to the Navy (1862-70), took charge and for a time was assisted by his brilliant pupil, Francis Elgar.[3] The main work of the yard was the building and repair of merchant ships, but there were also orders from the Admiralty and for foreign navies. Warships were built for Chile and Japan. In 1838, when Brownlow's Victoria first blew up, the steam-pressure was only six-and-a-half pounds,[4] and in 1843 the Hull and Leith packet still had a crankshaft rising above the deck.[5] With Reed and Elgar pressures of one-hundred-and-fifty pounds were common, there were proper engine-rooms, and everything was much more efficient.

By *c.* 1870 engines had become so reliable that some owners were no longer hiring real seamen who could handle the sails which were still carried. A ship was in distress if the propellor-shaft broke, or the coal ran out. The steamer *Joseph Somes* had a very stormy passage from Kronstadt in 1874, and sixty miles from Spurn her bunkers were empty. The master of a Tyne tug, cruising in expectation of a salvage job like this, demanded £600 to tow her into the Humber. The captain astonished everyone by bringing her in under sail, and was rewarded by the owners and underwriters.[6]

As soon as engines could take a pressure of seventy pounds or more per square inch it was uneconomic to use a single-cylinder engine, and it became usual to have a second cylinder taking the exhaust steam, still at a high pressure, from the first. Such two-cylinder engines, with a high pressure and low-pressure cylinder, were known as compound engines. Among the last in service were the engines of the Humber ferry-boats of the type of the *Lincoln Castle*, and in the middle years of the present century they were among the last in the world to burn coal. They served their purpose well. When the firm of C. D. Holmes in 1875 fitted the *Seagull* with 75-pound boilers and compound engines, she had a speed of eleven knots in the Rotterdam service and instead of fourteen tons of coal a day, she used only twelve-and-a-half.[7] When the *Louisa Ann Fanny*, a blockade-runner to the Confederate States of America, then later in the London-Rotterdam service, was taken over by a Hull firm and given compound engines, with less space needed for coal she could take another three-hundred tons of cargo and still do twelve-and-a-half knots.[8] Bailey and Leatham converted one of their ships, *La Plata*, in their own yard, which Brownlow had once owned. She was able to carry an additional six-hundred tons of cargo and with seventy-pound boilers used only fourteen tons of coal a day instead of twenty-five.[9] It was economy such as this which in 1877 took the *Louisa* from Hull to Tobolsk, deep in Siberia, by way of the river Ob, in sixty-five days from Hull, and brought her safely back again.[10]

Old ships were fitted with compound engines and new vessels were built to take advantage of the improved system. One of the first was the Wilson liner *Otranto,* launched in 1877, to bring live

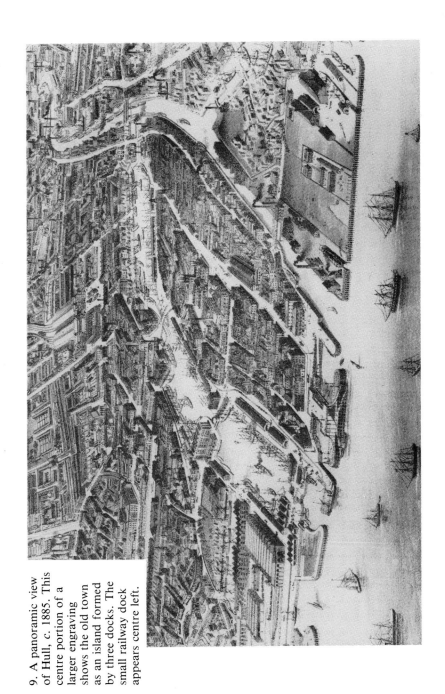

9. A panoramic view of Hull, c. 1885. This centre portion of a larger engraving shows the old town as an island formed by three docks. The small railway dock appears centre left.

10. Queen's Gardens (formerly Queen's Dock) 1980 and 1988.

cattle from New York.[11] To reduce corrosion, there were sewage-pipes from the stables, additional condensers to provide the cattle with drinking-water, longitudinal and transverse bulkheads, and pumps, winches, and steering-gear worked by steam. She was from Earle's yard, which also built four transatlantic liners for the North German Lloyd between 1873 and 1875. The latest, the *Hapsburg*, four-decked, with accommodation for a hundred-and-eighty first class passengers and eight hundred emigrants, had steam-heating throughout, to lessen the risk of fire.[12]

All the latest vessels for a decade or more were flush-decked, as if they were sailing-ships, and passenger-liners even had the saloon on deck. The top of the *Othello's* saloon was a promenade deck with the open bridge in the fore part. By 1885 there were modifications. Earle's built the SS *Eastwood* without a raised forecastle, but with a higher poop and quarterdeck. A more important innovation was in her engines. They were no longer two-cylinder compound, but triple-expansion, with three cylinders, an even more economical type.[13*] Soon Earle's had the reputation of having made more triple expansion engines than any other firm. One of their later vessels, fitted with ordinary two-cylinder compound engines, was the *Kongo*, a corvette designed by Reed for the Japanese Government. Japanese nobles and diplomats visited the yard in 1877, viewed the enormous quantity of timber in the yards and ponds, and were feted by the Mayor.[14]

Steel was taking the place of iron. The firm used it for boilers first. The *Marengo*, the fifty-third ship made by the yard for Wilsons, had steel boilers but the hull was iron, heavier but rusting much more slowly than steel. She was designed to bring either grain or cattle from New York, with 'turtle-backs' fore and aft, of the type seen in early destroyers, to prevent seas from sweeping the flush deck. There were special bulkheads to prevent grain from shifting in the holds, and steam-steering to the design of Wilson's marine superintendent.[15]

By 1885 they were building ships with steel hulls also. With their triple-expansion engines the *Finland*, built by them, did a Singapore voyage with a cargo of 2500 tons, averaging 202 miles a day on a daily consumption of ten tons of coal.[16] A. E. Seaton, succeeding Reed as general manager, had such enthusiasm for innovation that he told the St Andrews Mutual Improvement Society, at one of their meetings in Beeton Street, that steel was everywhere taking the place of iron and would in course of time be replaced by aluminium, then very costly but weighing far less. Beeton Street has gone and aluminium is cheap, but hulls are still of steel.

In 1899 Wilson's *Cito* and her sister-ships used steam at a pressure of 250 pounds,[17] and C. H. Wilson, senior partner in the firm and an MP for Hull twice spoke of the advantage of water-tube boilers which they were beginning to use.[18] By then Earle's had built several cruisers for the Admiralty with even higher pressures, and destroyers with speeds of over thirty knots. The higher the steam pressure, the greater the economy of fuel. One person who realised that technological change should lead to social betterment was William Saunders, formerly an industrialist, then owner of the *Eastern Morning News* at Hull and the *Western Morning News* at Plymouth. When he spoke to the *Hull Literary Club* in 1885 he was the Liberal member for Hull (East), too radical for many of his party. His subject was the changes which could be measured in the productivity of Hull merchant shipping since 1835, confining his attention to the Hull-New York trade. In fifty years the partnership of labour and capital had made these voyages six times more productive. The men whose work had produced the wealth ought to enjoy their share of prosperity, and he implied that they were not.[19] He was speaking to those who knew how hard the times had been in Hull.

The year 1884 was a bad one, but probably not as bad as 1848-9 when the Danes for a time prohibited access to the Baltic; but in its own way it was truly awful. In east Hull it was estimated that 1000 families were starving.[20] A lady who interested herself in the condition of the poor saw a mother of seven children taking pieces of bread from a swill-tub for her family; and Messrs Stone, who did what they could to relieve distress, found that children kept coming into their yard in Dansom Lane to raid the buckets where bread, bones, etc. were kept for pigs. A district then known as Little Ireland was near their sawmill. When one of the Stone brothers asked six people to come to his office for tinned meat he found a hundred waiting at the door.[21*] A soup kitchen in the Primitive Methodist schoolroom in Williamson Street provided 1000 loaves to go with 800 pints of soup; but in each pint there was no more than one-and-one-tenth ounces of meat and just over one-and-a-half ounces of vegetables. A ton of fish sent by Mr Sims, a smack-owner, must have done far more to lessen hunger. This is simply the chronicle of a few days in a famine no worse than that of the forties, but better recorded. Many winters were similar.

There may have been more hunger in east Hull than in the rest of the town. It was certainly better publicised because of the attempts at relief organised by Dr Holder and the Stones,[22] and a stoppage in the construction of the new Alexandra Dock, because the Hull and Barnsley had run out of money, must have made matters worse. There were 5000 navvies out of work, though many of them were not in Hull but further along the line, but in spite of their high earnings of about £2 a week they and their families were soon destitute.[23] All the guardians could do was to relieve the families of those who had gone off to look for work. A relief committee for the whole town was organised at a meeting in the town hall called by the mayor, Sir A. K. Rollit.[24] He referred to the depression in shipbuilding and in an appeal through *The Times* said:

> People with gaunt and hungry faces walk our streets. Candidates canvassing for votes at the municipal elections were met with the reply that such requests were a mockery to a breadless family, and by most distressing appeals for food, with which, in the face of the law on corrupt practices, they were unable to reply; and on every hand the signs of suffering from both hunger and cold are most heart-rending to those who witness them.

In the end nearly £6000 was raised, most of it locally, C. H. Wilson, MP heading the subscription list with £500. Just under £5000 was spent on bread, coal and blankets distributed by volunteers. The spring, as usual, was thought to bring a lessening of distress—and probably there was rather less unemployment as the first ships from the Baltic were expected—and the surplus was put in the hands of trustees for the next appeal. Even the Hull vegetarians had helped with an offer to supply soup and plum bread for a thousand dinners.

Things were a little better in 1885 and 1886, but for the poor the winter was still a terrible season. The great Alexandra Dock was open and all the navvies had gone; but in east Hull alone there were again a thousand men out of work, ship-carpenters, joiners, iron-workers, builders, general labourers and dockers. Credit from small shopkeepers and pawning of clothes and furniture helped many to survive, but this time there was no soup kitchen

Those who could buy food stuck to rice, oatmeal and bread. Weddings were postponed: 'Prosperous times are always indicated by a rise in the number of weddings, and hard times by a corresponding decrease. When Earle's shipbuilding yard is full the clergymen of the district are busy.' But nothing, as yet, could stop the birth and premature death of children, the corpse being carried by hand in an improvised coffin—a practice so common as to be thought to constitute a nuisance. A certain Mary Gray wrote in all seriousness:[25] 'It is to be hoped when we get new blood into the police force stone-throwing, sliding and carrying coffins at all hours of the day on the principal pavements will be abolished.'

For a time Wilsons turned a ship in the Railway Dock into a soup kitchen. First 250 people, with tickets issued by the firm, were given a quart of soup each and a loaf and then 350 others were fed on board the *Angelo*.[26] Those who had nothing else in which they could carry a quart of soup home used 'every conceivable utensil'. And perhaps for the first time the corporation began to recognise that some kind of public enterprise was needed to help the unemployed.[27] Some work was provided in the laying out of the new East Park, but some of the men employed were so weak from hunger that they collapsed and had to be sent away, their places being taken by single men, their bodies less weakened by the need to provide for a family, and men from the country who from childhood had known nothing but near-starvation and hard labour. It seems incredible that any place could be less desirable than the slums of Hull, but to workless labourers from the East Riding, if they could not afford to emigrate, Hull was their best hope. Many were coming into the town and because they could do a greater variety of jobs than the average town dweller, they sometimes got a job which would otherwise have gone to him. The 'Index' column in the *Eastern Morning News* said:

> The fact that the population of Hull has increased by more than 5000 people during the last year confirms that much of the distress in the east district arises from the numbers of country people. They are not all unskilled labourers but in many cases carpenters, blacksmiths and other mechanics. In some cases they have edged out the townsmen. Also the unskilled country labourer as he can no longer exist in the village where he was bred comes into town, and being in most cases a handy, hard-working chap, manages to pick up an odd job as a driver or hod-man or something of that kind.[28]

Poverty was always worst in the winter, when work was hardest to find. Cases such as the following were common:

> The report of another house visited is: 5 children; husband earned 1s 6d in six weeks; no fire, no bed-clothes, one pennyworth of bread to last the family of seven for that day, and do not know where more is to come from; baby eight weeks old wrapped in an old coat; the poor children starving inside and out. F. LORD, Holborn Mount, Hull. Jan 20th 1888.[29]

To add to the problem, visitors and emigrants from Europe thought Hull a place where some kind of living could be picked up. 'Index' was shocked by the Italian street musicians who carried their infant children with them through the streets for twelve or fourteen hours on a winter day, and even more shocked by the 'ragged, hooting mob of children and grown up girls and women with shawls on their heads' who chased a terrified small girl street singer 'whose national costume seemed all too inadequate'—an incident which he said could be seen almost any day.[30] In six months of 1888 over 41,000 emigrants from Gothenburg, Oslo, Copenhagen and Hamburg passed through Hull on their way to America.[31] An examining officer in the Hull customs thought that German Jews were the most numerous, but he also saw Hungarians, Rumanians and some Polish Jews. They had no luggage, but only a little bread and fish. He thought them dirty in their persons and in their habits generally, though some who came from Rotterdam were slightly better. One of his colleagues saw the Russian Poles from Hamburg as tall and thin, with haggard faces, and the Rotterdam arrivals as 'mainly German pork butchers'. Some of the emigrants got no further than Hull and the foreign population was increasing. The 1891 census showed that although Leeds had a larger alien population Hull had more Germans— 906.[32]

Somehow they managed to enjoy themselves and so bring themselves to the notice of the police. In Blanket Row a signboard, in German, showed that here was the Hull headquarters of the Communist International.[33] Assassinating Romanovs was then a sport without a closed season, and as one of them, in the person of the Duchess of Edinburgh, with her husband the Duke, was expected in Hull it was thought well to look at these dangerous persons. Their existence would not have been known but for their jollifications. Their *Bildungs Verein* was thought to mean that they formed a building society, but a string of sausages hung in the window and persons living nearby complained of the noise of their parties which went on up to 5 a.m. They had, however, found time to hold a discussion on socialism, in which a German pastor took part. The royal visit duly took place with a tour of the docks in the steam yacht *Mazeppa*, streets lined with flags and banners, a triumphal arch on the site of the old Beverley Gate to show how Hull had repented of its discourtesy to royalty in 1642, and brass bands performing a march, *Welcome to Hull*, composed for the occasion by Weber's pupil, Sir Julius Benedict—himself an immigrant.[34]

The pogroms of 1881 in Russia greatly increased the size of the small Jewish community and in the middle of the present century there were persons still living here who had literally fled across the snow from Russian Lithuania. It was not fully realised that these newcomers had fled to save their lives. They came, it was thought, because 'the poor Russian Jew has a notion that the British workman is overpaid and overfed and believes that he can live well where an Englishman would starve'.[35] This belief, for a Russian, did have some foundation, but the arrival of so many penniless Jews was for many years a heavy burden for the Hull Hebrew Board of Guardians, which they could not have sustained but for the efforts of a few successful Jews, such as Mr Cohen, the first Jewish town councillor, and Herman Bush, a learned jeweller and watchmaker who had travelled extensively in Europe, the U.S.A. and Canada before he settled in Hull.[36]

A good part of the population, especially the newcomers from the countryside, Ireland and the Continent, lived in the vilest slums. In 1883, largely stimulated by J. Malet Lambert, the Hull clergy and scripture readers investigated the housing of the poor. Though they appear to have uncovered evidence of a great deal of prostitution, sodomy and incest, they carefully omitted this from their report, believing that vice could not be eradicated until squalor had been abolished:

> So long as these crowded dwellings exist the poorest classes must necessarily be forced into them often in close contact with the most repulsive forms of vice. They are made constantly subject to influences which tend still further to depress and demoralise them. These influences must be so continuous and powerful as to render an improvement in their physical condition a necessary prelude to any general moral or religious improvement.[37]

In the oldest part of the town enclosed by the docks they found the worst conditions, with houses of three floors packed into courts between four feet and nine feet wide, entered by an archway from the street, often with a secondary court approached through a similar arch from the first. Most of the houses were let in single rooms. In the older parts of the town outside the ring of docks there were similar courts, but as the houses were smaller, letting off in single rooms was less common.

This led the *Eastern Morning News* to do its own investigation.[38] Streets off Hessle Road were found comparable 'with the foulest slums in Constantinople'. In all the slums of the town sewage was found overflowing from decrepit privies, lying in pools so that it was difficult to walk without treading in it. On open ground near Chiltern Street there were great pools, except in very dry weather, surrounded by 'long rows of piggeries which illustrate the fertility of resource among the pig-keeping class'. The writer does not seem to have realised that working-class families which could keep a pig were on their way up from the worst poverty. The interior of most slum houses was filthy and squalid, with plaster falling from the walls, gaps in the tiles and rags stuffed into the holes left by broken windows. Some houses had no furniture other than old boxes, and the people slept on straw. 'But even in such wretched lairs as these a cat or dog with a consumptive looking fowl or two may sometimes be found.' Everywhere animals and people were to be found living on top of one another. Pigs, cows and horses were put wherever they could be squeezed in. The medical officer of health, not yet a full-time official, found a lodging-house with sleeping quarters for twenty persons over a stable, 'and a nuisance arising from an accumulation of manure and the keeping of poultry'.[39] At 32 Hope's Place he found a six-roomed house let off in tenements, and a filthy cellar below where poultry were kept. The 1851 census recorded 93 cow-keepers in the town. Later censuses lump them with milk-sellers, but it is still (1988) among older Hull people common knowledge that even in this century milkmen often kept their cows in the town. The number of milk-sellers increased faster than the population, a possible indication of a somewhat higher standard of living. There were 92 milk-sellers and cow-keepers, mostly men, in 1871 and 311 in 1891.[40]

But in spite of the persistence of slums virtually indistinguishable from those of the forties, in the last twenty years of the century there were signs of improvement. The ratio of houses to people was the same in 1891 as it had been thirty years earlier but all reports show less overcrowding, presumably because there were more rooms. If we count those who came under the care of the boards of guardians as the least fortunate of all the inhabitants, even here there was improvement. Two of the Sculcoates guardians censured the master and matron for giving the paupers bad potatoes, though the rest of the food was good.[41] For both boards of guardians 1895 was a bad year. Sculcoates had 584 paupers in the house and 3448 on outdoor relief as against 528 and 3020 in 1894; but the guardians bought twenty-one acres at Hessle to start cottage homes for the workhouse children and began to convert their school into a hospital.[42] In 1888 the Hull board, which looked after the older and on the whole poorer part of the town, 'superannuated' their teachers and sent the children to the board-schools, but only by a majority of seventeen to fourteen.

In this atmosphere of improvement a new generation of reformers asked how it could be that in spite of forty years of sanitary legislation so many of the old evils were still there, and the answer was always the same: corruption—corrupt councillors and corrupt officials. No one then and certainly no one now can say just how large the corrupt minority was. It may be that in any society there are bound to be some who take an improper advantage of a privileged position, and certainly the old corporation from which the new took over in 1835 does not seem to have set high moral standards. The new councillors were often business men who probably saw no evil in protecting themselves and in using their special knowledge to make a profit. In their business affairs there would have been nothing wrong in such an attitude and in a society which still worshipped *laissez-faire* it was perhaps difficult for them to recognise that in public office higher standards should operate. In a series of articles entitled 'Squalid Hull' the *Eastern Morning News* said this:

> Much had been said i.e. in 1883 of the unhealthy dwellings of the Hull poor. Hull is not one whit in this respect better than most of the other large cities and towns. Improvements such as parks and promenades which are made at the public expense and enhance the rentals of property are much easier to carry out in a town council in

which property owners are most largely represented than are
improvements of a sanitary kind which tend to harass negligent
landlords.[43]

In a district off Charles Street, with 'men, women and children,
half smothered in filth wearing the form and semblance of
humanity but herding like savages', there were three property
owners. One was a town councillor, and he was agent for one of
the others.[44] In their own meetings, where their words were
privileged, the councillors so frequently implied that their personal
opponents were men of infamous character that trades-union
candidates standing for election spoke of 'the oppressors of the
poor, the speculative builders and owners of small tenements of
which the council is composed'.[45]

Feeling was heightened at the time as one elected individual had
been exposed in an attempt to swindle the school board. This was a
certain Thomas Haller who had bought land which he expected
would be required for the building of Westbourne Street school,
taking a commission from the vendors and then trying to make a
profit of £359, equivalent to not less than £11,500 in the money of
1988, by selling it to the board. The case against him seemed to be
so fully proved that the board demanded his resignation, which he
refused to give,[46] and at the Board of Guardians of which he was
also a member, a Captain Butlin, a retired master-mariner, refused
to be present while he was speaking. If he was guilty, his talk about
his philanthropy and his services to the poor also convicted him of
the nastiest hypocrisy; but the denunciation of some of his enemies
perhaps even now may win him friends. One particularly
scurrilous journalist, Richard Cook, of the *Hull and East Riding
Critic* wrote: 'Mr Haller is, I learn, a great Salvation Army man
and one of the most bigotted *sic* teetotallers in Hull'.[47] 'Index'
half-seriously suggested that he might prove to be, after all, the
hero of a melodrama with his innocence vindicated in the last act.

Actual exposures such as this were rare, and year after year the
atmosphere in council debates suggested to the innocent that
nameless villainies were all the time being concealed. Suspicion
was further increased. In 1899 the council administered 'a severe
castigation' to the Revd A. Allan who on Citizen Sunday at
Newington Presbyterian church had made allegations of council
bribery and corruption. Since everyone knew that any detailed
accusation he made would result in an action for libel it may have

been that 'some gossip in a railway carriage with an unknown gentleman purporting to be a contractor' was gossip founded on fact.[48*] Public confidence can hardly have been increased by the report of the asylum inquiry committee which after two years 'practically amounted to a vote of no confidence', since the chairman, who presumably did not know less than his colleagues, refused to sign the report.

It is not to be expected that the paid officials should have been better than their elected masters. Those of them who handled money were open to a particularly strong temptation, since no provision was made for their retirement. Some were eventually given a pension if they survived to serve the corporation to so advanced an age that they were no longer fit to serve. This was the case with Mr W. Bolton, the retired borough treasurer, who at the age of eighty, in 1876, though he had always been regarded as a man of the strictest probity, admitted that he had stolen about £10,000 in a period of twenty-five years: but his reputation did not suffer. The poor man was simply too old to understand the state of newly consolidated accounts when they were shown to him. For nine years a certain William Brooke had had complete charge of the accounts and after he had faced a committee he thought it best to go home and blow his brains out, an expedient relatively convenient for him since he was a captain of volunteers; and it may be that the avoidance of prison was the only advantage his commission ever brought him.[49] At this time some of his fellow volunteers were complaining that their commissions were costing them £200 a year.

The corporation could be a merciful employer, but the opposition usually insinuated that the majority, whoever they were for the time being, were acting from the blackest of motives—as they may have been in the case of the incompetent waterworks engineer.[50] In 1884 an enlargement of the borough boundaries made it necessary to pump more water, though some was taken from the Newington Water Company (whose bore still supplies the Albert Avenue baths). A tall, lonely building stands in the fields to the north of Cottingham, housing the engine which was set up to pump water from Sand-beck into the Springhead pipes. The boots and the habits of the workmen employed in laying the pipes led to a severe epidemic of diarrhoea. The engineer at first ridiculed the suggestion that the supply was polluted, but in the end he had to admit that more than one per cent of the supply was contaminated with sewage and resigned. He was reinstated, however, possibly because a more serious scandal was impending.[51]

The duties of the police were so difficult, sober constables so hard to obtain and keep sober and interference by the watch committee so petulant, that to run a truly efficient force would have been a thirteenth labour of Hercules. Strong drink percolated so far into the fabric of Victorian society that it was said that some blue-ribbon men habitually drank a pint of bitter, first sprinkling it with ginger to make it nominally ginger ale. Constables were frequently charged with being helpless with drink in the small hours and it was suggested that a prudent man should remember that a flask offered to him by a kindly stranger might be 'narcotized'. Naturally the more virtuous saw it as their duty to write anonymous letters about the less, and one consequence of this was that an inspector was accused of forgery in the making of a report. The watch committee and the Council by a vote of thirty-four to nine found that he was guilty of no more than an 'inadvertence'; but the chief constable had said it must have been forgery.[52]

The chief constable's fall came just over a year later. A poor-law guardian who was also a councillor on the watch committee pressed the police to prosecute the keepers of brothels under the Criminal Law Amendment Act of 1885, and in particular, since the age of consent was now raised from thirteen to sixteen, to stop juvenile prostitution. At the end of the year the chief constable was discovered in circumstances which suggested that he himself was the patron of juvenile prostitutes. The girl, at any rate, was sitting on his lap, and not at a good address. There was nothing left for him but resignation, utter disgrace and emigration with his family to Australia.[53] Richard Cooke, ever on the look-out for hidden scandal—and the services of a scavenger were certainly needed in the society of late-Victorian Hull—wrote:

> His defence may be quite as true as the girl's story. Mr Campbell's friends will no doubt think it hard that he should lose his situation especially as serious faults in superintendents and inspectors have been condoned or lightly punished by the committee and council. For some time past the chief and his committee have not worked harmoniously together. In the force matters have gone awry. Recently

> a serious complaint as to its management was made by Mr Justice
> Hawkins, and it is possible that some persons may look upon the
> incident as a lucky termination to an unfortunate appointment.
> Meanwhile every disreputable character in the town is rejoicing over
> Mr Campbell's downfall, for he was in truth a terror to evil-doers.

The same moralist had hinted that the police were neglecting their
duty to suppress vice:

> what about the gilded butterflies who openly traffic in champagne
> and who are known to the police? . . . Is there one law for a
> courtesan in silk and furs and another for one in rags? . . . Vice is
> rampant in this town of Hull . . . Why do not the police visit those
> houses at which courtesans assemble day and night and report the
> landlords to the magistrates? It cannot be for want of knowledge; the
> fact is notorious to everyone, and even if justice is blind, the police
> have eyes and only want instructions.[54]

Houses of ill-fame were to be found in all parts of the town. For a
time there was one even in 'sedate Linnaeus Street', and one
'monster' was known to have five houses in one street. His
speciality was the procuring of very young girls. In another house
five apprentice-harlots under fourteen were found.[55] From eleven
in the morning Paragon Street was a parade for prostitutes, the
numbers increasing all day until the night brought drunken
fights;[56] and to assist navigation after daylight, in many parts of
the town with a pub at every corner there were such signs as *back
way to the Beehive*—'and the red lamp at the end of the court
emphasises the tacit invitation'.[57] It seems very odd that the Revd
Parkinson Milson was shocked by his only visit to Paris, which,
not surprisingly, he thought very different from Hull: 'His delight
with much that he saw was unbounded and his pain at other things
he was obliged to see was great.'[58] It is more surprising that a
Times correspondent thought it worth while to write an article,
from a rather different point of view, on the contrast between Hull
and Paris. In Hull he had attended the meeting of the T.U.C. and
found that at social gatherings 'the first notion of enjoyment
consisted in the rigorous exclusion of wives and female friends'.
The songs were not so gay as in Paris—'The moral of *wait till the
clouds roll by* was taught in all these ditties.'[59]

Nevertheless, there was a capacity for innocent enjoyment, and
there can be no doubt that most people in late-Victorian Hull were
finding more pleasure in life. For coarse traditionalists there were

regular Saturday dog-fights at Stepney, off Beverley Road, with which the police thought it best not to interfere. By 1891 so many people were enjoying cycling that there were fifteen cycle dealers in the town, some of whom were also cycle makers. The Victorian love of photography supported sixty-two male and sixteen female photographers. Cooks in Lowgate offered passenger trips to Yarmouth and Norwich on the s.s. *Amelia*, built in 1894 and 'lighted throughout by electricity'; Tadmans & Co. of Paragon Street had installed electric light in the Palace theatre, the Theatre Royal, and the New Alhambra Palace and assured householders that if they had electricity installed it would preserve the health of the family and prevent the tarnishing of decorations, pictures and books.[60] In the streets there were German bands, often condemned as a nuisance;[61] and for those who could afford it there were recitals by such virtuosos as Pachmann and Adelina Patti,[62] with tickets obtainable from Gough and Davy. In the parks on summer evenings anyone could hear the police band performing selections from *Carmen* or *La Traviata*, and waltzes by Waldteufel, from 7.30 to 9.30.[63] There was even Sunday music, and at one concert in West Park by the artillery band, 10,000 people were present.[64] Plainly if so many people were enjoying themselves the devil must be there, and there were petitions to the Council against Sunday music in the parks.[65] As late as 1913 the watch committee recommended that the young might be more easily preserved from sin with 'better lighting in the parks and more attendants on band nights'.[66]

There was a wide variation in the innocence of pleasures. On Sundays as a respectable person walked to St Paul's church he found football being played and similar disgraceful proceedings 'by lads and even lasses of the very lowest and degraded type with shouting and cursing'.[67] Bookmakers on weekdays openly took bets on Drypool Green, since through some absurdity of the law it had not yet been proved to be a 'place', and when this was proved the bookmakers packed a parish election with their supporters and in a rowdy meeting elected two new overseers of the poor, believing that the former overseers had been responsible for their prosecution.[68] From 1885 great danger was seen impending over the morals of Hull from the project for a racecourse, and in 1888 it actually opened and was always known as Hedon racecourse (though actually in Preston).[69] When racing ceased it was used as an airport for Hull, and for a time in the 1930s KLM planes could be seen each day over the town flying from Manchester to Amsterdam via Hedon.

New swimming baths were opened for the people of Hessle Road at Madeley Street in 1885, on Holderness Road in 1898 and on Beverley Road in 1905.[70] For those less healthy in body and in mind it was possible, apparently from the age of five or six, for boys to wait outside the Theatre Royal to pick up the tab ends of cigars and cigarettes discarded by gentlemen going into the theatre.[71] Probably such children were among those who 'had not seen a piece of soap for some days' and who by hooting and hissing spoiled Saturday evening entertainments at St Mary's and the Porter Street schoolrooms;[72] or who, each August, for a halfpenny return went to Drypool feast on the carts of coalmen, so crowded together that they often fell off.[73] And coal carts were used, as many as a hundred on a fine Sunday, to take coalmen and their families out to Burton Bushes on the edge of Beverley Westwood.[74] There were also wagonettes for country rides, and until 1888 it was possible for those who took a ride in one out to Hessle to claim to be a *bona fide* traveller 'entitled to demand that a publican should serve him with intoxicants during closing hours'.[75]

There was a terrific struggle between drink and the temperance organisations for the soul of Hull; and though the temperance people often behaved with some absurdity and intolerance, no one who had ever talked with survivors from Victorian Hull can be sorry that on the whole temperance came out on top. Both politics and religion were affected by opinions on drink. Milson in one of his open-air preachings, in St John's Wood—the area north of Queen's Road and west of Beverley Road—had a large congregation because of the interruptions by a publican and a sceptic.[76] By 1898 there were six organisations devoted to temperance, which by this time always meant total abstinence: the Hull Women's Christian Temperance Association, under the patronage of the Quaker Priestmans; the British Women's Temperance Association; the Sons of Temperance; the Good Templars; the Independent Order of Rechabites; and the Band of Hope. The president of the last-named was Joseph Rank, already a wealthy miller. Drink and the devil would have rejoiced to know that a man of so austere a life and so convinced a Methodist was to be blessed with a son 'well known on the Turf'.[77] Charles Wilson, MP was at this time a much wealthier patron of the cause, though his younger brother Arthur could hardly have worn the blue ribbon when he entertained the Prince of Wales at Tranby Croft where, after a game of baccarat 'undeserved obloquy clouded the remainder of his life'.[78]

There were even temperance candidates in local elections. One was elected to the School Board in 1877 but lost his seat in 1880; and in 1883 the only man to stand as a temperance candidate was defeated, very near the bottom of the poll, while Edward Robson, a brewer standing as an Independent, topped the poll with over 15,000 votes,[79] with a Labour candidate in second place with 12,000. With an election address distributed from Hop Villa, Newland, Robson became a borough councillor in 1885, sheriff and JP in 1889, and mayor in 1891; but temperance men still occasionally got a seat on the school board. Even so, because of the strengh of Nonconformity, there, on the Council, in the boards of guardians and on the bench, they seem to have outnumbered the supporters of the 'trade'. At the brewster sessions of 1880 one new temperance hotel was licensed, but twelve other applications for licences were all rejected.[80]

However, no one had to go thirsty during the very extensive licensing hours, which were virtually unlimited except on Sundays, and there were recognised seasons of Saturnalia. Until it was stopped—by stopping the service—it was the custom until 1899 for a drunken and disorderly crowd to assemble with the more respectable congregation for the watch-night service in Holy Trinity; and a reference to 'the mockery which took place in the neighbourhood of the north door'[81] suggests a survival of something as ancient and obscure as the ritual of 10 October:

> the singular custom in Hull of whipping all the dogs that were found running round the streets on October 10th. Some thirty years since when I was a boy, so common was the practice that every little urchin used to consider it his duty to prepare a whip for any unlucky dog that might be seen on that day. The custom is now (1853) obsolete, those 'putters-down' of all boys' play in the streets, the new police, having effectually stopped the cruel pastime. 13, Savile Street, HULL, John Richardson.[82]

Though there is some indication of falling-off of church attendance in most denominations, matters of religion were still taken very seriously even by those who were only occasional church attenders. Even the most radical of Hull socialists and free-thinkers, Mr N. Billany, regularly attended the Anglican service at St James's where Christianity as interpreted in the sermons to him seemed to be socialism. And when the Archbishop of York said 'there were things existing in Hull which would not be tolerated for an hour in Manchester', the town council could not have been more hurt if it had been the Queen expressing her displeasure.[83*] Some of the clergy, and more particularly the Revd J. M. Lambert, gave a strong lead to social reform. His parish, St John's, Newland, was not sufficient to keep him occupied, and he threw himself strenuously into school-board affairs. This may be what drove him further to the right, until by the time he became an archdeacon he was in most matters ultra-reactionary and so great a snob that he turned his name into Malet Lambert, insisting that the accent was on the second syllable in each name; but in his middle years he was a scholar and a good man.[84] It is also to the credit of the clergy of all denominations that in relieving distress caused by unemployment they forgot about their differences; at other times they were as much aware of them as Christians at the Council of Nicaea.

School Board elections were largely sectarian. The first time elections were held for the board in 1874 the top three places were taken by two Wesleyans and a Catholic; five Anglican candidates got in, and five places went to men who were nominally unsectarian. At the second election in 1877 the Catholic Canon Randerson headed the poll, five Anglicans again got places and the rest went to two Primitive Methodists, two Wesleyans, three unsectarians, an independent and a temperance man.[85] The School Boards have often been condemned for their sectarianism, and the small interest taken in the elections; but sectarianism was the result of sixty years of Anglican domination of the schools, and the interest in the elections was greater than the small polls suggest. In 1886 only 1200 persons used their votes when up to 40,000 could have voted; but the polling booths closed at 7 p.m. This was far too early for most wage-earners who did not get home until after 6 p.m.:

> Large numbers remained unpolled who had gone to the booths for the purpose of voting. The clerks were unable to issue voting papers fast enough for the demand. This was notably the case at Waltham

Street, the Protestant Hall and Dansom Lane. If the loss to the candidates had been anything like equal the matter would not have been so serious. But the probability is that this was not so. The church men most likely polled their full strength. The candidates who would suffer the most were the labour and unsectarian candidates who depended most largely on the support of the working classes.[86]

The achievement of the School Board was remarkable. In spite of internal quarrels, by 1897 it had thirty-three schools, each of which provided for between 600 and 1000 infants, juniors and seniors, boys and girls and two which took juniors only. There were also three higher-grade schools, at Brunswick Avenue, Boulevard and Craven Street, each with more than 1000 places, and all at this date provided a free (or almost free) grammar school education. In all, forty new schools, some still standing and in use, had been built in twenty-seven years.[87] Even so, when the Progressives gained a majority over the sectarians in 1899 they maintained that not enough had been done. They raised the school rate from £27,000 to £40,000 a year, and it is even now very noticeable that some of the schools provided under the new regime, such as Southcoates Lane (in open country when it was built), did have something of sweetness and light about them. The new School Board also provided a new centre for pupil teachers.[88]

To understand the next brief crisis in the School Board we must again look at sectarian differences. The privileges of the established church were so resented by Liberals and Radicals that wherever they were in a majority they never lost an opportunity to push the church in the right direction. When Canon Watson moved to York on his appointment to a cathedral prebend, after fourteen years as chaplain to the Sculcoates workhouse, the progressive majority on the board of guardians defeated a resolution to congratulate him and then refused to appoint a salaried successor, but did appoint a dentist. The Nonconformist clergy of the town took the services in rotation without any pay but the established church refused to join in.[89]

The Anglican clergy were united only in defence of the Establishment. Two or more had been appointed by the ultra-Protestant Simeon trustees, to the churches of Drypool,[90] but at St Mary Lowgate, the vicar, Mr Carr was so High Church that he heard confessions, attended by no one except his female parishioners,[91] while from Holy Trinity Canon McCormick exuded Evangelical doctrine of such purity that the boys of the grammar school took up the holy war by attacking the poorer and on the whole smaller boys at the Catholic school in Pryme Street, who in their turn were discovered by their priest, Canon Randerson ready to counter-attack with sticks, stones and a bayonet.[92]

With the exception of the Revd Charles Overton, the learned but too-aged Vicar of Cottingham, all the Anglicans, lay and clerical, were united in their condemnation of the Salvation Army, reviving a notion almost as ancient as Christianity itself that religious heterodoxy and enthusiasm are linked with sexual orgies. This is an account of the Icehouse citadel in 1884:

> Nothing more disgusting or offensive to morality can be conceived than some hundreds of persons of both sexes and all ages, shut up with locked doors, a whole night, in a building, most of them in a state of fanatical excitement. Wives and mothers who should be at home with their husbands and families, and servant girls who should be in their beds . . . are clearly defying decency and order by attending such meetings, and it is high time that such preposterous proceedings should be prevented by the local authorities. No doubt many of the scandals we read of in connection with the Salvation Army are attributable to this 'all night of prayer' system.[93*]

Year after year the teetotal crusade went on. There were occasional defeats for the virtuous. When a Hull Wesleyan minister named Spicer took an Anglican curacy in Leeds Conservatives naturally assumed that he would join them and that the teetotallers of Hull had 'lost one of their most zealous and conscientious advocates'.[94] But as slum-clearances began the Council gleefully bought up licensed houses and demolished them without replacing them,[95] and the process of dessication went on to such effect that the 452 pubs of Hull in 1901 had become 288 in 1935.[96] Such houses as the *Earl of Durham*, the *Empress*, the *Anchor* and the *Lord Londesborough* are lost with the song the sirens sang.

And then, in 1904 the last School Board was dissolved, the first education committee was set up under Sir Alfred Gelder, and the Nonconformists saw with horror that the church schools were coming on the rates. Thirty years of fighting against parsons and publicans seemed to be lost. There was maybe some consolation to the Nonconformists in the fact that Sir Alfred was one of their own, the son of a small farmer at North Cave, a self-made architect who a few years earlier, before he was knighted, lived at 4 Chestnut Villas, Holderness Road, the manse of the Kingston circuit superintendent, and a few years later was to be the Liberal member for Brigg from 1910 until 1918.[97] As a matter of conscience there were those in Hull, as in most other places, who decided that they would not pay the education rates since to them this meant paying for church schools. Enthusiasm was aroused at a mass-meeting in May addressed by Dr Clifford, then regarded as perhaps the greatest of liberal-minded Nonconformists. In November an address by Sir George Kekewich to the Hull Free Church Council seemed to demonstrate that there was some official sympathy with them, since he had long been permanent secretary to the board of education before his retirement. Passive resisters appeared before the stipendiary in September to answer summonses for non-payment of rates, distress warrants were issued and a few decided to go to gaol rather than submit. The Revd W. Bowell, secretary of the Hull and District Passive Resistance League, and the Revd W. R. Wilkinson suffered a short spell of imprisonment in Hedon Road gaol, perhaps able to hear the choir which assembled outside to sing hymns, and on their release they were welcomed by a large crowd; and then the movement had spent its force, though the feeling to which it gave rise led to the Liberals again winning two seats at the general election of 1906.[98]

The new education committee remained strongly Protestant. The Board of Education overruled their decision that the Anlaby Road convent should not be recognised as a centre for the training of Catholic pupil teachers, but the committee decided by a vote of ten against five not to grant any of them bursaries. Soon, however, they transcended barren sectarianism. By 1906 there was talk of the need for a university college[99] and a year later they selected the site for a municipal training college on Cottingham Road, though it was not completed until 1913. Hopes were very high in 1908: 'It is confidently expected that in the near future the buildings will be extended, and that in size and equipment they will compare favourably with the universities of Leeds and Sheffield.'

The school medical service began in 1908—at any rate the children were given a medical inspection. Meals began to be provided for poor children, and the school playgrounds were kept open for the holidays to provide somewhere other than the street in which children could play.[100*] Under Councillor Stephenson a committeé was formed to help find work for school leavers, and the outlines of the welfare state, at any rate for children, were already there before 1914. It was even realised that delinquent children are not ordinary criminals, and to avoid the need to bring children into court the chief constable began meeting parents and offenders in his office on Friday evenings: 'In several cases the children had been helped with clothes and in some instances suitable employment had been found.'[101]

Before the close of the nineteenth century the progress of society was already slightly improving the position of women. It is true that drudgery was the lot of most working women, among whom in the 1891 census were the 7900 indoor domestic servants and the 1046 charwomen, but the 366 hospital nurses and the 863 teachers (there were more than twice as many women as men in the schools) were mostly on their way to better things. There were also 180 women music-teachers and musicians, two more than the men, and some of these may be assumed to have gained a partial liberation; probably a few of the 16 female civil servants and the 79 'commercial clerks' would live to see the day when women teachers, clerks, typists, with members of the ill-defined group in various professions were more numerous than the men of 1951 in those categories, or the unhappy domestics of 1891.

The beginning of the emancipation of women was in part the consequence of half a century of educational effort, principally for men, but, since women were not excluded, of some indirect benefit to them also. In the university extension society examinations of 1886, more girls than boys were successful, some from Board Schools, but some from Ellerslie House and Granville College, which admitted only fee-payers; and in the junior section of the examination, only one was from a Board School.[102] Some of those who attended the Saturday morning university extension lectures were less fortunate, and since they were nearly all pupil-teachers this could have been serious for them. One course included instruction on later Latin as used in Roman Britain, and this for children who knew no Latin at all! By the end of the century they were gaining nothing from the Mechanics' Institute, the proprietory members having in 1895 turned it into a private limited company with a share capital of £45,000—and considerable profit from the running of the Empire Music Hall, [103] but the School Board maintained five evening continuation schools which could have provided for 600 persons, though on an average only 106 attended. Nevertheless, in one way or another some Hull women had demonstrated that they were intellectually the equals of men. All the women who stood for election to the Sculcoates board of guardians in 1895 were elected: Annie Lawton, Martha Stephenson, Sarah Richardson, and Sarah A. Horton, all standing as Progressives. None was put on any committee of the guardians. Soon there were no more than three women guardians. Mrs Corrighan, who had won a place on the Hull board of guardians, was defeated in 1907, and Mrs Russell was left as the only woman guardian in the city. This, and an unsuccessful strike of working girls at a tin works in Stoneferry, were the Pyrrhic victories of a single year.

From the beginning, enlightened women and educated ladies were active in the Hull Society for the Prevention of Cruelty to Children, and the Sheltering Home for Girls. Between October 1885 and April 1886 the Society provided 1314 meals for children and dealt with 78 children affected by the death of the mother, parental neglect or immorality, drink and poverty, and with four children who were either wilful or vagrant. [104] After a few years the Sheltering Home, which at first was for 'unfortunates' only, dealt with all girls, fallen or not, who needed temporary protection. One of its patrons, Lady Reckitt, provided the main support for a working-girls' club and boarding house, which as Pashby House in James Reckitt Avenue still serves the community as a psychiatric out-patients department. [105] Even in the eighties those interested in self-improvement were provided for at the Church Institute in Albion Street, once the house of the physician Sir James Alderson (1794-1882) but now a place with a newsroom, library and lecture room where in a single session they could hear the Savillian Professor of Astronomy, the Boden Professor of Sanskrit and the President of the Society for Psychical Research. If his ghost stories advertised in the prospectus were not enough there were 'classes for ladies, and no pains have been spared to make the lectures popular'. There were also numerous technical classes there, presumably for men and boys, and if few women were likely to be found at the Hebrew or Greek Testament classes, some almost certainly attended the classes in music, elocution, shorthand and book-keeping.[106] It seems likely, however, that those who could not claim some kind of middle-class status would be excluded more by their own diffidence than by any real barrier other than their lack of 'respectable' clothes. When they were approached by the Trades Council the committee of the university extension society said they were prepared to send twenty free tickets and 'would not object to the enrolment of working women as well as working men eligible to attend the lectures', which in one session included Oscar Wilde on interior decoration at the Royal Institution, in October 1883.[107]

The fact that Hull began to look like a real city in the early part of this century was made possible by economic change—the place was more prosperous even if most of the poor were not. Most still dreaded old age and the threat and disgrace of the workhouse. There were many like this man:

> He was 68 years of age. Sitting upon a stone wall he showed me how he could put his boot toe to his mouth. He was bad in bronchitis. Said men ought not to live to be very old, for when their masters saw they were becoming aged, they turned them away for younger men. He worked in one shop 16 years. Got his affliction pushing his master's work under a contract, and saved him a £20 fine. And when his master died his son turned him off like a dog.[108]

All the same, there was real improvement. The building of more and more seed-crushing mills along the River Hull, where they could take in their raw material from barges, was a notable example of this. The trade began with a single horse mill. By 1840 there were ten and by 1878 forty-five mills. As they were highly inflammable, insurance was expensive or unobtainable, and the business was for a long time seasonal, the mills closing every summer. In most years almost as much linseed was imported as wheat. In 1881, 717,000 quarters of linseed came from the Baltic, the Black Sea and from Bombay and Calcutta.[109] 1885 was on the whole regarded as a bad year all round, but though the amount of linseed and rape-seed imported declined, linseed began to arrive for the first time from the River Plate and the loss was more than balanced by an increase in cotton-seed and the first arrivals of this from Peru: 'Although it is asserted that seed-crushing is unprofitable, yet whenever a mill is destroyed (i.e. by fire) one larger and finer springs from its ashes.'[110] In 1896 the quantity of linseed, rape-seed and cotton-seed coming to Hull had risen to one-and-a-quarter million quarters, or just under 80,000 tons.[111] As a consequence of the Japanese exploitation of Manchuria Hull received its first consignments of soya beans, 153,000 tons or nearly forty per cent of the total reaching Britain. The Chamber of Commerce reported: Without this large addition to the available raw material for the mills crushing must have been a lean business whereas this addition, combined with rising markets has on the whole proved to be fairly remunerative in 1909. There is reason to hope that the soya bean will be a regular article of import.[112]

The industry grew to such an extent that in the inter-war years it dominated east Hull, where the British Oil and Cake Mills Company had its own model village, until the mills were destroyed in the bombing of May 1941 and for several summers millions of crickets chirped among the half-burned seed.

The growth of the oil and oil-cake industry was paralleled by the growth of other imports. Much of the wheat imported— 1,400,000 tons in 1887, rising in nine years to 3,000,000 tons—was turned into flour by Ranks; and much of the timber also—81,000 loads in 1876, and 197,000 in 1897—went to the Hull saw-mills. The increased imports of iron, on the other hand, mostly went to Sheffield,[113] and the huge increases in food imports went mainly to the one-third of the population of the UK for which Hull was once believed to serve as the 'natural' port. Even when we remember that this was a period in which British agriculture was in decline, the six-fold increase in imports of high-protein foods—meat of all kinds, cheese, butter and margarine—between 1876 and 1897 reflects something more than the extent to which the growth of this port took trade away from others; and what it surely does reflect is the general improvement in the quality of life which is the theme of this chapter and in which Hull had its share.[114]

Sources

1. *VCH*, Hull, 368.
2. *EMN*, 26 Jan. 1894.
3. *DNB*, s.vv. REED, EDWARD JAMES; ELGAR, FRANCIS.

4. *R*, 16 June 1838.
5. Ibid., 27 Jan. 1843.
6. *EMN*, 22 Feb. 1875.
7. Ibid.
8. *HN*, 29 Sept. 1877.
9. *EMN*, 3 May 1875.
10. *HN*, 20 Oct. 1877.
11. Ibid., 11 Aug., 6 Oct. 1877.
12. *EMN*, 11 Jan. 1875.
13.* P. Kemp (Ed.), *The Oxford Companion to Ships and the Sea*, 479. This design, originally produced in Newcastle, proved so free from faults that 2270 engines were made in America for the workhorse liberty ships to replace tonnage sunk during the Second World War.
14. *HN*, 21 Apr. 1877.
15. *EMN*, 23 Aug., 27 Sept. 1879.
16. *Hull Critic*, 21 Mar. 1885, pp. 21, 27.
17. *EMN*, 28 July 1899.
18. Ibid., 22, 29 July 1899.
19. *DNB*, s.v. SAUNDERS, WILLIAM (1833-95); *EMN*, 27 Jan. 1885.
20. *Hull Critic*, 15 Nov. 1884, 6.
21.* Ibid., 22 Nov. 1884, 23. It seems impossible to write of this age without using the words 'lady' and 'gentleman' to indicate those thought to be better than the common herd.
22. *EMN*, 1 Jan. 1885.
23. *Hull Critic*, 23 and 30 Aug. 1884.
24. *The Times*, 15 Nov. 1884 and 26 Mar. 1885.
25. *EMN*, 14 Jan. 1886.
26. Ibid., 19 Jan. 1886.
27. Ibid., 9 Jan. 1886.
28. Ibid., 18 Jan. 1886.
29. Ibid., 23 Jan. 1888.
30. Ibid., 6 Feb. 1886.
31. BPP, Emigration, vol. 8, 185-7.
32. BPP, Population, vol. 23. Census of 1891, Table 9.
33. *Hull Critic*, 16 Aug. 1884, 10.
34. Ibid., 4 Oct. 1884 [not dated] *passim; The Times*, 2 Oct. 1884, 5f.
35. *EMN*, 11 Jan. 1888.
36. Ibid., 16 June 1888.
37. Ibid., 2 Nov. 1883.
38. Ibid., 19 Dec. 1883, 2 Jan. 1884.
39. Ibid., 20 Dec. 1883.
40. BPP, Population, vol. 18, 484; vol. 23, 439.
41. *EMN*, 28 Apr. 1886.
42. Ibid., 1 Jan. 1896; BPP, Industrial Relations, vol. 23, 260.
43. *EMN*, 5 June 1888.
44. Ibid., 1 Jan. 1884.
45. *Hull Critic*, 18 Oct. 1884, 13.
46. *EMN*, 22 Dec. 1884.
47. *Hull Critic*, 15 and 29 Dec. 1883, 3 and 11, 12 Jan, 3, 9 Feb. 1884, 17.
48.* *EMN*, 1 Jan. 1900. In 1943 the present writer heard men gossiping about corruption, on an enormous scale, in the construction by a firm belonging to a Hull councillor, of the perimeter track at R.A.F. Melbourne. This gossip is now known to have been true.

49. *The Times*, 21 Sept. 1876, 4a; 27 Sept., 4f.
50. *EMN*, 31 Dec. 1885.
51. Ibid., 1 Jan. 1884; *Hull Critic*, 18 Apr. 1885, 19.
52. *Hull Critic*, 16 Aug. 1884, 21.
53. Ibid., 5 Dec. 1885, 22.
54. Ibid., 13 June 1885, 21.
55. Ibid., 2 Feb. 1884, 16.
56. Ibid., 16 May 1885, 25.
57. *EMN*, 2 Jan. 1884.
58. *PM*, 278.
59. *The Times*, 14 Sept. 1886, 8c.
60. *ERB*, xxv, xli [advertisements at end of book] .
61. *EMN*, 31 Mar. 1886.
62. Ibid., 22 Mar. 1886.
63. Ibid., 18 June 1888.
64. Ibid., 24 Sept. 1888.
65. Ibid., 21 Sept. 1888.
66. *The Times*, 11 Aug. 1813, 5e.
67. *EMN*, 27 Apr. 1886.
68. Ibid., 1 Jan 1897.
69. *Hull Critic*, 25 Apr. 1885, 14; *ERB*, 16.
70. *EMN*, 31 Dec. 1885; *Kelly's* 1921, Hull, xii.
71. *EMN*, 16 Jan. 1888.
72. Ibid., 23 Mar. 1886.
73. *Hull Critic*, 16 Aug. 1884, 7.
74. Ibid., 9 June 1883, 13.
75. *EMN*, 28 Sept. 1888.
76. *PM*, 23.
77. *ERB*, 119; *The Times*, 14 Nov. 1943, 6e.
78. *DNB*, s.v. WILSON, ARTHUR (1836-1909).
79. *ERB*, 87, 42, 51, 83.
80. *The Times*, 28 Aug. 1880, 8b.
81. *EMN*, 1 Jan. 1900.
82. *County Folk Lore*, ed. E. Gutch, vol. 6, 108-9.
83.* *EMN*, 13 Jan. 1886. Neiles Billany, the radical, was the grandfather of Dan Billany, novelist and graduate of University College, Hull, killed in 1943 when fighting for the Italian resistance.
84. *Who was Who*, 1929-40, 773.
85. *ERB*, 86-7.
86. *EMN*, 21, 26 and 28 Aug. 1886.
87. *ERB*, 85.
88. *EMN*, 1 Jan. 1900.
89. Ibid., 1 Jan. 1897.
90. *ERB*, 149.
91. *Hull Critic*, 13 June 1885, 12.
92. Ibid., 29 Mar. 1884, 12.
93.* Ibid., 20 Dec. 35 and 22 Mar. 1884, 4. For similar libels on early Christians see Minucius Felix, *Octavius*, xxxi, 1, and *Fronto* (Loeb Edition, p. 284).
94. Ibid., 29 Mar. 1884, 8.
95. *EMN*, 1 Jan. 1900.
96. Evans, 171.
97. *Who was Who*, 1941-50, 427; *ERB*, 42, 122.
98. *EMN*, 2 Jan. 1905; *VCH*, Hull, 269.

99.   *EMN*, 2 Jan. 1908.
100.* Ibid., 1 Jan. 1909; *VCH*, Hull, 359. In the summer the old delighted pattern of parents sitting at their doors and children playing in the street can still be seen in a few streets.
101. *The Times*, 15 Mar. 1907, 4f.
102. *EMN*, 10 Mar. 1886.
103. Ibid., 1 Jan. 1897.
104. *EMN*, 2 Jan. 1908.
105. *EMN*, 1 Jan. 1909.
106. *Hull Critic*, 27 Sept., 7, 19, 4 Oct. 1884, 17. *Brown's Guide*, 162; *DNB*, s.v. ALDERSON, SIR JAMES.
107. *EMN*, 5 Feb. 1886; *Hull Critic*, 20 Oct. 1883, 3.
108. *PM*, 388, 6 July 1888.
109. *EMN*, 31 Dec. 1881; *TC*, Appendix, xv.
110. *EMN*, 31 Dec. 1885.
111. *ERB*, 139.
112. *The Times*, 13 Nov. 1909, 15f.
113. *ERB*, 139-40.
114. Ibid., Evans, 42; R.C.K. Ensor, *England 1870-1914*, 121.

25

'Pre-War'

The very few who can remember the town as it was before 1914 still tend to say 'pre-war' in much the same tone as Talleyrand used when he spoke of the sweetness of life which none could know who had not lived before the Revolution; but there is nothing in contemporary records to show that Edwardians and late-Victorians of Hull realised that they were living in the golden age of the city, and they were not. Quite apart from the picture of poverty and destitution which has been presented in previous chapters, the town was rent by factions as bitter as those of Dickens's Eatanswill, but less memorable.

The anger of factions could even at times quench what passed for patriotism. A Lt Col Humphrey commanded the Hull Artillery Volunteers, and superior persons preferred to be members of this body because the artillery was still sufficiently equestrian to enjoy almost the same prestige as the cavalry. In June 1880 the War Office called for his resignation, and in protest the men handed in their uniforms, and the War Office, not to be intimidated, responded by dismissing three captains and others of lesser rank. The men then planned a march-out as a protest apparently with some sympathy from Col Lord Londesborough who dissuaded them. He himself had resigned, but had been persuaded to keep his commission. Hull then had so many captains and colonels that only a study of the army lists distinguishes the very few who held regular commissions from those who were in the militia and the numerous professional and business men who were in the volunteers and habitually used their military titles. This snobbish custom lasted until the Second World War killed it. There was no impropriety in a Reckitt's manager styling himself captain since he had won the M.C. and served throughout the war; but there was surely something odd about a person still styling himself major in 1935 when he had fought the whole of his war from the new Guildhall. After the dismissals of 1880 a new group of patriots stepped forward, and the town suffered from no scarcity of officers;[1] in Sir A. K. Rollit it even had a colonel of submarine miners—though his knighthood made it unnecessary for him to style himself colonel. How an excellent solicitor could also excel in submarine mining is probably as incomprehensible to outsiders as Gödel's proof remains for most of us.

If the factions of Hull could be traced to any single origin it would probably turn out to be to disputes arising from the position of the Dock Company and the North Eastern Railway. By 1872 the business community was seriously dissatisfied with the railway and wanted a new company to break its monopoly and to relieve the growing congestion in the docks and the warehouses, and the Chamber of Commerce unanimously favoured the construction of a new line. Alderman Lumsden, a shipowner as well as a director of the North Eastern Railway 'said that the company was fully able to conduct the trade of the port', a defence which revealed the extent to which this railway had come to regard Hull as part of its private domain. Other shipowners did not share his opinion, and subscribed to promote a bill in Parliament for a new Hull railway. Wilsons', and Bailey. and Leetham, whom they were later to absorb, each contributed £20,000. The bill for a Hull South and West Junction Railway passed the Commons. Its rejection by the Lords may conjecturally be attributed to various interests which were as strong in the Dock Company as in the railway. It was probably from that moment in 1873 that the feud between C. H. Wilson and the Dock Company began. To the outside world it was necessary to show brotherly harmony, and when the associated Chambers of Commerce met here in 1877 they were told:

> The Dock Company may be said to hold the key of the general warehouse of the town. If the Dock Company prospers the entire community may be said to prosper. The chairman is devoted to the interests of the company. The company is in fact the whole object of his life.

But by then Wilson was an enemy of the company and in spite

of the acumen which enabled him, with his brother Arthur, to create a business empire of £2½ millions, he could hardly maintain his self-control in public when the question of the Dock Company arose. Politics also had something to do with the feud.[2] C. H. Wilson was a Gladstonian Liberal and until his sudden resignation in 1879 with Col Gerard Smith, the Liberals had a clear majority on the board; but their resignations, and the retirement of the chairman, Sir William Wright, to Sigglesthorne Hall and winters in Algiers, gave the Conservatives a majority.[3]

Wilson's argument that the docks were neither wide nor deep enough did not convince the Dock Company, which had seen the tonnage of ships entering the docks increase from 811,000 in 1850 to 2,258,000 in 1876,[4] but they may have felt some uneasiness. With forty-two steamers Wilsons' were now (1877) by far the largest owners in the port and during the next twenty years were to form the world's largest privately owned fleet. While Bailey and Leatham had only twenty ships of over a thousand tons, Wilsons had twenty-six, with another three exceeding 2000 and three more of over 3000 tons.[5] While it had long been the custom of Hull magnates to live in the country, no one had yet displayed the baronial splendour of Charles Wilson, MP, at Warter Priory, bought from Lord Muncaster, or of Arthur Wilson, his brother and master of fox-hounds, at Tranby Croft. It was said that many Conservatives voted for Wilson in spite of his being a Liberal, fearing that if defeated he would take his ships to another port, and on several occasions he did petulantly threaten to do this though never on political grounds. If there were such voters, their consciences must have been eased by the fact that although he was said to incline to radicalism, he was no low radical like poor Neiles Billany, who never got more than 735 votes: and Arthur in due course became a Liberal-Unionist and almost a Conservative. Nevertheless Charles opposed the Boer War, and then quixotically lent the *Ariosto* free of charge to transport men to the Cape. He married his eldest son to the daughter of a Marquis, setting them up in The Bungalow, Cottingham (now part of Cleminson Hall). In 1905 he was ennobled as Lord Nunburnholme, shortly after he had taken over the assets of Bailey and Leatham.[6]

After he had resigned from the board of the Dock Company, and before his success was assured, C. H. Wilson maintained such a feud that, even at a luncheon to celebrate the opening of the new buildings of the Hull Savings Bank, he attacked the Dock Company, and when its chairman made a pacific reply, told the guests 'that he had complained to the Dock Company until he was tired of it'.[7] A case was argued against him, elsewhere, by his political opponents:

> From the firm's business in the port Mr C. H. and Mr Arthur Wilson have realised enormous fortunes. . . We doubt very much whether it is to the interest of Hull and Hull people that Messrs. Wilsons should have created such a huge monopoly of the Baltic trade. Wherever there has been any attempt at competition . . . Messrs Wilson have ruthlessly driven their opponents out of their path . . . and are masters of the situation . . . they purchase the great bulk of their stores away from Hull, bringing them to their warehouse . . . while those stores which of a necessity must be bought in Hull are procured from a small circle of energetic . . . Radical supporters.[8]

In spite of propaganda of this kind, and hints that while standing for the new constituency of West Hull C. H. Wilson was planning to transfer his ships to the new dock in the east, in the general election of 1885 he defeated Dr A. K. Rollit by 5247 votes to 3697, held his seat until he became a peer, and them passed it on to his son.[9] He was so sure of his hold on Hull that, when his constituents asked him to take a more radical view of the Bradlaugh question, he could reply in the manner of Burke addressing the electors of Bristol—that he was a representative and not a delegate:

> There is no inducement for me to be in Parliament unless I have the sympathy and confidence of my supporters; and I beg you will convey to the Liberal association my sense of the undesirable relations which would exist between us if my conduct is to be criticised and my course of action dictated in such a spirit.[10]

The new dock was seen as the salvation of Hull. Before it was started the need for it could be questioned. The tonnage paying dock dues, 2,346,000, was very little greater in 1880 than it had been in 1876 and less than the 2,377,000 tons of 1878.[11] But the pattern was changing and even if the promoters of the new dock and railway did not make a fortune for themselves, their prediction of future needs was correct. Other trades were appearing to rival that with the Baltic. In a single week in May 1880 a Wilson liner and two other vessels docked from New York, one from Alexandria and two from San Francisco.[12] The trade of the port dropped in 1881, principally because so many Hull ships had been frozen up in the Baltic ports, but 106 ships arrived from beyond the Cape of Good Hope and Cape Horn, more than in any previous year.[13] With the decline of British arable farming, wheat had become the main article of import into Hull, twenty-five ships bringing it from San Francisco in 1880 and forty-nine in 1881, and others from North American ports as well as from India and New Zealand. By our standards the average size of the ships was ridiculously small—610 tons in 1883 and 554 tons in 1882; but the smallest ships entered the port a dozen times or more in the course of the year, while the much larger trans-oceanic vessels naturally could make fewer voyages in a year.[14] Sail was dying out, but the size and the length of passages of sailing vessels was increasing enormously. The only sailing ships to reach Hull in 1883 came from America, Australia and India, and for the first time one brought a cargo of more than 3000 tons. Such men of the future as the Wilsons had got rid of all their sailing ships but were in a sense parasites of sail since they wanted only deck officers with certificates in sail; and the last sailing merchantmen which docked in Hull in the 1930s were all fantastically undermanned by future captains and first officers. When war began in 1939 a full-rigged ship, the *Archibald Russell*, was trapped in Victoria Dock and for two years her topmasts and royals could be seen with the barrage balloons on all the approaches to the city.

These, then, were some of the complexities of the situation in which the Hull and Barnsley Railway and the Alexandra Dock were brought to birth by Col Gerard Smith, a member of the Hull banking family.[15] So much depended on breaking the hated monopoly of the Hull Dock Company, and on the construction of a deeper dock half as large again than any of the existing docks, that the enterprise had the backing of the corporation and there was a public holiday when the necessary bill passed the House of Lords and a public procession with the presentation of an illuminated address to the new hero.[16] The cutting of the first sod for the dock in 1881 was the occasion for more demonstrations and a banquet, and five months later the working men of Hull presented Col Smith with a commemorative silver plate. Soon there was a temporary line of railway as far as Eppleworth.[17] The Dock Company was stimulated into providing a new graving dock and starting work on St Andrew's fish dock, to be opened in 1883.

With the new line almost complete at the end of that year, C. H. Wilson was already pressing for the construction of yet another dock to the east of the Alexandra, which was not yet ready for the first water to be let in, much of which was to come from land drains with the intention of reducing the amount of silt to be dredged; and though the supporters of the dock were firm free-traders, there was some disquiet when Lucas and Aird, the main contractors, imported 1000 tons of steel rails while half-a-mile away Earles were using foreign steel plates.[18]

The dock was ready four-and-a-half years after it was begun, in spite of serious financial difficulties, and in July 1885 there was more public rejoicing. Now there was a dock which would take the largest ships through its locks even at low water, but at first it seemed that there would be no great change after all. Fewer ships arrived at the port in 1886 than in 1885. The Hull and Barnsley, however, was intended to bring south Yorkshire coal to Hull, and almost immediately there was a spectacular rise in the tonnage of coal brought by rail. The tonnage of coal brought by barge hardly changed and by 1897 was 577,000, but the rail tonnage, 2,077,000, had nearly tripled in twelve years.[19] The new coal hoists worked continually and until well into the twentieth century, at night, from many parts of Hull, the sound of steam engines shunting coal trucks on the dock sidings could be heard, with the occasional rumble of thunder as coal was dropped into the hold. Little more than half was exported in the ordinary sense, most of it for bunkering, but much of the rest was used for bunkering ships at Hull. The South Wales coal strike of 1898 brought much additional traffic, and vessels from the Continent as well as from other English ports came to load for Port Said, Santos, Rio de Janeiro and India.

But there were other things as important as coal. By 1896 wheat was arriving at the rate of 3,479,000 quarters a year, and two years later Wilsons' were bringing 'vast quantities of railway' material from New York to be trans-shipped for Russia and the Trans-Siberian railway. Granite from small Norwegian ports and redwood from Western Australia were being brought for the improvement of the city streets, and the Australian wool trade had already begun. At the old Albert Dock cold-storage sheds were opened for the increasing Argentine meat trade.[20]

Superficially the statistics would seem to show that the

Alexandra Dock was doing no harm to the others. The tonnage of ships coming to the port rose from 2,385,000 in 1884, the last year before the new dock opened, to 3,282,000 in 1892, the last year of the independent existence of the Hull Dock Company, the Alexandra Dock taking about a third of the traffic.[21] But actually the two companies were cutting rates in competition with one another, and the Dock Company was the first to go under, though the removal of James Stuart and four other Hull directors from the board of the Hull and Barnsley in 1889 showed that there was trouble there also[24] and Col Smith was no doubt glad to go off to govern Western Australia in 1895.[22] The earnings of the Dock Company fell from £232,000 in 1884 to £191,000 in 1890 and the dividend for the holders of ordinary stock was no more than 7s 6d for each £100 held, and the same in the following year.[23] The directors recommended that the docks should be sold to the North Eastern Railway Company.[24] They repeated their advice in 1892. C. H. Wilson had retained his stock and now advised that the offer of £30 of their stock for each £100 of Dock Company stock should be accepted—and it was accepted, and endorsed by the North Eastern.[25] An Act of Parliament was necessary to bring about this amalgamation. Waves of alarm spread as far as the Tyne, and Newcastle city council informed Parliament 'that the council views with great concern the proposal to purchase the Hull docks'.[26]

Hull was even more alarmed. There had long been a tendency to see the Dock Company and the North Eastern as concerned much more with their own interest than with that of the town. The union of two enemies was seen as potentially disastrous; but the trade of the port continued to grow and the tonnage of shipping paying dock dues was ten per cent greater in 1897 than it had been in 1892,[27] although for three years there had existed another factor tending to limit Hull trade. The long-feared Manchester Ship Canal opened in 1894, and as it was much nearer to most of the places served by the Hull and Barnsley, many of the cargoes which would have been loaded in the Alexandra Dock were exported via Manchester. Nevertheless it became part of the folklore of the town that the North Eastern, vastly stronger than the Hull and Barnsley, was the enemy. When Edward Bannister protested that the Hull and Barnsley's rates for coal left Hull at a disadvantage as against Goole, little attention was paid to him, but by 1904 feeling against the North Eastern was so strong that the Chamber of

Commerce readily adopted the proposal of Alderman Massey, a shipowner, and resolved that:

> It appears to this council to be necessary that a committee should be appointed to take such action as they may deem fit with the view of endeavouring to obtain active interest by one or more of the large railway companies other than the North Eastern Railway company in the development of traffic to and from Hull over the Hull and Barnsley Railway company's line.

He also said that in his opinion the joint-dock agreement could be torn up.[28] This agreement had been made six years previously, the North Eastern proposing to the Hull and Barnsley that they should together make an even larger dock in Marfleet, east of the Alexandra. The North Eastern abandoned the improvements which it had planned for the western docks. The advantages of the proposal to the port were obvious, and the Hull and Barnsley, instead of having to use the inconvenient Cannon Street station for its passenger services would be able to run from the Paragon station. But suspicion of the North Eastern was so deeply felt that many suspected a trick, and for several years events seemed to suggest that they were right:

> The chief thing to be thought of in the trade of Hull is the independence of the Hull and Barnsley railway. There are those who contend that the new proposal is simply a rope which the North Eastern is placing round the Barnsley company's neck.[29]

Nevertheless an agreement was reached between the two companies and an act of Parliament was obtained for the joint dock, with numerous amendments resulting from the opposition of the corporation, the chamber of commerce, and the corn trade:

> Those who remembered the North Eastern's action in the past were naturally anxious that anything might be left undone to prevent the North Eastern through the means of their partnership in the joint dock crippling or dominating the Hull and Barnsley.[30]

Three years went by and nothing happened. In reaching the agreement it had been estimated that the dock of fifty-five acres would cost £1,194,000, but some surprising miscalculation had been made since the lowest tender was over £2 million. The corporation protested vigorously when it was suggested that a dock of no more than thirty-two acres would have to do[31] and T.

R. Ferens, president of the Chamber of Commerce, insisted that there must be new and more dock accommodation. Arthur Wilson, of a different political complexion from Ferens, spoke up for the North Eastern and protested at the hostile attitude assumed by the Chamber and the corporation, sarcastically telling them: 'He did not think that the railway companies would object to the city's taking over the docks if terms could be agreed, but he scarcely thought the rate-payers would like to spend five or six millions on them'.

Ferens was too much of a radical to be taken in by so specious an argument, and a few years later, as Liberal member for East Hull, where he lived in Holderness House, he was to mention the nationalisation of the railways without a shudder; but the rest of the Chamber could do no more than agree tamely with Sir James Reckitt 'that the city had waited three years for a new dock and they were no nearer its realisation'. They were actually a little nearer than they thought and after they had waited another four years the contract was let to the firm of S. Pearson of Westminster in May 1906.[32] The work generated by this activity nevertheless could not prevent the total of unemployed from rising to somewhere, it was estimated, between 3000 and 4000 in 1908.

The new King George Dock was opened in 1914 by the King himself in time for the war. Already in 1910 the Chamber of Commerce had pressed the Admiralty to consider Hull as a naval base rather than the Tyne, and in this they showed more sense than their lordships who entered the war with no naval base for the Grand Fleet.[33] Up to 1914, with occasional slight fluctuations, the tonnage of vessels arriving at the docks increased from 2,258,000 in 1876 to 2,542,000 in 1886,[34] 3,471,000 in 1896 and 4,215,000 in 1900.[35] The only marked fall was in 1893 when the tonnage fell by 308,000 to 2,974,000 as a consequence of the clash between Wilsons' and the new unionism. C. H. Wilson had sincerely wanted to be a benevolent despot. He took his firm out of the Shipping Federation and even presided at the meeting convened by Ben Tillett to form a Hull branch of the dockers' union.[36] But this Liberal-Labour alliance which so elegantly suited his political career was found to conflict with his position as the leading shipowner of the port. He said that he found himself 'continually harassed by fresh demands' and believed that he would cease to be 'master of his own business' if he did not make a stand against the union.

The break came on 20 February 1893 when dockers refused to unload three barges because one of the crew was not in the union and others were in arrears with their subscriptions. They demanded that the employers should deduct the arrears from their wages and pay them to the union. This was refused, the men refused to carry on with unloading the coal and Wilsons' retaliated by returning to the Shipping Federation and insisting that none of their foremen or clerks should belong to a union.[37] They gave their support to a local branch of the self-styled British Labour Exchange which was opened on 4 April with a promise that men registering there would have the first chance of a job. As there was nearly always a surplus of dock labour this could have been fatal to the union and all its members came out on strike. Wilsons' had started it, but all employers of dockers were involved. They did not refuse to employ trade unionists but said that they would employ union men who were prepared to work with free labourers. At a later date these would certainly have been called blacklegs, but as the term was rarely used in contemporary references to the dispute it will be convenient in this chapter to use the language of 1893, which will do little to obscure the fact that free labour was an expression logically equivalent to cheap coal and that the men were treated simply as a commodity to be used when convenient and then discarded. On 5 April, 250 free labourers arrived from London and the next day a special train brought another 500. Police cordons made it possible for them to begin to discharge two ships, one a Wilsons' vessel moored against the shed in which they were housed. Facing a hostile mob of over a thousand, one hundred of the free labourers became aware of the situation in which they were involving themselves, accepted the union's offer to pay their rail fares, and went home.[38] A detachment of 160 men from the Royal Scots arrived from York to reinforce the police and were followed by a troop of dragoons.

Additional police were called in from Leeds and Nottingham and it was hoped that under their protection all the docks could be worked with a limitless supply of free labour from London and Liverpool. Wilsons' were able to use their clerks to discharge the *Montebello* and then other ships at the small Railway Dock which was relatively easy to protect, but even so the police had to make a baton charge[39] 'in gallant style' against a crowd of up to 2000 dockers who pelted them with stones; and the apparent success of Wilsons' clerks induced unemployed clerks to offer themselves as dockers at the Shipping Federation offices.[40] The number of free labourers was continually increased and later Wilsons's brought some from Holland and Sweden.

For the strikers, Ben Tillett and Joseph Havelock Wilson, MP, consistently urged non-violence, and Fred Maddison, who in Hull Central won 4462 Labour votes in 1892, and 3515 in 1894 even urged the men to go back and work with non-unionists since they had as yet no strike funds to support them, and Tillett was apparently willing to urge the same course if only the employers would give up their attempts to destroy the union through the free labour bureau. This conciliatory attitude in no way softened C. H. Wilson. He simply told union leaders that he would take his ships from Hull rather than concede anything to the strikers. He attended a meeting of the Shipping Federation at York where it was resolved: 'That while expressing every sympathy with the men no further communication should be held with the union leaders', and the leaders were now almost invariably called paid agitators. It was claimed that the strikers had no sympathy except in the working class, but the town council passed a resolution urging the Shipping Federation to negotiate and, when the strike still dragged on, Sir A. K. Rollit, making his first attempt at conciliation after consultation with his fellow MP John Burns, suggested to the employers that if the men went back to work on their terms they in return should agree not to reduce wages in 1893.

Ships went on being discharged, particularly at the Albert, Victoria and Alexandra docks, under the protection of police from Retford, Nottingham and Huddersfield and mounted police from London. The smaller docks which surrounded the old town could not be worked as they were accessible to strikers on all sides. Wilsons' were able to use their ships' officers to move lighters from one dock to another, but other owners do not seem to have enjoyed the same advantage.[41] The aim of Wilsons' and the Federation was to involve the watch committee in the dispute by inducing them to call in a large enough reinforcement of police to enable the older docks to be worked, but the watch committee declined to be drawn in any further[42] and *The Times* correspondent, always virulently hostile to the strikers, commented:

> The watch committee met this afternoon to consider the matter. A majority of one decided the fate of the resolution dealing with the matter, the argument of the opponents of extra protection being that while work was proceeding but poorly at the other docks it was not right that work should be attempted at these two docks. What lies behind all this is a desire on the part of some of the watch committee to coerce the masters into compromise, and also a fear of the rate-payer, for some day Hull will have a heavy bill to pay for this month of lawlessness.[43]

In the opinion of such friends of law and order the great fire, visible more than twenty miles away, in the Citadel timber yards on the night of 23 April was the climax of such lawlessness and an act of incendiarism. Strikers showed the extent of their bitterness by refusing offers of up to 10s. an hour to remove timber to safer sites, but this was not evidence that any of them had resorted to arson, though it was the case that there had been a similar but smaller fire during a dispute with the Wilsons in June 1881. Ben Tillett claimed that the fire must have been started by the utter neglect of smoking regulations, police, free labourers and soldiers being allowed to smoke even in the most dangerous places. Moderate contemporary opinion, exemplified by James Stuart, was that there had been no arson and that throughout the seven weeks of the strike the union had been far more conciliatory than the Shipping Federation,[44] and the chairman of the watch committee openly blamed the employers for their refusal to meet union representatives.[45]

Consideration of the evidence eighty years later suggests that it was more likely than not that the Citadel fire was a case of arson. The overwhelming numbers of the strikers and the probable desperation of a few were almost their only assets. No police force which could have been raised could possibly have contained them, and even if the council had been able to afford to pay for larger reinforcements, it would have had the greatest difficulty in finding them. Even as it was the Nottingham town council disapproved of the action of its watch committee in sending forty men to Hull, and they were brought home.[46]

Consequently, although everyone was agreed that most of the dockers were peaceable and law-abiding there was a good deal of violence both by the strikers and by the police. Strikers stoned railway carriages taking strike-breakers to Alexandra Dock. A union member who refused to strike had all his windows broken and had to go and live on the Wilson ship *Eldorado*, which also served as a police station. In spite of the presence of 350 additional police, 'Each night there is more or less disorder in the streets and the attitude of the crowds is very hostile to the police.'

Attempts were made to obstruct trains and possibly there was an attempt to blow up a bridge on the Hull and Barnsley line in the town.[47] Free labourers from Scarborough, met by a large horse-omnibus at Paragon station, were pursued and pelted by strikers all the way to the gates of the Victoria Dock. Another wagonette with free labourers crouching for cover was heavily stoned in Osborne Street. Women carried stones from road works in their aprons for the men to use as ammunition, until three charges by one hundred policemen dispersed the crowd. Many persons not involved in the strike were said to be going about armed to the teeth.[48]

At first the strikers must have survived as they already had done in a bad winter, by pawning and credit from the small shopkeepers who were almost as poor as themselves. From mid-April their credit was guaranteed by the union which had no funds but sent out a national appeal on behalf of the 12,000 men said to be involved. Before any money was raised by the appeal each man was given a ticket for 5s a week, later increased to 6s. In their own interests shopkeepers had to accept them, and the appeal by Ben Tillett, and the later appeal by John Burns, Michael Davitt and three other MPs, brought in enough money to leave only a deficiency of £750 at the end of the strike.

In the face of Wilsons' determination and wealth, however, it became apparent by the end of April that the strike could not succeed. In another effort to mediate, Sir A. K. Rollit and Alderman J. T. Woodhouse met the President of the Board of Trade along with union representatives and drafted terms for a settlement which represented almost complete capitulation. Virtually the only concession required from the employers was that they should import no more free labour; but they would concede nothing at all and the strike went on for another four weeks. And during this period the Wilson brothers began to realise that they were after all losing their cherished independence, not to the union, but to the Shipping Federation which was even more determined than they were to crush the union.[49] Now both sides had an interest in ending the struggle. Negotiations began between the shipowners and Tom Mann and other union representatives,[50] ending in an agreement signed in the Guildhall on 19 May. By agreeing to work with non-unionists and to molest no one the unionists recognised their virtually complete defeat, and C. H. Wilson kept his kingly prestige intact by leaving his brother, Arthur, to sign the agreement with Ben Tillett.[51] And the real position of free labourers became quite clear. As *The Times* said: 'Arrangements are being made to send away the free labourers whose time has expired and it is thought that the bulk of these men will be got rid of within the next week.' They were *got rid of*, but the relics of the union survived, and there was even a minor strike in 1894 over the unemployment of too many non-unionists.[52]

In that year the trade of the port was greater than it had ever been, and no permanent damage had been done by the struggle of 1893. In another six years the men were able to regain everything which they had lost.[53] In the spring of 1900 the port was busier than ever. Some dockers were army reservists and the South African War had therefore created a shortage of dock labour. Without any kind of organisation, and refusing all compromise, in a single day nearly 700 dock workers forced their daily wages up from 5s to 6s and the movement for higher wages spread to all the docks. Ben Tillett came to reorganise the union, C. H. Wilson was still in the south of France, and his brother had to give in along with all the other employers. Union members then refused to work with non-members, 1700 men re-joined within three days and soon all were in the union. The lions of 1893 now spoke with the voices of doves: 'The owners expressed the hope that in future the employees would give some notice of their intention to ask for an increase as much inconvenience had been caused on the present occasion.'

In 1913 there was a brief dock strike which from its very brevity demonstrated the new strength of the union.[54] On 17 July 10,000 men struck for an increase of $\frac{1}{2}d$—approximately .025p—per hour and the end of the working day at five instead of six. Work with loading coal was not interrupted and the union showed its conciliatory spirit by arranging for the unloading of perishable fruit. The master stevedores accepted the men's terms within four days, but they employed less than 4000 of the total labour force and there was no return to work until the shipowners also gave in, which they did almost immediately.

In 1901 Wilsons' took over Earle's shipbuilding and engineering yards. The firm had long ago established its reputation by constructing more triple-expansion marine engines than any other in the UK.[55] At the end of 1906 500 engineers were out on strike and C. H. Wilson, now Lord Nunburnholme, threatened from Nice to close the yard permanently, but although the strike went on until July 1907[56] labour relations generally were more harmonious than they had been. At the oil-and cattle-cake mills, the principal industry outside the docks, the workers demanded that wages should be increased and no non-union men employed. There was a month of negotiation before a strike closed twenty mills and only two were able to continue. With the support of the dockers and transport workers the strike went on for a month before a compromise settlement was accepted by a ballot of the men on strike. The employment of non-unionists was to continue, but wages were increased by amounts ranging from 1*s* to 2*s* a week.[57]

Labour and the unions gained their successes in spite of a good deal of unemployment and lack of relief for the unemployed. There was no way of knowing just how many men were actually out of work. In 1901 there were thought to be several thousand, but even so the men at Rose, Downs and Thomsons's stayed out on strike for twenty weeks until the dispute was settled by conciliation.[58] The city council in 1904 supported the local trades and labour council in asking for a national policy to relieve unemployment.[59] By then there were several Labour councillors and guardians, and at the suggestion of the two boards of guardians the corporation started a labour bureau and provided a modicum of relief by offering work at 6*d* an hour in East Park; and the Church Army helped to alleviate distress by opening a 'labour and lodging' home.[60] The first Labour alderman, Francis Askew, was elected in 1908 and the small Labour group in the council kept bringing forward proposals for the unemployed, then estimated at between 3000 and 4000, and again work was provided in East Park and on Cottingham Road, but even with a grant from the Local Government Board no more than £913 could be spent, though there was a prospect of spending another £1500 on what was really relief work disguised as improvement of the avenues and the parks.[61]

The corporation was involved in the negotiations which in 1905

induced an American firm to set up the plant of the National
Radiator Company, a British replica of its German works, on a
thirty-acre site in what became National Avenue, and work was
found for another 700 men.[62] The Chamber of Commerce invited
the Australian agents-general to the city for a two-day tour,[63] and
partly as a consequence of this considerable quantities of
Australian wool began to arrive by 1912, when the Hull and
Barnsley sent their men to Australia to find out whether it would
be possible to import Australian as well as Argentinian meat, for
which it had large cold-storage sheds—and in the city there were
six shops of the Argenta Meat Company.[64] The wool trade
expanded, was greatly reduced by the war, but was again well
established by 1920 when there were 100,000 bales in store at the
docks, 70,000 in sheds at Brough and 80,000 in transit at sea; and
new wool sheds, destroyed in the 1941 bombing, were being built
at King George Dock.[65]

Before 1914 there were already firms which took a paternal
interest in their workers. In East Hull a job with Reckitts was the
proletarian equivalent of a place in the Indian Civil Service. Sir
James Reckitt (1833-1924), a Quaker, expanded and diversified the
glue and starch works started by his father in 1840. By the turn of
the century he had what was then a liberal pensions scheme for his
employees and a few years later spent £140,000 in building for
them a housing estate to standards considerably better in most
ways than those of the last quarter of the twentieth century, and
for many years a tour of what came to be called Garden Village
was always included in the programme arranged for important
visitors to the city.[66] His close associate, T. R. Ferens, lived next
door to the estate in Holderness House, and like Reckitt was a
Liberal MP as well as the principal founder of the University
College. Ferens and his wife in 1911 presented twelve almshouses
to the city with pensions of 13*s* a week for each married couple;[67]
and in 1917 he gave the site of St John's Church, still to stand for a
few more years, with £30,000 in Reckitt's shares, for an art
gallery.[68] But the paint firm of Blundell Spence was several years
ahead of Reckitt and Ferens with its profit-sharing scheme,
distributing £936 to 326 of their men (45 of them in London), at
the first share-out in 1886. The oldest beneficiary had started work
with them in 1829.[69] Joseph Rank (1854-1943) was the greatest
and, oddly, the least popular of these benefactors. Beginning in his

father's windmill on Beverley Road, he later became a flour-miller on a huge scale and in 1934 he gave £300,000 to provide pensions for the Hull poor, and in 1939, £60,000 to the Hull Royal Infirmary. But among those who did not share his convictions his deeply pious Methodism was treated as hypocrisy and it was commonly reported that he had once said that £1 a week was a big enough wage for any man.[70]

Hull had the usual ramshackle system of government partly arising from its inheritence from the old corporation, from the poor law and sanitary legislation and from its private improvement acts. As urban sanitary authority it had its own rate collectors and from this rate could pay for drainage, lighting and street repairs, but for all other purposes it had to issue precepts to two quite separate boards of guardians. The guardians of the Hull Incorporation of the Poor, responsible for the old parishes of St Mary's and Holy Trinity, were elected by half-a-dozen or so ratepayers meeting about midday with the deliberate intention of excluding those who had to work. The Sculcoates guardians were elected by the ratepayers, though even here there were said to be irregularities in the collection of voting papers. This union contained the greater part of the working-class population of the city, and therefore had more poor and a poor rate usually about 5*d* in the pound higher than that of the 'Hull' union. The school board obtained its money by issuing its precept to the corporation which then issued yet another precept to the two poor-law unions.[71] Yet under this system a remarkable amount of improvement was made.

People were fond of boasting that they had 'the worst service of tramcars of any town of equal size in the UK'. When the cars were moving only a brisk runner could catch them, but they were so frequently held up that a horse-tram often took three-quarters of an hour to get to the city from Mile House (now the Crown Inn, near East Park). For many years hardly any kind of traffic or parking regulation was enforced. It has been said in 1883:

> Butchers' carts, rullies and shop-keepers' delivery carts drive at whatever speed they please; upon whichever side of the street they like; pull up and stand in the middle of the street or at right angles with the pavement for as long a time as they choose . . . while at such congested corners as the Market Place and Silver Street, Saville Street and Waterworks Street and Beverley Road and Spring Bank,

when a block does occur, there is no policeman to make the offending butcher or drayman move on.[72]*

For the horses and men working the trams conditions were dreadful, with a working day never shorter than fourteen hours and, for the men, one day off in alternate weeks. This was the system of the Street Tramway Company which the corporation acquired in 1893 so that it could replace it with its own system of electric trams.[73] These covered the ground at about the same speed as modern city transport. The first of the new trams began on Anlaby and Hessle Roads in July 1899 and during the following year started on Holderness Road and Spring Bank. With the lines laid on two roads only, in the first six months the trams carried four million passengers and on an average collected £640 a week in fares, whereas the horse-trams usually took less than £300.[74] There were quarrels with the North Eastern about level-crossings, and since on Hedon Road it was necessary to have some kind of bridge or subway the railway company unsuccessfully tried to blackmail the corporation into abandoning its rights in the foreshore up to Hessle.[75] When the trams started on Hedon Road also all the main roads had been surfaced with hardwood sets which had been in use in parts of the old town since 1877, and all the main roads were now fit for bicycles or the few motor cars. Here and there these sets can still be seen where the asphalt was worn off them.

With the speed and cheapness of the trams it was no longer necessary for so many people to live within easy walking distance of the place of work and the city began to spread out. Great numbers of houses, some of good quality, are still in use which were erected within a few years of the laying of the electric tram-lines—in such areas as Hawthorn Avenue, Alexandra Road and Westcott Street.[76] For those salaried and professional men who had leisure to walk some distance, larger houses began to spread in ribbon fashion along all the main roads and before 1914 had reached points about a mile beyond the tram termini. Fares were so low and services so frequent that even in the depression of the twenties and thirties it was quite usual for working-class people to take a tram even for distances of less than half a mile, and from 1908 the fare on any route was ½*d* (rather less than .25p) between 5 a.m. and 9 a.m., and the same amount for children at any time.[77] Even the pattern of courtship was changed. In its concern for the morals of the young the watch committee in 1913 asked for better police supervision of the unlit open spaces and lanes on the city outskirts, now accessible for a penny tram ride by 'boys and girls who secretly use the *poste restante*'.[78]

The following was written in 1883:

> There is one thing in which our works' committee exhibit a great amount of false delicacy, and that is in not placing urinals in our public streets and thoroughfares. We ought to keep pace with the times as do other towns. Hull is sadly in the rear in this respect. Nuisances in consequence are committed upon private property hundreds of times in a day.[79]

One way of dealing with it, particularly on walls and bridges near the docks, was to put up notices: *Commit No Nuisance*. To puzzled children of the twenties this looked rather like an eleventh and meaningless commandment. By then the town was provided with scores of smelly, green, iron, public conveniences about 8 feet high. For a time evil had been made visible by the use of electric-arc street lighting in some of the more important streets in 1881, but the carbon rods burned out so quickly that the system was abandoned in 1884 and slightly improved gas-lamps, now familiar from the paintings of Atkinson Grimshaw, took their place.[80] In 1896 electric street lighting was tried again with primitive versions of the modern type of glass bulb, in parts of the old town, with current generated at the corporation's own plant in Dagger Lane. There was another municipal power station at Sculcoates, some houses already had electric light, and the undertaking had a revenue of £6875. It was decided to spend another £40,000 on the system, and in 1911 another £99,000 was provided for the Sculcoates station.[81] The side streets, however, were still lit by gas-lamps, and for many years up to about 1939 lamp-lighters every evening cycled round the town poking their long poles into the lamps to turn on and light the gas.

By 1899 the corporation could be, or at any rate was, proud of its new cattle market, its main roads laid with wooden sets, the profitable working of the trams, a reduction in the price of electricity for householders and the laying of the foundation stone of 'the first and only municipally owned crematorium in the kingdom'.[82] A telephone system had existed since about 1880 and the Chamber of Trade was urging the corporation to take it over.[83] The telephone company was about to make the Fish Street Congregational Church its central exchange, and the corporation made a small beginning in 1903 with its own exchange,[84] and applied to the local government board for sanction to borrow £47,000 to enable it to take over the whole concern.[85] They met opposition from Sir James Reckitt and Arthur Wilson, but the municipal system was set up, though immediately in 1906 there was a strong pressure from Post Office officials for it to be sold to the National Telephone Company and some suggestion that their motives might not be pure.[86] But the enterprise survived, as it still does today, and by 1910, after paying government royalties, had in five years made a profit of £12,000 on an investment of £60,000.[87]

In 1888 a councillor of Dutch extraction had asserted that veal unfit for human consumption was being brought from the continent, but the council proposed to do nothing as their meat inspector satisfied them that 'such veal carcasses might have been passed on to inland towns, none of them being sold in Hull'. They had just spent £23,000 on replacing the old shambles, felt that they need do no more, and were to learn that to do nothing was often the safest policy.[88] In 1899 they tried to stop the sale of tuberculous meat at the cattle market, and the indignant farmers, followed by the auctioneers, even from the other side of the Humber, boycotted the market for eight weeks and took all the cattle for sale to Beverley, Driffield and Bridlington. Possibly they too were reformers at heart. At any rate they abandoned the boycott when they were promised that a municipal slaughter house would be provided, with cold storage at the meat market.[89] At the same time the sanitary committee was having to deal with an outbreak of small-pox, believed to have been brought by a seaman from Libau, with more than 700 cases in hospital and 120 deaths; and it was forced to begin the removal of the isolation hospital from its site on the Citadel estate, to West Carr Lane in Sutton: and all this happened when the corporation was in the middle of the largest project of demolition and re-planning of the centre of Hull which it had so far undertaken.

What was being done now had been contemplated for thirty years and was costing more than £200,000. In spite of the bombing of 1941, much of what was done then can still be seen, and until very recently no addition was made to the streets at the centre except for the opening of Ferensway in 1931. Victoria Square with the statue of that Queen, originally in a less elevated position, the City Hall, the Guildhall and law courts, the derelict Edwardian

Renaissance police station and most of Alfred Gelder Street, the post office buildings at its eastern end with the statue of Lord Nunburnholme in the open space in front of the Guildhall, as well as much of Paragon Square are all survivals of this effort to turn Hull (a *Times* writer in 1886 had spoken of the centre as consisting of 'small red-brick uninteresting houses' in a murky atmosphere) into a place of some pomp and circumstance. On the whole the effort was a brilliant success, though as with most places of its size the city seen from a distance in the pre-electric era simply looked like a collection of tall factory chimneys, all, unless the firm had closed down, pouring out vast quantities of soot and more or less illegal smoke (and even now from New Holland there are days when it looks like the City of Dreadful Night).[90] But for the traveller who did not look until he got there, or took what he saw for granted since he saw it everywhere, the new city centre could look, and was, magnificent—and no more could have been done.

To do what it had for so long thought of doing the corporation first obtained an improvement act in 1897, which also enabled it to build a third bridge over the river at Scott Street as an addition to Salthouse Lane bridge, planned twelve years earlier. What made it all necessary was the fact that the fine streets built parallel with the first (Queen's) dock to the north of the old town had not been matched by any similar development on the west, and the Dock Offices, and opposite them the Wilberforce monument in its original position, stood among a mass of mainly squalid buildings and streets, of which only Savile and Chariot Streets counted as respectable. In the other streets the police usually found it best to patrol that area in pairs. The four main roads into the city converged on to this and disappeared among it. The only advantage of the layout was that it helped the police to find those persons whose life-style depended on a high concentration of brothels and low public houses. The magnates of Hull suffered very little in the way of personal inconvenience since so many of them were Hull men only in the sense that they had seats on the city council or offices in High Street or Lowgate; but for the first time in a century they were intent on city improvement. Since then those who make their money in Hull and live elsewhere, with honourable but too few exceptions, have tended to see the improvement of the city merely as something which puts up the rates; and not rich men only, since it was a city council well to the left of centre which proposed, as a useful economy, to leave Scheemaker's lovely gilded statue of King William out in the country, where it had been taken for protection during the Second World War.

To compare small things with great, Alfred Gelder (1855-1943) did for Hull what Sir Christopher Wren had done for London. He was the son of a North Cave farmer, became a successful Hull architect, was elected mayor almost immediately on his entry into public life, was re-elected again and again, knighted in 1903, and was Liberal member for the Brigg division from 1910 to 1918. The new town plan seems to have been largely his and was certainly for the most part carried through during his mayoralty.[91*] By 1900 most of the clearance and demolition had been done, and the old Kingston gas works had been purchased in order to use the ground for a great western extension of the municipal buildings, behind the town hall, which was to cost another £120,000.[92] The next year the central library in Albion Street, still in use, was opened.[93] The ratepayers had repeatedly voted against proposals to adopt the Free Libraries Act and it was not until Sir James Reckitt had given a free library on Holderness Road that in 1892, in the fifth poll and by the narrowest of majorities, the ratepayers, most of them, of course, exceedingly poor, voted for municipal libraries.[94] In 1901 Jameson and King Edward Streets were opened, with the De la Pole statue, now at the pier, placed at their junction. The demand for new shop and office sites was so brisk that Jameson Street was said to have been built without any charge on municipal resources. The construction of Alfred Gelder Street had also begun and application made to the local government board for a new central police station there. Back in the eighties Councillor Elam had been demanding that there should be proper public rooms so that it would no longer be necessary to hold town meetings and other important functions in the artillery barracks, and T. B. Holmes had repeatedly protested that it was disgraceful that in a place of such size there was no public library, museum, art gallery, public hall, or technical and scientific college.[95] By 1903 some of these deficiencies had been supplied. For some years there had been a technical college under Dr J. T. Riley, and work had been started on the new City Hall, where the city would soon have its public meetings, concerts, exhibitions and conferences. Demolition had cleared the way to the new Victoria Square—never spoken of as anything other than City Square, and the extension of Jameson Street, creating Paragon Square, had been undertaken at a cost of £63,000. It had also been decided to extend Alfred Gelder Street across the river and make a direct connection with Holderness Road.[96]

In May 1903 the Prince and Princess of Wales (the future George V and Queen Mary) came from Lord Wenlock's seat at Escrick for the royal opening of Victoria Square, the unveiling of the Queen's statue, the laying of the foundation stone of the City Hall and other necessary ceremonies. William Alfred Gelder, as mayor, gave the civic dinner in the assembly rooms (now the New Theatre) and the Prince commended the wisdom of the city in making him mayor in five successive years, congratulated it on having laid out new streets and demolished slums, mentioned the royal interest in the welfare of the working classes, and applauded the martial and patriotic spirit which had produced so many Hull volunteers for the South African War.[97] During 1904 'a splendid piece of marble statuary, Hull's tribute to her sons who fell in the South African war', appeared in Paragon Square, and the laying out of Sir (William) Alfred Gelder's new streets was finished with the extension of Jameson Street to the square from George Street. A covered game market, burned out in 1941, was opened in Corporation Field, as well as the covered market, still mostly intact, on North Church Side, to supplement the New Market Hall (1887-1941) at the corner of Blackfriargate and Queen's Street, one of Gelder's earlier works. On Anlaby Road the College of Art building had commenced, and the contract had been let for the vast westward extension of the municipal buildings.[98]

The plan was virtually complete by 1908, except for the demolition three years later of Cuthbert Brodrick's Italianate town hall (1864) and its replacement by the present Guildhall in 1914 to harmonise with the new municipal buildings stretching along Alfred Gelder Street.[99] The city council wanted to launch yet another improvement bill in 1908, but the butchers opposed the clause for a municipal slaughterhouse, and by large majorities in a small poll the ratepayers rejected the whole scheme. At a time when only a very few could retire on pension they particularly disliked the proposal to set up a superannuation scheme for corporation officials.[100] The general suspicion of the probity of all officials, however ill-founded, had probably been strengthened by the arrest three years earlier of the corporation archivist who had pawned fifty-three articles of corporation property and had tried to sell their letters from Andrew Marvell.[101] This could hardly be taken as a sign of Edwardian laxity of morals—though perhaps the strength of organised religion was already undermined. The *Eastern Morning News* in describing the 'phenomenal success' of Joseph Rank's Queen's Hall and the Wesleyan mission there also wrote: 'It is significant that while the mission halls are filled to overflowing the churches and chapels are too often half empty.'[102] In the post-war period even Queen's Hall was to be full only for organ recitals and concerts, and is now demolished.

So, apart from the building of new schools and houses which went on into 1915, there were only minor changes. Museums and art galleries were opened on Sundays and the council in 1908 made regulations for taxis for the first time. The council was worried by the proposal of the electric light committee to buy German instead of English dynamos. The North Eastern was wiser. It had Airedales trained to assist the police: 'The dogs are taught to obey the calls of small trumpets which the policemen carry. They are even trained to upset bicycles.'[103] Alsations would have been better, but were too German. But for the prevalence of Germany, it seemed, all would have been well.

A trial which took place in 1909 had a long-lasting effect on the tone of Hull public life. A pillar of society was brought down. The Revd Joseph Malet Lambert, then a canon of York minster and rural dean of Hull, with Rose, his wife, at Dolgelly assizes was charged with gross cruelty to a girl, Mary Elizabeth Inman. At the time of the trial the husband was fifty-four and the wife forty-nine. The girl was the daughter of their charwoman. She was ten and had lived with them since she was four or five. The canon always treated her kindly, as if she had been his daughter, but his wife, perhaps temporarily deranged, for several years was madly cruel to her. In 1907 the whole family moved to Barmouth, the canon commuting to Hull, in spite of the great distance from Cardigan Bay to the Humber, for his duties in the church and local government. The change of scene failed to improve Mrs Lambert's conduct. The child might have died but for the fact that a doctor, summoned to attend one of the sons, caught sight of her and found her starved and covered with bruises. He at once had her taken to the workhouse, where she began to put on weight until she was well enough to give evidence at the trial which was the outcome of the doctor's observations. The canon could have been tried separately, but appeared with his wife. His reputation saved her and destroyed him. He may have been one of the Anglicans who was in favour of Welsh disestablishment. The evidence against Mrs Lambert was damning, and the judge's summing-up was unfavourable, but it took the jury only ten minutes to return with a verdict of not guilty, a verdict so popular that the judge had to suppress loud applause. Lambert then said how grateful he was for the support he had received from Welsh Nonconformists, but for many years, especially among a section of the Hull working classes, he was unjustly regarded as lucky to have got off so lightly. When the East Hull school which still bears his name was opened long after the trial, many repeatedly said that his name should for ever be held in dishonour. Though the trial was very fully reported in Hull, prejudice against an honourable man had extinguished all recollection that in his case the verdict had really been one of complete innocence. His work for social reform in the town was quite forgotten, and when the Archbishop showed his sympathy by making him Archdeacon of the East Riding, the family moved to Bridlington. T. R. Ferens continued to think well of him and, when the University College was founded, he saw to it that Malet Lambert, then near the end of his life, became the first chairman of its council, the most powerful element in its constitution.[104]

Two years after the Malet Lambert trial Sir Mark Sykes of Sledmere (1879-1919) became the Conservative member for Hull Central. Because of the numerous affairs of his mother, the wife of Sir Tatton Sykes II (and so known as Lady Satin Tights), neither he nor Sir Tatton was certain of his paternity, but Sir Mark's doubts seem to have served to spur his ambition. After a distinguished military career, in 1916 he was co-author of the Sykes-Picot agreement, one of the main elements in the emergence of the Palestinian problem. When he first launched himself into politics he held the anti-Semitic views then common among the landed gentry, but his experience made him a Zionist. Whatever her moral lapses, his mother was popular in Hull because of her charitable work among the poor. Sir Seymour King, who had represented Hull Central since 1885, was unseated after the 1911 election, because some of *his* charity could be regarded as an attempt to corrupt voters. At the by-election Sykes was returned with a majority of 278. It was a constituency with many owners of business premises who had two votes.[105] At the 1918 election he was returned with an enormous majority, which surely came from his personal popularity, since on his death in 1919 the Liberal, J. M. Kenworthy (later Lord Strabolgi) was elected. Hull thus came to have the honour of being represented by a man who was as far-sighted as Maynard Keynes. Kenworthy was the only member from an English constituency to vote against the ratification of the Treaty of Versailles.[106]

Madame Emily Clapham (1856-1952) about this time was at the height of her fame as a court-dressmaker. It was an indication of the poverty of Hull that she was able to pay her girls so little. Some must have been in desperate need, especially in the first year of their apprenticeship, when they were paid nothing. Jobs with her were nevertheless eagerly sought because her high prestige gave girls the best recommendation they could have. At the height of her prosperity she had 150 girls. But what did she do? Her sole achievement was to find a way of imitating Paris fashions without the risk of litigation; (but her girls were warned that they would be dismissed instantly if they were caught copying *her* designs). She was regarded as perhaps supreme amongst all British dressmakers.[107] Osbert Sitwell thought it was the patronage of the beautiful daughters of Charles and Arthur Wilson which first made her reputation. His mother, Lady Ida, and her cousin, the Countess of Westmorland, ordered their dresses for a court ball from her, travelling from Scarborough to her place at 1-3 Kingston Square.[108] It may have been from the Wilsons that Edward VII heard of the quality of Madame Clapham. His daughter, Queen Maud of Norway, summoned her to Sandringham, and until 1933 she made coats and dresses for her, and supplied her with jewellery.

Sources

1.   *ERB*, 14.
2.   *Hull Critic*, 8 Dec. 1883, 11.

3. Ibid., 15 Nov. 1884, 7.
4. *TC*, 39.
5. Ibid., 126-7.
6. *Complete Peerage*, vol. xiii, 65; *DNB* 1901-11, 685-7; *The Times*, 28 Oct. 1907, 8c.
7. *Hull Critic*, 9 Aug. 1884, 6, 8.
8. Ibid., 28 Mar. 1885, 9-10.
9. G. R. Park, *Parliamentary Representation of Yorkshire*, 278-9.
10. *The Times*, 8 July 1880, 13b.
11. *ERB*, 138.
12. *The Times*, 14 May 1880.
13. *EMN*, 31 Dec. 1881.
14. Ibid., 1 Jan. 1884.
15. *VCH*, Hull, 251.
16. *Brown's Guide*, 214.
17. *EMN*, 31 Dec. 1881.
18. Ibid., 31 Dec. 1885.
19. *ERB*, 140.
20. *EMN*, 6 Jan. 1889.
21. *ERB*, 137-8; *VCH*, Hull, 252.
22. *ERB*, 14, 17.
23. *The Times*, 30 Jan. 1891, 11f; 13 Jan. 1892, 10c.
24. Ibid., 30 Nov. 1891, 11a.
25. Ibid., 3 Feb. 1892, 11e.
26. Ibid., 4 Nov. 1892, 10f.
27. *ERB*, 138.
28. *EMN*, 31 Dec. 1904.
29. Ibid., 6 Jan. 1899.
30. Ibid., 1 Jan. 1900.
31. *The Times*, 21 Oct. 1902, 12f.
32. Ibid., 10 Apr. 1907, 3f.
33. R. C. K. Ensor, *England 1870-1914*, 472; *The Times*, 15 Apr. 1910, 10e.
34. *ERB*, 138.
35. J. M. Bellamy, 61.
36. *The Times*, 7 Apr. 1893, 4f.
37. *EMN*, 20 May 1893.
38. *The Times*, 8 Apr. 1893, 10a.
39. Ibid.
40. *The Times*, 12 Apr. 1893, 10b.
41. Ibid., 15 Apr. 1893, 11f.
42. Ibid., 3 May 1893, 5e.
43. Ibid., 25 Apr. 1893, 10b.
44. *EMN*, 20 May 1893.
45. *The Times*, 6 May 1893, 14a.
46. Ibid., 4 May 1893, 11e.
47. Ibid., 26 Apr. 1893, 5e.
48. Ibid., 1 May 1893, 6b.
49. *EMN*, 4 May 1893.
50. Ibid., 12 May 1893.
51. *The Times*, 20 May 1893, 9e.
52. Ibid., 9 Oct. 1894, 4d.
53. *EMN*, 1 Jan. 1901 and *The Times*, 3 May 1900, 12f.
54. *The Times*, July 1913; 18, 8b; 21, 10e; 22, 13e.
55. *EMN*, 3 Jan. 1906; *Hull Critic*, 21 Mar. 1885, 23.

56. *EMN*, 2 Jan. 1908.
57. *The Times*, 1911; 26 Oct., 12e; 27 Oct., 8d; 28 Oct., 8d; 30 Oct., 6c; 24 Nov., 10e.
58. *EMN*, 1 Jan. 1901.
59. Ibid., 31 Dec. 1904.
60. Ibid., 2 Jan. 1905.
61. Ibid., 4 Jan. 1909.
62. *The Times*, 1905, 29 Sept., 10d; 21 Nov., 6b.
63. Ibid., 1905, 12 Oct., 4e; 13 Oct., 4d.
64. Ibid., 23 Aug. 1912, 6c.
65. Ibid., 29 Nov. 1920, 15d.
66. Ibid., 20 Mar. 1924, 6a.
67. Ibid., 26 June 1911, 3d.
68. Ibid., 12 Jan. 1917, 9a.
69. *EMN*, 15 Feb. 1886.
70. *The Times*, 8 Nov. 1943, 6e.
71. *EMN*, 1 May 1886, 7 Nov. 1888, 6 June 1888.
72.* *EMN*, 1 Jan. 1886; *Hull Critic*, 21 July 1883, 14; *EMN*, 6 Feb, 1886. When the first horse trams ran on Beverley Road in 1875 each tram had four horses, two being rested while the others drew the tram.
73. *ERB*, 39; *EMN*, 1 Jan. 1897.
74. *EMN*, 1 Jan. 1900.
75. Ibid., 1 Jan. 1901.
76. Bacon's 1905 map of Hull.
77. *EMN*, 31 Dec. 1908.
78. *The Times*, 1913, 11 Aug., 5e; E. Partridge, *A Dictionary of Historical Slang*, 344, s.v. 'French letter'.
79. *Hull Critic*, 6 Oct. 1883, 16.
80. *EMN*, 31 Dec. 1881, 1 Jan. 1885.
81. *ERB*, 109, 58; *EMN*, 1 Jan. 1897; *The Times*, 1911, 7 Jan., 6b.
82. *EMN*, 1 Jan. 1900.
83. *VCH*, Hull, 382.
84. *EMN*, 31 Dec. 1904.
85. *The Times*, 1903, Aug. 29, 9f, 31, 4b.
86. Ibid., 21 Mar. 1906, 4d.
87. Ibid., 21 May 1910, 17d.
88. *EMN*, 1 Aug. 1888.
89. Ibid., 1 Jan. 1900.
90. Ibid., 1 Jan. 1896, 31 Dec. 1885; *VCH*, Hull, 276.
91.* *Who was Who 1941-1950*, 427. The scandals of land deals of a later date have caused many to believe that this great man was corrupt. There is no foundation for this belief. He laid the foundations of his fortune by allowing Rank to give him shares instead of cash for commissions executed for him. This was entirely proper.
92. *EMN*, 1 Jan. 1901.
93. Ibid., 1 Jan. 1902.
94. *The Times*, 12 Dec. 1892, 9f.
95. *EMN*, 1 Jan. 1885, 16 Jan. 1888.
96. Ibid., 1 Jan. 1903.
97. *The Times*, 13 May 1903, 12e.
98. *EMN*, 1 Jan. 1904.
99. *The Times*, 24 June 1911, 6d.
100. *EMN*, 31 Dec. 1908.
101. *The Times*, 1905, 21 Apr., 8f, 24 Apr., 7f.
102. *EMN*, 2 Jan. 1908.

103. *The Times*, 6 July 1908.
104. *EMN*, 30 Jan., 1, 3 Feb. 1909.
105. *DNB*, s.v. SYKES, SIR MARK; R. Adelson, *Mark Sykes, Portrait of an Amateur*, 11, 24, 141-3. For Lady Sykes, see C. S. Sykes, *The Visitors' Book*, 28-63, 196.
106. *VCH*, Hull, 278; A. J. P. Taylor, *England 1914-1945*, 183-4.
107. A. Crowther, *Madame Clapham, the Celebrated Dressmaker* n.p.
108. O. Sitwell, *Left Hand, Right Hand*, 233-4.

26

After the Bombardment

The outbreak of war in August 1914 aroused enthusiam in Hull in no way different from that seen in most places between Belfast and Petrograd. As unnaturally high spirits subsided, it was seen that glory too presented its problems. Within a few months those who so anxiously made the morals of Hull their concern were discussing what should be done about the many war babies expected by unmarried mothers; and for perfectly regular families there were problems which at first patriots were anxious to resolve. Within the first six months of the war 20,000 men had enlisted. Many, such as S. H, a clerk in the office of the Ellerman's Wilson line (whose reminiscences will be mentioned later) joined the new Hull Pals Battalion, virtually destroyed on the Somme in 1916. The battalion consisted mostly of young bachelors, but in other units, including those of the Territorial Army, three quarters were married and at first wives not in work had to look to charity and the poor-law for support. The Council heroically decided that in these cases the Education Committee should provide the children with three meals a day. Archdeacon Malet Lambert, once a Christian Socialist, thought that this would tend to pauperise the parents; and as there were 5872 such children the annual cost would be £67,000. Then the War Office produced a system of separation allowances and soon no more than 7 per cent of the children were taking free meals; but could there be some significance in the fact that the name of the chairman of the Finance Committee which had allowed this state of affairs was *Feldmann*, that he very soon died and that his widow was seen signalling to Zeppelins, which were not there, from an empty house in Linnaeus Street? Fevered imagination had taken the place of perhaps generous enthusiasm.

W. C. Dawson, Sheriff in 1916, was exposed to blasts of rage from the Finance Committee chairman and a few other councillors. He was a handsome man, in the prime of life, of what would then be called rather Bohemian appearance, and a great enthusiast for cultural and technical education. But one member of the Education Committee pointed out that culture was a Germanic concept, and the estimates had been exceeded by nearly £3600. It was to the credit of the majority of the Council that they gave Dawson their support and a fair hearing.[1]

The real patriotism of the young was shown in innumerable instances in the war. The heroic deeds which received official recognition are duly commemorated. Malet Lambert (formerly Craven Street) school still has the plaque recording the lieutenant who within a few years of leaving had won the Victoria Cross not long before he was killed in action. And all such heroes would say that there were many more whose gallantry had not been rewarded with any medal or ribbon. This was a common saying of one lesser hero, twice decorated, who, in his Hull accent, always called his Croix de Guerre 'groydiger', adding that he did not know how anyone in the infantry (he was an artillery sergeant-major) could have endured it. These lesser heroes, often through their own modesty, especially since most of them who survived the war are now dead, may be forgotten and probably already are. James Houston (1900-85), a Hull doctor, as a boy was staying with a French family in an area immediately overrun by the Germans. He wanted to avoid internment, and through the kindness of his hosts and the excellence of his French, passed himself off as a Frenchman until he reached the age for military service, when he walked home through Switzerland to join the Tank Corps. And there was a Quaker, Richard Evans, who, when actually serving on the western front as a stretcher bearer, was recalled to serve eighteen months in Wakefield gaol became he had not duly registered for military service. He became one of the founders of adult education in Hull. But these honourable men would agree that it was proper that they should be mentioned here not for what they themselves did but as reminders of the many more whose actual deeds will never be recorded. Even their names, except in those small places which erected public monuments listing them, are in danger of being forgotton. Formerly, especially in the poorer streets, there were wall-plaques, with the names, in gilt lettering, of those who had served in the forces, with two vases for flowers to honour those killed, who were listed separately. Now they can be seen, glazed over for protection, only in Dansom Lane, Marfleet Lane and Sharp Street.

For the business community 1914 was not a bad year, but naturally not as good as 1913 when 6,151,000 tons of shipping had used the port. In 1914 the decline went no further than 5,307,000 tons. With a full year of war, 1915 was worse and the tonnage was down to 4,060,000.[2] The Baltic was virtually closed, and the docks of the North Eastern felt the worst effects of this. Imports of hewn timber, which had reached a peak of 306,000 loads in 1910 went down to 164,000 loads in 1915. Russia could still be reached through Archangel and the Murman coast.[3] The outbreak of war had left ten Wilsons' ships at Petrograd, and in the winter of 1915-16 another nine of their vessels were ice-bound at Archangel and in the White Sea.[4] They had already lost six ships through enemy action, the largest being the *Urbino*, of 6650 tons.

The loss of the *Glengyle* on her second voyage from Vladivostock made it clear that there would soon be no more soya beans from north China, though in 1915 the Hull oil mills actually received 135,000 tons. The *Glengyle*[5] was one of three ships, all of 13,000 tons, intended for the China trade. Soon, to economise on shipping, soya beans were a prohibited import; but the Hull mills were kept going by the transfer of a Belgian Congo line from Antwerp and large imports of palm-kernels from the Congo.[6]

The fishing industry almost died and some fish was actually landed by neutral trawlers. Nearly all of the fish-and-chip shops were closed. Only ninety-three of the Hull trawlers were fishing, the Admiralty having taken 300 or more. Losses were made good by rapid building, and in spite of a shortage of labour, by the end of 1915 Earle's, with 600 men, had launched forty vessels, mostly trawlers, and other Hull firms had built thirty-five.[7]

In 1915 the Hull and Barnsley Railway Company was the only Hull concern to pay a dividend as low as 2 per cent. Most paid 5 per cent or more. British Oil and Cake Mills paid 15 per cent, British Gas Light 12¼ per cent, Hull Brewery 11 per cent and the Kingston Steam Trawling Company 18 per cent.[8] The language used by some Hull business men showed some anguish. A fruit merchant wrote, 'The German trade in soft fruits, which used to be considerable, is, of course, gone, and it may well stay gone'.[9] An editor who 'found that it ill accorded with the temperament of an old soldier to be launching salvoes of print' nevertheless managed to write, from Bishop's Lane, of 'The common enemy, the blood-gorged tribes of the Teutonic states. The sea and air around us are the media of stealthy raid and piratical outrage, causing wanton destruction of inoffensive women and children'.[10]

Because it was quite unlike anything before experienced, the bombing of the city by Zeppelins was especially terrifying and on two occasions highly demoralising. The attack by the L.9 on 16 June 1915 happened only because the wind prevented Kapitänleutnant Mathy from reaching London. From Bridlington he followed the railway to Hull. Just before midnight he dropped flares to light up the docks. There were no prepared defences, and no opposition except from the guns of HMS *Adventure* under repair at Earle's. Thirteen high explosives and 50 incendiary bombs destroyed 40 houses and shops and killed 24 persons. On the ground mobs retaliated by sacking shops, such as those of Kress and Wagner, believed to belong to Germans.[11]

On 9 August 1915 the L.9, having made a landfall at Aldborough, set a course for Hull, but through errors of dead-reckoning bombed Goole by mistake.[12] On 5 March 1916 there was an attack by two Zeppelins which had been intended to bomb Rosyth as their contribution to a combined operation with the High Seas Fleet. Winds prevented this. L.14 found Flamborough Head and since the ground was covered with snow was able to see Beverley and then Hull. She hovered in light winds for ten minutes and was able to take deliberate aim. L.11 came in about an hour later at Tunstall and reached Hull before L.14 had left. Clouds then covered the target but she remained until they cleared. From the ground between 3000 and 4000 feet below the interior, lights were seen as the bomb bay was opened. One bomb falling in the river near Earle's partly destroyed a 3000-ton ship on the stocks. Other damage was less severe than the commander of L.11 believed, but the effects of blast on the glass roof of Paragon Station were spectacular and seventeen were killed. The indignation caused by this raid turned itself against the authorities who had been unable to prevent two Zeppelins remaining un-molested for a whole hour. At Beverley, where the nearest bombs had fallen in fields, an officer of the Royal Flying Corps was mobbed and in Hull a transport was attacked. The GOC Northern Command met the Lord Mayor and Members of Parliament and promised anti-aircraft guns as soon as possible.[13] S.H., now a dispatch-rider on his own motorbike, saw the bomb doors of a Zeppelin open in one of the earliest raids, and driving with a message for the Chief Constable saw prostitutes in King Edward Street, terrified by the noise, on their knees praying to be spared.

In the next raid Hull was not the primary target but suffered worst. Nine Zeppelins dropped bombs at various points between Berwick and south of the Wash. The Hull anti-aircraft gunners could not see through the ground mist and forty-four bombs killed people.[14] The attack by the L.41 at 2.40 a.m. on 25 September 1917, with sixteen bombs, did little damage and was chiefly notable for the fact that she was held by the Paull searchlights and chased by a fighter until out of range of the lights.[15] The final attack was on the evening of 10 March 1918 when the L.63 arrived at Hornsea, followed the railway and dropped six bombs in Hull and six in fields at Sutton and Swine, causing only one death—from shock.[16]

Many graphic accounts can be heard from eyewitnesses who saw the destruction of one or more of these airships, but all stem from a single post-war accident. All aircraft were considered such marvels that it was still the custom to go outside and look when one was heard. The sound of an airship was particularly distinctive and so almost everyone saw the craft which at various times came over from the great hangar at Howden. Consequently there were tens of thousands who saw the collapse and explosion of the R.38 over the Humber in 1921.[17] The *Graf Zeppelin* and the *Hindenburg* were also seen at various times in the 1930s, and the enormous hangar at Howden was opened for those who wanted to go and see the R.100 in course of construction.

In the later stages of the war, hatred of everything German increased and showed itself in the most detestable ways. Baltic Russians, mostly Jews, were excoriated by the tribunal which sat in public to hear appeals against conscription, and the cruel witticisms of its old, safe members to Englishmen as well as aliens beggar description. A Hull-born man who probably did not know that he had a German father until he saw his birth certificate, was dismissed from his post in the workhouse, and a guardian found it necessary to confess that he had known him for twenty years as a docker but never suspected this 'Teutonic taint'. Coal merchants may have been something of an exception in looking forward to a resumption of German trade. By 1917 they were exporting only about one-third of the amount of coal which they had sold in 1913. Most of it was going to France in sailing and motor vessels not subject to requisitioning.[18] Their 1913 figure was reached again in one year only, during the French occupation of the Ruhr. Even in 1924 there were protests that 'largely at the instigation of the socialist element' the corporation had considered buying tram-rails from Germany instead of from Middlesborough and that 'Orders that are given to firms apparently belonging to countries that were our allies are being executed in Germany and sent here in German ships'.[19] When the war was over it was found that at least 7000 Hull men and women had been killed and 14,000 of the wounded were disabled.[20] Only ninety-one Hull-owned ships were still afloat, and nine of these had been built during the war. These losses were soon made good and in 1921 there were 122 Hull ships.[21]

Between the wars, unemployment in Hull was usually rather worse than the national average here given in brackets. In 1923 11.8 per cent (11.6) of the insured population were without work; in 1925 12.6 (11.1), in 1927 12.7 (9.7) and in 1929 14.1 (10.4). In the worst of the depression Hull was rather better off. In 1931 19.1 per cent (21.4) were out of work and in 1933 20.3 (22.0); but as the economic situation improved Hull again lagged behind having 18.2 per cent (16.6) unemployed in 1934.[22] Some sections of the working population suffered a great deal more than others. Dockers in 1934-5 were able on an average to get work for no more than three-and-a-half to four days a week although the tonnage of shipping entering the docks had risen from 6,030,000 in 1921 to 10,030,000 in 1934. Of the 10,320 dockers of 1924, 28.2 per cent were unemployed.[23] Nearly 2000 left the docks, but in 1931 half of the 8420 dockers were unemployed. For those who were then young and politically conscious it seemed that things were falling apart, but in fact they were simply experiencing a twentieth-century version of a situation which had affected generations of workers. The difference now was that the extent of unemployment was known, whereas in mid-Victorian times all dockers were unemployed for a considerable part of every year, and the out-of-work existed in a painful limbo between charity and starvation, whereas now most of those who could not find work were provided for, however meagrely. And the mobility of labour eased the situation. More and more men left the docks. There were 5188 dockers in 1951,[24] and in 1978 there were less than 3000.

Shipyard workers also had a very hard time. Earle's in 1926 built two ships, each of 1754 tons, for a Canadian firm carrying grain on the Great Lakes, and only one other vessel, of 1080 tons.[25] In its last year the yard launched two ships totalling 2295 tons and provided engines with a total horsepower of 3350 for others.[26] With 710 ships laid up in other UK ports and 18 at Hull the firm could not last. Shipbuilding Securities Ltd acquired the yard in 1930 and closed it, and in 1931 just under 40 per cent of the Hull shipbuilding workers were unemployed in a year when 60 per cent of all such workers in Britain had no job and could expect to remain on the dole for years.[27] Hull was lucky. Work on marine engineering and shiprepairing still went on, employing 2230 men. C.D. Holmes in 1932 made triple-expansion engines for six vessels, each averaging over 600hp,[28] in 1932 they made sixteen marine engines of 600-800hp, and Amos and Smith made another three.[29] But Earle's great crane, for so long visible from far outside Hull, had been dismantled and now stood in Hong Kong.

Many women found work in metal-box manufacture which had been established before 1901, and 2513 men worked in general engineering. They were employed at the large radiator works in National Avenue, in making excavators and grabs, chiefly at Priestman's, and in the manufacture of large castings and oil-seed crushing presses at Rose, Downs and Thompson's.[30] They were thought to have equipped most of the British seed-crushing factories, half of which were in Hull,[31] mostly on sites once occupied by firms dealing with whale-oil.[32] Since 1868 they had exported steam-driven crushing machinery to China, and they had opened a Shanghai office in 1909.

It was claimed that Hull was the 'natural' port for one-third of the population of England. Unfortunately trade took no notice of this, and Hull took about six per cent of all British imports and five per cent of the exports, ranking as the third largest port, but far behind London and Liverpool. The Humber drained a ninth of the area of England, and in the twenties, before road transport had become so horrifying, Bury and Oldham as well as the West Riding, Nottingham and Sheffield received goods from Hull in canal boats.[33] Oil and petrol were beginning to be sent inland in barges, a traffic which still continues. Visiting delegations from the 1925 British Empire (Wembley) Exhibition were impressed with the eighteen Hull mills of the British Oil and Cake Mills, at that time the largest seed-crushing concern in the world, and by the LNER woolsheds, built by the Government during the war at the King George dock. There were eleven acres of floor-space for Australian and New Zealand wool, of which 360,000 bales had been handled in 1924; and there were also the National Wool Sheds which, with eighteen sheds, had an even larger capacity.[34]

Seen in perspective, the years between the wars probably provided a better life than most of the people of the city had previously known. Something of the burden had been lifted from women. In 1901, 31,000 mothers had about 39,000 children under school age. In 1931 just under 40,000 mothers had 32,000 children not yet at school.[35] By 1971 larger families had again become popular and 29,400 mothers had 30,000 children under five.[36] The birth-rate figures express these facts in a more spectacular way and clearly show how knowledge of contraception began to have an effect after the beginning of the century. The Hull birth rate fell from 33.1 per 1000 in 1901 to 28.5 in 1911, 25.8 in 1921, 19.2 in 1931 and 17.5 in 1939. During the Second World War it never fell below 17.1.[37] The birth rate in the 1930s was above the national average and in 1931 among the large towns only Liverpool had a higher rate than Hull.[38]

The quality of school buildings was improving. In the twenties and thirties the Education Committee was responsible for more than thirty newly-built elementary and two new secondary (i.e., grammar) schools. The old School Board had built twenty-eight of the schools in use in 1914, and the local Education Authority five, all of a higher standard. The Hull schools were more seriously overcrowded than in some towns, but in a well-run school a class even of sixty was very pleasant for the children. In 1936 53.3 per cent of Hull children were in classes of forty or more, when in the whole country the number of classes of forty or more was 44.5 per cent of the total.[39] In spite of everything school was becoming popular. There were more than 150 acres of school playing fields, most of them at some distance from any school. On a cost-adjusted basis the city was spending ninety-three per cent more from the rates than the School Board had done. In 1911 it was necessary to prosecute 732 parents for not sending their children to school, but only fifty-four were taken to court in 1935;[40] and by then the schools contained many who were to be lucky enough to go on to the universities, and in some cases to distinguished careers.

The 603 new houses built in Garden Village between 1907 and 1916 set standards to which new houses were now tending to conform. In the worst parts of the town there were as many as 130 houses to the acre. The new standard was twelve. But there were some real advantages in very high densities. A Board of Trade report on the cost of living in industrial towns gave the following account of Hull.

> The characteristic feature of housing in Hull is the prevalence of what is called the *Terrace System*. The expression is rather misleading, since the word is used elsewhere to describe a long, unbroken row of houses, whilst in Hull it denotes a short, blind court, usually 18-20 feet in width, running out from the main street. Such a court or terrace usually has on each side a row of six to ten houses facing one another and is faced with cobble stones. The court is ended by a wall which divides it from the corresponding court running from the next parallel street. In the oldest types there is practically no back yard or back entrance, but in the newer a narrow pathway runs between the backs of these houses in two adjacent terraces, and sometimes there are forecourts or gardens and bay windows. The ends of the terraces do not abut on the main street. A row, usually of four houses, is built facing the main street, with a little narrow path at the back of them, and the terrace begins like this. It is because of this that 13 miles of tramway suffice for this town of 250,000 people and that such low rents obtain in Hull.[41]

This gave a density of 49 houses to the acre and rents were lower than in most towns, and only half as high as those of London. Terraces of this type had been built up to 1914, as, for example, in the New Bridge Road area. A few of the most primitive terraces can now still be seen and many of the front garden and bay-window type are still inhabited.

Much of the sanitation was rural, and earth-closets with their characteristic Oriental smell were to be found in many streets outside the middle-class districts. The size of the tank was limited, and though it took ashes the males had to urinate into a sink in the yard. Virtually all these houses had cold water only and no bath, with one tap inside and another over the outside sink, though many had a hot-water tank in the kitchen range not connected to the supply, from which water could be taken with a ladle. The ratepayers in 1903 had voted by 21,000 to 12,000 against any conversion to water-closets and the market gardeners of Cottingham continued to receive their supplies of highly fertilizing nightsoil from this cornucopia. In 1908, 33,000 houses had the earth-closet either within six feet of a door or window or actually indoors, and in over 10,000 the dustmen—called wet dustmen to distinguish them from the dry dustmen who merely removed household refuse—had to carry tanks through the house to empty them. Even in 1924 there were still more than 8000 of these houses; but within the next ten years the conversion to water-closets was completed at a cost of £249,000, of which private landlords contributed about 40 per cent.[42]

By 1935 there were 74,000 houses of which 19,000 had been built after the war. 8600 of the new houses had been built by the corporation which had become the landlord of about ten per cent of the population. Measured by the meagre standards of the 1935 Housing Act only three per cent of the houses were overcrowded. Actually in some respects overcrowding had become worse than in 1901 and by the saner but parsimonious definitions of the 1930 Act 17,000 houses with 100,000 inhabitants—then about one-third of the population—were overcrowded.[43] But even in 1932, 20,000 houses had electricity and the number went up every year.[44] Three years later the Hull electricity undertaking was connected with the national grid, and working a three-shift system was producing current more cheaply than the grid. The Sculcoates power station had high, rectangular, wooden cooling-towers which in 1975 could still be seen next to the tall, concrete tower which was not erected until after the Second World War. The wooden towers were demolished by 1976.

There were 30 cinemas in 1935 with 40,000 seats, and three variety theatres (Alexandra, Tivoli and Palace) as well as the Little Theatre with its repertory company. The Grand Theatre in George Street became a cinema in 1930. It was estimated that these were attended by about 200,000 patrons a week, but it was well known that whereas some went every weekday, others never went at all. Half the seats taken at the cinemas cost 6*d*, or less.[45] For the Saturday afternoon matinee children were admitted to the Cleveland for two jam-jars in lieu of cash. Most of the larger cinemas had a Wurlitzer organ, manned in one case by an unhappy FRCO who never saw the lights fully turned on because it was said that the manager's policy was to prevent faeces deposited under the seats by some. eccentrics from becoming visible. A single parachute mine eliminated this nuisance in 1941. The places of entertainment gave the public what they wanted. Taste in radio (there were about 70,000 sets) was indicated by a poll conducted by the Re-Diffusion company which showed that in 28 preferences light entertainment came first, drama fifteenth, religious services seventeenth, symphony concerts twenty-seventh and chamber music twenty-eighth.[46] But the size of the minority audiences was already very large. Orchestral concerts at the City Hall were usually full, and concerts of chamber music usually filled the hall of the University College.

Public houses were fewer than at the beginning of the century— 452 in 1901 and 288 in 1935, but there were a hundred or more clubs serving much the same purpose for their members. There were more clubs in proportion to the population than in any town except Leeds. The decline in off-licences was less marked, from 381 to 316.[47] Even so, there were fewer facilities for drinking than in most towns. The survival of Puritan feeling, in the Established Church as well as in the largely teetotal chapels, probably contributed to this; and the great Evangelical influence of the Simeon trustees strengthened the Anglican kind of Puritanism. They nominated the vicars of St Andrew's, Drypool; St Peter's, Drypool; St Columba's, Holderness Road; and St Giles's Marfleet; and the Vicar of Holy Trinity, always an Evangelical, in his turn selected the clergy of St John's, until it was demolished to make way for the Ferens gallery, St James's, off Hessle Road; St Luke's, off Porter Street; and St Matthew's, Anlaby Road.[48] The most muscular of this Evangelical group was Canon E. A. Berry of St Andrew's, and it was largely because of his influence that the prosecution of shopkeepers who opened their shops on Sundays still went on. Before the passing of the 1937 Sunday Trading Act there were in England and Wales 26,000 prosecutions every year for shops opened on Sundays, and all but 1000 of these were in Hull or Grimsby.[49] It was estimated that at this time there were no more than fifteen per cent and possibly as few as ten per cent of the population regularly connected with any church or chapel. It was probable that the seventy-three dance halls (there had been only twelve in 1903) drew more people than the churches, though no doubt some went to both.

Few strikes in Hull attracted more than local attention unless they affected fishing or the docks. The trawler engineers struck in 1919 and fishing was almost completely stopped until they returned to work after ten weeks on the owners' terms.[50] By 1923 the dockers were well enough organised to protest against the Ministry of Labour method of calculating the cost-of-living index which at that time determined their rate of wages. There was a strike in the following year affecting 8000 dockers and transport workers. The ordinary fish trade went on, but the strikers would not unload the boats bringing herrings from Norway; and consequently a large number of women and girls in Hull for the herring season, including many from Scotland, were left stranded, and uncertain whether to go home, or on to Yarmouth.[51]

When the General Strike came in 1926 Councillor A. Digby Willoughby seems to have felt that he alone could save the city from the horrors of a Red Revolution, which he felt to be imminent. His diagnosis was mistaken. He probably over-estimated his own abilities, but he had been an efficient chairman of the Tramways Committee and appears to have been a man with considerable talent and force of personality. For public transport Hull was still almost wholly dependent on the trams which, though they were being run without a profit, were not in serious economic difficulties and were generally both popular and efficient.

All the proper local preparations had been made for dealing with the strike. The Government had plans worked out in 1920, and their local administration was in the hands of a Voluntary Services Committee administered by Col James Walker, nominally under the direction of R. Chichester-Constable, probably the most autocratic of all East Riding landowners. Mr Rayner, manager of the tramways, was made Road Transport Officer, a duty which he seems to have discharged with great efficiency in spite of his other responsibilities, continually worsened by interference from A. Digby Willoughby. Though there was some obstruction by pickets, village bus services continued. Councillor Archibald Stark, highly respected in trade union and Labour circles, was imprisoned for three months. His offence was a peaceful attempt to stop Binnington's bus from Hornsea.[52] Fish could not be dispatched by rail, but the strikers did not interfere with the movement of essential supplies of food, and fish went by road. At the fruit depots, the presence of naval ratings with fixed bayonets from the cruiser *Enterprise* made it possible to continue the trade in fruit, which the strikers treated as non-essential. During a disturbance outside the City Hall on Friday, 7 May, five mounted policemen and fifteen on foot charged the crowd, injuring eight men and one woman.[53] The side-streets were still surfaced with water-bound macadam, which made it easy to get stones for pelting at any person felt to represent authority in any obnoxious form. It was therefore easy, and for some a pleasant diversion, to stone trams and buses, and the Withernsea train; so at the week-end there were more baton-charges and forty-one people, including two policemen, had to be treated for their injuries at the Royal Infirmary, then in Prospect Street. The innocent no doubt suffered with the guilty if they happened to be in the way. This was no Peterloo but the bitterness it caused was still alive as late as 1974 when the B.B.C. showed several clips taken at the time by newsreel cameramen.[54]

In mining areas the great sufferings of the miners kept the memory of the strike alive long after it was over in the rest of the country. In Hull the wounds were kept open by the victimisation of the tramway-men. Almost all were union members, and all but a few joined the strike. Because of their relatively high wages and fringe-benefits Councillor A. Digby Willoughby was under the illusion that they would remain 'loyal' to him. Rayner had expected half of them to stay at work, and consequently no preparations had been made to provide public transport during the strike. Not a single man turned up for the two meetings called by Rayner and from Tuesday, 4 May, they were with the 25,000 Hull strikers. They were told to report for duty by Thursday or hand in their uniforms.[55]

Efficient management was needed to get the trams running again. This was made almost impossible by the mistaken view of A. Digby Willoughby that he should take complete charge of the situation. In the Town Clerk's room there was an encounter with Rayner which almost developed into an actual fight.[56] Digby Willoughby was convinced that with a few volunteers he could run the trams as well as the few buses which Rayner had been able to put on to the roads. But was there enough steam for the turbines to provide current to move them? Rayner had been told by the superintendent of the tramways power-station in Osborne Street that the fires had been damped down and there was no steam. Though he did not know it, there was actually about half the full pressure needed, since for some time the boiler furnaces had been kept going in spite of a mob beating on the doors and yelling threats.

Since these episodes have been investigated by Dr Lee in great detail much more might be said about the trams at this time. They were eventually restarted with volunteer drivers and conductors. A minority were undergraduates who were provided with a daily bottle of beer and did not hesitate to stop for an emergency visit to a pub. Further, their driving methods were not good either for the trams or for the overhead equipment, but they were popular with non-strikers. It was the professional staff who managed an emergency service, though Digby Willoughby did good work in providing accommodation for the undergraduates at short notice. The start was chaotic, with one engineer narrowly escaping electrocution, and another badly burned when the current was turned on while he had overhead cable wound round him.

When the General Strike ended it was a long time before the trams were back to normal. The 254 undergraduates went back to their studious labour, and many of the 656 local volunteers were business men and clerical workers who went back to their normal occupations. Some of the strikers who were taken back—each had to apply individually—had served only for a short time, or were men without families to keep, while some with very long service, in one instance at least going back to 1899, and others with large families to feed, did not get their jobs back. What saved them was that many of the volunteers who stayed on were found to be altogether unsuitable and were soon replaced; but others did their work well and remained, one or two still being boycotted by the rest of the workers even forty years after the strike. The Council congratulated Digby Willoughby on his heroic performance as *supremo* in the emergency. They did not congratulate Rayner, who had done so much of the real work, and to add to his bitterness they did congratulate three of his immediate subordinates.[57]

As they travelled along the main roads the trams vibrated noisily on their track, with flashes of electric sparks which made any radio unusable within a hundred yards. Cyclists too, rather disliked them, since the lines were difficult to cross diagonally on two wheels. But they were among the safest forms of city transport ever used, injuring no one even when two volunteers had a head-on collision; and the guards provided at the front and sides made it almost impossible for even a dog to get under their wheels. They were cheap and frequent, usually appearing at five-minute intervals. In spite of them, however, until the mid-fifties, at rush hours the roads were taken over by thousands of cyclists. Especially before 1939 a great many workers went home for a midday dinner, which meant four rush hours every day. The crowds of cyclists were especially dense when they had been held up at a level-crossing. Collisions were remarkably few, and usually friendly.

Cyclists came out in thousands at the week-ends, many with much lighter machines than those ridden for work, which rarely moved at much more than 12 m.p.h. The light-weights, and especially tandems, moved at between 15 and 20 m.p.h. and often, especially in cycling clubs, would go as far as Whitby or Knaresborough. The riders were surprisingly tough. A group of sixth-formers on one occasion left at four for the York military tattoo, turned for home after midnight, and did not get to bed until four in the morning or later. One youth of twenty took the afternoon off to cycle twenty miles to Skipsea in February, to see what swimming in really cold water was like. Having found it not too bad he ate a scone for sustenance, had no warm drink until he reached home, and found that his soccer-worshipping friends did not regard this as in any way remarkable. The late C. H. Frankland once set out for his first trip to London via the ancient Boothferry, carrying a tent, on a heavy bicycle, so that he could camp on the way; but his map was so poor that he found himself in the outer suburbs of London before he could pitch his tent, and did the whole journey in one lap—and although he was a youth of quite exceptionally poor physique.

There was much family cycling, for those who could afford it, with the youngest child in a side-car which was detached for the rest of the week; and many children had a saddle on the crossbar of their father's bicycle. At week-ends a few cyclists and persons on tandems may still be seen making for the Wolds, but most have given up cycling as too dangerous. It was actually much more dangerous in the thirties. In 1937 there were 3176 accidents, with 29 deaths, and in 1938, 3306 accidents causing 39 deaths. It was not until 1965 that the number of deaths on the road reached 35 again.[58]

The bitterness caused by the General Strike, and a Labour victory at the polls in November 1929, led to a revival of political controversy about the trams and questions in the House of Commons when the Council was alleged to have victimised those who had stayed on as volunteers. Lady Houston raised a fund for them, but the cause roused little enthusiasm, and the campaign was dropped. After the Council had just returned from watching Hull City win a cup-tie in March 1930 they decided to re-employ all those who had lost their jobs as a result of their participation in the strike.[58] But the trams were in a bad way, and their decline was soon to begin. When D. P. Morrison came from Dundee to be transport manager in 1931, he was no enthusiast for trams. The trams themselves were in poor condition and some of the subordinate managers inefficient. There was some overmanning, and the track laid in Chanterlands Avenue in 1925-8 was not paying its way; and though much of the track had been relaid, it was in an unsatisfactory state. Buses had been in use for some years, but they too were becoming too old to be economical.[59] In 1932 trams were withdrawn from Alfred Gelder Street and the old town.[60] The first trolleybus route was opened in 1937. There were then still fourteen miles of main road with tram-lines, but by the outbreak of the war there were no more than seven miles.[61]

In spite of unemployment, there was a general but unspectacular improvement in health in the inter-war years. The death rate fell, as it did almost everywhere. Tuberculosis was not quite so deadly as it had been. When the population had been smaller, 424 Hull people had died from tuberculosis in 1908. Food shortages in the First World War brought the civilian deaths from tuberculosis in 1919 up to 538.[62] The hospital for tuberculosis, now the Castle Hill hospital, Cottingham, had beds for ninety men in 1920, but for no more than forty-two women and girls. Obviously most people infected were treated and died at home. As this tended to spread the disease, facilities at Castle Hill were being extended, and cases were being admitted where a cure was unlikely, simply to isolate sources of infection. There was also a small after-care colony at Walkington, supported by voluntary contributions and there those who had recovered sufficiently were trained for outdoor work as market gardeners and poultry and pig-keepers, while a few who could work in their own homes were trained as cobblers.[63]

In the thirties, improved care and the introduction of artificial pneumothorax brought the tuberculosis deaths down from 394 in 1930 to 285 in 1938. No drug had yet been produced which was both effective and safe for use in these cases, but some progress was being made already, and the local firm of Smith and Nephew made a notable contribution by the manufacture of PAS (para-amino-salicylic acid) which could be used in some cases.[64] At the same time Reckitts launched their pharmaceutical division, which under Dr Reynolds produced para-chlor-meta-xyelenol which when dissolved in essential aromatic oils produced a pleasant-smelling, dark-yellow liquid—the first effective disinfectant which was almost harmless to mucous membrane and completely harmless to the skin. Marketed as Dettol, it was soon used in the home, and its effects in midwifery would have looked spectacular if they had not been masked by the almost simultaneous introduction of gentian violet and the sulphonamides for the treatment of puerperal fever. The firm formed an amalgamation with Colmans in 1937 after a courtship which had lasted since 1909.[65]

Treatment of venereal disease was more effective than that of tuberculosis as a result of the discovery in 1913 of Salvarsan in Berlin—the first of the chemotherapeutic synthetic drugs. By 1922 Salvarsan was being supplied free to Hull doctors and 248 specimens were sent to Leeds University for Wassermann tests. In 1921 at the Mill Street V.D. clinic there were 968 new cases, of which 532 were of syphilis in men.[66] By 1930 in 1392 new, male cases there were only 294 of syphilis. The number of cases in women was smaller, but the decline in syphilis equally marked.[67] By 1939 there were no more than 92 new cases of syphilis in males.[68] The figures for the less serious forms of V.D. remained as horrifically high as they were in all seaports.[69]

Diptheria was a very serious illness throughout this period, though with a death rate well below ten per cent. In 1930 there were 856 cases and 47 deaths.[70] It was not until after the outbreak of the Second World War that the effects of diptheria immunisation became apparant. By 1943 there were only six deaths in 368 cases.[71]

Because the week's work did not end until about noon on Saturday, when wages were paid, the Saturday afternoon and evening crowds on the main roads were enormous, and hardly thinned out until after the pubs had closed at ten and the last shops had, literally, put up their shutters at about eleven. The town was less spread out than it now is, its population was larger, and people mostly enjoyed being in crowds. Early in the afternoon (they were at work in the morning) large numbers of men set out to walk to the football match, not so much because they could not afford the tram-fare as because no seats were available and queues resembled mobs. About the same time loud cheers could be heard as the cinemas opened for their Saturday matinee, and the children were let in. They would have got in in any case, but the custom was to wait outside for half an hour. Soon, away from the traffic noise, anywhere within a mile of the football crowds, immense cheers could be heard; and the side streets still heard the sound, more on Saturdays than at other times, of the peculiar mechanical piano-on-wheels locally called the hurdy-gurdy.

In Charles Street and on two of the main roads much of the road space was taken up by hand-carts with huge out-riggers which turned them into market stalls, piled high with fruit and vegetables. Moving on by the police was purely ritual. Naturally the pavements were congested, but no one regarded *that* as a crowd. With a little difficulty one could walk in either direction. In Whitefriargate, on the other hand, body was pressed close to body, to the immense advantage of fleas (flea-circuses procured much of their stock from Hull), and the crowd rather resembled a slow flow of lava, still thicker for those who went into Woolworths'. It thinned a little, but not much, in the Market Place, where a fine meal of peas and chips cooked to *cordon bleu* standards could be had for a few pence, within hearing of the cheap-jacks who at the other end of the market sold their goods (and not all were rubbish) by oratory and acting rather than by display. This was a survival from Victorian and perhaps even more ancient times, as those who have read Dicken's *Doctor Marigold* will know. One or two of these performers sold pills, not actually known to be harmful, but, according to them, possessing miraculous properties. One, a genuine plains Indian (called *Seekwa* since *Sequoia* was too much for a Hull tongue) sold prairie medicine, which he had manufactured for him in Hull. Another was able to endow his patrons with huge physical strength. He was a big man, with two photographs of himself, in one of which he was wearing what looked like the Lonsdale belt, while in the other, as a boy, he was what he called 'a certified weakling'. The bookstall was against Trinity Church, and one could still buy a good eighteenth-century volume for sixpence, while the religious bookstall seemed to do little business.

For those who could afford it, or had the nerve, Saturday night was the time for the pictures or the *palais de dance* (anglicised to pallydadance). Churches and chapels were more generally attended than they are now and much of Sunday was therefore very quiet in many streets while the effects of Saturday's beer were being slept off, and then the *News of the World* properly studied. In spring and summer, by the late afternoon and evening, in retrospect at any rate, it was as if all the flowers had suddenly come into bloom. Along the main road and especially near the parks there were parades of young men and girls, each in groups of their own sex, constantly moving up and down with cries of greeting and occasional pauses for a conference between the sexes, after which they again invariably segregated themselves. The girls wore their best, and actual silk stockings if they were lucky. If the boys belonged to a club or college which entitled them to a blazer or scarf, both then comparatively rare, they always wore them—and trousers which had probably been pressed under the mattress all week. This was undoubtedly a form of courting ritual, frustrating perhaps but in its way very enjoyable. The evening ended with 'seeing friends home' which might go on for a couple of hours, with the more earnest talkers going first to the one home, but never inside it, and then to the other. After the Second World War, though most of the participants had survived, they were six years older, and the ritual simply and sadly died.

But while it lasted, there were some celebrities among the Sunday evening walkers. Some, as fighter pilots, were killed quite soon, but one, who had a humble but then enviable job in the Guildhall, was soon a group captain, a rank in which he ultimately retired as a regular. Two were comrades of Richard Hillary. Others were notable boy-footballers, including the captain of Hull Boys F.C. killed as a corporal in the desert. There were some remarkable athletes too. One, later killed by a lorry, was, when he had passed the age of fifty, still able to do more than 400 miles on the road in the great annual North Road 24-hour time-trial for cyclists. Another, Jack Hale, an Olympic medallist, deserves to be better known as the inventor of the dolphin-kick breast-stroke now used internationally in racing. As long ago as 1885 a Hull fish merchant, as umpire, testified that a Mr Marquis Bibbero, swam a mile in the South Bay at Scarborough, with his legs tied and his arms fastened behind his back. He must have used the dolphin-kick, but as he earned his living as a 'professor of swimming' he apparently kept his method secret.

Nearly all of them were uninterested in the arts. Some, however, were members of the many dramatic societies which then flourished, and some were performers of high quality. The British Drama League organised contests, of which the semi-finals for the north were held in the City Hall. The performers really deserved the breathless hushes and the rapturous cheers which their supporters gave them; and some of the adjudications were memorable.

Much more fiction was read. There were numerous commercial libraries, well below the standard of Boots and Smiths, which provided the works of Edgar Wallace, Rafael Sabatini, Ethel M. Dell and similar novelists. For those who could not afford them, kindly librarians kept a stock of 'Love-stories for me mum' which children used to bring from the library. They provided fare of a much higher standard also. In the reference library there was much of the material for the history of the city. Both the young men who shared most of the desk duty, Woolley and Lawson, were killed in the war; and for those who were interested, the latter, who would probably have had a distinguished academic career, pointed out a Hull man, working at his table, who was already a Fellow of Keble. At Hymers, Redwood Anderson wrote and published poetry, and at the University College Professor W. S. Vines had produced several good novels, though few people in Hull seemed aware of either fact.

There were cultural things of which no one could be ignorant. The film actor Ronald Colman was born in Hull. The press told us every time one of his films was being shown, which was often. There was also a celebrated actress, Anne Croft[72] (1896-1959) who was believed to be a daughter of Edward VII by someone at Tranby Croft, though it is unlikely that he was ever there after the baccarat scandal became known in 1891. There is now a myth about her royal origins—that to promote her career, King Edward regularly attended her performances; but he died several years before her first appearance on the stage. She recorded that her parents were Michael Croft, of Skirlaugh, and Emma, his wife; but many speak of her having been boarded with Mrs Elizabeth Bridgeman at 230 St George's Road. Because Muriel, daughter of Arthur Wilson, so often visited her there from Tranby Croft, it is often said that she was Ann's mother. Though her great kindness to the girl may indicate some connection with Tranby Croft, it is unlikely in the extreme that she would have risked boarding an illegitimate daughter so close to her own home. Muriel Wilson was certainly in the Prince's raffish set.[73*] Royal paternity has been ascribed to a boy who, as a major in the First World War was awarded the DSO. There are circumstances which seem to confirm this. On one occasion his friends, sharing a taxi from Tranby Croft to Beverley, deferred to him as they would have done to the half-brother of George V. Because he gave a tip of £5, more than £100 in money of 1988, each of them gave the same—so much in fact that the taxi-driver was able to buy a bus. About the same time a man working on the roof at Tranby Croft, had his attention drawn to a figure walking in the garden and thought he was seeing Edward VII, long dead. This seems to have been the major.[74*]

If the young were, or professed to be, indifferent to culture, the middle-aged middle classes were not. They attended chamber concerts in evening dress in the acoustically fine assembly hall of the University College, and filled it, although it was hard to reach for those without a car, which then meant most people. Without evening dress, and with a strong reinforcement from other classes, they filled the City Hall for the concerts of the Choral Union, especially for the excellent annual *Messiah*, which had to compete with several other performances elsewhere in the city. Four times a year Sir Henry Wood came to conduct the Hull Philharmonic in classical works, and occasionally in works by Dohnanyi, or Delius, or other composers then regarded as outrageously *avant-garde*. For half the year too, almost every Saturday evening there were remarkably cheap, but very good, celebrity concerts at the now demolished Queen's Hall, where there was also a fine organ, vastly different from the Wurlitzers of several of the larger cinemas, still admired by many and lovingly preserved. After the end of the silent film had banished the highly accomplished pianists who had provided the incidental music, in one or two cinemas there was still an orchestra which played at the interval, and in these, and in some cafe orchestras, there were outstanding musicians who just missed the first rank, such as the late B. de Boer.

In the 1930s the Little Theatre in Kingston Square was at its height. Under the inspired direction of Peppino Santangelo its repertory company provided popular entertainment, and drama of high quality in several weeks of the year. Ibsen was performed occasionally, Shaw and Shakespeare regularly. One year a highly talented amateur, Joe Palmer, performed with the company for a whole week as Macbeth. Santangelo was a man of imagination, and he spent some of his time playing the cello with the Philharmonic. When he was well known as a film actor, James Mason was remembered as one of the best of the Hull repertory performers. Further, there were three variety theatres in which those traditions of the Victorian stage which the law still allowed, and occasionally a few which it did not, were honourably maintained; and one, the Palace on Anlaby Road, almost every year had a week of the Carl Rosa Opera Company presenting as many as four or five operas.

No one could enjoy these entertainments unless he could afford the price of a ticket, but there were two places where two very different views of life were presented free of charge. In the still-new Ferens Gallery, the director, Vincent Galloway, a good portrait painter, began to add to the permanent collection given by T. R. Ferens and Sir James Reckitt a fine collection of impressionists and others, while just down the road Samuel Hemming presided over the College of Art, where first Dudley Harbron and then Max Lock were also building up a school of architecture, which is now part of the Humberside College of Higher Education.

In the opposite direction one could find the magistrates' court, where less could be learned of the law than of the fruitful collaboration of the police with a stipendiary magistrate whom they loved, partly because his standard sentence for any assault on the police was three months. He was a clever man, and a real wit, who unhappily forgot that wit should never be exercised at the expense of those who will be committed for contempt if they join in the repartee. He knew as much law as a stipendiary needed to know, he tried to be just, and when he gave himself a chance he was fair. The gems of the day's wit were printed in the *Mail* and avidly read; but any person, knowing something of the law and waiting in his court as a witness, was likely to be saddened. At the court of the Recorder, there was less wit, more true law, and much more serious crime.

For people in a job and not afraid of losing it, the 1930s in Hull were fine, with a steadily improving standard of living. For the decreasing number of unemployed, and for the politically conscious, it was not quite so fine. At any rate from the time of Franco it seemed reasonably certain that there would soon be a war. Sir Oswald Mosley held a meeting at the Fulford Rooms, marked by much disorder, but was prevented from speaking on the Corporation Field by an indignant mob. Hull earned the distinction of producing the first member of the British Union of Fascists convicted for wearing an illegal political uniform.

There were numerous meetings, almost all of the left, addressed by Sir Stafford Cripps at the City Hall, and by the inimitable J. B. S. Haldane. For those who could take their punishment there were uninspiring meetings almost every Sunday afternoon at the Co-operative Institute in Kingston Square; but they performed a useful purpose, as did the more intimate meetings of the W. E. A., organised by Richard Evans and Frank Nicholson, above the shop tenanted by the Peace Pledge Union. At one of these, in 1937, a distinguished Conservative lady, not named here in case she should still be living and object to being reported, argued with some ability that since the two greatest enemies of this country were Russia and Germany, and since Hitler clearly intended to attack Russia, would it not be best for us to stand by and let him, so that each side would dispose of the other?

Problems of international relations were also treated impartially and academically, notably by Frank Darvall, in a series organised by the Hull Cambridge Extension Society. No one who has not heard a Cambridge or Oxford extension lecturer at work can possibly realise how brilliantly illuminating a fine lecture can be. Perhaps the very best of them was Louis Umfraville-Wilkinson, a friend of the poet J. C. Powys. The one person in Hull who could compete with him, in brilliance if not impartiality, was Norman Poole, whose life ended when he was an artillery captain in Malta in 1942. He had been the openly Marxist assistant registrar of the University College, and by far the most brilliant lecturer there until he joined the army as a volunteer. Without notes, or a moment's unnecessary hesitation, totally without drama, he could lecture in a rapid, exciting tone, but still with such clarity that it was possible to take notes of all his points.

It was his Marxism, and the European origin of two of his collaborators who have since attained the highest distinction, which made the University College unpopular with the hard-headed businessmen of Hull. Neither was wholly in agreement with him. Professor Roll, as Sir Eric Roll, became a Treasury knight and an outstanding figure in international economic affairs; he was awarded an honorary degree by the University of Hull in 1967, and entered the House of Lords as a Life Peer ten years later. Jacob Bronowski, assistant lecturer in mathematics, an almost unbeatable chess-player, and already an authority on William Blake, had become world-famous for his popular expositions of science and history when he died in 1974 in the USA. Both were more active than Poole in organising public opinion regarding the perils of Nazism.

Hull's justly acclaimed heroine of the 1930s, very often in the news, was Amy Johnson, a former pupil of the Boulevard Secondary (now Kingston High) school. In 1930, in a Gipsy Moth, a splendid but difficult aircraft, she became the first woman to make a solo flight to Australia. There was even a popular song about her. She subsequently made other remarkable flights and in the Second World War lost her life flying for Transport Command. At that time, almost completely forgotten, were four other heroes: J. Vincent, A. Holness, A. Cheetham and T. Green, who had been with Shackleton when the *Endeavour* was abandoned, crushed by the ice of the Weddell Sea, in the long march to Elephant Island, and in the camp there from which they were eventually rescued. Vincent, an able seaman and a fisherman in Hull vessels, was one of those chosen by Shackleton as fittest to join him in the open boat, the *James Caird*, with four others for the passage to seek help at South Georgia, which can now be seen in perspective as more remarkable than any flying venture. Vincent was judged one of the three men least likely to be able to cross South Georgia with Shackleton to the whaling station from which a rescue expedition could be organised, and remained with two others in the camp at King Haakon Sound. He served in and survived the First World War, but was killed by enemy action at sea in the second.[75]*

Much of the latter part of this history has been concerned with the sordidness of slum life, at which we may here take a last look. Such horrible late-Victorian slums as the place called the Rabbit Warren in Lower Union Street had been replaced by streets off Holderness, Hessle and other main roads with houses built to a higher standard under later bye-laws; and here the last traces of medieval social customs were to be found since these were the new slums. On Hessle Road there was a man who earned his living by fighting dogs, not with his hands but with his teeth, and it was generally believed that he had even killed a bulldog. In the same district there were pubs in which eating contests were sometimes held. These contests must always be taken as an indication that for many people getting enough to eat was a daily problem, and therefore there was an element of ostentatious waste, always a source of entertainment, in watching others eat far more than the normal amount. But the Hessle Road contests were essentially races. Meat pies were laid out on the floor and the contestants had their hands tied behind them. They then went down on their knees and the pie-eating race began, with the faces of all the contestants at the end covered in a mess of meat, gravy and pastry up to and sometimes beyond the forehead. But as the new corporation housing estates grew the population of the new slums dispersed, and there are now few persons living who have witnessed dog-fights or pie contests.[76*]

In the years between the wars many persons, perhaps mistakenly, entertained grave suspicions of the honesty of the members of the corporation, and some went so far as to believe that only two were under no shadow of suspicion. These were Sir Alfred Gelder and Francis Askew. It was soon to appear that in the case of three Councillors there was strong foundation for suspicions of improper practices which at that time were just within the limits of the law. Since the General Strike Councillor A. Digby Willoughby, though popular with his own party, was bitterly hated by many—so much so that for six months after the strike he had needed police protection. A meeting of the Municipal Reform Party, of which he was the leading member in 1926, was broken up by tramwaymen who sang 'The Red Flag', and, to the appropriate hymn tune, 'Tell me the old, old story/Of Albert and his chums'. His chums did not like it, but he so dominated the party that when he lost his Council seat in the November election a vacancy was immediately created for him.[77]

In 1932 the City Council signalised its relative purity by asking the Ministry of Health to hold an inquiry into the purchase of land for housing estates, and what the Lord Mayor described as 'rumours which have been circulated which reflected upon the integrity of members of this Council'.[78] This was at once seen to be aimed at Digby Willoughby, then chairman of the Housing and Town Planning Committee. Before the inquiry could begin he committed suicide. It was generally believed that he deliberately went to Scotland to end his life so as to avoid an inquest which might incriminate his associates. It was also generally believed that more were involved than the two who finally faced the commission of inquiry. If indeed this was the motive for Digby Willoughby's suicide he must be judged to have shown stoical bravery. He was about to be tried for demanding money with menaces from a reputable firm of Hull tailors. He was alleged to have threatened that unless they gave him £5 a month (about £100 in money of 1988) he would ensure that they had no more corporation contracts for police or tramway uniforms. The police claimed to have known this for some time, but it was not until 1931 that they were able to persuade the firm to give him marked notes. Oddly enough this ill-fated man first appeared in connection with land deals in 1918, as an enemy of what he saw as corruption. Christopher Pickering, who had already given the city Pickering Park and was to endow the Pickering Homes, was offering to the Council seventy-five acres for housing at £493 an acre. Councillor Digby Willoughby pointed out that Pickering had bought the land about the turn of the century for £120 an acre, that its current value was £250 an acre, and that the vendor would therefore realise a profit of £17,000 or more.[79] The Council nevertheless decided to purchase and he may well have decided that if business was done in that way he might as well join in. There was a group of Hull celebrities known as 'The Forty Thieves', proud of their sharp practice and grudgingly admired by a great many. Why should he not be one? He would be doing no more than many other members of the corporation had done since its first election in 1836.

When the inquiry was held and the Recorder of Blackburn made his report the extent of his malfeasance became known.[80] As committee chairman he had sometimes made an ostentatious display of disinterestedness, refusing to take any part in proceedings which affected his own personal interests. Now, however, it was shown that he was deeply involved with Councillor Frank Finn who as well as being a shipping agent and a timber merchant was also a papal baron, and with R. G. Tarran, a self-made builder and contractor who in a few years had done work for the Corporation amounting to £600,000, and who generally and correctly believed that he was allowed to get away with sub-standard work, and long afterwards motorists claimed they could feel when they were on a Tarran road. This official report[81] made on behalf of the Ministry said:

> There is no doubt, I think, of the role played by Councillor Digby Willoughby. Distasteful as it is to criticise the activities of an individual who is no longer able to explain his conduct the conclusion at which I have arrived is that Digby Willoughby, taking advantage of the information which came to him in his official capacity, and relying on his influence with the Council, used these opportunities to promote his own personal gain. The system of turning information into money had become a business pursued almost to recklessness. In less than a month he had made over £1100, and it should have occurred to him that discovery was inevitable.
>
> The part played by Councillor Frank Finn is not so readily apparent. According to his own story his contribution to the partnership was to find purchase money while it was Councillor Digby Willoughby's to develop the land at some future date. Councillor Finn entered into the speculation knowing full well that sooner or later the land must by reason of the proposals of the corporation appreciate in value.
>
> As regards Mr R. G. Tarran, I was not favourably impressed by the way he gave his evidence. I am unable to accept Tarran's evidence that he embarked on this transaction after seeing the land and reviewing its merits as a building proposition . . . Recalling Mr Tarran's intimate personal relations with Councillor Digby Willoughby I have come to the conclusion that his only real interest in the land was to hold it until such time as it should be required by the corporation. Tarran by his personal and business relations with Willoughby and Finn placed himself in a position in which he could hardly expect to escape comments of an adverse nature.

When Frank Finn died in 1940 it was found that he had established a charity under his will worth far more than anything he could possibly have gained in these land deals, and its assets in 1962 were valued at £77,000.[82] In spite of the adverse report R. G. Tarran continued to prosper, eventually became a Councillor, and continued to receive corporation contracts. It was his firm, commemorated on a plaque there, which built the pontoon at the

11. Hull under fire, 1941.

12. Hammond's store (now known as Binns of Hull) before and
after the bombing, 1941.

corporation pier. He lost none of his influential friends, who apparently put him in the category, to which he surely did not belong, of those innocents who do not understand finance. On the other hand, his group in the Council were willing to regard their opponents, then in power, as capable of any kind of misdeed. After a full inquiry in 1935 the Ministry of Health reported that there were serious inadequacies in the control of public assistance, and the opposition had their day:

> With reference to immorality it cannot be said under present conditions with any degree of certainty that prostitution is not being subsidised at the expense of the rate-payers . . . The refusal of the public assistance committee in many cases to institute proceedings against fraudulent claimants for relief may lead to the belief that the public can be robbed with impunity, and that lying and cheating may be made to pay.[83]

During the bombing of Hull, R. G. Tarran was sheriff and, according to at least one witness not prejudiced in his favour, behaved with very great gallantry.[84*] Unfortunately, however, he was still in business and his firm was swindling so monstrously on defence contracts that the police seconded to investigate were taken off the case on the grounds that a prosecution in time of war would affect morale detrimentally.[85*] The most that could be done was to force the firm to meet the cost of making good work, at Melbourne R.A.F. station, not performed according to contract. The cost would have bankrupted them if the true financial position had been disclosed, and the shareholders were therefore provided with false balance sheets for 1942 and 1943; but Tarran and his fellow directors were not prosecuted until 1947.[86] After forty-four days of committal proceedings[87] they were tried at a special assize in Hull, the trial lasting forty-two days. Two were dismissed from the case at an early stage.[88] The third, the secretary of the company, was found not guilty; but the cost of his defence had ruined him financially. Tarran was found guilty and sentenced to nine months hard labour but was bailed so that his appeal could be prepared.[89] The Court of Appeal found that there was no evidence that he knew the balance sheets were false, and the verdict was reversed.[90] Yet it was strange that this had never been found out in eighty-six days of legal proceedings during which lawyers earned about £30,000[91]—rather more than £300,000 in money of 1988. The law was surely brought into more discredit by this—at any rate in the eyes of non-lawyers—than was Tarran who emerges as something of a Till Eulenspiegel. His career was over, but he was perhaps not greatly depressed, and about this time was seen modestly but conspicuously enjoying life in the lounge of the George Hotel at Perth.

The traffic problems of Hull differed from those of other towns in two respects, the number of bicycles and the level-crossings on main roads. Each day the five principal level-crossings were closed 500 times for a total of about sixteen hours, during which they held up 80,000 vehicles. The corporation in 1928 prepared a scheme to abolish the worst of the level-crossings at a cost of £1,217,000, if the Government's unemployment grants committee could be induced to provide £500,000 and the L.N.E.R. would still give the £100,000 which it had promised in 1915.[92] Nothing came of this and no level-crossings were eliminated until the Hessle and Anlaby Road bridges were made after the war. Just before the Second World War, to make a new ring road, bridges were made in Marfleet Lane and Sutton Road, and both of these now carry heavy traffic over railways which are no longer there. Because of the extreme flatness of the site of the town, there were more bicycles per thousand of the population than in any other city, one consequence of which had been that Hull has produced many notable amateur racing cyclists. A traffic census taken in 1936 recorded 7302 cycles at a single point in sixteen hours;[93] and during the Second World War, even in the city centre which prudent cyclists avoided, they outnumbered all other vehicles by three to one.

Improvements carried out on the eve of the war were financed by a three-and-a-half per cent loan which the city added to its total debt of £12 millions. There was no difficulty in raising this sum secured by a rateable value of £1,764,000 and municipal enterprises with a gross revenue of £1,500,000 provided by the city's investment of £4,400,000 in housing and £4,000,000 in electricity, water, markets and transport.[94]

Though comparatively little of the corporation's investment was destroyed by the bombing of the Second World War, the total damage may have exceeded £20,000,000 calculated at prices of 1952. Corporation housing suffered its share of damage, but the principal loss suffered by the corporation was that of most of the buses in the central bus station, after which they were left each night on the roads in the parks. Over 5000 houses were destroyed, with half the central shopping area, 3,000,000 sq. ft. of factory space, including two of the three flour mills and several oil and cake mills, twenty-seven churches and fourteen school and hospital buildings.[95] This was trivial by German or Japanese standards, but serious for Hull, which was thought to have suffered to about the same extent as Plymouth, but rather more than Manchester.

The things which were changed in the town by the Second World War, though the loss of life was far less than for those who joined the forces, in the First, were so many and so permanent that they have masked other small but significant changes which may be forgotten. Until 1939 at least half the people of the town were able to hear the works' sirens, here always called 'buzzers', which ceased to be used as they might be confused with air-raid warnings. Every schoolchild home for the midday meal, and most still did go home, shortly after the one o'clock buzzer used to hear the ringing of at least one school-bell, and it was counted a privilege to be given a week's duty at the bell-rope; but bells meant gas, and so were never used again in the schools where they hung.

Though the majority of young men waited for their turn to be called to the forces, there was a rush of volunteers, consisting of those anxious for commissions, or for places in the R.A.F. or Navy, and veterans of 1914-18 who again felt that it was bliss in that dawn to be alive and even in their late fifties were sure their country needed them. Most but not all were turned away, though a few were young enough to be eligible for compulsory service. One noted volunteer who had been in the Merchant Navy in the First World War bravely decided that, in spite of a very notable handicap, he would do the same in the Second. His handicap, however, was amusing to his shipmates, and got him honourably ejected from two wars. It was a heart-murmur so loud that anyone who cared to listen could hear it, and the medical authorities took the view that it could not be taken to sea as a source of entertainment for bored seamen.

There was a small minority in this, as in other towns, who, as Fascists, were regarded as dangerous, though it is probable that most of them were misguided men who would never have betrayed their own country. One public official, of moderate importance, who had formed a Fascist cell, withdrew to Northern Ireland.

Having reached pensionable age, he applied to the appropriate committee of the council for his pension, and was told to return to Hull, nominally to claim it, but actually so that, like most members of his cell, he could be interned in the Isle of Man under regulation 18B. Naturally he did not come, ignorant of the fact that the Luftwaffe bomb which was to kill him in Belfast had already been manufactured. And there were others, chiefly Italians, who were even more unfortunate, and who in 1940 were deported to Canada. One, greatly respected for his wonderful ice-cream as well as for his undoubted integrity, joined the tens of thousands who, by enemy action, were drowned in the Atlantic.

For young people, not yet combatants themselves, the raids by the Luftwaffe were sheer and pure excitement. The first few were almost harmless. One Saturday night raid was followed by a lovely summer day which enabled hundreds to walk to a point near the Lambwath stream on the road to Wawne to see their first, scarcely credible bomb-crater. When the real raids came many, no longer young, experienced real terror. In the opinion of Mass Observation, then still usefully flourishing, morale in poor districts in St Paul's parish was shaken. This was never the official view, but it seems probable, and certainly not blameable, that people who had known the near-starvation of unemployment were shaken by the prospect of near-cremation, from living against an aiming-point.[96] From outside, for those few who had not yet felt any reason for fear, these fire-raids, with a great deal of high explosive as well, looked beautiful and exciting. The flames from the burning mills soared to incredible heights—the largest fires anyone had ever seen (and Hull had had several really remarkable ones in peace-time in timber-yards and at Saltend) and the brilliantly-lit smoke above them, fed by water from the N.F.S. hoses, formed a cumulo-nimbus which sucked up light debris and dropped it as far away as Kirton Lindsey in North Lincolnshire. There were also the very high-pitched and deafening barks of the A.A guns in and around the town, followed a few seconds later by the brilliant pin-point as the shell exploded at somewhere near the 15,000-feet level. And when the hail of shrapnel-fragments descended, to the lucky ones it meant not so much a narrow escape but rather the illusion of sharing the danger of the real combatants. Children on their way to school the morning after a raid collected pocketfuls of shrapnel, and few supremely fortunate ones were able to pick up a nose-cone. Few, in any, seem to have kept their mementoes.

A bomb which was going to fall near could always be recognised by its whistle, and noise-devices were attached to some to increase the terror. Most terrifying of all were the so-called land-mines, probably at first real mines which had missed the river. Because they hung from a large parachute, their characteristic moaning noises caused by their swinging could be heard long before the tremendous detonation on impact. One of these touched the roof of an air-raid shelter in Bean Street, killing everyone inside. Hull people were probably among the very few who, late in the war, were attacked by cannon-firing JU88s. Those who knew the sound dropped to the pavement in time, but thirteen people were killed outside the Savoy cinema on Holderness Road.

In the First World War many people had been in the habit of moving out of the town, or to the outer suburbs, on nights when raids were expected. In 1941 this happened on a larger scale, and it was believed that at one time a third of the population was moving out at night, though here, as almost everywhere, many remained in their beds in every raid, or only moved into a shelter for the sake of the dog and those who really were afraid. Women with a job to do showed as little sign of panic as the men, but those of middle age were often very frightened, though their ex-service husbands told them that this was really *safe* by comparison with the Somme and Passchendaele.

When the raids, but not the war, were over, the ruins were remarkable. Because so many tens of thousands of tons of rape and linseed had been half burned, grasshoppers and crickets bred in millions and every evening their sharp, faint scream could be heard from among the rubble and the glorious masses of rose-bay willow herb (*epilobium angustifolium*) which until then very few local people had seen unless they were botanists. And in the hundreds of Hull terraces running at right angles from the side streets, all the iron railings with fleur-de-lis heads had been taken for scrap, so that the terraces, where they survived, were never to look the same again. Where the tram-lines were no longer needed they too had gone, some for scrap, but many to be seen long after the war forming Home Guard tank traps, sticking up from beds of concrete next to great concrete blocks: and until the very end, the more official a place was, the greater the number of sandbags which shielded its entrance and its windows. Even the University College had its share, with an air-raid siren immediately on top of the attic roof where a minor administrator worked.

Hull's misfortune was that its position near the coast and on the River Hull made it easy to find, and it was therefore often used by the Luftwaffe for operational training, which A. A. command tried to discourage by a high concentration of searchlights to dazzle inexperienced crews. The Humber was defended by thirty-eight heavy A.A guns in 1940 until twelve were removed for the defence of London. This provided a comparatively light barrage from such sites as Spurn, Stone Creek and Little Humber before the planes had to face the fire of the city defences, keeping above the seventy-four balloons, of which twenty-four were on floating sites, of 942 and 943 squadron R.A.F.[97] Before the attacks on Hull had ceased two 'Z' batteries, manned by the Home Guard, were able to put up spectacular curtains of fire from the simultaneous launching of all their rockets. Up to 16 May 1941 in night attacks Hull received, or was intended to receive, 593 tons of high-explosive bombs. The worst raids were on 13 March 1941 when seventy-eight bombers were sent and on 18 March when 378 bombers carried 316 tons. A large proportion of bombs missed the target entirely. On 19 May 1942 the attacking force dropped everything on a fire started by incendiaries on an A.A. site well outside the target area.[98] In the raid of 25 July 1943 not one of the fifty aircraft dropped any of the seventy tons of bombs with which they were loaded, on Hull, and there was another completely abortive attack on 20 March 1944. After a more effective raid on the previous night by 131 planes, sixty-one tons of bombs were flown to Hull on 20 October 1942, but only thirty-seven tons were counted as having fallen on the target or within fifty miles.[99]

It was only in 1941 that the effects of the bombing were clearly reflected in the death-rate, which rose to 19.1 from 15.3 in 1940. Each rise in the death-rate was partly attributable to the absence of much of the younger population, evacuated or on war service. Soon most of the evacuees returned. For a time the Hull evacuation in the Spalding area overlapped with that of London. In spite of the war the death-rate fell to 14.2 in 1942, but rose to 15.5 in 1943.[100]

The University College, founded with a gift of £250,000 from T. R. Ferens and incorporated in 1925, almost became a casualty of the war which took away most of its staff and students. If it had succumbed, it would have been judged to have died of self-inflicted wounds. Inside the college there was a faction hostile to the Principal. One of their aims was to secure the suspension or dismissal of Professor T. E. Jessop, who, like several of the original staff of the College, had won the MC during the First World War and was an outstanding ornament of the institution. The Principal did not always enjoy the support of the University College council and there were Hull business and professional figures who looked forward to the extinction of what they saw as a community of Communists: but in spite of everything the University College survived to become a University in its own right in 1954. Some members of the staff performed special war services. One, now knighted and an F.R.S., was engaged in insect-pest research, and one of his colleagues from the same department was a brigadier. Others were concerned with radar and aeronautics, and Jacob Bronowski was called away to estimate the damage likely to be caused by the first atomic bombs. At the end of the war, after a visit by a party which included a grandson of Darwin, the University Grants Committee accorded recognition, which for more than thirty years virtually guaranteed the future of the College which in 1954 became a university in its own right. By 1952 the student body had increased from about 200 to 900, of whom 660 were in University residences.[101] A students' union with common rooms and refectories had been built and the chemistry block had been started. Within the next twenty years the assets of the new University approached £15,000,000 and it ranked as one of the most important employers in the city.

Post-war rebuilding of the city went on slowly, and although the total bomb damage was made good before 1960, even today there are several bombed sites still lying derelict and profitably used as car parks. The corporation during the war commissioned Edward Lutyens and Patrick Abercrombie to produce a plan for reconstruction, and their inspired but quite practical plans were presented in 1945. The almost equally inspired words of *The Times* ten years later should be recorded for its splendid mixture of metaphors and misuse of a passage from Hamlet:

> Municipal bickering over who should own the land for rebuilding undoubtedly delayed matters and in part the Abercrombie plan of 1945 stood somewhat in the style of a Chinese wall in the way of the

business men's idea of rebuilding his own property. In the future,
though not entirely jettisoned, the plan will appear as a palimpset,
more honoured in the breach, than in the observance.[102]

'Municipal bickering', though no scandals on the 1932 scale were
revealed, had included the activities of a councillor who for a time
had all the movements of the entirely blameless town clerk[103]
shadowed by private detectives, and a High Court injunction in
1947 to prevent another councillor from disclosing the contents of
a Home Office report on the conduct of the Chief Constable.[104]
The full reasons for the premature retirement of this officer
therefore remain obscure.

The river-side quay, a prominent feature of the port since late-
Victorian times destroyed in the bombing, was completely rebuilt
and modernised in 1957-8 at a cost of £1,750,000, and there was
once again half a mile of berths usable in any state of the tide,
mainly for embarking passengers for the Continent and
discharging fruit.[105] Now, however, except by trawlers, all the
berths west of the river are largely unused. The Victoria Dock, also
expensively re-equipped, is now filled in again; and in all several
millions of post-war investment have ceased to be productive.
Traffic is entirely concentrated on the river and the easternmost
modern docks. Vessels from the Continent can be seen moored as
far up-river as Stoneferry bridge. Work on a twenty-eight-acre
extension of the 1914 King George dock, costing £6,750,000 and
called the Queen Elizabeth Dock, was started in 1967, and there
was an official opening by the Queen in 1969.[106] The Saltend oil
terminal had also been greatly enlarged, but very much larger
tankers now discharge at Immingham.

Shipments of coal declined to 312,000 tons in 1957, but by 1965
cargoes were being dispatched at the rate of two million tons a
year, chiefly for the Thames power station. After a long period of
prosperity with few intermissions the fishing industry by 1978
found itself more and more hemmed in by a ban on trawling
within 200 miles of Iceland, and in the following year even stricter
limits were imposed. Each of the wars had allowed stocks of fish in
the North Sea to recover, and fishing there became extremely
profitable until the grounds were over-fished again. More distant
grounds were exploited and increased landings of fish—59,000
tons in 1919 and 197,000 in 1931 coincided with a fall in prices at
the quayside from four-and-seven-tenths of a penny per pound to

just under one-and-four-tenths of a penny; pennies then being 240 to the pound.[107] The shipping slump of the 1930s made it possible to purchase surplus merchantment at low prices. Three of these were converted into factory ships and went each summer to the west coast of Greenland for cod and halibut. This was a time when £3 a week was a good wage and eighty per cent of the workers of Hull earned less than £4 a week; but they could buy immature halibut at the fried-fish shops for 3*d* each. The actual catching of the fish was done by motor-dories, each with a crew of three or four, and the converted merchantmen simply acted as bases and provided refrigerated storage.[108] The bulk of the fish, however, was caught by 240 mainly Arctic trawlers manned by over 5000 fishermen.[109] After the Second World War trawlers became still larger and there were only 145 in 1956, with 3500 men, and the concentration of the industry still went on.[110] For a time, even after the war, all Hull trawlers were coal fired, though very soon a few began to use fuel oil and in the end all had diesel—instead of steam-engines. As more vessels were built to gut, wash, and freeze their catch at sea the 250 Hull fish-merchants of 1965 felt themselves far from secure. One of them, thinking of the fifty-two who had gone out of business in three years, called Hull a graveyard.[111] In 1978 the number of fish merchants, including such large firms as Ross, which also owned trawlers, had fallen to ninety-four, and of these only sixty were not limited companies.[112]

It seemed that the intransigence of Iceland (and the importance of Keflavik to N.A.T.O.) had destroyed the greater part of the Hull fishing industry. No trawler could fish within 200 miles of Iceland and no alternative source of cod had been found. What made matters worse was that it was now far more difficult for unemployed fishermen to find a job on shore. As the economic difficulties of Britain increased, the consequences were felt in Hull. By 1968 the Humberside unemployment rate among males was just under five per cent;[113] eleven years later the situation was a great deal worse and there were already many persons out of work for a year or more.

The situation was not as bad as it had been in the 1930s. The general rise in the standard of living meant that, for some unemployment pay was not seriously inadequate, and for many families the effects were lessened by the fact that while one member of the family was without work, others still had their jobs.

Shipbuilding had gone through a severe crisis, and came out much smaller than it went in, and several hundred persons lost their jobs, in spite of a much publicised workers' occupation of a factory on Hedon Road, following the closing down of Imperial Typewriters on the decision of the multi-national organisation of which it was a small part. And the decision was not made because the factory was uneconomic, but with the intention of killing competition with typewriters made elsewhere by the same group. In the summer of 1977 the works were bought by the light-engineering firm Armstrong's of Beverley, but this merely meant that 700 jobs were transferred, and that what Hull gained, Beverley might lose.

Hull was at last connected with the motorway network by a dual carriageway up to the eastern end of the M62, and the crossing of the Humber was made much easier by the fact that the new Ouse bridge, part of the motorway, was so much more accessible than the old Boothferry bridge which it replaced. The Humber bridge was visibly near completion, after long delays caused by geological difficulties on the south side. On fine Sundays large numbers of people came in cars to look at the enormous height of the piers, and from several miles away the cables could be seen stretching between the northern and southern towers. Very few persons, however, felt that the completion of the bridge would make much economic difference unless there were a general economic revival.

The bridge was well outside the Hull boundaries—but so was a good part of the working population. For years the adjoining and indistinguishable area called Haltemprice (now absorbed into the new borough of Beverley) had sixty per cent or more of its working population employed in Hull, and the inhabitants came into the city for many of their leisure activities.[114] This tendency for much of the higher-paid working population to move out continued. Many persons were coming into Hull daily from new, suburban houses as far away as Gilberdyke, Cherry Burton, Leconfield, Hutton Cranswick, and Thorngumbald; and it was not the professional classes only who were moving out. Because of the city's rehousing policy old neighbourhoods were destroyed without the slightest thought for the social consequences, and the former inhabitants moved into tower-blocks of flats or to the new housing estate of Bransholme, in the city, but so distant from the centre as to make travelling to work very expensive.

It was becoming very difficult to distinguish between Hull and not-Hull. No traveller coming by road could know when he had reached the city unless he was driving slowly enough to see one of its boundary signs. From most directions he would not come to one of these until he had driven a mile or more through a built-up area. In the old parts of the town many of the streets and landmarks referred to in this history had either disappeared or were hard to find. It was far from the days of Celia Fiennes when the walls and the town had been clearly visible from a distance, sharply standing out above the flat countryside.[115] As in most cities, few of the people living there, even if they had been born there had many Hull ancestors. As late as about 1920 the speech of the country people was very different from that of Hull, and surname research showed that twice as many of them were of Scandinavian descent. Neither appeared to be the case in 1978; but to develop this theme would merely be a historian's lament. As in the rest of Britain, most of the people, though far from perfection, had a better chance in life than their ancestors.

There is one place of which few of the people ever see the interior, the horrible Victorian gaol on Hedon Road—not only a gaol but also one of the relatively few formerly equipped for hanging, so that for more than a decade it seemed that Hull would have the dishonour of being the last town to hang an unhappy woman, one from the Horncastle district, who had poisoned her husband: but some attempt was always made to disguise or alleviate horror, and the Hull Ladies' Orchestra was brought to the prison to console her last Sunday afternoon.

This atrocious inhumanity has disappeared, one hopes for ever; but in 1976 the whole country learned of the Hull gaol riots. A reasonably observant person who visited the gaol a couple of years before the riot was impressed not only by the horror of the place, but much more by the efforts of an enlightened governor and staff to make it endurable. Probably no harm can now be done (everything was put back by the riot) by recording that, although nothing whatever on this subject was said, a prisoner was allowed to be alone with his wife in his cell during the time of the visit, and it was assumed that this was the small beginning of what is usually called connubial association. Since it appeared to be impossible for anyone to escape through the outer part of the prison, the inner part was amazingly free. It was then unnecessary to take any precaution to prevent prisoners from having access to the alarming armoury of murderous choppers and knives which a large institutional kitchen must have. Men were busy in the cabinet-making and joinery departments, where they acquired great skill, but rarely enough to enable them to be employed in civilian life. It seemed that no prisoner had to work unless he wanted to, and one whose crime was of such distinction as to afford him the prospect of a high standard of living after his release, was sitting in his cell with his courtiers, visibly extremely proud of himself. For years there had been no violence; and any man who found the strain telling on him could have largactil, or whatever other psychotrophic drug was most suitable for his condition.

The first hint of trouble came just before eight in the evening on Tuesday, 31 August. The police had an emergency plan for the situation which was about to erupt, and within a few minutes a strong cordon was placed round the prison. About 200 of the prisoners gained control of much of the prison, and some came out on to the roof while others built barricades inside. During the night fires were lit. The fire brigade was ready, but although a very great amount of damage was done to furnishings a prison is largely incombustible. So many police were needed for this emergency duty outside the prison that men had to be brought in from other parts of Humberside for ordinary duty in the city. The gaol riot was all the more spectacular in that the prison is bounded by Southcoates Lane and Hedon Road. Crowds gathered, and for several days television showed prisoners on the roof displaying their improvised slogans. As for some time they were uncertain whether they wished to pelt slates at everyone within reach, or make their grievances known to the outside world, it is unlikely that they gained many converts. The weather turned cold and wet, and late on Friday, 3 September, the rebels—not all the prisoners had joined them—surrendered. During the riot the internal control of the prison was, as a matter of policy, left to the prison staff. Hull had had the worst gaol riot in Britain for over forty years.[116]

Fortunately most police work in Hull has remained routine. An increasing number of people convinced themselves, medical evidence and the law notwithstanding, that drink makes them more proficient drivers. In 1964 no more than 123 motorists and cyclists were convicted of driving with an excessive amount of alcohol in their bloodstream. By 1973 this figure had increased to more than 300. It is still rising, but here Hull does not differ from most other places.[117] The rise in venereal disease statistics, too, is no doubt comparable with that of every place which has felt the effect of the contraceptive pill. The Mill Street clinic had 1261 new patients in 1965, and 1643 in 1971. In the latter year there were only eleven new victims of syphilis, though eighteen cases of congenital syphilis were still being treated.[118]

A port is a particularly complex social unit, and much of its history depends on factors and events on the other side of the world. A hundred years ago the weekly newspapers reported in the greatest detail every single consignment of goods arriving by sea; and this made sense, since the imports were largely for Hull merchants or Hull agents of West Riding men. Now, and this too makes sense, the *Mail* gives shipping reports only in the baldest outline, since nearly all the goods pass through the city by road for other destinations. Many ships now come from Nigeria, no longer a really poor country, and much cannabis is known to arrive via the docks, though the city, as yet, has no 'hard-drugs' problem. And the extent of unemployment depends not only on the E.E.C. but also on decisions made in the Pentagon on weapon systems (they are no longer aeroplanes), some of which are manufactured by Hull labour in the Brough plant originally set up by Blackburn's. Unemployment was still growing in the 1970s, but the picture was different from that of the 1930s when sad groups of men almost permanently out of work could be seen standing about in the streets, at such focal points as the railway level-crossings, or where there was a bridge to lean on, and the trains to be seen passing. Now there is T.V. to watch at home and excellent news coverage from local radio stations. Unemployment benefit, except for those with children, comes nearer to supporting a decent standard of living: and while the husband may be unemployed the wife may be supplementing the family income by doing housework for middle-class households (which appears in no statistics). As the number of jobs grew less, the proportion occupied by women increased. They appeared to have about thirty-three per cent of the Hull jobs in 1962 and thirty-seven per cent in 1972.[119] Hull was still almost a depressed area, and as the bridge was visibly almost complete it was commonly said that it would lead from nowhere to nowhere.

There could be no greater error, though early optimism has not yet been fully justified. It is not only that the Hull dock traffic no longer passes through the city centre, but with the completion of the new high bridge at the mouth of the River Hull and the south orbital road, there will be a real bond between two virtually-severed but highly-industrialised areas. The Humber has been such a barrier that few Hull people realise that Lincolnshire long ago ceased to be a rural county. From a few points just outside the city the northern tip of the Scunthorpe steel plants can be seen; but from what is left of the Victoria pier the petro-chemical complex of south Humberside can be seen. Its chimneys, none perhaps much nearer to Hull than twelve miles, are so high that across the water they look insignificantly slender. But the flames rising from some, and the smoke-plumes from others, indicate the rapid approach of a period in which Humberside, a name still very much resented, will seem no more unreal than Teesside. Perhaps they are prophetic of more than that, forcing one to ask whether the world can much longer sustain an industrial revolution which has now been increasing ever more rapidly for two centuries.

While the bridge was being built, the M18 motorway connected the Yorkshire section of the M62 with the M80 in the Isle of Axholme, providing a toll-free route to Scunthorpe, Immingham and Grimsby, used by many even after the great bridge was completed. It is only partly for this reason that the benefits expected from the bridge have not been realised and the tolls have been insufficient to service the loans raised for its construction.

For many years the great dock at Immingham seemed to be a failure, and the same may turn out to be true of the Humber bridge. The port of Immingham, however, seems to have taken much of the shipping which formerly came to Hull. Grimsby and Immingham together take a bigger tonnage than Hull, which in 1980[120] had only 2.58 per cent (estimated by value) of all United Kingdom imports and 3.1 per cent of the exports. It is only the King George and Queen Elizabeth docks, two sharing one entrance, which are in regular use, and as they are so far east of the Victoria Pier, the Humber usually seems empty, unless there are one or two vessels steaming with the tide for Goole. Occasionally fish is discharged at the otherwise disused Albert Dock, but not usually from British trawlers. In the 1988 *Hull Telephone Directory* only the Boyd Line Ltd and J. Marr Ltd appear as trawler owners, and there are about seventy fish-merchants. In 1921 Hull had fifty or more shipowners, all overshadowed by Ellerman's Wilson line.[121] That line has gone, and only four others remain.

At the end of 1987 the percentage of the working population registered as unemployed was 16.7 and had fallen considerably during the year.[122] The city did not yet display the economic growth so apparent in the south-eastern counties, but there were some signs of prosperity—the crowded Marina in the Humber Dock and the expensive flats in the Old Town (though house prices are increasing very slowly.) A history, by definition, has no concern with the future. Where some will see principally a degradation of the natural environment, others will point to the vast and mostly beneficial social changes of the last hundred years. The Humber can no longer support the enormous number of salmon which as late as 1877 were being pursued up-river by grampuses;[123] but it would be difficult to find many people as disinherited as the poor of 1877.

Sources

1. *EMN*, 27 Feb. 1915, and *passim; PHA*, 1916, 1.
2. *PHA*, 1916, 25.
3. Ibid., 78.
4. Ibid., 27.
5. Ibid., 78.
6. Ibid., 27.
7. Ibid., 1917, 35; Ibid., 1919, 39.
8. Ibid., 1916, 61.
9. Ibid., 51.
10. Ibid., 82.
11. Jones, iii, 103; *EMN, passim.*
12. Jones, iii, 110.
13. Ibid., 184-6, 188-9.
14. Ibid., 218.
15. Ibid., v, 80.
16. Ibid., 121-2.
17. *Annual Register 1921* (Chronicle), 11, 14.
18. *Port of Hull Monthly Journal*, Nov. 1924, 7.
19. *PHA*, 1919, 37, 69.
20. City of Hull Great War Trust, *A Great Opportunity* (1919) 5.(L361.53 in the local history collection at the Hull Central Library).
21. *PHA*, 1919, 39; Ibid., 1922, 23.

22. Evans, 51 (Table 25).
23. Ibid., 53-4 and Table 24.
24. *Census of 1951*, Occupation Tables, 313 ff.
25. *PHA*, 1927, 33.
26. Ibid., 1932, 31-3, 15.
27. Evans, 30.
28. *PHA*, 1933, 62.
29. Ibid., 1934, 59.
30. Evans, 31.
31. *Hull Trade and Transit*, May 1923, 15.
32. T. Sheppard, *Hull Civic and Empire Week*, 33.
33. Evans, 42.
34. *The Times*, 2 Sept. 1925, 9a.
35. Calculated from Evans, 92.
36. Calculated from *Census of 1971: East Riding of Yorkshire*, part i, 10.
37. Hull Medical Officer of Health, *Annual Reports, passim*.
38. Evans, 92.
39. Ibid., 118.
40. Ibid., 111-12.
41. Ibid., 73.
42. Ibid., 77.
43. Ibid., 81-2.
44. *PHA*, 1933, 45, 50.
45. Evans, 163-4.
46. Ibid., 170.
47. Ibid., 171.
48. *Kelly's Directory of the North and East Ridings of Yorkshire*, Hull section, iv-vi; *Oxford Dictionary of the Christian Church*, 1257, s.v. SIMEON, CHARLES.
49. Evans, 254.
50. *The Times*, 19 Aug. 1919, 7a.
51. Ibid., 20 Feb. 1924, 4c.
52. G. A. Lee, 'The Tramways of Kingston-upon-Hull' (Sheffield University Ph.D, 1967-8) 215, 188.
53. *The Times*, 6 May 1926, 3e.
54. Ibid., 10 May 1926, 2f.
55. G. A. Lee, op. cit., 193.
56. Ibid., 194.
57. Ibid., 190.
58. Ibid., 198.
59. Ibid., 200.
60. Ibid., 216.
61. Ibid., 217.
62. *Annual Report of the Hull Medical Officer of Health*, 1930, 28.
63. Ibid., 1920, 47-50.
64. Ibid., 1938, 98. Mr B. Foster supplied the information on PAS.
65. B. Reckitt, *The History of Reckitt & Sons Limited*, 83-8.
66. *Report of the Hull Medical Officer of Health*, 1925, 96.
67. Ibid., 1931, 112.
68. Ibid., 1939-43, 74.
69. Ibid., 74.
70. Ibid., 1931, 80.
71. Ibid., 1939-43, 42.
72. *Who was Who in the Theatre* 10th ed. (1947).

73.* The Prince mentioned her as being one of a party at Chatsworth in one of his letters to his mistress, the Countess of Warwick (T. Lang, *My Darling Daisy* (1966) 65).

74.* Information supplied by the taxi-driver and a son of the man on the roof.

75.* Information supplied by Mr B. Foster who knew these men.

76.* Information from Mr B. Foster who then worked in that district.

77. G. A. Lee, op. cit., 196, 198ff.

78. *The Times*, 22 Mar. 1932, 11c.

79. *EMN*, 21 July 1918.

80. *The Times*, 23 Mar. 1932, 11c.

81. Ibid., 2 May 1932, 11c.

82. *VCH*, Hull, 343.

83. *The Times*, 17 Feb. 1936, 14f; 21 July 1936, 14f.

84.* Information from the late Mr C. H. Frankland who witnessed the act for which it might have been expected Mr Tarran would have been awarded the GM.

85.* From a senior police officer, deceased, who investigated the matter.

86. *The Times*, 25 Mar. 1947, 2e.

87. Ibid., 30 July 1947,2e.

88. Ibid., 6 Nov. 1947, 2e.

89. Ibid., 4 Dec. 1947, 2d; 12 Dec. 1947, 2b; 16 Dec. 1947, 3c.

90. Ibid., 24 Apr. 1948, 2g.

91. Ibid., 5 Dec. 1947, 2c.

92. Ibid., 10 Dec. 1928, 9d; 12 Dec. 1928, 13d.

93. *Plan*, 12.

94. *The Times*, 30 Sept. 1937, 9d.

95. Ibid., 8 Oct. 1952, 3c; *Plan*, 17.

96. T. Harrison, *Living through the Blitz*, 265-9.

97. Collier, 301, 479, 447.

98. Ibid., 506.

99. Ibid., 515-16.

100. *Hull Medical Officer of Health Reports*, 1939-43, 4.

101. *The Times*, 8 Oct. 1952, 3c. The fellow of the Royal Society was a Hull man, now Sir Cyril Lucas CMG, then acting head of the Department of Oceanography set up under Sir Alistair Hardy, FRS.

102. *The Times*, 23 Aug. 1955, 5d.

103. Information from a town clerk of a neighbouring large town.

104. *The Times*, 11 Sept. 1947, 2f; 1 Oct. 1947, 4b; 5 Dec. 1947, 2a.

105. Ibid., 2 Dec. 1958, 6g; 13 May 1959, 13c.

106. Ibid., 14 Dec. 1966, 6b; 5 Aug. 1969, 2e.

107. Evans, 35.

108. *The Times*, 27 Sept. 1932, 16b.

109. Ibid., 4 Oct. 1933, 9a.

110. G. W. Horrabin, 'Community and Occupation in the Hull Fishing Industry', *British Journal of Sociology*, viii, No. 4, 344.

111. *The Times*, 11 Jan. 1965, 6c.

112. *Hull Area Telephone Directory*, classified section, 70-71. Mr Vernon Webber, for many years a fish-merchant, estimated that the tonnage of fish landed at Hull in 1978 was probably about 40,000 which was less than one-third of the quantity landed in 1972.

113. P. Lewis and P. N. Jones, *Industrial Britain—the Humberside Region*, 67.

114. *Local Government Commission for England and Wales* (1958); replies to questionnaires and proposals on behalf of . . . Hull, App, IX, iv, p. 17.

115. C. Morris, *The Journeys of Celia Fiennes*, 47.

116. *Humberside Police Annual Report* (1976) 44.

117. *Report of the Chief Constable of Hull* (1965) 40; ibid. (1973) 34.
118. *Report of the Medical Officer of Health for Hull* (1972) 31.
119. Ibid., 28, 33.
120. *Statistics of Trade through UK Ports in 1980*, Tables I, III and IV.
121. *Kelly's Directory Hull* (1921) 668.
122. *Hull Civic News*, No. 22, 8.
123. *EMN*, 7 July 1877.

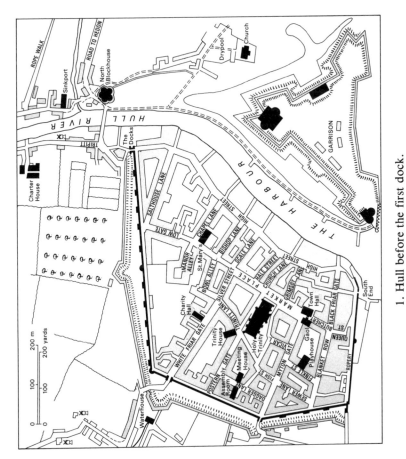

1. Hull before the first dock.

2. Hull - 1976.

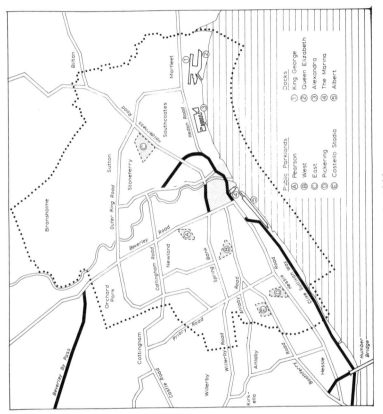

Public Parklands
Ⓐ Pearson
Ⓑ West
Ⓒ East
Ⓓ Pickering
Ⓔ Costello Stadia

Docks
① King George
② Queen Elizabeth
③ Alexandra
④ The Marina
⑤ Albert

3. Hull - 1988.

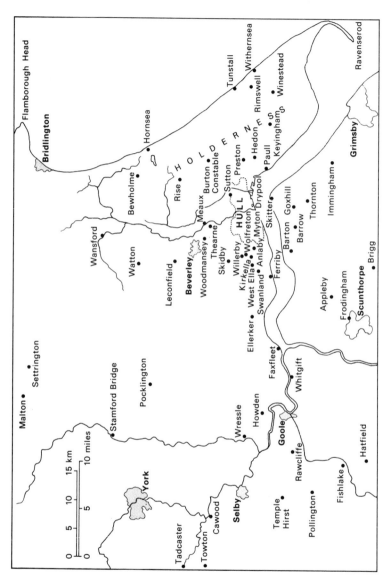

4. Hull and the Humber region.

5. Scandinavian and Baltic ports trading with Hull in 1865.

Index